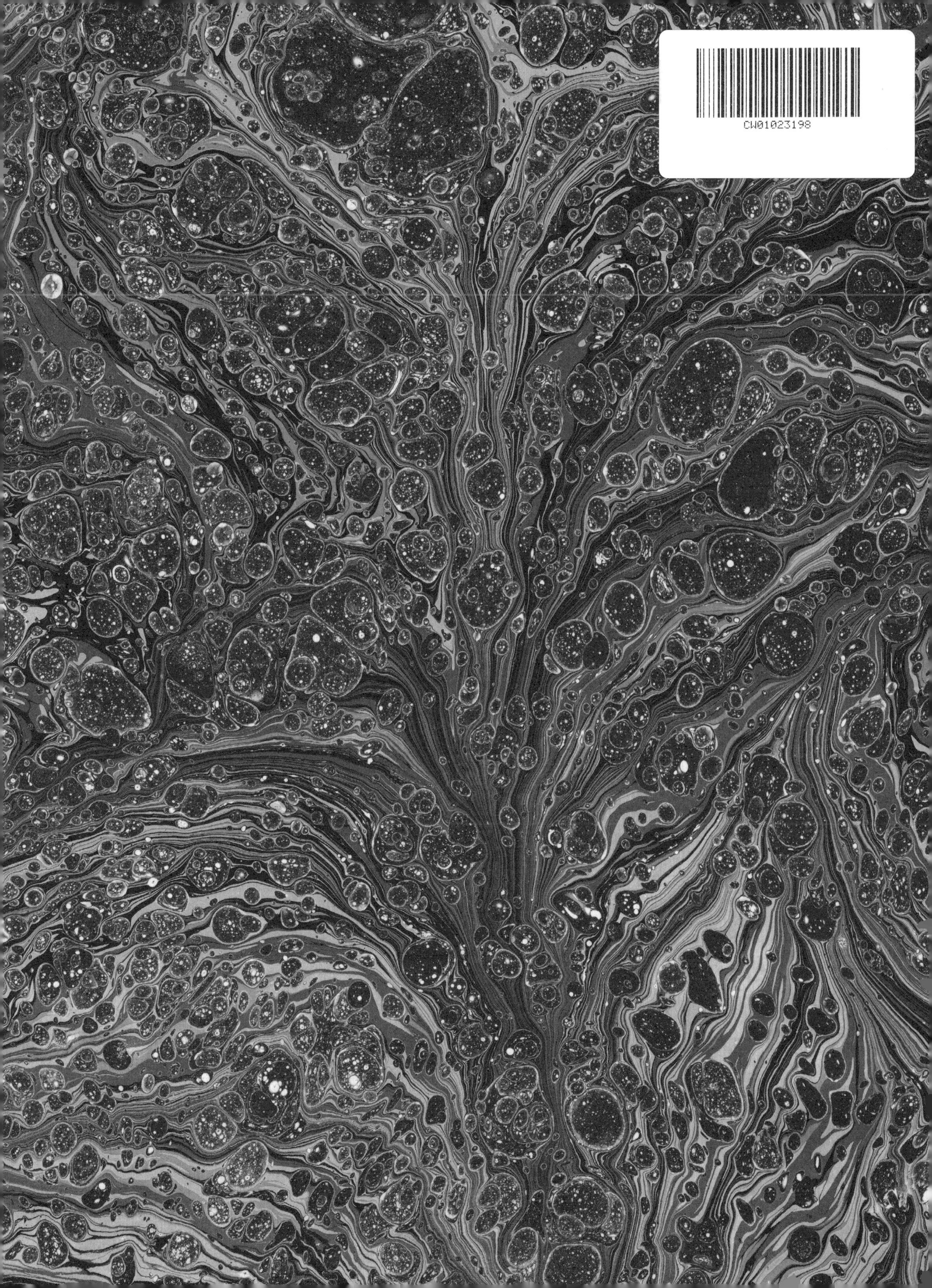
CW01023198

"We Wage War by Night"

SQUADRON
622
622
ROYAL AIR FORCE
BELLAMUS NOCTU

“We Wage War by Night”

erational and Photographic
y of No.622 Squadron
F Bomber Command

Howard J. Sandall

Schiffer Military History
Atglen, PA

Book Design by Ian Robertson.

Library of Congress Control Number: 2011929851

Printed in China.
ISBN: 978-0-7643-3814-4

We are interested in hearing from authors with book ideas on related topics.

Published by Schiffer Publishing Ltd.
4880 Lower Valley Road
Atglen, PA 19310
Phone: (610) 593-1777
FAX: (610) 593-2002
E-mail: Info@schifferbooks.com.
Visit our web site at: www.schifferbooks.com
Please write for a free catalog.
This book may be purchased from the publisher.
Please include $5.00 postage.
Try your bookstore first.

In Europe, Schiffer books are distributed by:
Bushwood Books
6 Marksbury Avenue
Kew Gardens
Surrey TW9 4JF, England
Phone: 44 (0) 20 8392-8585
FAX: 44 (0) 20 8392-9876
E-mail: Info@bushwoodbooks.co.uk.
Visit our website at: www.bushwoodbooks.co.uk
Try your bookstore first.

Contents

Foreword

Flight Lieutenant T.J. Maxwell DFC RAF (Ret'd)

Night after night, undeterred by the fury of guns
And new inventions of death, they battled their way across Germany
And paid a terrible price
Winston S Churchill

Early in the year 2001, after much research to find the crew of 622 Squadron Lancaster GI-J (LL828) who failed to return on March 16, 1944, I eventually located RAAF Pilot Peter Thomson in Perth, Western Australia, and telephoned him from Devon. The last time I had spoken to him was 57 years ago about 5000 feet over enemy occupied France, when all I said was "I'm off then, best of luck", and was whisked backwards from the rear turret in the slipstream into the black unknown night.

The telephone call was not easy; he was then aged 89 and in poor health, and was not to see 90. The conversation was short; I asked if he remembered me and there was silence, and I said that I would write to him, now that I knew where he lived. Next day his wife returned my call and said that he was very emotional, and that he said to her afterwards "Of course I remembered Tom, he was just a Boy." I was 19 then.

622 Squadron was just one of scores of other Bomber Squadrons whose crews nightly put their lives on the line for King and Country. Unknown to the cinema going public, for them no newspaper attention, celebrity status or media invented names, just numbers! But their losses were just as hard to bear; their lives were taken, injured beyond repair, blown apart before they had lived, consumed by fire, broken in twisted wreckage, dispatched with ignominy with no time for prayers, all now forgotten by their Governments.

Records of their lives and deaths are of little interest now and almost allowed to pass into oblivion, but for two things. The "Mildenhall Register", formed by Don Clarke, has kept their memory alive over the intervening years, and now 65 years on the Squadron's history is to be written as a lasting memorial to 622 Squadron and its dead: 215 of the Royal Air Force; 37 of the Royal Australian Air Force; 32 of the Royal Canadian Air Force; 20 of the Royal New Zealand Air Force; and one from the Royal Norwegian Air Force.

Fifty-six have no known grave:103 lie buried in Germany, 77 buried in France, 25 in England, 25 in Holland, 16 in Belgium, and 2 in Scotland.

Much credit is due to Howard Sandall, a nephew of John Gray whom I subsequently joined in Richard Allen's crew, for his perseverance and resolve over several years in painstaking research, and having the patience needed to get old men like myself to resurrect their failing memories. He has spent long hours of his meager off duty time, some at the expense of family life, in his ongoing research, and visits to study relevant archives at the RAF museum, Imperial War Museum, and National Archives also took much of his time and expense.

His completed history of 622 Squadron lifts his work well above a catalogue of events, and will be a permanent reference for friends and younger readers in future years to know that the aircrews of 622 Squadron RAF Bomber Command have left behind a heritage of dedication to duty in the two short years of its operational life.

622 brought with it a quality pedigree from XV Squadron when it formed in August 1943, converting its offensive operations against the enemy two years later to a humanitarian role in dropping food supplies to starving families in Holland and bringing Allied Prisoners of War back home.

I am honored and indeed humbled to be able to write this short foreword to Mr. Sandall's history of 622 Squadron, and proud to have been a part of it.

Thorverton, Devon, England, Spring 2010

Acknowledgments

Over the last five years, I have had the pleasure of meeting and corresponding with the most delightful people who have contributed enormously to this narrative. Without their memoirs and experiences, the personal story of 622 Bomber Squadron at war could not be relayed with any clarity. I am humbled to know these people who come from a generation, the likes of, I believe, will never be seen again. I would like to mention one person in particular who started me along the research journey after he expressed a desire to have a replacement copy of his lost Bomber Command logbook. That person is my Uncle, Flight Lieutenant John T. W. Gray, who won the Distinguished Flying Cross for gallantry against the enemy. His attributes were also recognized by his attendance at the Central Gunnery School, known then as the gunnery university. His help has been invaluable, and I spent many hours in his company, sharing his memories. Now in his ninety-first year, the respect for his fellow crew companions never fades. John's incredible story can be read in chapter twenty-two, and epitomizes the experiences of all those brave young men who volunteered for Bomber Command.

Whilst every effort has been made to list the original source of material, I apologize now if any material or photographs have been incorrectly credited. Every effort will be made to rectify any errors if the publisher decides to print further editions. In addition, I am indebted to the following people for allowing me to compile and reproduce their memoirs and for their assistance in gathering information. I would therefore like to thank the following contributors to this operational history (ranks as per end of hostilities): Mr. D. Bale; W/O C. E. Barclay; F/O J. Barker; Ms B. Beaumont;Sgt A. F. Belson; F/O W. Bishop RAAF; F/O T. S. Briggs; F/Sgt K.J. Boulton; Mr. R. Bright; F/O A.M. Bourne RAAF; Sgt 'Chick' Chandler; F/Sgt A. Cole; F /Sgt M. Coles; F/O G. Conacher RAAF; Mrs. Mollie Dawn WAAF new in(formally Nielsen); Mr. D. Clarke MBE; W/O J. Crago RAAF; F/Lt John Cox DFC; W/O R.R. Davie; Mr H. Dring; Sgt B. Dye; LAC E. Field; Sgt R. Francis; Ms. A.Gallop; F/Lt J. T. W.Gray DFC; W/O W. Hickling DFM;W/O R.V.Higgins; Dr. P. Irwin; Sgt E. Johnson; Mr. P. Jones; Mr. A. Kind; F/Sgt J. Kelly; Sgt R. Last; Mrs. A. Laws; Sgt W. E. Lister; F/Sgt A. Martin; Mr. A. Marshall; F/Lt T. J. Maxwell DFC; F/Lt J. McCahill RAAF; F/O W. A. Mildren; F/Sgt K. Monether; Mr.B. O'Connor; Ms. S. Ogilvy; Ms. J. Urwin; Mr. S. Patterson; Sgt E. Peck; Mr. A. Pender; W/C A. Pennington; F/Sgt R. Pepper; F/Lt R. Perry DFM; F/O H. Pam; F/Lt K. Pollard DFC; Ms. J. Potkins; Sgt G. Potter; Mr. C. Pratt; Sgt D. Pudney DFM; Sgt C. Pulman; Remco; F/O W.E. Richards RAAF; F/Sgt K. J. Ridley; W/O D. W. Shellock; F/O W.C. Sinclair RAAF; Sgt P.J. Simmonds; Sgt 'Swifty' Swallow RCAF; F/Sgt L. Shaw; Sgt E. Taylor; Sgt D. Thorman; Sgt J. Trend (XV); F/O E. J. Willis RAAF; James Willis; F/Lt (DR.) W. E. Woods RAAF; and F/O G. Wright.

Historians and official organizations: the Mildenhall Register, Imperial War Museum, Royal Air Force Museum, Public Records Office, Chris Ward, Martin Middlebrook, Martyn Ford-Jones, David Williams, Timothy O'Brien GAvA, Royal Air Force Museum Hendon, and Josselyne Lejeune-Pichon.

Their great generosity and kind permission to reproduce their memoirs and photographs have enriched this narrative.

Finally, I would like to thank my wife Carole and son Harry, whose encouragement and support have been an inspiration to me.

Howard John Sandall
622 Squadron Historian

Introduction

The expansion of Bomber Command during 1943 saw the emergence of several new squadrons, and 622 Squadron was one of those newly formed squadrons. To the majority of historians 622 may well be deemed as "just another squadron"; however, the squadron's contribution to the war effort was significant and worthy of remembrance.

Numerous books on the "Bomber War" have been published that depict heroic deeds, and some squadrons have received considerably more publication than others. 622 Squadron played a vital part in taking the war to Germany, orchestrated through 3 Group operations. There were over 60 Bomber squadrons operating the Avro Lancaster during WWII, and each and every one of them endured heavy aircrew casualties. These men deserve to be remembered for the sacrifices they made to keep us free from tyranny.

This operational and photographic history covers all aspects of the squadron's operations throughout almost two years of war and, to a degree, addresses the imbalance of published material.

Air and ground crew who served on the squadron have supplied many of the accounts herein, and the accounts provided by the Commonwealth and Dominion aircrew are particularly welcome. These young men freely volunteered to unite under the banner of freedom and democracy to strike a blow for the free world.

The young aircrew of World War II, in the main, arrived straight from school with no concept of what the future held. What was clear in their minds was the fact that they wanted to fly and make a difference in shortening the war. Revolutionary technology was being developed continuously, and the distance travelled by Bomber Command during five years of war, in technological terms, was astounding. The method of war that they were subjected to had never been employed before, and by the climax, No.3 Group was operating the G/H radar system that negated the need for "Pathfinder" assistance to find and bomb a target.

No words can describe the debt we owe to the air and ground crew of Bomber Command. However, for the purpose of this manuscript the focus will be on the exploits of those who served with 622 Squadron.

May we be worthy of their sacrifice.

Poem

John;
And when your wings are bright against the sky'
and all your guns are blazing crimson fire
Suspended there remote, In dangers span
Forget me not!
Think of these things
That here below we knew;
And I-
I will remember too.
The winding cobbled lane;
The river view and all the peaceful land that called to you.
Those hours we shared
The endless cups of tea
The plans you made while I would listen; quietly proud
You cared to tell your dreams to me.
Innumerable instances to live again
I'm all the silences-
Till you return-
Once more to touch the blessed loam and know, at last
That you are home.

Helen Wyn 1944

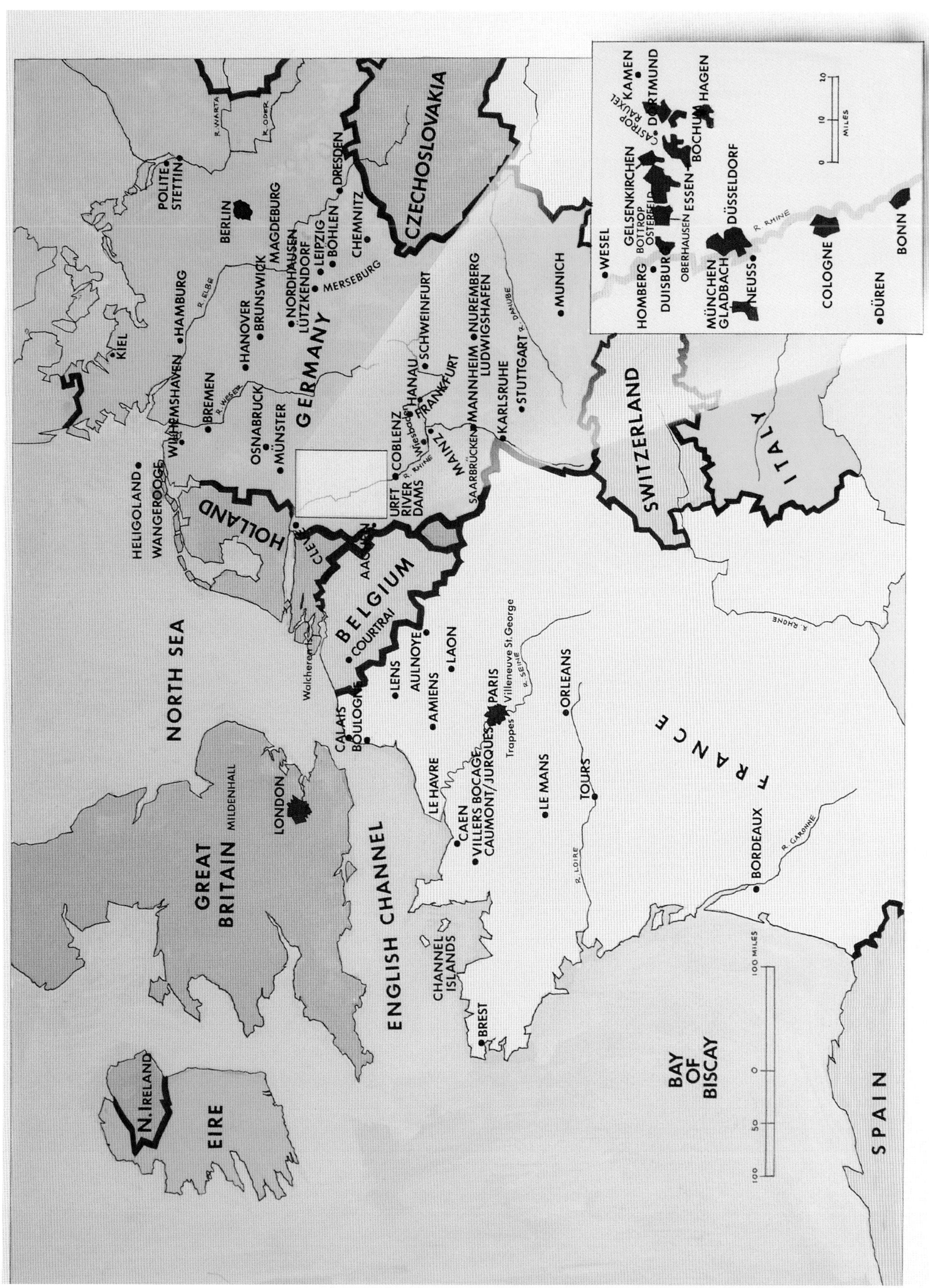

Map of Bomber Command targets in Europe. *Courtesy of Timothy O'Brien GAvA.*

1

No Parallel

In October 1943, Flight Sergeant Thomas Hargreaves and crew left No.1657 Conversion Unit at RAF Stradishall for their operational posting to a front line squadron. That squadron was No.622 based at RAF Mildenhall. Little did they know that over the next thirty operational missions they would experience the full spectrum of emotions and collect three medals for bravery. What is even more remarkable is that the crew would survive German fighter attacks, flak and bombs falling on them from above. Two of the bravery awards won by the crew were 'immediate' awards for outstanding devotion to duty.

By this stage of the war, Bomber Command was developing into a considerable force and in 1942, a full force of 1,000 bombers was sent out on a single sortie. The Commander in Chief of Bomber Command was Air Chief Marshall Arthur Harris and he believed that the bomber force could shatter the morale of the German people and seriously restrict their capacity to make weapons. In January 1943, Arthur Harris attended the Casablanca summit with all Allied leaders to discuss the way forward for the Allied forces. It was during this meeting that the Casablanca Directive was issued with clear instructions on what was expected from Bomber Command. The complete document was very lengthy however, for Bomber Command the following paragraph was the most significant: "Your primary objective will be the progressive destruction and dislocation of the German military, industrial and economic system, and the undermining of the morale of the German people to a point where their capacity for armed resistance is fatally weakened."

In June 1943 the 'Pointblank' directive superseded the Casablanca Directive but only in as much as the priorities had changed. The Americans were bombing by day and Bomber Command by night on a continuous basis. The Allied losses were mounting due to an advanced German day and night fighter force that had developed radar detection to new levels of efficiency. The result was increased losses for the Allies, especially the Americans who were bombing by day. Therefore the 'Pointblank' directive focused on the destruction of the Luftwaffe's fighter force and its industry upon which it depended.

Arthur Harris welcomed the new directive and recognized an opportunity to continue to bomb cities especially those that produced components for the aircraft industry. The primary objective for Harris was to wipe Berlin off the face of the map. He knew that to affect the morale of the German population he would have to destroy their capital city; however Berlin had proved to be a step too far on previous attempts. 'The Battle of Berlin', which raged from November '43-March '44, was not successful and the night fighter force reaped revenge on the bomber crews inflicting heavy losses. Berlin was at the outer limits for the aircraft deployed and a combination of weather conditions and improved night fighter techniques meant that the attrition rates could not be sustained indefinitely.

Usual practice for a new crew joining a squadron would be for the pilot to take a trip with an experienced crew as a 2nd 'dickey' pilot. The majority of crews hated taking a spare 'bod' with them and it was considered unlucky to do so, however on 19th November 1943, F/Sgt Hargreaves was the 2nd 'dickey' to F/Lt Watson and crew on a mission to Leverkusen. The rest of the crew felt very apprehensive whilst their skipper was away and they all waited anxiously for his return and news of what it was like on an actual mission. Whilst the crews were over enemy territory, thick fog descended over England, making landing very dangerous. A large proportion of aircraft were diverted to airfields that deployed the 'FIDO' system of runway marking. The runway had fuel lines running along the edge which were set alight to guide returning crews. RAF Mildenhall originally diverted all crews to Bradwell Bay airfield in Essex, however, this instruction was rescinded and Mildenhall was considered clear enough from fog for crews to attempt a landing. The crew piloted by Pilot Officer Hughes descended through the fog and crashed due to poor visibility seven miles from Ely in Cambridgeshire. The mid upper gunner, Sgt J McSpadyen was badly injured and never flew again. Six of his crewmates perished in the crash.

Tom Hargreaves returned safely none the worse from his experience and the whole crew sat him down so that he could recall all the details of the mission. On 25th November 1943 the crew was promulgated on the battle order for their first mission. They were assigned 'Stirling' RJ992, GI-O to carry out a mining mission to the Frisians Isles to drop parachute mines into the mouth of the river de Gironde. The mission did not go without incident and the 'Stirling' encountered severe icing making control difficult for the pilot.

The Battle of Berlin was not going well and the high attrition rates of the Stirling bombers resulted in Arthur Harris withdrawing the bomber from front line service in late November 1943. The Short Stirling suffered at the hands of the enemy due to not being

622 Squadron Lancaster LM477, GI-L. Crew L-R: Sgt C. H. Chandler F/E, F/Sgt G. R. Burns B/A, P/O R. L Urwin D.F.M. Nav, F/L T. Hargreaves D.F.C Pilot, F/Sgt S. S. Crawford W/op, F/Sgt H. R. Malpass M.U.G, F/Sgt F. D. Glynn D.F.M R/G. *Courtesy of C. H. 'Chick' Chandler.*

F/Lt Hargreaves and Crew pose for a photograph during early 1944.The photograph includes F/Sgt Williams (3rd from right) and F/O Urwin who were both injured during a mission to Berlin on 20th January 1944.After medical treatment, F/O Urwin returned to operations with the crew on their next mission to Stuttgart on 15th March 1944. F/Sgt Williams did not fly again with the crew; his replacement was Sgt 'Chick' Chandler who transferred in to join the crew from XV Squadron after a similar incident with a German night fighter. Crew L-R: F/Sgt Glynn D.F.M, F/Sgt Burns, F/Sgt Malpass, F/T Hargreaves D.F.C, F/Sgt Williams, F/O Urwin D.F.M, F/Sgt Crawford. *Courtesy of J. Urwin & Stefania La Bianca (Royal Navy)*

able to gain altitude over 17,000 feet when fully laden and the flak and fighter defenses took a heavy toll on the aircraft. F/Sgt Hargreaves and crew did not fly the Short Stirling again on operations. 622 Squadron converted to the much-improved Avro Lancaster, a revelation in aircraft engineering, during December 1943. Further conversion training took place during January 1944 and the winter weather was particularly bad with heavy snowfalls throughout January. However, by the second week of January, the weather had improved and the squadron commenced operations against the enemy in their new Lancasters on the 14th of the month on a trip to Brunswick.

On 20th January, the crew was detailed to attack 'The Big City' otherwise known as Berlin. Their Lancaster was L7576, GI-L from 'B' flight. Berlin was the nemesis for Bomber Command and the crews knew that the route there and back would be fraught with danger. Berlin was the most heavily defended target of any city with a flak belt stretching 40 miles across and a searchlight belt some 60 miles across. The flak defenses comprised of the very effective 88mm type artillery guns strategically placed around the city with three massive flak towers that contained eight 128mm heavy guns each. The eight guns could fire a salvo every ninety seconds and up to a height of 45,000ft. The exploding shells would send out a shower of molten shrapnel covering a diameter of 260 yards.

En route to the target, Flight Sergeant Urwin made his course calculations with the aid of 'Gee' navigational radar and dead-reckoning calculations to determine speed and distance to the target. Raymond Loraine Urwin was an above average navigator a fact recognized at No.6 Air Observer School at Starverton in Devon. He had completed the difficult navigational course with ease attaining an 85% pass mark and he had already proved himself a reliable and extremely capable navigator. He was an asset to the crew and they all appreciated his intellect and attention to detail.

The crew's Lancaster lurched and rolled in the slipstream of other aircraft flying in close proximity and they witnessed several air-to-air combats take place. The flak was extremely accurate and the searchlights probed the darkness for their next prey. Once a searchlight locked onto a bomber all the others converged onto that aircraft making the flak gunners target relatively easy to hit. Pilot Officer Urwin left the psychological safety of his navigation table and ventured into the cockpit to satisfy his curiosity. He was greeted by searchlights in the sky and explosions all around that showered shrapnel bursts against the aircraft like pebbles hitting a tin roof. He hurriedly made his way back to his navigation table and drew the blackout curtain behind him to blank out the chaos that was unfolding outside. Almost immediately after the words, 'bombs gone' had been spoken their Lancaster was hit by a flak burst adjacent to the cockpit that ripped out the side of their Lancaster hitting F/Sgt Urwin and the flight engineer, F/Sgt Williams. Raymond Urwin was badly wounded with shrapnel wounds to his neck and shoulder bleeding profusely. The wireless operator, F/Sgt Crawford made the navigator comfortable and attended to his wounds. F/Sgt Williams was not in a critical state so he was allowed to carry on with his duties after having assured them that he was alright. Ray Urwin was ordered to leave his post and go and lay in the rest area next to the main spar of the Lancaster leaving the rest of the crew to try and navigate the bomber home across enemy territory for around six hours. Urwin knew that it was imperative that he assisted with the navigation. Otherwise, the Lancaster may get lost and fly into heavily defended target areas on the route home, signaling almost certain destruction. He resumed his position as navigator and plotted a course for home, relaying

Flying Officer R. L Urwin DFM. *Courtesy of J. Urwin & Stefania La Bianca (Royal Navy)*

course alterations to the pilot all the way back to Mildenhall. By the time the crew reached Mildenhall, F/Sgt Urwin had lost a considerable amount of blood and he needed urgent medical attention. The skipper, Tom Hargreaves contacted ground control and requested a priority landing, which was granted and executed with his usual efficiency. The moment the Lancaster ground to a halt, F/Sgt Urwin collapsed from loss of blood, in the knowledge that he had brought the crew back to safety.

For his incredible actions on the night, Raymond Loraine Urwin was awarded an immediate Distinguished Flying Medal. His citation was 'gazetted' with the following citation:

> One night in January, 1944, this airman was the navigator of an aircraft which attacked Berlin. On the homeward flight, the aircraft was hit by an anti-aircraft shell. Sergeant Urwin was wounded in the neck and the shoulder. In spite of his injuries he insisted on fulfilling his duties and, although deprived of some of his equipment, he navigated the aircraft safely to base. This airman set a fine example of courage, fortitude and devotion to duty.

Recommended for immediate award of Distinguished Flying Medal

Due to the injuries to two of the crew, their next mission did not occur until 15th March when Stuttgart was the target. They were assigned the new GI-L, IM477 the replacement for the previous Lancaster that was written off. Various missions followed in quick succession to heavily defended places in the Ruhr Valley including Frankfurt, Dortmund, Düsseldorf, Berlin and Essen. During February 1944, Tom Hargreaves was informed that he had been awarded his commission to Pilot Officer, a proud moment for the whole crew.

On 18th March, the crew was on the battle order to fly IM477, GI-L to attack Frankfurt, the first of two consecutive trips to this German city. The route to the target was the usual mixture of searchlights and flak and the crew witnessed several aerial combats which resulted in aircraft being shot out of the sky. Over the target, they approached the bomb run and P/O Hargreaves received instructions from the bomb aimer, F/Sgt Burns to keep the Lancaster steady and on course. Just after bomb release their aircraft was hit by incendiary canisters from an aircraft above; luckily no damage to engines, crew or major areas of the Lancaster occurred. For some unexplained reason F/Sgt Williams, the flight engineer did not continue to fly with the crew and his replacement was Sergeant C.H. 'Chick' Chandler. Originally, with XV Squadron, Chick had completed several missions and had only just returned from 'survivors leave' when he was informed of his posting to 622 Squadron and a place in the Hargreaves crew. 'Chicks' first mission with his new crew was undertaken on 31st May 1944 against the railway marshaling yards at Trappes, a mission that passed without incident. On 5th July 1944, the crew of F/Lt Hargreaves were promulgated on the battle order to attack the flying bomb site at Wizernes in France (Chick Chandler's account of the Wizernes mission can be read later in the story).

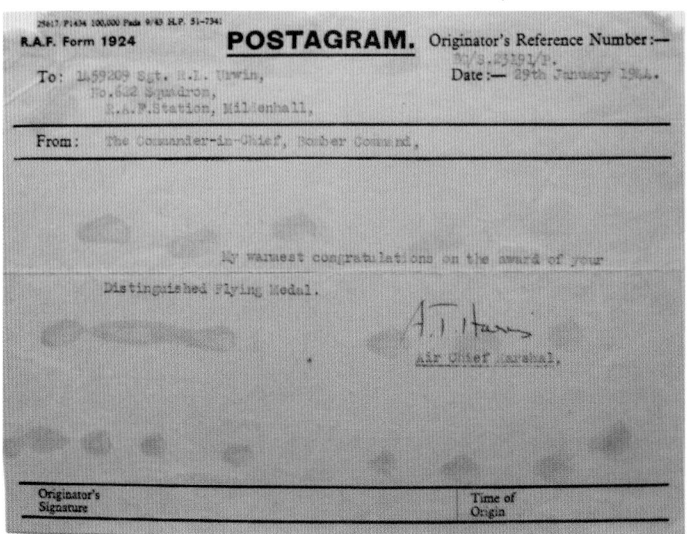

25617/P1434 100,000 Pads 9/43 H.P. 51-7341

R.A.F. Form 1924 **POSTAGRAM.** Originator's Reference Number:— [illegible]/S.25191/P.

To: 1459209 Sgt. R.L. Urwin,
No.622 Squadron,
R.A.F.Station, Mildenhall,

Date:— 29th January 1944.

From: The Commander-in-Chief, Bomber Command,

My warmest congratulations on the award of your Distinguished Flying Medal.

A.T. Harris
Air Chief Marshal.

Originator's Signature | Time of Origin

The congratulatory post gram from ACM Arthur Harris sent to acknowledge the award of the Distinguished Flying Medal. *Courtesy of J. Urwin & Stefania La Bianca (Royal Navy)*

Bomber Command was now placing great emphasis on destroying the launching sites of the V1 rockets codenamed operation 'Crossbow'. The build up to the 6th June and the D Day landings in Normandy had been considered a diversion by ACM Harris and he reluctantly agreed to divert his bombers from bombing German cities. The second diversion for Harris was now the flying bomb menace and Eisenhower, the Allied Supreme Commander, gave priority to the task of destroying the flying bomb launching sites. The launching sites were hidden in the countryside of the Pas de Calais usually in the center of wooded areas.

On one such mission to Nucourt France on 10th July, the crew carried a special observer on board, Wing Commander Cyril 'Mac' Baigent RNZAF, who was assigned to headquarters No.3 Group. W/C Baigent was the youngest Officer to command a bomber squadron and he had completed two 'tours' of operations. He was so well respected that he went on to command No.75 Squadron, comprised mainly of his fellow countrymen. By the end of hostilities he had been decorated with the DSO, DFC & bar.

The mission went without complication apart from slight flak over the target area troubling F/Lt Hargreaves. Although woods offered perfect concealment, it also acted as a beacon to bomber crews who were trying to identify launching sites. If the V1 sites had been built in open countryside then the bombers would have found it extremely difficult to locate them. Bomber Command attacked flying bomb targets until late August 1944 when the launching sites were captured by advancing Allied troops.

Sergeant 'Chick' Chandler poses for an official photograph around the time he was awarded his flight engineer brevet. He would endure eleven separate enemy fighter attacks with two pilots and successfully complete his 'tour' of operations. The odds of surviving one fighter attack were stacked against a bomber crew; remarkably, he would survive eleven attacks, a feat worthy of mention in any war record. *Courtesy of C. H. 'Chick' Chandler.*

'Chick' Chandler-Flight Engineer

Sergeant C. H. 'Chick' Chandler trained as a flight engineer at No.4 trade training school at St. Athens. He joined the other six members of a bomber crew at 1651 Heavy Conversion at RAF Waterbeach. His first skipper was Oliver Brooks, who demonstrated exceptional pilot skills on more than one occasion to save their stricken bomber while under attack. 'Chick' settled into the crew well and their first operational posting was to RAF Mildenhall to join XV squadron in October 1943.The squadron at the time shared the runway with 622 Squadron, and unbeknownst to 'Chick' Chandler at that time, it would be the squadron with whom he completed his 'tour' of operations.

The crew quickly settled into squadron life and the number of targets attacked included all the main cities in the Ruhr Valley. The Battle of Berlin would pose numerous challenges for the crew, as would the infamous Nuremberg raid on 30/31st March 1944 when they witnessed al least 50 bombers going down in flames. The crew themselves were attacked by a Ju88 night fighter en route and had an empty petrol tank holed by the fighter. 'Chick's' order to 'corkscrew' undoubtedly saved the Lancaster from almost certain destruction. By far the most memorable raid for Sergeant Chandler was the crew's seventeenth on 23rd April 1944 to Düsseldorf. The route to the target was the usual mixture of flak and vigilance against the fighters and after every mission the crew's confidence and belief in each other's abilities grew. 'Chick' had an unusual tendency to ignore the inferno that was raging below and stand in the cockpit blister straining his eyes for enemy fighter attacks. Just after releasing the bombs on the target, the aircraft was attacked by an enemy fighter. Cannon shells ripped through the Lancaster's fuselage and 'Chick' identified their attacker as a Me109 approaching at speed with its forward wing edges lit up from firing explosive shells. Almost instantaneously, 'Chick' shouted down the intercom to 'corkscrew' starboard. At that very moment the aircraft was struck by an explosion that knocked him from his feet, his fall being cushioned by his thick flying equipment and his Mae West life jacket. As he fell, his eyes caught sight of tracer fire passing closely above the cockpit where the Lancaster had been moments before the pilot commenced his corkscrew. The Lancaster was now in a screaming dive as Oliver Brooks fought to bring the aircraft under control. The aircraft lost 8,000 feet in the dive with Sgt Chandler pinned to the floor through 'G' force before the pilot managed to gain control at 14,000 ft.

'Chick' Chandler clipped on his parachute and noticed that it felt extremely loose compared to his usual preferred tight fitting harness. Almost immediately, the Lancaster went into another uncontrolled dive and lost another 7,000ft before Pilot Officer Brooks managed to gain control. The crew had trained for such an occurrence in the classroom and on training flights, and they started to take stock of their predicament. The port inner engine was feathered to put out the fire, the damage to the aircraft's structure was making life difficult for the pilot to control, and he gave the order to put on parachutes.

With no time to lose, the crew began to examine the aircraft and each other for damage or injury. The mid upper gunner dropped out of his turret to find his flying boots and three of the crew's parachutes on fire, making a 'bail out' impossible. The crew came to the consensus decision to attempt to fly to the emergency landing airfield at Woodbridge in Suffolk. With the Lancaster under control, P/O Brooks asked 'Chick' Chandler to check the aircraft for damage and he started at the front position of the bomb aimer. On first inspection, it was very clear that he had taken the full force of the explosion and he was dead from his injuries. Sgt Chandler systematically checked all the crew's positions as he ventured back into the fuselage and noticed that the wireless operator was not at his position. This fact did not immediately alarm 'Chick' because he knew that the wireless operator ventured to the rear of the aircraft at the time of bomb release, to visually check that the photoflash left the aircraft with the bombs. As Sgt Chandler reached the rear of the aircraft he found the wireless operator laying unconscious on the floor with severe injuries to his lower body and legs. He died before they reached England.

The situation was grim, and Sgt Chandler had to report that the hydraulic system had totally failed and that the starboard outer engine was only producing partial power. The damage to the port inner engine had rendered the hydraulic system useless and subsequently the bomb doors were still open and causing considerable drag to the aircraft. The journey home was long and stressful with the Lancaster gradually losing height all the way with a concerted effort by the pilot to gain the height of 500 feet to clear the English coast. On reaching the emergency landing strip at Woodbridge it was time to attempt to lower the wheels by pulling the toggle to release the emergency undercarriage. The Lancaster was in such a poor flying condition that they had to land on their first attempt, and with the undercarriage failing to work, they had to crash land with the bomb doors open. Pilot Officer Brooks ordered the crew to take up crash positions and he skillfully put the Lancaster down on its belly and they careered down the runway at 120mph until eventually they ground to a halt.

Shortly after this incident the crew was sent on survivor's leave. Whilst on leave from Mildenhall the crew was split, and Pilot Officer Brooks was assigned to a crew that had lost their pilot. 'Chick' Chandler and the rear gunner, 'Whacker' Marr were posted to 622 Squadron to fill vacancies in two other crews. Fortuitously, Sgt Chandler joined the crew of F/Lt Hargreaves in May 1944 and before his tour concluded, he would endure more contacts with enemy fighters.

Target Wizernes (Flying Bomb Site) 5/6th July 1944, Lancaster GI-P, LM 466.

'Chick' Chandler picks up the story:

"It is being written from memory nearly fifty years after the event and whilst some things are crystal clear in my memory others are rather vague. Flying with this crew, (on my 27th op), we had a 'hairy do'.The date was the night of 5/6th July 1944, and we were on the return trip from Wizernes, time around midnight in Lancaster GI-P LM466. Unusually our navigator was F/Lt Nicholl, the squadron Navigational Leader. Our usual navigator, P/O Urwin was on sick leave. The outward trip and bombing run had been comparatively uneventful; we were cruising along at 8,000ft in very bright moonlight with not a cloud in the sky.

Sometime after leaving the target another Lancaster formatted on us at about 500yds: slightly below us on our starboard side, and slightly astern. We were not too happy with the situation since there were rumors floating around that the Germans were repairing some of our shot down aircraft and mixing them in our bomber stream and shooting down our unsuspecting aircraft. Since the other Lancaster was on our starboard side my position as flight engineer put me in a very good position to keep an eye on its movements. Its position relative to ours remained unchanged for seven or eight minutes. Suddenly, without any warning whatsoever, it disintegrated in a vast explosion and ball of fire. Almost immediately, the gunners and I saw a Me110, which seemed to appear from nowhere. Without doubt the Lancaster had fallen to the night fighters 'Schräge Musik' armament."

'Schräge Musik' is a German codeword given to the Nachtjagd night fighter planes equipped with two MG ff's or MG 151/20s 20mm cannons mounted in the cabin or fuselage at a 70-80 angle which were aimed by a second Revi C12/D or 16B gun sight mounted on the canopy roof. 'Schräge Musik' proved to be lethal and took a fearsome toll of heavy bombers in the night". At the time the appearance of the Me110 was a complete mystery and when 'Schräge Music' was discovered it explained the sudden explosion of our formating Lancaster.

"The Me110 positioned itself for an attack on our aircraft, as it came in we corkscrewed violently and both gunners opened fire on our attacker. Unfortunately, only one gun was firing in the rear turret and one of the guns in the mid upper was loaded with daylight tracer. Result, a blaze of light and loss of night vision until such time as the mid upper gunner was able to disconnect the offending belt of ammunition he restricted himself to a running commentary of the enemy aircrafts position. The Me110 made three attacks before breaking off and was claimed destroyed by our rear gunner. Almost immediately, we were attacked by a Ju88 and by now the mid upper gunner had managed to return fire from his one good gun. Again, three attacks were made before our assailant broke off the engagement and the rear gunner claimed the attacker as damaged, probably destroyed. The rear gunner, F/Sgt Glynn was given an immediate award of the Distinguished Flying Medal."

F/Sgt Douglas Frank Glynn's citation was 'gazetted' with the following citation:

'This airman has completed numerous sorties as rear gunner, most of which have been against targets in Germany. On a recent occasion his aircraft was attacked by a fighter soon after the target had been bombed. Flight Sergeant Glynn defended his aircraft with great skill and drove off the attacker which turned away with one engine on fire. Shortly afterwards he drove off another enemy aircraft which attempted to close in. His good work contributed materially to the safe return of the bomber'.

Recommended for immediate award of Distinguished Flying Medal

'Chick' Chandler continues the story:

"Hindsight is a wonderful thing and after nearly 65 years I wanted to clarify if my version of events was accurate. Having had time to consider the incident, I am not too convinced that we did in fact shoot down both, or even one of our attackers. There is little doubt that we were all very euphoric that we had survived a determined enemy attack and our assessment of the situation may have been biased. However, I cannot recall either of our attackers being on fire or spinning out of control.

"When settling down to write this and having several theories expounded about why attacks were not pressed home as they might have been, I made a big effort to contact any survivors of my crew. Mainly I hoped to contact the mid upper gunner who of course had the best view of the incident, but without success. With all these factors in mind, I made a concerted effort to confirm my memories of that July night back in 1944.

On the night of 5/6th July, Target WIZERNES, height 8,000 ft., an ME.110 was claimed as destroyed by F/Sgt Glynn. A JU.88 which attacked immediately afterwards was also claimed as destroyed.

Gunnery Leader.

F/Lt Ward, 622 Squadron Gunnery Leaders report describing the action during the Wizernes mission. *Courtesy of C. H. 'Chick' Chandler*

The above photo depicts F/Lt Derisley D.F.C & crew posing for an end of tour photograph in front of Lancaster GI-P LM466. This photo was taken shortly after 'Chick' Chandler and crew encountered enemy fighters on their mission to Wizernes in France. The discerning eye will notice the repaired bullet holes in the fuselage just above the crew's heads near to the 30 mission bomb symbol. *Courtesy of R. Bright*

"My endeavors enabled me to trace and contact the W/op F/Sgt Crawford. I asked him to tell me his recollections of the incident with absolutely no prompting from me. He sent me a copy of his original combat report that he filed on the night. That account is below".

Flight Sergeant Crawford's account of enemy fighter attacks during the raid on Wizernes

Report filed on 6th July 1944-Wizernes-8,000ft-622 Squadron.

"I first saw combat on starboard beam approx 100 yards. After destroying the Lancaster the enemy aircraft came into attack from starboard fins quarter 800 yards. Rear gunner identified enemy aircraft as Me110 at 800 yards and opened fire giving corkscrew starboard. Enemy aircraft came within 400 yards firing.

"The enemy aircraft's port engine was seen to burst to flames and broke away to port. Enemy aircraft attacked port quarter 500 yards, rear gunner again ordered corkscrew port and opened fire.

"Enemy aircraft broke away in flames to port. The enemy aircraft was diving in flames but another attack from a Ju88 prevented gunners from seeing result of this combat".

Second combat:

"Immediately after Me110 broke away in flames a Ju88 attacked from port quarter from 500 yards. The rear gunner and enemy aircraft opened fire simultaneously. By this time only one gun in rear turret was firing. Enemy aircraft again attacked from starboard quarter 600 yards.

"Rear gunner and mid upper gunner opened fire and corkscrew starboard ordered. Hits were observed on enemy aircraft which broke away 400 yards to port quarter.

"Enemy aircraft attacked again from port quarter 500 yards. The rear gunner and mid upper immediately opened fire and gave order to corkscrew port. By this time the mid upper had one gun serviceable. Hits were again observed on enemy aircraft which broke away starboard 300 yards. Enemy aircraft resumed attack from dead astern 800 yards. Rear gunner opened fire 500 yards and gave order to corkscrew starboard.

"Enemy aircraft broke away starboard quarter again. Enemy aircraft attacked from starboard quarter from 600 yards.

"Rear and mid upper gunners opened fire at 500 yards and enemy aircraft's port engine was seen to catch fire.

"Enemy aircraft broke off attack diving to port burning well and trying to reach east coast. During this combat enemy aircraft was firing on all attacks but our aircraft received no hits. Between each attack our aircraft was flying straight and level".

'Chick' Chandler's comments on reply from F/Sgt Crawford

"Unfortunately, I have mislaid the original copy of my reply to Stan Crawford's account of the incident; however, I can recall the main gist of it. I disagree with his assessment regarding the destroyed Lancaster that we witnessed. Stan stated that the action occurred only 100 yds away when I believe that it was more likely 500 yards away. My thoughts on why the mid upper gunner had only one gun firing were not confirmed. However since he could give no opinion, I will stick to my recollection of the incident. The only person who can finally settle the mystery would be F/Sgt. Malpass the mid upper gunner.

"Since I was only able to see action on the starboard side of our aircraft, I had to rely on intercom 'chatter' to assess what was happening on the port side. The wireless operator had a better view of the incident from his position in the astrodome and I believe that his is the most accurate account. As previously stated I did not see an aircraft on fire and I am sure that if I had, then it would have been most memorable. Because Stan states quite clearly that both our attackers were seen to break away to port in flames, I now believe that my initial doubts were unfounded and that, unlikely as it would appear, we did in fact shoot down both enemy aircraft. You will see that I have amended my assessment of six attacks to seven as F/Sgt Crawford described. Having gone through Stan Crawford's account again, it is clear that he disagreed with my version of only one gun firing in the mid upper turret since initially both guns were firing. Only the mid upper gunner can finally resolve this matter".

During a remarkable spell with Bomber Command, 'Chick' Chandler endured eleven separate fighter attacks surely a feat of endurance unsurpassed by many. By his own admission, they were all eventful as he outlines below:

"In any combat situation against an enemy fighter, the advantage is always with the fighter. Therefore, I consider myself extremely fortunate to have survived eleven individual strike attacks by fighters. The encounters were as follows:

No.1 Nuremberg 30/31st March 1944. Attacked by Ju88 in one attack, petrol tank holed, no casualties.

No.2 Düsseldorf 22/23rd April 1944. Flak and Me109; two crew members killed, two wounded. Port inner engine on fire; starboard outer severe loss of power. Complete loss of hydraulics i.e. gun turrets, undercarriage, flaps and bomb doors stuck open. In addition, we had H2S on fire; dinghy shot away, 3 parachutes burnt. Crash landed at RAF Woodbridge. Immediate awards of two D.F.C's and one D.F.M.

No.3 & 4 Karlsruhe 25/26th April 1944. Two separate attacks were made, both from the port side so that I was unable to see our attackers. Our corkscrew maneuver evaded the tracer that passed over our aircraft. On this operation our depleted crew was made up of 'spares' the deceased bomb aimer's position being filled by W/C Watkins, XV Sqdn Commanding Officer.

These last four incidents happened whilst I was flying as flight engineer with P/O Oliver Brooks on XV Sqn. At about this time XV Sqn lost F/Lt Amies flying with a 'sprog' crew, and decreed that P/O Brooks was to take over the 'Amies'crew. My rear gunner, 'Whacker' Marr and I were moved to 622 Sqn to replace vacancies in two separate crews.

No.5-11 Wizernes 5/6th July 1944. Witnessed Lancaster blow up from Schräge Musik. Me110 turned its attention on us attacking from astern on three separate occasions. On last attack, Me110 broke away in flames claimed destroyed. Ju88 commenced attacking from astern on four separate occasions. On the last attack, it broke away in flames and the Ju88 was also claimed as destroyed."

Fate Intervenes

F/Lt Thomas Hargreaves was awarded the Distinguished Flying Cross on completion of his operational tour of operations. The award is documented in the squadron's operational records books as effective from week commencing 8th August 1944. He stayed in the RAF to further his career and found himself in India flying the Lancastrian, the transport derivative of the Lancaster. Tragically, during a routine flight on 2nd August 1949 the aircraft crashed near Manipur (Karachi) killing all three of the crew on board. Thomas Hargreaves originated from Burnley in Lancashire and throughout his tour of duty showed extreme courage and fortitude against the enemy. The whole crew stand as a shining example to the resilience and determination in defeating the enemy and liberating all from oppression. The following words from Sir Arthur Harris epitomises the 'Hargreaves' crew in every respect:

> "There is no parallel in warfare to such courage and determination in the face of danger over so long a period...It was, furthermore, the courage of the small hours, of men virtually alone, for at his battle station the airman is virtually alone. Such devotion to duty must never be forgotten".
>
> Air Chief Marshal of the Royal Air Force
> Sir Arthur Harris
> Commander in Chief Bomber Command
> 1942-1945

F/Lt Hargreaves and crew pose for the end of tour photograph. Sgt 'Chick' Chandler can be seen at the back of the three aircrew, sitting on the bomb. *Courtesy of C. H. 'Chick' Chandler*

2

Danger in the Shadows

Pilot:F/Sgt G.Marsh
Nav: P/O A.C. Richards D.F.C
F/E: Sgt S. E. Meaburn
B/A: Sgt J. C. Bailey RCAF C.G.M
MUG: F/Lt L.F. Berry (Station Gunnery Leader) replacement for Sgt Smith rested by MO
R/G: Sgt H.J. Hynham
W/Op: Sgt G. M. Wright

On the night of 23/24th August 1943, F/Sgt Marsh lifted the Short Stirling into the air totally unaware of the drama that would unfold as the night went on. This was the crew's eighth operation and occupying the bomb aimer's position was Sergeant Calder Bailey of the Royal Canadian Air Force. By the end of the mission, Sgt Bailey would show extreme courage and fortitude culminating in the award of the Conspicuous Gallantry Medal.

The expansion of Bomber Command during 1943 was a result of increasing demand to attack numerous targets. The directive issued at the Casablanca Conference called for the 'progressive destruction and dislocation of the German military, industry and economic system and the undermining of the morale of the German people'. Air Chief Marshall Arthur Harris, Commander in Chief of Bomber Command, had successfully attacked the Ruhr industry over a sustained period and launched the 1,000 bomber raids against Hamburg. However to sustain this level of commitment, several new bomber squadrons were formed during the latter half of 1943, and subsequently 622 Squadron was formed on 10th August 1943.

Air Chief Marshall Harris knew that to really affect the moral of the German population he would have to destroy their capital city; however Berlin had proved to be a step too far on previous attempts. Berlin was the most heavily defended target of any city with a flak belt stretching forty miles across and a searchlight belt some sixty miles across. The flak defenses comprised of mainly the very effective 88mm type artillery gun strategically placed around the city. In addition three massive flak towers contained eight 128mm heavy guns each. The eight guns could fire a salvo every ninety seconds up to a height of 45,000ft. The exploding shells would send out a shower of molten shrapnel covering a diameter of 260 yards.

Unbeknownst to F/Sgt Marsh, he was taking part in the build up to what would historically become known as 'The Battle of Berlin'. This particular period for Bomber Command (November 43- March 44) was not successful and the night fighter force reaped revenge on the bomber crews, inflicting heavy losses. Berlin was at the outer limits for the aircraft deployed and a combination of weather conditions and improved night fighter techniques meant that the attrition rates could not be sustained indefinitely.

The increase in efficiency and number of the German night fighter force was a growing concern. The Germans utilized new night radar systems such as the Himmelbett system of ground radar, controlling a series of imaginary boxes of space in the sky and night fighters were vectored into position within the radar box sections. The mainstay of the German night fighter force (Nachtjagd) was the Me110 and the Ju88 twin engined fighters. These fighters were equipped with the Lichtenstein and SN-2 airborne radar devices.

Picture showing the deadly Junkers 88 night fighter. Note the camouflage, the black crosses and the Schräge Musik 20mm cannon. These twin upward firing cannons in the mid fuselage of the Ju88 were sighted by a periscope and employed low-illumination ammunition to make RAF crews believe that they were being engaged by flak. The deadly Ju88C was equipped with a large radar array and worked within a co-ordinated structure using radar and searchlights. The ground radar system was known as Himmetbett and utilized twin Wurzburg radars for fighters and target tracking coupled with Freya radar for overall surveillance. Such was the accuracy of the radar equipment, skilled controllers were usually able to bring a fighter crew to visual identification of a target. By mid-1941, the chain of night fighter zones or 'boxes' extended from west of the Ruhr, as far north as the Danish coast. All that was required was the provision of airborne radar to make the system almost perfect. *Courtesy of ww2images.*

The destruction of the bombers was due to the inroduction of the 'Schräge Musik' upward firing 20mm cannon assembly. This armament was mounted in the fuselage or in the rear of the crew's cabin. In practice, the night fighter would approach the bombers by way of radar detection aides from slightly below so that the aircraft was silhouetted against the night sky. The bomber's gunners were at a disadvantage by looking down into the dark night sky. Once in position the fighter would fire into the bombers fuel tanks situated in the wings, causing almost certain fire and destruction. In addition, the Ju88 was fitted with a standard 20mm cannon armament in the nose which when fired tore open the thin metal of a bomber like a tin opener.

Flight Sergeant Marsh had originally joined XV Squadron also based at Mildenhall in late June 1943. He undertook his first mission on 5th July to the Frisian Islands as part of a mine laying operation in the waters surrounding the Islands. A few more operations followed before his immediate transfer to 622 Squadron on 10th August along with Stirling BK816, which displayed the XV Squadron codes of LS-X and was christened as *'Madame X'* by the crew. The Stirling was initially given the 622 Squadron code letters of GI-X and Marsh and crew were promulgated on the battle order for 10/11th August to attack the city of Nuremberg, a round trip of seven hours and fifteen minutes. Due to the arrival of two more Stirlings on the 12th and 14th August, BK816 was assigned the new squadron code letters of GI-B, and so it was on the night of 12th August Flight Sergeant Marsh and crew took the aircraft to bomb Turin in Italy.

On 16/17th August the crew took the same Stirling to attack Turin again and Marsh had trouble en route gaining the required height out of their aircraft to fly over the Alps. With the Alps successfully negotiated, the crew met with little resistance from the cities defenses. Intelligence reports suggested that the Fiat motor works was damaged delaying production.

It was no great surprise to F/Sgt Marsh and crew when it was announced at the briefing on the evening of 23rd August that the target for that night would be Berlin. The crew had test flown their aircraft earlier in the day and the ground crew had advised them that it would be a maximum effort deep into the enemy heartland. Flight Sergeant Marsh gradually coaxed the Stirling up to an operational height of 14,000 ft en route to the target. The crew followed a direct course to thirty miles south of Berlin, and then turned to the north for the run in and bomb. The return journey was programmed to take them home via the Baltic, south across Denmark and across the North Sea. The journey to the target had been plagued with minor problems associated with venturing this deep into Germany. As the crew came to the turning point the 'Pathfinder' marking flares were clear to see. The enemy's response was instant with hundreds of searchlights being switched on simultaneously turning night into day in an instant, there was no place to hide from the probing beams. The wireless operator, Sergeant George Wright, remembers vividly the utter fear of being exposed in the night sky to the German night fighters who were lurking ominously amongst the dancing searchlights, ready to pounce on a bomber caught in the probing lights.

The Stirling released its heavy load of bombs at just after midnight with Flight Sergeant Bailey calling 'bombs gone' over the intercom. Almost simultaneously, a Ju88 came in and opened fire from 500 yards taking the whole crew by surprise. The gunners, Flight Lieutenant Berry and Sgt Hynham, opened fire instinctively hitting the night fighter several times claiming a 'probable' kill in the process. F/Sgt Marsh flung the Stirling bomber into evasive action in one instinctive movement plummeting several thousand feet in an attempt to avoid further night fighter attention.

Flight Lieutenant Berry had only just arrived on the unit and volunteered to deputize for the crew's usual mid upper gunner, Sgt. Smith who had been sent to his sick bed by the Medical Officer. Another night fighter attacked caused the controls of the Stirling to become unresponsive and seriously wounded F/Sgt Marsh in the pilot's seat. The force of the cannon shells were equivalent to an almighty blow, which hit him with full force almost rendering him unconscious. The cannon shells had caused a large hole at the top of his leg, severing his sciatic nerve. Another shell passed

On the right in this photograph is F/Sgt Gil Marsh who was severely wounded by a night fighter over Berlin on 23/24th August 1943. His wounds were so severe that he would not fly again operationally. On the left of the photograph is Sgt Hynham the rear gunner who fired off several bursts at the attacking Ju88. *Courtesy of George Wright.*

Unidentified 622 Squadron Short Stirling increases engine power with full brakes applied ready for take-off. C4017 *Courtesy of IWM.*

through his right hip shattering the bone. Marsh lost consciousness momentarily and when he came around he found the Stirling in a dive, plummeting from 12,000 to 1,500ft. Fighting frantically to pull the aircraft out of the dive, Marsh managed to pull it out and climbed back to 4,000ft, as the tail plane and elevators had all been severely damaged.

F/Sgt Marsh called to his bomb aimer, 'Jack' Bailey for help, but there was no response. During the evasive action, Bailey had been thrown around the aircraft and hit his head, knocking him unconscious for a while. There had been no warning of the attack and therefore no time to get strapped in. Marsh needed help desperately and he called upon the navigator, Pilot Officer Richards for assistance. Richards's aircrew training had involved the basics of piloting an aircraft and between him and Marsh they were able to steady the aircraft and set course for the Baltic. Sgt Meaburn, the flight engineer evaluated the situation and found the port engine pressure had gone. In addition, the engines were overheating and could have caught fire at any moment. Marsh was informed of the situation and in the confusion; he feathered the port inner engine by mistake. When they tried to restart it, the blowback through the exhaust manifold lit up the night sky with flames, so they carried on with three engines.

F/Sgt Marsh was taken out of his seat; he was in a poor state having lost a lot of blood. It was then that Jack Bailey, having regained consciousness, took over the pilot's seat. The navigator, P/O Richards was unsure of their position and instructed George Wright the wireless operator, to obtain a 'fix', which he duly did via a SOS signal. As they reached the coast of Denmark, some flak ships opened fire so Marsh ordered Bailey to turn away and fly further north before crossing the Danish coast. When they got out over the sea Bailey and Sgt Meaburn managed to get the fourth engine going aiding the flight home. Bailey was fine flying the Stirling straight and level, however he was concerned about putting the Stirling on terra firma. An assessment on F/Sgt Marsh soon established that he was too ill to be pushed out by parachute, therefore the only option available was for Marsh to remain on board whilst Bailey attempted to land. The English coast appeared and a course was set for Mildenhall. The airfield was informed of the predicament on board and crash crews were brought to readiness. The crew decided to move Sgt Marsh to the rear door, but he had lost copious amounts of blood by this time and he was very ill indeed. Gil Marsh kept crying out for water to quench his thirst and George Wright gathered together all the crew's flying rations and gave them to Marsh. Any further movement could be life threatening, so he was left in the forward section of the aircraft. All the escape hatches were opened in readiness for a quick exit.

Sgt J.C. Bailey RCAF, seen here on the left in the photograph with Sgt G.Wright W/op. The magnitude of Bailey's actions of bringing home and landing the stricken bomber were recognized when he was awarded an immediate Conspicuous Gallantry Medal. Only 110 were awarded to aircrew throughout the war. *Courtesy of George Wright.*

F/Sgt Marsh had no recollection of the landing due to the fact that his body had gone into shock at this stage. However he does recall that Jack Bailey had been on a pilot course but failed the exams, and the navigator had a similar experience. Jack Bailey made a perfect landing and all were safe. Later inspection of the Stirling showed only 75 gallons of fuel left in the tanks. The scenario could have gone either way, but due to the endeavors of Jack Bailey and the other members of the crew; they all survived to fight another day. Jack Bailey was immediately recommended for a well-deserved award of the Conspicuous Gallantry Medal on 25th August 1943.

F/Sgt Marsh did not return to operational flying, his injuries were too severe; instead he was posted to a training unit teaching aircrew the idiosyncrasies of the link trainer. F/Lt Berry would become the squadron's 'Gunnery Leader' and be involved with another incident on 31st/1st June 1944 when he was again a stand in gunner in the crew of F/Lt Randall attacking the railway yards at Trappes. On the return journey a Junkers 88 night fighter attacked the Lancaster and F/Lt Berry was blown out of his turret as the bomber exploded. He was the only survivor, successfully evading back to 622 Squadron and the award of a D.F.C.

The events of 21st August over Berlin were traumatic for the crew and endemic to all bomber squadrons at this juncture of the air war. The remaining crew were without a pilot, so Flying Officer Kenneth Stoddart was posted into Mildenhall on 30th August 1943 to join the depleted crew. Ken Stoddart was an amenable and assured character whose skill as a pilot would be demonstrated to the extreme before his tour of operations was complete.

It was customary on arrival to an operational squadron for the pilot to undertake a mission as a second pilot. Therefore, on 8th September F/O Stoddart boarded Short Stirling EF126, GI-Q as the second pilot to Wing Commander Gibson, with their objective to bomb the German coastal gun positions at Boulogne. The arrival of Ken Stoddart as pilot was not the only change to the original crew. The bomb aimer position was now assigned to Pilot Officer Ashton with Jack Bailey CGM posted to Canada to undertake pilot training as acclaim for his actions over Berlin and his subsequent award of the CGM, a prestigious award indeed. Flying Officer Burrows RNZAF joined the crew in the navigator's position.

The Short Stirling bomber was an ideal aircraft to drop mines in shipping areas around the German fortified costal areas. Interspersed with missions into the Ruhr Valley, were missions to drop anti-shipping mines to counteract the threat from German warships and submarines. The Royal Air Force was immensely successful at destroying enemy shipping. Official figures suggest

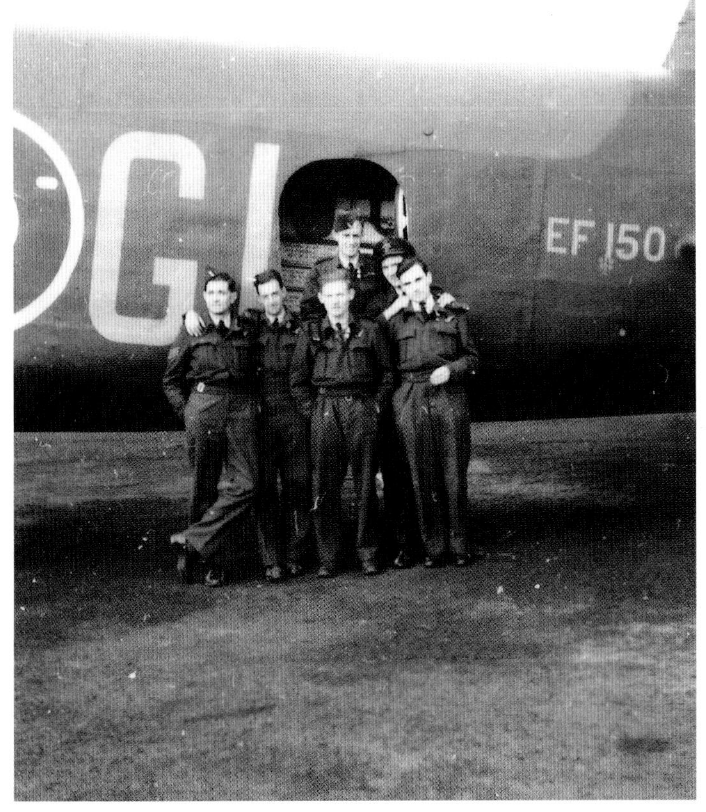

The reformed crew of F/O Stoddart. L-R: Sgt Hyman (R/G), Sgt Smith (MUG), Sgt Meaburn (F/E), P/O Ashton (B/A), F/O Burrows (Nav).Standing to the rear is F/O Stoddart. When this photograph was taken George Wright (W/op) was being interviewed regarding the Berlin mission by AVM Don Bennett who formed the Pathfinders. On hearing of the crew's exploits on that night, Bennett immediately commissioned George Wright to Pilot Officer.The 'Stirling' in the photo is GI-E, EF150 which was lost on the night of 22/23rd November 1943, shot down by flak over Hanover. F/Lt Denham & crew parachuted into captivity. *Courtesy of George Wright*

that Bomber Command laid mines up and down the shores of Europe preventing enemy shipping leaving harbors. In total approximately 759 German vessels of all types were sunk (figures supplied by the Enemy Shipping Assessment Committee).

The crew were promulgated on the battle order on 18th September for the first time as a complete crew. The target was Hanover and they were assigned 'Stirling' BK816, GI-B, the same 'stirling' that they brought home from Berlin on that fateful night. The omens were not good, new pilot, same aircraft and a trip deep into Germany's Ruhr Valley. The crew's apprehension was justified when the aircraft suffered an engine failure en route to the target forcing them to bomb the secondary target of Emden and return on three engines.

A series of further missions followed without incident and Flying Officer Stoddart was recognized for his abilities by being promoted to Flight Lieutenant. Manheim was the target on the night of 23rd September and another two mining missions followed to the Frisians Isles on 27th and again on 7th October. The following evening saw a return to the Ruhr Valley with the target being the industrial heart of Bremen a round trip of three hours and forty minutes in 'Stirling' EF128, GI-D. Unbeknownst to the crew, their final mission in the Short Stirling bomber took place on 6th November '43 when they dropped mines along the Baltic coast in EF150, GI-E.

The catalyst for the withdrawal of 'Stirlings' from front line service was the Berlin raid on the night of 22/23rd November 1943 when fifty Stirlings were part of the bomber force and 10% of those were lost. ACM Harris knew that the Stirling losses could not be sustained and relegated the Stirling to secondary roles. The Short Stirlings replacement was the superb Avro Lancaster that had been introduced to operational squadrons during 1943 and surpassed all expectations. The superlatives associated with the Lancaster are too numerous to mention in this story however, perhaps the most qualified person to heap praise on the Lancaster was the Commander in Chief of Bomber Command, ACM Arthur Harris. In a letter to the Lancaster production team at Avro, Harris put into words the sentiments of every aircrew member:

> "As the user of the Lancaster during the last three and a half years of bitter, unrelenting warfare, I would say this to those who placed that shining sword in our hands: Without your genius and your effort, we would not have prevailed- the Lancaster was the greatest single factor in winning the war."
>
> Sir Arthur Harris.
> Chief of Bomber Command

With the Short Stirling now relegated to secondary duties, 622 Squadron commenced the process of converting to the Avro Lancaster with ground lectures and familiarization visits to other

Pilot Officer George Wright. *Courtesy of George Wright*

3 Group squadrons locally. At around the middle of December the first Lancasters began to arrive at Mildenhall and equip both squadrons. The first Lancaster to arrive on 622 was W4163, a veteran deployed from another squadron. It was common practice for new squadrons to receive other squadrons' cast offs.

On New Year's day the last of the squadrons' Stirlings were flown out to commence duties at Operational Training Units and special operations units. The business of working up to operational status continued but was hindered by the severe winter weather, which brought a high degree of snow and frost to the airfield. The Lancaster was immediately thrust into operations and the Stoddart crew experienced a baptism of fire in the new aircraft on the night of 28th January 1944. The crew's first mission was to Berlin in Lancaster JA876, GI-E and the crew successfully navigated there and back whilst contending with the considerable flak and fighter defenses. Berlin was again the target on 15th February in the same aircraft and the crew returned in tact, although their resolve was again tested against Berlin's defenses.

During March 1944 the crew attacked Stuttgart twice (1st & 15th) and a single mission to Frankfurt on the 22ndMarch. April commenced with the usual missions into the German industrial Ruhr interspersed with shorter trips into France. The invasion of Normandy was growing nearer and Arthur Harris wanted the supply routes to the German front lines seriously disrupted. For the crews of Bomber Command the missions to France were a welcome relief from excursions to the heavily defended cities of Germany. However, the German night fighter force was based in France and it could deploy numerous fighters every night to attack the bombers. The night fighters had become very adept at hunting down the bombers, they were equipped with the latest radar detection devices and the 'Himmelbett' system of vectoring night fighters was proving very successful. The night fighters had the advantage over the heavily laden bombers. They would approach from underneath the bombers so that the bomber was silhouetted against the night sky. In their turrets looking down, the gunners' view was nothing but pitch-blackness. The only chance a gunner had of spotting a night fighter was if it was reflected against the searchlights over the target.

F/Lt Stoddart DFC sits in the rear entrance door of 'Stirling' GI-L, EH921 in late 1943. The original crew completed 12 missions in Short Stirling bombers with F/Lt Stoddart being the pilot on 7 of those missions. The crew commenced missions in the Avro Lancaster from January 1944. *Courtesy of George Wright*

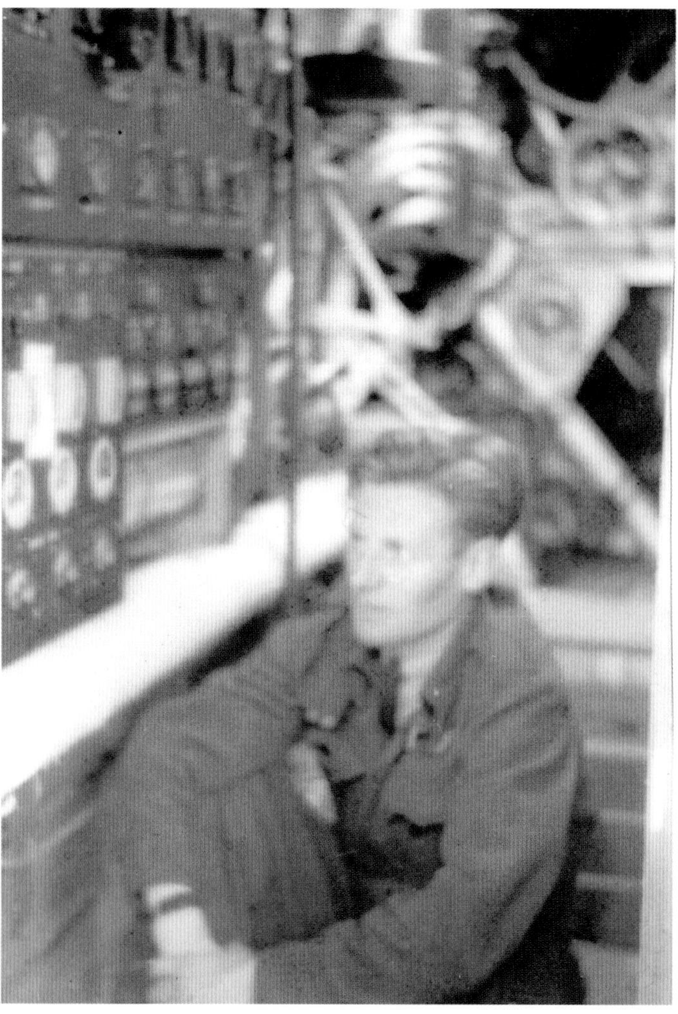

Sgt Meaburn the flight engineer, monitors the controls and settings of the Short Stirling. The flight engineer's duties were to monitor the boast and fuel flow from the four Bristol Hercules engines and switch fuel tanks once empty. *Courtesy of George Wright*

On the night of 10th April the crew supported the impending invasion force by bombing the railway yards at Laon in France, although raid reports suggested the damage was quickly repaired by the Germans. A return to Germany was on the cards on the night of 11th April when a large force of aircraft of all descriptions attacked Aachen's industrial manufacturing areas. Impressive results were reported of the bombing of the railway yards at Rouen on 18th April, although the 'Stoddart' crew reported that the Pathfinder force marking appeared scattered. Subsequently the haze over the target made bombing difficult. The crew took part in a large scale attack on Karlsruhe on the night of 24/25th April and returned without incident to a welcome tot of rum and a warm bed.

The crew was now counting down to their end of tour target of thirty missions. Although they were assured of each other's abilities, they never afforded themselves the luxury of relaxing whilst flying. This alertness to duty was tested to the full on the night of 26th April when they lifted Lancaster IM491, GI-E off the runway at Mildenhall destined for Essen. The new 'Signals Leader', F/Lt Noonan RNZAF who had just arrived on the squadron, covered George Wright's position as wireless operator. By this time, all on the squadron held George Wright in high esteem and he was given the task of 'Signal leader' for the Essen raid. The role involved briefing the wireless operators for the night's mission and offering advice and guidance to inexperienced crews.

The route to Essen was relatively uneventful for the crew minus their usual wireless operator. However, it was no time to relax and the crew witnessed several combats, obviously from night fighter activity. The crew's navigational log recorded the crew witnessed five aircraft on fire and tumbling to earth. F/Lt Stoddart checked his final course with navigator F/O Burrows and checked that the bomb aimer, P/O Ashton was making final adjustments to his bomb release gear. Shortly before bomb release time, a Ju88 night fighter attacked the Lancaster without being spotted by the gunners. The Ju88 lit up the night sky with his cannon tracer shells and peppered the Lancaster along the fuselage. The mid upper gunner, Sgt Smith returned fire instinctively but recorded no hits on the night fighter. The smell of cordite filled the Lancaster and F/Lt Stoddart threw the aircraft into a corkscrew maneuver in an attempt to lose the fighter. The maneuver worked and the crew all reported in from their respective workstations, except the rear gunner. The wireless operator was sent back to check on the rear gunner. The Lancaster had suffered some damage but responded to the controls.

F/Lt Noonan reported to the skipper that the night fighter's bullets had severed the hydraulics to the rear turret and cut the intercom link. With the damage appraised, the crew jettisoned the bomb load and nursed the damaged bomber back to Mildenhall. The target area over Essen was full of night fighter activity and the decision to continue and bomb the target with a u/s rear turret was foolhardy and extremely dangerous.

L-R: S/Ldr L.E. Chapman W/AG, F/Lt Signals Leader DFC DFM (name unknown) P/O George Wright, S/Ldr Markins W/AG. This photograph was taken when P/O Wright was given the opportunity to become the squadron's 'signals leader' in April 1944. *Courtesy of George Wright*

With P/O Wright reinstated to the crew, they were promulgated on the battle order to attack Friedrichshafen, a site manufacturing engines and gearboxes for German tanks. Compared to the Essen mission, the trip was relatively uneventful although the night fighter activity was intense and the crew were apprehensive throughout. Official figures show that eighteen Lancasters fell victim to night fighters during the raid. On 19th May, the railway yards at Le Mans were successfully bombed and on the 21st May the crew undertook their final mission of their tour when they attacked Duisberg as part of a force of 510 Lancasters.

With the required numbers of operations completed, the crew were assigned to training duties which coincided with the good news that F/Lt Stoddart had been awarded the Distinguished Flying Cross. For George Wright tour completion was something of a relief. He was glad that the danger had passed for the immediate future and he looked forward to a period of training at No.12 OTU. The crew were now firm friends and the bond between them would last a lifetime. After his lucky escape over Berlin in late 1943 George Wright never expected to complete his tour of operations, he knew the dangers that lay ahead and that the odds of coming through were no better than 50/50. What he had not factored in to his thoughts was the resilience and fortitude of his crew and the exceptional ability of his pilot. The crew had survived through the most dangerous period of the bomber campaign when the German night fighter force and flak defenses were at their most effective. A lesser crew would surely have perished!

3

Esprit de Corps

Pilot: F/Lt R.T. Hussey D.F.C
Nav: F/O R.L. Simpson RAAF, D.F.C
B/A: F/Sgt G.C. Dalton RAAF
W/op: F/Sgt R. May
MUG: Sgt C. O'Connor
R/G: Sgt G. Potter
F/E: Sgt R. Hand

Glyn Potter answered the call to arms in November 1940 when he walked into a recruitment office in Cardiff. Due to a backlog of prospective aircrew candidates, he was referred to the Air Training Corps to become accustomed to Royal Air Force practice and procedures. In September 1941, Glyn received his medical and 'call up' papers and after numerous literacy and numerical tests, he achieved an above average marking. Glyn always wanted to be a pilot however, the waiting list for the training was of considerable length, therefore Glyn decided to take the fast track to flying and he chose to become an air gunner. Eventually he was sent to Paignton in Devon to commence his RAF life in earnest. Whilst at Paignton Glyn was taught the necessary discipline and physical fitness disciplines for him to progress in the RAF and he also commenced classroom lessons on Morse code and aircraft mechanical systems.

Glyn was now sporting a white flash in his forage cap signifying aircrew under training and it was with a sense of pride that he reported to No.14 Initial Training Wing at Bridlington on the Yorkshire coast to commence his gunnery training. Initially, the role of the air gunner was an amalgamation with other aircrew trades and not given the recognition it deserved. The early war daylight bombing campaign taught Bomber Command a lesson with the nimble Luftwaffe fighters ripping the bombers out of the sky with far superior armaments and cannons. Through the lessons learnt from the early war years, the role of the air gunner changed from aggressor to the defender of an aircraft. Primarily the air gunner was there to protect the bomber and act as an early warning system to the pilot so that he could take evasive action such as the 'corkscrew' maneuver. The skillful air gunner soon established almost an extrasensory perception with the pilot and saved many crews from being shot down with his quick reactions.

The air gunner was recognized as a specialist and graduated with the rank of sergeant. The intensive air gunnery training included a great deal of ground lectures on the theory of gunnery and the hands on approach of stripping a machine gun down and reassembling it blindfold. Interspersed throughout the course were aircraft recognition and the theory of bullet trajectory. The syllabus also covered basic armament, Morse code and the unpleasant mathematic classes mixed in. By far the most enjoyable aspect of the training for the majority of the candidates was the live firing exercises. Students were issued with a drum of ammunition that contained several hundred rounds of bullets dipped in paint; each student was given 200 rounds each in his designated color so that his score could be evaluated. The drums of bullets were loaded into the aircraft's machine gun turret. The objective was to fire rounds into a drogue being towed by another aircraft and score as many direct hits as possible. Glyn was classified as an average gunner at the conclusion of the course, a status that he was proud to achieve considering the hurdles that he had to surpass.

The next stage of Sergeant Potter's training took him to No.12 Operational Training Unit at Chipping Warden near Oxon in May 1944. It was here that he teamed up with his crew in the usual RAF method of putting the exact numbers of aircrew designations into a room and telling them to come out as a full crew.

Flying Officer Reginald Hussey from Surrey chose his crew well and selected an Australian from Sydney, Ross Simpson to be his navigator and Gordon Dalton a fellow Australian from Melbourne to be his bomb aimer. The wireless operator was Roy May from Bath and the two gunners were Welshmen, the mid upper gunner was Cecil O'Connor and the rear gunner was Glyn Potter. Finally, John Hand, a Scotsman from Edinburgh occupied the flight engineer's position. The crew developed an immediate affinity with each other and became firm friends.

The role of the OTUs was to continue specialist training and to convert aircrew to the aircraft that they would take to war. Throughout the course trainee aircrew learned to become proficient in their respective roles which prepared them for life on an operational squadron. The pilot was subjected to a series of flights on instruments by day and night and the navigator was expected to reach an acceptable level of navigation and wireless operation. The duration of the course was 8 weeks and included a minimum of 32 flying hours. The gunnery content was a repeat of the live air firing exercises that Glyn Potter endured whilst at Bridlington.

The standard course content covered a mixture of the following:

Link trainer experience including bombing techniques.
Gunnery combat maneuvers, air to-air firing, fighter affiliation
Bombing. High level bombing by day and night, bombing on cross-countries.
Navigation. Cross countries including wireless fixes.
Operational training. Night and day exercises. Drills; dinghy & parachute practice, fire, oxygen, crash drills.

Battle Ready

With the crew's training complete, they eagerly awaited news of an operational posting. They believed in each other's ability and their reliance on each other would be essential to come through 30 operations with Bomber Command. Eventually Flying Officer Hussey informed the crew that they had been posted to RAF Mildenhall in Suffolk an essential part of 3 Group Bomber Command. In late September 1944, the crew arrived at the gatehouse at RAF Mildenhall, a pre-war station with a proud heritage.

On arrival, Flying Officer Hussey and crew were allocated to 'B' flight with the Officers amongst them moving into Officers quarters and the NCOs moving into peacetime married quarters. The first seven days concentrated on more intensive training starting with fighter affiliation, air tests and practice bombing runs whilst fully laden. In addition, the crew endured a series of loaded climbs with dummy bombs that were dropped in the North Sea. Finally, several practice flights were undertaken in the art of formation flying.

The crew were now considered ready to commence operational flying which meant flying missions against the enemy involving every ounce of their training to be utilized if they were to survive a 30 mission tour of operations. It was customary for the pilot to complete a second 'dickey' trip with an experienced pilot before he would take his own crew into action. F/O Hussey returned from this trip to a barrage of questions from the crew who were eager to hear his feedback.

On 3rd October 1944 the crew was promulgated on the battle order for the first time. The target was significant to the war effort and history would consider the operation essential to the Allied armies' progression in defeating the Germans. The crew attended briefing to be told that the target was the sea wall at Walcheren Island on the Dutch coast. Tactically the port of Antwerp was a prized target for the Allies and the advantage gained by its capture from the hands of the Germans would be infinite. Replenishing the troops with food and munitions was a growing concern and one that was holding up inevitable defeat for the enemy. The lack of a strategically placed sea port meant that supplying the front line troops was down to the Air Force. Delivering the essential supplies was an arduous task which diverted resources away from important other Air Force directives. The consensus decision by all the Allied Commanders was to focus on opening up a supply port closer to the front lines.

The port of Antwerp is in an ideal location and presented an opportunity to address the Allies' dilemma. Unfortunately after Antwerp was captured it was still relatively useless to the Allies due to the Island of Walcheren still being occupied by a strong German Garrison of troops and their artillery. Walcheren is situated at the mouth of the river Scheldt and it was considered to be a 'fortress' by Hitler who ordered his troops to fight to the death in the defense of the Island; such was the strategic benefit to whoever was the occupier.

The task of capturing Walcheren and clearing the anti-shipping mines from the river Scheldt would be no mean feat and an assault by sea would surely fail due to the entrenched German troops. After considerable deliberations the Allied Supreme Commander General Eisenhower, called upon Bomber Command to pave the way for a concerted Allied land and sea assault.

Sgt C.O' Connor, mid upper gunner. *Courtesy of Glyn Potter.*

Sgt R. May, wireless operator. *Courtesy of Glyn Potter.*

Sgt G. Potter, rear gunner. *Courtesy of Glyn Potter.*

F/O R. Hussey D.F.C., pilot. *Courtesy of Glyn Potter.*

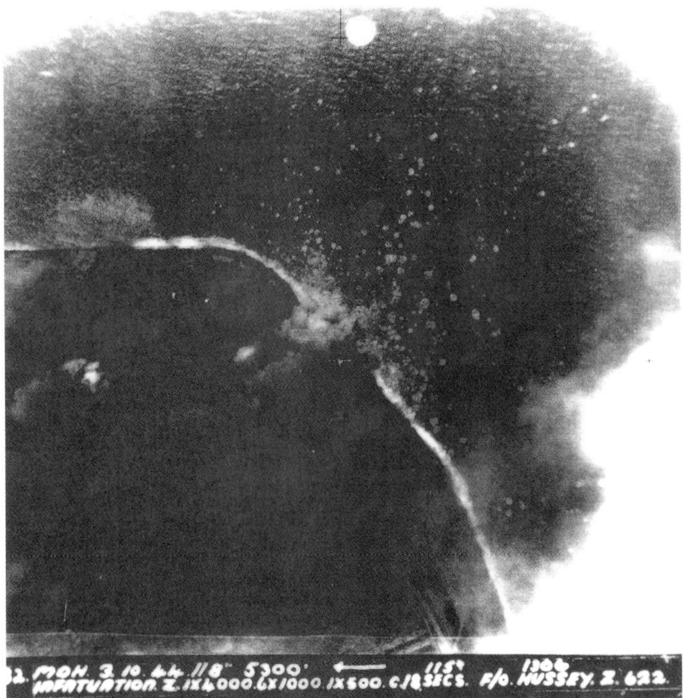

Bombing photograph taken by the crew on 3rd October whilst attacking the sea wall at Walcheren. The photograph clearly shows that the bomb aimer, F/O Dalton was spot on. The Lancaster utilized on the mission was HK615, GI-Z. *Courtesy of Glyn Potter.*

Walcheren Island is unique with its saucer shape and rim consisting of a bank of high sand dunes to keep out the North Sea. Once over the extremities the land is flat and lying below sea level. It was decided that the dyke near Westkapelle had to be breached to allow the North Sea to flood the Island and make it practically impossible for the Germans to move their soldiers and equipment around.

On the afternoon of 3rd October 1944, 252 Lancasters (12 from 622 Sqdn) and mosquito bombers took off to attack the sea wall at Westkapelle. On approaching the target the aircrew received very little anti-aircraft defenses and attacked in waves of thirty bombers. Flight Lieutenant Hussey and crew were flying in HK615,GI-Z as a part of the first wave of bombers over the target. F/Sgt Dalton RAAF in the bomb aimer's position had a perfect view of the target and released his bombs at 5,300ft resulting in a direct hit and recoded for posterity on the crew's bomb photograph.

Bombing in daylight can be extremely accurate and so it proved on this mission, the sea wall was breached to such an extent that the sea burst through with tremendous force flooding the Island and causing considerable disruption to the German defenses. The enemy did not surrender immediately; in fact Bomber Command would have to pay the Island a few more visits before the enemy capitulated.

A recent photograph of Walcheren Island clearly shows the magnitude of the bombers' task to breach the sea wall. *Courtesy of Glyn Potter.*

Sgt Potter makes his final preparations to the rear turret shortly before departing on a deep penetration raid into the Ruhr Valley in late 1944. *Courtesy of Glyn Potter.*

After successfully bombing the target a sense of euphoria spread throughout the crew. With the adrenalin still flowing through their veins, Flying Officer Hussey dropped the Lancaster down to 100 feet where the gunners could have some fun. Glyn Potter sat in the rear turret, strafing the German troop positions until almost all of his ammunition was expended. At the debriefing Sgt Potter was chastised by F/Lt Berry the squadron's Gunnery Leader who emphasized that a gunner's responsibility was to defend the aircraft from attack, not use up all the ammunition leaving the aircraft vulnerable to fighter attack on the return journey.

The Supreme Commander had returned to the task set out in the Casablanca Directive. The contribution made by Bomber Command to the Allied invasion and subsequent support of the land forces had been immense. By early August, the Allied forces were firmly lodged on the Continent and on their way to Brussels slowly pushing the Nazi war machine back into Germany. Lord Portal and the combined chiefs of staff agreed that the new objective would be to progressively destroy the German military, industrial and economic systems. Therefore, the German oil, ball bearing and motor transport industries would become priority targets once more.

Operations continued thick and fast for the crew and during October 1944 they attacked, Dortmund, Bonn, Stuttgart, Essen (twice) and Bottrop, all industrial targets situated deep in the Ruhr Valley and very heavily defended. During November Bomber Command called for concentrated daylight attacks on oil installations with the intention of starving the German war machine of vital fuel. Therefore the 'Hussey' crew attacked the oil installations at Homberg (2/11/44) Solingen twice (4/5th 11/44) and Castrop Rauxel on 11th November.

The Allied army advance into Germany allowed G/H radar stations to be erected on the continent. Three Group Bomber Command had been designated to specialize in the use of G/H radar bombing and the 3 Group squadrons utilized the device to full effect on 18th October 1944 to bomb the industrial city of Bonn. The radar device worked by receiving signals from two ground stations to accurately plot the aircraft's position. The advantage of G/H was the fact that several aircraft could use the device at the same time without interference. A large number of attacks that used G/H were conducted in daylight and a certain number of Lancasters within a squadron would be fitted with the device with their tail rudder painted to distinguish them. These selected aircraft would lead three to four other aircraft to the target and when they released their bombs, the others would follow suit.

November merged into December and at the beginning of the month the 'Hussey' crew had completed eighteen missions and they had achieved considerable experience. Sergeant Glyn Potter in the rear turret position was starting to believe that the crew could complete the full thirty missions required to become 'tour expired'. The rear turret was the loneliest place in the sky, and the rear gunner would be cocooned in his small space away and most vulnerable to fighter attack. Concentration whilst searching the night sky was essential if Glyn was to warn the skipper of an approaching fighter and this task was made all the more difficult by the monotony of the engine drone. For long periods, the only sound he could hear above the engines was the hiss of the oxygen being fed to his facemask. The rear turret was fitted with four .303 Browning machine guns with an effective range of 300 yards

Photograph taken by the crew en route to Solingen on 4th November 1944. There were fireworks when the crews Lancaster (HK617, GI-Y) received a direct hit from flak guns. *Courtesy of Glyn Potter.*

Serial No. ....190. 1st Battle Order for 5th Nov 1944. No. 622 Squadron.

A/C NO.	LETTER.	CAPTAIN & 2ND PILOT	NAV. & W/OPERATOR.	A/B & M.U.GUNNER.	R/GUNNER & F/ENGINEER.
HK.621	G.	F/O Curling	F/S. Murdin. W.O. Bisbop	F/S Middleditch Sgt. Robinson. & F/S McRae	Sgt. Wallace. Sgt. White.
NN.709	H.	F/Lt. Armitstead.	F/S Brewster Sgt. Foulkes.	Sgt. Daniels Sgt. Keylock	Sgt. Borne. Sgt. Peck.
LL.885	J.	F/O Peck	F/S Barchard. F/O Cargill	F/O Long. Sgt. Brisey	Sgt. Pudney. Sgt. Bowyer.
PD.239	K.	F/S Francis	F/S Steeden Sgt. Kelly	Sgt. Traylen Sgt. Baxter	F/S Stott. Sgt. Soames.
HK.645	Z.	F/O Thomson	F/S Ward. W.O. Aland.	F/S Malley Sgt. Smith.	Sgt. Woolloff. Sgt. Boulton.
HK.623	F.	F/O Phillips	Sgt. Lowry F/S Hopewell.	Sgt. Smart Sgt. Morgan	Sgt. York. Sgt. Barber.
HK.628	X.	F/S Waigh	F/O Briggs F/O Morrison	F/O Lister Sgt. Simmons.	Sgt. Mitchell. Sgt. Evans.
HK.644	D.	F/O Barnett	Sgt. Grimsey F/S Sullivan	F/O Harditch Sgt. Staplehurst	F/S Nicholls. Sgt. Murrell.
PD.225	C.	F/O Baxter	Sgt. Parsons Sgt. Brooker	F/S Hopkinson Sgt. Smith. Gun.445	Sgt. Ramsey. Sgt. Rossiter.
DM.288	V.	F/S Rudenko	F/S Mckeown Sgt. Vollmer.	Sgt. Sleigh Sgt. Syvelos	F/S Ross. Sgt. Lucas-Garner.
HK.646	M.	F/S Thomas.	F/O Berry Sgt. Charlesworth	F/S Gambell. Sgt. Kingston	Sgt. Davies. Sgt. Ralph.
PA.164	P.	F/O Campbell.	Sgt. Galt. F/S Hozzard.	F/S Shepley Sgt. Fallows.	Sgt. Hickling. Sgt. Hill.
HK.614	R.	F/O Richards.	F/S Kidd Sgt. Doyle	F/O Mildren Sgt. Pappe	Sgt. Nicholson. Sgt. Martin.
HK.616	W.	F/Lt. Woods.	F/S Groat. Sgt. Johnson	Sgt. Taylor Sgt. Henderson & W/O Davis.	Sgt. Gantley. Sgt. Cooney.
HK.617	Y.	F/O Hussey	F/O Simpson Sgt. May	F/S Dalton Sgt. O'Connor.	Sgt. Potter. Sgt. Hand.
PD.332	N.	P/O Gilmore.	F/O Tomsett F/S Austin	F/S O'Loughlin Sgt. Davies.	Sgt. Firth. Sgt. Davidson.
LM.449	T.	F/O Richards.	F/O Isbell. F/S Martin	F/O Carter Sgt. Brierley	Sgt. Campbell. Sgt. Burnard.

Rations to be collected by F/Commanders and distributed to aircraft.

Briefing Meal 0715
Nav. 0745
Main 0815
Trans. 0830.

GUARD ROOM TO COMMENCE EARLY CALLS 0600 hours.

(Sgd) G.K. Buckingham W/Cdr.
Commanding No. 622 Squadron.

W/C Buckingham F/Lt. Allen. F/Lt. Dean. F/L Nicholl F/Lt. Noonan F/Lt. Middleton F/Lt. Berry F/Lt. [illegible]

Battle order for the mission to Solingen oil installation on 5th November 1944. F/O Hussey has been assigned Lancaster HK617, GI-Y. The crew would complete nine missions in this particular aircraft. *Author's Collection.*

Sgt Glyn Potter loads his ammunition into the Browning .303 machine guns prior to a daylight mission to Cologne on 27th November 1944. Due to an engine failure that cut off his electrically heated suit, he suffered frostbite and was hospitalized. *Courtesy of Glyn Potter.*

therefore the principal role of the gunners was to warn of enemy attack. To aid night vision rear gunners removed the small Perspex panel in front of their view, and Glyn Potter was no different in this respect. The temperature in the rear turret would go down to well below sub zero and the gunner would take some solace from his electrically heated suit, which offered a small degree of warmth.

On 27th November the crew attacked the German city of Cologne and their allotted Lancaster NG299, GI-O had a port inner engine failure en route to the target. The crew knew that a failed engine would mean that they would fall behind the Bomber stream and become vulnerable to German night fighters however, the crew made the consensus decision to press on to the target. The port inner engine operated the electrical system which sent warm air to the rear gunner's heated suit and subsequently Glyn Potter endured the rest of the mission in extremely cold temperatures. On arrival back at base, Sgt Potter was in a poor condition and he was sent to hospital suffering from frostbite.

Gathered intelligence from previous missions alerted the crews of Bomber Command to the latest technology deployed by the German night fighters. By far the most successful method of attack for the night fighter was to attack from underneath a bomber and approach from out of the darkness. The rear gunner would see nothing but darkness below unless the searchlights and explosions over the target silhouetted an approaching fighter. It was here that the night fighter had the advantage over the bombers. Looking up into the night sky a bomber would be visible against the moonlight and the slightly lighter sky making a stealthy approach plausible. The most deadly weapon deployed by the night fighters was an upward firing gun configuration that comprised two cannons known as 'Schräge Musik'. The night fighter would position itself under the bomber after being guided in by its sophisticated radar detection system. Once in position underneath the bomber, the gunner would aim for the bombers wings which were full of aviation fuel and quickly caught alight, ultimately causing the destruction of the bomber.

The railway yards at Siegen were the target for the crew on 15th December and they lifted off the runway at Mildenhall in NG299, GI-O at 11:20 hours. It was customary at this stage of the war for a fighter escort to join the bombers as they approached the enemy coast, but on this occasion, the fog closed in over England and the Mustang fighter escort could not take off. The crews received the radio communication to abort the mission and they turned for home setting course for the designated bomb dump zone fifty miles south of Beachy Head in the English Channel. Shortly after receiving the order to abort the mission, Flying Officer Hussey was taken ill rendering him unable to fly the aircraft. The obvious replacement was Flight Sergeant Dalton the bomb aimer who had some experience of flying Lancasters during his training. Under guidance from the pilot, Dalton successfully flew the Lancaster to the bomb dump zone and back to base whilst completing a relatively good landing. Due to the mission being aborted the usual debriefing was not conducted and the exploits of F/Sgt Dalton were not officially reported which may be the reason that he did not receive a well deserved gallantry medal. Flying Officer Hussey filed a report to the base commander recommending him for a medal however, it never materialized.

The 15th December was eventful for another reason that may explain the disappearance of the renowned American bandleader, Glen Miller. Major Glen Miller boarded a Noorduyn 'Norseman' C-64 airplane bound for Paris and took off never to be seen again. Several theories have been put forward to explain his disappearance however; the most plausible one is that he flew under the weight of 100,000 incendiary bombs being jettisoned by returning bombers from the aborted Siegen raid. Eyewitness reports from 3 Group Bomber Command crews state that they saw an aircraft that fitted the description of Miller's plane struck by overhead bombs, which crashed into the sea. In later years, researchers placed Miller's plane on the exact course and place as the eyewitness accounts of

Lancaster NG299, GI-O depicted on the dispersal point at RAF Mildenhall in late 1944. This particular aircraft became the regular aircraft for the 'Hussey' crew. *Courtesy of B.O' Connor.*

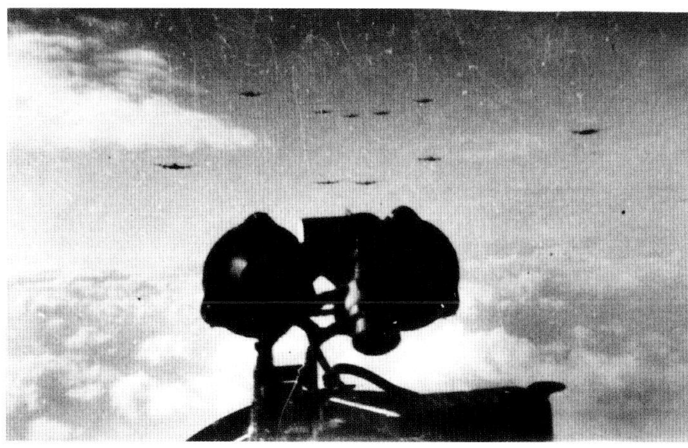

En route to the target during a daylight mission in late 1944. This photograph was taken from the bomb aimer's position in NG299, GI-O. *Courtesy of B. O' Connor.*

those crews disposing of their bombs that day, they have no doubt that the reason for Glen Miller's demise was from falling bombs.

Speculation will continue to surround his death, but there can be no doubt that the world lost a fine musician and icon of American swing music.

Due to the failure of the mission to Siegen the previous night Air Chief Marshall Harris ordered another attack to the same target on 16th December and the 'Hussey' crew bombed the target successfully. The month of December was seen out with further missions to Cologne on 28th, an attack on the railway yards at Koblenz on 29th, and on the last day of the month an attack on railway yards at Vohwinkel.

The year of 1945 commenced with Bomber Command very much on the offensive with the advantage in the hands of the Allied Forces. The D-Day landings in early June 1944 had seen the start of the end for German forces. After initial strong opposition from the German's ground forces, the Allied bombing campaign concentrated on supporting the Allied forces advance and on the destruction of industrial centers, in particular the oil industry. The skies had practically been cleared of German fighters and daylight missions were a common practice with fighter support just in case the enemy did send up a few fighters. By far the greatest threat was from the German flak guns that claimed so many aircraft during the Second World War and daylight missions increased the accuracy of the German flak gunners. In addition, the new German Jets had entered the war with a vengeance and their air speed totally outclassed the best of the Allied fighters. However, the jets were unpredictable and difficult to fly which meant only the most experienced German pilots got their hands on this potent weapon.

On the 1st January 1945, the crew again attacked the railway yards at Vohwinkel successfully and without incident. The next night the target was Nuremberg a seven hour plus trip deep into the heart of Germany. The raid was memorable for Glyn Potter when he saw a Me 262 jet fighter streak past his turret at high speed and disappear from sight. The crew was now on 29 missions and with the end in sight, Reg Hussey was promoted to Flight Lieutenant in recognition of his crew's proficiency and their valiant efforts to deliver the enemy a deadly blow. In total, the crew completed 32 missions culminating in their final trip to bomb the benzol plant at Recklinghausen.

The crew were all called to meet the Commanding Officer, and with trepidation they stood before Wing Commander Buckingham. He congratulated them on successfully completing their 'tour' of operations in such a commendable manner. Each member of the crew was asked in turn if they wanted to volunteer for additional operational duties and they all declined. The alternative was a posting to a training unit and a period free from operational stress.

It was with heavy hearts that the crew said their final goodbyes with their respective futures uncertain at this juncture. However, one thing was certain, the esprit de corps between them would last a lifetime.

Tour of operations complete, the crew pose for their 'tour' completion photograph. The crew were finally recognized when F/Lt Hussey and F/O Simpson were awarded the D.F.C for gallant service. Back L-R: F/O Dalton RAAF (B/A), Sgt Potter (R/G), F/Lt Hussey D.F.C (pilot), F/O Simpson RAAF, D.F.C (Nav), Sgt O'Connor (MUG), Sgt Hand (F/E), F/Sgt May (W/op). *Courtesy of B.O' Connor.*

4

Leap of Faith

Pilot: F/Lt K.H. Denham DFC
(2nd pilot): F/S G.E Bartholomew
Nav: F/O D.E. Woodward
B/A: Sgt E. Johnson
W/op: F/O J.Carter D.F.M
F/E: Sgt A. Littlewood
MUG: Sgt D. W. Shellock
R/G: Sgt W. Hoggan

Bomb load: 1X 1,000Ib 4X 8X30Ib 7X90X4Ib. Special equipment: Identification Friend or Foe

It had been some months since Donald Shellock had walked through the door of the RAF recruiting office to volunteer his services and he had resigned himself to a long wait. Eventually he was summoned to the 'Burtons' building in Chatham Kent in early 1943 for a medical where the doctor gave him a good examination and asked various questions. He was delighted to be passed fit 'A1' and he was told to wait for his call up for aircrew training. When the call up papers finally arrived, Donald Shellock reported to the Aircrew Reception Center at Lords Cricket Ground in London. He was provided with a train ticket to St Johns Wood, which apparently was the nearest station to Lords. When the day came to join up Don was, as usual running late and subsequently arrived late at St. Johns Wood station. He departed the train in a hurry and ran down the streets towards the ACRC at Lords. On approaching his destination a Corporal who was standing outside shouted at him "don't run you're in the RAF now". Once inside he joined several other new recruits in the famous 'Long Room' for a further medical and various inoculations. Donald and the rest of the recruits were told to strip completely naked and stand in a line and a Sergeant and Officer entered the room. The Officer was the stereotypical RAF officer type with a stick under his arm and handlebar moustache. The Officer walked past each new recruit in turn and examined them. If he pointed at any they were approached by the Sergeant with paintbrush in hand, and their private parts were painted with a dark colored liquid. When the officer approached Don Shellock he pointed at him which perturbed him a little. Don asked why he had selected him and his reply indicated that he had a sweat rash which Don put down to all the running that he had done to arrive on time.

Don Shellock and the rest of the recruits were posted to No.14 Initial Training Wing at Bridlington on the Yorkshire coast for the duration of a twelve week course. On arrival, they were all billeted in houses along the streets just behind the sea front. Don shared a house with eight other aircrew in two rooms and shared the bathroom. The initial stages were mainly focused on discipline and 'square bashing' and being shouted at by the Warrant Officer. They marched for hours on end up and down the sea front and through the town and then changed into their gym kit for running along the beach. The local residents often gave encouragement to the recruits during this period and their warmth was especially welcome. Eventually all recruits were assembled into a team worthy of being in His Majesties Royal Air Force.

With the discipline now at an acceptable level, all progressed onto intensive classroom work on technical and air related subjects. In general, Don enjoyed himself during the course however, he found the lessons in Morse code very difficult and so did several others. Don remembers that there was somebody on top of a tall building flashing an 'Aldis' lamp message in Morse and they had to decipher the message. Finally the course was at an end and they were dispersed to various Gunnery Schools around the country, Don was destined for North Wales and No.7 air gunnery school in Penrhos Wales.

No.14 I.T.W. Bridlington Yorkshire February 1943. No.2 Squadron 'A' Flight Don Shellock AC2, 2nd row from rear 5th from left. Front row L to R: NCOs & Officers. Cpl Watson, P/O West, F/O Shouten, F/Lt Feham, F/O Handy, Cpl Courtney. *Courtesy of Don Shellock.*

No.7 Air Gunnery School, Penrhos, North Wales

When Don Shellock arrived at air gunnery school, he felt that he was well and truly on his way to becoming an air gunner. The instructors were experienced gunners who had either completed a tour of operations or had some operational experience. Almost immediately the students were subjected to considerable lessons in arithmetic and they learned how to strip a .303in Browning machine gun in their sleep. The theory of a bullet's trajectory was studied and the capabilities of defensive armament were compared with the formidable firepower fitted to the German fighters, which they all learned to distinguish through aircraft recognition lessons. Early recognition of friend or foe could be the difference between life and death. Familiarization exercises continued with the technicalities of the various turrets in production including the hydraulic systems and how to fix blockages and malfunctions whilst in potential combat positions. The aircraft that was utilized was the Bristol Blenheim which had a mid upper turret comprising just two .303 Browning machine guns. Initially all students flew familiarization trips and practiced air-to-sea firing which all really enjoyed. No matter how often Don fired the 'Brownings', the sound of the guns always startled him, however firing a few hundreds rounds into the sea was most gratifying. The next stage of the training was shooting at drogues towed by Lysanders over the sea at a distance of about 4-700 yards. It was very difficult to see the bullets hitting the target and Don had no idea of his success until he landed and his strikes on target were counted. Each trainee had the tip of his bullets marked with different colour paint to identify who had the most success.

Whilst Don Shellock was at Penrhos he witnessed a Vickers Wellington bomber in difficulty during a night training trip. It was on Easter Sunday 1943 and it was evident from the alarm and hurried activity from ground staff that the Wellington and its crew were in difficulty. Accident rates among training crews were extremely high and official figures record that over 8,000 aircrew lost their lives during training. The course instructors came to the billets and told everyone to switch the lights on and open the curtains to assist the pilot's orientation. Don could hear that the bomber was on one engine and that engine sounded as if it was racing to keep the bomber in the air. After a short time, the Wellington crashed into a hangar killing all the crew on board. Don was only in his initial weeks of RAF service and he was already destined to attend a funeral. The station Warrant Officer on any airfield was usually a man to be feared who barked out orders and anybody who failed to carry out his orders would regret the day. However, the Warrant Officer in charge was a weak character who had no authority and Don can remember his technique at reveille was to burst in shouting obscenities. His routine always failed and as he went out the door a hail of boots followed quickly behind him. As station Warrant Officer he was to lead the funeral parade and this involved a degree of ceremonial duties with a band stick. He made a complete fool of himself leading the procession and the trainees had a good laugh at his expense. Don successfully completed his initial air gunnery training with an average assessment and gained his sergeant's stripes.

No. 26 Operational Training Unit

No.26 OTU at Wing in Buckinghamshire was an operational training unit. It was here that Sergeant Don Shellock crewed up with Wing Commander Gibson who would later become Commanding Officer of 622 Squadron at RAF Mildenhall. Don and all the other aircrew present were all thrown into a room and told to crew up. Nobody wanted to be placed with the aircrew that were left over to form a crew. Don cannot actually remember how he crewed up, but he believes that W/C Gibson approached him with Sgt Johnson (B/A) and Sgt Hogan (R/G) and asked him his preferred gunnery position, Don had no real preference therefore he was assigned to the mid upper turret. The three of them then ventured around the packed room and collected the rest of the crew. The complete crew were:

Studio photograph of Sergeant D. W. Shellock, fully qualified air gunner. *Courtesy of Don Shellock.*

W/C Gibson (arrowed) instructing pilots on Whitley bombers whilst at an Operational Training Unit. *Courtesy of D. W. Shellock.*

Pilot: W/C G.H.N. Gibson DFC AFC (destined to become Commanding Officer of the newly formed 622 Sqn), Nav, Jimmy James- sent on navigational course at OTU as a development measure. He was never seen again, his replacement was F/O D.E. Woodward. W/Op: F/O J. Carter DFM (second tour), Sgt A. Littlewood F/E, Sgt E. Johnson B/A, Sgt D. W. Shellock MUG, Sgt W. Hogan R/G.

W/C Gibson was a very quiet unassuming character who was a gentleman in every respect. He had just arrived back from a tour in the Middle East where he was in command of 104 Squadron.

At 'Wing' the trainee aircrew flew in the Vickers Wellington twin engined bomber and Don Shellock assumed the position of rear gunner. The Wellingtons at OTU were aeroplanes that had seen considerable service and had been retired to training units. It was evident that the aircraft at 'Wing' were past their best and there was often an emergency landing, with sometimes fatal consequences. It never ceased to amaze Don just how many young aircrews went to their deaths in these old crates. It was a tragedy that the Air Ministry did not appreciate that inexperienced, training aircrews would have had a greater survival rate if they had been provided with serviceable aircraft. So many Wellingtons were lost at Wing that there was not enough aircraft to go around and aircrews were given two weeks leave on an alternate basis to allow for the lack of aircraft. It was whilst the crew were at 'Wing' that their navigator, Jimmy James failed to make the grade. During one cross-country night flight, W/C Gibson spent the entire training flight with him to assess his capability. He proved unsatisfactory in the role of navigator and he was sent back to ITW to repeat the navigational course.

The role of the OTUs was to continue specialist training and to convert crews to the aircraft that they would take to war. The gunnery content for Don Shellock was again shooting at targets being pulled by Lysanders. Registering any hits on the targets was difficult due to the Wellingtons tendency to lurch around the sky when the rear turret was operated. The rear turret moved by using a pressurised hydraulic system that was linked up to one of the Wellingtons engines. Every time Don Shellock moved the turret left or right the pilot would have to correct the engines performance drop off and re-establish level flight. Wing Commander Gibson and crew eventually passed the course and moved to 1651 Conversion flight at RAF Waterbeach in Cambridgeshire on 18th August 1943

1651 Conversion Flight

The crew arrived at RAF Waterbeach on 18th August 1943 in readiness for their familiarization onto the Short Stirling. At Waterbeach the crew experienced very little ground training and concentrated on flying in four engined heavies for the first time with a lot of ditching practice thrown in. Tuition included practice with the Aldis lamp and on how to use 'Very' cartridges.

The Short Company had produced some great aircraft including the renowned Sunderland flying boat that equipped air sea rescue squadrons around the world. The Stirling was born out of a desire for the RAF to have a four engined bomber that was capable of carrying a substantial bomb load into Germany. The original design of the Stirling allowed for a wingspan of 112 ft, but this length would not fit the standard RAF hangar and the wingspan had to be reduced to just under 100 ft. The crew arrived at RAF Waterbeach full of apprehension about the indifferent performance regarding the Stirling. Their introduction to the Stirling focused around continual take offs and landings both in daylight and at night and sometimes on three engines. The Short Stirling was a handful for any pilot on take off and landing because it had a tendency to swing which had to be controlled by the engine throttles being opened in varying degrees. With an instructor on board the crew went on 'bullseye' exercises. These exercises were at night across country with a loaded aircraft to simulate a bomb load and practiced evasive maneuvers, although they didn't actually do any 'corkscrewing' because it had apparently been tried before at conversion flights and crews were lost due to inexperience and the poor condition of some of the Stirlings. The theories of evasive maneuvers were taught during the numerous classroom lectures. It is amazing to think that through all the excitement of flying a Stirling and the preparation for an operational squadron, Don Shellock's lingering memories of Waterbeach concern the long spells of inactivity waiting for the damaged or unserviceable aircraft to be made ready to fly again. At the time he had no idea that he would return to Waterbeach in the very near future to undertake the same training again with a new pilot.

A Bomb Aimer's Perspective

Eric Johnson took a very different training route to that of Don Shellock. His particular story is indicative of the period and emphasises exactly how difficult it was to complete all sections of aircrew training.

Eric joined the RAF on 27th December 1939 and he was posted to RAF Padgate near Warrington, Cheshire, for six weeks basic training. From here his next destination was RAF Benson, near Oxford, where his ambition to become a pilot was encouraged by the station education Officer who gave him extra tuition in Maths. The extra studying paid off and Eric was invited to attend a selection board to become a pilot in Oxford with eight other potential candidates. The first part of the day consisted of an interview in front of senior Officers and in the afternoon the recruits were subjected to intense numerical and literacy exams. At the end of the day Eric Johnson was delighted when he was told that he had passed the selection board and within four weeks he turned up at the Aircrew Reception Center (ACRC) in St John's Wood London. From here, his posting was to the Initial Training Wing at Newquay in Cornwall.

The training at Newquay was very intense and aircrew numbers gradually diminished due to the physical and mental intensity of the course. Eric Johnson proved himself well and excelled in subjects such as, Morse code, navigation (including stars & clouds), aircraft recognition, flight plans and mathematical elements. After three months Eric and others passed the course and were posted to commence flying training. Gurrock, in Scotland, was the embarkation point for those destined for Canada and training under the Empire Training Scheme. Unfortunately, Eric Johnson missed the boat and ended up at a small airfield near Swindon called Clyffe Pypard. The objective here was to fly solo in six hours in the trusty Tiger Moth trainers, an objective Eric achieved. The circle was complete when Eric Johnson was again posted to Gurrock to catch another boat to Halifax, Nova Scotia, Canada. On arrival, the trainee aircrew caught a train to Moncton, New Brunswick, and endured four weeks more classroom based tuition. Eventually he boarded a train to Turner Field, Albany, Georgia for a month long acclimatization course to get used to the ninety-degree heat in the shade. Another train journey took Eric and others to Suther Field, Georgia to commence actual flying instruction in Boeing Stearman aircraft. The course consisted of sixty hours of flying without the use of instruments interspersed with ground lectures. To Eric Johnson the course was really designed to ascertain the candidate's ability to fly by the seat of their pants, or in other words their natural ability.

The next part of his training took him to Cochran Field, Macon, Georgia and an introduction to the Vultee 13 monoplane. It was here that the candidates had to fly aerobatics, instrument flying, cross country flights, and formation flying. It was whilst at Cochran Field that Eric Johnson took off on a solo cross country flight navigating by map reading. Shortly after take off, he looked up and saw another Vultee trainer coming straight at him on a collision course. Eric took evasive action narrowly missing the other aircraft. Once under control again, he discovered that his maps had blown into the rear of the aircraft and beyond reach. He was now in a dilemma, navigating on instinct and the desire not to turn back and admit defeat. In retrospect, he took the wrong decision to continue with his training flight and he headed for the coastline to try and establish a navigational reference point. After some time of flying he became worried that he was lost, he tried unsuccessfully to contact Cochran via radio whilst he was flying blind. Fortunately, he spotted an airport and landed at what he later discovered was Jacksonville airport in Florida. From here he was able to contact Cochran and the next day an instructor arrived to ferry him home in formation.

Eric received no recognition for averting disaster and using his initiative. The uncertainty surrounding the incident had a marked affect on his confidence and for the next four days he could not concentrate on his flying. His hesitancy culminated in a period of assessments which he failed and he was subsequently informed that he had failed the pilot's course.

After getting over the disappointment of failing the pilot's course, Eric and another candidate were posted back to Moncton where he requested he be allowed to complete the pilot's course again. He was told that the wait for pilot training was considerable; therefore he decided to re-muster to a bomb aimer's course. Picton, Ontario, was the home of No.31 Bombing & Gunnery School, and it was here that Eric arrived in the autumn of 1942. Yet another intensive course followed this time relative to bomb aimers and another posting to the Bombing & Navigational School at Mount Hope, Hamilton followed shortly afterwards. Just before Christmas 1942 Eric Johnson was informed that he had passed his bomb aimer course with flying colours and he was awarded his sergeant's stripes and air bomber's brevet. An immediate return to Moncton for two weeks was followed by a train journey to New York where he boarded the Queen Elizabeth liner destined for England. The journey aboard the famous ship allowed Eric the time to reflect on his training and overcome his disappointment of failing the pilot course. He was now a fully trained bomb aimer a position of respect and some importance within a bomber crew.

The journey had come full circle when the Queen Elizabeth docked at Gurrock, in Scotland, and after another three weeks at Wigtown Scotland undertaking bombing exercises over the sea, Sergeant Johnson was posted to No.26 OTU at Wing Buckinghamshire. It was here that he experienced the same 'crewing up' process as Don Shellock and joined the crew of Wing Commander Gibson.

The crew received the news that they were posted to join the newly formed 622 Squadron at RAF Mildenhall and they were ready to join a front line squadron. They had endured just about all the training they could and all were ready to do their bit for King and Country. Collectively they knew nothing about 622 Squadron but quickly found out that it was formed from 'C' flight out of XV Squadron who were also based at Mildenhall. The squadron was equipped with the Short Stirling, an aircraft that they had become accustomed to during their training. At the squadron's initial formation, seven Short Stirling aircraft were immediately transferred from 'C' flight of XV squadron with the expectation that the squadron would reach sixteen operational Stirlings with four in reserve. The crew had hoped that they would be joining a Lancaster squadron for they knew that in comparison the Stirling was an inferior aircraft to the Lancaster. The crew had heard the stories about the Stirling struggling to gain the sufficient altitude over the target and the stories about how they were shot out of the sky by fighters and flak because of their low operational height. The official statistics confirm the stories; the Stirling suffered considerably more at the hands of the Germans than its counterparts the Lancaster and Halifax, in fact the night Don and the crew were shot down over Berlin (22/23rd November 1943) was the last time Stirlings went to Berlin. They were withdrawn from front line service due to their poor attrition rates.

The Short Stirling was the first of the four engined 'heavies' that was restricted by the officialdom at the Air Ministry. The original design allowed for a wingspan of 112 feet however, the wingspan would have to be reduced to 100 feet to allow the Stirling to fit into the standard RAF hangar. The Stirling suffered from developmental and operational problems from the start and the majority of the problems can be attributed to a lack of operational experience and political interference. Officials criticized the Stirling's maximum operating height of 17,000 feet with a payload of just 3, 500lbs of bombs, compared with 14,000 lb of bombs carried by the Lancaster, in addition the bomb bay would not cater for the large 4,000lb 'cookie' blast bomb which was the mainstay of the RAF's arsenal.

From a personal point of view, Don Shellock considered the Stirling to be a majestic looking aircraft that took the war to Germany at a time when the country needed a boost after defeat at places like Dunkirk. Don never flew in a Lancaster to compare the characteristics of each; however, as a crew they came to love the Stirling and appreciated the aircraft's manoeuvrability and rugged design. W/C Gibson would throw the Stirling around the sky on fighter affiliation trips and very often turned inside some of the fighters on their tail.

After the crew's demise in November 1943, the Stirling was relegated to second line duties which mainly concerned special operations. The Stirling was very manoeuvrable at low altitude and it could conduct covert operations in the dead of night with ease. Towards the end of the war later versions of the Stirling were used to tow troop-carrying gliders into the fray during operation Overlord, Market Garden and Varsity, the Allied invasion of France. At the end of the war the Stirling proved invaluable as a troop carrier, bringing back POWs from the European theater.

W/C Gibson was quickly appointed the Commanding Officer of the newly formed 622 Squadron on 20th August 1943, which meant that the crew no longer had a skipper. He was kept extremely busy with the formation and continued growth of the squadron and the crew never actually flew an operational mission with W/C Gibson. Rumors and apprehension grew amongst the crew regarding the loss of their skipper and they wondered what was to become of the them. They quickly had a solution to their quandary when they were all called to the station adjutant's office. The adjutant was F/Lt Goode who was your quintessential Englishman complete with a monocle. When they walked into the room one of them burst into laughter and they all were sent packing, only to return when they could show him a little respect. Eventually returning to his office, they were informed that their skipper was far too busy with squadron business to fly operationally and therefore they were to be sent back to OTU at Waterbeach to crew up with a new skipper. The disappointed crew returned to RAF Waterbeach on 20th September 1943 to complete the whole course again with their new skipper P/O R.H. Denham. They returned to Mildenhall again on 9th October 1943, keen and apprehensive to commence their tour of duty.

On their return back to RAF Mildenhall the non-commissioned aircrew amongst them were billeted in a brick built, house type quarter with four of them to a room. Don Shellock was the youngest of the group which included W. Hogan (R/G), A. Littlewood (F/E) and E. Johnson (B/A). The whole crew bonded very well and if Don misbehaved, he was locked in the cupboard to teach him a lesson, only being let out after some considerable time. During their leisure time in the evenings they went to the local café called 'Dorothy's' which gave them the opportunity to have some female company and talk shop with the other aircrews. It was here that they really learnt the measure of their task to come, through listening to accounts of bombing trips. Occasionally P/O Denham joined them for a tipple. The skipper and navigator, F/O Woodward were officers and stationed within the officer's quarters which were far more lavish than the NCO billets and of course NCOs were not allowed in the officers mess.

The first few trips in the 622 Stirlings were associated with circuits and bumps and familiarization with the surrounding countryside. RAF Mildenhall was a part of 3 Group and in amongst a concentration of airfields that were all very close together. On one training trip the rear gunner shouted down the intercom that there was a four engined fighter on our tail. The aircraft on our tail turned out to be a special Stirling with 'POBJOY' engines fitted giving it a totally different perspective from the front. Usual practice for a new crew joining a squadron would be for the pilot to take a trip with an experienced crew as a 2nd 'dickey' pilot. The majority of crews hated taking a spare 'bod' with them and it was considered unlucky to do so, however on 8th October 1943, P/O Denham was the 2nd 'dickey' to F/Sgt Clarke and crew on a mission to Bremen. Don can remember that all the rest of the crew were very apprehensive whilst their skipper was away, they had already replaced their original skipper and they didn't want to start all over again. Fortunately, their skipper returned safely none the worse from his experience and the whole crew sat him down so that he could tell them all the details of the mission.

17th October 1943- Frisian Isles

True to form, the crew's first mission was to be a mining sortie to the Frisian Isles to drop anti shipping mines into the sea at strategic points around the enemy coast. They flew in GI-D EF123, a Stirling that had originally served on XV Squadron. A group of naval officers were on the station to teach aircrews about the precise nature of mine laying. The mines were dropped from low level about 1,000 ft and they had parachutes attached to them to ensure

Stirling GI-H, BF521 being prepared for a mine laying operation. In the foreground are two Naval Officers who briefed the crews on the correct procedure to drop the mines and the degree of precision needed to successful deploy. *C4016 Courtesy of IWM*

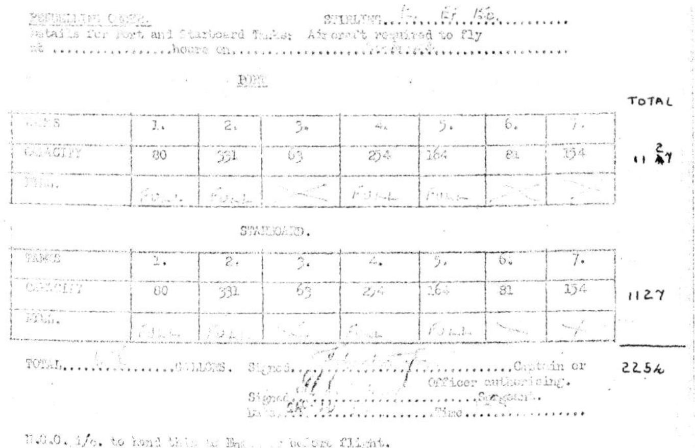

REFUELLING ORDER. STIRLING ...EF 150...

Details for Port and Starboard Tanks: Aircraft required to fly at ....hours on..............................

PORT

TANKS	1.	2.	3.	4.	5.	6.	7.	TOTAL
CAPACITY	80	331	63	254	164	81	154	1127
FUEL.	Full	Full	—	Full	Full	—	—	

STARBOARD.

TANKS	1.	2.	3.	4.	5.	6.	7.	
CAPACITY	80	331	63	254	164	81	154	1127
FUEL.	Full	Full	—	Full	Full	—	—	

TOTAL..............GALLONS. Signed..............Captain or Officer authorising. 2254

Signed..............Sergeant.

Date..............Time..............

N.C.O. i/c. to hand this to Eng... before flight.

Poor quality copy of the refuelling order for the raid to East Frisians on 24th October. *Courtesy of D. W. Shellock.*

that their decent was controlled. Mine laying operations called for a high degree of precision and an accurate altimeter which was very susceptible to barometric pressure. The mission was eventful through poor visibility and bad weather, however they found their target and dropped the stick of bombs in the set area, returning to Mildenhall glad to have completed their first trip.

On 18th October F/O Denham was granted the rank of Flight Lieutenant and features in the 622 operational records book monthly summary for October.

24th October- East Frisians

Return trip to the East Frisians to complete another mining sortie this time in GI-E, EF150. The trip was uneventful and the crew's confidence grew.

7th November 1943-Bay of Biscay at La Rochelle

The crew again flew in GI-E, EF150 on another mining operation this time to the Bay of Biscay at La Rochelle.

18th November 1943-Manheim

First venture into Germany and to the heavily defended target of Manheim, an industrial center contributing to the Nazi war effort. This was an introduction to the German defenses, and the whole trip was a nerve wracking experience with all of the crew flying by the seat of their pants. F/S Morecombe and crew in GI-D, EF128 crashed at Lachalade west of Verdun, in France, killing all but one, who was taken POW. F/S Owen and crew in GI-Q EJ113 crashed at Bussy-le-Chateau, France, killing all eight crew members. At the debrief Dame Laura Knight was sitting, painting in pastels all the crew members who had returned from the night's operation.

19th November 1943 - Leverkusen

Stirling GI-E, EF150 to Leverkusen in atrocious conditions. Numerous searchlight banks on the way to the target and the flak was intense. The target was bombed and a course set for home without seeing any fighters, presumably the foggy conditions had kept them grounded. The conditions were so bad that crews were being diverted to other airfields to land safely. The Stirling being flown by P/O Hughes GI-A, EF123 was originally given the order to land at Bradwell Bay, in Essex, due to a fog bound Mildenhall. However, the order was rescinded and a course for Mildenhall was set. Whilst letting down in poor visibility, the Stirling crashed killing all the crew with the exception of the mid upper gunner. On the return journey, the Denham crew's Stirling developed a fault and they landed at a small airfield called Hern. Inconceivably, if the crew had continued onto Mildenhall then they may have suffered the same fate as P/O Hughes and crew.

The Stirling's fault could not be fixed and it was left at its temporary base along with the crew's parachutes whilst they returned to Mildenhall in full flying gear on the train. Don Shellock believes that this turn of fate saved all their lives when they all had to bail out on their next trip to Berlin. The parachutes at Mildenhall were kept in damp lockers within the hangars and they would have been wrapped and locked together in the damp conditions for some considerable time. Eric Johnson recalls that prior to the mission his parachute had been used as a football amongst the crew and that a WAAF driving a large truck ran over his parachute. On arrival back at Mildenhall the crew drew freshly wrapped parachutes that hadn't had time to become damp in the hangar, and when used on the next mission, they all opened without fault. To this day Don is convinced that their original parachutes would not have opened at their time of need.

22/23rd November 1943- Berlin

Very apprehensive about the trip to Berlin after the previous raids to Berlin had proved costly in the number of Stirlings lost. On this particular night five Stirlings failed to return from the nights mission out of the fifty which set out a 10% loss rate which was not sustainable and Bomber Harris withdrew the Stirlings from front line service.

The Big City

Being detailed for 'ops' meant a busy day ahead with the various briefings to attend, routes to plan and the latest intelligence to consider. Eric Johnson can recall chatting to Nick Carter the wireless operator in the changing room prior to the mission. Flying Officer Carter had completed a previous 'tour' of operations on another squadron and he proudly wore the DFM ribbon on his tunic. F/O Carter relayed his apprehension over the impending mission, he had been married the previous week whilst on leave and Sgt Johnson thought that he was being overly concerned now that he was married.

The route to the target was relatively uneventful and F/Lt Denham guided the Stirling bomber towards Berlin on schedule. Over the Frisians Isles Eric Johnson, sitting in the bomb aimer's position in the nose section, heard the tinkling of flak shell bursts striking the Stirling. The approach to Berlin took the bombers close to the defenses at Hanover, and it appeared to Eric Johnson that they were slightly off course, because he knew that they should pass two miles south of Hanover. The result was that they were subjected to considerable flak which was extremely close. On the approach to Berlin Sgt Johnson could see the fires burning intensely below, and the sky was a mass of searchlights and flak bursts, a sight to strike fear into the heart of any man. Sgt Johnson reported to Ken Denham in the pilot seat that he could see the target markers, and that they were starting their bomb run and he would guide the pilot to the bomb release point. Eric Johnson reached for the handle that would open the bomb doors, and after several attempts had to report that the bomb doors would not open. The flight engineer, Sgt Littlewood, tried to wind them open manually without success. A decision now had to be made to either go around again and risk the flak and searchlights, or turn for home with the bombs still on board. Eric Johnson argued that the crew had come a long way to not try again and the opportunity to drop the incendiary canisters in the wings was still an option. The consensus decision was to go around again and drop the incendiaries, which was accomplished without a hitch.

The skipper turned for home and after leaving the target area, they were coned by searchlights over what they believed to be Hanover. Sgt Johnson was looking down through his bomb aimer's position and noticed a blue searchlight which indicated that the flak was predicted and determined by locking onto the blue master beam. Almost immediately all hell broke loose and the crew was bombarded by flak bursts from all angles. F/Lt Denham commenced evasive action by corkscrewing out of the danger zone with the help of Sgt Johnson who was trying to give instructions on which way to corkscrew. The buffeting and constant corkscrewing resulted in the Stirling hanging on its back and Sgt Johnson found himself looking up at the stars instead of looking into the caldron below. He immediately went up into the cockpit where he witnessed F/Lt Denham fighting the controls in an attempt to bring the large bomber under control. The pilot gave the bomb aimer the thumbs up and he returned to his position lying prone in the front of the aircraft. Suddenly there was a tremendous thud and the 'Stirling' lurched momentarily across the sky as a result of a direct flak hit. The batteries fastened around the bomb aimer's compartment fell all around Sgt Johnson indicating to him that either they had stalled or they were out of control. The 'G' force pressed Eric Johnson hard into the floor and F/Lt Denham was fighting to bring the Stirling out of a dive. The 'G' eased and it appeared that the pilot had gained control however, it was short lived and the skipper gave the order to 'bail out'. Sgt Johnson immediately started clearing the batteries off the escape hatch and Pilot Officer Woodward stumbled down and stood directly on top of the hatch. A state of controlled panic ensued and Sgt Johnson tried frantically to clip on his parachute whilst fighting the increasing 'G' forces. He managed to clip on one side of the parachute and contemplated jumping out with only one side attached but his persistence paid off when he was able to clip on the other side.

At the rear of the aircraft the drama was no less dramatic and unbeknownst to Don Shellock in the mid upper gunners position, the aircraft had also been hit in the port wing setting the fuel tanks on fire. It was apparent that they were in dire straits and the Stirling appeared to be in an uncontrolled dive and the skipper gave the order to bail out. Don released himself from his oxygen supply and dropped down out of the turret position into the aircraft fuselage. Don had an intense fear of parachuting and he decided to take his chances with the aircraft on crashing. He slumped down the side of the aircraft and waited to hit terra firma. He had always had a strong religious belief and he had no fear of dying and resigned himself to meeting his maker. It was a surreal moment for Don who accepted the fact that he was going to die in the burning aircraft and he felt no fear, accepting his fate and passage into the next world. Don recited the Lords Prayer and tried to blank out the noise and confusion going on around him.

After a relatively short period, F/O J. Carter (W/op) brought the mid upper gunner back to reality by shaking him out of what had become an acceptance of death. He continued to shake Don Shellock and asked, "What are you doing, let's get out of here." Don remembers being pushed towards the rear fuselage door and dropping out into the dark unknown. He immediately reached for his ripcord as he went out head first through the door. Almost immediately, he pulled the parachute ripcord and the parachute opened with the straps cutting into him as it broke his fall. It was so peaceful after the drone of the aircraft's engines, and he could see a flaming object falling away in the distance, assuming that this was his Stirling. Don's thoughts suddenly went to the other members of the crew and he hoped that they all made it out. The Short Stirling crashed 1km south of Derstenhausen and south of Fritzler.

Don Shellock slowly drifted down and came to earth with a bump, finishing up in a heap after hitting the ground somewhat harder than anticipated. He immediately dug a hole in the corner of a field and buried his parachute the best he could. He had no real idea where he was therefore he started to walk until he came upon a railway line and he followed the track until he came upon a wood which he entered in search of shelter. Don continued to walk through the wood and out the other side and eventually he reached a farmhouse where he entered the backyard and filled up his water bottle from a tap. All the excitement and tension suddenly flooded back and Don felt exhausted and looked for a place to sleep. He entered a barn and found a pile of straw, which he crawled into and covered himself. Don was startled out of his sleep in the morning by a barking Alsatian dog and he could saw women working in the nearby field. The farmer took him into the house and prepared him some hot water in a tin bath in front of the fire. Don stripped in front of his wife and had a strip wash whilst the farmer disappeared and returned with two German soldiers as company. The German soldiers gestured to Don with their guns to get dressed and to go with them. The group walked for some considerable time until they reached their camp where Don was delighted to be reunited with the rest of the crew except Sgt Littlewood. The soldiers handed them all over to the German Air Force and they marched through Hanover on foot where they witnessed the destruction caused by previous RAF bombing raids. The locals were hostile towards them spitting and punching them as they marched, thank heavens their captors were doing their best to protect them from the civilians. Eventually they reached a checkpoint where they boarded a truck that transported them to Frankfurt and into an interrogation camp. On arrival in the camp Don was placed in a room on his own for a period of time and eventually a man came into the room declaring himself to be a Red Cross member concerned for his welfare and wanting to help him make contact with his family back home. It was obvious to Don that he was an imposter and he told him his name rank and number. Eventually Don Shellock was placed in a single cell with several other cells around him. In the next cell, an American kept singing 'we don't get around much any more', which was a popular tune at the time. The next few days dragged and Don was glad when they were woken up early one morning and put on an armed train towards Leipzig, south of Berlin and the notorious Stalag Luft 4B at Muhlberg (Elbe). It was here that the photograph below was taken and Don was given the POW No. 263623.

Back in the burning bomber, Sergeant Johnson opened the escape hatch and with a quick look around dropped out of the Stirling into the dark night. His immediate thoughts were that of remorse, his mind drifted towards what his parents and girlfriend would think that he was dead. He looked up to check that his parachute was open and as he approached what he thought was the ground he pulled on the lines to ease his fall, in fact he was dropping through the cloud base and the sky went black again. He hit the ground with a bump which thrust him flat onto his back in the middle of a field. What follows is Eric Johnson's account of being on the run from the enemy and his eventual capture:

> "After landing in the middle of the field I immediately gathered up my chute, ripped the insignia off my tunic and buried them along with my flying kit. I then lit one of the three cigarettes I had left in the packet and tried to think calmly what to do next. I got my button compass out and started to walk and quickly discovered that my left boot was missing, obviously falling off during the parachute decent.
>
> I took the socks off my right foot and put them over those on my left foot to keep them dry, and carried on walking all night avoiding populated areas. When it stared to get light, I found a heap of 'stuff' by a windmill and buried myself in it. I could not settle down and I was very cold so I got out and moved into the barn that was close by. There was a large platform covered in straw, so I covered myself in the straw and fell asleep. I was rudely awakened by a loud thudding noise and the floor shook at each thud, accompanied by several voices. After a considerable period the noise and voices ebbed away and I looked through the straw and saw large bails of straw with large hooks lying around. I soon realized that the men moving the bails around caused the loud thudding. I eventually fell asleep again and when I woke up it was dark and quiet. I commenced walking for some time and then I heard faint voices so I approached carefully. I realized that I had stopped right on the edge of a very large round deep pit that was about twenty feet deep. In the center of the pit was a very large anti-aircraft gun with six German soldiers drinking tea. I crept away and round the pit and carried on walking until I came to a small village and decided to try to find some footwear. By now I was very hungry and I entered a house through the unlocked door, got some socks from a table and started to look for some shoes. A small dog with a very loud bark appeared and forced me out of the house with several voices coming from upstairs.
>
> I ran down the village street with the dog in hot pursuit being joined by more dogs intent on waking up the whole village. When I reached the outskirts of the village the dogs turned back thankfully, I was finding it difficult to run in one boot and one bare foot. I continued walking until daybreak and I found a hedge to hide in. Sometime later a group of people walked by and one man looked straight into the hedge and I feared that I would be discovered, fortunately he continued to walk on. When darkness fell, I started to walk again and came across a goods yard at a railway and I climbed into a wagon with a wooden hut attached. The door would not close properly and it kept banging open and shut drawing attention, I therefore moved to another wagon. My new hiding place was a wagon carrying planks of timber covered by a tarpaulin sheet, which I covered myself with. The train started to move and I began to freeze in the chill wind due to me being wet. The train stopped and I peeled my frozen body out of the tarpaulin and started to walk again in great discomfort from the cold until daybreak. By this stage, I was feeling extremely low in mood and the cold was biting however, I hid again all that day until dark. The onset of darkness brought another period of walking until I came across another railway yard, this time I dare not enter any of the carriages so I took up a position between the carriages standing on the carriage couplings. People walked by without noticing me until a young boy clearly spotted me and ran down the platform. I ran to a large goods yard and stood under a large floodlight on a metal pole.
>
> A group of German soldiers approached the floodlight and to my amazement, walked right past me as I slid around the pole as they passed. The soldiers eventually gave up and I approached the train again to find a hiding place in one of the carriages. I opened the door of one which contained small field guns and decided not to travel in this wagon. As I was climbing into the wagon, I fell off and hurt my hip on the rails, giving off a scream of pain. I was quickly surrounded by a group of men who were working in the goods yard who handed me into the main office where I was confronted by a man in a red tunic. He told me to empty my pockets onto his desk,

An official photograph taken by the German authorities at the time of Don Shellock's capture. The reality of starting life as a POW shows on his face. *Courtesy of D. W Shellock.*

which he examined. I discreetly put the things back in my pocket and he never challenged me over the issue. Soon after two soldiers arrived and told me to undue my braces forcing me to walk with my hands in my pockets to keep my trousers up with a pistol stuck in my ribs. We walked for a few minutes and then entered another office full of German soldiers and an Officer offered me a cigarette and a cup of awful coffee, which I was very grateful for. I was forced to board a train with two German soldiers and sit amongst the German civilians who were hostile towards me. Eventually I arrived at a Luftwaffe aerodrome and they accepted me as their prisoner. It was here that I received some kindness from two Luftwaffe Officers who were in solitary confinement as punishment. They told me to ask to use the toilet and whilst I was gone, they lit me a cigarette and placed it in my cell. I endured another train journey until I arrived at Dulag Luft, at Frankfurt, which was the main interrogation center. During the journey, I shared the compartment with German soldiers who were wounded from the fighting with the Russians. They made my journey very uncomfortable and did not disguise their dislike for me often arguing with my accompanying soldiers who were obviously stopping them doing something unthinkable towards me. At Dulag Luft, I was questioned about the course we flew as they showed me a map; I made up a course and said it was correct. In total, I was questioned on three occasions by different interrogators who waved a pistol at me and threatened to shoot me if I failed to co-operate, they even produced my lost flying boot, which I was allowed to keep. Soon afterwards I was moved to another part of the building where I was put into a room with the rest of the crew apart from Sgt Littlewood. I was greeted by all present and Don Shellock gave me a piece of chocolate, which I believe came from a Red Cross parcel.

After a while we were all marched to the railway station and loaded into cattle trucks and made several stops on route. On one occasion, the railway yard we were in was being bombed. Eventually we arrived at Muhlberg situated on the River Elbe and we were marched to the prison camp, stalag 4B. My first impression of the camp was the large gates with the inscription above in large letters, 'ARBIT MACH FR'."

Warrant Officer Eric Johnson standing on the right in the photograph. Eric's training to become a bomb aimer took a precarious route. He is seen here with his brother who was serving with the Royal Navy. *Courtesy of Mr Eric Johnson.*

There were 15,000 prisoners in the prison camp and all were billeted in huts that catered for 200 men, sleeping on bunks that were three high. Don Shellock grabbed the top bunk and his 2nd pilot, F/Sgt Bartholomew (Bart), was directly underneath him. Bart was a trainee doctor before the war studying at St Andrews Hospital in Edinburgh and he returned to finish his studies after the war. The rear gunner, Sgt Hoggan and Sgt Johnson were allocated another billet. The officers in the crew, F/Lt Denham, F/O Carter and F/O Woodward were sent to a camp for officers in Barth on the Baltic Coast. The flight engineer Sgt Littlewood, joined Don and the others at the camp about six weeks later, he was still in a terrible state with a massive scar on his forehead and he had difficulty walking unaided. Sgt Littlewood had jumped with a loose parachute harness that clipped onto the chest, and it had come up and virtually scalped him. The harness between the legs had cut into his flesh down to the bone and the Germans had stitched up the external wound neglecting to treat the internal wound. The result was constant pain and the crew would take turns to escort him around the prison camp as support.

The camp was made up of several nationalities including Russians, Dutch, Italians and French. The camp itself was a community and operated as such with football and rugby pitches, a running track, swimming pool, and a theater for each nationality. Dissecting the middle of the camp was a road on which supplies were brought into the camp. In general, the Germans treated prisoners well, although the prisoners never pushed the boundaries too far for fear of the consequences.

The daily routine was roll call at 0600, which took place outside the hut. The prisoners would line up in rows of five and the Germans counted them. Every week the prisoners received Red Cross parcels retrieved from the stores on the camp and issued by what would become known as 'men of confidence'. These prisoners were trusted to issue the parcels without taking items for themselves, although they usually did. The parcels had been packed in either Scotland or Canada and the contents contained, powdered milk, one pound tin of butter, tea, coffee, sugar and a tin of corned beef. The Red Cross parcels supplemented the meagre meals that the Germans supplied. The daily meal usually consisted of a bowl of millet, sometimes some mouldy cheese and about one inch of bread, the prisoners were always hungry. On Don's return home, his mother told him that she used to send him cigarettes every week. He never received even one. It was thought that the 'dockers' helped themselves to the bounty. Prisoners wore the same clothes for 18 months and looked forward to a shower every 3 months in a communal shower area with adjoining hot air driers. After a while, Don was admitted to the camp hospital or Lazarette as it was known. He had contracted impetigo from the blankets and he needed treatment.

The doctors were from the British Army captured during the Italy campaign, with support from orderlies of all nationalities. The hospital was only guarded by one soldier and the exit was through the wash room and out the other side. Whilst in the hospital Don made friends with a Canadian spitfire pilot who was having treatment for appendicitis. He was a real character and worked for an undertaker in Winnipeg, Canada. Don can remember that he gave the camp a talk on the undertaking business and he described the method of punching a hole under the arm of the body to shoot in formaldehyde to preserve the body.

Passing the time in the camp was difficult due to inactivity and boredom. Idle hands makes the devil's work and the prisoners of war participated in numerous dangerous activities. Many of the prisoners used to lie on their bunks virtually all day and become depressed. Eric Johnson and Bill Hoggan were not used to inactivity and were mixed up in all the activities to annoy their captors. This resulted in them being moved to a billet that was notorious for housing the known troublemakers. The inactivity was broken at times by organized physical exercise, which made the prisoners even hungrier. Eric Johnson picks up the story again:

> "We used to raid the coal shed at night (it wasn't real coal, like round balls of coal dust molded into balls). This provided us with excitement and heat for cooking but was rather dangerous, as we would have been shot if caught. Some of the guards were trigger happy and all were armed at all times in the camp.
>
> I remember one day the potato cart passing the door of our hut where I was stood. As it passed a Russian prisoner reached up and took a potato. The guard instantly shot him in the chest, the bullet passed right through the prisoner and out of his back hitting an RAF prisoner in the shoulder about twenty yards away. As the Russian lay on the ground blood was pouring from his mouth, so a few others and I went to help him, but the guards threatened to shoot us if we did not leave him.
>
> The camp was surrounded by a very high barbed wire fence with guard boxes, machine guns and searchlights situated at different points of the outside fence. Inside by about forty feet was another very high fence and between the two fences was the camp commander's greenhouse where he used to grow very good tomatoes. About twenty feet inside the inner fence was a trip wire about eighteen inches high, which we were not allowed to cross on threat of being shot. Sometimes we would play football and the ball would go over the trip wire, then we had to wait for the guards in the gun towers to wave us permission to retrieve the ball. In the summertime when the tomatoes were ripe, Bill Hoggan and I used to wait until dark and go through the inner wire and trip wire to help ourselves to the tomatoes. One night nearing dusk as we walked round the compound we spotted a German guard that we recognized dressed in a French uniform standing adjacent to the place where we used to go through. This was obviously a trap, we never went through the wire again, and this probably saved our lives.
>
> On another occasion Bill Hoggan and I went to the ablutions part of the hut and started to cut a piece of metal to be used as a part of a radio when a German corporal walked in. He went ballistic ranting and wanting the hacksaw whilst waving his pistol at us. He motioned that we should follow him at gunpoint, which we did whilst passing the hacksaw to another prisoner who quickly dispersed it amongst the others. In the confusion I made a run for it and hid under a bunk, the corporal took Sgt Hoggan to solitary for five days. Bill asked me to bring him some socks to darn because he was bored stiff in solitary, which I gladly did.
>
> Another incident springs to mind when Sgt Littlewood was caught in possession of a radio. He was taken out of the camp for about a month and on his return he was placed in solitary, which he stated, was a welcome relief to being in a Gestapo prison where he had been.
>
> News was in short supply in the camp and the best place to receive news was in the 'shithouse'. The toilets were a series of about 10 circular holes dug in the ground with drainage attached on both sides of the building with a low brick wall straight down the middle. Prisoners would shout out news to each other from different huts and take it back to our own hut. These stories supplemented the radio that had been built in nearly every hut on which war reports would be received every night. The radio was broken into pieces and dispersed around the hut to make it harder for the Germans to find the equipment."

Tunnel Digging

"Stalug Luft IV was no different to any other POW camp, it had an escape society and a tunnel was dug under the chapel floor. Don never actually got involved with any of the tunnel digging but he was hoping that the plan would be successful and that several of the lads would escape back to England.

Nearly all the floors in Stalag Luft IV were constructed out of bricks compressed down, similar to the house driveways that you see today. The chapel floor was of the same construction and the bricks had to be lifted to gain access to the tunnel and a false floor was made out of wood and placed under the floor and then the bricks were compacted down hard to form a uniformed pattern with the original. The Germans used to come around the huts and buildings, usually the same soldier who we christened 'Pickaxe Pete', with a pickaxe handle and tap the floor to see if there was a hollow sound, which would signify a tunnel below.

The tunnel was under construction for some weeks and it got all the way to the base of the fence before it was discovered by 'Pickaxe Pete' and all hell was let loose around the camp. There was a full roll call and the senior officer in the hut was taken away for interrogation. The Germans ordered the Russian prisoners to fill in the hole with human excrement from the toilet block. The Russians used a bowser pulled by two horses to pump out the excrement from the toilet block and pump it down the hole of the tunnel, which took them several days. The Russians prisoners were given extra rations to undertake the work and they were ridiculed for helping the Germans. Shortly after the hole was filled in the German High Command ordered that photographs should be taken of the tunnel and the Germans instructed the Russians to empty out the excrement from the hole, which they duly refused. Eventually the Germans had to empty the tunnel themselves to the amusement of all prisoners and 'Pickaxe Pete' was up to his neck in human excrement. This was the end of our hut's tunnel building days, although rumor control kept us updated on the tunnel attempts of several other huts."

Liberation

On 23rd April 1945 the whole camp woke up to find the German prison guards had gone and the gates were left open. All knew that the liberating armies were close at hand, but they did not know just how close they were. The whole camp was in a state of shock and there was a lot of activity and discussion about what course of action to take, should they all sit tight and wait for the Allies or should they march towards the nearest town. All questions were answered when the Russians turned up in celebratory mood. They had obviously consumed a lot of Vodka and they were shooting their guns into the air and dancing, which filled the prisoners full of alarm because of their indiscriminate firing of their weapons into the air without caution. Eventually the prisoners were gathered together and commenced marching towards Rizza and Don tagged along with an Army pilot until they came across a group of Russians in a field. Don went over to the crowd and discovered that they had shot a cow for its meat and through gestures and pigeon English it was understood that they were asking for some butter. Don and several others went off, found a farmhouse, obtained some butter, and returned to the location of the dead cow. They found just one Russian soldier remaining with a large gun and several empty bottles of spirits on the ground. He was clearly the worse for wear and waved the gun around in everybody's general direction so they left very quickly. The march continued until they reached Halle where they met up with the Americans and they gave them some bread, which tasted like cake and a pleasant experience after the food they had been used to over the last few years.

On 25th May 1945 Sergeant Don Shellock boarded a C47 transport plane to Brussels and on the 26th May he boarded a Lancaster with other POWs for the flight home. He landed in England at a place called Oakley in Bedfordshire and he was given immediate access to a telephone on which he contacted his mother to let her know that he was home safely and that he had been given six weeks leave to spend some time with the family.

After his six weeks leave had expired, Don Shellock was called to West Malling to re-muster as the rank of AC1 in the role of a driver on transportation duties. He was sent to Blackpool for two weeks training with the British School of Motoring driving 15cwt trucks. Don eventually got a posting to Lynton on Ouse where he commenced his driving duties. From here, Don was posted to Stradishall doing Ambulance duties picking up returning POWs from the runway and taking them to the hospital. His other duties at Stradishall included driving the fire engine which was quite an experience, Don remembers that nobody who rode on the fire engine had any training in firefighting and he was glad that he never responded to an actual emergency.

Don Shellock's RAF service came to an end in 1947 at Neatherhaven when he was de-mobbed back into 'civvy' street after nearly five years; it had been an unforgettable experience and he survived the war in readiness for another leap into the unknown.

Sergeant Johnson's experience of the Russian liberators was quite different to Don Shellock's as described below:

> "One day I broke into the records office to get the crew's records, I was just about to leave when I heard firing close by, then a Russian Officer appeared and told me and one of the others that we would be kept back in the camp. I was put into a solitary cell and felt very apprehensive. Very soon afterwards, Sgt Littlewood thrust a roasted chicken through the bars into my cell. During the next couple of days, various food items came the same way and Sgt Littlewood chiseled around the grilled window so that I was able to remove the window in case of emergency. One day the door was thrust open and a soldier was thrown in. To my utter surprise, I recognized the soldier as Harry Hackett, a classmate

A disheveled looking Don Shellock on his arrival back in England after spending time as a prisoner of war. *Courtesy of D.W Shellock.*

Don Shellock looking refreshed after six weeks home leave. *Courtesy of D. W Shellock.*

from the same school that I attended. He was captured at Arnhem. Eventually we were let out and told to march as a group. We marched for some time and finally entered a large camp full of Russian Army and civilian personnel. Inside the camp we were seated at long trestle tables and female interpreters asked for all our details. I was very suspicious of the interrogation by the Russians and I wondered off around the camp where I met up with a British soldier and we found a large hole in the fence and got out. We started to walk away unchallenged towards the Allied lines. The war was still going on so we had to be careful not to be shot and we stayed at German homes on a couple of nights. They fed us well, probably aware that we were now winning the war and the British were preferable to the cruel Russian soldiers.

During our walk to freedom we came across three Russian soldiers maintaining a machine gun overlooking a wood, they informed us that some Gestapo solders were holding out there. We carried on walking and eventually came across an American motor patrol led by a Major. We explained our plight and where we had come from; he was particularly interested to hear of the American soldiers being held by the Russians at our old camp. The Major turned his convoy of men around and headed straight for our prison camp and on arrival the major argued with the Russian Officers. We were ordered back into the camp and the Americans were turned away much to the annoyance of us both. Not content to stay in the camp I wandered back to the same hole in the fence that I had previously escaped from and got out again and started walking. After a few days I met up with some more Americans and they treated me to good food and a warm bed. After a couple of days I was taken to Halle and then flown to Brussels in a Dakota transport plane. From here I was flown to RAF Cosford in a Lancaster. As we climbed down from the Lancaster the Commanding Officer and a host of others greeted us. We were immediately deloused with white powder and then allowed a shower. Our uniforms were reissued and we were allowed to send a telegram home to our families and then given railway warrants to go on leave. A long period of inactivity followed which came as second nature to a POW and I was eventually demobilized on 9th January 1946. To say that my period in the RAF was eventful is an understatement but also typical of the experiences of many whom joined up to serve their country. It was the end of a long and sometimes arduous adventure, personally I would not have missed it for anything; these memories last a lifetime."

5

"Toying" with Berlin

Pilot: F/O G. E. Toy M.I.D– KIA
Nav: P/O F. M. Carter-KIA
B/A: P/O G.F. Ritson-POW
W/op: Sgt R.P. Benham-POW
MUG: Sgt F. Poyser-POW
R/G: Sgt S. Mackrell-KIA
F/E: Sgt F.H.M. Smith-POW

In the latter half of 1943, the Air Ministry authorized the expansion of Bomber Command to continue with the 'Pointblank' directive of destroying strategic military targets in Germany. Subsequently on 10th August 1943, 622 Squadron was formed from 'C' flight of XV Squadron. Seven crews from XV Squadron were immediately posted to the squadron, although they did not have far to travel, 622 Squadron was to share RAF Mildenhall with XV Squadron. Seven Short Stirling bombers and their ground crews were assigned to 622 Squadron with the intention that the squadron would build up to its quota of sixteen 'Stirlings', with four in reserve.

One of the newly trained crews that initially formed 622 Squadron was that of Flying Officer Toy. Posted into Mildenhall from 1665 HCU, Woolfox Lodge on the 9th August 1943, the crew was, for administrative purposes, temporarily allocated to 15 Squadron but transferred the following day onto their new squadron. With a scarcity of aircraft the crew did not fly immediately, only Flying Officer 'Chunky' Toy (as he was affectionately known by the crew) as second pilot to F/Sgt Batson, flew in the first week of the squadron's existence. Finally, after a number of false starts, the crew flew their first operational mission on 22nd August, dropping mines over the West Friesians. Lasting just over 4 hours, of the three aircraft dispatched, HK816, GI-B flown by Toy and crew were the only ones to complete an otherwise uneventful 'gardening' trip, the other 2 aircraft turning back due to 'Gee' failure.

Mine laying operations were always preferable to deep excursions over heavily defended enemy territory and Bomber Command suffered few losses whilst undertaking these missions. The German capital city of Berlin was at the other end of the spectrum, the most heavily defended target in the world with rings of flak towers around the perimeter of the city. In addition, the crews had to successfully negotiate a six hour round trip in which intense night fighter activity was a very real danger. At the time of the squadron's conception, Bomber Command was participating in what was to become known later as 'The Battle of Berlin'. Berlin was soon to become a regular destination for the crews of Bomber Command and aircrew would often refer to this target as 'The Big City'. Air Chief Marshall Harris believed that destroying the German capital would seriously dent the morale of the German people and bring home to them the realization that the war could be brought to them in devastating ways. Harris wanted the assistance of the American 8th Air Force and he stated that together the Allies could "Wreck Berlin from end to end".

The night of 23rd August 1943 is considered to have been the start of the Battle of Berlin. The order was given mid-morning by ACM Harris for an 'all out effort' and by teatime the bomber crews of 622 Squadron knew that their destination that night would be the feared 'Big City'. Flying Officer Toy and crew were promulgated on the battle order to attack Berlin on the night of 23rd August. Taking off at 2030hrs, the crew witnessed several aircraft being shot down as they cleared the Dutch coast, flew north of Hanover and approached Berlin from the southeast. As EH490, GI-F and crew lined up on the green marker flares exploding flak shells jolted and buffeted their Stirling. At 15,000 feet above the city,

Sgt R.P Benham, wireless operator who was taken POW when a night fighter attacked the Short Stirling they were flying on the route home. Tragically, three members of the crew were killed when they failed to parachute to safety from the doomed aircraft. *Courtesy of Anthony Marshall.*

Sgt Frank Poyser, mid-upper gunner. Survived the shooting down of his aircraft and was reunited with Sgt Dick Benham in Stalag IVB. *Courtesy of Anthony Marshall.*

Sgt Benham showing the scars of parachuting out of a stricken bomber at night. The parachute straps caused the markings on his face when the 'chute' opened as he was tumbling through the sky. This photograph was taken on 2nd September 1943 on arrival at Dulag Luftwaffe Interrogation camp. When the camp was liberated in April 1945, Sgt Benham managed to grab the photo from the camp admin hut before it was ransacked. *Courtesy of Anthony Marshall.*

and identified as being over the target, F/O Glen Ritson released the bomb load and 'Chunky' Toy made for the Danish coast. F/O Fred Carter wrote in his diary on return to base, "...It was a tough assignment for our first operation...we were the only 'green' crew flying." The 23rd August is significant because Bomber Command lost the highest number of aircraft to date with 56 aircraft going down, 16 of which were Stirlings and 622 Squadron suffered its first loss with Flight Sergeant Rollett and crew perishing on German soil. Considered to be a highly successful 'op' on the night, later reconnaissance photos confirmed that most of the bomber stream had turned too early onto their north-easterly bombing run and had consequently bombed the southern suburbs. With airframes once again at a premium, F/O Toy and crew found themselves without an aircraft and on the morning of 24th August and they were assigned six days leave. While away, the Stirling losses continued to mount and on the 27/28th August Bomber Command attacked the city of Nuremberg. 622 Squadron received no causalities on this raid however; the total Stirling losses amounted to 10% of the force.

Whilst on leave in the Medway Towns, Sgt Dick Benham, experienced what it was like to be on the receiving end of a bombing raid. A couple of evenings into his leave, Dick heard Luftwaffe bombers overhead on their way to bomb the nearby Chatham Naval dockyards. Urging his family to immediately join him in the 'Anderson' shelter at the bottom of the garden, his younger sister Muriel dawdled on the path looking up at the night sky. Urged again to hurry up by Dick, she replied, "they can't see us, they are too high". Probably remembering his trip to Berlin of only a few days before, he replied sharply "They can see bloody everything...I know I have been up there."

Fate Intervenes

The final week of August saw raids on various targets and Berlin was again the target on the night of 31st/1st September. Flying Officer Toy and crew had returned from leave to discover they were going back to Berlin and would be flying in the newly arrived Short Stirling EF119, GI-Q. Taking off from Mildenhall at 20:20 hours, six heavily laden Stirlings fought to gain height and join the rest of the mixed bomber stream of Halifaxes, Lancasters and Stirlings over the North Sea.

This time coming in over the Belgian coast, the stream of bombers flew a more northerly course than the week previously. As was his duty on crossing the coast, Dick Benham began throwing out chaff (or Window) in order to blind the ground based radar used by the Germans to guide their night fighters. Flying slow and low, illuminated by the flames spitting from the exhausts of their four Bristol Hercules engines, EF199, GI-Q was however soon picked up by a marauding night fighter that proceeded to position itself underneath and slightly behind the bomber. Racked with cannon fire and with its front section set alight, Hauptman Wilhelm Telge

Crew mates. Pilot Officers Ritson, Carter and Toy shared a room in the Mildenhall Mess. Glen Ritson survived the war, Frank Carter and 'Chunky' Toy dying in the stricken Stirling aircraft, 1st September 1943. *Courtesy of Anthony Marshall.*

of 5/NJG 1, flying a 2-man Bf110, claimed his thirteenth victim northwest of the Harz mountains at just after midnight. Flying Officer Toy knew that they were doomed and ordered his crew to bail out. Smith, Poyser, Benham and Ritson parachuted to safety; however, the remaining three were to lose their lives when the fully laden Stirling crashed near Wollerhausen, Osterode Am Harz just after midnight, 1st September 1943. Initially knocked unconscious by the chest-mounted parachute pack opening into his face, Sgt Benham drifted down and landed with quite a jolt in a potato field. Burying his parachute immediately, Dick Benham lay down in a furrow until it got light. As he made his way along the field in the early light of morning he was soon spotted by an old man carrying a pistol. Taken into captivity and marched to the nearest police station, Dick was soon reunited with Glen Ritson who had also been recently captured. After the obligatory stay at the Dulag Luft, both were eventually transported to prisoner of war camps, Ritson to Stalag Luft III and Benham to Stalag IVB (where he was reunited with Frank Poyser).

A Caterpillar Club membership card presented, along with a 22ct gold Caterpillar Badge, by the Irvin Parachute Company after the war. *Courtesy of Anthony Marshall.*

The mission had been disastrous for Bomber Command, with a massive 47 crews paying the price for a disappointing raid and the Stirling loss rate was a massive 16%. This mission was the catalyst for the withdrawal of Short Stirlings from front line service. ACM Harris knew that the Stirling losses could not be sustained and relegated the Stirling to secondary roles. 622 Squadron was also mourning the loss of F/Sgt Young and crew with six of the crew perishing. Sergeant Benham would remain a prisoner of war until Russian Cossacks liberated him on 23rd April 1945.

For his actions on the night Flying Officer Toy was awarded a posthumous Mention In Dispatches, an award that fell just short of a gallantry medal Flying Officer TOY M.I.D, Pilot Officer Carter & Sgt Mackrell are all buried in Hanover War Graves Cemetery.

6

Here by the Grace of God

Alan Martin was notified on 6th October 1941 that in accordance with National Service Acts 1939-1941, he had to attend a medical examination at Congregational Hall, Little Castle Street, Exeter, on 9th October. He volunteered for the Royal Air Force Volunteer Reserve in November 1941 and was interviewed as a National Service Aircrew candidate on 4th December 1941 eventually being called up for duty on 2nd July 1942 with the service No.1602539.

Alan's training began when he was enlisted at RAF Padgate and issued with his kit along with a white flash in his cap signifying that he was aircrew under training. Almost immediately he was posted to his Initial Training Wing at Blackpool for the usual square bashing and physical training. He also endured similar training at Yatesbury and Western Zoyland before being called forward for flying training.

No.4 Radio School RAF Madley

The first part of his aircrew training was at No 4 Radio School at Madley where the flying element started on 8th June 1943. Alan first flew in De Havilland Dominie aircraft eventually completing 11 hours and 25 minutes on the type. Alan spent a total of 9 hours and 55 minutes in Percival Proctors culminating in his course finishing on 12th August 1943. Aircrew at the time were taught to learn another aircrew designation and Alan commenced his air gunnery training on 21st August 1943 at No.8 Air Gunnery School at Evanton, Ross and Cromarty approximately eleven miles north of Inverness. The training was conducted in Blackburn Botha aircraft, which had been designed for anti-shipping and reconnaissance. It was an operational failure by all regards.

The training started in earnest on 1st September 1943 on bullet trail exercises which were on a beam trace, relative speed, cine camera gun, quarter cross over and air to ground. During September Alan Martin flew 16 hours 45 minutes at Evanton on the Botha qualifying as an air gunner on 8th October 1943. Alan's overall assessment was a credible 78% and classed as an average student, and the instructor commented that Alan was very keen, good in all subjects.

No.86 Wireless Operators/Air Gunners Course

On 20th October Alan Martin started his wireless operator and air gunnery course at Staverton in Gloucestershire and at Moreton Vallance flying predominantly in Avro Ansons. The course consisted of flying cross country exercises simulating actual operating conditions at both night and day culminating in Alan Martin completing twenty seven hours and fifteen minutes in total.

F/Lt Ivor Richards RNZAF D.F.C. makes a landing in Lancaster LM433 GI-T on return from a daylight mission to Essen on 25/10/44. Bottom center crew are as follows: Back L to R: Sgt. T. Bernard (F/E) F/O F. Carter (B/A) F/O B. Lubell RCAF(Nav) F/Sgt A. Martin (W/op) Front; Sgt M Campbell (R/G) F/Lt Ivor Richards RNZAF (pilot) Sgt J.Brierley (MUG). *Courtesy of Alan Martin.*

The course reached its climax by candidates flying a 3 hour cross country exercise to No. 8 Observers Advanced Flying Unit at Mona in North Wales. On 20th February 1944 Alan Martin progressed his training to No.12 Operational Training Unit at Chipping Warden. The aircraft here were the twin engined Wellington bomber and a vast improvement on the previous types flown. Alan was initially assigned to 'B' flight as a wireless operator in the Wellington on various training exercises. On 6th March he was assigned to an exercise with 'A' flight and he flew for the first time with his future skipper F/Sgt Ivor Richards RNZAF. The final exercise at 12 OTU was on 19th April 1944 with a 4 hour 5 minute night special exercise to St. Evreux with F/Sgt Richards again his pilot. In total Alan Martin had completed 58 hours and 10 minutes by day and 37 hours and 5 minutes by night at No.12 OTU.

It was whilst the crew were at an operational training unit that they formed into a crew in the traditional RAF manner. Aircrew of all trades were placed in a large room and told to form up into crews, otherwise the 'brass' would assign them to what was left over. Alan Martin had flown with Ivor Richards and he knew that he was a quiet proficient fellow so he joined his crew. Before the war, Ivor Richards had been a tomato grower in New Zealand. The navigator was Flying Officer Ben Lubell from Montreal Canada who had a Russian father. The bomb aimer was Flying Officer Frank Carter an accountant from Poltimore Devon. Both Carter and Lubell had been instructors before joining the crew and brought considerable experience to their first operational tour. The mid upper gunner was Jim Brierley a redhead from Burnley Lancashire and the rear gunner was Mick Campbell from Kilmarnock in Scotland and he stood just over 5' tall. The flight engineer was Tom Burnard who had given up an engineering apprenticeship in Dursley Gloucestershire to volunteer for aircrew duties.

After forming into an operational crew they moved to Wratting Common in Cambridgeshire to No.1651 Heavy Conversion Unit. The main role here was to convert aircrew onto four engined heavies by practice flying the Short Stirling bombers. On 25th May the course started with circuits and landings in the tricky Stirling whilst on the best of occasions concentrated the pilot's mind to counter the swing on takeoff and landing. Once in the air the Short Stirling was a joy to fly and extremely maneuverable. The highlight of the course for Alan Martin was flying as second pilot to Ivor Richards on a four hour day flight. The reason for the training was to familiarize one of the crew to fly an aircraft straight and level in case the pilot was incapacitated. The final trip on a Short Stirling was on 15th June 1944 after enduring 15 hours and 55 minutes night flying and 25 hours by day. The final stage of the crew's preparation for an operational squadron was a posting to No. 3 Lancaster Finishing School at Feltwell in Norfolk. The purpose of the finishing school was to familiarize the crews with the Lancaster bomber and on 7th and 8th July the crew flew a total of 45 hours and 20 minutes including a loaded climb.

An Operational Station

The story continues here in the words of F/Lt Ivor Richards, an account of his operations kindly sent to the author by Alan Martin:

"You have seen fit to ask me to write some memories of a couple of outstanding operational sorties in our Lancaster GI-T, LM433. Just one of thousands of those mighty machines of war that had the ability to fill the crew in temporary charge of her with awe and fear, but a wonderful confidence that 'if you leave it to me, I will never let you down'. I was one of many Bomber Command aircrew who on surviving a tour of operations and the end of the war could not get home quick enough to marry the girl of my life. To put all thoughts of those times of day to day living completely behind me and erased it all, as far as possible from my mind. My wife, family and work became my life, war was never mentioned and I could not face up to flying again for many years. It was not until I attended the third RAF Bomber Command N.Z. reunion at Rotorua from 21st-23rd March 1994 with my English flight engineer, that I realized just how many other aircrew members had been affected in a similar way."

Vivid Operational Memories

"Memories of incidents that were so vivid and soul chilling at the time are now, after fifty plus years of being purposefully pushed to the back of my mind, almost impossible to recall in detail. At the time of writing I have just returned from England after 53 years and a reunion with three surviving crew members of 'T' Tommy. The steps taken to trace all the members of the crew were fruitful in finding everyone apart from Frank Carter (bomb aimer) and Ben Lubell (Canadian navigator). After our reunion, my thoughts about what happened on our last operational flight have been completely revised due to the input of the other crew members present. I will leave the account of this eventful last mission to the end of this account because it is a fitting end to our clash with the enemy.

The usual practice for any new crew arriving on an operational station was for the pilot to go on a mission as 2nd 'dickey' pilot. The purpose of these exercises was to familiarize a new pilot to the actual rigors of an operational mission especially experiencing the flak and searchlight batteries. I was assigned as 2nd 'dickey' to a Canadian pilot by the name of F/O Clarke who was on his last mission of his tour and our target was the heavily defended city of Stuttgart deep in the Ruhr. The Lancaster we flew in was LM443, GI-T the Lancaster that we were destined to inherit. My most vivid memories are of a raw inexperienced pilot, sick with nerves and apprehension at the start of his first operational flight as a second pilot to an experienced veteran and his crew on their last trip. I can't describe my feelings and I guess that only another pilot in the same situation would know how I felt at that time. Numb, useless, would probably be the best way to describe it. As we crossed occupied French territory we were evidently low enough to be reached by light anti-aircraft fire from German defense positions and, in my

The crew assembles behind GI-T, LM443. *Courtesy of Alan Martin.*

ignorance, I remember admiring the beauty of the red, white, green and amber tracer shells as they climbed slowly into the sky on our starboard side. I imagined an illuminated water fall slowly flowing the wrong way. How naïve can one be in this situation? I was suddenly brought back to reality when we were hit on the starboard wing by one of those innocent looking lights which, fortunately, passed right through but severed the fuel lines to the outboard motor on that side. It was fortunate that the shell passed through without exploding but still deadly serious as it became apparent that we were losing fuel at an alarming rate. F/O Clarke immediately closed down the starboard outer motor and ordered the engineer to cut of its fuel supply. Cool calm efficient team work, and the long term effect of this move had not yet registered on my mind, but I am sure there was never any thought or discussion about scrubbing the 'op', and heading for home.

We were a long way from the target and obviously not high enough to be out of range of that deadly light anti-aircraft fire, so the skipper and engineer had the problem of how to maintain or even gain height with only three engines and to conserve fuel to get us home. The revs had to be increased on the remaining motors to even maintain height and we steadily lagged behind with our loss of airspeed. We did, however manage to reach and bomb the target but received another hit that took out our starboard inner motor and also our radio communication. Now in dire straits we set course for an emergency landing at Stoneycross in the south of England. Entirely on our own, slowly losing height, saving every drop of fuel available by cool and calculated airmanship between pilot and engineer they were able to transfer fuel to the two remaining engines. F/O Clarke, completely in control of the aircraft and the situation, decided to cut the port outer motor at 15,000ft and to maintain height with just one, which he was able to do without any trouble.

I can remember re-crossing occupied France at that height in the dawning light of day without attracting any interest from the defense batteries. We crossed the French coast and headed out into the Channel and about half way across on a heading towards our emergency landing field, F/O Clarke decided that we were maintaining height and that we had enough fuel to reach Mildenhall. He changed course and made a perfect one engined landing in the bright morning sunshine after being posted as missing."

This was F/Lt Richards initiation to operational flying and although many details have been forgotten over the years, he learned valuable lessons that would be essential in completing a 30 mission tour of operations. Aircrews were very superstitious about carrying a 2nd 'dickey' pilot and many crews were lost whilst carrying out this duty. What makes this story even more remarkable is the fact that it was the 30th and last operation of F/O Clarke's tour. The 29 previous missions for the Clarke crew had been completed with only minor incidents; it was this final mission with a 2nd 'dickey' on board that nearly cost them their lives.

F/Lt Richards picks up the story again:

Down To Business

"With my familiarization trip out of the way, we were on the battle order for 3rd August 1944 for a trip to L'Isle Adam in the French countryside adjacent to the Pas de Calais. This was our first trip as an operational crew and

Lancaster LM433 GI-T, the trusty mount of F/Lt Richards & crew showing signs of wear. Shown here with Alan Martin in the pilot's seat and a tally of 75 'ops'. *Courtesy of Alan Martin.*

the objective was to combat the V1 flying bomb menace that was terrorizing London. The German high command hoped the rockets would avenge the Allied bombing of their cities. Destroying the launch and refueling sites for these terror weapons had suddenly become an important strategic target for Bomber Command. The raid went without incident and we were glad to have successfully completed our first mission as a crew. Our next three targets were concentrated on V1 sites at Bassens, Foret de Lucheux and Port de Englos, ironically in Lancaster LM443 GI-T, the Lancaster that F/Lt Richards had his 2nd 'dickey' experience within. F/O Clarke had finished his tour and GI-T was now the aircraft assigned to the Richards crew.

On 12th August 1944 our attention was focused on the industrial city of Russelsheim in the Ruhr Valley on one of two trips we would make to the city. Our target on the first 'op' was to bomb the Opel factory that was making vital supplies for the German military machine and the second trip on 25th August was along the same lines. The next night (26th) we were on the battle order to attack Kiel and the mission went without incident considering the considerable German defenses around the city."

It was around this time that Ivor Richards was promoted to Pilot Officer and moved into the Officers mess:

"The early part of September saw us take LM443 to Le Harve, Kamen, Calais and Frankfurt mainly in support of the Allied invasion forces and to soften up the German resistance on the ground, interspersed with the occasional trip back to the industrial Ruhr. On 23rd September we were on the battle order to attack Neuss and in particular the dock area. The months of October and November 1944 saw us undertake various missions into the German heartland all without major incident. The raid to Homberg on 2nd November was eventful for us being hit by flak and two other 622 Lancasters being lost to the considerable defenses around the target area. The 15th November was to be our last trip in LM433, the 'old lady' had used up her operational hours and she was posted to 1653 Heavy Conversion Unit at RAF Chedburgh until June 1945. Our replacement was a brand spanking new mark one coded NG300 but assigned the same squadron prefix of GI-T and coincided with my promotion to Flight Lieutenant. The old 'Lanc' had served us well and NG300 was destined to be a disaster for us.

Our first trip in the new kite was to Heinsberg to support the ground forces to break the German resistance on the ground. En route, all went according to plan until we came to the point of releasing the bombs, which would not release so we had to dump them in the Channel on the way home. The ground crews carried out extensive testing on the faulty mechanism and we were assured that the fault was rectified for our next trip to Homberg again on 20th November. Once again the bombs failed to release and eventually the fault was identified as an electrical circuit that didn't show up during normal testing.

Here by the Grace of God–'op' 34 Gelsenkirchen

"On 23rd November 1944 we took off at 12:40 hours in our relatively new kite hoping for a better performance and a mission without incident. The mission was a daylight sortie led by GH bombing techniques. Certain Lancasters had G/H radar sets fitted to enable them to positively identify the aiming point. All other Lancasters would format on the G/H equipped Lancasters in a 3 'vic' formation and release their bombs on visually seeing the G/H 'Lanc' release its bombs at 19,000ft. We missed the old Lancaster and her characteristics of crabbing slightly to the port, climbing slowly but surely above any other 'Lancs' and her amazing turn of speed on the downhill run home. All went well until nearing the target and then the usual problem of the Halifaxes arriving early and above us. Too close for comfort, I decided to break formation and climb to another lanc 'V' formation above us and away from the offending Halifaxes. All went well as I put this, done it before practice into operation. I had a deadly fear of being knocked out of the sky by friendly bombs, an unfortunate but not unusual happening.

Climbing away to the selected formation we suddenly and so quickly took on so much thick ice the aircraft just couldn't handle the extra weight and stalled, nose down, where I held her to regain flying speed. I had problems and plenty of them. Once in a dive the ice began breaking off with loud frightening noise. All the instruments had been affected and the windscreen iced over so I was forced to fly by sound. Nose down until I could tell we were traveling too fast and then pulling her out of the dive into a climb until she lost flying speed and began juddering before the stall when I had to push her over the top and into another dive. The 'G' forces going over the top were terrific so everything not restrained was in the top of the aircraft including parachutes and their owners. Then the opposing 'G' force as I pulled her out of the dive when everything returned and was glued to the floor. We went through three of these maneuvers fighting for our lives but there was no time for fear or thought of crashing. Perhaps I was speaking to myself as things were happening so fast there was no time to think of anything but the survival of the aircraft and the crew."

Time To Reflect - The Reunion

"It was from the time of the icing up and the first stall and dive that our respective memories of the incident were so different as we saw and remembered them from the different jobs we were doing and our positions in the aircraft at the time."

F/O Ben Lubell RCAF (Nav) & F/Sgt Alan Martin (W/op) who both assisted in the drama that unfolded when their Lancaster iced up over Gelsenkirchen. *Courtesy of Alan Martin.*

Tom Burnard and the two gunners had 'chewed over' this incident years later when they met up at a 622 Squadron reunion at Mildenhall:

"The reunion of Tom, Alan and I on 3rd July 1997 was, for all of us, quite amazing, as our thoughts concentrated on the events of that last and dramatic mission. After a time lapse of 53 years memories for me that had receded into one incident gradually began to unfold into so many different events that made up the whole. It came to life for the three of us as we shared our different thoughts and how each one was affected and remembered in different ways. For me, although I knew, as skipper, most of the incidents the other two were talking about, I was completely amazed at how far back in the memory they were, never to have returned without our reliving of the incident. Not just by the three of us but also with crew members no longer with us but who had played such an important part in the whole episode. At the start of the emergency I evidently ordered the crew to put on their parachutes and bail out, already an impossibility as the 'chutes' had scattered from the first stall. Ben, the navigator, was the only one left with his 'chute' and the maneuvers were so violent nobody could have made it to the escape hatches anyway. But Ben must have tried and was forced into the top of the aircraft and then hurled down again as the 'G' forces changed, his head colliding with the sharp corner of his 'Gee' set which opened up a severe cut above his right eye, leaving him badly injured and concussed. As the drama unfolded with Alan Martin (W/op) caring for Ben Lubell, I began to remember asking him to also check on the two gunners. The mid upper gunner had fallen out of his turret and was sure that he had a broken leg but fortunately soon forgot about it when he found he was able to stand. The rear gunner, Mickey Campbell was shaken but OK. I had no memory of that incident or that the ammunition had been thrown out of the trays and tracts. Without visibility through the windscreen and no instruments working the situation was desperate but Frank Carter (B/A), calm and responsible as ever, was able to wet a cloth with glycol, clear part of his screen to get a visual horizon and give me instructions how to fly the aircraft straight and level again.

During the drama we had lost height from 19,000 to 6,000ft but things began to return to normality as my screen cleared enabling me to fly visually and the bomb aimer with his screen clear to see that we were nearing the target. He immediately started me on the bombing run at 6,000ft in clear visibility and some minutes ahead of the main force. We had a good run in with no opposition at all, dumped our bomb load and immediately climbed away and set course for home."

Crew photographed in October 1944 in front of LM433. From left, Ben Lubell, Tom Burnard, Ivor Richards, Jim Brierley, Frank Carter, Alan Martin, Micky Campbell. The dog in the photo was the station unofficial mascot named 'Bill Prune'. Apparently, the dog belonged to an aircrew member who failed to return and aircrew considered him a good luck omen, especially when he wandered into this photograph uninvited. *Courtesy of Alan Martin.*

"As soon as the violence stopped Alan was able to take care of Ben who was in a dazed state and he has been crawling between Tom's legs on his way to carry out my orders to bail out. They got him back onto the rest bed where Alan Martin was able to dress his wound, give him morphine and make him as comfortable as possible with extra oxygen. In the heat of the emergency, and then having to concentrate on the bombing run I don't believe I ever knew of Ben's crawl forward into the cabin.

So far so good we were free of ice, survived the ordeal, dumped our bomb load and were climbing away on course for home. Unfortunately, it was not over yet as the 'Gee' set caught fire. It was quickly extinguished by Alan Martin but left us without instruments and without Ben and our navigational aid. The responsibility once again fell on Alan Martin who had to break radio silence to inform group of our predicament. Their response was immediate to give us a course to steer and orders to land at our emergency aerodrome at Woodbridge on the east coast and even having a Mustang fighter escort to avoid enemy attention whilst still over their territory. What a relief to us all as the Mustang approached and stayed on our wing tip until we cleared the French Coast. Getting nearer to home and finding that Ben was comfortable and recovering from his confusion and the aircraft instruments had returned to normal, with strong pressure from the crew to return to base, as none of us wanted the extra trauma of the emergency landing at Woodbridge. The request was granted in part but to land at Newmarket racecourse that had an undulating grass runway for emergency landings and an ambulance would be waiting there for our navigator. It was a good try but there was no way they wanted us landing at Mildenhall and blocking the runway when there was 29 other Lancasters due to land with the dark rapidly closing in.

Without knowing our airspeed and fear of stalling, I erred on the safe side and came into land in the semi darkness, too fast, bounced off the top of an undulation, narrowly avoided digging the starboard wing into the ground at the recorded time of 17:40 hours. The Lancaster then took over and settled and I was able to taxi over to the control tower."

A very good walk away landing

"The ambulance and transport was waiting for us. After seeing Ben Lubell off to Ely hospital, I reported to the control tower Duty Officer and we were quickly on our way by road back to Mildenhall. The normal debriefing session must have finished before our arrival and I don't believe that we were ever debriefed. My thoughts were confirmed by Tom and Alan as we shared our memories recently. It was an unfortunate error because Frank and Alan deserved well earned recognition for their devotion to duty well beyond the norm and would have automatically been picked up by the debriefing officers and the necessary medal recommendation put in place. As the pilot I should have made it known that our survival was clearly due to the quick thinking of Frank Carter our bomb aimer who cleared the screen enabling me to bring the Lancaster into a normal flying position. Then the wonderful work by Alan Martin caring for Ben Lubell, checking on the gunners, putting out the 'Gee' set fire, then making the emergency call to Group. Without that outstanding devotion to duty by both of them, we could never have made it.

On inspection of our Lancaster the ground crew reported that nearly all the coolant fluid had been forced out of the engine vents by the pressure of the violent maneuvers. The ground crew was under the opinion that we must have been upside down at some stage and that the coolant had drained out, a theory confirmed by all the crew who went through the ordeal. I was amazed that a fully laden Lancaster with bomb load still on board could fly upside down and recover. Official reports suggested that five aircraft had been lost on the operation however; there were no defensive opposition so I can assume that the icing affected these other aircraft also.

Our final flight together was to bring 'T' for Tommy back from Newmarket to Mildenhall and so ended our 34th operational trip and the end of our tour. That night we had a celebratory dink in the 'Bird in the Hand' pub, a stones thrown away from the officers quarters and invited our ground crew along. We were all sent on a period of leave and Ben Lubell returned to Canada never to be seen again. Our Lancaster GI-T NG300 was passed into the hands of F/O Clarke DFC the pilot that I had taken on his first trip and they successfully completed their tour in the winter of 1944/45. NG300 was transferred to No.39 M.U. in February 1945 and struck off charge in November 1946."

F/Lt Ivor Richards was awarded a well-earned DFC for completing 34 operational missions over enemy territory and for gaining control of a seemingly doomed Lancaster. The rest of the crew were not recognized for the part they played in saving the doomed aircraft, surely an injustice to a proficient and brave crew that risked all for our freedom.

7

"Sparks"

The route to Bomber Command for Australian John Crago began in early 1942 when he walked into the recruiting office in Perth, Australia, determined to become an airman of whatever denomination. At the time he enlisted there was a waiting list for training and he began his Royal Australian Air Force career as a temporary guard on 4th August 1942. However, by 5th December of the same year he commenced his initial training at No.5 ITS at Clontarf, Western Australia. After several weeks of physical fitness and education courses, he graduated to No.35 course Wireless and Gunnery training followed by attendance at No.1 Bombing and Gunnery School (WAG) at Ballarat Victoria.

In some respects, the role of wireless operator was considered by many to be less glamorous and the role was very often overlooked for promotion and any awards for bravery. The role was similar to that of the flight engineer in as much as the role required an all-round ability and involved a variety of duties within a bomber. For example, the W/op was expected to have a working knowledge of navigation and the navigational equipment in case of death or injury to the aircraft's navigator. This was no easy task because the navigator on a bomber had to pass stringent educational tests to qualify for the role and they underwent extensive training to become competent. In addition the W/op was responsible for checking for bomb 'hang ups' and for switching on the Identification Friend or Foe (IFF) or firing off the colors of the day to trigger happy Allied defense gun batteries. By far the most important role of the wireless operator was to listen out for communications and new instructions from command and to obtain an accurate radio 'fix' for the aircraft to assist the navigator.

The training associated with the role was intensive and began with the basics of radio communications and how to strip and repair a damaged radio set coupled with the mandatory 18 words per minute of transmitting and receiving messages by Morse code. Once the basics were mastered, John Crago learned how to contact ground stations whilst flying. Each stage of the training was assessed and when the required level of competence had been reached, John and the rest of the pupils would move onto an aircraft on their own, quite a different experience. The radio sets used for this instruction were quite basic and usually the R1082 and T1083 radio sets were used to contact a series of ground based operators whilst the aircraft flew within a set radius of the airfield. On completion of the 24 week course graduates were awarded a 'sparks' badge worn on the tunic sleeve.

The next posting for John Crago was to No.3 Bombing and Gunnery School at Sale for air gunnery training, principally air to air and air to ground firing. The aircraft utilized were the Fairey Battle fighter-bombers with two trainees in the rear cockpit

Nineteen year old Sergeant John Crago RAAF. Seen here after just receiving his wireless operator/air gunner's brevet for completing his I.T.S. course. He would attain the rank of Warrant Officer before the time his operational 'tour' was completed. *Courtesy of John Crago.*

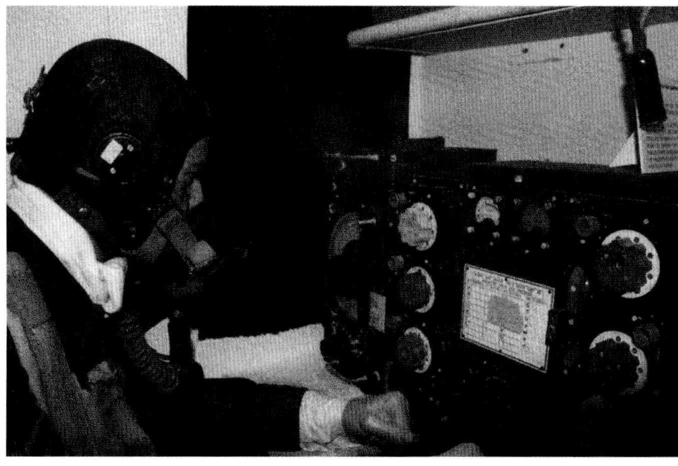

Model of W/op's position and radio receiver. The mannequin is wearing battledress rather than a heated suit. The W/Op position was situated next to the aircraft's heating system and many wireless operators found the heat unbearable, whilst other crew members such as the rear gunner experienced extreme cold. *Courtesy of John Crago.*

Flying Officer Frank Stephens RAAF and crew at No.26 OTU June 1944. L to R: F/Sgt Deacon RAAF (Nav), Sgt K.J. Moran (R/G), F/Sgt J.D. Crago RAAF (W/Op), F/O F. Stephens RAAF (pilot), Sgt A. Young (B/A). *Courtesy of John Crago.*

with a Vickers gas operated machine gun for practice. The three week course was completed on 19th August 1943 and John was awarded his air gunner wings and promotion to sergeant. The successful conclusion of air gunnery training signaled a period of pre-embarkation leave which started with a four day train journey home to Perth and a further nine days before another train journey took John back to Melbourne. It was here that Sergeant John Crago joined approximately 200 other aircrew by embarking on the troopship 'Nieuw Amsterdam' on 27th September 1943.

The route to Great Britain took the ship via Wellington New Zealand finally arriving in San Francisco where the aircrew disembarked and caught a train to New York and they enjoyed five days leave in the 'Big Apple'. After five days exploring and enjoying the American hospitality, John Crago boarded the converted troopship 'Queen Elizabeth' together with approximately 15,000 US Army personnel finally arriving at Greenock Scotland on 9th November 1943.

Eventually Sergeant Crago found himself in Brighton, a seaside town on the south coast of England where he was billeted for three months whilst waiting to continue his training. A posting to No.6 Advanced Flying Unit at Staverton, Gloucestershire followed, with his arrival on 2nd February 1944. John Crago was there for an eight week course designed to familiarize aircrew to English flying conditions and more importantly the extremes of the English weather. The fundamentals of the course were to train and familiarize aircrew on the type of equipment that was fitted to the squadrons of Bomber Command and included operating the Marconi T1154 transmitter and the R1155 receiver in Avro Anson aircraft. A series of training flights ensued mainly for establishing communication with ground stations requesting QDM's (magnetic course to steer to reach base) and position fixes on the MF (low frequency) band. A 'fix' involved two or more ground stations taking bearings on the aircraft's transmission, plotting the 'fix' and transmitting the position back to the aircraft.

After successfully negotiating the course Sergeant John Crago and fellow course members were re-categorized as wireless operators (air) and entitled to wear the 'S' wing and would no longer undertake gunnery duties. The significance of John's training could only mean that he was destined for multi-engine aircraft and the inevitable posting to Bomber Command.

On 4th April 1944 John Crago was posted to No. 26 OTU at Wing in Buckinghamshire for 'crewing up' and final preparations to join a bomber squadron. A posting to an OTU was a natural progression for all aircrew after completing individual instruction in their respective specialism. Now at an OTU, the air 'trades' were brought together as one crew. Eight weeks of instruction usually in Vickers Wellington bombers honed individual skills into a team ethos. Each member of the crew were dependent on the other for survival. Crews would be expected to achieve a certain level of competence during training exercises both during the day and at night. These exercises tested the newly qualified aircrew to their limits, essential if they were to survive on an operational squadron.

It was at the Operational Training Unit that the 'crews' were formed and they would normally stay together throughout their full 'tour' of operations, usually thirty. The process for crewing up was unique and although the process was nonsensical, the Royal Air Force had every confidence in its aircrew training and every person in the room had reached the required standard. At this stage aircrew consisted of six members, and the seventh member of the crew, the flight engineer, would join the crew at Heavy Conversion Unit prior to joining an operational squadron. Each pilot would wander around the room selecting the required people to make up his crew and after the Air Force's usually high level of assessment this process was rudimentary to say the least. John Crago was approached by Flying Officer Frank Stephens a fellow Australian pilot and asked to join his crew, to which he readily accepted. The 'pick and mix' continued until Frank Stephens had selected his crew, which are pictured above.

Continued Training

After successfully completing the course at Operational training Unit, F/Sgt Crago and his new crew were posted to 1653 Heavy Conversion Unit at RAF Chedburgh in Norfolk. It was here that crews first experienced the four engined heavy bombers and the aircraft used at Chedburgh were the Short Stirling. Compared to the Vickers Wellington bomber the 'Stirling' was a massive machine towering over 30 feet from the ground point to the top of the cockpit. The Short Stirling had been withdrawn from front line operations due to its inability to reach heights above 17,000 feet when fully laden and the result was easy pickings for the German flak and night fighters. However ungainly on the ground, in the air the Short Stirling was very maneuverable and pilots appreciated its capabilities and tight turning characteristics. It was at Chedburgh that the flight engineer joined the crew. It was his duty to manage the fuel and mechanical systems in the four engined bombers to relieve some of the pressures that were placed upon the pilot. F/O Frank Stephens quickly mastered the art of circuits and bumps and each aircrew designation got his chance to practice his new found skills. This came via exercises such as cross country, fighter affiliation and bombing practice culminating in night flying and navigation skills. Once competent on the Short Stirling the crew was posted to No.3 Lancaster Finishing School at Feltwell in Norfolk to be introduced to the machine that they would take to war, the Avro Lancaster. RAF Feltwell was the 'finishing' school for 3 Group Bomber Command and therefore gave F/O Stephens and crew an early indication to their eventual operational posting. More familiarization trips took place only this time in a Lancaster, which was a wonderful aircraft to fly in and quite comfortable for a bomber. Towards the end of the course, Flying Officer Stephens informed the crew that they had been posted to 622 Squadron at RAF Mildenhall in Suffolk.

Mildenhall was a pre-war base and also home to XV Squadron and provided the luxury of houses for crews to stay in as opposed to the usual hastily built billets. The crew was introduced to the Commanding Officer 'Blondie' Swales DSO, DFC, and DFM who was a Wing Commander and held in high regard by all on the squadron. F/O Stephens completed a 2nd 'dickey' trip with an experienced operational pilot and the crew found themselves assigned to 'A' flight under S/Ldr Richard Allen DFC the Flight Commander. On 17th September 1944 the name of Flying Officer Frank Stephens and crew appeared on the battle order for the first time to attack German gun sites at Boulogne in France. The aircraft that they were assigned was GI-C, HK621 a Lancaster that became associated with the crew and one in which they completed the majority of their missions. Several missions followed in quick succession and on the 3rd October 1944 the crew was briefed to attack the Sea wall at Walcheren Island on the Dutch coast. The following narrative has been provided by F/Sgt John Crago and describes the mission to destroy the German defenses:

"After D day and the breakout from the Normandy area, Allied armies in the northern offensive were held up by the Germans guarding the Scheldt Estuary and the approaches to the Dutch port of Antwerp. The port was essential to supply the Allied Armies and although Antwerp had been captured, it was useless until such time as the Schedlt Estuary was cleared of German gun positions commanding the sea lanes. Following several conferences the Allied commanders determined that the best means of achieving the desired result was to flood the island of Walcheren by breaching the sea wall. Approval to this action was given by the Allied Supreme Commander, General Eisenhower. The island is on the western side of the estuary, most of the land being about six feet lower than the surrounding water. On the western side of the island near the town of Westkapelle the sea wall, or dyke, was about 200 feet wide with a gradual slope down to the sea."

"The task of breaching the dyke was given to Bomber Command, advance warning being given to the civilian population through BBC broadcasts and leaflet drops. As the operation was an experimental one, nobody knew whether the attack would be successful. A fairly large strike force of 240 Lancasters was arranged to attack in eight waves with a bomb load of 10, 500lbs 94.74 tons) including one 500lbs time delay bomb to discourage any attempt to repair the breach. The date of the operation

Serial No. ....154. 1st. Battle Order for 16th. September, 1944. No. 622 Squadron.

A/C. NO.	LETTER	CAPT. & 2ND. PILOT.	NAV. & W/OPERATOR.	A/B. & M.U. GNR.	R/GNR. & F/ENGINEER.
[illegible]	B.	F/O. Barnett	Sgt. Grimsey F/S. Sullivan	F/O. Hurditch Sgt. Staplehurst	Sgt. Nicholls Sgt. Murrell
[illegible]. 621	C.	F/O. Stephens	F/S. Deacon F/S. Crago	Sgt. Young Sgt. Fitzsimmons	Sgt. Moran Sgt. Green
D. 225	D.	F/Lt. Stratton	F/Lt. Nicholl F/O. Chapman	F/O. Thurston F/Lt. Ward	W/O. Summerton Sgt. Clifton
[illegible]	G.	F/O. Neilson	Sgt. Perry F/S. Silbert	F/O. Blundell F/S. Lean	F/S. Drury Sgt. Williams
[illegible]. 709	H.	F/O. Thomson	F/S. Ward F/S. Aland	F/S. Dilley Sgt. Smith (184)	Sgt. Woolloff Sgt. Boulton
D. 229	K.	F/O. Locke	Sgt. Bell Sgt. Hoy	F/S. Robertson F/O. Maxwell	Sgt. Hawkes Sgt. O'Donnell
[illegible]. 617	Y.	F/O. Armitstead	F/S. Brewster Sgt. Foulkes	Sgt. Daniels Sgt. Haylock	Sgt. Borge Sgt. Peck
K. 619	Z.	F/O. Bourne	F/S. Bourne W/O. Taylor	P/O. Brown Sgt. Heffron	F/S. Humphrys Sgt. Vincent.
L. [illegible]	M.	F/O. Jones	Sgt. Westbrook Sgt. Keatley	Sgt. Gibson Sgt. Geddes	Sgt. Desbresque Sgt. Dryland
[illegible]. 283	O.	F/Lt. Orton	F/O. Simpson Sgt. Collins	F/O. Humphreys Sgt. Strong	W/O. Prince Sgt. Davis
[illegible]. 164	P.	F/O. Cox	F/O. Taylor F/S. Shine	F/O. Titchener Sgt. Matthews	Sgt. Gilroy Sgt. Hughes
[illegible]. 614	R.	F/O. Ionson	F/S. Wood F/S. Clarke	F/S. Berkley Sgt. Welsh	Sgt. Dodson Sgt. Ross
[illegible]. 413	T.	F/O. Richards (NZ)	F/O. Lubell F/Lt. Noonan	F/O. Carter Sgt. Brierley	Sgt. Campbell Sgt. Burnard
[illegible]. 915	U.	F/O. Fomer	F/S. Brooker F/S. Vaughan	F/O. Ward F/S. Lothian	F/S. Hogan Sgt. Beechem
[illegible]. 202	V.	F/S. Myles	F/S. Aveyard W/O. Mills	Sgt. Reily F/S. Field	F/S. Scholl Sgt. Crawford
[illegible]. 616	W.	F/O. Woods	F/S. Grebt Sgt. Johnson	Sgt. Taylor Sgt. Henderson	Sgt. Gentley Sgt. Cooney

Officer i/c. Flying Rations : F/O. HEAD. (To report to Sqdn. Adjutant at 16.00 hours).
Briefing to be notified later.

(Sgd). I.C.K. Swales, D.F.C., D.F.M. W/Cdr
Commanding, No. 622 Squadron, R.A.

W/C. Swales. S/Ldr. Allen. F/Lt. Dean. F/Lt. Gillies. F/O. Smith. F/O. Williams. F/Lt. Ward

Battle order for F/O Stephens and crew's first operation to the gun sites at Boulogne on 16th September 1944. *Courtesy of John Crago.*

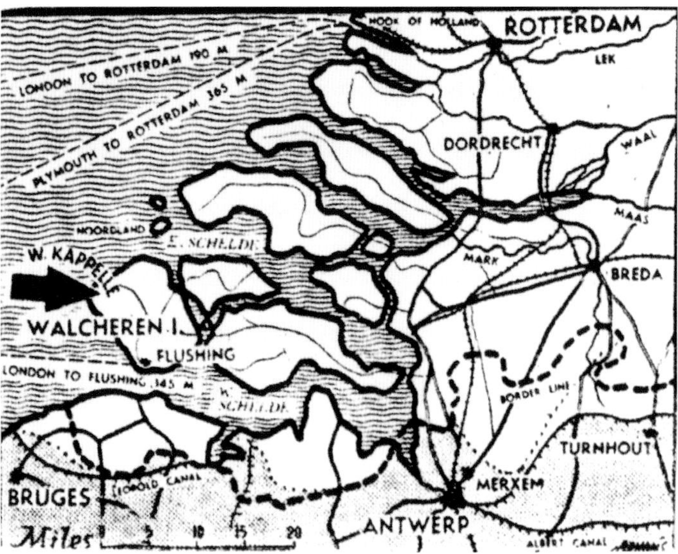

Map showing the exact position of Walcheren Island and the intended aiming points (marked by the arrow) specified to breach the sea wall defenses. The result would be to flood the Island and force the German occupying forces to retreat. *Courtesy of John Crago*

was 3rd October 1944, H-hour set at 1300hrs (near to high tide) the aiming point being the large breakwater south of Westkapelle, to be identified by nine 'Pathfinder' force aircraft under instructions from a master bomber.

Twelve aircraft from 622 Squadron led the first wave with our aircraft HK621 GI-C, being the ninth over the target. As the weather was clear we were able to bomb visually from a height of 4, 600feet at 1304 hrs, the bomb aimer reported a direct hit on the aiming point. Very little flak was encountered and all aircraft returned safely, most within three hours of take-off.

The operation was a success, photo reconnaissance showing a complete breach in the sea wall of 100 yards, later enlarged to 130 yards with flooded areas extending from the breach. A few days later further attacks with lesser numbers of aircraft were made on the sea wall near Flushing, Rammekens and Veere resulting in further breeches in the dyke. By 17th October most of the island was inundated. On 4th October a daily newspaper reported the initial attack under the headline 'RAF "Sinks" an Island'."

"Although it was a military success, in spite of warnings, post war reports indicated that 159 civilians had lost their lives in the operation. The general consensus of Walcheren residents was that they held no hard feelings against the Allied crews, accepting the bombardment and flooding as a necessary part of the liberation.

On November 1st 1944 British troops landed near West Kapelle and Flushing and by 9th November German resistance ceased. Fifteen days later, the first Allied supply ships were unloaded at Antwerp. Eventually the breaches in the dykes were repaired and the island again reclaimed. However, it is understood that the island again disappeared for a second time because additional reclamation has been carried out so that it is now an integral part of mainland Holland. It is ironic that although the operation was probably one of the easiest carried out by Bomber Command, it has been publicized more than most."

WEDNESDAY OCTOBER 4 1944

RAF 'SINKS' DUTCH ISLAND TO SILENCE NAZI GUNS

LANCASTERS have struck two surprise blows with their 5½-ton block-busters, letting in the water of the North Sea's high tide yesterday to menace German batteries on Walcheren Island, which block the way to Antwerp, and letting out the water along miles of the great Dortmund-Ems Canal, North-West Germany's most vital waterway.

THE LETTING-IN must have given the Germans one of their biggest surprises of the war. The garrison and gun crews, comfortably settled behind the great dykes which, are 200 feet wide at the base, and with the sea between them and the Allied armies, felt snug and secure.

But at 1 p.m. yesterday the first wave of Lancasters flew over West Kapelle, the western tip of the island, and started blasting a 125-yard gap in the great sea wall.

The headlines on 4th October in a daily newspaper announcing the success of the raid to Walcheren Island. *Author's Collection*

Crash Landing

Operations continued for Flying Officer Stephens and crew, and they became a proficient crew in a short space of time. Eight operations later the crew was on the battle order to attack the Marshaling Yards at Koblenz. The crew for this mission were a mixture of replacements with the addition of a mid under gunner. By this stage of the war the Allies attempted to stop the German night fighters from attacking from beneath the bombers by fitting a .5 caliber machine gun in the underside of the fuselage slightly to the rear of the mid upper gun position. A percentage of each squadron's aircraft were modified to accommodate the new defensive gun and an eighth member of aircrew was added to operate the gun. The idea was that a small number of these Lancasters with the underside defensive gun would fly in the bomber stream, identify night fighters attacking from below, and subsequently defend the aircraft. These spare gunners were usually volunteers from other crews or aircrew that had lost their crew due to unfortunate circumstances. One such Lancaster was HK621, GI-C the usual Lancaster that Flying Officer Stephens flew when serviceable. The eighth member of the crew was F/Sgt W. (Jock) McRae and he had the uncomfortable job of searching the night sky below for German night fighters attacking from below whilst lying prone in the fuselage. The crew for this particular mission was as follows:

Lancaster HK621, GI-C at RAF Mildenhall dispersal. Delivered to 622 Squadron in August 1944 this Lancaster had only completed 115 hours flying time when it was crash landed by F/O Stephens near Florennes in Belgium. *Author's Collection.*

Pilot F/O Stephens RAAF
Nav P/O Deacon RAAF
W/Op F/Sgt Crago RAAF
B/A Sgt Young RAF
F/E Sgt Green RAF
MUG Sgt Fitzsimmons RAF
M/Under G. F/Sgt McRae RAF
R/G Sgt Barclay RAF

John Crago picks up the story of this fated mission:

"On Monday 6th November 1944, having completed 14 operations, we were briefed for our 15th attack on the German town of Koblenz on the Rhine.The operation was limited to aircraft of No.3 Group comprising 128 Lancasters. Our bomb load was one 4,000lb HE bomb plus incendiaries to be aimed at sky markers dropped by aircraft fitted with G/H radar equipment. It was a night operation, time on target 1930 hrs.

We took off at approximately 1700 hrs, route Reading. South coast, France, Belgium, approaching the target from the north. At this stage of the war, the front line was near the border of Belgium and Germany and we crossed at about 19,000feet, saw flashes on the ground followed by flak bursts, some of which were close. Shortly before the 1900 hours Group broadcast, the flight engineer who had gone off intercom to attend to an oxygen problem, returned with an alarming exclamation that the starboard outer engine was unserviceable. Following a brief discussion the skipper said that they would attempt to feather the propeller. As there appeared to be no cause for concern and it was time for the 1900 hrs Group broadcast I went off the intercom.

Returning at 1903 hrs to the intercom, I was greeted by the skipper giving the order 'prepare to abandon aircraft'. My immediate reactions were bewilderment and horror. How could the situation have deteriorated to such an extent? Then I could only think of clipping on the parachute and getting to the nearest escape hatch as quickly as possible. Removing the helmet and oxygen mask, I realized that the cabin was full of smoke which did nothing to ease my state of mind.

Getting out of the seat and moving towards the front escape hatch I noticed our navigator Fred talking on the intercom and indicating that I should return to my position. It was a great relief to learn the immediate danger was over, that we were turning back from the target to attempt a landing at an emergency airfield at Juvincourt in France. Later I learned that the pilot and engineer were unable to feather the engine and it had caught fire. Attempts to cut off the fuel supply to the engine failed leading to cutting fuel to both starboard engines. The outer propeller was 'wind milling' causing considerable drag and with the port engines running at full power, the port outer overheated and had to be throttled back.

Operating on one and a half engines meant that the aircraft could not maintain height. The skipper ordered that guns, ammunition and movable non-essential equipment be thrown out and the bombs jettisoned in order to lighten the load. He agreed to me attempting to advise base that we were making a landing in France. We had been given the position of Juvincourt only a few days beforehand but at that stage radio facilities were not available. I endeavored to make contact with Group HQ using both fixed and trailing aerials on the HF band without success. Retuning the transmitter I received an answer from the MF base station normally reserved for emergency situations and transmitted the message. The base station also asked for a position fix requiring a continuous signal to be sent for lengthy periods. After what seemed an age, probably due to our rapidly losing height, I received the fix. Returning to the intercom to advise the navigator I heard the bomb aimer's voice 'Do you want me to jump now skipper?' Dismay returned as the skipper confirmed my query and that I should also get out. Being off the intercom most of the time, I was unaware that the gunners and navigator had previously jumped. Later I learnt that despite the lessening of the load, the aircraft was still losing height and was approaching a critically low level, so crew members not required were told to bail out.

Moving forward to the front escape hatch my main thought was that what couldn't happen to me was in fact happening! Not a happy thought! Passing the engineer's seat I noticed that his parachute had been pulled and the silk canopy had billowed out of its covering. It was obvious that for him to get out safely would be very unlikely. There was a blast of air coming up through the open escape hatch and I pondered on how to go out, aware that one should go head first. At training, we had limited practice in such a procedure. Fortunately the approved method came to me, sitting on the rear ledge facing forward until dragged out by the slipstream. I was clutching the 'D' ring of the chute and experienced a rush of air, a sharp crack, (presumably the chute opening) then being suspended in the harness looking at the aircraft disappearing into the night.

Realizing the chute had opened was an immense relief and I was conscious of swinging from side to side. Thinking that I may be sick if it continued I tried to control the swing, felt overhead for the straps but couldn't find them. The situation was resolved when, with a terrific crash, I hit the ground. Having no idea of the aircraft height when I jumped and being pitch black meant that I was unaware of the proximity of the ground. The time in the parachute seemed only a few seconds but was probably about a half minute which would make the height less than 1,000 feet.

On landing, all parts seemed to hit the ground at once. There was a fairly strong wind and I was dragged along by the chute. I hit the harness release but apparently only the top straps released, the leg straps slipped around my ankles and I was pulled along by my legs. Eventually extricating myself I got to my feet and was relieved to find everything seemed alright. Having been off the intercom I had no idea whether my landing was on our side of the front line or the enemies. Advice given to aircrew that came down behind enemy lines was to either bury or hide the parachute so as to conceal ones presence and, if possible avoid capture. I could see nothing, but appeared to have come down in an open field. There was no means of burying the chute and I couldn't see anything let alone a place to hide, so I left it where it lay.

I started to walk into the unknown and shortly came to a road where after a few minutes, in the distance; I saw the lights of a vehicle approaching. Thinking it could be Germans, I hid behind some bushes at the side of the road. It was a truck but I could not determine whether it was theirs or ours. Soon after resuming walking there was a noise at the side and I was challenged by a guard who appeared to be an American. With some relief I said that I had bailed out of an aircraft. He looked at me incredulously and said "Are you from those British bombers? You wear a tie in combat?" I managed to convince him and he led me into the base to one of his officers who took me to the MO's tent. The doctor produced a bottle of whisky and poured out half a mug, he must have thought I needed it! I was asked what had become of my parachute and when I explained, a couple of them set out to retrieve it. Parachute silk was much sought after and had saleable value."

"The base was a US Air Force base near the town of Florennes in Belgium and I learned that our Lancaster had crash landed with the skipper and engineer safe. I was taken to a RAF unit at Rosee and there met other members of the crew who had all bailed out safely. It transpired that just after I had jumped the airfield lights were turned on so that one of their aircraft could land. By this time our skipper was down to under 1,000 feet and too low to bail out successfully. The skipper lined up on the runway and brought the aircraft in without the benefit of either wheels or communication with the base. With the

F/Sgt W. 'Jock' McRae who occupied the mid under gun position during the fated mission to Koblenz on 6th November 1944. F/Sgt McRae and F/Sgt Crago were the only members of the crew to return to operational flying with 622 Squadron. Tragically Jock McRae was killed on his very next operation on 6th January 1945 when on a mission to lay mines in Danzig Bay. He had volunteered to be a spare gunner in the crew of Pilot Officer Eoin Francis RAAF. *Courtesy of John Crago.*

runway blocked the returning aircraft had to be diverted. Damaged beyond repair our Lancaster was written off. On our return to England instead of being sent back to the squadron as expected, we were taken to No.107 Personnel Dispatch Center at St. Johns Wood London and treated as evadees. Following medical examination all our regular crew except me and the spare mid under gunner F/Sgt Jock McRae, were declared medically unfit for operational flying. McRae and I returned to the squadron where, as a spare W/op, I was fortunate to complete a further nine operations before the war ended. 'Jock' McRae, on his next operation, was killed along with the crew of another Australian pilot P/O Eoin Francis, failing to return from a mine laying 'op' in Danzig Bay on 6th January 1945."

When John Crago returned to 622 Squadron it was a little uncomfortable because the squadron did not know what to do with aircrew members that were surplus to needs. It was traditional for 'spares' to fit in with other crews when they had a vacancy due to illness or injury from operations. In this way 'spares' would either become accepted into new crews on a permanent basis or go from crew to crew. Established crews would consider that taking a new aircrew member on operations was a bad omen and therefore it was very difficult for the spare airmen to form a bond with a new crew and the original airmen would quickly return where possible. After some consideration he was advised that he would be retained as a 'spare'.

On his arrival back at Mildenhall John Crago lacked confidence after his ordeal and wished for a return to operations to confront his fear. On 29th December 1944, he was selected to replace the W/op in the crew of Flying Officer Waigh and it was with great apprehension that he entered the briefing room. The Commanding Officer entered the room with all the briefing officers and the target was revealed as Koblenz, the same target that he was shot down attacking back in November. On this occasion the raid was successfully completed although the Lancaster returned with a few flak holes for repair.

F/Sgt Crago completed a further nine operations acting as a spare wireless operator and through his level of competence in the air his confidence returned. The remainder of his 'tour' was uneventful except for the one to Potsdam when his skipper was F/Lt Arkins. The rear gunner claimed a Me109 shot down, although this was never confirmed. In the last month of the war John Crago now a Warrant Officer was placed in the crew of F/O Clement and completed another four missions with this crew including their last operation to Bremen on 22nd April 1945. When the German surrender finally came John completed three trips under the operation 'Exodus' guise to bring back prisoners of war to England.

In total, John Crago completed 23 operations against the enemy and these were achieved with determination and courage after having a nerve shattering experience with his original crew. Only one member of John Crago's original crew returned to active service and John's courage is testament to all aircrew that fought bravely with Bomber Command during the Second World War. Without the sacrifice of the many thousands of Commonwealth airmen fighting for a belief in humanity we would have surely lost the war.

Serial No.....................40. 1st. Battle Order for 18th. February. 1945. No. 622 Squadron.

[illegible] NO.	[illegible]ER.	CAPT. & 2nd. PILOT.	NAV. & W/[illegible]R.	A/[illegible] GUNNER.	R/GUNNER & F/ENGINEER.
HK. 651.	B.	F/S. Fiedler	F/S. Elliott F/S. Fitch	F/[illegible] Doherty Sgt. [illegible]lmer & F/S. Boone	Sgt. Smith 498 Sgt. Taylor.
PD. 366.	E.	F/O. Darville	F/S. Lisle F/S. Keough	F/S. Pearce Sgt. Dunn	Sgt. Beckwith Sgt. Godfrey
HK. 787.	F.	F/S. Ray	F/O. Boyle F/S. [illegible] CRAGO	F/S. Lewis Sgt. Heywood	Sgt. Armitage Sgt. Ormshaw
PD. 225.	G.	F/O. Thorbecke	F/L. Westbrock Sgt. Adams	F/O. Villiers Sgt. Staels	Sgt. Smith 445 Sgt. Hogan
LL. 885.	J.	F/O. Morrison	F/S. Orr Sgt. Totman	F/O. Pollard F/S. Stock	Sgt. West Sgt. Chambers
PB. 819.	K.	F/O. [illegible] 3	Sgt. Morgan Sgt. [illegible]	Sgt. Brabazon Sgt. Dewey	Sgt. Jones Sgt. Eastwood
HK. 628.	X.	F/O. Willis	F/S. Walters F/S. Robinson	F/O. [illegible] Sgt. Hawkins & F/S. Boyce	Sgt. Farthing Sgt. Campbell
PA. 218.	L	F/L. [illegible]	F/S. [illegible] F/O. Dixon	F/S. Brown Sgt. Morris	Sgt. Williams Sgt. McCue
HK. 646.	M.	F/Lt. Thomas	F/S. McKay F/S. Charlesworth	F/S. Cambell F/S. Kingston & Sgt. Mitchell 222.	F/S. Davies 950 Sgt. Ralph
NG. 299.	O.	F/Lt. Ogilby	F/Lt. [illegible] F/O. [illegible]	F/O. Tanner Sgt. Reed	Sgt. Watkins Sgt. Barton
PA. 164.	P.	F/Lt. Cook	F/O. Parry F/O. Sherry	F/O. Gough Sgt. Savage 610	Sgt. Hogerty Sgt. McLaren
NG. 447.	U.	F/O. [illegible]	Sgt. [illegible] Sgt. [illegible]	Sgt. Wood Sgt. Stone	Sgt. Savage 800 Sgt. Gough
PB. 795.	V.	F/L. [illegible]	F/S. McKeown F/S. Weller	F/O. Sleigh F/S. [illegible]	F/S. Ross. Sgt. Lucas-Garner
HK. 615.	Z.	F/O. [illegible]	Sgt. [illegible] Sgt. [illegible]	Sgt. Gross Sgt. Pearce & F/S. Chapman	Sgt. Nairne Sgt. Chittock

Rations to be collected by F/Commanders and delivered to Aircraft.
Briefing to be notified later.
F/O. Robbins & Crew to stand by for Radar. G.H. Air craft. E. K. L. V.

(SGD) J.A. Brignell. S/Ldr.
Commanding, No. 622 Squadron.

F/L. Arkins. F/L. McHugh. F/L. Johnson. F/O. Arben. F/L. Noonan. F/O. Gowan. P/O. Hills. P/O. [illegible]. P/O. Glasspool.

Battle order for 18th February 1945 showing F/Sgt Crago as the W/op in the crew of F/Sgt Ray. John Crago completed nine operations in total whilst acting as a replacement wireless operator. The pilot F/S Ray and his crew were killed shortly after this mission on 2nd March 1945 (Cologne) being shot down by a direct flak hit that was witnessed by several other aircrew in the formation. *Author's Collection*

8

Against the Odds

Pilot: F/O H. P. Peck RAAF- D.F.C
Nav: F/Sgt J. W. Barchard RAAF
B/A: F/O A. G. Long RAAF
W/op: F/O R.T Cargill RAAF
MUG: Sgt J. Rumsey D.F.M
R/G: Sgt D. C. Pudney D.F.M
F/E: Sgt R. C. Bowyer

Denis Pudney's ambition to join the Royal Air Force as an aircrew member was achieved through sheer determination and endeavor. What is remarkable about his story is that he is one of only a few air gunners to confront a German night fighter and shoot down that fighter whilst defending his crew and Lancaster. For his considerable skill and bravery, he was awarded an immediate Distinguished Flying Medal.

War was declared on the 3rd September 1939 and the conscription age was set at twenty years of age. Denis Pudney was not twenty until February 1940 therefore he missed out on the first call to arms. The time Denis spent waiting was not wasted and it gave him the opportunity to volunteer for the RAF after being impressed by the sight of a friend on leave from the RAF with his smart uniform, sergeant's stripes and air gunner's brevet.

It was not until the summer of 1943 that Denis Pudney reported to an aircrew selection center and passed the required tests to become an air gunner. Within a week, he received a telegram telling him to report to St. Johns Wood to receive his uniform and the coveted white flash to place in his forage cap, denoting aircrew under training. After the formalities of the Aircrew Reception Center, he was posted to Bridgenorth in Shropshire for the start of his air gunnery training. The town of Bridgenorth is split in two, known as upper town and lower town. Most of the instruction was aircraft recognition, dissembling and assembling the Browning machine gun, the obligatory classroom lessons in bullet composition, trajectory and turret maintenance. A posting to an initial training wing at Bridlington in Yorkshire followed in November 1943 and the course instruction intensified with considerably more theory and exams to contend with. In early December, Denis Pudney was posted to No.2 Gunnery School at Dalcross near Nairn on the Moray Firth in Scotland for continuation of his air gunner training. It was at Dalcross that he received his flying equipment and got his hands on live ammunition. The candidates utilized mock turrets whilst films of enemy aircraft moving from all angles were shown against a wall with the objective of firing imaginary rounds at the enemy aircraft.

Eventually the trainees were allocated to flights and in early January 1944 Denis Pudney and three other gunners climbed aboard an Avro Anson twin engined aircraft and took it in turns to fire the Lewis machine gun out into the sea. This progressed onto each candidate being given 200 rounds of ammunition that were painted an individual color applicable to each candidate. Armed with their own pan of bullets, the trainee gunners would fire at a drogue being towed by another aircraft, any hits on the drogue would register in the color applicable to the candidate, and individual scores would be assessed. To add to the assessment process, on occasions the guns would be removed and replaced with a camera and 25 feet of film to expose. Each time the trigger was pulled the camera would record the action and the instructor would play back the camera action to the candidate and analyze his performance.

After eight weeks Denis Pudney successfully passed his Air Gunnery training and he was issued his sergeant stripes and air gunner's brevet which he proudly sewed onto his tunic. After a short period of leave he received instructions to report to No.84 Operational Training Unit (OTU) at Desborough in Northamptonshire for an introduction into the bomber aircraft that he would take to war and to join a bomber crew as an air gunner. The aircraft utilized at OTUs were time served bombers, usually the Vickers Wellington, that had seen considerable service and were a challenge for the ground crews to keep operational. It was at Desborough that Sergeant Pudney joined the crew of Pilot Officer Harold Peck of the Royal Australian Air Force along with three other members of the crew from Australia, three of them being commissioned officers.

RAF Chedburgh in Suffolk was a heavy Bomber Conversion unit and the next destination for Flying Officer Peck and his newly formed crew. Four engined Stirling bombers were based at Chedburgh and there was now a requirement to have a seventh crew member in the form of a flight engineer. Sergeant Robert Bowyer joined the crew and it was his job to assist the pilot and to balance the fuel and engine management systems associated with a large bomber. The majority of the training at Chedburgh was focused around circuits and landings by day and night designed to allow every crew member to become familiar with their own position within the aircraft. A period of cross country and fighter affiliation practice followed along with high level bombing culminating in a final flight on 29th June 1944. Next, the crew moved to RAF Feltwell in Norfolk which was the designation of a Lancaster Finishing School (LFS). The Lancaster was the mainstay of bomber command and a wonderful aircraft with its own characteristics, which the crew had to master before they could be posted to an operational squadron. The crew again experienced a series of circuits and landings, similar to the course content to that experienced at the OTU, designed to familiarize them with the Avro Lancaster, the bomber that they would take to war. Harold Peck soon mastered the superb Lancaster and the crew were informed of their posting to a front line squadron. .

622 Squadron

RAF Mildenhall was a pre-war station with permanent buildings that offered aircrew a degree of comfort compared to what they had previously experienced whilst training. On arrival Flying Officer Peck and crew were allocated to 'A' flight with the Officers amongst them moving into Officers quarters and the NCOs moving into peacetime married quarters. The first seven days concentrated on more intensive training starting on 16th July with fighter affiliation, air tests and practice bombing runs whilst fully laden. In addition, the crew endured a series of loaded climbs with dummy bombs that were dropped in the North Sea. Finally, several practice flights were undertaken in the art of formation flying.

The crew was now considered ready to commence operational flying which meant flying missions against the enemy involving every ounce of their training to be utilized if they were to survive a 30 mission tour of operations. It was customary for the pilot to complete a second 'dickey' trip with an experienced pilot before he would take his own crew into action. On 17th July Flying Officer Peck joined the crew of Flying Officer O'Brien RNZAF for a trip to bomb the railway yards at Vaires on the outskirts of Paris. Unfortunately, the master bomber recalled all the bombers and Harold Peck failed to complete his mission. The next night he was on the battle order to join the crew of Flying Officer M.T. Thomas RAAF on a mission to bomb the railway junctions at Aulnoye in France, which was successfully carried out. F/O Thomas and crew would all lose their lives on the night of 24/25th July when a German night fighter intercepted the bomber stream en route to Stuttgart.

F/O Peck returned from this trip to a barrage of questions from the crew who were eager to know what the experience felt like, they would shortly know for themselves on the night of 23rd July, target Kiel.

Denis Pudney picks up the story:

> "Each member had a preliminary meeting with their own job section because we had been informed we would be going on operations that day or night, but we never knew the target until the main briefing. The ground staff of each aircraft meanwhile had quite a massive task of preparing the Lancasters for the mission including fitting the bomb load, ammunition and fuel. Each ground crew member was highly trained in their respective duties and they gained the respect of all aircrew for they toiled in all weathers on an open airfield. We were then transported to the aircraft allotted to us for that particular 'op'. We each checked everything was serviceable, the pilot running up the engines, the gunners checking the guns and each crew member checking their respective equipment.
>
> All crews who were going on the night's operation would be assembled in the main briefing room awaiting the arrival of squadron Commanding Officer, Wing Commander Ian Swales affectionately known as 'blondie'. We all stood to attention until he took his seat in the front row. On the platform, each trade 'leader' took his turn to deliver their briefing. For example, the navigators were told course and deviations to the course to avoid the German defenses, the wireless operators were informed of code words and operational codes in case of emergency. Eventually the weatherman stood up and told all present about what weather was predicted to the target and back. In general, weathermen took the brunt of the ridicule from around the room, although this was always good humored as a reflection of their inability to predict the weather to any degree of accuracy. At the

The crew Denis Pudney joined comprised four Australians. L-R: F/Sgt Barchard RAAF (Nav), Sgt Rumsey (MUG), F/O Long RAAF (B/A), F/O Peck RAAF (Pilot), F/O Cargill RAAF (W/op), F/Sgt Pudney (R/G), Sgt Bowyer (F/E). *Courtesy of Denis Pudney DFM*

end of the briefing, the crews would walk noisily to the locker rooms to collect their flying gear.

The gunners were in the coldest part of the aircraft so were clothed accordingly. Long sleeved vest, long johns, thick white roll neck pullover, battle dress, thick white socks over ordinary socks, electrically heated suit with studs at the back to connect to electric slippers and studs on sleeves to connect to the gloves. An inner kapok flying suit, an outer canvas suit, long leather gauntlet gloves, long suede flying boots, leather helmet incorporating intercom for listening, goggles, oxygen mask, and finally 'Mae West' on the chest in case of ditching. There was no room for the parachute, so that was left in the fuselage near the turret. There were plugs in the turret to connect to electric suit and intercom and a rubber concertina tube fixed to the oxygen mask and the other end with a bayonet fixture to fit in a recess in the turret.

Shortly before the allotted take off time, the crews were transported in covered vans around the airfield to the aircraft they were designated to fly in for that mission. The crews would then climb aboard and go through the preflight checks. There were many Lancasters around the perimeter and we would follow each one round to the takeoff runway with approximately one minute between each aircraft taking off. Once airborne a triangular course would be taken at a predetermined height and all aircraft would pass over the airfield through crossed searchlights heading for the coast. From this point onwards, the aircraft climbed to the required height and we settled down to the job in hand keeping intercom chatter to a minimum. I was always apprehensive as we crossed the North Sea en route to the target due to the risk of collision and the enemy night fighters who lurked in the dark striking at will any unsuspecting crew. The tension surrounding a mission was endless and exhausting and as a rear gunner, I always felt isolated from the rest of the crew. Once an hour the skipper would call and say, "Are you alright Pud"? This was a reassuring measure to me and one that had immeasurable content.

When we reached the target everything seemed to be happening at once. Green and red flares were floating down as markers dropped by the Pathfinders, as well as white flares dropped by the enemy to guide their fighters onto a target. I described the scene as Dante's inferno, with all the flashing, the light was not constant, and more like a disco. As we came near to the point of bomb release, I could hear the bomb aimer giving the skipper instructions –left, left, steady, right steady-bombs gone. The silhouette of other aircraft could be seen above and below us and the chances of collision and being hit by another crew's bombs was very high. Gradually we left the fires and flak behind as we set course for home whilst diving hard out of the target area. As I looked back from the comparative darkness to the scene we had just left, I thought 'how did we ever get through that in one piece'? A thought that would reoccur on every mission that followed. The return journey followed a similar theme to the outward one, the tension was still high and the likelihood of being attacked by a fighter on the return journey was just as high. I would scan the sky for the slightest indication of a fighter or danger to the aircraft.

On arrival back in the landing circuit for Mildenhall, we were notified by a WAAF in the control tower to circle at a thousand feet and each subsequent aircraft would circle another thousand feet higher. The skipper of the aircraft on the bottom of the pile would inform the control tower when he was flying upwind and he was given permission to land. The control tower would then inform each individual aircraft to come down a thousand feet and the process would continue until all aircraft had landed. After we landed, we would taxi around the perimeter to our allotted parking position and disembark into the waiting transport, back to the debriefing room. The debriefing teams were intelligence officers, of both sexes, who were specially trained to extract as much information as possible. This information was vital to assess the success of the mission and passed to Bomber Command headquarters. When eventually we fell into our beds exhausted the flashing lights over the target came back into my mind and only exhaustion allowed me to sleep.

Two nights later on 25th July, we were on the battle order to attack the heavily defended target of Stuttgart a trip that would last for nine hours and twenty minutes. All of the heavily defended targets in the Ruhr Valley had searchlight batteries with a master searchlight, which had a deeper blue color. If the master beam picked out an aircraft all the other beams would focus on the aircraft and pass it from one searchlight to another making the aircraft vulnerable to fighters and flak. For some unexplained reason we lost our course and I could see the target area on the rear of our starboard bow well alight from the concentrated bombing that was now underway. The skipper did a 'U' turn and came in on the right course and we bombed the target. On the journey home our fuel was running low and the flight engineer had to run on a weak mixture to economize the fuel being used. Running on a weak mixture caused damage to the engines and once we had successfully landed at base the skipper was punished via a short disciplinary course."

Several other targets were bombed during the remainder of July and August 1944 and Flying Officer Peck and crew had evolved into an efficient crew with a high degree of accuracy over the target. The crew was brought down to earth with a bump on the night of 11th September when they were detailed to attack Rostock Bay by dropping mines against enemy shipping. At approximately 1930hrs, Harold Peck lifted LM291, GI-F off the runway for what would become an eventful evening for all the crew, but in particular for the two gunners. Denis Pudney picks up the story again:

"We were one of six crews detailed to attack Rostock in the Baltic. From what I can remember it was pretty dark and after roughly three hours we were attacked by an enemy night fighter who deployed his cannons. The noise of the cannon shells striking home is frightening and very loud. Night fighters tracked their prey by means of a sophisticated radar system that allowed the fighter to accurately track a bomber right up until near enough to open fire. I never saw the fighter approaching and only realized he was there when he opened fire. I immediately fired back but I was too late and three out of my four guns jammed. Our mid upper gunner was also caught by total surprise and never had time to fire his two guns. As the enemy fighter broke upwards and away to port, I could see the silhouette against the sky, which was a bit lighter than the level below. I immediately identified the fighter as a Ju88, a formidable fighter with extensive armament that could blow us out of the night sky. I instructed the skipper to corkscrew starboard a little late which allowed me to re-cock my guns and to clear the jam. I searched for the Ju88 in the night sky and knew that it was inevitable that he would try to finish us off. I could not see the enemy aircraft until his guns were firing bright cannon shells towards us and as predicted, he commenced another attack. This time I was ready, I fired in front of his line of flight, and he flew right through my hail of bullets and tracer, immediately turning over under the impact of my bullets and dived down. Unbeknownst to me at the time the mid upper gunner Sgt Rumsey was also blasting away at the fighter. We claimed a probable kill due to not being able to confirm if the fighter crashed or not. We had overcome the odds and repelled a night fighter attack and continued with our mission and dropped our mines. At the debrief, we relayed our account and our story was backed up by another crew who witnessed the event and saw the fighter go down and crash. For my part in the incident, I was awarded an immediate DFM along with the mid upper gunner. The skipper was awarded the DFC for his skill in handling the Lancaster under battle conditions. The mission was tinged with tragedy when we were informed that the Lancaster being flown by Pilot Officer Devine and crew were lost without trace. There is a strong possibility that the night fighter we dispatched was the same aircraft that attacked P/O Devine and retribution was served. The next night GI-F was lost on a mission to Frankfurt resulting in the deaths of Flying Officer Alexander and crew."

It was customary for crews to be assigned an aircraft that they would complete the majority of the operations within. After ten missions, Flying Officer Peck and crew were allocated Lancaster LL885 GI-J and the crew would complete 21 missions in this aircraft. This particular Lancaster would become a centurion completing a total of 113 operations by the end of the war and became one of only 34 Lancasters to reach the magical one hundred missions.

On 20th September Denis Pudney completed one of his most memorable missions on a daylight operation to bomb the heavy guns at Calais. This mission would be memorable for all the wrong reasons and result in the loss of 15 aircrew men in tragic circumstances. The mission was led by S/Ldr Allen and he climbed away from Mildenhall over a patch of cloud meaning those behind would have to fly through the cloud. The Lancasters were in formation and a slight mistake could result in a collision. Reduced visibility through the clouds created a dangerous situation. Two lancasters broke through the cloud locked together in a deadly spiral towards earth near Wormington, Colchester. The official investigation concluded that the pilots should have 'opened out' in

Picture depicting the incident on 11th September 1944 when Denis Pudney shot down a Ju88 night fighter whilst en route to Rostock. Denis and the mid upper gunner were both awarded immediate Distinguished Flying Medals. *Courtesy of Denis Pudney DFM*

Lancaster LL885, GI-J completed all of its 113 missions with 622 Squadron. This photograph was taken shortly before its first mission on 30/31st March 1944, target Nuremberg. The aircraft was hit by a falling incendiary over the target which cracked the main spar. Denis Pudney & crew was the most prolific user of GI-J completing 21 missions during their operational tour. *Author's Collection*

cloud and the collision was attributed to pilot error whilst in cloud, a harsh and unfair judgment.

The operations came thick and fast for the crew and every single one of them wondered if they would successfully complete their tour. Denis Pudney would look at the white cliffs of Dover en route to a target and wonder if he would see them again.

On 31st October, the crew's usual Lancaster had to undergo essential maintenance and they were allotted NF939 GI-B as a replacement. The target on this night was the synthetic oil plant at Bottrup and the crew suffered flak damage over the target area. The bomb aimer, F/O Long had removed his gloves while he prepared his sights for bombing and the gloves were holed by a piece of shrapnel from the flak guns. Two nights later the crew took the same Lancaster to another oil target, this time at Homberg, a heavily defended target. The flak over Homberg was very accurate and heavy and the aircraft was again peppered by flak resulting in damage to the controls. The skipper asked Denis to look at the extent of the damage and Denis was able to rotate his turret allowing him to spot a large hole in the fuselage. F/O Peck nursed the aircraft home with sluggish controls and once they had landed the extent of the damage became clear. A piece of flak had damaged the connecting rods to the ailerons and was almost cut through holding together by a mere quarter of an inch thickness, a complete cut of the aileron connecting rods would have brought the aircraft down.

Denis describes just what it was like flying on operations:

> "Every operation had its moments of tension and if I am honest, moments of fear. It was a strange unreal life, one day or night it would be operations and wondering no matter how good or dedicated we were, luck played the biggest part in the means of survival. Then the next day back at base we would see the military police taking away the kit bags and belongs of crews who never returned. We could not afford to be sentimental at the time; it was a case of so and so got the chop last night. It did not pay to dwell on the fact, it was war and we had to carry on like all other services in the front line, and families like my parents who lived in vulnerable areas, subjected to enemy bombing. In the camp we would spend our own time individually, Red, Bob, Jack and myself usually in the billet or in the Sgt's mess. Likewise in the Officers mess Harry, Ron and Alan. Now and again, there would be a drinking night in the Sergeant's mess in which all Officers were invited; there was no class distinction just mutual respect."

Serial No. ....190. 1st Battle Order for 5th ~~October~~ Nov. 1944. No. 622 Squadron.

A/C NO.	LETTER.	CAPTAIN & 2ND PILOT	NAV. & W/OPERATOR.	A/B & M.U.GUNNER.	R/GUNNER & F/ENGINEER.
HK.621	G.	F/O Curling	F/S. Murdin. W.O. Bisso.	F/S Middleditch Sgt. Robinson. & F/S McRae	Sgt. Wallace. Sgt. White.
NN.709	H.	F/Lt. Armitstead.	F/S Brewster Sgt. Foulkes.	Sgt. Daniels Sgt. Keylock	Sgt. Borne. Sgt. Pook.
LL.885	J.	F/O Peck	F/S Barchard. F/O Cargill	F/O Long. Sgt. Brissy	Sgt. Pudney. Sgt. Bowyer.
PD.229	K.	F/S Francis	F/S Steedman Sgt. Kelly	Sgt. Traylen Sgt. Baxter	F/S Stott. Sgt. Soames.
HK.645	Z.	F/O Thomson	F/S Ward. W.O. Aland.	F/S Dalley Sgt. Smith.	Sgt. Woolloff. Sgt. Boulton.
HK.623	F.	F/O Phillips	Sgt. Lowry F/S Hopewell.	Sgt. Smart Sgt. Morgan	Sgt. York. Sgt. Barber.
HK.628	X.	F/S Waigh	F/O Briggs F/O Morrison	F/O Lister Sgt. Simmons.	Sgt. Mitchell. Sgt. Evans.
HK.644	D.	F/O Barnett	Sgt. Grimsey F/S Sullivan	F/O Burditch Sgt. Staplehurst	F/S Nicholls. Sgt. Murrell.
PD.225	C.	F/O Baxter	Sgt. Parsons Sgt. Brooker	F/S Hopkinson Sgt. Smith. Can.443	Sgt. Ramsey. Sgt. Rossiter.
LM.288	V.	F/S Rudenko	F/S Mekeown Sgt. Vollmar.	Sgt. Sleigh Sgt. Syvolos	F/S Ross. Sgt. Lucas-Garner.
HK.646	M.	F/S Thomas.	F/O Berry Sgt. Charlesworth	F/S Gambell. Sgt. Kingston	Sgt. Davies. Sgt. Ralph.
PA.164	P.	F/O Campbell.	Sgt. Galt. F/S Howard.	F/S Shepley Sgt. Fallows.	Sgt. Hickling. Sgt. Hill.
HK.614	R.	F/O Richards.	F/S Kidd Sgt. Doyle	F/O Mildren Sgt. Papps	Sgt. Nicholson. Sgt. Martin.
HK.616	W.	F/Lt. Woods.	F/S Grest. Sgt. Johnson	Sgt. Taylor Sgt. Henderson & W/O Davis.	Sgt. Gantley. Sgt. Coney.
HK.617	Y.	F/O Hussey	F/O Simpson Sgt. May	F/S Dalton Sgt. O'Connor.	Sgt. Potter. Sgt. Hand.
PD.332	N.	F/O Gilmore.	F/O Tomsett F/S Austin	F/S O'Loughlin Sgt. Davies.	Sgt. Firth. Sgt. Davidson.
LM.443	T.	F/O Richards.	F/O Inball. F/S Martin	F/O Carter Sgt. Brierley	Sgt. Campbell. Sgt. Burnard.

Rations to be collected by F/Commanders and distributed to aircraft.

Briefing Med. 0715
Nav. 0745
Main 0815
Trans. 0830.

GUARD ROOM TO COMMENCE EARLY CALLS 0600 hours.

(Sgd) G.K. Buckingham W/Cdr.
Commanding No. 622 Squadron.

W/C Buckingham F/L Allen. F/Lt. Dean. F/L Nicholl F/Lt. Noonan F/Lt. Middleton F/Lt. Berry

Battle Order for a mission to Solingen on 5th November 1944. Flying Officer Peck & crew can be clearly seen to have been allocated GI-J, LL885 for the trip. *Author's Collection.*

Denis Pudney completed 33 operations during his time with 622 Squadron, completing his last mission as a spare gunner in the crew of F/Lt Richards RNZAF. The camaraderie amongst the crew lasted a lifetime, the close bonds established through fear, and adversity brought a reliance on each other's abilities. Nobody let the crew down and the admiration for each other would outlast all other emotions and the passage of time. A tour of operations with Bomber Command was an experience that could never be forgotten. Denis Pudney had beaten the odds and survived a full tour of operations.

The author is indebted to Denis Pudney for allowing him to use his personal recollections throughout this story.

Lancaster NF939, GI-B taxis out for a daylight mission in late 1944.This is the aircraft that F/O Peck & crew flew on two consecutive missions suffering flak damage on both occasions.The discerning eye will notice the mid under gun protruding out of the bottom of the fuselage. During the autumn of 1944, Bomber Command squadrons utilized Lancasters with the mid under gun configuration to combat the threat from the German night fighters who approached from below. The intention was that these specially adapted Lancasters would fly in the bomber 'stream' and act as a deterrent against the night fighters. In reality, the new gun position was less that effective with just a hole being cut in the bottom of the aircraft to facilitate a .5 machine gun. The mid under gunner experienced many painful hours lying prone on his stomach looking into the dark night. *Author's Collection.*

9

Conspicuous Bravery

As an Australian Allan Nielsen was determined to play his part in the war effort and after a long and grueling journey to England he fulfilled his ambition to become a pilot. After completing considerable aircrew training in readiness for combat over Germany, Allan and his crew were posted to RAF Mildenhall in May 1944. The crew had formed a bond during their respective training that would last a life time and that special bond would be a contributory factor in saving their lives on the night of 29/30th August 1944. The crew's 'tour' up until then had been a mixture of luck and good fortune and a near miss when returning from Stuttgart on 25th July on two engines.

The Stettin raid was the crew's 27th mission and one that would be remembered for the rest of their lives. To place things into perspective, Bomber Command sustained heavy losses on this particular mission to night fighter activity. The final toll of Lancasters lost on the night was twenty three with 161 aircrew either dead or POWs. The morning of the operation began just like any other day on a Bomber Command airfield with crews reporting to their respective flight offices. This was an apprehensive time and nerves increased when the crew were promulgated on the battle order. If operations were on for the crew they would go to their designated Lancaster and check on the serviceability of the aircraft. If the ground crew had rectified an identified fault then the crew would air test the Lancaster, often with the ground crew on board. The confirmation that operations were on meant the airfield became a buzz of activity with petrol dowsers pumping the aircraft full of fuel and ground crew checking the Lancaster's instruments and radio communications. The most important task for Allan Nielsen was to have a chat with the Flight Sergeant in charge of the ground crew whilst the crew would check their respective positions on the aircraft.

Briefing

Shortly before the night's operation the 'Nielsen' crew would gather outside the large briefing room until finally being given permission to enter. The wall in front of them was dominated by a large map of northern Europe covered by a large curtain. A roll call would ensue and all the 'skippers' would account for their crews and then stand to attention whilst the Station Commander and Commanding Officers entered the room. The curtain covering the map of Northern Europe would be drawn back revealing the night's target. A red ribbon pinned to the map depicted the route to the target. It was at this point that all the crews burst into discussion about the target and were told to be quiet whilst enemy tactics were discussed. Known flak and searchlight batteries were identified. The intelligence and Met officers who would inform the crews

The 'Nielsen' crew depicted on arrival at RAF Mildenhall. L-R: 1.F/Sgt A. K. Nielsen RAAF DFM Pilot, 2.Sgt J. I. P. Bevan, MUG 3.F/Sgt T. T. L. De-Guerin, B/A, 4.Sgt T. J. Thorman F/E, 5.W/O T. E. Farquharson RCAF DFC, Nav, 6.F/S A. Cole C.G.M., W/op, 7.Sgt S. A. Nicholls R/G. Quite unusually, there was another Australian pilot with the same surname of Nielsen on the squadron named Ron Nielsen who was posted to the Pathfinder force in September 1944. *Courtesy of Mollie Dawn.*

on the importance of the target and the expected wind speed and cloud heights gave by far the most important briefing. Finally, the wireless operators would be given the night's radio frequencies and colors of the day on rice paper for easy disposal.

With all the necessary intelligence details for the mission gathered, Allan and his crew would collect their parachutes and 'Mae Wests'. Next, their personal belongings were placed in their lockers. These items could be useful to the enemy if they were taken captive. Once all the preliminaries were completed Allan and his crew would catch the crew bus that would take them to their Lancaster which could be on a distant dispersal. For most crews the waiting before take off was the most nerve racking and surreal. On summer nights, the crew would enjoy the last rays of the sun going down and enjoy the birdsong of the English countryside. Unbeknownst to Allan Nielsen and his crew at this time, was that in a few hours he and his crew would be fighting for their survival after a sustained enemy fighter attack. Once aboard the aircraft all the crew would go to their respective positions and do their preliminary equipment checks. Allan Nielsen would signal to the ground crew for the battery cart to connect to the first engine to assist starting the Merlin engine. Allan would press the starter button on each engine in turn and the propeller would start to rotate with puffs of smoke emitting from the exhaust stubs until finally the engine burst into life. Sergeant Thorman the flight engineer, would check all the engines oil pressures and magneto drops. When satisfied Allan would sign the Form 700 and pass to the ground crew.

Eventually the green 'Aldis' light would be flashed and Allan would maneuver his Lancaster to line up at the end of the runway awaiting his turn to take off. Final checks were made and the brakes were applied whilst the four Merlin engines were run up to maximum power straining against the brakes. Finally Allan released the brakes and the Lancaster surged forward gathering speed until the tail wheel came up and the Lancaster became airborne. Lancaster GI-L, PD219 lifted off the runway at RAF Mildenhall at approximately 21:10 hours. Once airborne Allan would steadily climb the heavily laden aircraft to the Group's assembly point on the English coast usually at Cromer in Norfolk and W/O Farquarson would give Allan a course to steer. As they crossed the Kattegat, en route to attack the port of Stettin, the crew was warned of the presence of enemy fighters by seeing three aircraft go down after combat. Shortly afterwards, when approximately fifteen miles west of Sweden, they were attacked by an He219 which was seen in the moonlight some distance away on the port quarter. The recorded time was 01:30hrs at a height of 8,000 feet. The Enemy aircraft closed in, crossing to starboard and the rear gunner gave "corkscrew starboard". At the bottom of the corkscrew, the He219 opened fire at 400 yards hitting the aircraft and wounding five of the crew. The short burst of cannon fire damaged the airframe, rendered the W/T Gee and intercom u/s and holed the Perspex in the cockpit near the pilot's face. The astro dome and the Perspex in the navigator's position was blown out and the D/R compass was rendered u/s. Five members of the crew were wounded, with the navigator having been peppered with cannon fire. Sixty two pieces of shrapnel were taken from him after landing. A piece of shrapnel cut the wireless operator's thigh, baring it to the bone. The flight engineer was hit under the right eye and although suffered no serious injury, blood gushed from his nose. The mid upper gunner was cut on the face with Perspex and the pilot got some small pieces of Perspex and metal under his right eyelid. After ascertaining the damage, Allan Nielsen decided not to go to the target or try landing in Sweden due to the navigator being seriously wounded. In addition, the weather conditions were poor and it would be too dangerous to bail out, especially over the sea.

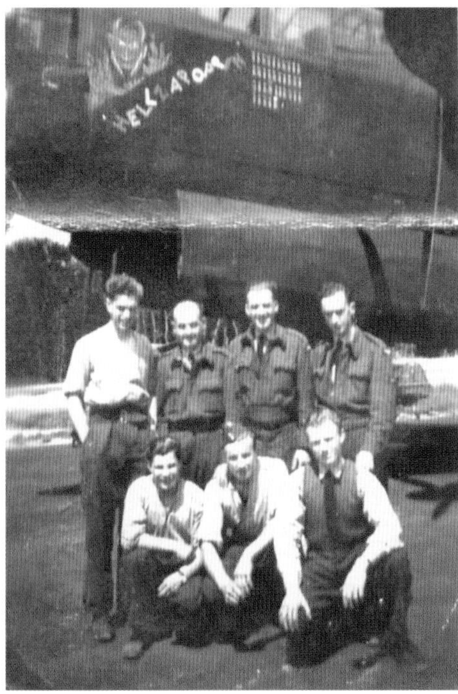

Lancaster PD219, GI-L 'Hellzapoppin', sustained heavy damage at the hands of a German night fighter on the night of 29/30th August 1944. *Courtesy of C. H Chandler.*

Allan Nielsen decided to return to base, flying west over Denmark at 4-6,000ft. The W/op had not disclosed the seriousness of his wound and was given the task of navigating. He worked the 'Gee' set constantly attempting to get fixes on the way home, carrying out his duties cheerfully and without complaint. With no intercom the pilot had to communicate with the crew verbally through the flight engineer or, by slips of paper which the W/op carried to the two gunners. Eventually landfall was made but uncertain of their position, they landed at the first available aerodrome, which turned out to be Hardwick. As he left the aircraft the W/op removed the detonator from the IFF set. For their actions this night, the W/op, F/Sgt Cole was awarded the Conspicuous Gallantry Medal, second only in merit to the Victoria Cross. The pilot, F/Sgt Neilsen was awarded the DFM and the navigator W/O Farquharson, was awarded the DFC.

During his time at Mildenhall Allan Nielsen was going out with a WAAF called Mollie who assisted with the essential ground operations in her role as wireless operator. Mollie eventually married Allan Nielsen and vividly remembers the aircrew when they returned from operations. She would volunteer to serve them tea and rum shortly before de-briefing. On one occasion

Mollie gave almost a full cup of rum to one 'flyer' and he was rendered unfit for de-brief, quite a serious offence at the time. The airman was not disciplined on this occasion. There was another Australian pilot on the squadron called Ron Nielsen and Mollie remembers him well. Both 'Nielsens' would spend their spare time together enjoying the English countryside with other members of the squadron (Ron Nielsen was posted to No.7 Squadron PFF on 24th September 1944 and went on to complete 52 operations). He married another WAAF at Mildenhall at the time by the name of Carol Strivens at the local church. Mr. Norman was a farmer and therefore in a reserved occupation forbidding him from joining the armed forces. He was most kind to Mildenhall personnel and invited as many around as possible to his home for dinner. He was so well respected by Allan and Mollie that they invited him to their wedding.

Mollie's recollections of the 29/30th August 1944

"The night of the raid, I was on duty (wireless operator) and of course, I knew the letter of the kite was 'L' for love and when it came through followed by a few letters everything went blank. I took off my headphones and said to the duty officer "that was Allan's plane" and was promptly told to put my headphones back on. I was very emotional when I came off duty at 8am and went back to my billet. No way could I go to bed and decided to go for a coffee at the NAAFI. As I stepped out of the door, Allan came riding up the pathway on his bike. Now WAAF billets were totally out of bounds to all males and the first thing I said to Allan was "you are not allowed here", Allan's reply was unprintable but a big hug put it right. We then went off to sick quarters to have Perspex splinters removed from his eyelids. Only people who actually worked on an operational station knew the fun and laughter we had together and also the terrible sadness and tears that we shed. We often stood at the side of the runway and watched those heavy aircraft thundering down the runway to take off for a raid and as we waved them off, we wondered how many would return. No one can imagine the bravery of those young men knowing as they flew into the night that it could be their last night alive."

Flying Officer A. K. Nielsen RAAF proudly wears his DFM ribbon awarded for his action when he brought back a badly damaged Lancaster from Stuttgart on two engines. *Courtesy of Mollie Dawn.*

Allan Nielsen poses proudly in his RAAF uniform for this studio portrait. *Courtesy of Mollie Dawn.*

A Day To Be Proud Of

During July 1944, the King & Queen of England visited RAF Mildenhall for a field investiture and inspected the airmen on parade. The King stopped in front of Allan Nielsen and asked him how many operations he had completed. When the King received his reply, he turned to the Senior Commanding Officer accompanying him and asked 'why is this man not commissioned'? The next day the Commanding Officer called F/Sgt Nielsen into his office and offered him a commission. Allan Nielsen was very close to his crew and shared the same living quarters, to accept a commission would mean that he would have to move into the Officers quarters and away from his crew. He refused his commission on these grounds, a true measure of friendship and respect for his crew. Despite all his protests Allan's commission was awarded. The bond developed between aircrew on operations over Germany was eloquently described by Wing Commander Leonard Cheshire VC, DSO & 2 bars, DFC, OM when he wrote the following about his crew:

> "These men have etched themselves on my memory for all time. We have lived, flown fought, experienced danger, felt elation, sorrow and fear, taken leisure and done our drinking together. We are now a closely knit aircrew who trust each other when in the air and are happiest when in our own company on the ground. There is a mutual respect and a sense of comradeship that will make these days supreme in our lives, days that we will remember always, or for as long as we live."

Sadly, Allan Nielsen died in his late forties of a heart attack; he left behind a devoted wife and two children.

Postscript-Conspicuous Gallantry Medal

Extract from HM King George VI's approval of the institution of the medal, November 1942:

> Whereas Her Majesty Queen Victoria was graciously pleased by her Order-in-Council dated 7th July 1874, to establish a medal designated the Conspicuous Gallantry Medal for such Petty Officers and seamen of the Royal Navy and non-commissioned Officers and privates of the Royal Marines as distinguished themselves by acts of conspicuous gallantry in action with the enemy. And whereas we deem it expedient to provide for the award of the Conspicuous Gallantry Medal to members of our military and Air Forces for acts of conspicuous gallantry whilst flying in active operations against the enemy…

F/Sgt Cole was awarded the Conspicuous Gallantry Medal on 10th September 1944, along with the award of the Distinguished Flying Cross to W/O Farquharson. Both men were cited for their medals in the London Gazette with the following text:

'In August 1944, Warrant Officer Farquharson and Flight Sergeant Cole were navigator and wireless operator respectively of an aircraft detailed to attack Stettin. On the outward flight the aircraft was intercepted and severely damaged by an enemy fighter. Although seriously wounded and in great pain, Warrant Officer Farquharson continued his navigational duties but was finally persuaded to be removed to a rest bed where he was given an injection of morphine. Meantime, Flight Sergeant Cole, although injured in the thigh by a piece of shrapnel, concealed the seriousness of his wound and took over the task of navigating the aircraft back to base. The English coast was eventually crossed and a landing was made at the first available airfield. Weak from loss of blood, Flight Sergeant Cole was on the verge of collapse and was removed to a hospital. These airmen have completed many sorties and their gallantry and devotion to duty have been of a very high order'.

Courtesy of the London Gazette.

10

Luftwaffe Retribution
The Nuremberg Raid 30/31st March 1944

On 30th March Air Chief Marshall Harris ordered a maximum effort on the city of Nuremberg a center for the Nazi party and a favorite city of Hitler. The city was full of architectural beauty but beneath the façade, it was manufacturing vital components for the German Radar defense systems. The confirmation of the attack came as a surprise to all Bomber crews because it came right in the middle of the full moon period and a moonlit sky was happy pickings for the German night fighter force. 795 aircraft were dispatched to the target. When the bombers had reached the Belgium border, the night fighters made first contact and on the route to the target, 82 bombers were shot out of the sky. A major factor in the high losses was the technological advances with radar that had been developed by the Germans. Unbeknownst to the British the German night fighters were fitted with new bomber detection radar called SN-2 which actually homed in on the bomber force defensive radar sets. In addition, the forecast winds were grossly underestimated and a fierce crosswind caused many navigators to be off course and out of the bomber stream. The strong winds also caused the Pathfinder marking aircraft to drop their target markers well to the east of the city and such was the confusion over the target area that many crews actually bombed the nearby city of Schweinfurt in the heat of battle. On the route from the target, the night fighters had further success although due to the need to refuel, only 13 bombers were lost on the return journey.

622 Squadron dispatched sixteen Lancasters to Nuremberg; the squadron would suffer the loss of two crews with fourteen men killed. One Lancaster would lay strewn on its belly at RAF Woodbridge due to battle damage.

En route to the target Pilot Officer Ken Derisley and crew in GI-P, LM466 could not believe the sight befalling their eyes. In his Frazer Nash rear turret, F/Sgt Bright sat cocooned and frightened whilst witnessing some of the carnage. He saw several bombers going down in flames, with fighters darting in and out of the bomber stream. The Me110s and Ju88s sprayed cannon and machine gun trace into the bombers. F/Sgt Bright lost count of the bombers he saw falling out of the bomber stream trailing flames eventually to leave a burning pyre on the ground. The 'Derisley' crew released their bombs at 22,000 ft at 01.26hrs and the pilot threw the Lancaster into a diving turn anxious to start the journey home immediately. On the return flight, the enemy contacts were less frequent and the crew came through unmolested. At the first opportunity the W/op F/Sgt Hollings, obtained a fix for the navigator and he received a communication instructing them to divert to the emergency landing strip at Woodbridge due to RAF Mildenhall being fog bound. After landing, the crew could see many wrecked planes around the aerodrome and they thanked their lucky stars that they had returned safely.

Pilot Officer Jack Lunn and crew were also witnessing the carnage and his thoughts concentrated on getting his Lancaster to fly higher than any other to stay out of the way of the enemy night fighters. He was piloting a brand new Lancaster on its first mission and therefore he anticipated that the aircraft would perform better than any other and obtain the height. To the crew's surprise falling incendiaries hit their Lancaster over the target, which cracked the main spar resulting in a flight home that required all Pilot Officer Lunn's skill as a pilot. The Lancaster he brought home that night was GI-J, LL885 and by the end of the war, it would notch up 113 operations, one of only 34 Lancasters to achieve this goal.

Flight Lieutenant Ray Trenouth DFC was an Australian pilot from Adelaide and his crew was experienced with regards to the

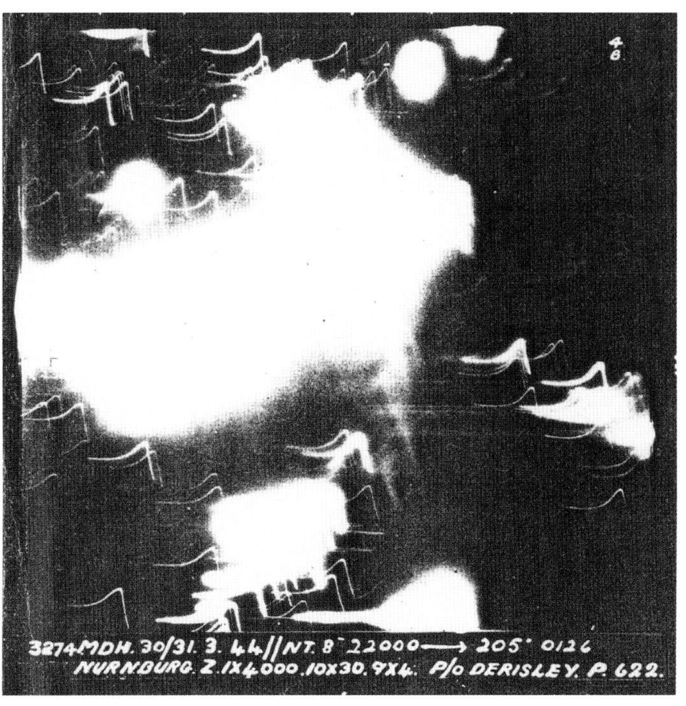

Pilot Officer Derisley's bombing photograph for the Nuremberg raid. *Courtesy of Robert Bright son of Charles.*

German defenses, having been on the squadron since December 1943. The 'Trenouth' crew flew their usual Lancaster GI-B 'Beer' with a foaming pint of beer proudly painted on the nose section along with the numerous bomb tally markings. The mission was no different to any other that they had previously done apart from the fact that their wireless operator F/Sgt Atkins was in his sick bed with colic and Sgt Hopewell was his replacement. Whilst, still climbing over the English Channel the bomb aimer, Flying Officer Good RAAF reported the first combat. Ray Trenouth initially thought that the bomb aimer must be mistaken until very shortly afterwards he witnessed another combat and as a crew they all realized that they were in for a hard night.

B 'Beer' was on course flying at 19,000 feet over France when the flak opened up and F/Lt Trenouth weaved skillfully through the flak barrage. Streams of red tracer became frequent, seeming to hang in the air until arching over and down like water from a hose. Alarmingly the Lancasters started to go down with regularity, starting with a flash of fire, growing in intensity until the stricken aircraft exploded into a mass of blazing clumps. With the danger increasing, Ray Trenouth called upon all his experience and he decided that the safest place would be above all other aircraft. The whole crew was now living on their nerves and they realized that to survive this mission they would have to conjure up every ounce of their training and comradeship as a crew. The gunners, Sgt Pulman in the mid upper and Pilot Officer Harvey RAAF in the rear turret rotated their turrets ceaselessly in an attempt to spot the enemy fighters first. Sgt Ray Francis, the flight engineer stood beside the pilot and searched the night sky to port and starboard in readiness to warn his skipper of impending danger. Sgt Pulman spotted the first of the enemy fighter encounters in the mid upper turret and he ordered an immediate corkscrew starboard. He was unable to fire because of the cutouts on his guns, which prevented him from shooting off the tail of the Lancaster. There were no such gun restrictions with the four browning machine guns in the rear turret and P/O Harvey fired off a burst of tracer that mingled with that of the enemy fighter as it dived away into the night sky. The rear gunner who gave the pilot the instruction to corkscrew starboard announced the second encounter. F/Lt Trenouth threw the Lancaster into a violent corkscrew maneuver, the 'G' forces pinned the rear gunner down in his turret and subsequently he was unable to fire. The evasive maneuver had forced the belted ammunition in four tanks halfway down the fuselage into the chutes and jammed the servo feed at the bottom of the turret, blocking the guns from firing. The skipper sent the wireless operator, Sgt Hopewell back into the fuselage with a portable bottle of oxygen to pull the belts of ammunition back into their tanks. Some time passed and Ray Trenouth decided to check on the wireless operator's progress via the intercom. On receiving no response his sent Sgt Francis back to investigate. Sgt Francis found the wireless operator unconscious from lack of oxygen and he dragged him back to the rest bed and plugged him in to the main oxygen supply.

The crew eventually reached the run in for the target with a height of 25,000 feet showing on the altimeter. The bomb aimer identified three blazing areas and he skillfully guided the pilot to the bomb release point. With the temperature outside reaching 40 below zero, F/Lt Trenouth carefully steered 'B' Beer out of the target area. Pilot Officer Harvey in the rear turret reported the sensation of the aircraft diving down however; the cockpit instruments suggested that they were not. The sudden realization that the Lancaster had 'iced up' brought another danger to the already stressed crew and F/Lt Trenouth called for the flight engineer to help. When Ray Francis did not respond, the now recovered wireless operator went to investigate. In a reversal of the earlier incident, Sgt Francis was found unconscious on the floor and he was dragged to the rest bed and plugged into the main oxygen supply.

The flight engineer quickly recovered and joined Ray Trenouth in the cockpit still fully aware that the crew had three and a half hours of flying time back to Mildenhall. The violent maneuvering over the target had severed a pneumatic brake line just below the pilot's seat and Sgt Francis skillfully repaired the damage enabling them to land at Mildenhall and not on an emergency airfield. Finally the crew started to descend over the Channel and F/Lt Trenouth called base with the usual code word of "hello redcoat, hello redcoat, this is Hogsfoot, turn to land please". The response was instant and the WAAF radio controller instructed them to join the circuit at a designated height.

Lancaster 'B' Beer touched down on the runway at Mildenhall after seven hours and twenty-five minutes of intense combat action. As the crew dropped out of the Lancaster they took off their parachutes and lit up their cigarettes. The flight engineer and wireless operator were taken away to be treated for oxygen starvation the rest of the crew would attend a de-briefing. That night the crew could not sleep as they recalled their lucky escape and contemplated images of the mission.

The following aircrew accounts feature in the book 'The Nuremberg Massacre' by Geoff Taylor and vividly describe the fact that other 622 Squadron Lancaster crews were also living on their nerves:

"Pilot Officer Raymond Curling, an Australian Lancaster pilot assigned to 'A' flight, and flying GI-A, ED430 was on his sixth mission. His crew was a typical Bomber Command amalgam

F/Lt R.Trenouth DFC RAAF & crew experienced one of their most eventful missions against Nuremberg. In the background is Lancaster ED437, GI-D and the Officer's mess at Mildenhall. ED437 originally served with No.617 (Dambuster) Sqdn and was used for low level practicing L-R: F/Sgt Atkins (W/op), F/Lt Trenouth RAAF (pilot), F/O Good DFC RAAF (B/A). Front L-R: Sgt Francis (F/E), Sgt Pulman (MUG), P/O Harvey RAAF (R/G), P/O West (Nav). *Courtesy of Ray Francis.*

comprising, navigator, F/Sgt Featherstonehaugh RNZAF, bomb aimer, F/Sgt Short RNZAF, flight engineer, Sgt Humphrier RAF, W/op, F/Sgt Smith RAAF, mid upper gunner, Sgt Harris RAF, rear gunner, Sgt Russell RAF. The five previous trips they had already flown together had not been uneventful. In 42.30 operational hours they had experienced flak damage, fighter attack and a mid air collision.

Referring to his wartime diary, Ray Curling recalls:

"On this occasion, 'Butch' Harris decided to take a risk on the moon which was almost full and ideal for enemy fighters. By 22:00 PM, we were well on the way. As soon as we reached the enemy coast the enemy defenses went into attack. We were equipped with an instrument called 'Boozer'. This was a warning device in the form of two lights in the pilot's cockpit. One, a yellow light, would blink on if an enemy aircraft picked the aircraft up on his radar beam and the other light, a red one, would warn of anti-aircraft defenses. In the event of either coming on we would immediately go into evasive action. The instrument had a reputation of going haywire.

As soon as we reached enemy territory I thought that Boozer had gone berserk but convincing puffs of black smoke behind us confirmed that the ack-ack indicator was working OK. From that point to the target, enemy fighters seemed to be on us in swarms and the sky was continually criss-crossed with tracers. It was truly grim and we were extremely tense. Every second I was waiting for the word from my gunners to weave. We were not attacked. All we could see was my little light blinking from time to time, streams of tracer and the all too frequent sight of a dead aircraft diving to earth in flames."

"By the time Curling reached the target at 01:25 he estimated that he had about six to seven tenths of cloud cover at 20,000 feet. (Taylor 1980, 58-59).The way out of the target had been quite a sight; as Curling recalls from the pilots seat.

"We didn't need a navigator, he reported, the moon lit the sky like daylight and vapor trails of aircraft ahead of us left a road like a modern highway. I just kept above this roadway in readiness to dive into its cover should the need arise. Fighter attacks seemed to have eased off considerably. We were not permitted to land at our base, Mildenhall, and were diverted to the emergency airfield on the coast, Woodbridge. Landing there was no problem. There were plenty of other aircraft badly shot up. The various other air crews we spoke to had confirmed our opinion that it had been a shocking raid." Curling's aircraft was undamaged. It had been airborne for eight hours. (After the war, a RAF medical officer expressed to Curling the opinion that the plan of the Nuremberg raid had been known to the Germans. 'Their attacks certainly seemed to confirm this," commented Curling.(Taylor 1980, 123).

London born Sergeant E.C. Hazelwood was also en route to Nuremberg in GI-U. With the exception of Canadian bomb aimer, Flying Officer Burnett, the crew of the Lancaster were all English and all non-commissioned. F/Sgt McQueen pilot, Sgt Mattingly flight engineer, Sgt Blakes W/op, Sgt Quinlan mid upper gunner and F/Sgt Chivers the rear gunner.

Conscious of his responsibilities as a navigator and anxious to do his job well, Seargeant Hazelwood had, once airborne, previously always kept himself shut off from the activity outside the aircraft. This allowed him to concentrate on his navigation (a task that he did not find any easier when he was suffering from airsickness as a result of evasive corkscrewing by his pilot, McQueen, to escape enemy attack). On this night however, in view of the crew's comments on the intercom, he left his navigation table to look out for once to see just what was happening. Near Bonn, south of the fabled but infamous industrial complex of the Ruhr, what Hazlewood saw was not reassuring:

"A lot of our aircraft seemed to be drifting north into the Ruhr defenses as I saw a lot of activity over the Ruhr with searchlights and gunfire. I thought at the time that the winds might have changed and drifted a lot of the aircraft off track."

From his position in the nose of the Lancaster, prone above the forward hatch in the floor, the Canadian bomb aimer, Flying Officer Burnett, remarked how bright the moon was and that he could see for miles. The gunners and the rest of the crew who were looking out all agreed that it was a lovely night with nobody voicing the thought that was in their minds, for German night fighters. After passing the high flak glittering over the misted gloom of the Ruhr Valley it was Hazelwood's time to feel that his aircraft was either being followed or being waited for.

In front of us, he recalled, anti-aircraft shells were being shot into the air and, on exploding, looked like aircraft being shot down. With a blithely British calmness that no doubt would have infuriated the sweating Luftwaffe flak gunners far below, Hazelwood added, almost as an afterthought, "I suppose this was to upset aircrew morale". On several occasions, Sgt Quinlan in the two gun mid upper turret and F/Sgt Chivers in the four gun rear turret saw enemy fighters but held their fire in case the muzzle flashes from their guns betrayed the Lancaster's position in the bomber stream. 'Our orders were to bomb the target, not to engage in fighting enemy aircraft, ' Hazlewood recalls. Though unlikely to have inspired paeans of patriotic praise, this tactic nevertheless had about it a certain cold and brutal logic, which was entirely in keeping with the bloody business of bombing Germany out of the war.

On the long leg eastward across the bitterly contested line of the Rhine and on to the target, the gunners of Hazelwood's Lancaster were to see many more enemy aircraft including Dornier 17s, probably flare droppers and observers plotting the track of the bomber stream, and many Messerschmitt Me210 fighters. None of them though, were to stop Hazlewood's Lancaster from reaching Nuremberg. (Taylor 1980, 85-86).

It was fog over England, not flak or fighters over Europe that was nearly the undoing of Lancaster GI-U on its return from Nuremberg. F/Sgt Edgar Hazlewood navigated the aircraft back to base only to find the airfield blanketed by fog. The pilot, F/Sgt McQueen, was then instructed to divert to Docking, north of Kings Lynn, on the Wash.

"We landed with enough fuel in our tanks for a further five minutes flying, Hazelwood noted, I understand a number of our aircraft crashed over England due to lack of fuel and being unable to land at their bases because of fog." (Taylor 1980, 150).

Flight Lieutenant Randall and crew in Lancaster IM443, GI-G were not as lucky as their squadron colleagues. On the return journey they were attacked by a night fighter and severely damaged. Again, the narrative is extracted from 'The Nuremberg massacre' (Taylor 1980, 148):

"At 02:17 rear gunner reports fighter to port quarter at 1000 yards but it makes off, At 02:21 our aircraft is violently attacked, without warning, and cannon shells smash through the port side of the fuselage penetrating the navigators' neck and chest killing him instantly. The navigational instruments are wrecked. The flight engineer's panel is unserviceable. The bomb aimer and I struggled aft to the rest bed with the navigator's body. The bomb aimer then binds the wounds to stop the blood dripping onto the floor of the aircraft. (Fluids such as blood, vomit, coffee spilled from in flight ration flasks or oil gushing from the ruptured pipelines of a shot up hydraulic system could make the metal deck above the Lancaster's bomb bay slippery and dangerous to walk on, particularly when the aircraft was engaged in evasive maneuvers.)

"When we were hit, the aircraft lost 7000 feet, out of control, but the skipper kept his head and with difficulty regained control and set course on DR. The bomb aimer makes a reasonable effort at navigating. The port outer motor is practically shot out. Number three fuel tank is holed. A test on the undercarriage fails to extend the legs. Flaps also fail to extend.

The English coast is a welcome sight. Called up Woodbridge for priority landing and warned them to stand by for crash landing.....whole crew bruised on aircrafts violent impact with ground. The aircraft is a total wreck and we have difficulty getting the dead navigator out owing to a floor spar, which is pinning him down. We thank the skipper and shake his hand. The mid upper gunner has disappeared. The bomb aimer found him out

Lancaster GI-G, IM443 lays forlorn after crash landing at RAF Woodbridge on return from the Nuremberg raid. The pilot, F/Lt Randall skillfully flew the damaged aircraft back to England after it suffered severe damage at the hands of a German night fighter. In the attack, the navigator was killed and during the crash landing the mid upper gunner lost his life. *Courtesy of the Mildenhall Register.*

on the concrete dispersal. He was dead." (Taylor 1980, 148-149).

F/ Lt Randall and his replacement crew members would lose their lives attacking the railway marshaling yards at Trappes on the night of 31st May 1944. On the return journey a Me110G night fighter piloted by Hptm Fritz Sothe of NJG 4 attacked them. Their Lancaster exploded under the enemy fighter's cannon fire and the rear gunner was thrown clear of the explosion and survived. Standing in for the crew's usual rear gunner was F/Lt Berry DFC the squadron Gunnery Leader.

Tragically two more 622 Squadron Lancasters were to be lost on the return journey, firstly Pilot Officer Pickin in Lancaster GI-D, ND767 (5th op) and crew collided in mid air with a Halifax bomber from 427 Squadron in the southeast corner of Belgium close to the French border, killing 13 crew members. The rear gunner in the Halifax escaped death by parachuting to tell his story of how his aircraft cut across the top of Pilot Officer Pickin's aircraft. He witnessed both aircraft fall away in a deathly spiral.

Airborne 22:30 from Mildenhall. Homebound, collided with a 427 Sqdn Halifax (LV923) and crashed, both crashed near Rachecourt (Luxembourg), 13 km SW of Arlon, Belgium. All are buried in Hotton War Cemetery.

Pilot: Pilot Officer E. Pickin RAF
Nav: W/O J.P. Merritt RCAF
W/Op: Sgt R.J. Asplen RAF
B/A: F/Sgt C.J. Scmidt RAAF
MUG: Sgt G.R. Collins RAF
R/G: Sgt J. Coup RAF
F/E : Sgt H.F. Page RAF

The other Lancaster lost on this night was GI-T, ED619 piloted by P/O Sutton (12th op) and crew, their demise being credited to

Pilot Officer Pickin acts as best man for Warrant Officer John Percival Merritt RCAF, the navigator in his crew. This photograph was taken on 27th March 1944; three days before all the crew were tragically killed. *Courtesy of Mrs. A. Laws.*

night fighter activity. Airborne at 22:20 from Mildenhall. Shot down outbound, by a night-fighter and crashed 1 km E of Baumbach and approx 7 km NW of Montabaur. All are buried in Rheinberg War Cemetery.

Pilot: Pilot Officer J. Sutton RAF
Nav: F/Sgt J. A. McClean RAF
W/op: F/Sgt L.E. Read RAF
B/A: W/O D.J. Laberge RCAF
MUG: F/Sgt E.F. Jarvis RCAF
R/G: J. F. Richardson RAF
F/E: Sgt P. Newman RAF

On analysis, the whole raid was a complete failure; the German strategic plan had been well executed. The German ground direction finding stations were not fooled by spoof attacks by Mosquitoes and they established the bomber stream's course by accurately tracking the H2S radar signals being transmitted by the bombers. In addition, the forecast winds issued to the bomber crews at briefing were inaccurate and grossly underestimated the wind strength. Many crews were blown off track and out of the protection of the bomber stream. Before the navigators realized this fact, they became the target of the night fighters. Those aircraft who managed to stay in the bomber stream were far from safe and Junkers Ju88s released strings of parachute flares marking the bomber stream to the waiting night fighter force. A 200 mile running battle ensued with the free hunting tactics (Zahme Sau) employed by the Germans, reeking havoc on the terrified bomber crews.

Due to the constant attacks from night fighters and the strong winds many crews missed their turning points along the plotted route. Nuremberg was situated very close to Regensberg and Schweinfurt and hard to identify for bomber crews. Therefore, considerable bombs fell on Schweinfurt and the bombing was dispersed across a large area. The return journey was not so traumatic for the crews, many night fighters had returned to base to refuel, although another 14 bombers were lost on the return leg with another 12 crashing on or near their bases due to battle damage or the dense fog which had set in. In total 107 heavy bombers were lost and another 34 returned with serious battle damage. ACM Harris and his senior staff were left to mourn the loss of the crews and equipment.

Eric Pickin captured in this photograph immediately after completing his first solo training flight in America. He had originally joined Bomber Command as an air gunner, re-mustering to a pilot. Courtesy of the Mrs. A. Laws.

11

Resilience

Shropshire, born Charles Eric Barclay, volunteered for aircrew at his earliest opportunity. He would endure the same trials and tribulations as other aircrew, albeit Charles Barclay would test his immortality to the limit during his aircrew service. Many men strongly believed in fate and luck to bring them through an operational 'tour' of 30 missions and Flight Sergeant Barclay used both to the ultimate degree.

Having joined the RAF as an air gunner in 1943 at Hall Road close to the Oval Cricket Ground in London, he was soon posted to No.14 Initial Training Wing at Bridlington in Yorkshire for some 'square bashing'. Then a move to Elementary Air Gunnery School (EAGS) at Bridgenorth in his home county of Shropshire followed. More of the same followed with a splattering of Morse code thrown in for good measure. His aircrew training began in earnest when he was posted to Stormy Down in South Wales for his air gunnery training.

At this stage of the war, the air gunner was recognized as a specialist and graduated with at least the rank of Sergeant. The intensive air gunnery training included a great deal of ground lectures on the theory of gunnery and the hands on approach of stripping a machine gun down and reassembling it blindfold. Interspersed throughout the course was aircraft recognition and the theory of bullet trajectory. The syllabus also covered basic armament, Morse code and the unpleasant mathematical classes mixed in. By far the most enjoyable aspect of the training for Sgt Barclay was the live firing exercises. Charles Barclay takes up the story:

> "We were issued with a drum of ammunition that contained several hundred rounds of bullets dipped in paint; each student was given 200 rounds each in his designated color so that his score could be evaluated. We loaded our drum of bullets into the Vickers machine gun which was situated in the turret of the 'Avro Anson' aircraft. Our objective was to fire our rounds into a drogue being towed by another aircraft and score as many direct hits as possible. I was classified as an average gunner at the conclusion of the course, a status that I was proud to achieve considering the hurdles that we had to surpass."

The next stage of his training took him to No.84 Operational Training Unit at Desborough in Northants. It was here that he teamed up with his crew in the usual RAF method of putting the exact numbers of aircrew designations into a room and telling them to come out as a full crew.

Unbeknownst to the crews at the time was the fact that they were being assessed constantly. The expectation was that they should form into proficient crews, all gelling together and realizing that they depended on each other's abilities.

Sgt Charles Eric Barclay Proudly poses for a studio portrait on completion of his aircrew training in 1943. *Courtesy of Charles E. Barclay.*

The gunnery content was again shooting at targets being pulled by training aircraft usually Lysander, Ansons or Whitleys. Whilst at OTU Charles Barclay and crew completed an operational mission to Chartres in France on a nickel raid (leaflet drooping).

1678 Conversion Flight-RAF Waterbeach

Sergeant Barclay and crew arrived at Waterbeach during the early part of May 1944 in readiness for their familiarization onto the main stay of Bomber Command the Avro Lancaster. At Waterbeach the crew focused almost entirely on flying the four engined heavies interspersed with the odd lesson on ditching in the sea and survival techniques.

The Avro Lancaster had by this period of the war been in service for over a year and its reputation for being a wonderful aircraft was now well established. The crew arrived at Waterbeach full of anticipation and delight to be finally converting to the Lancaster after the old Wellington bombers they were used to. The Lancaster fulfilled their expectations and the crew, especially the pilot, soon respected the Lancaster's performance and record for durability. The training intensified with instructors on board and combined sessions on 'bullseye' exercises in the dark across country with a loaded aircraft to simulate a bomb load and practiced evasive maneuvers. The most stimulating experience was the fighter affiliation exercises where RAF fighters would pretend to attack the aircraft and they had to take evasive maneuvers in the form of the 'corkscrew'. This maneuver involved the gunner identifying the attacking aircraft and giving the pilot the instruction to dive either port or starboard to restrict the enemy fighter's ability to gain an accurate shot. Once the gunner gave the instruction to 'corkscrew', the pilot would put the Lancaster into a severe dive and pull up and down again in an attempt to shake off the fighter and make him select an easier target. The maneuver was very violent and aircrew endured considerable 'G' force, often inducing vomiting.

With Conversion Unit successfully mastered the crew were posted to an operational squadron in their case to RAF Witchford and 115 Squadron, a part of 3 Group Bomber Command. The first few days on the squadron amounted to familiarization of the airbase, attending briefings and getting acclimatized to their surroundings. The crew were interviewed by the Commanding Officer and informed that the pilot would carry out a '2nd dickey' trip with an experienced pilot and then the whole crew would commence operations over enemy territory. Having successfully completed his 2nd dickey trip, F/Lt Norbury and crew found themselves on the battle order for the first time as a crew. Unfortunately, F/Sgt Barclay was confined to his sick bed and under orders not to fly; his place in the mid upper turret was taken by Sgt K. Moore. Charles waited for the crew's return with great anticipation he had so many questions to ask about the trip, he was quite envious that they had completed a mission and he had not. The crew never returned,a having been shot down killing all the crew; they were all buried at Les Breviaires Communal Cemetery in France. Flight Sergeant Barclay completed his first mission as a spare gunner in the crew of F/O Burgess on 10th June 1944 on a mission to Dreux, which lasted three hours and fifty five minutes.

A Fresh Start

Charles Barclay was now in the unenviable position of being a spare gunner who was utilized as and when a crew needed a replacement gunner. As a deeply superstitious person, Charles realized that he had more chance of surviving a full tour of operations if he could join a regular crew. The bond of friendship and camaraderie gave aircrews at least a chance of survival. With this in mind, he jumped at the opportunity of being posted to 622 Squadron at Mildenhall in late June 1944 in the hope that he would join a regular crew. Mildenhall was a pre-war RAF station and aircrew had considerably better facilities than at the hastily built wartime

F/Sgt Barclay's original crew was formed at Desborough OUT. The crew was tragically killed on their first operational mission. L-R: Sgt M. Thomas (W/op), F/Sgt Barclay (MUG), F/O R.N Elwin RCAF (nav), F/Lt P.W. Norbury (pilot), F/O M. Dodds (B/A), Sgt. W.E. Astley (A/G). *Courtesy of Charles E. Barclay.*

stations. F/Sgt Barclay was assigned to the crew of Pilot Officer Clark, a Canadian who had been on 622 Squadron since February 1944 and was nearing his 'tour' completion. Charles never asked what happened to his original gunner but strongly suspected that he had been killed on operations. At this point of the war Bomber Command was concentrating all its efforts on bombing the V1 flying bomb sites that had sprung up across the Channel in France. It was from these sites that the Germans launched their lethal flying bombs on England's capital city bringing considerable devastation and loss of life.

On 6th July 1944, Charles took up the mid upper gunner's position in Lancaster LM443, GI-T for a mission to the flying bomb site at Wizernes along the coast of France. The mission went without a hitch and a further eight missions would be completed with P/O Clarke. The most memorable moment was a raid to Paris on 16th July, which was aborted due to the weather. On the return journey, a bomber in front dropped its bomb load onto a German airfield in France. The anti-aircraft fire opened up and caught their Lancaster with small holes in the bomb bay doors. On another trip to Stuttgart on 25th July 1944 one of the engines failed and the raid was completed on three engines causing considerable consternation for fear of lagging behind the bomber stream and straight into the hands of the German night fighter force. On 28th July 1944 Charles conducted an air test in LM443; this was to prove his last trip with Pilot Officer Clark. It is worth mentioning at this point the operational tour of Pilot Officer Clark who was awarded the French Croix de Guerre medal for his contribution to the Normandy invasion and the Distinguished Flying Cross. The citation for his DFC medal reads as follows:

'Pilot Officer Clark has been a member of No.622 Squadron since February 1944, and has established himself as a resolute captain and an admirable leader. On the opening of the Normandy offensive on the 6th June 1944, and also prior to the invasion, he engaged the enemy in all stages of the attack and undoubtedly contributed greatly to the operational success of his squadron. By his inspired leadership and total disregard of personal danger he was always a source of encouragement to the personnel of his flight. His devotion to duty and gallantry in action were outstanding'.

Courtesy of the London Gazette

With the departure of Pilot Officer Clarke, Charles Barclay again found himself classified as a spare gunner. He completed another eight missions during August and September 1944 in support of the advancing Allied Armies as a spare gunner without any real identity to a crew. On 24th September 1944, F/Sgt Barclay's name appeared on the Battle order for 'ops' to Calais, his pilot was an Australian, Flying Officer Frank Stephens. The original gunner in the Stephen's crew needed replacing and Charles welcomed the opportunity to join a regular crew again. Operations continued to be focused on supporting the Allied forces progressing towards Germany's capital. Bomber Command's focus returned to the industrial Ruhr Valley in October 1944 and F/O Stephens and crew flew to some of the most heavily defended targets such as Stuttgart, Essen, Cologne, Bonn and Dortmund without serious incident.

The 'Pointblank' directive agreed by the Allied Air Force Commanders in June 1943 called for the following objective:

'The mission of the United States and British bomber forces as prescribed by the Combined chiefs of staff at Casablanca is to conduct a joint US-British air offensive to accomplish the progressive dislocation and disruption of the German military, industrial and economic system, and the undermining of the morale of the German people to a point where their capacity for armed resistance is fatally weakened'.

Pilot Officer J. Clark DFC, RCAF and crew in front of LM443, GI-T at Mildenhall. Note the nose art depicting 'Clarkies Ark'. F/Sgt Barclay is standing on the left in the photograph. P/O Clarke is 5th from the left. *Courtesy of Charles E. Barclay.*

The Allied air forces had long considered that German oil supplies were a major contributory factor to their ability to wage war and under the guise of the 'Poinblank' directive several missions were concentrated on the German oil storage depots. Charles Barclay found himself on one such mission on 2nd November 1944 when the daylight target was the synthetic oil plant at Homberg, a raid lead by the G/H equipped Lancasters of 3 Group. On 4th November Solingen was the target, both objectives were successfully bombed restricting the plants output for some considerable time.

An Abrupt End

On 6th November 1944, Flying Officer Stephens and crew were on the battle order to attack the town of Koblenz, again using a G/H equipped Lancasters to mark the target, this time at night. The Lancaster assigned to them was HK621, GI-C an aircraft that they would leave resting on its belly at a forward Allied air strip. Charles Barclay picks up the story:

> "The night we went down did not start well and whilst the ground crew were bombing up our Lancaster, a hydraulic pipe burst in the aircraft releasing a 4,000lb bomb from its rack which fell onto the bomb carrier trolley without exploding. This was the start of things to come and I remember clearly the route out over Germany was littered with small flashes from the ground which were obviously flak guns firing up at us. The flak bursts were exploding all around us showering the surrounding air space with fragments of shrapnel. From the rear turret my vision of what occurred was somewhat restricted. The intercom chatter alerted me to the fact that our Lancaster had been hit in the port outer engine and that the skipper was attempting to feather the propeller. All attempts to feather the damaged propeller failed and the fuel supply to the port engines was unable to be cut. Therefore, the skipper cut the power to the port inner engine causing the outer engine to windmill out of control. By this stage the cockpit area was filling with smoke and the Lancaster was increasingly difficult to control by Frank Stephens. We jettisoned the bombs to lighten the load in an attempt to keep us airborne and we turned for home gradually losing height when the starboard outer engine cut out. Eventually the skipper gave the order to bail out and I climbed out of my turret and clipped on my parachute, which was stored directly outside my turret in the fuselage. By this time we had plummeted down from 18,000ft to just 2,000ft and I made my way to the rear door which was already open indicating to me that other members of the crew had jumped. At this stage one feels very lonely and self preservation quickens your stride, I was panicking and quickly exited the Lancaster by sitting with my back to the door and dropping backwards out. Almost immediately I pulled the parachute cord and my 'chute' opened up with the harness nearly cutting me in half, a most uncomfortable experience. My fall was brought to an abrupt end when I landed in a field near a small farm. After some hesitation, I walked towards the door where I was met by the farmer. I introduced myself to the farmer and he took me into the farm house to meet his wife and daughter and I eventually made him understand that I wanted to contact the Allies. The farmer took me a short distance to a big house where we were greeted by what appeared to be a butler who took me to the lady of the house who was remarkably from Herefordshire. She made me very welcome and obviously contacted someone because two Americans in a jeep arrived to pick me up and they took me to their camp. I was made very welcome and I spent considerable time drinking with American Officers and I drifted off to sleep. When I woke up I was surrounded by several American figures laughing at my predicament."
>
> "Our Lancaster was not the only one from 622 Squadron to go down that night. My best friend on the squadron was Flying Officer Harold Jones who was the rear gunner in the crew of flying Officer Leake. Harold had already completed a tour of operations, he was a great confidant to me, and we both had the same number of 'ops 'completed on our respective 'tours'. Apparently, their Lancaster, HK644, GI-D had only arrived on the squadron in September and only had seventy one hours of flying time. Harold Jones and the rest of the crew are buried in Rheinberg War Cemetery Germany."

The journey home for Charles Barclay took a few days and his parents were notified of him being 'missing from operations' via telegram. On his return to England, he was immediately sent

Lancaster HK621, GI-C the aircraft that F/O Stephens and crew crash landed behind Allied lines in France. At the time of the crash, the Lancaster had completed just 115 flying hours. *Author's Collection.*

Charles Eric Barclay in full flying gear, 622 Squadron 1944. *Courtesy of Charles E. Barclay.*

on home leave and ordered to report to a medical center in London periodically. It was here that he was evaluated through the course of several visits and eventually sent to a convalescent home in North Wales for three months. The intention for Charles was to recover from the shock of his experience and the stresses and strains of a tour with Bomber Command.

By the time Charles Barclay was passed 'A1' fit the war was fast approaching its conclusion and he never undertook another operational mission against Germany. The experiences of Charles Barclay are typical of life on a Bomber squadron, however what is commendable was his inner strength and resilience to continue after losing his first crew. Charles Barclay still vividly remembers his experiences with Bomber Command and especially all those that lost their lives fighting 'Nazi' tyranny. His mind always returns to his good friend Flying Officer Harold Jones and this tragic loss on the same night as his brush with death. Memories ingrained through personal tragedy always remain vivid.

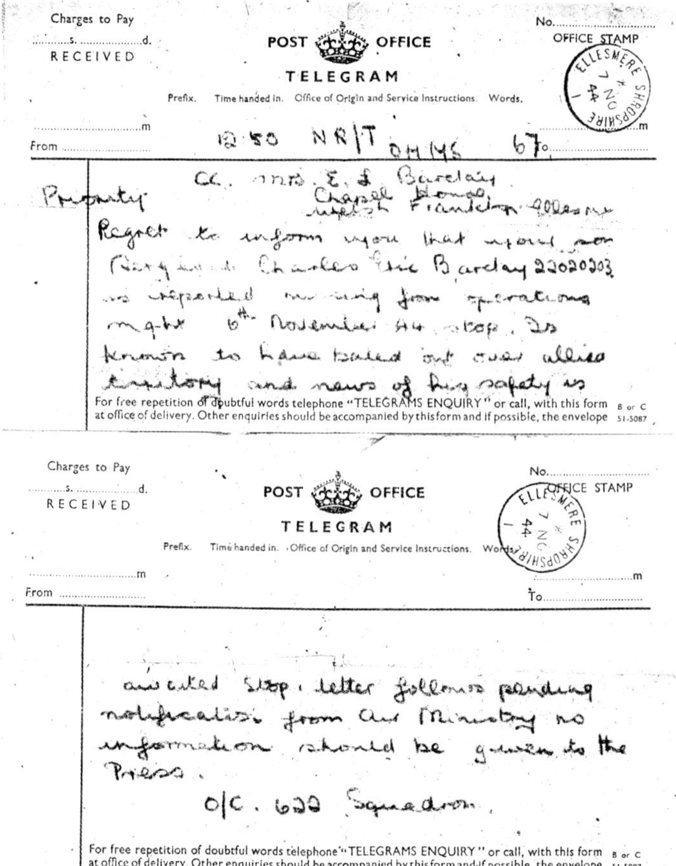

Charges to Pay
........s. ....d.
RECEIVED

POST OFFICE
TELEGRAM

Prefix. Time handed in. Office of Origin and Service Instructions. Words.

OFFICE STAMP
ELLESMERE 7 NO 44 SHROPSHIRE

From ....
12.50 NR/T OHMS 67.

Priority CC. Mrs. E. L. Barclay
Chapel House
Welsh Frankton Ellesmere

Regret to inform you that your son
Sergeant Charles Eric Barclay 2202020[3]
is reported missing from operations
night 6th November 44 stop. Is
known to have baled out over allied
territory and news of his safety is

For free repetition of doubtful words telephone "TELEGRAMS ENQUIRY" or call, with this form at office of delivery. Other enquiries should be accompanied by this form and if possible, the envelope B or C 51-5087

Charges to Pay
........s. ....d.
RECEIVED

POST OFFICE
TELEGRAM

Prefix. Time handed in. Office of Origin and Service Instructions. Words.

OFFICE STAMP
ELLESMERE 7 NO 44 SHROPSHIRE

From .... To..................

awaited stop. letter follows pending
notification from Air Ministry no
information should be given to the
Press.

O/C. 622 Squadron.

For free repetition of doubtful words telephone "TELEGRAMS ENQUIRY" or call, with this form at office of delivery. Other enquiries should be accompanied by this form and if possible, the envelope B or C 51-5087

Telegram received by the parents of F/Sgt Barclay informing them that he was missing on operations. *Courtesy of Charles E. Barclay.*

12

Superstition and Tragedy
Two Lancasters Crash

Bomber Command suffered the highest casualty rate of any armed force during the Second World War. Of the volunteers who flew almost sixty per cent (over 55,000) were killed. The bravery of the young aircrew cannot be overstated because they were all well aware of the high casualty rate among their own squadron and Bomber Command in general. Every night the squadron Adjustments Officer would go through the kit of young men who had 'failed to return'. These young men were either dead, struggling to evade capture, or taken prisoner to be interned in a POW camp for several years of deprivation. The grisly task of the Adjustments Officer would include gathering up personal possessions of the missing person(s) and vetting letters and the contents of wallets to send home to the next of kin. Inevitably, mistakes were made and occasionally wives would receive her husband's personal effects with photographs of him with other girls as company. Such was life on an operational squadron during the Second World War.

For any given 100 aircrew in Bomber Command, 1939-1945 the statistical breakdown was:

Killed on operations 51.
Killed in crashes in England 9.
Seriously injured 3.
Prisoner of War 12.
Evaded capture 1.
Survived unharmed 24.

Every day was treated as one's last and young men looked for a release from the realities of war through beer and song. There were no counselors lurking behind locker doors to deal with the trauma experienced on a daily basis by aircrew fighting for their lives against the enemy. Occasionally the stress of war became too much and the unfortunate person would be branded as 'Lack of Moral Fiber' (LMF) and have this abbreviation adorned across the front of his personal file. Aircrew who fell into this category were stripped of their rank and 'ghosted' out of the squadron as quickly as possible so as not to set a bad example to others. The medical advances since the war have recognized the trauma experienced by aircrew as a genuine illness equivalent to 'shell shock' experienced by soldiers on the front line of the battle field. LMF was a label of ignorance, which would not be permitted today and seen as unjust.

The aircrews at RAF Mildenhall were no different to any other squadron, off duty pursuits were drinking and girls, not necessarily in that order. The majority of aircrew who were not on operations that night would venture down to the local pub called 'The Bird in the Hand', a stones throw from the official Officers Mess at Mildenhall and it was suitably labeled 'The number two Mess'.

Invariably, anyone with blond hair got the nickname Blondie. There were two people at Mildenhall in 1944 with blonde hair at extremes of the social spectrum. Wing Commander 'Blondie Swales' DSO DFC DFM was the Officer commanding No.622 Squadron. The other 'Blondie' was the barmaid at the Bird in Hand hotel. If there was an end of tour party or a crew went 'missing' the beer was brought in by Blondie in large half or one gallon copper jugs. Nobody at eighteen was experienced at this drinking pastime and it was strictly an exercise in forgetting operations either previous or to come. Blondie was always the center of attention and plenty of aircrew wanted to take her home, despite her reputation as the 'chop blonde'. She worked hard cleaning up after rowdy aircrew and resisting their advances, with one night off in ten if she was lucky. The unfortunate label attributed to Blondie was born from superstitious aircrew who had noticed that whoever she became involved with failed to return soon after. Aircrews were very close companions and if one member had a perceived bad omen in tow, then the whole crew would feel the strain of this irrational belief. To counteract this superstition crews would carry out various rituals such as relieving themselves against the tail wheel shortly before boarding the Lancaster for operations. Others simply carried a lucky charm such as a rabbit's foot or some part of their girlfriend's underwear such as a silk stocking. Great emphasis was placed on superstitious ritual and any interruption to this ritual was considered fatal.

Fatal Collision

On the night of 19th September 1944, the 'Bird in Hand' was bursting at the seams with aircrew enjoying themselves by singing and dancing. Blondie, now established with her unfortunate title as the 'chop blonde' was dancing with a Flying Officer Hooker DFM from another squadron who was destined to fly on operations with 622 Squadron the following day. The Flying Officer was discreetly informed of 'Blondie's' reputation and he laughed it off as superstitious nonsense. The following day (20th) crews were

LL802, GI-M one of the Lancasters that collided en route to Calais on 20th September 1944 killing F/O James & crew. Keen eyes will notice the Monica tail and wing aerials. Monica was a radar device designed to warn aircrew of approaching fighters. *Courtesy of Mildenhall Register*

briefed to attack the German gun batteries at Calais in daylight and Flying Officer Hooker was a 'spare' in the crew of Flying Officer Hogg. A rear gunner in another formation of Lancasters that day can vividly recall what occurred.

On 20th September the Campbell crew was on the battle order to attack the German gun batteries at Calais on a daylight trip. For Bill Hickling this trip would be one of the most memorable of his operational tour for the futile and tragic waste of aircrew lives. Bill Hickling recalls the event that left fifteen aircrew dead on British soil:

> "At briefing we were told to attack German positions around the port of Calais. Our assigned Lancaster was HK614, GI-R the usual mount of the 'B' flight Commander, S/Ldr Mitchell DFC who for some reason was not on 'ops' this day. On daylight raids we were instructed to fly in three 'vic' formations which were extremely difficult to maintain due to pilots up until this point of the campaign, never having been trained in close formation flying. The degree of pilot skill necessary to keep a fully laden Lancaster in close formation was intense and physically and mentally draining. Our skipper could not see anything to his starboard side and had to rely on instructions from the mid upper gunner and the bomb aimer to keep him in position in relation to the other Lancaster on our starboard side. On instructions from both of them we were constantly moving from port to starboard. After forming up we set course for Calais and whilst climbing we entered very thick cloud, which restricted our ability to keep in formation. We kept losing sight of the Lancaster on our starboard side when we veered too much to port. It was the most intense and frightening experience imaginable and it felt like ages before we finally broke through the clouds. What happened next is etched in my memory and at the time it was a surreal incident that I could not believe was happening. Two Lancasters appeared out of the clouds together in the leading formation slightly ahead of us clung together in a grotesque embrace after obviously colliding in the cloud. The two Lancasters appeared to hang in the air for a brief period and then fall backwards out of control and start spiraling down. All I could think was that the crews would have time to put on their parachutes and bail out, however inside the planes the crews would have been totally unprepared for an incident of this nature and the 'G' forces and panic stricken crews were unable to leave the doomed aircraft". The two Lancaster's LL802, GI-M & LM167, GI-N crashed near the village of Wormingford near Colchester in Essex killing fifteen young men. Unluckily the crew of LM167 had been carrying an extra crew member who was visiting from another station." The 'Chop blonde' had struck again!

The crew members who died that day are as follows:

Lancaster LL802 GI-M
F/O. C.R. James (pilot)
F/Sgt R.S. Westbrook
Sgt J.A. Dumareque
Sgt P.I. Geddes
F/Sgt J. Gibson
Sgt E.J. Dryland
Sgt R.S. Keatley

Lancaster LM167 GI-N
Sgt J.A.J. De Angelis
F/O L. Hogg (pilot)
F/Sgt G. W. Fitness
F/Sgt Robinson
F/O H.E. Prichard
F/O A.T. Gill
F/Sgt J.M Adams
F/O E.L Hooker –Spare

A full RAF investigation was commissioned and the crash was attributed to pilot error in cloud. Apparently, due to the high cumulus of cloud both pilots should have opened out in cloud to avoid collision.

Four of the aircrew killed on that fateful day are buried in the war graves cemetery at Beck Row Church in Mildenhall, a stones throw away from the runway where they would have departed. Five others are buried in the War Graves Cemetery at Cambridge while the remainder were taken home to local church yards to be near to their family.

F/O Gill, Beck Row Cemetery. *Author's Collection*

Sgt De Angelis, Beck Row Cemetery. *Author's Collection*

Sgt Dryland, Beck Row Cemetery. *Author's Collection*

F/O James Beck Row Cemetery. *Author's Collection*

F/Sgt Frank Robinson, Holbeach Cemetery Lincolnshire. *Author's Collection*

The War Graves Cemetery at Beck Row Church Mildenhall, Suffolk. *Author's Collection*

Commonwealth War Graves Cemetery in Cambridge. *Author's Collection*

F/Sgt G.W. Fitness RNZAF. *Author's Collection*

F/Sgt J.M. Adams RNZAF. *Author's Collection*

F/O H. E. Pritchard RNZAF. *Author's Collection*

F/O M.L. Hogg RAF. *Author's Collection*

Sgt J.A. Dumareque RAF. *Author's Collection*

Five aircrew lay together in a row in their final resting place. *Author's Collection*

13

God Speed

Pilot: F/Lt. K. Derisley DFC
Nav: F/S D. McCrone
B/A: F/S E. Harrison
W/op: F/S E. Hollings
Mug: Sgt W. E. Crow
R/G: Sgt C. J. Bright
F/E: Sgt H. Terry

The fascinating story that unfolds below is the personal account of Mr. C.R. Bright, an air gunner in Bomber Command. However, his understated account of his operational tour must stand as a testament to one of the most difficult of operational 'tours' for several reasons. Firstly, his 'tour' commenced in earnest in January 1944 during the 'Battle of Berlin' when Bomber Command losses were at their highest and the odds of successfully completing a full tour were less than one in two. During this time Bomber Command was taking the war deep into enemy territory and German night fighter defenses had taken the upper hand with electronic counter measures which culminated in 96 out of 795 (12.07%) Bombers being lost on the Nuremberg raid on 30/31st March 1944.

Early Recollections
Charles Bright recalls his memories:

"Before I joined the Royal Air Force, I had been a member of the Air Training Corps based at Catford in south London. I remember that there was a Hawker Hart which was used for training purposes. It was one of the few biplanes that I encountered at close hand. It was removed during the war and taken to somewhere in Wales, after which I assume it was scrapped. I actually joined the RAF in late February 1943. I wanted to be a pilot, but instead I was offered the choice of being a tank driver or an air gunner, I chose the latter.

I was sent to Bridlington in Yorkshire for my initial training. I recall that there was an air sea rescue unit based locally which was equipped with high speed launches and Supermarine Walruses, though I only saw these from a distance. On 22nd May I was posted to No.9 Advanced Flying Unit (AFU) for my initial gunnery course. This was based at Penrhos. My first flight was on 12th June in Avro Anson No.941 piloted by a Sgt. Carter. This lasted for 40 minutes. All the initial training was done in Ansons using both camera guns and live firing. I remember all too well the manually retracting undercarriage on the Anson (52 turns, one for each week of the year). The target tugs were Westland Lysanders. As far as I can recall, all these aircraft were in normal camouflage colors, certainly on their upper surfaces. There were also long nosed Blenheims at Penrhos. These were not very popular as they had the reputation of being rather temperamental and potential death traps due to their restricted escape hatches (approx 14" wide). They were equipped with a twin turret, which meant they were mark Vs, rather than IVs. Fortunately, I never flew in one. After 20 hours 25 minutes of daylight flying, I completed the course with an examination mark of 83.5 % and the comment, 'with more experience should prove an efficient gunner'.

From 9 AFU, I moved to No.82 OTU flying a mixture of Wellington IIIs and Xs. The IIIs were rather worn out and seemed very sluggish in the climb. On both marks, when the rear turret was rotated it caused the airplane to yaw, necessitating the pilot to take corrective action. The planes I flew in most regularly were BK129, BK399, HE919 and LN282. To begin with, the pilot was F/Sgt Henry, but later Sgt Ken Derisley came on the scene and I became one of his crew. We were based at Bircotes. Training consisted of 'Bullseyes', fighter affiliation exercise with Tomahawks, bombing practice, live air to air firing with drogue towing Martinets. The last flight at Bircotes was on the 26th September. By this date I had flown 78 hours 50 minutes, 39 hours and 25 minutes of this was at night. I mention these figures to give some idea of how much training was involved.

The next posting was a short spell at 1483 Flight based at Newmarket. This was for 4 days of intensive live air to air firing. It was on this course that I first flew in a Short Stirling. While it was a new plane, it was still a Frazer-Nash turret. Whilst ungainly looking on the ground, I remember the Stirling could turn quite sharply, on one occasion we turned so tightly that we were contrailing from the wingtips. Again Martinet target tugs were used rather that Battles of Defiants. This course added another 6 hours 50 minutes to my flying time."

Charles Bright. *Courtesy of Robert Bright son of Charles.*

"My next posting was to 1651 Heavy Conversion Unit at Waterbeach and Wrattling Common. Here I was reunited with F/Sgt Ken Derisley. Night flying training was now the order of the day, culminating in a 5 hour 20 minute long 'Bulls eye'. All this training was done in Stirlings (R9643, W3722, BF385 and W3722).At the end of November 1943, when I left 1651 Heavy Conversion Unit (HCU) I had flown 121 hours, 50 of which were at night. One vivid memory of this period is of a Stirling flown by a chap called Runciman. He brought the plane in as if to land, then proceeded to retract the undercarriage and flew the Stirling straight and level. Needless to say he climbed away, but it says something about the Stirling's controllability and Runciman's skills as a pilot. I believe he was the same Runciman who once stood a Stirling on its tail in flight, a remarkable feat of flying."

Operational Posting

"In December 1943, we were posted to 622 Squadron flying the Short Stirling on active operations. Our first 'op' lasted 2 hour 50 minutes and took the form of mine laying just off the Frisian Islands in Stirling RP461 'C'. We were fired on by a flak ship and noted its position which we duly reported on our return. The Royal Navy near the Felixstowe coast fired on us on our homeward journey; this was despite firing off the 'colors of the day'. Given the distinctiveness of a Stirling and the fact that the Germans did not own a four engined aircraft, it suggested to us that some aircraft recognition training was required. This trip was to be our first and last operational trip in a Stirling and 622 Squadron began to convert to the vastly superior Avro Lancaster around the turn of the year. On New Year's day 1944 we completed over 2 hours on circuits and landings and the very next day we spent over 3 hours at night doing the same thing. The squadron's conversion and our training continued for the rest of January and on 30th January 1944 the squadron was deemed to be fully conversant with the Lancaster and therefore operational on the type.

The majority of operational stations attributed a particular Lancaster to a crew and subject to service and repair; the crew usually flew the same aircraft. For our second 'op' (first in a Lanc) on 30th January 1944 we were on the battle order to attack Berlin in W4248 'T'. We considered this to be a baptism of fire because the 'big city' was Germany's most heavily defended target and Bomber Command was taking heavy losses. We never realized that we were taking part in the Battle of Berlin. The Battle of Berlin was a major offensive to destroy the morale of the German population and send a message to the Third Reich that we could destroy targets deep in enemy territory. Air Chief Marshall Harris had promised with the aide of the US bombers to 'Wreck Germany from end to end', however Berlin was to prove a challenge too far at this stage of the war.The offensive began on 18th November 1943 and climaxed on 24th March 1944.

Over Berlin we were buzzed by a single engined fighter which we assumed to be a Me109, presumably a Wilde-Sau aircraft. Our mid upper gunner fired at it which seemed to dissuade it from further action and we returned safely to Mildenhall after 6 hours and 20 minutes in the air. Quite a trip considering that it was our first deep penetration raid and in a relatively new aircraft. To our surprise our third mission was also to Berlin (15/16th Feb) over 7 hours this time with no combats just the usual heavy flak and searchlights. Leipzig on 19/20th February followed our Berlin forays. During this raid Bomber Command suffered heavy losses, 78 bombers falling to mainly night fighter activity. The bomber stream had become too spread out which enabled German fighters to pick of the stragglers. When we landed back at Mildenhall, a very senior officer was waiting who I believe was Robert Saunby, deputy to ACM Harris. For some reason he asked for my opinion of the raid and I replied that it seemed to be a shambles, he appeared unhappy and shocked at my assessment. I upset the de-briefing officer that night by offering the opinion that smoke from the fires was reaching up to 18,000 ft. He was of the opinion that this was not possible; however, by knowing our height and distance, it was quite straightforward to obtain a reasonable accurate estimate from the angle of my guns. On 20th February we were on the battle order for Stuttgart and the operation went by without incident and only 1.5 % (5) of the bomber force was lost.

We were really being tested as a crew and the deep penetration raids were exhausting, although we carried these out with a team spirit and great determination. On 24th February Schweinfurt was on the battle order. Schweinfurt was seen as a major manufacturer in the ball-bearing industry, which distributed its components to all aspects of the German military machine. Our mount for this particular raid was GI-S, R5846 a seasoned Lancaster which had seen considerable service. The route into the target was the usual hot bed of flak and searchlights and over the target we were coned by searchlights. When an aircraft is coned by a searchlight the only way to survive is to dive through the air to escape the deadly beam. Ken, our pilot threw the plane into a steep dive and almost immediately we were nearly hit by an accurate burst of flak, the sky lit up with vivid red and pinks. At the time I reported it as a 'scarecrow' a German spoof intended to resemble an exploding bomber. The blast was so close that it ripped away the underside of the Lancaster directly beneath me in the rear turret and also damaged our oxygen supplies."

After the war, it was officially denied that scarecrows existed and no evidence has ever been uncovered to suggest that they did. What F/Sgt Bright actually saw was most likely to have been a bomber that had received a direct hit from flak which dispersed the aircraft's target markers into the night sky.

Another member of the crew F/Sgt Harrison, the bomb aimer, witnessed the Lancaster's demise in a more vivid fashion. He was in the nose section of the Lancaster and observed the flak strike split the Lancaster in half and 3 crewmembers literally just fell out of the stricken bomber. Charles Bright continues:

"We continued in our steep dive and at one stage our skipper called over the intercom that we had reached 410 mph! After losing considerable height, F/L Derisley successfully pulled us out of the dive and although extensively damaged we headed for home. The return journey took us over the Alps and two Fw190's formatted behind on each side and slightly behind. With the battle damage inflicted earlier, we were sitting ducks. However the Fw190's must have been low on fuel because they waggled their wings in recognition and flew off. We eventually made it back to Mildenhall and eggs and bacon. The Lancaster was examined for battle damage, the shape of the Lancaster's wings had become distorted and several rivets had popped. The main spar had suffered damage in the dive and the Lancaster was driven away by road for repair. R5846 eventually returned to active service with 75 Squadron at Methwold however, on 18th December 1944 it collided in mid air with another Lancaster and it was written off. I have often wondered if our diving speed of 410 mph was a record for a Lancaster."

"Our reward for wrecking one Lancaster was to be issued with a brand new Lancaster LM 466, which again displaying the squadron identification markings GI-P. From the outset, the Lancaster felt and performed beautifully and we were able to fly higher and faster than anything we had flown before. This was confirmed when we bombed a target at 22,000 ft and left it at over 300 mph once bombs had gone. Even allowing for inaccurate instrument readings, we knew that it was a 'hot' ship.

Our 7th trip was again to Stuttgart and thankfully went without incident. On the 18th we set course for Frankfurt but returned early because the ammunition feeds to my rear turret were faulty which was cured by changing the ammunition. Frankfurt did not escape our attention and we attacked the target again on 22nd March and on the 26th we attacked the heavily defended Ruhr target of Essen."

F/Lt Derisley & crew in front of LM466, GI-P. F/Sgt Bright is far right. *Courtesy of Robert Bright son of Charles.*

The Nuremberg raid 30th March 1944

On 30th March 'Butch' Harris ordered a maximum effort on the city of Nuremberg a center for the Nazi party and a favorite city of Hitler. The city was full of architectural beauty but beneath the façade, it was manufacturing vital components for the German Radar defense systems. The confirmation of the attack came as a surprise to all Bomber crews because it came right in the middle of the full moon period and a moonlit sky was happy pickings for the German night fighter force. 795 aircraft were dispatched to the target and when the bombers had reached the Belgian border, the night fighters made first contact. On the route to the target 82 bombers were shot out of the sky. A major factor in the high losses was the technological radar advances that had been developed by the Germans. Unbeknownst to the British, the German night fighters were fitted with new bomber detection radar called SN-2 which actually homed in on the bomber force defensive radar sets. In addition the forecast winds were grossly underestimated and a fierce cross wind caused many navigators to be off course and out of the bomber stream. The strong winds also caused the

Pathfinder marking aircraft to drop their target markers well to the east of the city. Such was the confusion over the target area that many crews actually bombed the nearby city of Schweinfurt in the heat of battle. On the route from the target the night fighters had further success although due to the need to refuel, only 13 bombers were lost on the return journey.On analysis, the whole raid was a complete failure the German strategic plan had been well executed and ACM Harris and his senior staff were left to lick their wounds.

In his Frazer Nash rear turret, F/Sgt Bright witnessed some of the carnage and witnessed several bombers going down in flames although as a crew they came through unmolested. On the return flight they were diverted to the emergency landing strip at Woodbridge due to Mildenhall being fog bound. After landing, they could see many wrecked planes around the aerodrome.

By the end of March 1944, Charles Bright had flown 227hrs (126 of these at night), been buzzed by a German fighter, nearly shot down, fired upon by the Royal Navy, survived the Nuremberg raid and all this in just a year since joining up! Charles picks up the story again:

> "April 1944 saw us attacking further German cities such as Cologne on 22nd, Karlsruhe on the 24th and Essen again on the 26th. On the Essen raid we took the squadron bombing leader F/Lt Middleton along as our bomb aimer was unwell. He was not happy with the approach to the target so he ordered the skipper to go round again! Our second run was successful and when we returned to Mildenhall, the bombing leader came in for a fair amount of stick for us having to go around again. The odds on being hit by flak or attacked by a fighter on the first run were considerable, however to go around again in the target area was practically suicide. Our trip to Dusseldorf on 22nd was another early return with mechanical failure, this time the engine driven pump to the turrets hydraulic systems had malfunctioned. We never experienced any difficulties when we returned early because our technical problems were justified. Only justifiable reasons for turning back were acceptable. For every 'turn back', we had to make up our total with other raids. I mention the turning back justification because there was a lot of talk on the station about Bomber Command crews dumping their bombs early and returning to base with alleged technical problems. I was obviously aware of the RAF's 'lack of moral fiber' description for airmen refusing to fly or turning back before reaching the target. I had immense sympathy for these airmen because I had witnessed real fear and often wondered if I would survive to complete my full tour. At the time of our tour Bomber Command was suffering heavy losses to the German defenses and at the end of March 1944 the bomber force was switched to supporting the D-Day invasion preparations and targets would now be mainly focused on France.
>
> During the month of May 1944 all our 'ops' were against French targets, again in preparation for D-Day. On the very first day of the month we attacked the railway yards at Chambly at low level. On 8th we attacked the gun position at Cap Griz Nez with poor results. The 10th saw us heading for Louvain again railway yards were the target and extensive damage and disruption was achieved. On the 24th May we attacked two railway yards at the German town of Aachen and suffered a total of 25 bombers being lost. The 27th brought us to attack the coastal batteries at Boulogne as a part of 5 costal batteries to be attacked, results were reported as good. Our final 'op' during May was against railway yards at Trappes. I remember the raid to Trappes well and I have vivid memories of bombs thoroughly wrecking the marshaling yards. Mixed in amongst the operations was a scattering of training exercises and on 6th May we visited Cosford. A prominent memory was the sergeant's mess at Cosford which had an orchestra playing and the tables had white starched table linen. When we left our skipper was invited to do a low level flypast. At the end of the runway was a railway embankment with a station. F/Lt Derisley had put the Lancaster down a little too low and he hurriedly pulled up over the station, which resulted in the rear wheel passing very close to the roof of a building, which sent the

F/Lt Derisley DFC & crew pose for this shot on the wing of GI-P with the ground crew who were responsible for the maintenance of the aircraft. *Courtesy of Robert Bright son of Charles.*

The crew pose for another photograph with a slightly different perspective. *Courtesy of Robert Bright son of Charles*

awaiting passengers scurrying for cover. Our training at this time was concentrated on low flying and on another occasion, we were flying along the 'Hundred Foot' drain with our wingtips about level with the dykes on either side. A young land army girl was walking along one of these and didn't bat an eyelid as we flew past, perhaps this was a sight that she had seen before and associated it with 'flyboys' showing off again."

6th June 1944 D-Day

"The 6th June is synonymous with the commencement of the historic invasion landings on the Normandy beaches. We awoke to find ourselves on the battle order to attack the coastal batteries at Ouistreham, our first daylight raid. On the way to the target, I looked down at the sea and I have never seen so many ships together before, it was a sight that I will always remember. On this raid I witnessed a friend's Lancaster being hit by flak and begin its spiral death plunge. The guns in the rear turret seemed to be firing all the way down. On our return to Mildenhall the ground crews sprung quickly into action refueling and rearming our Lancaster, it did not take a genius to guess that we would be on another mission very shortly. That mission was again in support of the Normandy battle area and we were sent to attack the railway and road centers at Lisieux, just behind the front lines. Our targets now were all concentrated on the support of the invasion and on the 8th & 10th June we were set to attack railway yards at Fougeres and Dreux respectively."

"Just when we were adjusting to the relatively short trips to French targets, we were sent back to the Ruhr and Gelsenkirchen to attack a synthetic oil plant. The post raid reports were very optimistic and it was confirmed after the war that the Pathfinders using Oboe sets had marked the target very accurately and all production was halted at the plant. Our foray back into Germany was short lived and on 15th June we were detailed to attack a French target again, this time Le Harve. Our objective was to destroy the light Naval forces that were threatening the Allied shipping near the Normandy beaches. This daylight trip was very distinctive for me because we were escorted by a group of spitfires as fighter escorts. The sight of the spitfires was a delight to behold and offered a reassuring element to the operation. Over the target we encountered accurate flak from a flak ship in the harbor/estuary.

The railway yards at Valenciennes were our next operation and it was a memorable one. We were approaching the target when we were stalked by a twin engined fighter which I believed to be a Me110. I reported its presence to the skipper and I began to give a commentary on its movements. F/Lt Derisley had seen two more Lancasters flying together ahead of us, and slightly higher than us. We formatted on these two 'friendlies' and the Me110 moved off. He obviously knew he had been seen and the prospect of 12 or more Browning machine guns, even .303's was evidently a powerful deterrent. The night of the 17th saw us raiding the railway yards at Montdidier without incident.

On the 19th June we had a welcome respite from 'ops' and took LM466 on an air test, to see how high it would go. Over the Solway Firth we clocked 29, 250ft on the altimeter. The sky was a deep indigo blue and the view was marvelous; Scotland, the English Lakes and Ireland could all be seen from our vantage point. I have often wondered if our altitude was a record for a Lancaster.

Our second daylight operation and also the last of our tour was a trip to Domleger. The raid went by without incident and we were elated at having completed a full 30 operations and the first 622 Squadron crew to do so. I had personally flown 330hrs, 190 of those at night, endured two trips to Berlin, two to Essen and survived the carnage of the Nuremberg raid and I had not yet reached my 20th birthday."

August 1944 saw not only Sgt Bright's 20th Birthday, but also a return to 1651 Conversion Unit. The CU was still operating 'Stirlings' but he was now returning as an instructor. The use of Stirlings at Wrattling Common continued from August to October 1944. By this time, the Stirling was definitely outmoded as a bomber. November brought substantial changes, a move to Woolfox Lodge and re-equipping to the Avro Lancaster. In February 1945 Sgt Bright came across Ken Derisley again. By now, he was a Flight Lieutenant and he had been awarded the D.F.C. One final flight together in a Lancaster was arranged and once airborne the emotions of operational flying were far removed.

The next occasion that Sgt Bright saw his old skipper was 40 years later at a Mildenhall reunion and they spent considerable time in each other's company catching up on the last 40 years. Sadly, Squadron Leader Derisley died of a brain tumor in 1989. Sgt Bright ends his story:

> "At the end of June 1945, I moved to 1668 Heavy Conversion Unit to begin training for 'Tiger Force' to operate against Japan. It was here that I first came across the infrared night sights and we undertook exercises and experiments with the new devices. Around this time aircrew were offered what became to be known as a 'Cooks Tour', which was an opportunity to fly over German cities and see the destruction delivered by 5 years of Bomber Command attacks. We flew over Coblenz, Frankfurt, Karlsruhe and Stuttgart. The damage to the German cites was immense and my most vivid memories was of the huge number of people who seemed to be camped out in the open along the banks of the River Rhine. Japan surrendered with a little persuasion from the Atom Bombs and the whole country celebrated. However, our training continued on H2S navigation exercises, high level daylight bombing practice and some daylight formation flying. We also undertook fighter

The crew again pose near the rear entrance door to LM466. The repaired bullet holes above the Lancaster's serial number are clearly visible. *Courtesy of Robert Bright son of Charles.*

The end of tour photograph taken alongside GI-P, LM466. The two German swastikas on the aircraft signify two German fighters shot down on a raid to Wizernes on 5th July 1944. The pilot on this occasion was F/Lt Hargreaves and the two gunners shot down their attackers with both of them being awarded immediate DFM's. If you look slightly to the left of the 30 bomb symbol you will see the bullet holes inflicted by the German fighters during the attack. LM466 was eventually lost on the night of 12th August 1944 after completing 303 operational hours. *Courtesy of Robert Bright son of Charles.*

affiliation with Mosquitoes, which were much faster than Tomahawks and Hurricanes; they were in and out very quickly. My last flight was a 6 hr long night time 'Bulls eye' on 16th November 1945. By this time I had flown 487 hrs, 230 by day, 257 by night, virtually all of this as an air gunner and the majority in Frazer Nash turrets."

Postscript

The following has kindly been shared with the author by Mr. Robert Bright, the son of Sgt Charles Bright. The contents are poignant and extremely moving, but also act as tribute to a generation that gave freely and many paid the ultimate sacrifice of losing their lives:

"My father died on 28th November 1998 after a long illness, a combination of angina, Parkinson's disease and cancer. He was 75. Before he died, he had checked my writing, which triggered further comments about events that he remembered. Since my father died, I have come across several accounts whilst sorting through his documents and he often supplied authors with detailed accounts of his operational tour of duty. I can remember that he supplied an account of his Nuremberg experiences to the renowned aviation author, Martin Middlebrook and I viewed a detailed account of the raid on Leipzig.

My father talked a great deal about his wartime experiences. It was only after I had grown up that it became clear how fortunate he was to have survived physically unscathed. I cannot say that the war did not take an emotional toll on him. After two or three heart bypass operations, he suffered from severe hallucinations as he came out of the anesthetic. On both occasions, these seemed to embody wartime experiences with oxygen masks and fighter attacks. I was present when he gave a running commentary involving a Me110 from his hospital bed in an intensive care unit at Guys hospital. He met these adversities with great courage; only towards the end of his life did he show signs of despair"..

14

Photographic Section

A segment from the Chapel's commemorative stained glass window at RAF Mildenhall. The segment depicts part of the 622 Squadron crest and motto. *Courtesy of Elizabeth Cox*

The Squadron personnel gather for a group photograph in front of a Short Stirling bomber. This photograph was taken on 13th August 1943, three days after the squadron was formed. *Author's Collection*

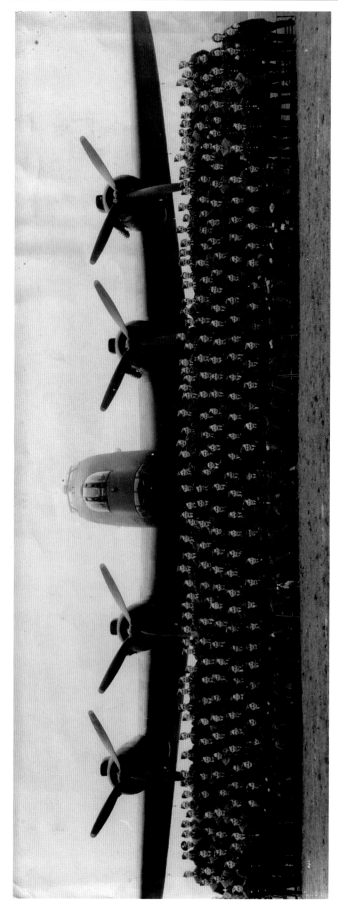

Another full squadron photograph in from of a Short Stirling bomber. This photograph was taken in October 1943. Front row from left 12th F/Lt Stoddart, 16th W/C G.H.N. Gibson (C/O) 17th S/Ldr Martin, 13th F/O Grainger, 2nd from right F/O Fielding. 2nd row back from front standing 7th from right P/O Pollard, 8th from right Sgt Rigby (next to P/O Pollard) 9th from right Sgt Towns. 2nd row from back, 18th from left, F/Sgt C. Thomas RNZAF (KIA). Back from left: 12th Sgt MaCilroy, 13th Sgt Bradshaw, 14th Sgt Belson, 15th Sgt Samson, 17th Sgt Gookey, 18th Sgt Hines, 21st P/O Jackson 32nd F/O Urwin, F/Lt Hargreaves. *Author's Collection.*

Full squadron photograph taken on 19th July 1944 in front of a Avro Lancaster. Front row seated on ground from left: 6th F/Lt J. T. W. Gray, 9th F/O J. Clarke RCAF, 11th S/Ldr Mitchell, 14th P/O Horton, 5th from right F/Lt Woodall RCAF, 6th F/Lt Taylor . Front row seated from left: 3rd F/Sgt Barclay, 9th F/Lt Derisley, 10th F/Lt Maxwell, 12th S/Ldr Allen, 13th P/O Drake 14th P/O Brunton, 15th, F/Lt Middleton, 18th S/Ldr Tilson RCAF, 19th W/C Swales (C/O), 20th S/Ldr Murgatroyd, 21st F/Lt Nichol RCAF, 22nd F/Lt Wishart, 23rd F/Lt Noonan RNZAF, 24th F/Lt Hargreaves, 27th F/O A. Neilsen RAAF, 28th F/O Lunn. Front row seated from right: 3rd F/O O'Brien RNZAF, 6th P/O Harvey RAAF, 7th F/Lt Trenouth RAAF, 8th F/O Good RAAF. Middle row from left: 1st P/O Paton, 2nd F/O Barker, 4th F/Sgt Bright, 13th F/O Bishop RAAF, 14th F/Lt Mason, 15th F/O Pennington, 16th Sgt Thorman, 18th Sgt De Gurin, 23rd Sgt Nicholls. 29th Sgt Farrow 2nd row from top & left: 8th Sgt Parsons, 9th F/Sgt White, 14th F/Sgt Jurgens RNZAF, 15th O'Brien crew air gunner, 16th Sgt Pulman, 18th Sgt Hall, 19th O'Brien crew air gunner, 11th from right F/Sgt J.T.Hargreaves, 15th Sgt Trennery, 16th Sgt Lister, 18th Sgt Hughes . Top row from left: 3rd Sgt Haynes, 4th F/Sgt Redshaw, 5th P/O Fenwick, 6th F/Sgt Roberts, 7th W/O Higgins, 8th F/Sgt Pearcy, 9th F/Sgt Hankinson, 10th Sgt Grant, 11th F/Sgt Featherstone, 12th F/Sgt Hardy , 16th F/Sgt Dye, 17th F/Sgt Monether, 18th W/O Gray RAAF, 21st Sgt Fagg, 22nd Sgt Fellow s, 24th F/Sgt Burns, 25th Sgt C. Chandler, 26th F/Sgt Glynn, 27th F/Sgt Malpass, 28th F/Sgt Crawford Top row from right: 5th Sgt Francis, 6th Sgt West. Author's Collection.

Sergeant Sidney L.W. Kelly (F/E) who was killed in action on the night of 31st May 1944 whilst attacking Trappes in France. Lancaster GI-D, ND926 was shot down by Hptm Fritz Sothe (4/NJG4) in his Ju88 night fighter claiming F/Lt F.R. Randall and crew as his 10th victory. All the crew apart from the stand in rear gunner, F/Lt L.F. Berry DFC was killed on impact. F/Lt Berry was thrown clear of the crash on impact and successfully evaded back to the squadron. Sgt Kelly and the remainder of the crew are buried in the war graves cemetery at Marissel in France. *Courtesy of John Guiver.*

A great photograph of 622 Squadron Lancasters 'running up' their engines prior to a daylight mission in the Autumn of 1944. *Courtesy of B. O' Connor.*

During the latter stages of the war RAF Squadrons turned their attentions to the repatriation of prisoners of war back to England as part of operation Exodus. The photograph above was taken on 10th May 1945 at Juvincourt in France and depicts the crew of Flying Officer G.Thurn RAAF assisting POW's to put on life jackets prior to the flight across the English Channel and home. These trips were very emotional for both the aircrew and the former prisoners, some of whom had been incarcerated since 1940.*Courtesy of R. Pepper*

The view from the rear turret en route to the target during a daylight mission in late 1944. This photograph was taken by Sgt G. Potter, the rear gunner in the crew of F/Lt Hussey DFC. *Courtesy of B. O' Connor.*

Two photographs depicting the crew of F/Lt Ray Trenouth, DFC RAAF. The crew completed a 'tour' of operations from January- August 1944, usually flying Lancaster GI-B 'Beer'. The crew's exploits are featured in chapters 10, 19, and 22.

L-R: P/O D. Harvey RAAF (R/G), Sgt C. Pulman (R/G), Sgt R. Francis (F/E), F/Sgt W. Atkins (W/op), F/O B. Good DFC RAAF (B/A), P/O D. West (Nav), F/Lt R. Trenouth DFC RAAF (Pilot)

L-R: Sgt C. Pulman (MUG), P/O D. West (Nav), F/Sgt W. Atkins (W/op), P/O D. Harvey RAAF (R/G), Sgt R. Francis (F/E), F/Lt R. Trenouth DFC RAAF (Pilot), F/O B. Good DFC RAAF (B/A). *Courtesy of Ray Francis.*

The O' Brien Crew

Pilot Officer William George O'Brien of the Royal New Zealand Air Force arrived with his crew at 622 Squadron in May 1944 and commenced operations almost immediately. He completed a mission on 21st May to Duisberg as second pilot to S/Ldr Tilson RCAF, the 'A' flight commander. The next night the crew started their operations in earnest when they bombed the German city of Dortmund after a year's absence from the attentions of Bomber Command. The crew's arrival on the squadron coincided with the build up to the D-day invasion on 6th June and on the morning of the invasion they attacked the coastal gun batteries at Ouisterham. Missions against the enemy continued at a pace for the crew and their targets during June to August 1944 were in support of the Allied Armies advance through France interspersed with industrial targets within the Ruhr. Bremen was the crew's final target on 18th August 1944 and signaled the end of their operations against the enemy.

F/O W.G. O'Brien RNZAF & crew photographed in front of LM577, GI-E in the late spring of 1944 with their ground crew. Center back, F/Sgt T. G. Jurgens RNZAF (B/A). Center row far left, P/O H. Brunton (W/op), Sgt R. H. Hall (F/E). Seated center, F/O W. G. O'Brien RNZAF (Pilot), 2nd from right, P/O B. W. Drake (Nav). Seated on the ground are the two air gunners, Sgt W. Lock (MUG) & Sgt J. E. Dyke (R/G). The author has been unable to positively identify the two gunners. *Courtesy of Philip O'Brien.*

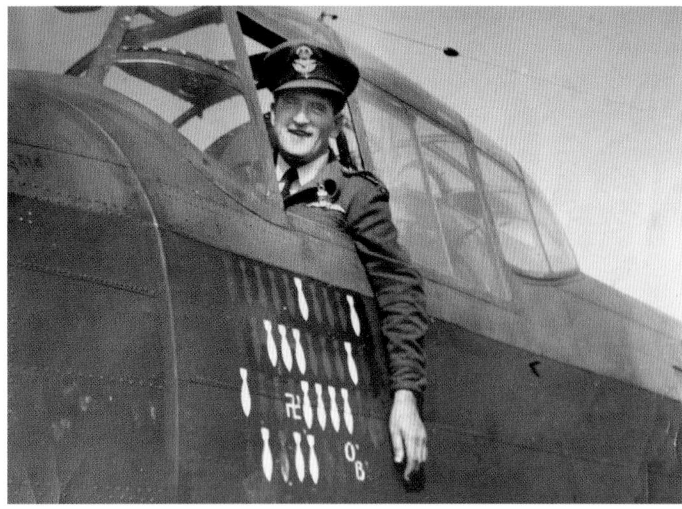

Great photograph depicting F/O O'Brien RNZAF in the cockpit of LM577, 'E' easy. The nose art clearly shows the number of missions completed by the Lancaster and the letters O & B signifying the surname of the pilot. The crew claimed a Germen fighter shot down during their 'tour' hence the swastika. *Courtesy of Philip O'Brien.*

Bombing photograph showing the crew bombing the railway yards & junction at Angers in France on 28/29th May 1944. The objective was to restrict the German's capacity to supply their front line troops by rail. *Courtesy of Philip O'Brien*

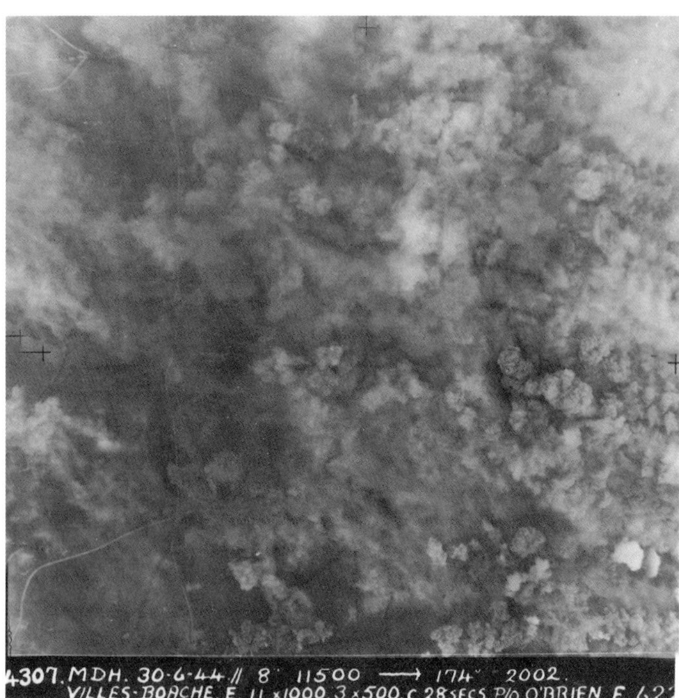

Villers Bocage was the target on 30th June 1944. The crew were briefed to bomb a vital road junction that was allowing German Panzer tank divisions an easy route towards the Allied troops. *Courtesy of Philip O'Brien.*

Target Bassens adjacent to the River Gironde. The objective was to disrupt the enemy forces stronghold. Please note that 'O'Brien' is now a Flying Officer after receiving his promotion in July 1944. *Courtesy of Philip O'Brien.*

Two bombing photographs of the attack on the German night fighter airfield at St. Trond in Belgium. These before and after the attack photographs, show the destructive power of Bomber Command. This was the penultimate mission for the O'Brien crew therefore, their accuracy over the target is clear to see with their bombs falling directly on the concrete runway. *Courtesy of Philip O'Brien.*

With their tour of operations complete, the crew pose for one last photograph together as a full crew in August 1944. In the background is Lancaster PD228, GI-A the Lancaster usually flown by the 'A' flight commander. The keen eye with notice the gas detection patch just in front of the mid upper turret. L-R: F/O O'Brien, P/O Drake, P/O Brunton, Sgt Hall, air gunners Sgt's Lock & Dyke, F/Sgt Jurgens. *Courtesy of Philip O'Brien.*

Studio photograph of Flying Officer William George O'Brien RNZAF. He was awarded the Distinguished Flying Cross for his bravery against the enemy during his thirty missions. A well respected pilot on the squadron. The operational record books show that he took a significant number of new pilots on their 2nd 'dickey' missions on arrival. This was a measure of his esteem on the squadron and the faith bestowed upon him by the Commanding Officer. After the war, he married an American girl and after a brief spell living in New Zealand, he returned to live in America until his premature death in 1959 aged just 45 years of age. *Courtesy of Philip O'Brien.*

F/Lt W. E. Woods RAAF and Crew

Two photographs depicting the crew of F/Lt W. E. Woods RAAF. The crew completed a 'tour' of 32 operations from July- December 1944, usually flying Lancaster GI-W, HK616. F/Lt Woods returned to Australia after the war and became a Doctor eventually retiring in his 80th year.

L-R: Sgt T. Gantley (R/G), F/Lt W. E. Woods RAAF (Pilot), Sgt A. Johnson (W/op), Sgt J. Cooney (F/E), F/Sgt J. Taylor (B/A) missing, F/Sgt J. Greet (Nav), Sgt P. K. Henderson (MUG). *Courtesy of W. E. Woods.*

This particular Lancaster (HK616, GI-W) was modified to take the mid under gun position. This comprised of a single .5 calibre machine gun protruding just aft of the bomb bay. The mid under gunner's position was very uncomfortable with the gunner having to lie on the floor of the Lancaster peering in the night sky below for many hours. *Courtesy of W. E. Woods.*

GI-W-'Bill The Conk' seen here with four members of the ground crew. On the far right is Corporal Keith Atherton. *Courtesy of W. E. Woods.*

F/Lt W. E. Woods RAAF (far right) & crew walk away from their Lancaster GI-W HK616. Sgt Henderson (MUG) applied the name of 'Bill The Conk' to the Lancaster. The crew equated their pilot's aptitude to that of William The Conqueror, F/Lt Woods Christian name was William and the aircraft identification letter was 'W' for Willie. *Courtesy of W. E. Woods.*

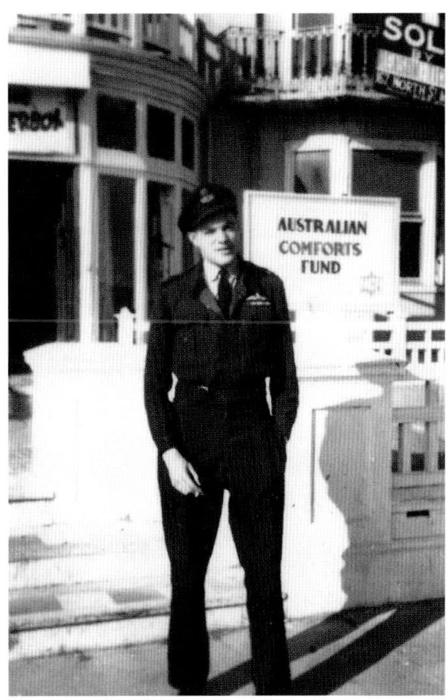

F/Lt Woods in Brighton 1945 shortly before his return to Australia in 1945. *Courtesy of W. E. Woods.*

Flight Commanders Autumn 1944

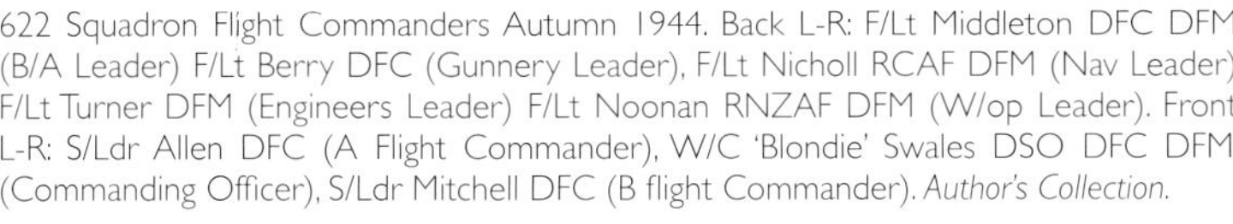

622 Squadron Flight Commanders Autumn 1944. Back L-R: F/Lt Middleton DFC DFM (B/A Leader) F/Lt Berry DFC (Gunnery Leader), F/Lt Nicholl RCAF DFM (Nav Leader) F/Lt Turner DFM (Engineers Leader) F/Lt Noonan RNZAF DFM (W/op Leader). Front L-R: S/Ldr Allen DFC (A Flight Commander), W/C 'Blondie' Swales DSO DFC DFM. (Commanding Officer), S/Ldr Mitchell DFC (B flight Commander). *Author's Collection.*

Pilots from the squadron share a lighter moment in the briefing room. The keen eye will spot the large map of Europe on the briefing room wall. Once the mission briefing was over the pilots would prepare their flight plan in readiness for the mission. Back L-R: F/O J. Lunn DFC, F/O H. Peck DFC RAAF, unknown. Front L-R: S/Ldr Hank Tilson DSO, DFC, RCAF, F/O A. Nielsen DFM RAAF, F/O W. G. O'Brien DFC, RNZAF. Courtesy of Ms B. Beaumont.

Miscellaneous

S/Ldr George E. Mitchell DFC and crew pose for their end of 'tour' photograph in the autumn of 1944. 'Mitch' Mitchell was the 'B' Flight Commander and well respected amongst aircrew. L-R: P/O G. Summers (F/E), F/O D.W. Ansell (Nav), F/Sgt R. Featherstone (W/op), S/Ldr G.E. Mitchell (Pilot), Sgt L. Fellows (MUG), Sgt W. H. Fagg (R/G), F/Sgt A. R. Hardy (B/A). Author's Collection.

The nose art of PD336. The outline of the "Baby in a nappy" which was the "Trademark" embedded into a bar of 'Fairy' washing Soap. *Courtesy of 'Swifty'622.*

Sgt 'Swifty' Swallow RCAF stands under the bomb bay of Lancaster GI-E, PD 336. *Courtesy of 'Swifty'622.*

F/Lt J. F McCahill RAAF and crew, who completed a tour of operations from December 1944-April 1945.

The crew took part in the infamous bombing of Dresden and Chemnitz in February 1945. Jim McCahill originally started his pilot training in 1942 but he was involved in a flying accident whilst in Canada. He was a passenger in a Harvard when it became lost in a snowstorm and whilst descending to establish their position, the aircraft clipped a tree and had to make a crash landing. On impact, Jim McCahill was thrown forward smashing his head against the instrument panel knocking him unconscious. The accident delayed his pilot training by six months and delayed his arrival onto 622 Squadron by about one year (Dec 44). Rather philosophically, Jim McCahill reckons that the delay most probably saved his life.

L-R: F/Lt Jim McCahill RAAF, F/O J. Hill (Nav), F/O D. Hulme (B/A), W/O J. Jenkins (W/op), Front: F/Sgt A. Harris DFM (F/E), Sgt H. Gay (MUG), Sgt E. Smith (R/G). *Courtesy of James McCahill.*

F/Lt McCahill RAAF & crew pose for another photograph near the rear turret. *Courtesy of James McCahill.*

F/Lt Jim McCahill RAAF sits on a bomb trolley in front of Lancaster GI-L, PA218. *Courtesy of James McCahill.*

L-R: F/Lt Jim McCahill RAAF stands proudly beneath the bomb bay of Lancaster GI-K, PD819. F/Lt McCahill flew this Lancaster on most of his operations. *Courtesy of James McCahill.*

Daylight formation flying en route to the target. In the foreground is Lancaster GI-K, PD819 and in the background is GI-A, PD228. Both these aircraft display the two yellow bar markings on the tail rudders that signifies these Lancasters are G/H leaders. Lancasters equipped with G/H radar would lead 'vic' formations of three aircraft to the target. When they released their bombs the other aircraft in the formation would follow suit. *Courtesy of James McCahill.*

Flying Officer 'Max' Bourne RAAF and crew

The 'Bourne' crew arrived at Mildenhall on the last day of July 1944 and commenced operational flying in early August. During early October, Max Bourne collided with another Lancaster whilst taxiing causing considerable damage to both Lancasters. A board of enquiry established that the other Lancaster should not have been parked in that position on the airfield. Ultimately, Max Bourne was found culpable for the accident and he was posted to the Aircrew Refresher Course at Sheffield as a disciplinary measure for one month. The crew commenced flying again on 11th November '44 and finally finished their 'tour' just before Christmas.

Flying Officer A.M. (Max) Bourne RAAF & crew, completed a 'tour' of operations during 1944 mainly flying the Lancaster depicted in the photograph, PD336, GI-E. L-R: F/Sgt R. Humphrys RAAF (R/G), W/O P. Taylor RAAF (w/op), F/O A. M. Bourne (pilot), F/Sgt A. Bourne (Nav), Sgt W. Vincent (F/E), F/O T. Brown (B/A), F/Sgt R. Heffron RAAF (MUG). *Courtesy of Max Bourne.*

Three of the 'Bourne' crew. L-R: Sgt W. Vincent, F/O 'Max' Bourne RAAF, F/Sgt R. Heffron RAAF. *Courtesy of Max Bourne.*

Miscellaneous

622 Squadron crews entertain their American Allies during a visit to Mildenhall in the spring of 1944. The Lancaster used for familiarization was GI-F, ME693. The discerning eye will notice the silver colored 'window' chute just in front of the bomb bay doors. This particular Lancaster was lost on a mission to Karlsruhe on 24/25th April 1944 killing the entire crew of F/Lt Jameson. All are buried in Rheinberg Cemetery in Germany. *Courtesy of IWM.*

Pilot Officer John Hall

The crew of Pilot Officer John Hall who were all tragically killed on 7/8th June 1944 whilst on a mission to Massy Palaiseau. The crew was shot down and are buried in the graveyard at Tacoignieres Seine-et-Oise. The bodies of the crew were extracted from the wreckage by the local population and buried by the Germans. Sadly, the 20 strong local Resistance group were betrayed to the Germans and arrested on 5th August 1944. All of its members were transported to Buchenwald prison camp, where all but one of them perished. Monsieur Roland Lejeune M.M., a former Officer in the French Air Force, was one of the Resistance men who died in Buchenwald, leaving behind a wife and an infant daughter.

Pilot Officer Hall & crew seen here standing in front of a Short Stirling bomber whilst at Operational Training Unit. L-R: Sgt Till (W/op), Sgt Cunningham (MUG), P/O Hall (Pilot), P/O Norris RCAF (B/A), P/O Smith RCAF (Nav), P/O Mayhead RAAF (R/G), Sgt Jarvis (F/E). *Courtesy of 'Swifty'622.*

Flying Officer W. E. Richards RAAF and Crew

The crew pictured in front of Lancaster GI-R, HK614 in early December 1944 on completion of their 'tour' of operations. Bill Richards & crew were hit by anti aircraft fire on 17 occasions during their 'tour' of operations. L-R: Sgt H. A. Papps (MUG), F/O W. A. Mildren (B/A), F/O W. E. Richards RAAF (Pilot), F/Sgt R. D. Kidd (Nav), Sgt R. Martin (F/E), F/Sgt J. Doyle (W/op). Absent is Sgt K. Nicholson the rear gunner who was injured in the leg by a flak burst on a mission to Cologne on 27/11/44. *Courtesy of Bill Richards.*

A fresh faced eighteen year old Bill Richards just after he joined the Royal Australian Air Force as a pilot. F/O Richards & crew joined 622 Squadron in August 1944 and completed day and night attacks against the enemy. His missions included support for the Allied Armies advance into Europe after 'D' Day and industrial targets deep in the Ruhr. Memorable moments included being coned by searchlights on a mission to Frankfurt followed by a night fighter attack, which called for skillful evasive action. *Courtesy of Bill Richards.*

F/O W. E. Richards RAAF & crew. L-R: Sgt R. Martin, Sgt H. A. Papps, F/O W. A. Mildren, F/O W. E. Richards RAAF, F/Sgt R. D. Kidd, F/Sgt J. Doyle. Sgt K. Nicholson is absent due to be hospitalized by a flak burst. The frost on the ground in early December 1944 shows considerable ground crew activity. *Courtesy of Bill Richards.*

Two bomb photographs taken by F/O Richards during his time at Mildenhall. The mission to Homberg on 21/11/44 was part of a series of three missions during November to destroy the oil refinery. This daylight mission was memorable for the intensely accurate flak barrage. Luckily out of the seventeen 622 Lancasters deployed only P/O Bonner returned early due to engine failure. The mission to Bonn on 18th October 1944 was notable because it was the first operation by the squadron under its new independent role. The Lancaster's of 3 Group had been fitted with the navigation device called G/H, which allowed accurate bombing of a target even through cloud without the assistance of the Pathfinders. 3 Group would specialize in G/H bombing from this point onwards.

The mission to Homberg on 21/11/44 was part of a series of three missions during November to destroy the oil refinery. This daylight mission is memorable for the intensely accurate flak barrage. Luckily of the seventeen 622 Lancasters deployed only P/O Bonner returned early due to engine failure. *Courtesy of Bill Richards*

The mission to Bonn on 18th October 1944 was notable because it was the first operation by the squadron under its new independent role. The Lancasters of 3 Group had been fitted with the navigation device called G-H, which allowed accurate bombing of a target even through cloud without the assistance of the Pathfinders. 3 Group would specialize in G-H bombing from this point onwards. *Courtesy of Bill Richards.*

Flying Officer J.H. Jones and Crew

Bombing photograph taken by F/O J. H. Jones & crew flying PD229, GI-K on 27th September 1944 during a daylight mission to bomb the German defensive positions at Calais. The 'Master Bomber' brought the bomber force below the cloud cover to increase accuracy. This resulted in the crews' releasing their bombs at a height of 5, 000 feet. The Lancaster in a precarious position below (bombing at 4, 500 feet) is S/Ldr W. E. M Dean & crew in HK617, GI-Y. S/Ldr Dean & crew would all lose their lives on 3rd January 1945 whilst attacking Dortmund. *Courtesy of K. J. Ridley.*

Squadron Leader J. A. Brignell DFC & Crew pose for a crew photograph in early 1945. The crew joined 622 Squadron in September 1944 and by the end of their 'tour' of operations in January 1945, 'Brignell' had aspired to 'A' Flight Commander. At the cessation of hostilities S/Ldr Brignell remained in the Royal Air Force attaining the rank of Group Captain by the end of a distinguished career. His impressive list of honors included; OBE, DFC, MA. The crew members are standing in front of Lancaster HK700,GI-Y are L-R: F/Sgt J. Harris (W/op), F/Sgt M. Davis (MUG), F/O K. Lewis RAAF (Nav), S/Ldr J. A. Brignell DFC (Pilot), F/O M.J. McDonnell RAAF (B/A), F/Sgt M. Coles (R/G), F/Sgt J. Irving (F/E). Courtesy of Mike Coles.

Pilot Officer Jeff Nicholls & Crew - Tour of Operation Aug-Nov 1944.
The majority of the missions undertaken by the crew were to bomb the German industrial cities deep in the Ruhr Valley, visiting, Essen, Kiel, Dortmund, Rostock, Bremen & Cologne to name but a few. The two trips to Duisburg on 14th/15th October 1944 became known to the crews as the 'Double Duisburg'. Once landed from the first mission, the Lancasters were checked over and refueled for the same target again. Back row L-R: P/O I.W. Pender RAAF (Nav), Sgt R. Smith (R/G) far right P/O J. Nicholls (pilot), Front row, far right, Sgt G. Cross (W/op). Other crew members depicted are: F/S S. Avrith RCAF (B/A), Sgt F. Bond (MUG), Sgt H. Lawson (F/E). *Courtesy of Mr A. Pender*

Flying Officer Gordon Thurn RAAF & Crew pose for a photograph in early 1945. Whilst at Lancaster Conversion Unit, F/O Thurn fell off his bicycle and broke his arm delaying the crew's progression for six weeks. On eventually reaching the squadron, the crew was on the 'Battle Order' on 9th March 1945 for their first mission to attack the industrial heart of Datteln. Just after take-off, at around fifty feet in height the starboard outer engine burst into flames and the Lancaster dipped its starboard wing. At this height any loss of control by the pilot would signal almost certain death, fortunately F/O Thurn gained control and the bombs were jettisoned and the mission aborted. In total the crew completed fourteen eventful missions including Sgt Carrol in the mid upper gun position being wounded in the arm and hand by a flak burst on a mission to Emscher on 14th March. On 4th April the crew experienced another engine failure over the target area of Merseburg; they carried on and bombed the target. L-R: Sgt A.A. Allen (F/E), F/O G.P. Thurn RAAF (Pilot), F/Sgt W.F. Jones RAAF (W/op), Sgt R.J. Pepper (R/G), F/Sgt A.E. Bale (B/A), F/Sgt J. Kelly (Nav), Sgt J.Carrol (MUG). Courtesy of Mr R.J. Pepper.

Miscellaneous

It was customary at Mildenhall for the air and ground crews to wave off the Lancasters as they departed on their mission. This great photograph depicts F/O Peck RAAF & crew in Lancaster GI-J, LL885 as it starts down the runway on a daylight mission to Essen on 25th October 1944. By the end of hostilities, this Lancaster would complete 113 operations and become one of only 34 lancasters to achieve this feat. *Courtesy of Bill Richards.*

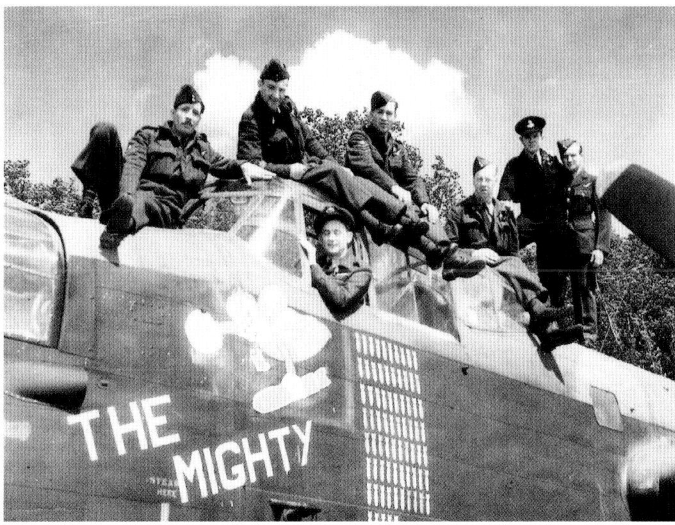

Photograph taken in May 1945 of an unknown 622 Squadron crew. Worthy of note are the seventy five bomb symbols. *Author's Collection.*

S/Ldr F.C. MacDonald & crew at Mildenhall 1945. McDonald had completed a tour of operations with 620 Squadron at Chedburgh flying Short Stirling bombers prior to commencing his second tour. It was whilst with 620 Squadron that he was awarded a DFC. The W/op in the crew was F/O W. Sinclair an Australian. He and the McDonald crew originally arrived on 622 Squadron in December 1944 with P/O Gillespie RAAF as their pilot. They completed their first mission to Osterfeld on 11th Dec. The Ruhrstahl steel works at Witten was their second target where they lost an engine and were forced to land in Allied held territory at Antwerp, being flown back to England in a Dakota transport plane. Ironically the Lancaster they were flying on this mission was, GI-W, HK616 the Lancaster depicted in the photograph. The 'Lanc' was repaired and eventually returned to the squadron. The navigator in this photo (2nd from left) was a replacement. F/O W. Sinclair RAAF is pictured 3rd from the left with S/Ldr McDonald 2nd from the right. *Courtesy of W. Sinclair.*

Pete Ryan RAAF & Crew pictured in the rear door entrance of Lancaster GI-N in April 1945. The crew arrived on the squadron in time to take part in operations MANNA & Exodus. L-R In doorway: B. Harris (R/G), P. Ryan RAAF (Pilot), J. Middleton RAAF (B/A). Front: F. Hughes (F/E), T. Graham (MUG), A. Mallen (Nav), S. Figg (W/op). *Courtesy of B. Harris.*

Informal group portrait of members of 622 Squadron returning from Essen on 26th October 1944. Identified are: back row, left to right: unidentified flight engineer (sixth from left, immediately beside the bus); unidentified mid-upper gunner (eighth from left, face partially obscured); unidentified bomb aimer (tenth from left); Flt Sgt 417704 Eoin Francis RAAF, pilot (standing back right) later KIA 6 January 1945. Middle row: Flight Sergeant T. Stott RAF (second from left smoking); Flt Sgt Kelly, wireless operator (third from left, smoking and wearing a 'Mae West'. *Courtesy of Australian War Memorial Negative Number P03363.001*

Flight Sergeant Hugh Dickson Patterson who was a navigator in the crew of Flying Officer C.B. Moore RAAF. The crew's first mission was to bomb Gelsenkirchen on 23rd February 1945. On 5th March, the crew had the honor of taking GI-J, LL885 to bomb the Wintershall oil refinery at Salzbergen, this was GI-J's 100th mission. *Courtesy of Steve Patterson.*

Flight Sergeant Ernest Herbert George Potkins, the wireless operator in the crew of Flying Officer C.B. Moore RAAF. On 2nd March 1945 whilst attacking Cologne, their Lancaster was hit by flak over the target. The result was a fire in the starboard outer engine which had to be extinguished and feathered with a subsequent loss of the use of hydraulics. The damage to the aircraft resulted in a forced emergency landing at RAF Woodbridge in Suffolk. *Courtesy of J. Potkins.*

Squadron pilots pose for a photograph in April/May 1945. Center back is S/Ldr Ogilvy & second from right is F/O J.W. Armfield. The keen eye will notice the lack of guns and the covers applied to the engine cowlings. *Courtesy of S. Ogilvy.*

Victory in Europe is celebrated in style at Mildenhall with Wing Commander Buckingham DFC center stage. Directly in front of him are S/Ldr Ogilvy and the Squadron's Flight Commanders. S/Ldr McDonald can be identified two to the right of Ogilvy partly obscured by an airman's arm. From the map of Europe in the background, it is safe to assume that this was the briefing room. *Courtesy of S. Ogilvy.*

622 Squadron Flight Commanders 1945. Wing Commander Buckingham DFC in doorway with F/Lt P. Turner DFM (Engineers leader) directly to his right in the photo. Far right is S/Ldr Ogilvy. Lancaster NG224 didn't serve with 622 Sqdn. This photograph would have been taken when several 3 Group squadrons converged on Mildenhall at the end of the war in 1945. *Courtesy of S. Ogilvy.*

Another shot of 622 Flight Commanders in 1945. Second from left F/Lt Turner, 4th from right W/C Buckingham (sqdn C/O), 3rd from right S/Ldr Ogilvy. *Courtesy of S. Ogilvy.*

Sgt Roger Last, the navigator in the crew of F/O J.W. Armfield, recalls his first experience of flying on operations on 9th March 1945, target Datteln: "First trip with W/C Buckingham, all were keen to impress him. The H2S and G/H systems were playing up and therefore we had to bomb through cloud on ETA. Once bombs were dropped, the 'Winco' pulled the Lancaster up above the cloud to avoid collisions. This was the only occasion when I ventured into the cockpit to have a look out. It was bright sunshine, the sun dazzled me with its brightness after being cocooned away behind my navigator's curtain, and I returned to my plotting table. The W/C asked me for a course to steer home and I couldn't see my charts until my eyes adjusted to the light, this made the W/C very agitated and he could see other Lancasters in the distance that he believed were from our Squadron. However, when we drew close the Lancasters were from 90 Squadron, also 3 Group and close to our base at Mildenhall. I eventually gave the W/C a course to steer and I believe that he had already formatted on other lancasters to get us home and I don't believe that he was overjoyed with my navigation skills."

Great end of 'tour' photograph with S/Ldr Ogilvy at the controls of an unidentified 622 'Lanc'. L-R: Air Gunner? F/O Tanner, Sgt Barton (F/E-also trained as pilot), S/Ldr Ogilvy (pilot), F/Lt Speed, Air gunner?, F/O Gloyne. Due to an abundance of trained aircrew during the latter stages of the war, trained pilots such as Sgt Barton volunteered to re-muster to flight engineers to see active service before the war ended. *Courtesy of S. Ogilvy.*

Squadron Leader C. E. Ogilvy and Crew

The 'Ogilvy' crew pose on the wing of a Lancaster which makes a great photograph for the album. *Courtesy of S. Ogilvy.*

622 Squadron Commonwealth pilots 1945. S/Ldr Ogilvy depicted sitting in the center of the group. *Courtesy of S. Ogilvy.*

S/Ldr C. A. Ogilvy sits proudly on the steps with his crew during 1945. Ogilvy saw action as a fighter pilot with 610 Squadron. A German fighter shot him down on 19/11/44 and he parachuted from his burning Spitfire. This made him eligible to be included in the records as a pilot who served during the Battle of Britain. After a period at Training Command, he converted to Bomber Command and joined 622 Squadron in February 1945. The exact positions of the air gunners in the photo are unsure however, the author can identify the majority. Doorway Back L-R: F/O J. W. Tanner (B/A), Air Gunner-either Sgt L. D. Watkins or Sgt R. A. H. Reed. Front doorway L-R: Sgt E. H. Barton (F/E), Air Gunner? Front L-R:F/Lt G. J. Speed (Nav), S/Ldr C. A. Ogilvy, F/O P. M. Gloyne (w/op). *Courtesy of S. Ogilvy.*

Flight Lieutenant W. K. Thomas DFC and Crew

Flight Sergeant Ken Thomas and crew arrived at Mildenhall in September 1944. Almost immediately the navigator, Sgt J.O'Toole was sent back for additional training. His replacement was F/O S. L. Berry who had lost his crew in early 1944 whilst he was in hospital with Tuberculosis. During a mission on 8th November 1944 to bomb the oil plant at Homberg, his navigator's position took the full force of a flak hit seriously wounding him. Despite his injuries, he continued to navigate the badly damaged Lancaster back to England. He was awarded an immediate Distinguished Flying Cross.

Flying Lieutenant W. K. Thomas DFC & crew. L-R: Sgt W. D. Ralph (F/E), F/Sgt J. N. Gamble (B/A), F/Lt W. K. Thomas (Pilot), Sgt J. T. Kingston (MUG), F/Sgt A. C. Davies (R/G). Chapter 28 provides more details of operations completed by F/Lt Thomas & Crew. *Courtesy of Ken Thomas DFC.*

Flying Officer S. L. Berry DFC. *Courtesy of Ken Thomas DFC.*

Photo taken on arrival at Mildenhall with original navigator. Standing L-R: Sgt Charlsworth, Sgt Kingston, Sgt Ralph, F/Sgt Thomas. Sitting L-R: Sgt J. O'Toole, Sgt Gamble, Sgt Davies. *Courtesy of Ken Thomas DFC.*

Photo taken at Mildenhall. Standing L-R: Sgt Ralph, F/Sgt Thomas, Sgt Gamble. Sitting L-R: Sgt Davies, Sgt Kingston. *Courtesy of Ken Thomas DFC.*

United States Army

Army Air Forces

Be it known that

1320471, LAC. A. R. Taylor, (RAF),

has satisfactorily completed the course of instruction

prescribed for

Pilot Training

at the Advanced Flying School.

In testimony whereof and by virtue of vested authority

I do confer upon him this

DIPLOMA

Given at Moody Field, Ga., this 16th day

of February in the year of our Lord one thousand

nine hundred and Forty-three.

Colonel, Air Corps,
Commandant.

Attest

Major, Air Corps,
Adjutant.

U. S. GOVERNMENT PRINTING OFFICE : 1942

A studio photograph of Flight Lieutenant A.R. Taylor who was an accomplished pilot on the squadron during the middle of 1944. His tour of operations included targets deep in the Ruhr Valley and his aircraft was damaged by German defenses on several occasions. His attributes were rewarded with the award of the Distinguished Flying Cross and this medal ribbon can be seen in the photograph directly below his pilot's wings. *Courtesy of Mrs. M.C. Taylor.*

Flight Lieutenant A.R. Taylor completed his pilot training at 'Moody Field' in Georgia USA. Moody Army Airfield was the home of the 29th Flying Training Wing and named after Major George Putnam Moody, who was an Air Force pioneer. F/Lt Taylor was awarded a diploma on completion of his pilot training on 16th February 1943. The discerning eye will notice that he still held the rank of Leading Aircraftsman (LAC). *Courtesy of Mrs. M.C. Taylor.*

F/Lt Taylor and crew pose for a photograph at RAF Mildenhall dispersal. The crew positions are: From top: Sgt L.S Shaw (MUG), 2nd from top, F/Lt A.R. Taylor DFC, Standing in front of 'Taylor' is F/Sgt R.E. Johnson (W/op), Sitting on ground, Sgt J.H Gregson (F/E), Standing left in photo (no cap wearing a life jacket) P/O F. Woodhall (Nav). On the left right in the photo is F/Sgt G. Hutchinson (R/G). Not in the photo is the crew's bomb aimer, F/Sgt F. Harriott who refused to have his photograph taken considering it bad luck to do so. P/O Woodhall was a replacement for the crew's original navigator and he had already completed several missions with another crew. Once his 'tour' of operations was complete he was replaced by P/O E.J. Insull RNZAF. Courtesy of Mrs. M.C. Taylor.

'Bud' Cawsey RCAF and Crew

Flight Sergeant E. H. 'Bud' Cawsey RCAF and crew arrived on 5th February 1944 after successfully completing their training course at No.3 L.F.S. F/Sgt Cawsey completed the obligatory '2nd dickey' trip on 19th February and arrived back to a barrage of questions from his crew. On 23rd February the bomb aimer in the crew, Flying Officer Hayter, was assigned the temporary duty of 'Viceroy Court'. This may account for the crews delayed first mission, which was not completed until 18th March when they attacked Frankfurt. The crew completed seventeen missions in total whilst with 622 and 'Bud Cawsey' was promoted to Pilot Officer during April 1944. The crew completed two missions in LM491 GI-E, the Lancaster depicted in the photographs before they were selected and posted to No.7 Squadron Pathfinder Force. The crew completed another 38 missions with the PFF with 'Bud Cawsey' being promoted to Flight Lieutenant and being awarded the DFC. This particular Lancaster was delivered to 622 on 13th March '44 and initially assigned the code letter 'C' before adjustment to 'E' Easy. The Lancaster was lost on a mission to Massey-Palaiseau on 7/8 June '44 with the loss of P/O Hall and all his crew.

Pilot Officer E. H. Cawsey RCAF & crew. L-R: Sgt F. N. Poynter (F/E), Sgt G. Pratt (R/G), F/Sgt E. Panton (Nav), P/O E. H. Cawsey (Pilot), F/O G. Hayter (B/A), Sgt W. E. Mayes (MUG). Not included in the photograph is Sgt I. Waters (W/Op). The crew photos were taken on 7th June the day before the crew's departure to the P.F.F. *Courtesy of C. Pratt.*

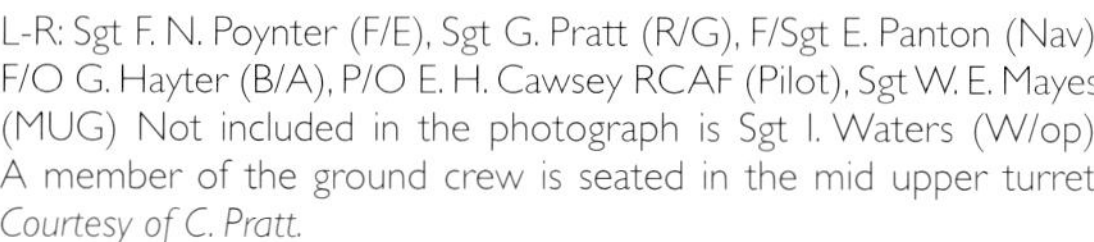

L-R: Sgt F. N. Poynter (F/E), Sgt G. Pratt (R/G), F/Sgt E. Panton (Nav), F/O G. Hayter (B/A), P/O E. H. Cawsey RCAF (Pilot), Sgt W. E. Mayes (MUG) Not included in the photograph is Sgt I. Waters (W/op). A member of the ground crew is seated in the mid upper turret. *Courtesy of C. Pratt.*

Pilot Officer E. H. Cawsey RCAF sits proudly in the cockpit of LM491, GI-E. *Courtesy of C. Pratt.*

Flying Officer G. Hayter, bomb aimer in the 'Cawsey' crew. Assigned as 'Viceroy Court'. *Courtesy of C. Pratt.*

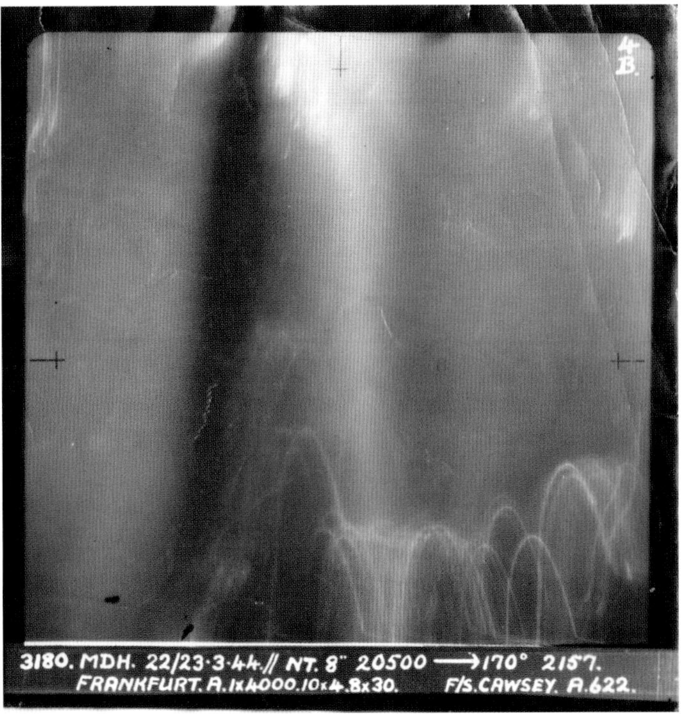

Frankfurt was the target for the crew on 22/23 March 1944 when a force of 816 bombers were sent to disrupt the manufacturing factories. 33 aircraft were lost to the German defenses. *Courtesy of C. Pratt.*

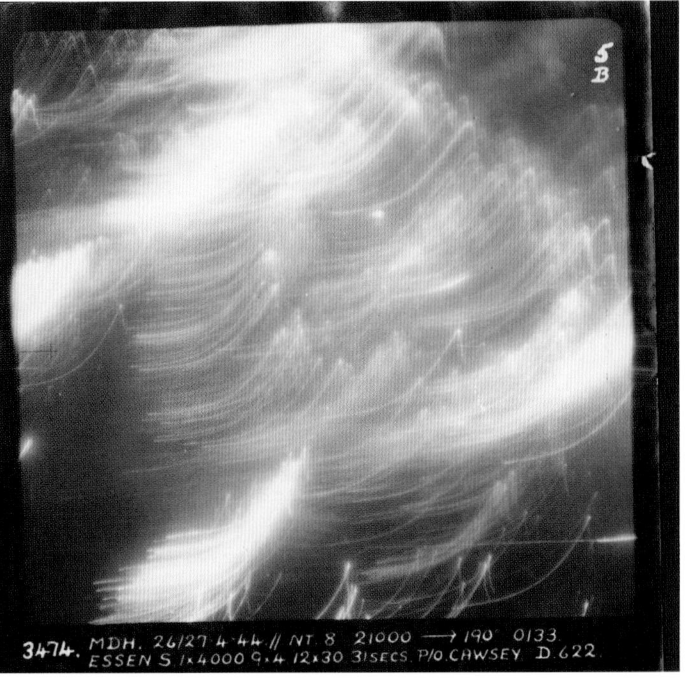

The crew joined forces with 492 aircraft to attack the industrial center of Essen on 26/27 April and seven aircraft were lost. The keen eye will note that on the mission to Frankfurt 'Cawsey' was a Flight Sergeant and on the Essen mission he had been promoted to Pilot Officer. *Courtesy of C. Pratt.*

Wing Commander I.C.K 'Blondie' Swales, DSO DFC DFM. Commanding Officer 622 Squadron from February 1944-October 1944.

An Emotional Farewell!

During October 1944, Wing Commander Swales was promoted to Group Captain and posted to 3 Group Bomber Command Headquarters. His fair hair earned him the nickname 'Blondie' and his decorations reflected his outstanding operational record. In total he completed three 'tours' of operations, the last being with 622 Squadron. All who knew him held him in high esteem and the support and encouragement he gave to new crews arriving on the squadron was second to none. When morale was at a low point he would place himself on some of the most dangerous missions, an inspirational act that inspired confidence in others when their confidence waned.

As a mark of respect, the aircrew NCOs organized a leaving party for their inspirational leader, an occasion that lasted long in the memory.

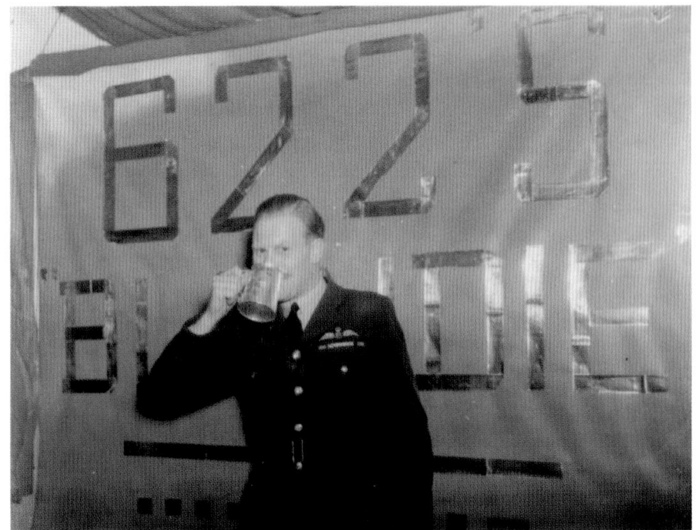

On his arrival at the party, 'Blondie' was presented with a tankard and told to return to his quarters and dress more informally. However, there was just enough time to christen the tankard in front of a banner made from 'window' tin foil used to deceive German radar frequencies. The banner reads '622's Blondie'. *Courtesy of Ted Peck F/E 622 Sqdn.*

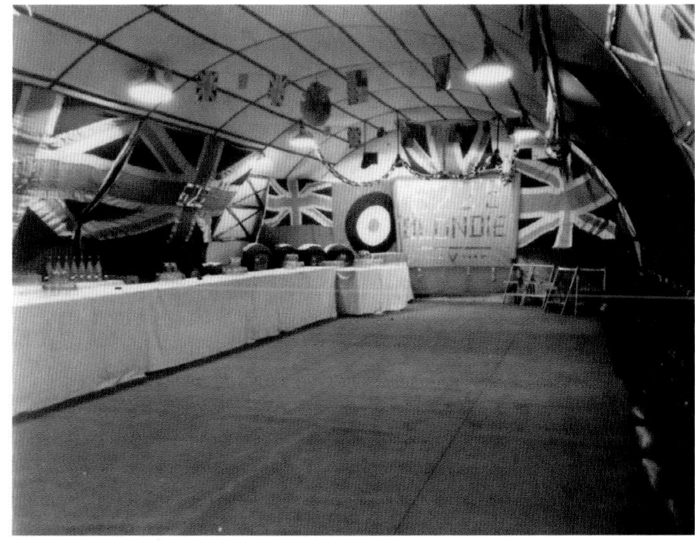

The briefing room suitably decorated for the occasion. The commemorative banner can be seen at the far end. *Courtesy of Ted Peck F/E 622 Sqdn.*

Joining the party in their dress uniforms before the party gets into full swing are L-R: Wing Commander 'Lofty' Watkins, Commanding Officer of XV Squadron and to his left Group Captain Young, The RAF Mildenhall Station Commander. *Courtesy of Ted Peck F/E 622 Sqdn.*

n more casual attire, 'Blondie' serves drinks to the lower ranks. F/Sgt Drummond waits with anticipation whilst F/Sgt Peck looks at the camera. *Courtesy of Ted Peck F/E 622 Sqdn.*

The section 'Leaders' were assigned the task of serving the drinks for the NCO's. F/Lt Pete Turner can be seen in the foreground. *Courtesy of Ted Peck F/E 622 Sqdn.*

The Officers who ran the squadron pose for a photograph with their departing Commanding Officer. L-R: F/Lt Pete Turner DFM (Engineer Leader), F/Lt Mac Middleton DFM (Bombing Leader), S/Ldr 'Mitch' Mitchell DFC ('B' Flight Commander), W/C Swales, F/Lt Gill DFC, S/Ldr Richard Allen DFC, ('A' Flight Commander). Seated left to right are F/Lt Noonan DFC (W/op Leader), F/Lt Nicholls DFM (Nav Leader). Far right is W/O Crisp the station Warrant Officer. *Courtesy of Ted Peck F/E 622 Sqdn.*

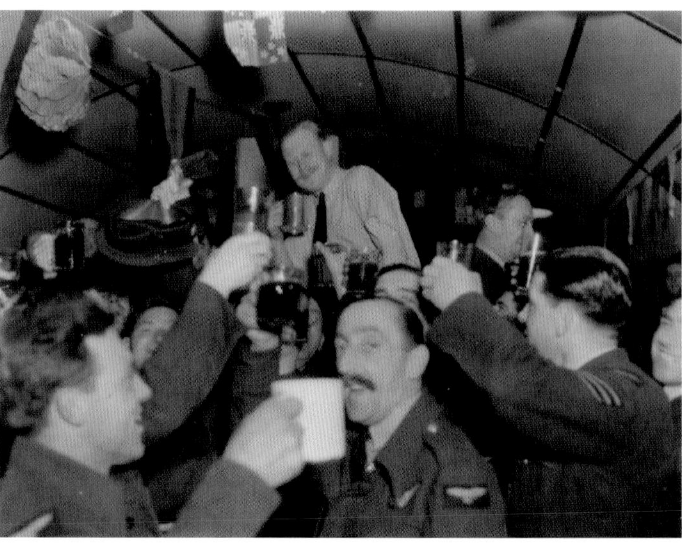

The aircrew lift up 'Blondie' and chant 'for he's a jolly good fellow….' *Courtesy of Ted Peck F/E 622 Sqdn.*

W/C Swales mingles with the crews who all exchange best wishes for the future. *Courtesy of Ted Peck F/E 622 Sqdn.*

Being covered with beer was part of the celebration and taken in good spirit. The high ranking Officer standing to 'Blondie's right is Air Commodore 'Square' McKee RNZAF. *Courtesy of Ted Peck F/E 622 Sqdn.*

One for the album at the end of the night. *Courtesy of Ted Peck F/E 622 Sqdn.*

Miscellaneous

Photograph depicting aircrew that flew with either XV or 622 Squadrons. Flying Officer Toy & Pilot Officer Hunt RAAF were assigned to 622 Squadron and both crews were shot down within weeks of their arrival. Flying Officer Toy and his crew were shot down by a German night fighter whilst attacking Berlin on 31st August 1943 with the loss of three crew and four taken POW (see Chapter 5). Pilot Officer Hunt and crew all perished on the 27th September 1943 when their Short Stirling bomber was lost without trace whilst on a mission to attack Hanover. The 'Toy' crew depicted in the photo are: F/O Toy KIA (pilot), F/O Carter KIA (nav), Sgt Mackrell KIA (R/G), Sgt Benham POW (W/op), P/O Ritson POW (A/B), Sgt Smith & Poyser are missing. 'Hunt' crew depicted are: P/O Hunt RAAF KIA (pilot), P/O Chandler RCAF KIA (nav), Sgt Meadow KIA (W/op), P/O Hall RCAF KIA (B/A), Sgt Tebbutt KIA (R/G), Sgt Weaving & McLeod are missing. *Courtesy of Anthony Marshall.*

1651 Conversion Unit RAF Waterbeach, Course 44. Nov-Dec 1943. Aircrew who joined 622 Squadron: Back Row L-R: X X X X X White 622, P/O J. A Harris RAAF pilot 622, X X X X Humphries 622, Short 622, P/O R. Curling RAAF pilot 622, Smith 622 X X Featherstonhaugh 622. 2nd from back L-R: Cornish, Lemky, Trend, Stubbs X X Zacharides, Emmott, Gill, Murphy X Lewis, Bourne, Baker, Duncliffe, Ward 2nd from front L-R: Thompson, McMillan, X X Baker X Musson 622, Murgatroyd pilot 622, Blott, Nabarro, Harrison X X X X X Front Row L-R: X, Nash, Kirkpatrick, X McGhee, Wilde, Butting. The crew on the back row left are flying with skipper P/O J. A Harris RAAF. Therefore it is possible to surmise that the first five are members of the 'Harris' crew. The back row right shows the crew of Ray Curling RAAF. Also present are the crew of S/Ldr Murgatroyd. *Courtesy of J. Trend.*

Flying Officer Geoff Conacher RAAF & crew 1945. Back row L-R: F/Sgt F. Hogan (F/E), F/O G. Conacher RAAF (Pilot), F/Sgt E. Thompson (Nav). Front row: F/Sgt D. Shorter (mid under gunner), F/Sgt J. Green (B/A), F/Sgt J. 'Duke' Marlborough (R/G), F/Sgt J. Llewellyn (mid upper gunner), F/Sgt A. Edwards (W/op). The crew had an eventful first operation on 1st February 1945 after they set off to attack Mönchengladbach. One the aircraft's engines caught fire and the flames spread throughout the aircraft forcing the crew to bail out. Unfortunately their mid under gunner, Sgt Baxter, was killed in the descent. Eyewitnesses saw his parachute on fire as he descended to his death. The full account of the fateful mission can be found within chapter 27. *Courtesy of Geoff Conacher.*

F/Lt Jordan RCAF (center) & crew stand in front of Lancaster LL885, GI-J in December 1944. The only other Officer in the crew at the time the photograph was taken was F/O R. S. Riley (B/A). Therefore, it is safe to assume that he is standing far right in the photo. Other members of the crew were: F/Sgt W.H. McDonald (Nav), Sgt M. C. Robertson (W/op), Sgt L. Eyre (F/E), Sgt T. H. Gregory (MUG), Sgt P. C. Laymore (R/G). *Author's Collection.*

Flying Officer A.H. Thomson RAAF and Crew

Alex Thomson and crew joined the squadron in August 1944 and were assigned to 'A' flight. The crew's first mission on 26th August was to attack the heavily defended industrial city of Kiel. The Lancaster utilized for the mission was LL885, GI-J that would eventually complete 113 missions, one of only 35 Lancasters to achieve this feat.

The mission would end in tragic circumstances with the death of the rear gunner, Sergeant P.S. Withers, due to a fighter attack. The German fighter, a Fw190 attacked from the starboard bow. The opening fire went between the flight engineer and the navigator, turning over the head, of the wireless operator, under the mid upper gunner and out through the rear turret. The mid upper gunner opened fire at the enemy fighter which broke off and did not return.

After the attack, no word came from the rear turret and the bomb aimer and flight engineer went aft to find the rear turret riddled with bullet holes. The bomb aimer had to chop away the rear turret doors because of the damaged lock. Sgt Percy Withers lay slumped over his guns, he was just 18 years old and a popular character on the squadron. At the time of his death, there was a famous American film actress called Jane Withers and Sgt Withers was nicknamed 'Jane'.

In tribute, Wing Commander I.C.K. Swales DSO DFC DFM wrote:

"You will always treasure the thoughts and indeed the knowledge that your son engaged in action against the common enemy, gave his life in the cause of freedom which you may be sure will not be in vain."

The replacement gunner was Sergeant D. Smith, and between August to December 1944 the crew attacked various targets. These targets included a mixture of support for the Allied Armies advance across Europe and industrial targets deep in the Ruhr.

Flying Officer A.H.Thomson RAAF & crew. L-R: Sgt D. Smith (MUG), Sgt K.J. Boulton (F/E), F/Sgt W.S. Ward RAAF (Nav), F/O A.H. Thomson RAAF (Pilot), Sgt E. Wolloff (R/G), F/Sgt R.J. Dilley RAAF (B/A), W/O R.V. Aland RAAF (W/op). The crew's first mission ended in tragedy with the death of their original rear gunner, Sgt P.S. Withers to a night fighter attack. *Courtesy of K.J. Boulton*

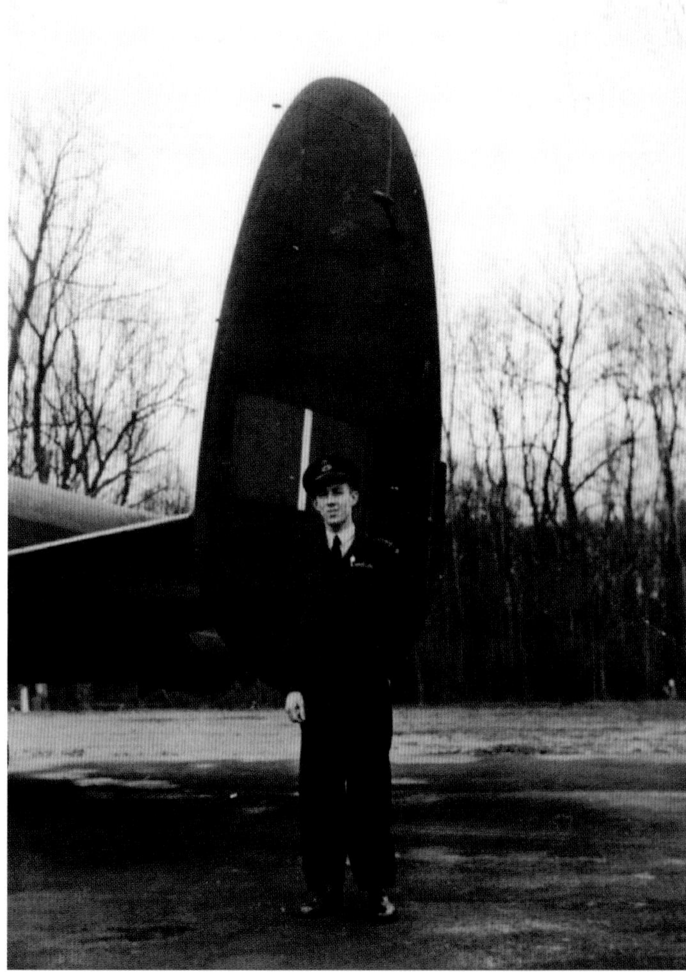

With the mandatory 30 missions complete, Flying Officer Alex Thomson poses for a photograph in late 1944. *Courtesy of K.J. Boulton*

A very relieved crew enjoy their first cigarette after returning from a night mission deep into the Ruhr Valley. From left: Sgt Eddy Wolloff, Ron Dilley. In the background are Sid Ward (face obscured), Denis Smith, Kenneth Boulton & Alex Thomson. Missing is Richard Aland. *Courtesy of K.J. Boulton*

Miscellaneous

Flying Officer Graham (Mac) Baxter & crew pose for an end of tour photograph in front of the rear turret of Lancaster GI-G, PD225. The crew completed 31 missions from August-December 1944 at RAF Mildenhall before commencing a second tour of duty with 99 Squadron flying Consolidated B-24 Liberator bombers in Northern India. L-R: Sgt G.C. Brooker (W/op), F/Sgt L.G. Parsons (Nav), Sgt J.W. Scoular (MUG), F/Sgt R.A. Hopkinson RAAF (B/A), Sgt E.J. Rossiter (F/E), Sgt F. Ramsey (R/G). Seated: F/O M.G. Baxter (Pilot). *Courtesy of Mrs. E. Parsons.*

End of 'tour' photograph of Flying Officer C. Barnett RAAF & crew taken on 1st February 1945. The crew completed all their missions during the latter half of 1944 and flew the depicted Lancaster, GI-B HK651 for most of those missions. The crew are back row L to R: F/O I. Hurditch (B/A), Sgt F. Murrell (F/E), F/O C. Barnett RAAF, F/Sgt J.P. Sullivan RAAF (W/op). Front row L to R: Sgt L. Nichols (R/G), Sgt G. Stapelhurst (MUG). *Courtesy of* Australian *War Memorial negative No.045306*

Studio portrait of Flight Lieutenant John Sydney Edward Allwright RAAF. In January 1945 the squadron attacked Ludwigshafen in daylight. The anti-aircraft fire was very accurate and F/Lt Allwright's Lancaster was badly damaged over the target area. He used his flying skills to successfully bomb the target and bring home his aircraft to base. He was awarded the Distinguished Flying Cross for his bravery. *Courtesy of* Australian *War Memorial negative No. P04357.001*

Studio portrait of Flight Lieutenant Richard Gerald Godfrey RAAF. On the night of 8th June 1944, he attacked the railway target at Massey-Palaiseau in Lancaster GI-C, ND765. The German night fighters shot down 17 bombers, one of which was being flown by F/Lt Godfrey & crew. All the crew rest in Viroflay Communal Cemetery. *Courtesy of Australian War Memorial negative No. P07868.001*

Pilot Officer A.E.W. Waigh and Crew

Anthony Waigh and crew joined the squadron in October 1944 commencing operations on 4th November when they attacked the industrial city of Soligen. The crew had an eventful 'tour' of operations including having to feather the starboard inner engine on a mission to Dortmund on 16th November. The loss of the engine resulted in a complete loss of hydraulics. The odds were stacked against them and on arrival over England, they were diverted to the emergency landing field at RAF Woodbridge. The crew managed to get the undercarriage down and locked into position. Woodbridge was equipped with the fog dispersal system called 'Fido', which was basically long lengths of fuel filled pipe laid the length of the runway. In foggy conditions, the fuel was ignited, burning away the low lying fog which enabled aircraft to land in relative safety.

On Christmas Eve, the crew attacked Hangelar Airfield near Bonn and they were hit by flak over the target. Due to the weather conditions and the damage to their aircraft, they were diverted to RAF Little Snoring in Norfolk. Christmas day lunch was at the pleasure of the Commanding Officer.

On 9th February 1945, the crew were assigned to a fighter affiliation exercise with an inexperienced pilot, F/Sgt Fielding. All went well with the exercise until they landed. The pilot's approach was all wrong and he placed the Lancaster down too hard causing a lower back injury to the rear gunner. This accident ended the flying for Sgt W.A. Mitchell, F/Sgt K.E. Boone DFM took over the rear turret until their 'tour' of operations was over in April 1945.

Flying Officer A.E.W. Waigh & crew pose for the customary end of 'tour' photograph in April 1945. The crew are R-L: F/O Waigh, F/O T.S. Biggs (Nav), W/O T.E. Allan RAAF (W/op), Sgt P.J. Simmonds (MUG), W/O T. N. Hayday (spare gunner). Sat on wing L-R: F/O T.M.R. Lister (B/A), F/Sgt K. E. Boone DFM (replacement gunner). The crew's usual rear gunner, F/Sgt W. A. Mitchell, was recovering from a broken bone in his back and therefore missing from the photographs. *Courtesy of P.J. Simmonds.*

The 'Waigh' crew stand in front of GI-B, HK615, with members of the ground crew who conscientiously maintained the Lancaster in flying condition. This photograph was one of three taken to signify the end of operations for the crew. This particular Lancaster arrived on 622 Squadron in September 1944 and at the time this photograph was taken had completed over 60 operations. Signs of wear and tear can be seen from the missing paint on the leading edges of the wings. HK651 was handed over to No.44 Squadron at the disbandment of 622 Squadron in August 1945. Like so many other 'Lancs' it was 'struck of charge' in October of the same year. The crew are standing L-R: Sgt P. J. Simmonds, ground crew, P/O E. Evans, F/O T.S. Biggs, F/O T.M.R. Lister, F/Sgt Boone D.F.M., F/O A.E.W. Waigh, W/O T.E. Allan RAAF, 2 ground crew members. Front L-R: Three ground crew members and W/O T. N. Hayday, spare gunner. At this stage of the war crews carried a spare gunner to work the mid under gun position. HK615 was fitted with this facility. *Courtesy of P.J. Simmonds*

The rear door of Lancaster GI-B, HK651, provides a good photographic setting for the 'Waigh' crew. The discerning eye will notice the battle damage repair directly above the top right corner of the door. The crew are, standing in doorway L-R: W/O T. E. Allan RAAF, F/O T.S. Biggs, Sgt P.J. Simmonds. Front L-R: W/O T.N. Hayday (spare gunner), F/O T.M.R. Lister, F/Sgt K.E. Boone D.F.M., (replacement gunner for F/Sgt Mitchell), F/O A.E.W. Waigh, P/O E. Evans. *Courtesy of P.J. Simmonds.*

Flight Lieutenant John Wesley Stratton DFC and Crew

The 'Stratton' crew joined 622 Squadron in early June 44 and were assigned to 'A' flight. The crew took part in supporting the Allied invasion immediately after D-Day on 6th June. They completed missions to destroy the launching sites of the V1 flying bomb menace throughout the month. The crew comprised of F/Sgt M.L. Reidy NZ (Nav), F/O L. Chapman (W/op), P/O E.P. Thurston NZ (B/A), Sgt R.N. Pittaway (MUG), W/O H.G. Summerton RAAF (R/G) and P/O F. Williams (F/E).

The mission to Gelsenkirchen on 12/13th June 1944 was eventful. They took off in GI-D, PD225 and whilst over the target area they were coned by searchlights. This alerted the night fighters to their presence and they were attacked twice in quick succession. The second enemy fighter was identified as a Me110 night fighter. According to the combat report, the fighter attacked from the port quarter and opened fire at 600 yards. Sergeant Pittaway opened fire from the mid upper turret and the enemy fighter burst into flames. F/Lt Stratton, and F/O Thurston saw the enemy fighter crash. Sergeant Pittaway was awarded an immediate DFM for his actions.

On 27th June the crew attacked the Flying Bomb site at Biennais in France. The mission went like clockwork apart from a trigger-happy air gunner in another Lancaster who registered 13 hits on the 'Stratton' aircraft. Luckily, no essential components were hit and John Stratton was able to land at base without incident.

The month of July 1944 brought numerous missions, some against the heavily defended targets in the Ruhr Valley including two consecutive missions to Stuttgart on 24/25th July. Shortly before the Stuttgart raid on 20th July, the crew attacked the oil installation at Homberg. They experienced heavy flak over the target area and were attacked again by a night fighter. Cannon shells from the enemy fighter badly damaged the port wing fuel tanks, flaps and ailerons. According to official records, this was a successful night for the German fighters who shot down twenty bombers.

John Stratton was an accomplished pilot and he quickly attained the rank of Flight Lieutenant for his tenacity and bravery against the enemy. His devotion to duty was epitomized when he attacked the enemy fortified positions at Calais in daylight on 24th September 1944. The target area was completely covered by cloud and F/Lt Stratton came down below the cloud base to bomb accurately from 2,000ft. On the first bombing run, his Lancaster was struck by three 88mm shells, which damaged the starboard wing and fuel tanks making the control of the aircraft difficult. Unperturbed, he immediately turned the Lancaster around for another bombing run and successfully dropped his bombs on the target area.

For his action on the day F/Lt Stratton was recommended for the award of the Distinguished Flying Cross. His citation was printed in the London Gazette on 15th December 1944:

'Flight Lieutenant Stratton is a keen, capable and devoted captain of aircraft. He has participated in a large number of sorties and has invariably pressed home his attacks with great vigor, often in the face of intense anti-aircraft fire. On one occasion he piloted an aircraft detailed to attack a target in the Calais area. His first bombing run proved unsuccessful. Although his aircraft had been repeatedly hit by light anti-aircraft fire, Flight Lieutenant Stratton made a second and successful bombing run. He displayed great courage and determination throughout'.

Courtesy of the London Gazette

John Stratton was posted to No.6 British Flying Training School (BFTS) Ponca City Oklahoma to undertake his pilot training. He sailed from Gourock in Scotland across the Atlantic ocean to New York. After a short tour of the city he departed by train into Canada arriving in Canada in August 1942. His first port of call was No.31 Personnel Depot at Moncton in New Brunswick, where he spent around two weeks. Another train journey took him to No 6 BFTS. John Stratton was one of approximately 50 trainee pilots to arrive and commence pilot training under the collaboration.

The photographs that follow are all associated with the time John Wesley Stratton spent in Canada and America training to be a pilot. The Empire Air Training Scheme (EATS), renamed the British Commonwealth Air Training Plan, provided a partnership with England to train aircrew in great numbers. These young airmen were a long way from home and more often than not the people of Canada and America opened up their homes and welcomed in the young airmen.

En route to No.6 BFTS, John Stratton's first official stop was at No.31 Personnel Depot at Moncton New Brunswick. This photograph depicts a view of Moncton Bridge. *Courtesy of Mrs. P. Stratton.*

Another shot of Moncton Bridge this time from the Golf Links.

John Stratton poses on Moncton Bridge. *Courtesy of Mrs. P. Stratton.*

En route for Ponca City. A Canadian National train provided the transport. *Courtesy of Mrs. P. Stratton.*

Situated along the route to Ponca City was Montreal. The passengers were allowed six hours to explore the sights. Dominion Square was the first scene for the camera. *Courtesy of Mrs. P. Stratton.*

The bank of Montreal. *Courtesy of Mrs. P. Stratton.*

The entrance to No.6 British Flying Training School at Ponca City Oklahoma. Some of the recruits christened the camp Stalag 6. *Courtesy of Mrs. P. Stratton.*

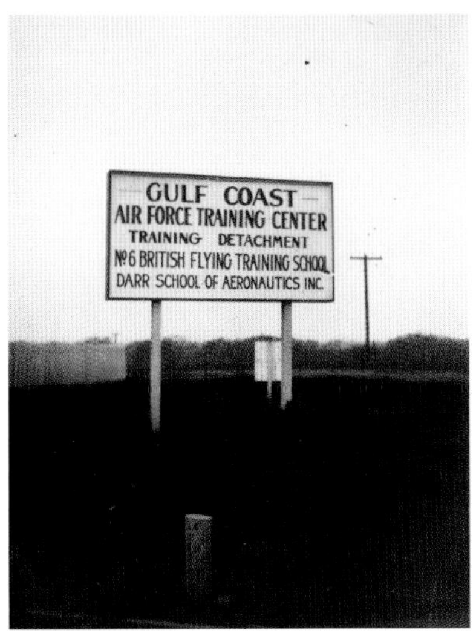

The welcome sign to the training center bearing reference to the 'Darr School of Aeronautics'. Harold S. Darr was the president of Braniff Airlines and he was under contract to provide the services at the training schools. *Courtesy of Mrs. P. Stratton.*

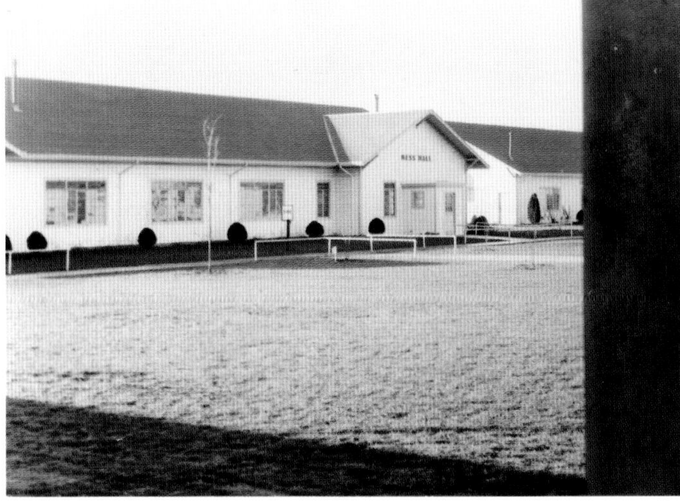

The 'Mess Hall' on the camp, to some the most important place of all. *Courtesy of Mrs. P. Stratton.*

It was not all work as this photograph portrays. A 24 hour pass allowed John Stratton and others attending the course to see Ponca City at night. *Courtesy of Mrs. P. Stratton.*

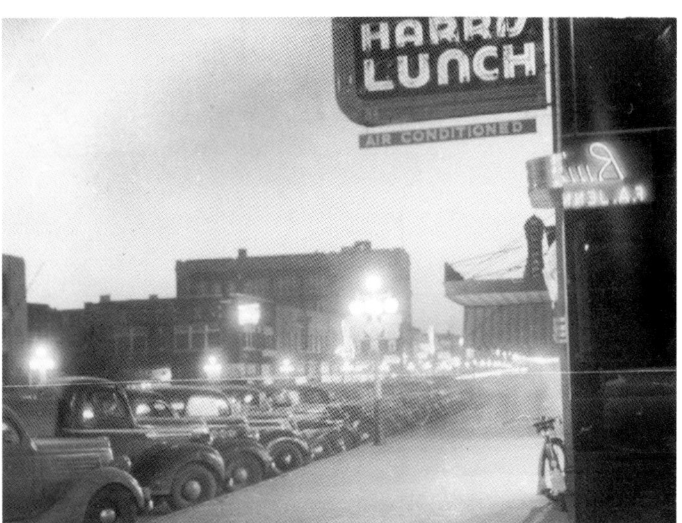

Grand Avenue at dusk. *Courtesy of Mrs. P. Stratton.*

The 'Pioneer Woman' a statue dedicated to all pioneering women of the United States, stands tall in Ponca City. *Courtesy of Mrs. P. Stratton.*

Down to business, the trainees on the flight line. John Stratton (standing) waits for his turn to fly. *Courtesy of Mrs. P. Stratton.*

Mr. A. Newman, the flight instructor. *Courtesy of Mrs. P. Stratton.*

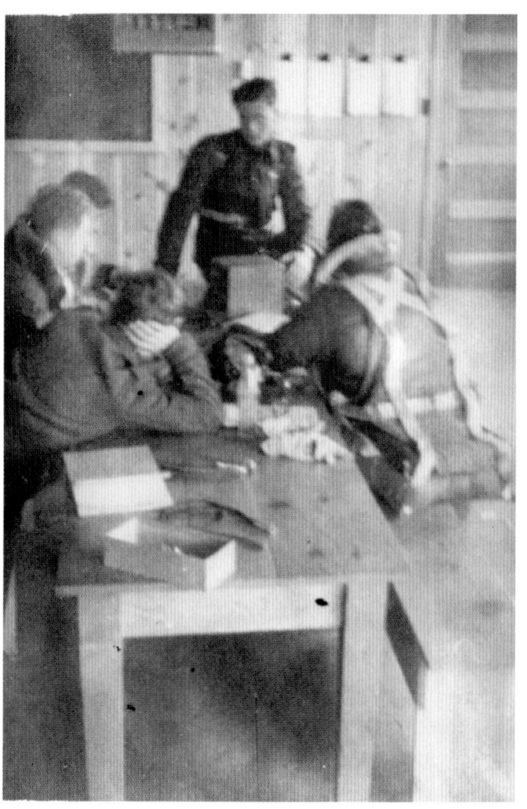

In the ready room sharing experiences. *Courtesy of Mrs. P. Stratton.*

Waiting for his turn, John Stratton and a friend wait patiently for their turn. *Courtesy of Mrs. P. Stratton.*

A great photograph of John Stratton and friend in full flying gear relaxing and sharing a joke. John is standing on the left in the photograph. *Courtesy of Mrs. P. Stratton.*

Finally the moment arrives and John Stratton takes the rear seat for his first flying training session. *Courtesy of Mrs. P. Stratton.*

It was not all the joy of flying, considerable planning was necessary before a flight. John Stratton is seen here planning his route for a cross country flight. *Courtesy of Mrs. P. Stratton.*

'Newman's Nondescripts'. The flight section poses for a photograph with their instructor. L-R: John Stratton, G. Williams, Mr. Newman, P. Legard, A. Thomas, P. McIntosh. *Courtesy of Mrs. P. Stratton.*

From 12th- 19th December 1942, John Stratton and friends were granted seven days leave in Ponca City. It was a welcome respite from the intensity of studying and flying. As a group, they visited Houston Texas. This picture captures a Chapel in Houston. *Courtesy of Mrs. P. Stratton.*

The front view of Houston Museum. *Courtesy of Mrs. P. Stratton.*

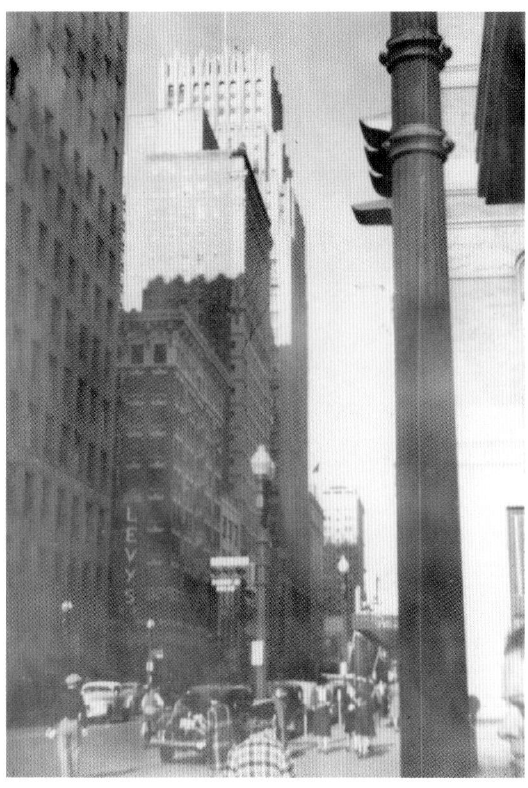

Main Street Houston 1942 style. *Courtesy of Mrs. P. Stratton.*

The tall buildings seemed amazing to the English visitors. An unidentified building in the middle of Houston. *Courtesy of Mrs. P. Stratton.*

St. Paul's Church Houston, Texas. *Courtesy of Mrs. P. Stratton.*

A great shot of the Court House in Houston. *Courtesy of Mrs. P. Stratton.*

Samuel Houston's statue in Hermann Park. A prominent figure in the history of Houston, Samuel Houston was a 19th Century American Statesman whose achievements inspired the city to be named in his honor. *Courtesy of Mrs. P. Stratton.*

The visitors first view of mighty Mississippi River. It was dusk when the group arrived and John Stratton just managed to take this photograph on a paddle steamer near Baton Rouge. *Courtesy of Mrs. P. Stratton.*

Canal Street, New Orleans offers a great photo opportunity. *Courtesy of Mrs. P. Stratton.*

Andrew Jackson's Square, New Orleans. General Andrew Jackson was the 7th President of the United States. *Courtesy of Mrs. P. Stratton.*

Another photograph of Canal Street showing the transportation of the period. *Courtesy of Mrs. P. Stratton.*

A close up shot of Andy Jackson's statue. *Courtesy of Mrs. P. Stratton.*

The Customs House, New Orleans. *Courtesy of Mrs. P. Stratton.*

The Cabildo, New Orleans

Canal Street showing two modes of transport in 1942. The vehicle appears to run across the path of the tram. *Courtesy of Mrs. P. Stratton.*

Customs House on the corner of Canal Street, New Orleans. *Courtesy of Mrs. P. Stratton.*

The French Quarter of New Orleans. *Courtesy of Mrs. P. Stratton.*

St. Louis Cathedral, New Orleans. *Courtesy of Mrs. P. Stratton.*

The next port of call for the visitors was Dallas Texas. This photograph shows the visitor's first view of Dallas, the railway station. *Courtesy of Mrs. P. Stratton.*

The First Mercantile Building photographed from the National Bank roof. *Courtesy of Mrs. P. Stratton.*

Elm Street Dallas, Texas. *Courtesy of Mrs. P. Stratton.*

Straight off the train and out of the exit. The first photograph had to be of the railway station frontage. *Courtesy of Mrs. P. Stratton.*

Pegasus the 'Flying Horse' statue on top of one of the tall buildings in Dallas. Originally the logo for the Magnolia Petroleum Company. *Courtesy of Mrs. P. Stratton.*

Trams were the most favored American mode of transport in Dallas. *Courtesy of Mrs. P. Stratton.*

Roof top view of the skyscrapers in Dallas. *Courtesy of Mrs. P. Stratton.*

The inevitable 'Coca Cola' factory. *Courtesy of Mrs. P. Stratton.*

It was not all the joy of flying. John Stratton is seen here revising for a navigation exam. *Courtesy of Mrs. P. Stratton.*

With the vacation over, the trainees returned to Ponca City for more training. A moment of fun is captured for posterity; John Stratton is featured on the far left in the photograph. *Courtesy of Mrs. P. Stratton.*

Flying was usually curtailed at the weekends allowing the trainees to visit Ponca City and enjoy the company of the local people. As usual the first stop was the railway station. *Courtesy of Mrs. P. Stratton.*

Grand Avenue Ponca City. *Courtesy of Mrs. P. Stratton.*

Ponca City's Civic Hall. *Courtesy of Mrs. P. Stratton.*

John Stratton enjoys the sights of Ponca City. *Courtesy of Mrs. P. Stratton.*

Pete Legard became a close friend of John Stratton whilst at No.6 B.F.T.S. He is seen here on the left with John Stratton. *Courtesy of Mrs. P. Stratton.*

A weekend in Oklahoma City was a welcome respite. *Courtesy of Mrs. P. Stratton.*

The first view of Oklahoma City after exiting the station, Main Street. *Courtesy of Mrs. P. Stratton.*

During his time in the city John Stratton and friends met up with a group of U.S. Sailors from the Naval Air Base at Norman. *Courtesy of Mrs. P. Stratton.*

State 'Capotol', the seat of Government and the meeting place of the Oklahoma Supreme Court. *Courtesy of Mrs. P. Stratton.*

Oklahoma's Court House. *Courtesy of Mrs. P. Stratton.*

View form the U.S.O. *Courtesy of Mrs. P. Stratton.*

South 4th Street Oklahoma. *Courtesy of Mrs. P. Stratton.*

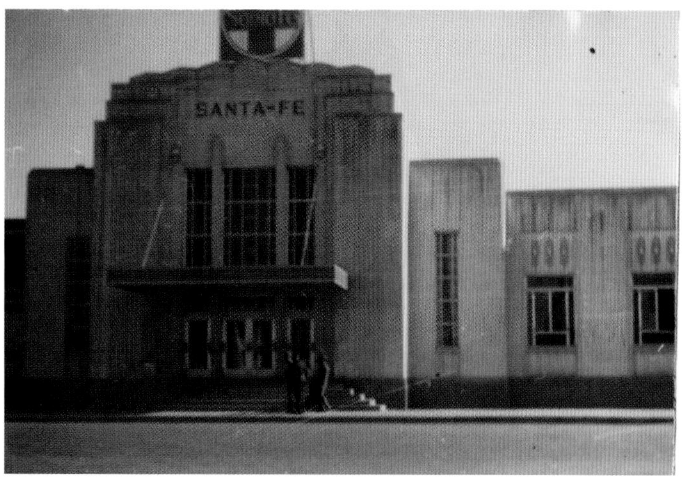

With the weekend over, the group head back via the station. *Courtesy of Mrs. P. Stratton.*

Back to the serious stuff. Activity on the flight line made everyone both excited and apprehensive to do well. This photograph shows the flight room activity in preparation for flying. *Courtesy of Mrs. P. Stratton.*

With flight logs in hand, No.10 course, 'H' flight pose for a group photograph. *Courtesy of Mrs. P. Stratton.*

One of the aircraft utilized at No.6 B.F.T.S. was the AT6A North American Harvard mark two. B402 is seen here with wheels down, locked, pressure up, reserve on. *Courtesy of Mrs. P. Stratton.*

Advance flying was undertaken in the AT6A Harvard trainer. John Stratton spent 122 hours on this type before graduating as a pilot and receiving his 'wings'. *Courtesy of Mrs. P. Stratton.*

Primary training was accomplished in the PT17 Stearman. This great photograph shows John Stratton going solo for the first time after 78 hours of guidance. *Courtesy of Mrs. P. Stratton.*

The cockpit of a AT6A Harvard. *Courtesy of Mrs. P. Stratton.*

The flight instructor for advanced flying was Mr. Minon, seen here second from the left with John Stratton immediately to his right in the photo. *Courtesy of Mrs. P. Stratton.*

Final discussions before flying. The trainees would compare flight routes and flying techniques. *Courtesy of Mrs. P. Stratton.*

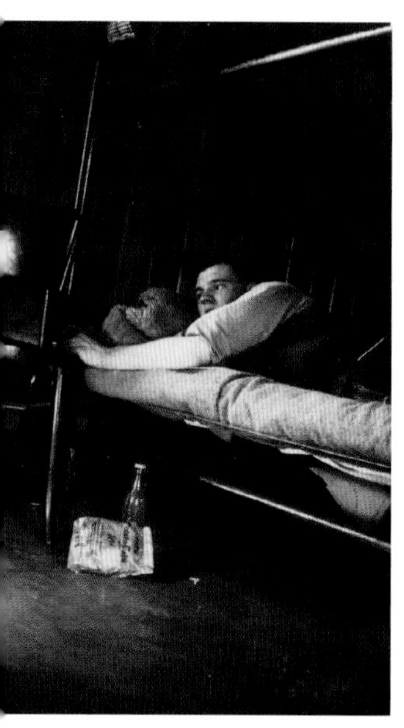

This is the life! The accommodation was basic to say the least. John Stratton relaxes during a rest period. *Courtesy of Mrs. P. Stratton.*

The first of a series of photographs of John Stratton's fellow trainees. C.B. Sandland from Wallasy, England. *Courtesy of Mrs. P. Stratton.*

M.J. Igglesdon form Hyde in Kent. *Courtesy of Mrs. P. Stratton.*

G. Sanders from Birmingham England. *Courtesy of Mrs. P. Stratton.*

Left: D. Morley from Brighton England. *Courtesy of Mrs. P. Stratton.*

Center: J. Leggett from Littleport, Cambridgeshire, England. *Courtesy of Mrs. P. Stratton.*

Right: J. Pearson from Blackpool, England. *Courtesy of Mrs. P. Stratton.*

J. Lett from Northampton, England. Jimmy Lett was eliminated from the course. *Courtesy of Mrs. P. Stratton.*

A. Keith-Thomas from Ealing, England. *Courtesy of Mrs. P. Stratton.*

L. A. Penfold from Hove in Sussex, England. *Courtesy of Mrs. P. Stratton.*

Mr. Fothergill, a trainee from Durham, England standing on the left. On the right is W.J. Henniken from South Carolina. *Courtesy of Mrs. P. Stratton.*

C. Allen from Ceylon. *Courtesy of Mrs. P. Stratton.*

P. Legard formed a close friendship with John Stratton at No.6 B.F.T.S. *Courtesy of Mrs. P. Stratton.*

P. Greaves. *Courtesy of Mrs. P. Stratton.*

A proud John Wesley Stratton poses for a photograph with his pilot wings sewn onto his tunic. His good friend Mrs. Peck sewed the 'wings' and sergeant stripes onto his tunic. John Stratton only wore his 'stripes' for 48 hours because he received his commission to Pilot Officer. *Courtesy of Mrs. P. Stratton.*

John Stratton pictured on the left in the photograph stands proudly on Ponca City station with his fellow newly qualified pilots. Saying good bye to the 'Peck' family was emotional for John Stratton and he never forgot the kindness afforded to him by the local people and especially the 'Peck' family. *Courtesy of Mrs. P. Stratton.*

The final moments before departure for some of the newly qualified pilots. What would they experience at an operational bomber squadron? Would they see each other again? *Courtesy of Mrs. P. Stratton.*

Boarding the train, final destination England and operations against a determined enemy. John Stratton's good friend Pete Legard stands in front of him in the doorway. *Courtesy of Mrs. P. Stratton.*

The route home took them to Boston Massachusetts railway station. *Courtesy of Mrs. P. Stratton.*

Photograph taken from the 'Chicago loop'. *Courtesy of Mrs. P. Stratton.*

The locomotive that would pull John Stratton's carriages. *Courtesy of Mrs. P. Stratton.*

An eight hour stop over in Chicago Illinois was a welcome break. A view from the lakeside. *Courtesy of Mrs. P. Stratton.*

Part of the skyline on Lake Michigan. *Courtesy of Mrs. P. Stratton.*

A bird's eye view of the outskirts of Chicago with the lake in the background. *Courtesy of Mrs. P. Stratton.*

During John Stratton's training at No.6 B.F.T.S. Ponca City, he was afforded a very warm welcome every time he visited 507 W. Atoe. He spent most of his free weekends staying with the 'Peck' family and enjoying their hospitality. John Stratton described the 'Peck' family home as virtually 'home from home'. Mr & Mrs Peck and one of their sons can be seen in this photograph outside their home in Ponca City. Pete Legard is on the far left and John Stratton far right. *Courtesy of Mrs. P. Stratton.*

A resplendent Flight Lieutenant John Wesley Stratton D.F.C., poses for a studio photograph in full dress uniform. *Courtesy of Mrs. P. Stratton.*

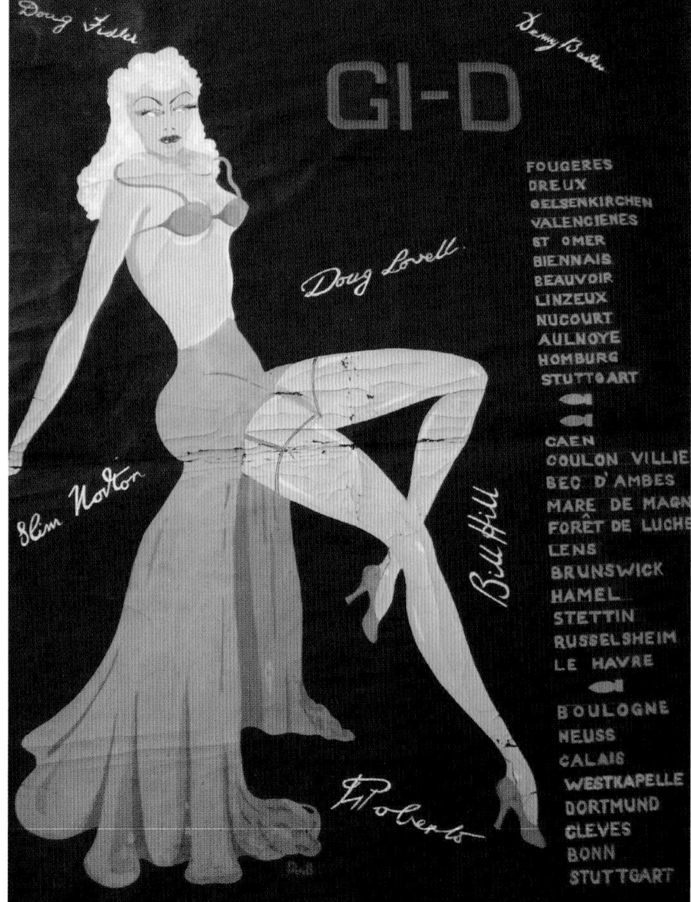

The bond between the air and ground crews who maintained the bombers was second to none. Each respected each other's abilities and the aircrew depended on the professionalism of the ground crew to keep the aircraft in prestige condition. During his time on 622 Squadron, F/Lt Stratton flew the majority of his missions in Lancaster GI-D, serial No.PD225. After each mission was completed, the ground crew would take great pride in painting a bomb symbol onto the area under the cockpit and keep a tally of the number of missions. To personalize a particular Lancaster, the aircrew would very often paint some form of nose art on the Lancaster and the 'Stratton' crew were no different. The Stratton crew chose to have a beautiful woman painted onto GI-D. At the end of the crew's operational 'tour', the same member of ground crew who painted the nose art, painted an exact copy of his work onto a canvas using oil paints. Each ground crew member signed the canvas and all the missions completed by the 'Stratton' crew were added. This is a photograph of that very canvas. *Courtesy of Mrs. P. Stratton.*

15

Target Acquired

Target: Homberg 8th November 1944-Synthetic Oil Plant. Time: 08:10-12:15.
Bomb load: 1x4000, 116x30, 1155x4Ib.
Fuel load: 1, 366 Gallons. All up weight: 58,000 Ibs.

Debriefing

Bombed on radar instruments at 10:35 from 17000ft. Pilot hit by flak, observations therefore difficult but appeared to be a good attack. Squadron summary: Flak very heavy over target, several crews bombed visually. Radar instruments and 'Gee' fixes coincided.

Intelligence Report: Just under half the aircraft received damage by flak, which was intense. Attack carried out by 136 aircraft, one lost to flak but 5 parachutes seen.

The following is the account of Sgt C.H. Hughes the flight engineer, who was awarded an immediate DFM for flying the Lancaster back to Mildenhall after the pilot had been hit by flak:

> "Predicted flak was very intense on the run up to the target and bursting very close on the starboard side of the aircraft. After dropping our bomb load a burst of flak on our starboard side severely damaged the starboard side main frame and ripped through the Perspex canopy tearing most of the starboard side and top of the canopy away. Without informing any member of the crew the skipper was taking violent evasive action, until a very severe burst of flak on the port side ahead seriously injured him resulting in slight concussion, necessitating me taking control of the aircraft."
>
> "After clearing the flak area, I put 'George' in and saw to the injured skipper who was bleeding profusely from a severed artery in his hand and Perspex splinters over his face. I applied a tourniquet on his elbow and dressed his wounds around his head and face, and then made him rest. I then set course for base after checking the controls and engines etc on the aircraft. On arrival at base we informed base of our plight and they made us aware of the emergency landing procedure. On coming into the circuit we found the undercarriage would not come down so under the stress and urgency we used the emergency air release. The skipper who had recovered slightly from his daze assisted and instructed on the landing, which was executed without a hitch. I switched off the engines and did my necessary duties in the aircraft. The skipper was rushed off for medical attention and then to hospital. The medical officer congratulated me on the first aid carried out.
>
> Air Commodore McKee recognized the part I played in bringing the aircraft back to base and I was recommended for the Distinguished Flying Medal, which was announced in the London Gazette on April 19th 1945 supplement to April 13th 1945."

Back L to R: F/O Titchener (A/B), Sgt K.J. Matthews (MUG), Sgt A. Gilroy (R/G), Sgt C.H. Hughes DFM (F/E). Front L to R: F/Sgt D.B. Shine (W/Op), F/Lt J.L Cox DFC (Pilot), F/O J. Taylor (Nav). *Courtesy of J. L Cox DFC.*

Lancaster HK614, GI-R fly's serenely over the Suffolk countryside in late 1944. *Courtesy of Mildenhall Register.*

GI-R HK614 being made ready by the ground crew for another operation. *Author's Collection*

The following is a brief account that appeared in the Mildenhall Register newsletter. It was written by Sgt Matthews the mid upper gunner and appears here courtesy of the association:

"We attacked Homberg on 8th November 1944 with skipper John Cox in Lancaster HK614 GI-R 'Roger' and it was our worst experience. John was badly hit in the face and hand over the target. He lost a lot of blood and kept passing out but our flight engineer Taffy Hughes, flew the aircraft but John sat in the seat for landing (with one overshoot) and we walked away except John who was obviously carried. John got the DFC and 'Taffy' the DFM. The rest of us were happy to come away with our lives."

Target: Rostock Bay 19th December 1944
Bomb load: 4x1800Ib Mk VI mines.
Debriefing: Mines dropped on instruments (H2S) at 19:23 from 10000ft. Squadron summary**:** Due to fog at base, two squadron aircraft diverted to RAF Lossiemouth and returned two days later. Mines dropped by twelve aircraft, all returned safely. F/Lt Cox's account of mission:

"On 19th December 1944 we were briefed to drop four 1800Ib mines in Rostock Bay, this time in Lancaster GI-N, PD332. The route from Mildenhall was to cross the North Sea to a position 56 N 7 E, and then eastwards along the 56th Parallel which entailed crossing part of Sweden; then south to Rostock Bay, dropping the mines ten miles off the German coast. The return route was across Denmark and then the North Sea. The flight took 7 hours and 25 minutes. There were two aircraft from 622 Squadron and a total of twelve aircraft from the Command. Navigation was by the newly installed H2S (an early form of search radar which gave a picture of the ground highlighting land mass and water), which showed us the coastlines. Mines were dropped from 1,000ft.

We saw nothing of the other aircraft; not surprising as it was at night and we were in and out of cloud all the time. There was no reaction from the Germans but quite a lot from the Swedes. Both times as we crossed the Swedish coast we could see numerous searchlights just north of our track. They were all pointing more or less vertically upwards and their anti-aircraft guns seemed to be firing in the same direction, they were certainly not trying to damage us. On the way back we received a radio message to say that Mildenhall was covered with fog and that we should divert to Lossiemouth. We landed there after a tiring flight and received a warm welcome and the usual bacon and eggs. We returned to Mildenhall two days later."

Target Westkapelle Sea Wall.
On 3rd October 1944, F/O Cox and crew were on the battle order to attack and breach the sea wall at Westkapelle. Their designated Lancaster was again HK614, GI-R loaded with 1X40000, 6X1000 & 1X500(DA) lb bombs. They lifted off from the runway at Mildenhall at 11:25 hrs along with twelve other Lancasters from the squadron being led by W/C Swales as a part of a force of 252 Lancasters and 7 Mosquitoes in total.

The rationale behind the raid was to assist the Allied forces in putting out of action the coastal gun batteries at Walcheren, which dominated the approaches to the port of Antwerp. The facilities could handle 40,000 tons per day of much needed supplies when ships could safely use the approaches. The intention was to flood the island, most of which was reclaimed polder below sea level. The flooding would submerge some of the gun batteries and hamper the German defense against eventual ground attack. The target for this first raid was the sea wall at Westkapelle, the most western point of Walcheren. The main bombing force was composed of 8 waves, each of 30 Lancasters, with marking provided by Oboe Mosquitoes and Pathfinder Lancasters; the whole operation being controlled by a Master Bomber. The attack went well and a great mass of high-explosive bombs, mainly 1,000- and 500-pounders but with some 4,000-pounders, forced a gap during the fifth wave of the attack. Later waves widened the breach until the sea was pouring in through a gap estimated to be 100 yards wide. Eight Lancasters of No.617 Squadron which were standing by were not needed and carried their valuable Tallboy bombs back to England. No aircraft were lost from this successful operation.

Leading elements of the British 11th Armored Division entered the Belgian port of Antwerp on the 4th September 1944 after a frantic 250 miles advance through Northern France and Belgium. The important Antwerp docks were captured virtually intact. This port was crucial in the plan to resupply the Allied Armies for the coming advance further into German held territory. The Germans were, however, still holding on to the south and north of the Scheldt estuary including Dutch island Walcharen.

The German defenses on the island were formidable and amongst the strongest on the European coast. They included 18 major gun batteries, mostly of 105mm and 150mm weapons, but also some 220mm guns. These were supplemented by 88mm, 50mm and 47mm anti-tank guns and numerous mine fields, skillfully laid along the coast, beaches and inland by the German engineers. The German garrison numbered 10,000 and was well equipped. Anti-aircraft defenses were highly organized with five radar stations and numerous heavy and medium flak weapons. Finally 85 small German warships including 15 'E' Boats and 10 'R' Boats were based at the main island port of Flushing.

The capture of the island was likely to prove a difficult and costly undertaking but the Allies needed to open up Antwerp quickly. Field Marshall Montgomery demanded that an all out effort be made to dislodge all German troops in the around the Schlelt estuary including Walcheren. Much of Walcheren was below sea level having been reclaimed from the sea by the industrious Dutch over many hundreds of years. The opening phase of the Allied plan was to breach the islands sea walls in various places and flood many of the German defenses along the coast and inland prior to landings by troops. The first site attacked was Westkapelle, where the sea wall was 200 feet wide.

FLOOD THE GUNPITS

For two hours the block-busters came crashing down, and Germans looking out saw the high tide—six feet above the level of most of Walcheren—surging in to flood their gunpits and dug-outs.

Pilots saw the waters reach the town of West Kapelle (pop. 2,227), most of whose peace-time workers had the job of keeping the dyke nder repair. An hour after the attack ceased the sea had run more than half-a-mile inland.

This great stroke, which threatens nearly the whole of the eight-miles-by-ten island, turns their own trick on the Germans, who have flooded other parts of Holland to hinder our troops.

The Walcheren floods menace Flushing (pop. 40,000), the island's port, and Middelburg (pop. 30,000), its capital—picturesque peace-time tourist resort.

Much of the land is three feet below sea level at low tide.

Some of the Germans' big guns are already likely to be under water.

So successful was the attack that Lancasters in the later waves saw there was no need to strike, and brought their bombs back. Not one plane was lost.

DYKE REFUGE

The blow follows General Eisenhower's warning to the Dutch on Monday to get out of the island.

Those who have not got out will be able to take refuge on the tops of dunes and other dykes round the island.

West Kapelle dyke is two miles long and has a road 39 feet wide along its top.

Years of post-war labour will be required for rebuilding the dyke and pumping sea water from the island. Parts of the dyke were first built 500 years ago.

Courtesy of John L Cox.

DAM-BUSTERS

Sea Pouring Through Huge Gap In Dyke

RAF LANCASTERS yesterday "sank" the enemy-held Dutch island of Walcheren by blasting a huge gap in its sea wall and flooding it. At the same time it was revealed that Germany's greatest inland waterway, the Dortmund-Ems, was bombed dry eleven days ago.

It is more than likely that all the big guns on Walcheren, which had prevented the Allies from using Antwerp as a supply port, are now completely submerged.

Timing their attack to coincide with high tide, between 1 and 3 p.m., 250 bombers struck in waves below 5,000-ft. cloud. Their target was a 200-ft. wide sea wall at Westkappelle, the westernmost town in the island.

Their 12,000-lb.—five-ton—bombs tore a gap 120 yards wide through the dyke, and the waters of the North Sea cascaded through to engulf the defences.

As nearly the whole of the island is below sea level the German garrisons must have fled for their lives.

Every bomber returned safely.

Photographs taken within an hour of the attack showed that the flood had extended over an area of 1,000 yards by 700 yards—with nothing to stop it.

First Town Inundated

The raid followed by only a few hours General Eisenhower's broadcast to the Dutch people on Walcheren to take warning of imminent bombing.

"On our first run we could see that five-tonners had already cratered the dyke," said one R A F officer.

"As we left we saw the water flow through and reach Westkappelle, which is 700 yards from the shore."

Another said. "I saw a stick of bombs fall along the dyke and a moment afterwards a growing lake of water forming on the landward side."

Walcheren is roughly square, about eight miles by ten, with the great port of Flushing at its southern corner. It has served as a stepping stone for Germans evacuating the south bank of the Scheldt.

Picked Canadian troops threw the Germans out of the Antwerp suburb of Merxem yesterday.

The enemy had turned Merxem into a fortress from which he dropped shells on to the Antwerp airport and the city generally.

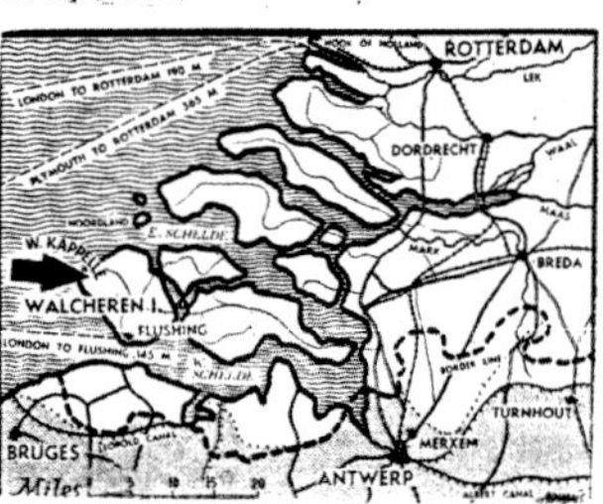

Courtesy of John L Cox.

RAF Bomber Command was given this task but it was appreciated how difficult this task was because the wall was constructed of sand. The plan was to bomb in two phases the first aircraft dropping 1000lb and 4000lb HE bombs with 617 Squadron in the second phase to drop 12,000lb Tallboy bombs if the first was unsuccessful.

This unusual and resourceful scheme was also controversial and would have long term effects for the local Dutch people. The breach in the sea walls and consequent inundation of salt water would ruin much of the island's excellent farm land which had taken hundreds of years to reclaim and also put the lives of the local inhabitants at considerable risk. It appears now that the Dutch government in exile was not given full details of the extent of the plan although they were informed and gave permission for a raid on Westkappelle. Leaflets were dropped on the island on the 2nd October 1944 warning the local people that an attack was imminent and they should take shelter.

The operation took place on the 3rd October and Bomber Command detailed 252 aircraft for this task led by seven Oboe equipped Mosquitoes and a number of Pathfinder Lancasters. The main attack was to be in eight waves of approximately 30 aircraft each. 617 Squadron made the final wave and were only to attack if the main force failed to make a breach in the sea wall.

The raid was a major success for Bomber Command as can be seen from the newspaper reports on the previous page.

F/Lt Cox and crew completed a full tour of operations with 622 Squadron from August 1944 to January 1945. F/Lt Cox was awarded a well deserved DFC for bringing his Lancaster home after he had sustained injuries on a mission to Homberg in November 1944.

On 14th November 1944 he was promoted to Flight Lieutenant and also made 'B' flight Commander an honor befitting his considerable leadership talents. After the war ended, John Cox continued to fly civil airliners for BOAC and British Airways, rising to senior captain on the Boeing 747 aircraft.

16

Joining the Caterpillar Club

Pilot: F/Sgt R. A. Deacon (KIA)
Nav: F/Sgt P. J. Irwin (POW)
B/A: F/Sgt W.S. J. Mckee (replaced by F/L Miller due to sickness - POW)
W/op: Sgt A.W. Woodcock (KIA)
MUG: Sgt J. Cunningham (KIA)
R/G: Sgt J.H. Kidman (KIA)
F/E: Sgt J. B. Strange (KIA)
2nd Pilot: Sgt N. Butler (KIA)

When the Second World War commenced in 1939 Patrick Irwin decided to join up and wanted to be in the RAF. Unfortunately, there were too many applicants and he was enlisted instead into the Territorial Army, Royal Artillery division in 1940, assigned to defending the coast positions. However, by 1941 the RAF was so short of trained aircrew that Patrick Joseph Irwin was transferred to the Royal Air Force to begin aircrew training. After attending the Aircrew Reception Center at Lords cricket ground in London, he was posted to No.11 Initial Training Wing at Scarborough on the Yorkshire coast where he undertook physical fitness training and experienced his first taste of 'square bashing'. He was billeted in the Prince of Wales Hotel on Scarborough sea front, one of a number of commandeered holiday resort hotels scattered the full length of the country.

He successfully completed the six week course in basic navigational techniques and Royal Air Force discipline. At the course conclusion he was posted to the pre discharge center at Heaton Park Manchester ready for his embarkation to Canada as a part of the Commonwealth Air Training Plan. With the preliminaries complete Patrick Irwin was sent to Gourock in Scotland where he set sail to Canada on HMT Montcalm. In early January 1942 he arrived in Canada and commenced his navigational training at Turner Field and various other locations within Canada.

The duration of the navigational course was about twelve weeks long and in the last week candidates would endure extensive exams both in the classroom and in the air. By far the most important of the exams to pass was navigation theory and then meteorology. Any aircrew candidate failing these exams was either re-mustered as an air bomber or some other aircrew discipline. In addition, candidates had to pass tests in Morse code and Aldis lamp recognition. The benchmark was set at twelve words per minute for the Morse test and eight words per minute for the Aldis lamp. In Canada the flying training really increased and pupils flew in pairs, one navigating and the other using a sextant at night and an

Aircrew under training at No.11 Initial Training Wing at Scarborough. Patrick Irwin can be seen top row immediate left displaying the 'white flash' in the cap denoting aircrew under training. *Courtesy of Patrick G. J. Irwin.*

Patrick Irwin (Front row 3rd from right) whilst in Canada undertaking his navigator training. *Courtesy of Patrick G. J. Irwin.*

astro compass by day taking bearings. All candidates were taught the basics of navigation using applied mathematics and how to navigate by the stars, a system that if used correctly could place an aircraft in theory in the right vicinity. However, in practice the plane bouncing about and the dimly illuminated sextant bubble made accurate reading very difficult and over heavily defended targets an accurate bearing to steer would have been practically impossible. At this stage of aircrew training the later radar inventions of 'Gee' and H2S were not in use so the fundamental techniques of navigation were essential learning.

The aircraft used on flying exercises were the Avro Anson two engined trainer which was very reliable and forgiving. Aircrew had to complete approximately 100 hours in both day and night flying conditions. At the end of the course, Patrick Irwin took his exams and passed easily and he was awarded his navigators brevet and sergeant's stripes, a very proud moment.

Sgt Irwin arrived back in England and was immediately posted to No.18 Operational Training Unit at Finningley near Doncaster in Yorkshire flying obsolete Wellington two engined bombers. It was here that newly qualified aircrew 'formed up' into a fully operational crew of six members suitable to operate a heavy bomber. At the time the RAF had an unusual method of 'crewing up'. An equal number of all aircrew designations were all thrown into a room and told to 'crew up', if they didn't they would be placed with aircrew that were left over to form a crew and nobody wanted to be a 'left over'. The system worked and Patrick Irwin 'crewed up' with Ronnie Deacon (P), Bill Mckee (B/A), Albert Woodcock (W/op.), Jim Kidman (R.G.) and J. Cunningham (M.U.G.) to form a heavy bomber crew.

It was whilst at the OTU that the nucleus of the crew was formed. They began training immediately after 'crewing up' in the most simplistic manner. All thrown together in a large room and selected on instinct and perception rather than knowledge of each other. Remarkably, this process worked in the majority of cases, aircrew had all qualified to the highest standard in their respective roles. Ground lectures were combined with hours of flying in obsolete twin engine bombers. Instruction was delivered by 'tour expired' aircrew who had been posted to Training Command. Flying exercises honed the skills of all and the compulsory night flights and 'bullseye' trips were essential to pass.

The next and final stage of Sgt Irwin's training took him and his crew to1651 Conversion Unit at Waterbeach in Cambridgeshire on 27th August 1943 where his crew acquired their flight engineer, J. Strange, and where they were introduced to the Short Stirling four engined bomber, the aircraft that they would eventually take to war. The squadron they were destined for was 622, which had only been formed on 10th August out of 'C' flight of XV Squadron at Mildenhall in Suffolk. The squadron was equipped with the Stirling bomber. The short four week course comprised a series of 'cross country' exercises where Sgt Irwin and crew fine tuned their flying skills by day and night.

At this point it is worth mentioning that the front line operational days of the Short Stirling were numbered due to increasing losses and the development of greatly improved bombers such as the Lancaster and Halifax. The Short Stirling was the first of the four engined 'heavy' bombers that was restricted by the officialdom at the Air Ministry. The original design allowed for a wingspan of 112 feet; however the wingspan would have to be reduced to 100 feet to allow the Stirling to fit into the standard RAF hangar. The Stirling suffered from developmental and operational problems from the start and the majority of the problems can be attributed to a lack of operational experience and political interference. Officials criticized the Stirling's maximum operating height of 17,000 feet with a payload of just 3, 500lbs of bombs, compared with 22,000lb of bombs carried by the Lancaster, in addition the bomb bay would not cater for the large 4,000lb 'cookie' blast bomb, which was the mainstay of the RAF's arsenal.

By late 1943 the German night fighter and Flak defenses had increased their efficiency by the introduction of revolutionary new radar systems. Stirling losses continued to mount and on the 27/28th August Bomber Command attacked the city of Nuremberg. The Squadron received no casualties on this raid; however, the total Stirling losses amounted to 10% of the force. Raids continued to varying targets and Berlin was again attacked on the night of 31st/1st September 1943 with the loss of two 622 Stirling crews piloted by F/O Toy and F/Sgt Young. A massive 47 crews paid the price for a disappointing raid and the Stirling loss rate was a massive 16%. The catalyst for the withdrawal of Stirlings from front line service was the Berlin raid on the night of 22/23rd November 1943 when 50 Stirlings were part of the bomber force and 10% of those were lost. The Stirling piloted by F/Lt Denham and crew was hit by flak near Hanover and the crew parachuted into captivity. AVM Harris knew that the Stirling losses could not be sustained and relegated the Stirling to secondary roles to be replaced in the main by the Avro Lancaster.

The 'Deacon' crew arrived at Mildenhall on 24th September 1943 and were immediately introduced to the Commanding Officer who welcomed them to Mildenhall and told them to settle in quickly. RAF Mildenhall was a permanent station that had been improved dramatically during the years prior to the war. It comprised of mainly two storied brick buildings, a large cinema, and many other facilities not found on a temporary station. When the 'Deacon' crew arrived they were assigned to a house together because they were all non-commissioned Officers, if one of the crew had been an Officer then he would have been assigned a bed in the Officers quarters.

It was customary for the pilot of a new crew to act as second pilot for their first mission, and F/Sgt Deacon was on the battle order to attack Hanover on 27th September with the crew of Pilot Officer Batson. (Rather unusually, Sgt Deacon would complete another '2nd dickey' trip on 31st October after he had already completed two missions with his crew).

With this first test of character behind him, Sgt Deacon and crew were on the battle order on 2nd October 1943 to lay anti-shipping mines around the Frisians Isles. It was usual practice for crews on their first few missions to undertake relatively easy missions of this nature to build up confidence and self-esteem. The mission was successfully carried out and the crew were duly assigned another mine laying trip to the Bay of Biscay on 8th October; again all went without incident. On 18th November the crew were on the battle order to attack the city of Mannheim deep in the German industrial Ruhr, a trip of over four hours evading the night fighters and heavily defended ground positions. The raid was not a success with the night fighters scattering the bombers across a wide area and shooting down 23 aircraft, nine of which were Stirlings and two from the squadron. Although they did not know it at the time it would be the last operational mission that the crew would undertake in the Short Stirling; due to their increasing loss rate they were withdrawn from front line service.

During December 622 converted to the Avro Lancaster, which was undoubtedly the most famous bomber of World War II. The aircraft's initial design specification was almost perfect and the Lancaster went on to surpass many milestones including having its bomb bay modified to enable the aircraft to carry the massive 22,000lb 'Grand Slam' bomb. Throughout December and the first two weeks of January crews were subjected to training exercises in the new aircraft all designed to prepare them to take the Lancaster to war. During this period Sgts Irwin, Deacon and McKee were promoted to the rank of Flight Sergeant. On 14th January 1944, the crew were assigned Lancaster R5915, GI-P to attack Brunswick for the first major raid of the war on this city. The German radar system picked up the bomber stream as soon as it crossed the English coast and the night fighters were ready and waiting. The result was that 38 Lancasters were lost during a disappointing night for Bomber Command.

Missing In Action

The 20th January again saw the crew promulgated on the battle order to attack Berlin, 'The Big City', in the same Lancaster. Berlin was undoubtedly the most heavily defended city in the world. ACM Harris, Commander in Chief of Bomber Command thought that the destruction of Berlin would severely damage the morale of the German public and bring the war to an end quickly.

The period in history known as 'The Battle of Berlin' commenced on 18th November 1943 and would end on the night of 31st March 1944 without the success wished for by Arthur Harris. Throughout this period, Bomber Command would mount thirty two raids on Berlin and cities in the region and the high attrition rate can be attributed to the success of the night fighter force, the severe winter period of 43/44 and the distance to Berlin, which exposed bombers to the enemies' defenses for longer periods. Aircrew were extremely superstitious and the night did not begin well with their usual bomb aimer, F/Sgt McKee again confined in hospital in Ely with a serious chest infection, having already missed the previous raid to Brunswick. His replacement was again F/Lt Miller, the squadron's bomb aimer leader. In addition, the crew were also assigned a 2nd 'dickey' pilot, Sgt N. Butler. The journey to the target was uneventful until the crew reached the area of Hamburg and its many flak guns that showered the sky with deadly exploding shrapnel. Shrapnel from a flak shell could disintegrate a bomber instantly if it hit the fuel tanks or bomb load. Lancaster R5915 was buffeted and bounced across the sky by flak bursts exploding nearby until it received a direct hit in the starboard wing setting the fuel tanks on fire. After an evaluation of the situation F/Sgt Deacon gave the order to bail out. F/Sgt Irwin followed F/Lt Miller out of the forward escape hatch, but as he bailed out, the aircraft exploded, temporarily stunning him and killing the rest of his crew. When F/Sgt Irwin regained consciousness he found himself free-falling to earth. However, he felt a slight pulling on one of his harness straps and looking up he could make out his unopened parachute pack. With great presence of mind he pulled the pack down towards him and managed to pull the rip cord, thus deploying the parachute. However, as the parachute was only attached to him with one strap, not two, F/Sgt Irwin was left dangling sideways and landed on the back of the head, badly wounding him.

The death of six of the crew was a tragic loss, and one that saddened F/Sgt Irwin deeply. With the exception of Albert Woodcock (W/op), his crew now rest in the Becklingen War Graves Cemetery in Germany. The body of Albert Woodcock was never found, but his name is commemorated on the Runnymede Memorial. Both surviving crew members, Sgt Irwin and F/Lt Miller were captured. F/Lt Miller was sent to Stalag Luft L3 at Sagan Beleria, while Sgt Irwin, after recovering from his injuries at a hospital in Lüneburg, was sent to Stalag Luft 6 at Heydekrug, near the Lithuanian border. With the rapid approach of the Red Army in the summer of 1944 Stalag Luft 6 was evacuated. F/Sgt Irwin was initially transferred, first to Thorn in Poland, and then a few weeks later to Stalag 357 at Fallingbostel, which is between Hamburg and Hanover.

F/Sgt Patrick Irwin spent the remainder of the war as a POW in Stalag 357 at Fallingbostel, before this camp was also evacuated in April 1945, and its inmates moved away from the advancing Allied forces.

R.I.P.
My Crew
They smile in death, for they have given
All that man can give
For freedom was their target, and
By dying, it shall live.
Requiescant in Peace.

What follows is an account of the forced march Sgt Patrick Irwin endured at the hands of the Germans to avoid the Allied Armies' advance.

Patrick Joseph Irwin
Camp-Stalag 357
POW No.923
Service No.657279
Force-RAF.

Transcript of written log of forced march from Stalag 357, Fallingbostel, to Lassahn in Schleswig-Holstein (now in Mecklenburg- Vorpommern), from Friday 6th April-Thursday 3rd May 1945 (PGJI: Lassahn is in the Naturpark Lauenburgische Seen, north of Laurenburg and east of Hamburg):

April 6th. After multitudes of rumors and counter rumors, the Deutsch officially informed us that we would have to march! Chaos reigned supreme while we gathered together as much of our belongings as we could carry, and destroyed that which we could not. They gave us one of their horrible loaves and some margarine each, and in drenching rain we were lined up, counted, and marched in groups of 150 from the camp at 15:30 hrs. Each group took a different route, and in view of the fact that we occasionally passed another group going practically in the opposite direction, any German plan seemed not only vague, but nonexistent. The policy of panic seemed, obviously, to be, that we were to be shepherded, at any cost, away from the oncoming Allied Armies. Only the sick in the camp hospital were left behind.

So tired, hungry, weak and wet, we were forced at the point of a bayonet, to tramp in a northerly direction for 14 Kilometres. In darkness, we arrived at a state owned farm in Bleckmar, where we had to find a place to lie in for the night. There was no food or cooking facilities, so each manor 'combine' had to fend for himself.

April 7th. Today we remained on this farm, trying to improve our conditions as best we could by pilfering anything and everything we could find. The wreckage of a Mosquito, which crashed near us last night in a special low flying sortie, was brought in amid the satisfied grins of our barbarous captors. Spent another night here, sleeping in huddles like animals.

April 8th. A short march today of 6 km to nowhere in particular. Tonight we slept in the open in wet fields, in hungry, cold misery.

April 9th. Today at about 07:00 we marched to Marbostel (actually there are two, Marbostel bei Soltau bei Wietzendorf), a distance of 16km. Here again we had to sleep in an open field, on beds of leaves which we industriously gathered from a nearby wood. We found two dying Russians in a shed; how they got there, we were unable to find out. They were dying of typhus.

April 17th. Our arrival at the above place had the feeling of zero hour. We were herded together in a small field amid the confusing clamouring of Germans. We settled uneasily to sleep, but were awakened about midnight and told to prepare to move on! In the closing stages of exhaustion we headed for the river Elbe, one man goes mad and is taken in a commandeered cart.

April 18th. Remained here in the open today. Now almost impervious to all weather, at least we take anything as a matter of course. Contacted by Dixie Dean, BBC news and promise of Red X food parcels from LUBEK.

April 19th. Today we marched 20km to Gallin. Got two red X parcels each on way at a fatal place called Gresse. All converged to get parcels. Five minutes after we passed one of the groups on ten roadside, they were shot up by Typhoons. Three of our fellows and six Germans killed, very many injured. E. Bardsley a victim, horrible. Some had been POWs since Dunkirk!

April 20th. We remained here today; the strain is beginning to tell on many. Our wretched feet are in a sorry state, we can't even get a wash.

April 21st. Again today we march 18km through Zarrentin to Techin. Only the spirits keeps us going now, and the glorious prospect of release.

April 22nd. We remain on this farm today. We are now sick at the closing stages of our physical resources, our wretched feet are painfully, and mishapenly blistered. The number of marching 'casualties' is increasing, and we feel that the end of the tether is near. German authority also is obviously on the wane, the guards are more concerned now with saving their own skins than indulging in their usual brutality.

April 23rd. Today we did our final march as prisoners, 3km to a little village called Lassahn where a 'lagarette' has been started! This consists of a small village hall, where our Australian doctor, severely handicapped by practically having nothing to work with except a few paper German bandages, tries to organize things. My feet are in a hell of a state, my chest aches and I have a horrid cough and a nasty attack of rheumatism completes my unhappiness.

April 24th. With the aid of a little straw, we endeavor to make our plight a little less intolerable. Our German rations are almost nonexistent, but we survive on the remnants of our Red X parcels.

April 25th-May 2nd. We still hold out despite all manner of illnesses. No bread and rampant diarrhea and dysentery. Dixie brings us the BBC news regularly. This has been our staff, our rod, our support throughout all of these dark days. The frantic comings and goings of German soldiers raise our hopes of an early release and Dixie, as Red Cross representative, actually gets across the Elbe to meet the Allied Commander. Like thermometers (only there is more coloring of blood in them), our temperatures rise and fall with hope and disappointment.

May 2nd. A wonderful day!! One 6th Airborne trooper, pistol in both hands, takes the village without a single shot. RELEASE AT LAST!

May 3rd. Taken by lorry past a column of German prisoners about 15 miles long across the Elbe again to Luneburg. Made comfortable in a hotel and de-loused. Now that freedom is here we can't believe it. This is my birthday, the most wonderful I will ever have.

May 4th. At 1700 we leave Luneburg and Germany forever I hope, by Dakota. About 1930, ENGLAND before us! Land Oxfordshire at 2130. THANK GOD, back to England, freedom, hope and Christianity.

Postscript

On the fateful night of 20th January, F/Sgt W.J McKee of the RCAF was confined to his sick bed in a hospital in Ely with a serious chest infection and classified by the medical officer as unfit to fly. His replacement was F/Lt K.R. Miller who joined the squadron as the 'bombing leader' instructor on 1st October 1943. Luckily, for him he parachuted safely, albeit into the enemy's hands becoming a prisoner of war along with F/Sgt Irwin.

F/Sgt McKee was now without a regular crew and after he got over the shock of losing his original crew, he joined the crew of F/Lt J. A. Watson RCAF. F/Lt Watson had arrived from 1657 Conversion Unit on 4th September 1943 and when F/Sgt McKee joined him, he was well into the twenties with missions completed. The squadron's operational record book starts to feature F/Sgt McKee with the Watson crew on 24th February 1944 when the target was the ball bearing factories at Schweinfurt. The original bomb aimer in the Watson crew was Flying Officer W. A. Crawford and for some unknown reason he stopped appearing on the battle order with the crew. Therefore, the opportunity arose for F/Sgt Mckee to join a regular crew. Various other targets followed including two trips to Frankfurt and one to Essen, which established F/Sgt Mckee as the regular bomb aimer, and of course he was also flying with a Canadian pilot, navigator and rear gunner, who made him feel welcome.

On 27/28th April 1944 F/Lt Watson lifted Lancaster ND781, GI-R off the runway at Mildenhall to attack Friedrichshafen on his 28th mission. The crew were a part of a contingent of 332 Lancasters to attack this relatively small town that specialized in making engines and gearboxes for German tanks. The route into the target was uneventful. However, whilst the bombers were releasing their deadly cargo, the night fighters arrived. The conditions were ideal for the German night fighters with a clear moonlight sky and they subsequently shot down 18 bombers, one being F/L Watson and his crew.

According to post-war reports from the survivors, at least four night-fighters converged on the Lancaster, which was flying at 17,000 feet. Two kept station about 1,000 feet overhead, while the others took up positions on the port and starboard quarters below. On fire, the bomber crashed near the railway station at St.Hippolyte (Haut-Rhin), 18 km north of Colmar.

Flight Lieutenant James Andrew Watson M.I.D of the Royal Canadian Air Force is buried in Choloy War cemetery in France. He was just 21 years of age.

POW

F/O W.V. Ranson RCAF- Nav, P/O W.H. Russel RAF –W/op, F/S W.S.J McKee RCAF-A/B, Sgt R.J. Hayes RAF-MUG, F/S M.D. Mackinnon RCAF-R/G, Sgt R.C. Eames RAF-F/E

17

Fortunes of War
Pathfinder Crews

Crew: Pilot P/O D. Jackson
Nav: P/O J. G. Sampson
B/A : Sgt S. M. Hines
W/op: Sgt T. S. Gookey
MUG: Sgt P. MaCilroy
R/G: Sgt C. Bradwell
F/E: Sgt A. F. Belson

Group Captain Hamish McHaddie was a distinguished and widely known member of the elite Pathfinder Force. He was on the headquarters staff of 8 Group under the inspirational leadership of Air Commodore Don Bennett. Part of his responsibilities was to visit squadrons and select crews who had operational experience and were deemed to have the potential to excel with the Pathfinder force.

The Pathfinders were always scouting squadrons for the best crews to join them and in late 1943, Flight Sergeant Derek Jackson and crew were at somewhat of a crossroads in their 'tour' of operations. Initially the crew had joined XV Squadron during early August 1943 and immediately transferred to 622 on its formation on the 10th. On the very first day of its existence, 622 sent its Stirlings to bomb Nuremberg, the Jackson crew had to return early in EF391 due to engine failure. The missions continued to build for the crew with two trips to Italy in August negotiating the Alps with the Stirlings struggling to gain sufficient height to clear the large mountains. On 23rd October the news reached the crew that, their pilot had been promoted to Pilot Officer in recognition of his missions achieved to date. During late 1943 the crew attacked the major industrial targets in the Ruhr and beyond including four missions to Berlin and two to Hanover. It was whilst on a mission

F/Lt Phillips & crew whilst with No.7 Squadron PFF, note the eighth member of the crew who assisted with navigational duties. Thomas Jones is 2nd from the right. *Courtesy of P. Jones*

to Hanover on 28/29th September 1943 that the crew flew Short Stirling EF123, GI-Q. This mark III aircraft had only just arrived on the squadron on the 14th of the month and whilst the crew was over the target they were struck by falling incendiaries from above. The extent of the damage was unknown and various systems were tested on the long route home. On nearing Mildenhall the crew reported the damage to the control room and rather surprisingly they were cleared to land as normal on the main runway. The undercarriage stood up on impact with the runway but it was quickly established that the Stirling had no brakes resulting in the aircraft over shooting the runway and collapsing on its belly in an agricultural field. In December 1943, the squadron converted to the Avro Lancaster and with nineteen missions under their belt, the crew was selected to join No.7 Squadron Pathfinders. A tour of operations with Pathfinders was a minimum of forty five and acceptance of the offer would have to be a consensus decision. Whilst the crew was deliberating their future they were automatically posted to training duties at Heavy Conversion Units. The story does not have a happy conclusion; Pilot Officer Jackson had a desire to return to operations in the de Havilland Mosquito. His wish was granted and he began his conversion onto the 'wooden wonder' in early 1945. On 4th February 1945 Pilot Officer Jackson was taking off in a Mosquito when an engine failure resulted in the death of himself and his instructor.

In March 1944, Hamish McHaddie paid another visit to the squadron selecting potential candidates. One of the crews that he instantly recognized was that of Flight Lieutenant Phillips DFC who had been with the squadron since September 1943. The crew had shown a remarkable resilience to the most heavily defended German targets. Once a crew was selected for the PFF, they would be asked to volunteer knowing that if they declined the offer, then they would be ordered to go. With this in mind the 'Phillips' crew volunteered for what would be a tour of forty five operations instead of the standard Bomber Command thirty. The crew knew that they were a proficient crew and accepted the challenge ahead. On 22nd March 1944, Flight Lieutenant Phillips and crew left Mildenhall for their new home at RAF Oakington in Cambridgeshire and No. 7 Squadron PFF.

What follows is a copy of the operational logbook of the flight engineer in the crew, Sergeant Thomas Jones. It is included as an example of the 'operations' that the crews of Bomber Command undertook in late 1943 and early 1944. The Battle of Berlin was raging during the crew's arrival in September 1943 and the Short Stirling bomber was nearing the end of its front line operational experience. The head of Bomber Command, ACM Arthur Harris withdrew the Stirling bomber after a sustained period of heavy losses culminating in five Stirling bombers being lost on the night of 22/23rd November 1943.

Essentially the logbook of Sgt Jones is testimony to many crews' attempts to take the air war to Germany in late 43 early 1944. By the end of their operational tour, the crew would become known as the 'lucky crew'. The experiences detailed in the logbook bear testimony to several near misses against the enemy in a period where the enemy defenses were at their most effective. In particular, look for the mention of engine failure, fuel tank holed, home on three engines, hit by flak and large fighter opposition. Keen eyes will spot the rapid promotion of the pilot and the transition during late December 43 and early 1944 from the Short Stirling to the Avro Lancaster.

Pilot: F/Lt F.A. Phillips RAAF
Nav: P/O D.G. Goodwin RNZAF
B/A : F/Sgt H.C. Thurston RNZAF
W/op: F/Sgt S. Williamson RAAF
MUG: Sgt R. Wyme
R/G: Sgt J.W. Naylor
F/E : Sgt T.J. Jones

F/Lt F. A. Phillips was awarded the Distinguished Flying Cross during his service with 622 Squadron and a bar to his DFC whilst with the Pathfinder force.

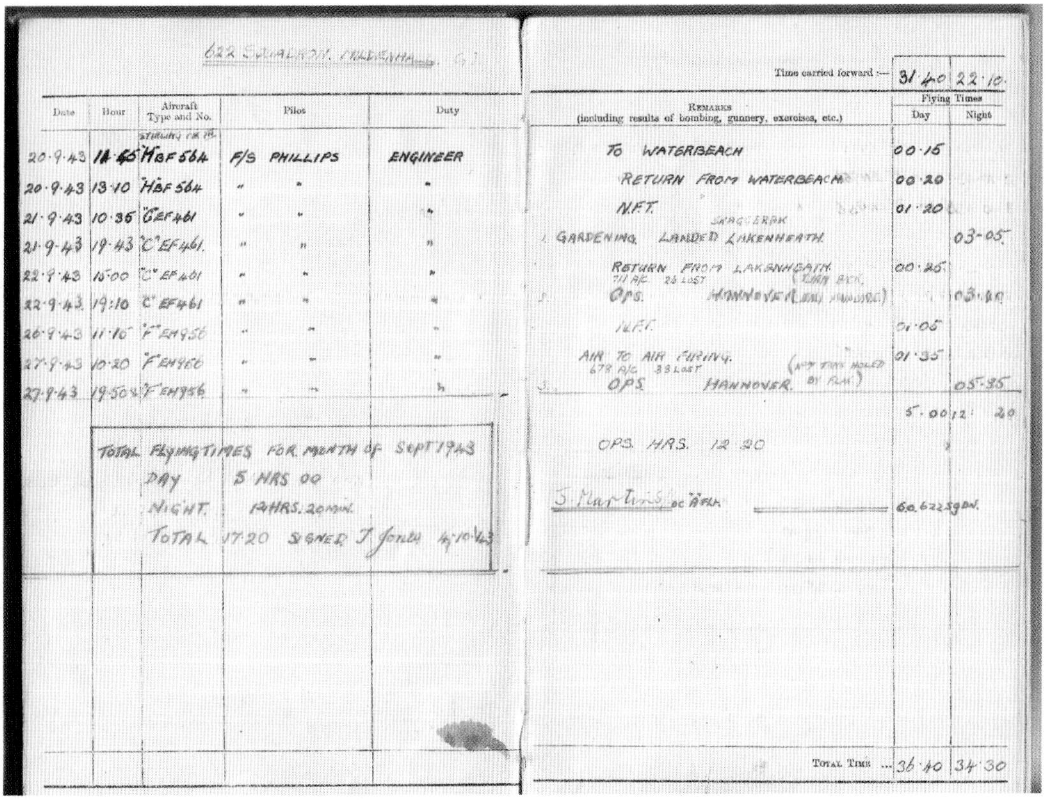

622 SQUADRON, MILDENHALL.

Time carried forward :— 31·40 | 22·10

Date	Hour	Aircraft Type and No.	Pilot	Duty	Remarks (including results of bombing, gunnery, exercises, etc.)	Flying Times Day	Flying Times Night
		STIRLING Mk III.					
20-9-43	11·45	"H" BF564	F/S PHILLIPS	ENGINEER	TO WATERBEACH	00·15	
20-9-43	13·10	"H" BF564	"	"	RETURN FROM WATERBEACH	00·20	
21-9-43	10·35	"C" EF461	"	"	N.F.T.	01·20	
21-9-43	19·43	"C" EF461	"	"	SKAGGERAK GARDENING LANDED LAKENHEATH		03·05
22-9-43	10·00	"C" EF461	"	"	RETURN FROM LAKENHEATH	00·25	
22-9-43	19·10	"C" EF461	"	"	711 A/C 26 LOST OPS. HANNOVER (TURN BACK ENG. FAILURE)		03·40
26-9-43	11·10	"F" EH956	"	"	N.F.T.	01·05	
27-9-43	10·20	"F" EH956	"	"	AIR TO AIR FIRING	01·35	
27-9-43	19·50	"F" EH956	"	"	678 A/C 33 LOST OPS HANNOVER (NO 7 TANK HOLED BY FLAK)		05·35
						5·00	12·20

TOTAL FLYING TIMES FOR MONTH OF SEPT 1943
DAY 5 HRS 00
NIGHT 12 HRS. 20 MIN.
TOTAL 17·20 SIGNED T. Jones 4-10-43

OPS. HRS. 12·20

J. Martin OC 'B' FLT — C.O. 622 SQDN.

TOTAL TIME ... 36·40 | 34·30

First mission on 21/09/43. Note the pilot as still being a F/Sgt. The difficulties facing aircrew in late 1943 become apparent as the months progressed. On the crew's second mission to Hanover, they had to turn back due to engine failure. On 27/09/43, the crew attacked Mannheim again and had their No.7 fuel tank holed. *Courtesy of P. Jones.*

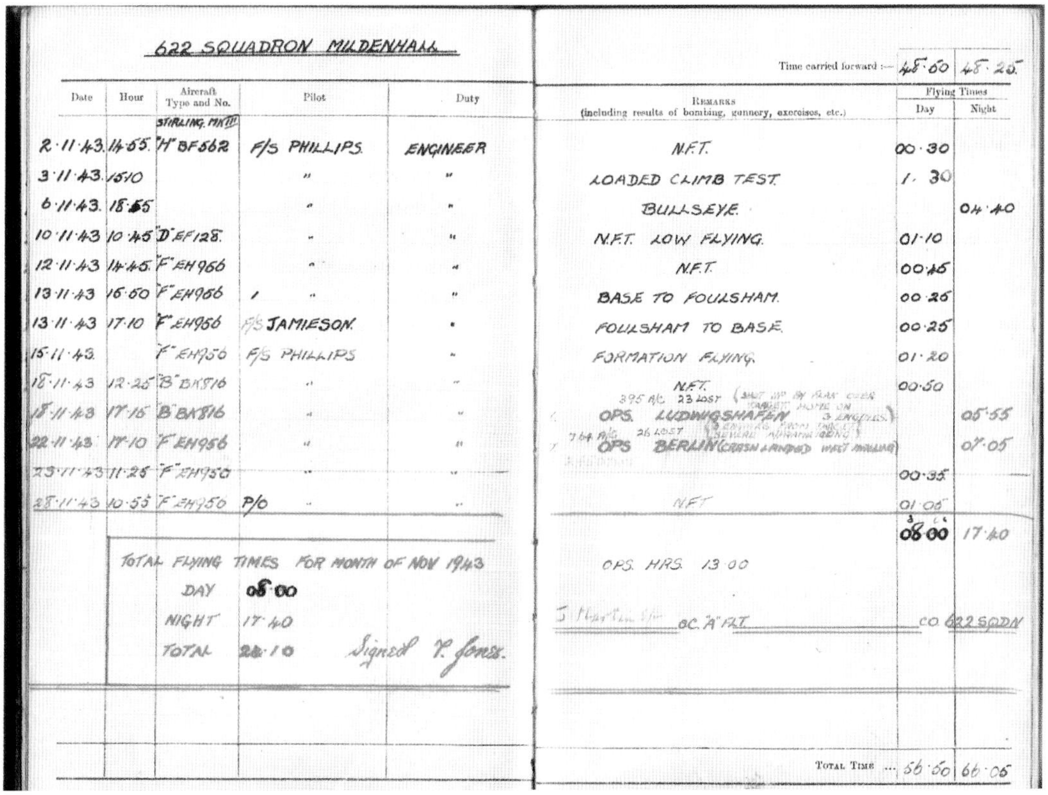

622 SQUADRON MILDENHALL

Time carried forward :— 48·00 | 48·25

Date	Hour	Aircraft Type and No.	Pilot	Duty	Remarks (including results of bombing, gunnery, exercises, etc.)	Flying Times Day	Flying Times Night
		STIRLING MK III					
2-11-43	14·55	"H" BF562	F/S PHILLIPS	ENGINEER	N.F.T.	00·30	
3-11-43	15·10		"	"	LOADED CLIMB TEST	1·30	
6-11-43	18·55		"	"	BULLSEYE		04·40
10-11-43	10·45	"D" EF128	"	"	N.F.T. LOW FLYING	01·10	
12-11-43	14·45	"F" EH956	"	"	N.F.T.	00·45	
13-11-43	15·50	"F" EH956	"	"	BASE TO FOULSHAM	00·25	
13-11-43	17·10	"F" EH956	F/S JAMIESON	"	FOULSHAM TO BASE	00·25	
15-11-43		"F" EH956	F/S PHILLIPS	"	FORMATION FLYING	01·20	
18-11-43	12·25	"B" BK816	"	"	N.F.T.	00·50	
18-11-43	17·15	"B" BK816	"	"	395 A/C 23 LOST OPS. LUDWIGSHAFEN (SHOT UP BY FLAK OVER TARGET. HOME ON 3 ENGINES)		05·55
22-11-43	17·10	"F" EH956	"	"	764 A/C 26 LOST OPS BERLIN (SEVERE ICING. FROM TARGET 3 ENGINES) (CRASH LANDED WEST MALLING)		07·05
23-11-43	11·25	"F" EH956	"	"		00·35	
28-11-43	10·55	"F" EH956	P/O	"	N.F.T.	01·05	
						08·00	17·40

TOTAL FLYING TIMES FOR MONTH OF NOV 1943
DAY 08·00
NIGHT 17·40
TOTAL 26·10 Signed T. Jones.

OPS. HRS. 13·00

J. Martin OC. 'A' FLT. — CO. 622 SQDN

TOTAL TIME ... 56·00 | 66·05

Ludwigshafen on 18/11/43 shows 'shot up by flak over target, home on 3 engines'. Berlin on 22/11/43-severe icing, 3 engines from target. Crash landed West Malling'. Phillips promoted to Pilot Officer on 28/11/43. *Courtesy of P. Jones.*

622 SQUADRON MILDENHALL

Date	Hour	Aircraft Type and No.	Pilot	Duty	Remarks (including results of bombing, gunnery, exercises, etc.)	Flying Times Day	Flying Times Night
					Time carried forward :—	62·00	66·05
		LANCASTER	P/O PHILLIPS DFC.	SCREEN			
1·1·44			F/S CRAIG	ENGINEER	DUAL CIRCUITS + LANDINGS.	00·55	
2·1·44	10·55	"F" ED425	" "	"	" " " "	01·55	
4·1·44	12·05	"C" N4272	P/O PHILLIPS DFC	ENGINEER	LOADED CLIMB.	03·50	
4·1·44	19·40	"F" ED425	" " "	"	NIGHT CIRCUITS + LANDINGS.		02·15
14·1·44	19·40	"C" R4272	" " "	"	BULLSEYE		04·40
25·1·44	11·15	"F" ED425	" " "	"	N.F.T.	01·15	
30/1·44		"N" LL782	" " "	"	534 A/C 33 LOST (...) OPS BERLIN. 1880·3 TONS		06·25
						07·55	13·20
					OPS HRS. 06·25		
					TOTAL TIME ...	69·55	79·25

TOTAL FLYING TIME FOR JAN 1944
DAY 07·55
NIGHT 13·20
TOTAL 21·15
Signed T. Jones.

[signature] OC. 'A' FLT

In early December 1943, P/O Phillips was awarded the DFC. During December 43 & January 1944, the squadron converted to the Avro Lancaster. The crew's first mission in a Lancaster was on 30/1/44 to Berlin. The logbook records 33 lost. *Courtesy of P. Jones.*

622 SQUADRON MILDENHALL

Date	Hour	Aircraft Type and No.	Pilot	Duty	Remarks (including results of bombing, gunnery, exercises, etc.)	Flying Times Day	Flying Times Night
					Time carried forward :—	69·55	79·25
		LANCASTER					
6·2·44		"D" ED437	P/O PHILLIPS DFC.	ENGINEER.	FIGHTER AFFILIATION.	01·20	
6·2·44		"F" ED425	" " "	"	LOCAL FLYING.	00·45	
7·2·44		"B" ED631	" " "	"	TO WESTCOTT AND RETURN.	01·20	
13·2·44		OXFORD V 3502	" " "	PASSENGER.	TO GATWICK AND RETURN (PRACTICE MAP READING)	01·45	
15·2·44		LANCASTER "J" LL812	" " "	ENGINEER.	N.F.T.	00·40	
18·2·44		"E" JA876	" " "	"	N.F.T.	00·20	
20·2·44		"T" W4265	" " "	"	598 A/C 9 LOST (HANG UP INCENDIARIES BURNED ON DISPERSAL) OPS STUTTGART		06·50
22·2·44		"F" ED425	" " "	"	N.F.T.	00·35	
24·2·44		"F" ED425	" " "	"	734 A/C 33 LOST (TROUBLE GETTING HEIGHT LARGE FIGHTER OPPOSITION) OPS SCHWEINFURT 2,263·2 TONS		07·45
28·2·44		"F" ED426	" " "	"	N.F.T.	00·50	
						7·40	14·35
					OPS. HRS. 14·35		
					TOTAL TIME ...	77·35	94·00

TOTAL FLYING TIMES FOR FEB 1942.
DAY 7·40
NIGHT 14·35
TOTAL 22·15
Signed T. Jones

[signature] OC 'A' FLT.

20/2/44 - Stuttgart - 'Hang up of incendiaries, burned on dispersal'. 24/2/44-Schweinfurt-'Trouble getting height large fighter opposition'. In early March 1944, P/O Phillips was promoted to Flight Lieutenant and selected to join the PFF with No.7 squadron. *Courtesy of P. Jones.*

18

Tried & Tested
The Memoirs of Flight Lieutenant R. Perry

Pilot: F/Lt Ron Nielsen RAAF
Nav: F/Sgt Reg Perry RAFVR
B/A : F/O John Blundell RAFVR
W/op: F/Sgt Rick Silbert RAAF
MUG: F/Sgt Knowle Lean RAAF
R/G: F/Sgt David Dury RAAF
F/E: F/Sgt Frank Williams RAFVR
Radar Operator: F/O Mungo Parkes RAFVR-Joined crew on Pathfinders.

Navigator Flight Sergeant Reginald Perry joined up with his crew at the Operational Training Unit at Wing near Leighton Buzzard in February 1944, duly flying twin engined Wellington bombers. The natural aircrew training progression took them next to Wratting Common and 1651 Conversion Unit where they were introduced to the four-engined Short Stirling bomber. After approximately four weeks of adjusting to four engined bombers as a team, they were posted to No.3 Lancaster Finishing School at Feltwell for familiarization on to the mighty Avro Lancaster.

On successful completion of LFS the crew was posted to 622 Squadron to join an operational squadron and enter the war in earnest. On arrival at Mildenhall on 23rd July 1944, it was unusual to hear that they were the second crew to have a skipper with the surname of Nielsen, the other pilot, F/Sgt Allan Nielsen DFM had arrived on the squadron shortly before. Both the pilots shared Australian nationality but were not related; however, this did not stop them from becoming firm friends.

On 27th July the crew conducted an air test on Lancaster L7576, GI-K after some considerable maintenance on the aircraft. It is worth mentioning at this point that this particular Lancaster was earmarked to become the squadron's first aircraft to reach the one hundred mark for operations. On 24/25th July, F/Lt Allen DFC, the 'A' flight commander had taken GI-K to Stuttgart and reported the aircraft as sluggish and difficult to obtain the desired performance from its engines. The squadron Commanding Officer was keen to achieve the magical one hundred mark and L7576 was well overdue essential maintenance. Fate would play a part in this particular Lancaster not reaching the 'ton up' when it was again sent to attack Stuttgart on 28/29th July with Flying Officer Peabody RCAF and crew at the helm. A night fighter shot down the Lancaster en route over France, crashing in a forest at Petitmont with the loss of five crewmembers and two prisoners of war.

F/Sgt Ron Nielsen completed a second 'dickey' trip on 28th July to Stuttgart with F/Lt Gill at the controls. The whole crew were promulgated on the battle order for the first time on the 5th August to attack the oil tanks at Bordeaux in France that were supplying the German war machine. The crew was issued two small tins of orange juice to sustain them for the eight hours plus trip. En route to the target the Lancaster flew at 1,000ft to Lands End and then climbed to 12,000ft to bomb and return home via the Brest Peninsula.

On 16th August, the crew set course for Stettin on the Baltic coast to attack the port region in Lancaster LL803, GI-G. Stettin was a return trip of some eight hours and to maintain concentration and remain objective for that period was extremely difficult. On the route home the bomb aimer reported that he could see an island below to which Sgt Perry stated that it was not possible because they should be over the North Sea. It was confirmed that they were flying over an island and established that it was Heligoland, some way off true course. Sgt Perry could not obtain a 'Gee' signal so he picked up his sextant and searched the night sky to locate the pole star to steer by. The skipper spotted the pole star and the Lancaster was aligned so that the star was on the starboard wing until eventually a 'Gee' signal was established and the crew successfully navigated back to Mildenhall.

Stettin Again!

At the briefing on 29th August the target was again revealed as Stettin on the Baltic coast. On this occasion, the crew of Ron Nielsen was again assigned Lancaster LL803, GI-G on a deja vu operation to the same target. The crew was driven to the dispersal point and climbed aboard the Lancaster where all preflight checks were conducted. Unfortunately, one of the engines would not start and the crew had to 'stand down' due to no other spare aircraft being available. At the time, the crew was unaware of the incident that would unfold on this operation for their counterparts, the crew of Allan Nielsen. The Following is an account of that eventful incident:

> "Over the target their Lancaster was attacked by a fighter who caused extreme damage to their aircraft and wounded five of the crew. Five members of the crew were wounded, with the navigator having been peppered with cannon fire and 62 pieces were taken from him after

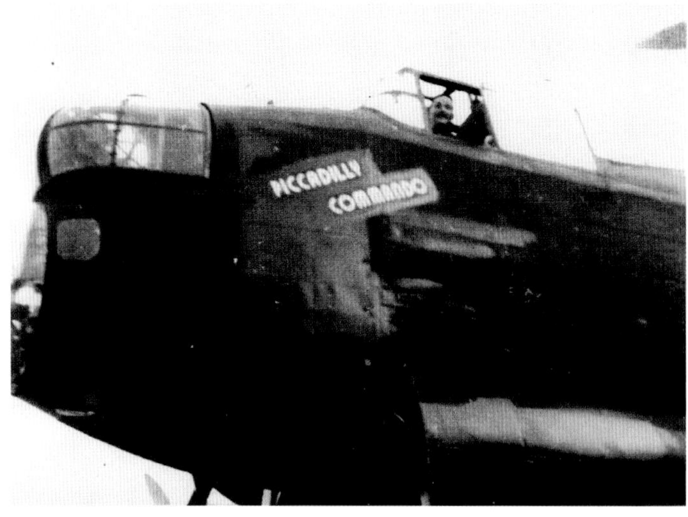

Lancaster LL803 GI-G adorned with *'Piccadilly Commander'*. The wording describes the 'ladies of the night' who frequented Piccadilly in London. LL803 also wore the squadron identification letters of 'M' & 'S'. Whilst in the latter guise, the aircraft was lost due to flak on a raid to Homberg on 2nd November with the loss of the entire crew. Out of the fourteen missions that F/Sgt Perry undertook, six were in this particular Lancaster. *Courtesy of R. Perry.*

landing. A piece of shrapnel cut the wireless operators thigh, baring it to the bone. The flight engineer was hit under the right eye and although suffered no serious injury, blood gushed from his nose. The mid upper gunner was cut on the face with Perspex and the pilot got some small pieces of Perspex and metal under his right eyelid. After ascertaining the damage the pilot, with the navigator seriously wounded, decided not to go to the target or try landing in Sweden because of the weather conditions and that it would be too dangerous to bail out, especially over the sea. He decided to return to base, flying west over Denmark at 4-6,000ft. The W/op had not disclosed the seriousness of the wound and was given the task of navigating. He worked the 'Gee' and constantly attempted to get fixes on the way home, carrying out his duties cheerfully and without compliant. With no intercom the pilot had to communicate with the crew verbally though the flight engineer or, by slips of paper, which the W/op carried to the two gunners. Eventually landfall was made but uncertain of their position, landed at the first available aerodrome, which turned out to be Hardwick. As he left the aircraft the W/op removed the detonator from the IFF set. For their actions this night, the W/op, F/Sgt Cole was awarded the Conspicuous Gallantry Medal, second only in merit to the Victoria Cross. The pilot F/Sgt Nielsen, was awarded the DFM and the navigator W/O Farquharson was awarded the DFC."

On 3rd September the crew was assigned to bomb the airfield at Eindhoven in daylight. This was the first time that the 'Nielsen' crew had flown in formation and found the whole experience nerve wracking. The Lancasters were flying in tight 'vic' formations and the slightest error could result in a fatal collision. Shortly after take off the crew entered some cloud and opened out to avoid collision and account for blind flying. The Lancaster immediately started to pick up ice on the wing surfaces so F/Sgt Nielsen took the Lancaster below the clouds to remove the icing. When the crew broke out under the cloud they had lost the rest of the formation and they were totally alone and vulnerable to fighter attack. The decision was made to proceed to the target and bomb alone which was successfully carried out with a large slice of luck used up.

In a matter of eight weeks the crew had completed fourteen operations and they were selected to go to the Pathfinder Force. The crew was apprehensive and Reg Perry was questioning his ability as a navigator. The consensus decision was that the skipper would go and see the commanding officer and tell him that they did not want to go to Pathfinder Force. The result was a posting to Pathfinder training with immediate effect.

Before they could join No.7 Squadron at RAF Oakington, they had to attend the Pathfinder Navigation Training Unit at Methwold in Suffolk for additional training. The Pathfinder squadrons selected the crème de la crème of aircrews and so it was in October 1944, Flight Sergeant Perry and his crew became 'Pathfinders'.

Whilst with the Pathfinders the crew continued to hone their flying skills and they became one of the most proficient crews on the squadron. By the end of their operational tour, the crew had been awarded four distinguished flying crosses and four distinguished flying medals for completing fifty missions against the enemy.

End of tour photograph taken in May 1945 at RAF Oakington, No.7 Squadron Pathfinders. Sitting in rear turret: F/Sgt D. Dury. Back row L-R: F/O J. Blundell, F/Lt R. Neilsen, F/Sgt K. Lean, F/O M. Parkes. Front: F/Sgt R. Perry, P/O R. Silbert, F/Sgt F. Williams. *Courtesy of R. Perry.*

19

"Q" for Queenie

In 1943 Bernard Dye was approaching the age where he would have to choose which military service to join to defend his homeland. For Bernard there was only one service that he would volunteer for, the RAF. At this time the realities of war were a million miles away and flying seemed heroic to young men who listened intently to aircrews' combat experiences.

Bernard Dye assessed his options and volunteered for the role of an air gunner and he was duly accepted for training. The air gunner position in an aircraft was the most vulnerable to attack and more gunners lost their lives throughout the war than any other crew position. Bernard had no delusions of grandeur; it was going to be one big adventure, how right that statement would prove to be.

No.9 Air Gunnery School, Penrhos, North Wales

On 7th July 1943 Bernard Dye was posted from the initial training wing at Bridlington to No.9 Air Gunnery School at Penrhos North Wales. For Bernard this was where the real training would begin along the road to being fully operational. The ITW at Bridlington had been several weeks of intensive marching and drill in an attempt to mould trainees into men worthy of wearing the King's uniform. The marching was interspersed with classroom activities which mainly focused on the theory of flight and aircraft dynamics. In addition, several hours were spent learning the rudimentary elements of Morse code.

The instructors at the Gunnery School were experienced gunners who had either completed a tour of operations or had some operational experience. Bernard was immediately subjected to considerable lessons in arithmetic and he learned how to strip a .303in Browning machine gun in his sleep. The theory of a bullet's trajectory was studied and the capabilities of our defensive armament were compared with the formidable firepower fitted to the German fighters, which he learned to distinguish through aircraft recognition lessons. He was taught that early recognition of friend or foe could be the difference between life and death. He familiarized himself with the technicalities of the various turrets in production including the hydraulic systems and learned how to fix blockages and malfunctions whilst in potential combat positions. The aircraft that the crew flew in was the Bristol Blenheim which had a mid upper turret comprising just two .303 Browning machine guns. Initially Bernard flew familiarization trips and air-to-sea firing which was really enjoyable. He progressed onto shooting at drogues towed by Avro Ansons who released the drogues over the sea at a distance of approximately 4-700 yards away. It was very difficult to see the bullets hitting the target and Bernard had no idea of his success until he landed and his strikes on target were counted.

End_of tour photograph with Lancaster GI-Q, LM241. Photo taken on 12th August 1944. This Lancaster suffered the same fate as the five previously allocated the 'Q' Squadron identification letter. LM241 was lost two weeks after this photograph was taken over Russelsheim. L to R: Sgt Grant (rear gunner), unknown, F/O Horton (pilot), F/Sgt White (W/op), Sgt Parsons (F/E), Sgt Monether (Nav), unknown, W/O Gray (B/A), unknown, Sgt Dye (MUG). *Courtesy of Bernard Dye Air Gunner.*

A newly qualified air gunner. Sgt Bernard Dye proudly poses for an official photograph after successfully completing his initial gunnery training. *Courtesy of Bernard Dye Air Gunner.*

Each trainee had the tip of his bullets marked with different color paint to identify who had the most success. The guns were fitted with a camera that recorded the gun action and crew watched back their particular performance. At the end of the course Bernard was pleased and proud to be awarded his Sergeants' stripes and to achieve a favorable instructor's report, which read 'Has worked hard, but requires experience. Should be a good gunner'.

The next stage of Bernard's training would take him to No.82 Operational Training Unit at Ossington just north of Newark in Nottinghamshire. It was at Ossington that Bernard Dye first realized that he had a guardian angel. His very first training trip ended in the death of two of his crew. The crew were allocated Vickers Wellington HE332 which was piloted by Flight Sergeant Shaw, an Australian. They undertook a night cross country exercise and they had been airborne for over two hours when disaster struck. Shortly before midnight they were making a low approach towards Ossington's runway and by all accounts the crew were destined to make a good landing. At this stage they had no idea that the ground controller had given them an incorrect QFE which had resulted in the aircraft's barometer being set incorrectly. As the aircraft descended lower they hit the tops of some trees adjacent to the end of the runway which resulted in the aircraft being flung to the ground rather abruptly. Pilot Officer Ingham the navigator and Sergeant Hughes the bomb aimer sadly died from their injuries. Four other members of the crew including Bernard Dye were taken to the station sick bay. Accident rates among training crews were extremely high and official figures show that over 8,000 aircrew lost their lives during training accidents.

Sergeant Dye did not sustain severe injuries, although he was treated for shock. Bernard's recovery progressed well and a few days later he heard a commotion break loose on the airfield. All airfield emergency services were deployed and the emergency vehicles with alarm bells blaring raced past the sick quarters. Curious for an explanation as to what was happening, Bernard asked a male nurse for an explanation. It transpired that a Wellington was sitting at dispersal with the engines running ready for take off on a training flight. One of the aircrew squeezed the trigger to the 'Very' pistol which went off with a loud bang. The Vickers Wellington was constructed of an aluminium geodetic fuselage, covered with fabric that was fixed with dope. The exploding 'Very' pistol set the bomber ablaze with ammunition exploding all over the aircraft, fortunately all the crew escaped without injury. Bernard was astounded at the report of the incident and respectfully said to the nurse 'good grief, I don't think I would want to fly with a crew like that'. Fate would have other ideas!

After a period of recuperation Bernard was declared fit and released from sick bay with the instruction to report to the Chief Ground Instructor (CGI). Bernard was now in the position of looking for a new crew to join and the CGI informed him that there were several crews who were looking for a new mid upper gunner. The photographs of the crews concerned were pinned to a notice board and the CGI told Bernard to choose a new crew. Bernard gave the photographs a good perusal as if trying to judge the capabilities of a crew from their photograph. Finally Bernard picked the crew captained by Sergeant Wheeler due to the fact that the rear gunner was Joe Hayes and he and Bernard had trained together. Fate had dealt her hand; this was the crew that had inadvertently burnt out the Wellington with the 'Very' pistol. Trepidation filled Bernard's heart however he remained silent and resolutely stuck by his first choice. Would it be a lucky choice?

1651 Conversion Flight-RAF Waterbeach

Sergeant Wheeler and crew arrived at Waterbeach on 13th August 1943 in readiness for their familiarization onto the Short Stirling. At Waterbeach the crew experienced very little ground training and concentrated on flying in four engined heavies for the first time with a lot of ditching practice thrown in. Tuition included practice with the Aldis lamp and on how to use Very cartridges.

The Short Company had produced some great aircraft including the renowned Sunderland flying boat that equipped air sea rescue squadrons around the world. The Stirling was borne out of a desire for the RAF to have a four engined bomber that was capable of carrying a substantial bomb load into Germany. The original design of the Stirling allowed for a wingspan of 112ft, but this was too wide for the standard RAF hangar and the wingspan had to be reduced to just under 100ft. The crew arrived at Waterbeach full of apprehension about the indifferent performance regarding the Stirling. Their introduction to the Stirling focused around continual take-offs and landings both in daylight and at night and sometimes on three engines. The Stirling was a handful for any pilot on take off and landing and with a tendency to swing which had to be controlled by the throttles on each side of the aircraft being opened in varying degrees. With an instructor on board, they went on 'bullseye' exercises in the dark across country with a loaded aircraft to simulate a bomb load and practiced evasive maneuvers, although they did not actually do any 'corkscrewing'. Apparently, this had been tried before at conversion flights and

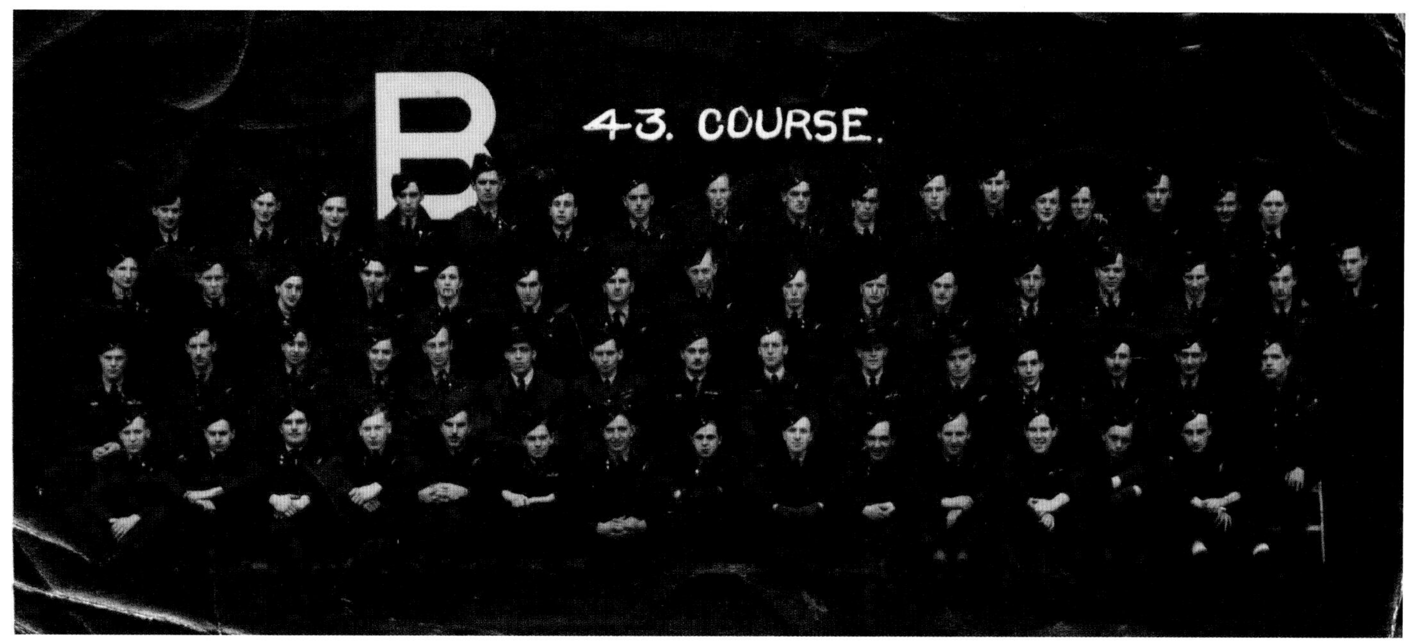

No.43 course 1651 Heavy Conversion Unit RAF Waterbeach. Top from left: Row one 10th Sgt Woods XV Sqn R/G. 12th F/Sgt Clarke 622 pilot. 13th Sgt Westaside 622 MUG, 16th Sgt Ashmore 622 R/G, 17th F/Sgt Lorimer 622 WOP. Row two from left: 2nd Sgt Bright 622 R/G, 3rd F/Sgt Woods XV Wop, 4th Sgt. Hayes DFM XV R/G, 6th W/O McKinley XV Nav. Row three from left: 1st F/Sgt Derisley DFC 622 pilot, 3rd Sgt Dye XV & 622 MUG, 4th F/Sgt Wheeler XV pilot, 8th F/Lt Soper XV pilot. *Courtesy of Bernard Dye Air Gunner.*

crews were lost due to inexperience and the poor condition of some of the Stirlings. The theories of evasive maneuvers were taught during the numerous classroom lectures. The only excitement at Waterbeach was landing on three engines after the port inner cut out and Sergeant Wheeler carried out a successful landing.

RAF Waterbeach trained aircrew predominantly for dispersal to 3 Group Bomber Command. The majority of the aircrew depicted were sent to squadrons within 3 Group. Over 55,000 aircrew lost their lives whilst serving in Bomber Command and at the height of the German defensive capabilities an airman stood only a 50% chance of successfully completing a full tour of 30 operations. This fact is exemplified by the fact that out of the 62 aircrew depicted in the photograph above only 17 survived their tour of operations.

In December 1943 the crew were posted to XV Squadron at RAF Mildenhall in Suffolk. The squadron was in the midst of re-equipping to the Lancaster bomber from the Short Stirling and they were immediately sent to No.3 Lancaster Finishing School at Feltwell for a conversion course. The course finished in early January 1944 and Sergeant Wheeler and crew were posted back to Mildenhall. Flying out of Mildenhall commenced on 8th January and a series of trips focused on circuits and bumps and familiarization with the surrounding countryside. RAF Mildenhall was a part of 3 Group and in amongst a concentration of closely located airfields.

On the 20th February Sergeant Wheeler and crew appeared for the first time on the battle order. Following the training this moment was expected and the realization of the task ahead registered in the minds of the crew, Bernard could not help feeling the normal apprehension and butterflies in the stomach. Prior to any mission the aircrews attended their respective specialist training briefing usually taken by the respective 'Leader' for the particular aircrew designation. Bernard attended the briefing for the air gunners where the latest German fighter techniques were discussed and likely interception points explored. Finally the crew would attend the mission briefing led by the Commanding Officer where the final touches were put to the nights mission. Each aircrew member climbed aboard the Lancaster one hour before take off and went through the various equipment checks that could ultimately save one's life against an attack. With the preflight checks completed the time arrived to start the Merlin engines. Sergeant Wheeler went through the cockpit checks eventually guiding the Lancaster around the perimeter track towards the runway. Bernard had a panoramic view from the mid upper gunner's position and his line of vision took in lancasters in front and behind awaiting their turn to thunder into the air. At this stage of proceedings fate struck another blow, the navigator and bomb aimer, both Canadians torn up their maps and charts and refused to fly. That was the end of the crews supposed first trip and the two Canadians were charged with lack of moral fiber and ghosted out of Mildenhall.

The Reality of War

Without actually flying an operational mission with XV Squadron, Sgt Dye was posted to 622 Squadron based at the same station. He was chosen to be the mid upper gunner for a pilot who he recognized from his time at Ossington as wearing white gloves when he flew. Bernard affectionately named him 'The Duke of Purduker' and he thought that he had a lucky face. He was in his early thirties, very different to the majority of aircrew who were early twenties.

Flying Officer Arthur Horton. *Courtesy of Bernard Dye Air Gunner.*

Arthur Horton had experienced an indifferent training period prior to 622 Squadron. His initial training had taken him to an airfield near to the Mojave Desert near a small town called Lancaster in California, America. The airfield was affectionately known as War Eagle Field and was the home to No.2 British Flying Training School (BFTS). Arthur Horton completed his training on 23rd December 1943 when he was presented with his 'Wings' and Sergeant's stripes. On his return to England he was posted to Lulsgate Bottom for conversion onto twin engined aircraft. It was here during a solo training flight that the rudder jammed and he crashed the Airspeed Oxford aircraft into the apex of a house roof sustaining minor injuries. As previously mentioned Arthur's training eventually led him to Ossington along with Bernard Dye.

On 4th February 1944 Flight Sergeant Horton reported for duty at RAF Mildenhall and was subsequently assigned to 622 Squadron. He completed the mandatory 'second dickey' trips with Pilot Officer Sutton (KIA with his crew on the infamous Nuremberg raid when bomber command lost 97 aircraft) and he completed his first two trips as skipper to Stuttgart and Schweinfurt both heavily defended targets that led Arthur to believe that it was a real baptism of fire. The seven man crew of a Lancaster quickly formed a team that depended on each other for survival and anybody that did not complete their duty to the best of their ability could endanger the rest of the crew. Unexpectedly Arthur Horton had to replace two of his original crewmembers almost immediately. His original navigator was flight sergeant Flavell who was considered old at the age of thirty. However, he was an accomplished navigator and invented a navigational instrument that he named the 'Dangleometer'. This device was designed to calculate 'drift', unfortunately, he developed conjunctivitis and he had to stand down from aircrew duties at this time. The new mid upper gunner was nineteen year old Bernard Dye and Ken Monether the new navigator. Bernard had finally begun his operational tour in earnest and lady luck or fate would play a major part in the crew completing the required thirty missions.

On 10th April 1944 the newly formed crew were on the battle order for an attack on the marshaling yards at Laon. Bomber Command had recently directed all its attention towards the preparation of the forthcoming invasion in a few weeks time. The overall objective was to weaken the German's ability to resist an invasion force and cut off the supply routes to their troops in the front line. With this in mind specific targets such as marshaling yards and defensive targets along the invasion coast were targeted. The crew's second mission took them to the heavily defended Ruhr target of Essen on 26th April which was vitally important to the German war industry. In contrast to Laon, the searchlights over Essen were very active along with the night fighters. In his mid upper turret Bernard Dye fired his two 303 Browning machine guns at a Messerschmitt 110 that strayed too close to their Lancaster and the Me110 disappeared into the night. After successfully bombing the target F/O Horton set course for home being ever watchful for night fighter attack. What occurred next is recalled by F/O Horton:

> "Suddenly, we were attacked by what appeared to be four stubby winged rocket projectiles. I did not know what they were or what they contained and I told the gunners not to fire in case they exploded. Whatever maneuver I put the aircraft through the projectiles followed. One of them disappeared, but for at least fifty miles, out of France and over the coast, I put the Lancaster through twists and turns that it was never designed to do. The throttles were through the 'gate' and over fifty miles we lost some 14,000 feet of height. At one point, I called Dave Parsons the flight engineer, 'what about the engines, Dave?' I asked, concerned for we were not supposed to run them at full power for more than three minutes. His typical and laconic reply filtered back through my headphones, 'F... the engines'. The Lancaster was vibrating and shaking due to the speed which must have reached 300mph. Shortly after crossing the coast, the projectiles lost speed and fell

The newly formed Arthur Horton crew with Bernard Dye sitting centrally on the tail wing. *Courtesy of Bernard Dye Air Gunner.*

out of sight, much to our relief. Once again, the crews luck had held and we landed at Tuddenham adjacent to Mildenhall."

Bernard's first mission in May 1944 took him to Mantes-La-Jolie and in particular to a suburb of Gassicourt to inflict damage on the railway yards. The crew were slightly damaged by flak but returned safely to base. On the 8th May the target was the coastal gun positions along the French coast at Cap Griz Nez. On 11th May the crew reverted back to the railway yards at Louvain. The railway yards at Le Mans were the target on 19th May and the crew were again subjected to flak, some of which damaged their Lancaster. Sergeant Dye, eagle eyed as usual, sighted a Junkers 88 which luckily turned its attention towards other unsuspecting victims.

Duisberg was the target on 21st May and it signalled a return to the Ruhr Valley. En route to the target the searchlights were very active conning other Lancasters. Bernard again sighted two Ju88's and opened fire at one of them apparently driving them away to choose an unsuspecting target. Over the target the Lancaster was conned by searchlights and once locked on the predicted flak would surely follow. In a matter of seconds, the flak opened up and they were hit in one of the self sealing petrol tanks. The skipper threw the Lancaster into evasive corkscrewing action and eventually escaped the beams attention. The subsequent missions in late May and June were focused on destroying the launching platforms of the deadly V1 flying bomb. For the last few weeks the flaming rockets had been launched to deliver their deadly payload into the heart of London and the morale of the British public was wavering. Bomber Command made the destruction of these weapons on the ground a priority.

On 27th May, the crew were assigned Lancaster LL859 marked with the letter 'Q' for Queenie. Had fate finally dealt the Horton crew the fateful blow that would result in them failing to complete their tour? 622 Squadron had lost more Lancasters marked with the letter 'Q' than any other aircraft and the superstition surrounding this letter of the alphabet was almost tangible.

The month of June 1944 brought an intense challenge for Bomber Command on three fronts. Firstly, the Allied invasion on 'D' Day needed the support of the bombers to assist in defeating the enemy strongholds in and around the invasion area. Secondly, the enemy launched their terror weapons, the V1 rockets against London six days after the invasion and the destruction that they reaped had to be stopped. Thirdly, the bombers renewed their attacks on the German oil industry as first outlined in the Casablanca Directive back in 1943. To identify the flying bomb and German troop positions a high degree of accurate bombing

On 5th July 1944 RAF Mildenhall received a visit from His Majesty the King, Her Majesty the Queen and Her Royal Highness Princess Elizabeth. The purpose of the visit was to attend a Field Investiture Ceremony and present aircrew with their awards and decorations. Throughout the day, the Royal party were introduced to aircrew who were allowed to parade in battle dress in readiness for the day's mission. The photograph above depicts H.M. Queen Elizabeth and H.R.H. Princess Elizabeth with the following 622 Squadron aircrew: 1. Sgt Hayes F/E 2. F/Sgt White W/Op 3. Sgt Grant MUG 4.Sgt Dye MUG 5.W/O Gray B/A 6. Sgt Chandler F/E 7. F/Sgt Glynn R/G 8.F/Sgt Farrow MUG 9. Sgt Ashmore R/G. Far left is Air Commodore 'Square' McKee the King's aide-de-camp. *Courtesy of Bernard Dye Air Gunner.*

was essential, therefore a return to day bombing was instigated. ACM Harris was apprehensive about a return to daylight bombing after the experiences earlier in the war when the bombers suffered heavy losses against the more nimble enemy fighters. On this occasion, the bombers operated within the range of the Allied fighter escorts and subsequently they were well protected against enemy fighter attack.

The attacks against the V1 launching sites posed numerous problems due to their camouflaged positions within wooded areas and their constantly changing locations. The POWs could erect the launch sites in a matter of days and their locations were moved to avoid the attention of Bomber Command. The attack on Biennais on 27th June was noteworthy for an attack by a Me110 on the crew's Lancaster. Both gunners blazed away at the fighter and it was seen to fall away damaged and claimed by the gunners.

On 30th June 1944, the squadron was briefed to attack a position in Normandy at Villers Bocage. The Germans were planning to move two Panzer tank divisions through a road junction that would lead to the Allied forces. At the briefing for this particular raid were the crew of F/Lt Trenouth RAAF who were nearing completion of their tour of operations. The mission for the crew would be eventful because they would take a passenger with them to report on the mission. This passenger was a war correspondent named Ronald Walker who worked for a popular newspaper publication called the 'News Chronicle'.

The bombing was extremely close to the Allied troops on the ground and therefore it was necessary for the bombers to bomb from low level under the instruction from the master bomber. Over the target area, the cloud hindered positive identification of the target and quite suddenly F/Lt Trenouth and crew dived through the cloud and identified the colored aiming points. The crews Lancaster was extremely low and the aircraft was battered from the bomb blasts below resulting in the whole aircraft trembling from the impacts. The next day Ronald Walker produced a full report for the newspaper.

Back at dispersal, the ground crew inspected the Lancaster for damage from the previous raid and found a flak hole in the wing that had narrowly missed the main fuel tanks in the starboard wing. The passenger had come close to writing his own epitaph.

Two Ju88s Destroyed

At around this period of the Horton crew's tour of operations, they witnessed two enemy fighters being shot down by the 622 Squadron Lancaster being flown by F/Lt Hargreaves. Through further research it was possible for the author to have an account of the attack relayed to him by the flight engineer in the Hargreaves crew, Sergeant Chandler. Both aircrews' accounts of the combat are identical and witnessed by other crews belonging to the squadron. However both crews have conflicting dates for the incident. F/O Horton and crew record the incident happening on 14th June whilst returning from a mission to Le Havre. Sergeant Chandler records the incident occurring on 5th July whilst returning from Wizernes. The official squadron operational records books record the incident occurring on 5th July and the rear gunner in S/Ldr Allen's crew (F/Lt J. Gray) confirms that the incident happening on 5th July, target Wizernes. The anomaly surrounding the date recorded by F/O Horton and crew is unexplained and conjecture would suggest that an error occurred whilst the crew filled in their logbooks at the end of the month. Whatever the actual date of the actual shooting down of two German fighters in succession, it was an incredible feat and one worthy of mention in the squadron records books. The two gunners in F/Lt Hargreaves crew were awarded immediate DFM's.

Sitting in his mid upper turret on the night in question Bernard Dye could see the other Lancasters flying in formation on either side to them. Sgt Dye's account of the incident follows:

> "Suddenly two enemy fighters dived in from astern to attack a Lancaster about 600 yards off 'Queenies' rear port quarter. I reported the sighting to our skipper and continued to watch intently. I could not see any tracer emanating from the rear turret, but I could clearly see the mid upper gunner blazing away. The first fighter was clearly hit and started to trail smoke which almost instantly turned to fire. The fighter dived down in flames and crashed into the sea. The second fighter, a Ju88, now made an attack presumably to avenge his comrade's demise. The mid upper gunner continued to fire and to my astonishment, it too burst into flames and spun down to the same watery grave. The action was recorded in 'Queenie's' log. When we were being debriefed back at Mildenhall, F/Lt Hargreaves and crew entered the room in jubilant fashion and claimed that they had shot down two German fighters. Subsequent checks on the coordinates were confirmed from all crews and they were found to correspond".

Paradoxically the Wizernes raid on 5th July has also gone on record as another attack by a German single engined fighter, this time a Focke-Wulf 190. Flight Sergeant White the W/op obtained a contact on 'fish pond' radar and moved to look out in the astro dome when he spotted a Fw190 emerging from the clouds. The enemy aircraft was on a reciprocal height and course to that of the Lancaster and it gave no indication of seeing F/O Horton's aircraft. Bernard Dye traversed his turret towards the fighter, readied his guns for action and opened fire. Flight Sergeant White witnessed Bernard's bullets hitting the Fw190 and in his excitement yelled 'you've hit him, keep firing'. The flashes from the gun muzzles began to destroy Bernard Dye's vision as he continued to fire, but he was able to see the Focke-Wulf dive down apparently out of control into the cloud below.

The jinx of 'Q' Queenie struck on the night of 20th July when LL859 was taken to Homberg by F/L Smith and crew. The Lancaster came down over occupied territory killing all seven crew members. On 25th July the skipper was promoted to Flying Officer and he was also assigned a new 'Q' Queenie which carried the serial No.LM241. The crew air tested the new Lancaster prior to that night's target of Stuttgart. Over the target the new aircraft was hit by flak but F/O Horton successfully nursed the Lanc back to base and repairs. Stuttgart was again the target on 28/29th July.

A relieved looking crew pose for the end of tour photograph with 'Q' Queenie. *Courtesy of Bernard Dye Air Gunner.*

The navigator miscalculated the wind and they had to dogleg to lose time resulting in the crew coming in behind the main bomber force. The bomb aimer reported that there were target markers going down behind them and that there was intense activity in the form of bomb bursts, guns firing and searchlights. F/O Horton turned the Lancaster onto a reciprocal course to join the bomber stream but by the time they were over the target the raid was over. Bombs were dropped from 22,000 feet and a course set for home. The crew were left unmolested by fighters on the return journey and witnessed a beautiful summer's morning over Normandy. Unbeknownst to the crew at the time the German night fighters had enjoyed great success and recorded one of their most devastating blows to Bomber Command. 39 Lancasters were shot down en route to the target due to a perfect moonlit night, which created perfect conditions for the fighters to approach from underneath the bombers undetected.

By this stage the crew started to believe that the end of the tour was in sight and during the first week of August 1944 they completed several more trips into France to destroy oil and flying bomb targets. The last mission for the crew was to attack the marshaling yards at Lens and after dropping their bombs from 15,000 feet they turned for home. Back at dispersal, Flying Officer Horton shut down the Merlins for the last time and breathed a sigh of relief. Each member of the crew had been through an experience unwittingly forming a bond of friendship that would last throughout their lives. For Bernard Dye the realization of completing a tour had yet to register with him. Fate appeared to be against him from the very start of his RAF career, however in retrospect that fate or luck had brought him through. His guardian angel would sit on his shoulder for many more years to come. Perhaps 'Q' was his lucky letter?

LM241 'Q' Queenie was assigned to another crew and took then to their deaths two weeks later over Russelsheim. The jinx had struck again.

20

Through it All

Pilot: S/Ldr J. Martin DFC
Nav: P/O J. Vaughan
B/A: F/O L. Granger
W/op: P/O K. Pollard
MUG: Sgt W. Rigby
R/G: Sgt J. Towns
F/E: Sgt H. Fielding

Ken Pollard's Royal Air Force service commenced, in earnest in May 1942 when he reported to RAF Wing Operational Training Unit. His initiation did not last long and he was required almost immediately to take part on a mission to Cologne. The Commander in Chief of Bomber Command, Arthur Harris wanted to strike hard at Germany and put on a show of strength that would break the resolve of the German public and their will to continue the fight. 'Bomber' Harris, as he would become known, wanted to send one thousand bombers to a target in one night and obliterate that target. The code name for this operation was appropriately 'Operation Millennium'. To achieve this feat the bombers and crews at the training units would be required to fly to make up the numbers. Therefore shortly after commencing his wireless operator training, Ken Pollard was on the battle order to attack Cologne on 30th May 1942 in a training unit Vickers Wellington twin engined bomber piloted by Pilot Officer Wilson. This mission was quickly followed by two more missions to Essen on 1st June and Bremen on 25th June, both successfully carried out. July followed a similar theme and Ken Pollard finished his training whilst undertaking missions to Hamburg on 28th July (recalled) and to Düsseldorf on 31st July 1942.

On 21st June 1943 Flight Sergeant Ken Pollard arrived at RAF Mildenhall having been assigned to No.XV Squadron as his first operational squadron. He was immediately signed up to join the crew of Squadron Leader John Martin who was the 'C' flight commander and an experienced pilot. XV Squadron was operating the Short Stirling bomber. At this period in the war the Stirling was taking heavy losses due to its restricted operational height and the vast improvement in German defenses such as radar and night fighter units. XV Squadron had a proud heritage being formed before the First World War and it was considered an innovative squadron that carried out its duties in an efficient and effective manner.

S/Ldr Martin and crew were quickly in action and on 22nd June they were detailed to attack Balstrum in Stirling EF351 and again on the night of 25th June when they completed a mine laying operation in the Bay of Biscay. June finished with a trip to Cologne on 28th with Wing Commander Stephens at the controls. Operations in July included Cologne again on the 3rd July, Aachen on the 13th and Hamburg on the 24th. The heavily defended targets of Essen (25th), and Hamburg on 27th and 29th concluded a busy month for the crew. August commenced with a trip to Hamburg again on the 2nd followed by fighter affiliation, air tests and night flying training. Unbeknownst to Ken Pollard the operation to Nuremberg on the night of 10th August would be his last with XV Squadron.

New Posting

622 Squadron was formed on 10th August 1943 from 'C' flight of 15 Squadron as a bomber squadron equipped with Stirling Bombers. The formation of the squadron came about due to the expansion of Bomber Command after the successful campaign against the Ruhr and Hamburg. Its formation also coincided with the beginning of the long and costly 'Battle of Berlin', which would see the Stirling Bomber withdrawn from front line operations due to unsustainable losses.

Seven Stirling bombers and their crews were immediately transferred from XV Squadron to 622 Squadron to form 'A' flight. The squadron code letters were changed to GI. Among the transferred crews was S/Ldr Martin, Ken Pollard's pilot who took immediate charge of the squadron for the first ten days. The squadron was in action on the first day of its formation when it dispatched seven Short Stirlings to Nuremberg. Berlin was soon to become a regular destination for the crews of Bomber Command with the up and coming "Battle of Berlin", and aircrew often refer to this target as 'The Big City'. ACM Harris believed that destroying the German capital would seriously dent the morale of the German people and bring home to the people the realisation that the war could be brought to them in devastating ways. Harris wanted the assistance of the American 8th Air Force and he stated that together the Allies could "Wreck Berlin from end to end".

On 20th August Squadron Leader Martin stepped down as the Squadron Commander, relinquishing his duties to Wing Commander G.H.N. Gibson DFC and reverting back to flight commander. The experience for John Martin would prove invaluable. Secretly he

A FLIGHT AUGUST 1943

Date	Hour	Aircraft Type and No.	Pilot	Duty	Remarks (including results of bombing, gunnery, exercises, etc.)	Flying Times Day	Flying Times Night
					Time carried forward :—	899.25	365.10
12.8.43	2120	STIRLING MK III BK-766	S/LDR MARTIN	W/OP	(17) OPERATION - TURIN		8.15
15.8.43	1135	"	" "	"	N.F.T.	1.05	
16.8.43	1500	"	" "	"	AIR TEST	.10	
16.8.43	2005	"	" "	"	(18) OPERATION - TURIN (DIVERTED - HURN)		8.10
17.8.43	1335	"	" "	"	HURN - BASE	.55	
19.8.43	1145	"	" "	"	N.F.T.	.35	
22.8.43	1140	"	" "	"	N.F.T.	1.10	
23.8.43	2045	"	" "	"	(19) OPERATION - BERLIN		7.40
27.8.43	1125	"	" "	"	N.F.T.	.35	
"	2135	"	" "	"	(20) OPERATION - NURN'BURGH		7.05
29.8.43	1505	"	" "	"	N.F.T.	1.00	
						905.00	396.20
					TOTAL TIME ...		

SUMMARY OF FLYING TIMES
"A" FLIGHT AUGUST 1943.
DAY - 5.35 hrs.
NIGHT - 31.10 hrs.
SIGNED. J. Martin S/LDR.

Page from Ken Pollard's logbook showing that he was quickly in action after being posted to 622 Squadron on 11th August 1943. The mission to Berlin on 23rd August was significant for Bomber Command who lost 56 aircraft 7.9% of the attacking force. *Courtesy of K. Pollard.*

was relieved to be able to concentrate of flying and completing his tour of operations without the added pressure of setting up and managing a new squadron.

On 23rd August 1943 a force of 727 bombers set out to bomb Berlin including 622 Stirlings. The German defenses were considerable and the casualty rate was 13% including the loss of the Stirling flown by F/Sgt Rollett and serious damage to another Stirling by a night fighter. Remarkably the damaged Stirling was skillfully brought back to base by its crew.

Berlin was again the target on 23rd August. The 'Martin' crew attacked the German Capital in Stirling BK766, GI-G as a part of Bomber Harris's commitment and passion towards the destruction of the 'Big City'. The raid did not go entirely to plan and the Pathfinders had difficulty in identifying the center of the city with the result of bombing being spread out across the city. On a positive note, analysis suggested that it was the most effective raid on the capital to date with over 2,600 buildings destroyed or damaged. At 04:25hrs, seven hours and forty minutes later the crew touched down at Mildenhall exhausted after their ordeal. The de-briefing was a formality that they all had to endure, all the crews' wanted was a good meal and to fall into bed for a well-deserved sleep.

The Stirling losses continued to mount and on the 27/28th August Bomber Command attacked the city of Nuremberg with S/Ldr Martin again on the battle order. No casualties were received by the squadron on this raid however; the total Stirling losses amounted to 10% of the force. Raids continued to varying targets throughout September totaling six heavily defended targets in the Ruhr Valley for the Martin crew. Ken Pollard was appointed to a commission as a Pilot Officer on 11th September.

The month of October was inactive for the crew in an operational sense with only one mission to Frankfurt on the 4th and a period of well deserved leave and time to see family and friends. It is worth noting that the latter half of 1943 was a very difficult and challenging time for Bomber Command with the German night fighter defenses becoming truly formidable. A string of radar stations known as the 'Kammhuber Line' were used to detect incoming raids and the night fighters were directed to 'boxes' away from the flak defenses in which they would seek out the stream on bombers flying to or from the target. The bombers' gunners would

The target was Mannheim on 23/24th Sept 1943 when this bombing photograph was taken by Stirling BK766, GI-G. On the return journey the Starboard outer engine developed a fault and had to be feathered resulting in the crew diverting to land at RAF Tangmere. *Courtesy of K. Pollard.*

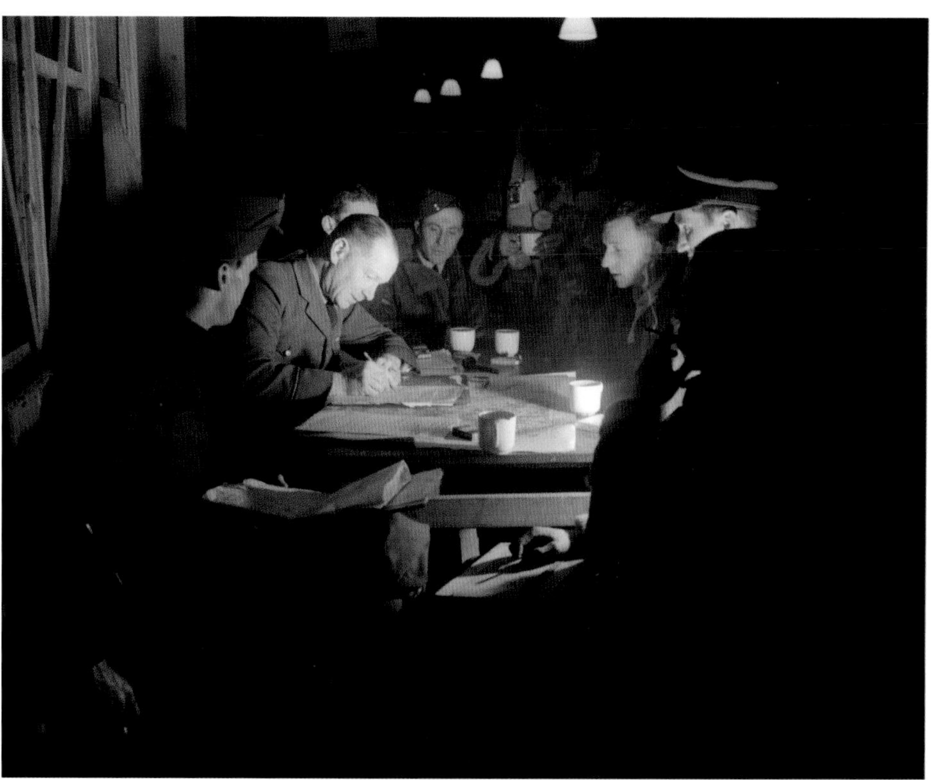

This amazing photograph captures the moment when S/Ldr Martin and crew are debriefed after a mission to Berlin on 22/23rd November 1943. L to R: F/Lt Mackay (Nav), F/O Dunbar (Intelligence off), Sgt Towns (R/G, partly hidden), P/O Pollard (W/op), F/Sgt Stevenson (2nd pilot standing), S/Ldr Martin (pilot), Sgt Rigby (MUG), F/O Grainger (B/A), Sgt Fletching (F/E). *Courtesy of K. Pollard.*

search the night sky intently for any signs of night fighters and instruct the pilot to carry out the 'corkscrew' maneuver.

The attacks on Berlin infuriated Adolph Hitler and he ordered the city's fortification to be increased. By late 1943 Berlin was the most heavily defended target of any city with a flak belt stretching 40 miles across and a searchlight belt some sixty miles across. The flak defenses comprised of mainly the very effective 88mm type artillery gun strategically placed around the city with three massive flak towers that contained eight 128mm heavy guns each. The eight guns could fire a salvo every ninety seconds and up to a height of 45,000ft. The exploding shells would send out a shower of molten shrapnel covering a diameter of 260 yards.

Berlin was the target again on the night of 31st/1st September 1943 with the loss of two 622 Stirling crews piloted by F/O Toy and F/Sgt Young. A massive 47 crews paid the price for a disappointing raid and the Stirling loss rate was a massive 16%. The catalyst for the withdrawal of Stirlings from front line service was the Berlin raid on the night of 22/23rd November 1943 when 50 Stirlings were part of the bomber force and 10% of those were lost. Again, S/Ldr Martin and crew were on the battle order and flew in their usual Stirling BK766. The crews' again successfully bombed the target witnessing the awesome defenses from many miles away. Collectively they wondered how long their luck would hold out whilst attacking Berlin. ACM Harris knew that the Stirling losses could not be sustained, and relegated the Stirling to secondary roles. On arrival back at Mildenhall they were debriefed by Flying Officer Dunbar and the moment was recorded for prosperity on film and depicted below.

With the Short Stirling now relegated to secondary duties, the squadron commenced the process of converting to the Avro Lancaster with ground lectures and familiarization visits to other 3 Group squadrons locally. At around the middle of the month the first Lancasters began to arrive at Mildenhall and equip both squadrons. The first Lancaster to arrive on 622 was W4163, a veteran deployed from another squadron and common practice for new squadrons to receive other squadron's cast offs. The Lancaster was immediately assigned the squadron code letters of GI-A and the crews began flying tests, including circuits and bumps to enable them to adjust to the Lancaster. S/Ldr Martin and crew completed two training flights during December, one on 21st December in

RAF Mildenhall received many distinguished guests. After debriefing from the Berlin raid on22/23rd November 1943, S/Ldr Martin and crew were introduced to two Saudi Amirs. L-R: F/Sgt Craig (2nd pilot), Sgt Rigby, Emir Feisal, P/O Pollard, S/Ldr Martin, F/O Grainger, Emir Khalid, Sgt Towns, Sgt Fielding, F/O Vaughan. *Courtesy of K. Pollard.*

Lancaster W4248, GI-Z and the other on 29th December in W4163, GI-A.

On New Year's day the last of the squadron's Stirlings were flown out to commence duties at Operational Training Units and special operations units. The business of working up to operational status continued but was hindered by the severe winter weather, which brought a high degree of snow and frost to the airfield. The first operation with the Avro Lancaster was promulgated on the battle order on 14th January 1944, target Brunswick. S/Ldr Martin and crew were allocated W4163, GI A. Flight Sergeant Thompson was assigned as a '2nd dickey' pilot under training. Brunswick is situated near to Hanover and had proved a difficult target for Bomber Command the year before due to the surrounding cities and the defenses deployed in that region. Almost 500 hundred Lancasters took off at 17:00 hrs and set course for the target. Shortly after crossing the north west coast of Germany the bomber stream were picked up by night fighters who enjoyed rich pickings all the way to the target and back.

John Martin and crew bombed on schedule and quickly left the target area which was infested with night fighters. The crew had witnessed several aircraft going down in flames and the utmost vigilance was necessary to survive. Ken Pollard was standing in the astrodome of the Lancaster facing aft and suddenly witnessed a streak of flame strike their Lancaster in the port outer engine putting it out of action. The skipper immediately feathered the propeller and went into a series of corkscrew maneuvers until he was happy that the night fighter had been lost. The crew continued on their course for home gradually losing height on three engines down to 15000ft where the Lancaster was comfortable and able to maintain height. On arrival at base the skipper tried to lower the under carriage and found that only one wheel would go down. He operated the emergency air bottle, which failed to lower the other wheel and unfortunately would not bring the retracted wheel up, forcing the pilot to attempt to land on one wheel. Mildenhall control was informed and the crew took up crash positions behind the main spar. John Martin put W4163 down on the runway as light as a feather and as the Lancaster lost speed the dead wing dropped and dug into the ground swinging the Lanc off the runway and onto the grass surrounds. The crew scrambled out unharmed and suddenly realized that their skipper was still on board. As they ran to the front of the aircraft they called out to him and received a reassuring "I'm OK, just waiting for a ladder".

Ken Pollard never flew with the crew again, having been ordered to stand down from operations. His previous missions whilst at the training units counted towards his total of thirty and High Command ordered him 'tour expired'. He remonstrated with the commanding officer to no avail and he therefore had to sit back and watch the crew complete another five operations before they were tour expired.

On 22 February 1944, Ken Pollard said his good byes to his crew and left Mildenhall for his new posting to 1657 Conversion Unit at Stradishall, a short distance down the road. Being tour expired he was now due a six month period at a training unit teaching others the skills he had learned. Ten months later in December 1944, he was posted to No.186 Squadron to commence another tour of operations. Between 9th February 1945 and the end of hostilities, he completed a further six operations against the enemy. His last mission was on 1st March 1945 to Cologne, the same target as his first mission back in May 1942. He had come full circle and endured a tour with Bomber Command that was commendable in every sense. When Ken Pollard joined the RAF the attrition rate for aircrew was at its highest with three out of every five members losing their lives. Over 55,000 aircrew were killed, 9,000 injured and over 10,000 became prisoners of war. Pilot Officer Pollard has beaten the odds and to quote a phrase, 'He had been through it all!"

21

Ground Crew
Unsung Heroes

Whenever aircrew talk about life on an operational bomber squadron, great affection is always shown towards the members of the ground crew staff. Without the diligence and professionalism shown by the ground crew, a great number of aircraft would not have reached the target and back. The Lancaster was a mass of mechanical engineering that required various specialists such as engine and airframe fitters, armorers and electrical engineers. Working in all weathers, the ground crew ensured that the aircraft was in first class condition on every sortie into enemy territory and maximized the chances of survival for the aircrew. Often referred to as 'erks', the ground crew would work from dawn to dusk servicing their allotted aircraft to the required standard to take to war. The methodical nature of their endeavors belied a dedication above and beyond the call of duty. The crews knew that a well serviced aircraft would contribute greatly to the lives of the aircrew and the respect for each other's proficiency was tangible.

The ground crew showed considerable distress at the loss of a crew and their aircraft and a great many aircrews owe their lives to the unsung heroes of Bomber Command. The pilot and crew would arrive on the dispersal and receive the Lancaster from the ground crew by signing the form 700 and the 'chief' would release the aircraft into the crew's custody for the duration of the mission. On the aircraft's safe return home the process of repairs and 'bombing up' would commence again. When a crew had finished their tour of thirty operations, it was customary to have their photograph taken. These photographs nearly always included the ground crew that they had built an affinity with; this was a measure of the mutual respect for each other.

Sergeant Ted Peck was a flight engineer and completed a tour with 622 Squadron during 1944. His appreciation for the ground crews epitomizes all aircrew sentiments when he makes the following statement:

> "We never forgot the devotion of the ground crew to our aircraft and to us. We depended on each other and we quickly established that if we were to complete a full tour of operations, we would need our aircraft operating at its maximum efficiency. The ground crews attained a standard of pride in their work that will never be bettered in any future theatre of war. They took the loss of 'their' aircraft and crew personally and grieved as though they had lost a brother. The most welcoming sight back on the dispersal at Mildenhall was the ground crew who extracted us from a battle weary Lancaster. We often brought the Lancaster back in a terrible state with gapping flak damage holes and burnt out engines. This never daunted the ground crews, they were just glad that we had returned home in one piece. The camaraderie built between us has stood the test of time, how many crews owe their lives to these unsung heroes."

A New Aspect of Service Life

Ernie Field served as a member of the ground crew at RAF Mildenhall. He has kindly contributed the following narrative about his experiences:

> "Mildenhall, pre-war, was a show place of the Royal Air Force. Not only was it Headquarters of 3 Group covering East Anglia but many early trials were held there. For instance, the first airborne lifeboat was dropped at Mildenhall using three parachutes and this idea was copied when man first came home from space. When I arrived at Mildenhall it was home to No.XV heavy bomber squadron currently flying the Short Stirling, and the new Lancaster planes. A Dinghy Section was being built in order that safety equipment could deal with dinghies in plane wings and other aspects of equipment coming into service. WAAFs would deal solely with parachutes. Also, a new Squadron was forming to be called 622 and I became part of this. All planes were kept at dispersal points and a crew bus made a continual circuit carrying servicing personnel too and fro. Every so often equipment had to be removed and inspected. The hardest part was removing the wing dinghy, so important should the plane ditch in the sea. The plane wing was covered with oil from the engine, it was a very precarious job to remove the dinghy for inspection, and one had to be roped to the wing. Furthermore, the longer a plane survived it became increasingly difficult to ensure the now worn rubber flange of the lid remained intact in flight. Every piece of safety equipment inspected both inside and outside the plane had to be signed for. So vital were these inspections a Court Martial loomed should negligence be proved.

While ground crew had to be meticulous in their approach to safety, aircrew themselves were rather nonchalant. Having been fitted with a harness to accommodate their parachutes they threw it in their lockers often taking out others. Consequently, when needed in flight they either fell out of their harness or were ruined for life. The Air Ministry took a dim view and consequently chose Mildenhall to create a Cloak Room system. For this purpose they built a hut on to the crew room so that crews collected their equipment on each flight and handed it back on return. No one wanted the job so we drew lots and I drew the short straw. It would mean almost permanent night duty!

The actual mechanics of the system was left to the person chosen. I set about sealing the concrete floor with isinglass to stop the dust, got racks for storage plus a large Perspex sheet on which to enter crew details. Every crew was then fitted properly and drew out equipment and handed it back after each flight. I got to know the crews of both squadrons quite well and each evening we would meet before operations in the tea hut and they would hand me letters to send to their parents should they not return. Losses were sometimes great and I remember the night when some forty nine men did not get home. Amid the American paraphernalia today the crew hut still stands proud and each year at our reunion, I stand outside and remember those young men who went through those doors never to return!

Even permanent night duty had compensations. Most nights the squadrons were active and I was allocated an assistant in the form of a WAAF from The Parachute Section. Especially when targets were long distant and

Ground crew servicing a 622 Squadron Lancaster prior to the night's mission. The front Perspex turret is receiving a thorough clean, aiding vision. Ground crew worked in all weathers to make sure that the 'maximum effort' was achieved for every mission. The aircrew never underestimated the dedication shown by these men and women, although they received little recognition from official quarters. The ground crew were assigned to individual Lancasters and after the aircraft returned from a mission they would set about overhauling the aircraft thoroughly. The serviceability of an aircraft could mean life or death to aircrew. *Courtesy of Mildenhall Register.*

Two photographs taken in March 1945 depicting 'B' flight ground crews who worked under considerable strain to maintain the aircraft in airworthy condition. *Courtesy of Mildenhall Register.*

H.R.H. the Queen speaks with Mildenhall aircrew during an official visit on 5th July 1944. Princess Elizabeth (now Queen Elizabeth II), stands near to her father, King George VI. The pilot who has blinked at just the wrong moment is F/O O'Brien RNZAF. *Courtesy of Philip O'Brien.*

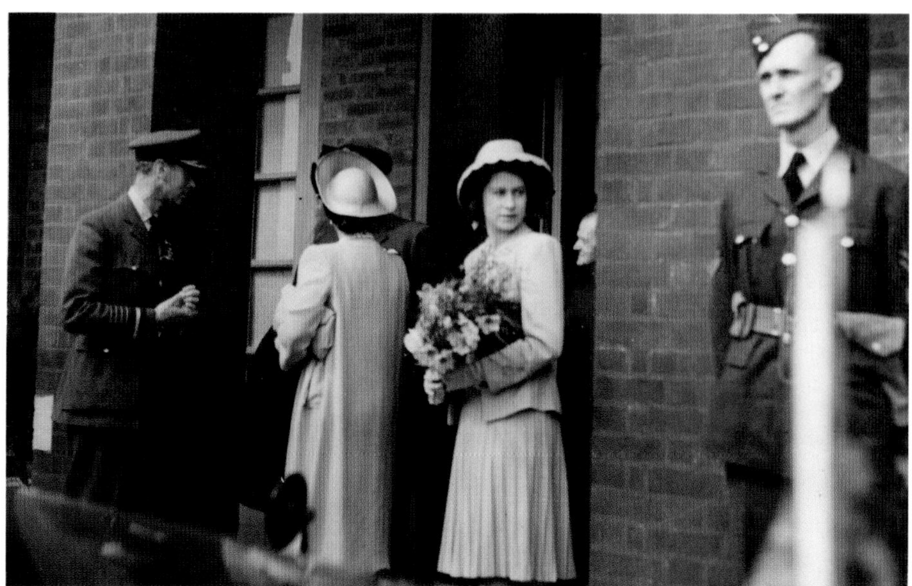

Princess Elizabeth holds a bouquet of flowers whilst her parents engage in conversation. *Courtesy of B. Dye Air Gunner.*

routine servicing was completed there was time to spare. Two beds were provided and we lay side by side hence my boast that I have slept with a WAAF many a time!

This procedure may have sounded romantic but one never knew when the Duty Officer would appear or a crew had to turn back. Returning aircraft from a raid was a busy time. Each item of equipment handed back was inspected closely for damage before placing on racks. The strain on the crews was only too apparent. They usually refused a tot of rum, so haggard were they; one can only say they were young men on departure but returned as old! It was standard procedure should a parachute ripcord be pulled a charge of 2s 6d was made and this was placed in a fund for aircrew dependents. Some were so pleased to get back they would pull the cord on return and pay up immediately!

Every crewmember wore a 'Mae West' a life jacket that contained a gas bottle and a dye block. In the confines of the aircraft, these often came adrift and much repair work had to be done to make them serviceable again. It was remarkable how an experienced crew survived yet 'rookie' crews were continually being replaced. Each crew had a number on my board and night after night, we were giving replacement crews the same number when their predecessors did not return. Obviously, no crew was given number 13!"

"I was at Mildenhall during the 1000 bomber raids when the sky was black with aircraft. What a morale booster it was for this country when these were coupled with American daylight raids also. An abiding memory; having been on night duty I was sauntering towards the cookhouse at mid-day complete with mug and eating utensils. A dispatch rider swept in followed by a royal car which came to a juddering halt. Inside sat the King and Queen who gave me a withering look. Apparently, they had followed the wrong despatch rider and the welcoming party was waiting at the main gate complete with top RAF 'brass'. After taking their fill in the Officers Mess the King asked for his hat. An attendant went to the cloakroom to find a row of similar gold braid ones. Nervously he approached his Majesty who, in a stuttering voice, said 'look in each one. King is written in mine'!

My pilot cloakroom system having been voted a success and was shown to the King and Queen and I understand the system is still used by the RAF today. The Commanding Officer was also very generous with praise when I was posted to Langar near Nottingham in August 1944. I will always treasure memories of my involvement in an operational station during a crucial period of the Second World War not forgetting the sacrifice in human life that ensued!"

Royal Visit

On 5th July 1944 RAF Mildenhall received an official Royal visit from King George VI, his wife H.R.H. Queen Elizabeth and H.R.H Princess Elizabeth. The purpose of the visit was to perform an investiture in the field and present medals to aircrew. Aircrew from both squadrons were told to assemble in No.1 Hangar and shortly after the Royal Party arrived with both squadron commanders for company. The names of the aircrew to be honoured were read out and the recipients from XV and 622 Squadrons marched proudly to stand in front of the King.

Following the investiture, the Royal Party inspected the parade and then joined members of both squadrons for an informal gathering. Both squadrons had been made aware that they were on operations that night and they had just been briefed for a mission to attack the flying bomb site at Wizernes. Due consideration was given to this fact and the crews were allowed to wear battle dress to greet the Royal Party.

King George VI listens intently to the gathered aircrew during his official visit. The airman trying to listen in is F/Lt T. Hargreaves DFC. *Courtesy of B. Dye Air Gunner.*

22

When Prayers are Answered

Pilot: S/Ldr R. G. Allen D.F.C
Nav: F/O W. Bishop RAAF
B/A: F/O C.D. J. Pennington DFC
W/op: P/O T. Paton
MUG: F/Lt D.B. Mason AFC, Résistance Medal, Dunkirk Medal
F/Lt T. J. Maxwell DFC (Replacement air gunner)
R/G: F/Lt J. T. W. Gray DFC
F/E: F/O J. Barker
(Ranks as per end of hostilities)

The 'Gray' family was very much a working class family at the outbreak of the Second World War and this reflected in the family struggling to sustain itself during ever increasing economic hardship. George and Beatrice were both hard working parents from large families that had endured the hardships of little food to eat and clothes to wear. The couple settled in a quiet hamlet named Dyke (Taken from the Roman word 'Cardyke' which signified the canal systems that they built in Britain during their occupation) in south Lincolnshire and were blessed with three children; John the eldest born in 1919, Arthur and Una.

The author's mother was Una and Beatrice was his grandmother. Beatrice Gray was a wonderful mother whose care and compassion for people and animals was only exceeded by her strong beliefs. Some years after the war, whilst watching hymn singing on a Sunday afternoon, the author asked his grandmother about her strong faith. She gave a very emotional and poignant reason for her strong beliefs. "God took care of my two boys during the war and brought them back to me, there were not many families that sent two boys to war and saw them both return unharmed". Whilst her two sons were away in different theaters of war, John over European war torn skies and Arthur serving as a Mosquito navigator with 82 Squadron over Burmese skies, she was saving money that she could ill afford as a donation to the Church on their safe return home.

This story will focus on the RAF career of John Gray, the eldest son who joined up at his earliest opportunity by walking into the recruiting office in Oakham Leicestershire (now Rutland) where he was working on a local farm. Originally, from humble beginnings, by the end of the war he would rise to the rank of Flight Lieutenant and receive the award of the Distinguished Flying Cross for bravery in action against the enemy. In total, he would spend thirty years in the RAF.

After the initial examinations and tests were completed for RAF entry, John Gray showed an aptitude to be trained as an air gunner, a designation originally amalgamated with the wireless operator training program and later established as an outright specialist position within an aircraft. After a period of frustrated waiting, John Gray received a telegram to report to the Aircrew Reception Center at Lords Cricket Ground in London where he underwent medical and physical examinations to assess his suitability to become aircrew. He was billeted in nearby flats commandeered by the RAF for the purpose of housing new recruits and the daily meals were served in Regent Parks Zoo cafeteria. Most of the three weeks spent there focused on the aircrew being kitted out with their uniform and being given the various inoculations that were deemed necessary. For John Gray, the proudest moment was when he was issued the white flash to go on his cap denoting aircrew under training.

A three month period at the Initial Training Wing in Morecambe Lancashire followed and it was there that the trainees were introduced to a series of physical fitness exercises including running down the sea front and along the beach. The academic exercises included the dreaded course in Morse code and candidates were expected to achieve 12 words per minute or fail the course. In addition, the candidates had to endure lessons in English and arithmetic and they got their first taste of how to strip down and reassemble a .303 Browning machine gun. After some initial trouble with the Morse code, John Gray qualified and was sent on indefinite leave, being told that he would be contacted when required to attend air gunnery school. The RAF had a surplus of aircrew waiting to be trained and only a limited number of training facilities that could be utilized.

In early January 1944, John Gray received a communication from the air ministry informing him to report to No.3 Air Gunnery School at Castle Kennedy in Scotland. On arrival at Castle Kennedy John was allocated to a tent along with two other trainee aircrew and that is where he spent his entire six weeks under canvas. The weather during January was extremely cold and all aircrew slept in full uniform with numerous blankets. John Gray described Castle Kennedy as being very bleak and depressing in the middle of winter. He spent the entire six weeks feeling frozen to the bone and marching everywhere at double pace on the orders of over zealous instructors. In between the cold, there was occasional flying and several ground lessons to undertake. The flying was completed in obsolete Blackburn Botha aircraft that were underpowered and reputed to be highly dangerous in inexperienced hands. Several hours were spent in the air firing at air to ground targets and drogues towed by light aircraft. At the end of the course, John Gray was awarded his sergeant's stripes and air gunner's brevet, which he proudly sewed onto his tunic. Due to the backlog of aircrew training programs, the airmen were forced to endure an undisclosed period of absence before the next part of their training. The aircrews were given the opportunity to complete the air gunnery training again whilst waiting to be posted to an Operational Training Unit, or simply go on a prolonged period of leave or ground duties. John Gray accepted the challenge of completing the course again and he made the short journey to No.10 Air Gunnery School at Walney Island, already having qualified as an air gunner.

The instructors at Walney Island were an improvement on those at Castle Kennedy and they were experienced gunners who had either completed a tour of operations or had some operational experience. John was immediately subjected to more in depth lessons in arithmetic and he learned how to strip a .303in Browning machine gun in his sleep. He studied the theory of a bullet's trajectory and the capabilities of defensive armament compared to the formidable firepower fitted to the German fighters. John learned to distinguish between the two through aircraft recognition lessons. He was also taught that early recognition of friend or foe could be the difference between life and death. He familiarized himself with the technicalities of the various turrets in production, including the hydraulic systems and learned how to fix blockages and malfunctions whilst in potential combat positions. The aircraft that he flew was the Boulton and Paul Defiant which had a mid upper turret comprising just two .303 Browning machine guns.

Initially John flew familiarization trips and air-to-sea firing which was enjoyable. He progressed on to shooting at drogues towed by Avro Ansons which released the drogues over the sea at approximately 4-700 yards away. It was very difficult for the trainees to see the bullets hitting the target and they had no idea of their success until they landed and their strikes on the target were counted. Each trainee had the tip of his bullets marked with different color paint to identify who had the most success. The guns were fitted with a camera that recorded the gun action for crewmembers and they watched back their particular performance. At the end of the course, John qualified again but this time with an above average marking as an air gunner.

No.12 Operational Training Unit RAF Edgehill, Warwickshire 8th March 1944-18 April 1944

On 8th March 1944, John Gray arrived at No.12 Operational Training Unit at RAF Edgehill in Warwickshire to commence the next stage of his training and to 'crew up' with five other newly qualified aircrew as a bomber crew. John Gray remembers that Edgehill was a hive of activity with large numbers of aircrew newly qualified in all disciplines including pilots, navigators, wireless operators and gunners all milling around together. After a couple of days, a meeting was called and all the aircrew were to attend in a hangar. The time had come in their training to form themselves into a bomber crew and all assembled were in no doubt that if they did not 'crew up' then they would be placed together. John Gray recalls looking around the room and seeing complete strangers approaching each other and asking to join a particular crew. Whilst observing the free for all, John was approached by another gunner and asked to join him in a crew that only needed another gunner to have a full complement. The confident gunner was Flight Lieutenant Denis Mason and John wondered how he had achieved his rank so quickly. Denis had already completed one tour of operations on Wellington bombers with 102 Squadron. He was an experienced gunner that was to the liking of John who thought that he could learn from his experience. John agreed to join the crew but almost immediately stated that he wanted to be the rear gunner or he would look for another crew. Denis Mason admired his obstinacy and stated that he had already completed a tour in the 'rear seat' and that he did not mind being a mid upper gunner. With that established, he was introduced to the rest of the crew which comprised the pilot, Flight lieutenant Richard Allen, a South African who had been instructing other pilots to fly since 1942. The navigator was an Australian called Wally Bishop, a Flight Sergeant from Brisbane Queensland with a dry sense of humor and a more than adequate navigator he proved to be on several

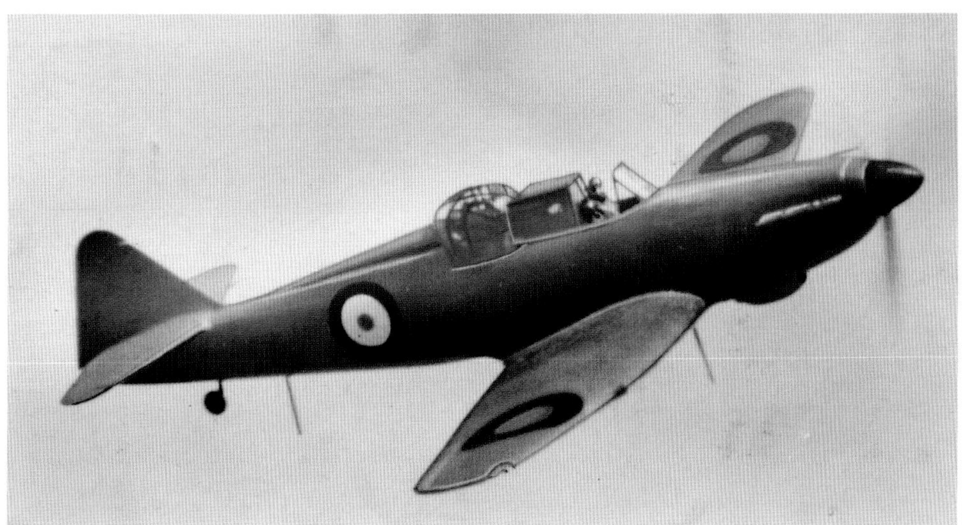

The single engined Boulton & Paul Defiant aircraft used by trainee aircrew at Walney Island, for air to ground gunnery practice. The Defiant was originally classed as a fighter with the RAF. During the early stages of the war, the Defiant saw action against the German fighters and discovered that the more agile and faster Me109's outclassed it. Subsequently it was removed from front line service and placed in a training role. *Courtesy of J. Gray DFC.*

occasions. The bomb aimer was Pilot Officer Cliff Pennington who had trained under the empire training scheme in Canada achieving high marks and an above average final assessment. Finally, the wireless operator was Flight Sergeant Tom Paton, a Londoner who was passionate about hitting back at the enemy after he witnessed the Luftwaffe bombing London on more than one occasion. The crew immediately had an affinity with each other and had faith in each other's ability to fit into a team ethos. John Gray was especially happy to be joining a crew with an experienced gunner who had already completed a tour of operations. This experience would prove essential as they progressed through their tour of operations and undoubtedly saved their lives on more than one occasion. No.12 OTU operated the Vickers Wellington twin engined bomber that by this stage of the war and been relegated to training duties. Nearly all the Wellingtons at OTU had seen considerable front line service and they were becoming increasingly difficult for ground crew to keep flying. Many aircrews lost their lives on training missions due to antiquated dangerous aircraft being utilized at training establishments. F/Lt Allen had no problems mastering the Wellington due to his previous experience and his circuits and bumps were almost perfect gaining the respect of all the crew. John Gray received the news that his commission had come through just before the end of the course and he was made a pilot officer, a very proud moment indeed. On 18th April, the crew successfully passed the course and was sent on leave awaiting a posting to a Heavy Conversion Unit.

The newly formed bomber crew at No.12 OTU at Edgehill in March 1944. The Vickers Wellington Bomber can be clearly seen in the background. L-R back row: F/Sgt T. Paton (W/op), F/Lt D. Mason (MUG), P/O J. Gray (R/G), F/Lt R. Allen (Pilot). Front L-R: F/Sgt W. Bishop RAAF (Nav), P/O C. Pennington (B/A). *Courtesy of J. Gray DFC.*

No.1678 Heavy Conversion Flight, RAF Waterbeach, Cambridgeshire 14th May 1944-29 May 1944

The Lancaster was a fantastic aircraft in every respect and its symmetry flowed over the human eye like a rainbow in the sky during a heavy shower of rain. The Lancaster had already established an aura of its own and its achievements to date made it a favorite airplane for bomber crews. In flight, the Lancaster was a delight to fly and its four Rolls Royce Merlin engines simply hummed in perfect pitch whilst delivering staggering performance.

Pilot Officer John T.W. Gray proudly wearing his Officers uniform on arrival at RAF Mildenhall in late May 1944. Whilst being fitted for his uniform at Greaves in London he bumped into ACM Harris and exchanged pleasantries. *Courtesy of J. Gray DFC.*

The Lancaster was crewed by seven crewmembers and it was necessary to have a flight engineer join the already established crews. The flight engineer's role was to ensure that the engine and fuel management systems were operating correctly within the Lancaster and this involved switching fuel tanks in flight once they had been drained by the four Rolls Royce Merlin engines. Therefore, F/Sgt Jim Barker augmented the crew as flight engineer. Jim Barker had joined the RAF in 1940 initially as a ground crew member spending time in Canada working on Harvard trainers. Eventually in 1943 Jim was sent back to England to join the OTU at Market Harborough, servicing the Wellington aircraft engines. Jim Barker took the opportunity to complete a conversion course to aircrew and his obvious choice was that of a flight engineer, his forte. The crew was extremely fortunate to have Jim Barker join the crew because his experience of mechanical systems was second to none.

Whilst at HCU the crew took part in exercises on high-level bombing, fighter affiliation and cross-country exercises during the

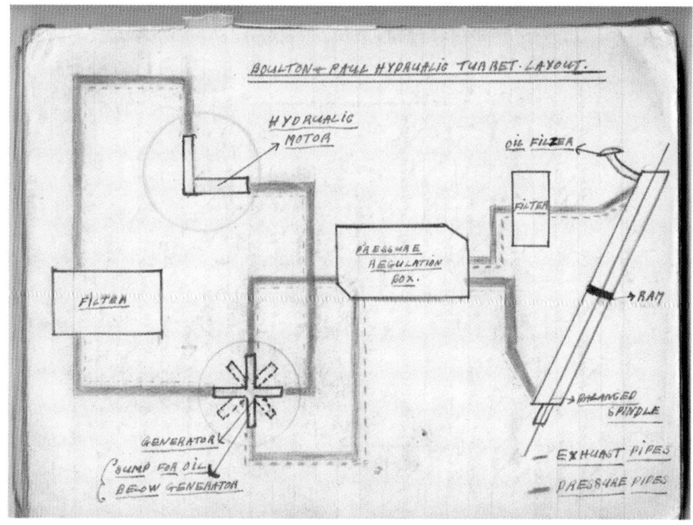

Page from the training notes of John Gray whilst at Gunnery School at RAF Walney Island. *Courtesy of J. Gray DFC.*

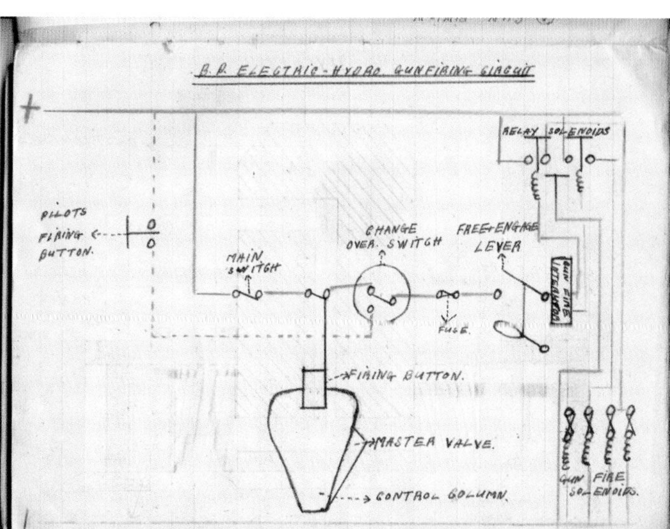

Training notes depicting the Boulton & Paul Hydraulic Turret Layout. *Courtesy of J. Gray DFC.*

day and night. These exercises were designed to test each aircrew specialist in turn, however by far the most challenging role was that undertaken by the navigator who had to ensure that the aircraft flew to the rendezvous point and back again without running out of fuel. F/Lt Richard Allen's previous experience on four engined bombers at Operational Training units allowed him to quickly master the Avro Lancaster bomber, its flying characteristics a joy compared to the ageing Wellingtons that they had experienced at Edgehill. On 29th May 1944 the crew was notified that they were now ready to commence operational flying with a front line bomber squadron. For John Gray this was a welcome relief after all the training he had endured. Therefore, it was on 30th May that

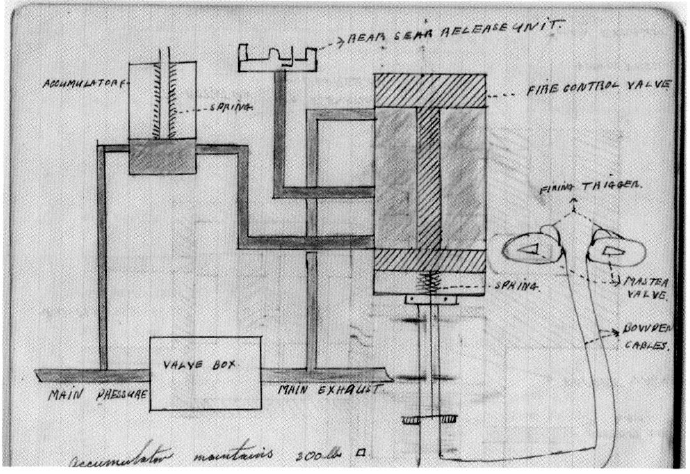

Palmer Hydraulic Gun Firing Mechanism. *Courtesy of J. Gray DFC.*

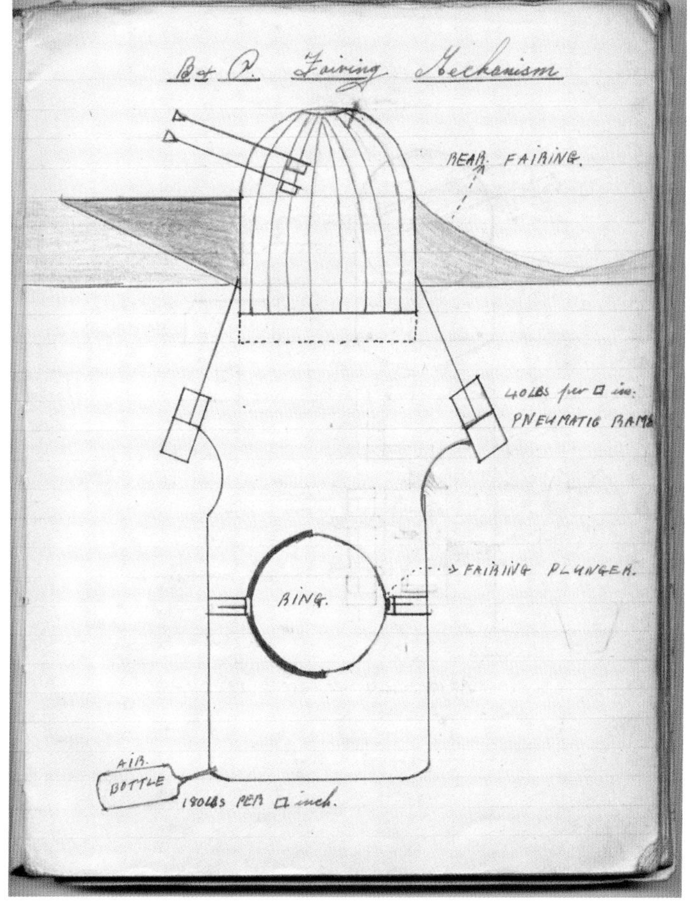

Training notes depicting firing mechanism. *Courtesy of J. Gray DFC.*

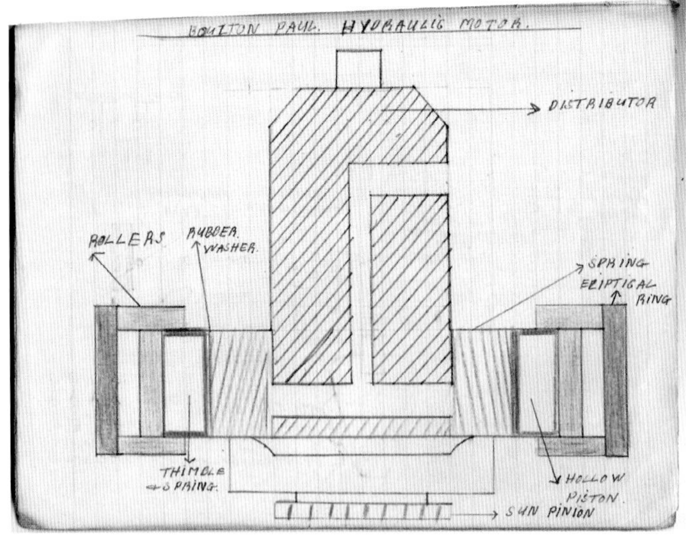

Hand drawing of Boulton & Paul Hydraulic Motor. *Courtesy of J. Gray DFC.*

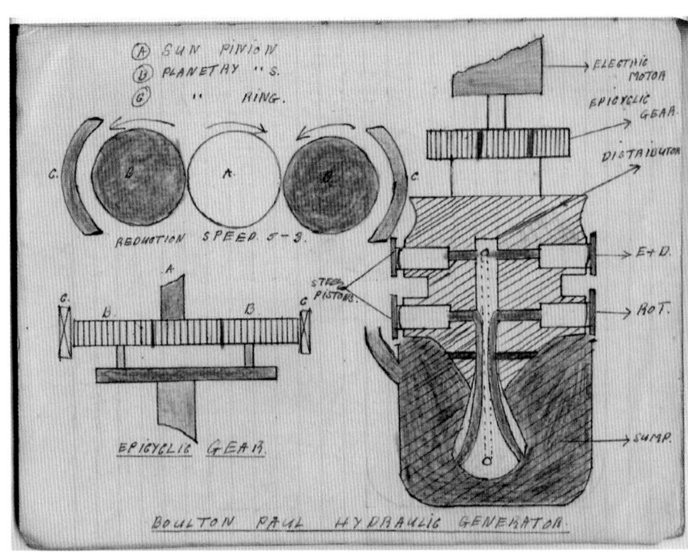

Hand drawing of Boulton & Paul Hydraulic Generator. *Courtesy of J. Gray DFC.*

the 'Allen' crew turned up at the main gate of RAF Mildenhall to join 622 Squadron.

Mildenhall was a pre-war base and home to XV and 622 Squadrons and provided the luxury of houses as opposed to the usual hastily built billets. The crew was introduced to the Commanding Officer 'Blondie' Swales DSO, DFC, and DFM who was a Wing Commander and held in high regard by all on the squadron. F/Lt Richard Allen had been posted to Mildenhall to replace an experienced operational pilot who was coming to the end of his operational tour. That person was a Canadian pilot called S/Ldr Hank Tilson DSO DFC. Before the crew could become operational as a unit, Richard Allen had to complete a 2nd 'dickey' trip with an experienced pilot which took place on 7th June to bomb the railway yards at Massy Palaiseau. The pilot who would take F/Lt Allen on his first mission was F/Lt Trenouth DFC RAAF who's skill and ability as a pilot would save the crew from death on this particular mission. The rear gunner in the 'Trenouth' crew was Pilot Officer Don Harvey an Australian from Maryborough. Some years after the war he recalled the take off on 7th June 1944 and his account is transcribed below:

> "With a second 'dickey' on board (F/Lt Allen) our skipper turned 'F' Freddie onto the end of the runway fully laden with bombs and fuel. The skipper applied maximum power to the engines and released the brakes and we started to roll. Almost immediately, after we had started to gather speed, a controller ran out of the control caravan and fired a red 'Very' flare just behind out tail. This indicated to us that there was another aircraft in the 'funnel', which could possibly be an enemy fighter. Sgt Pulman in the mid upper and I were both fully alert to the threat, we continued to gather speed and I noticed a stream of sparks flying past my turret on the starboard side. At the same time, I informed the rest of the crew that the other aircraft in the circuit was a four engined bomber of some description that was coming into land on top of us. The skipper knew that at this point of the take off his only option was to continue to take off or crash at the end of the runway and certain death. However, our skipper had another problem with a starboard engine on fire and Sgt Francis was trying to keep full power to the engine for as long as possible before he had to deploy the fire extinguisher. Sat in my rear turret, I could see the aircraft getting lower in the sky and gaining on our Lancaster with the distinct possibility that it would land on top of us. I shouted down the intercom to keep going and maintain maximum power to get us into the air. Our Lancaster struggled off the runway brushing some trees as it slowly gained altitude. We were clearly in no position to carry out our mission therefore we dumped our bombs on Rushford bombing range and turned for home. We were diverted to Newmarket to land, where we found numerous American bombers that had landed due to damage, fuel shortage or just lost from the days mission."
>
> "We were collected from Newmarket by coach and by the time we returned back at Mildenhall all the other crews had bombed the target and were back at base. Wing Commander Swales approached F/Lt Trenouth and explained that it was an American Liberator bomber that had nearly landed on top of us. The Wing Commander asked for an explanation as to why the gunners had shot out the tyres of the Liberator to which our skipper replied that it was not bullet tracers that you saw, it was an engine on fire. F/Lt Trenouth was congratulated on his successful take off with an engine out."

Aborted missions did not count as a mission and subsequently F/Lt Allen joined the same crew on 12th June 1944 as a second 'dickey' pilot when Gelsenkirchen was successfully bombed.

The crew's arrival on 622 Squadron coincided with the final preparations for the D-Day landings on 6th June and attacks against the German oil industry by night. By far the most supporting role for the invasion by Bomber Command was that against military positions in the invasion area. Bomber Commands' resources would be further stretched with the continuing destruction of railway, communication and oil targets in support of the advancing Allied forces. Continuous bombing by Bomber Command had reduced the threat to bomber aircraft allowing them to commence daylight bombing again in relative safety, although the Germans could, and did send up opposing fighters in large numbers. A further objective was added to the target lists when the Germans launched their flying bomb campaign around the middle of June, raining V1 rockets down on the inhabitants of London until late into August. On a happier note, John Gray received the news that he had been promoted to Flying Officer from 22nd June.

In mid August Bomber Command was removed from the control of the Supreme Commander and returned to the task set out in the Casablanca Directive. The contribution made by Bomber Command to the Allied invasion and subsequent support of the land forces had been immense. By early August, the Allied forces were firmly lodged on the Continent and on their way to Brussels slowly pushing the Nazi war machine back into Germany. Lord Portal and the combined chiefs of staff agreed that the new objective would be to progressively destroy the German military, industrial and economic systems. Therefore, the German oil, ball bearing and motor transport industries would become prominent targets once more.

On 14th June 1944 the crew was promulgated on the battle order for the first time to attack the 'E' boats and naval forces at the port of Le Harve as a part of the second wave of bombers. The mission was completed in daylight with fighter escort and initially thought of as an experiment for a return to daylight bombing for Bomber Command. The crew bombed the target successfully and was relieved to have come through their first mission unscathed. Several missions followed in quick succession to Valenciennes (railway yards) followed by seven attacks on flying bomb sites ending on 10th July. The attack against the V1 site at Beavoir on 2nd July was memorable for their Lancaster (GI-J, LL885) being hit by flak over the target area and the crew returned on three engines. Stuttgart was the target on the 24/25th July and the first of three eventful trips that the crew undertook to this well defended city during their tour of operations. The Lancaster for the mission was GI-K, L7576 an aircraft that was on its 98 mission and showing signs of considerable wear and tear. The Commanding Officer, Blondie Swales wanted the Lancaster to be the squadron's first centurion aircraft and told F/Lt Allen to take care of the 'old girl'. The mission went without incident for the crew apart from their first taste of the Ruhr defenses that brought a cold reality after the relatively easy trips to the V1 sites in France. Throughout the mission the pilot struggled to gain height in the Lancaster and the whole crew was worried that they would be struck with bombs falling from above. On arrival back at Mildenhall they filed a report to make everyone aware that the engines were extremely worn and due for an overhaul. On the next mission, to Stuttgart again on 28/29th July, GI-K was lost to a night fighter with the eventual loss of five crewmembers.

Stuttgart 28/29th July 1944

F/Lt Allen and crew lifted off the runway at RAF Mildenhall in Lancaster GI-J, LL885 at 21:55 hrs en route to Stuttgart. This particular Lancaster was destined to become a centurion Lancaster and complete 113 operations. Due to the actions of the crew on this particular night repelling a night fighter attack, three members of the crew were awarded the DFC. The following extract is taken from an account of the evening and recited to the author by his Uncle F/Lt John Gray DFC, the rear gunner on this particular night:

F/Sgt Jim Barker who joined the crew at 1678 Conversion Unit at Waterbeach. He had previously trained as ground crew, re-mustering to aircrew as a flight engineer. An extremely knowledgeable man in aircraft mechanical systems, he was a welcome addition to the crew. *Courtesy of G/C A. J. Pennington.*

The crew enjoy the peaceful countryside of Suffolk whilst not required for operations. The sports car belonged to Denis Mason. The two gunners, left F/Lt D. Mason & right F/O J. Gray. *Courtesy of G/C A. J. Pennington.*

Right: F/O C. Pennington, bomb aimer and John Gray. *Courtesy of G/C A. J. Pennington.*

F/Sgt Jim Barker, flight engineer. *Courtesy of G/C A. J. Pennington*

"On 28/29 July on our way to Stuttgart, having reached the Orleans area of France, we were attacked by a German night fighter, which suddenly appeared out of the darkness. The night was shrouded in bright moonlight and made the whole crew feel vulnerable and although I could see nothing down below the rear turret, I knew only too well that a Lancaster would stand out quite clearly to the German night fighters from below. We had already witnessed one Lancaster go down in flames which we believed to be GI-K piloted by F/O Peabody RCAF and crew, which was later confirmed on our arrival back at base."

Josselyne Lejeune-Pichon established the fate of the 'Peabody' crew more recently whilst she was researching her book entitled, 'Nous Combattons de Nuit au Squadron 622'. Lancaster L7576 GI-K crashed in an area known as the Vosges mountains in Alsac. The aircraft ploughed into a deep ravine known as the 'Noir Trou' (Black Hole) filled with giant fir trees, embedding pieces of metal into the trees on impact. The French locals retrieved three bodies from the wreckage and buried them with around 500 locals attending the funeral. Some of the crew had bailed out of the stricken Lancaster and F/O Peabody and his navigator, F/O Doe also Canadian, were hidden in the Maquis de Viomboid. The airmen were found by the Germans and shot where they stood. F/O Wishart (POW) was also in hiding and discovered by the Germans who shot the father and son who were hiding him. The young girl of the house was sent to a camp where she died. The seventh member of the crew, F/O Fiddick evaded back to England with the help of the French Résistance. The story continues:

"The night fighter a Junkers 88, came from underneath and the first thing we knew about the attack was when the bullets began to lacerate the rear part of the fuselage, tail and elevators. There was a terrific smell of cordite and some flares were set on fire. I ordered a 'corkscrew' and our pilot put the Lancaster into the maneuver, rising up, and then plunging down earthwards. I heard the call to put on parachutes so disconnected the radio transmitter and climbed back out of the turret. The mid-upper gunner must have misinterpreted this precautionary instruction for he immediately clipped on his 'chute' and bailed out! Reconnecting my radio in the fuselage, I noticed the rear door was open, so I knew the mid-upper had gone. I

F/O C.D. J Pennington. *Courtesy of G/C A. J. Pennington*

L-R: F/Lt D. Mason (MUG) P/O Paton (W/op) S/Ldr R. Allen DFC (pilot) F/Lt J. Gray DFC (R/G) P/O W. Bishop RAAF (Nav) F/O J. Barker (F/E) F/O C.Pennington DFC (B/A). Ranks as end of hostilities. *Courtesy of J. Barker.*

checked with the skipper about what was happening, and was told to hang on.

Our skipper and the flight engineer F/Sgt J. Barker, were both struggling to pull the bomber out of its headlong dive, and managed it at 1, 500ft, then jettisoned the bombs. We had lost the fighter, and the damaged Lancaster was turned for home with the bomb aimer operating the mid upper turret. One third of the elevators had been shot away and all the trims, and there were large holes in the tail plane. The skipper made as assessment of the damage and managed to obtain a degree of control of the Lancaster whilst heaving back on the stick to keep her level and decided to head for home, although alone and vulnerable to further attack. The concentration of the bomber stream was a major protection factor for a Lancaster against the individual interception controlled from the ground stations, and GI-J was now appearing as a neat little mark on the German radar tubes on the ground, a clear target for the German night fighter force."

"After about 30 minutes something blew off from the tail section and our pilot was able to ascertain a greater degree of control and we climbed up to 10,000 feet and removed parachutes. On reaching the Channel, the wireless operator sent out an S.O.S. so that we would be plotted over the sea in case we had to ditch. We crossed the Channel and then came the question whether to jump out or try to land. At this time I was giving the skipper constant updates on the state of the elevators, which we suspected would gradually strip. The whole crew had the utmost confidence in our pilot and we decided to stay with the damaged aircraft and attempt a landing back at Mildenhall. Our Lancaster was still shuddering in the turn and the pilot was having difficulty turning to the left, staying on course and reducing height to land, but eventually reduced height to 1,500ft. There were about 5 circles of aerodromes round Mildenhall so as we came near to base, skipper asked base to flash their lights on and off so that we could identify which was our landing strip.

Picture depicting GI-J LL885 the Lancaster that S/Ldr Allen and crew took to Stuttgart. This particular Lancaster completed 113 missions with 622 Squadron. GI-J's first mission was on the infamous trip to Nuremberg on 30/31st March 1944 when Bomber Command lost 97 bombers to the enemy defenses. This aircraft was almost a casualty when it was hit over the target by falling incendiary bombs from an aircraft above, which cracked the main spar. *Courtesy of Mildenhall Register.*

We crossed the boundary of our airfield at 140m.p.h. and the throttles were closed and the skipper very skillfully controlled the aircraft as long as he could and with one big bounce we were running along the runway. GI-J, LL805 landed back *at* RAF Mildenhall at 02.35 with extensive battle damage.

We slept soundly in our beds that night and the next day had a look at the damage. The Lancaster was a wreck around the tail and we were lucky to get back."

On examining his parachute on terra firma, John Gray discovered that it was full of bullet holes, and if he had bailed out then he surely would have been killed. Bomber Command lost 39 Lancasters that night, 7.9% of the force.

A night fighter in the Orleans area of France had attacked Richard Allen and crew en route to Stuttgart at approximately 01:14 hrs. Over the years, the research opportunities to establish just who shot at the crew have been greatly enhanced. The release of the Oberkommando der Luftwaffe and the Abschusse Kommission, the organization responsible for victory confirmations, has narrowed down the possibilities of who actually attacked the crew. Night fighter unit victory boards, rudder markings, personal accounts, supplement the listings along with logbooks and diaries. By far the most revealing research material was the 'Nachtjagd' official records, which revealed that an accomplished German pilot attacked Richard Allen and crew. That pilot was Hauptman Heinz Rökker, who attacked their Lancaster at 00:14 hours in the Orleans area of France. He recorded seeing the bomber spiral down towards earth without seeing it crash.

Hauptman Heinz Rökker was already an adept and proficient sharpshooter with 35 victories to his name and claimed GI-J, LL885 as his 36th kill after seeing its death plunge. By the end of the war, Heinz Rökker's total tally was 65 bombers destroyed including six in one night in February 1945. For his achievements, he was awarded the Knights Cross and Oak Leaves.

Sitting in the mid upper turret during the night fighter attack was F/Lt Denis Mason, an Englishman who at the time of volunteering for aircrew duties was residing in Australia. After the

Schräge Musik upwards-firing cannon installation with two MG/FF 20mm cannon, fitted to German night fighters. Initially, the Bomber Command crews' thought that the aircraft losses were due to flak guns. However, it soon became apparent that the fighters were firing non-tracer ammunition. A great many aircraft were lost to this weapon before the truth was discovered. *Courtesy of David Williams.*

Hauptmann Heinz Rökker 2/NJG. Based at Coulommieries in France, he finished the war with the award of the Knights Cross with Oak Leaves for destroying 65 enemy aircraft. *Author's Collection.*

Damage caused to GI-J, LL885 by a German night fighter in the Orleans area of France, en route to Stuttgart. *Courtesy of J. Barker.*

The JU 88 used its cannon shells to good effect as can be seen from the gaping holes in the fabric of the Lancaster. *Courtesy of J. Barker.*

death of his father during World War one, Denis moved to Australia in 1938 in anticipation of a new life and experience. As a boy his grandfather, now his legal guardian used to take him sailing on the Thames Estuary and effectively introduced him to a love of sailing and boats. He trained as an air gunner on the Isle of Man and completed a first tour of operations in Wellington bombers with 102 Squadron, which led to him being commissioned as a gunnery instructor at the end of his operational tour of duty. Denis' love of sailing was tested when he sailed a small boat to rescue soldiers trapped on the beaches of Dunkirk during a period of leave.

Denis Mason's first recollections of the night fighter attack en route to Stuttgart was when the enemy fighter's bullets struck the aircraft with sheer intensity and forced the Lancaster into a steep dive, presumably a dive that was unrecoverable. The pilot issued the instruction over the intercom to prepare to bail out which was misinterpreted by Denis and he clipped on his parachute and bailed out. He landed in a field at Montcresson near to Montargis in France where he was totally lost and confused. The Germans

F/Lt Denis Mason seen here relaxing beside a Suffolk river in early July 1944. His exploits after bailing out are worthy of remembrance and the award of the Air Force Cross and French Resistance Medal was some recognition of his bravery. *Courtesy of J. Barker.*

The Schräge Musik gun configuration utilized considerable firepower whilst firing from below. The force of the cannon shells exiting through the upper surface of the tail fins can clearly be seen. *Courtesy of J. Barker.*

The rear flaps are shredded as a result of the attack. *Courtesy of J. Barker.*

The house at Pressigny les Pins where the local teacher, Mme Marcelle Jouis, kept Denis Mason safe overnight. *Authors Collection*

did not send any soldiers to find him because his Lancaster had not crashed and he made his way to the village of Pressigny Les Pins. The local teacher, Mme. Marcelle Jouis, an extremely brave woman and a member of the local resistance found him and offered help after assuring herself that he was an Allied airman and not a German imposter. Satisfied as to his identity, the teacher took Denis to the Mayor the next day who provided him with false identity papers and instructed him not to speak in the presence of Germans. Denis was then moved to Ochamps Chateau in Thimory, which was used by the Alliance Maquis. It was here that Denis Mason met up with a 464 Squadron mosquito crew that had been shot down on the night of 25/26th July 1944. The crew, F/O John Walton RAAF (pilot) and F/O Charles Harper (Nav) had been on an offensive patrol over Orleans when their Mosquito was hit by flak, forcing them to bail out. A prominent member of the Maquis was a woman by the name of Mme Alcala whose codename during the war was 'Belette' and she took care of Denis, the Mosquito crew and several other airmen at great personal risk to herself.

Denis Mason was destined to stay in France and fight with the resistance until his liberation in late 1944. During this time, he took part in undercover operations with six other airmen designed to disrupt the Germans and rescue other Allied servicemen who had suffered a similar fate. One such rescue mission involved an English Commando and sixty SAS soldiers who were fighting valiantly against overwhelming odds. These soldiers had orders to harass the Germans and they had been fighting for some time causing them to become hungry and exhausted. They were all taken to Ochamps for shelter and to gather their strength. Once fit and well Denis Mason and six other airmen took the soldiers to a wood nearby to return to combat where they were engaged by the Germans and a bloody battle ensued. Initially the Germans captured the area, found an English uniform button, executed the forest guard, and burnt his body. The SAS soldiers returned with the airmen for company and recaptured the area taking several German soldiers prisoner, forcing them to bury the casualties. This allowed Mme Alcala to collect the burnt body of the forest guard and place him in a bag for burial. The battle took place around mid August, the Resistance lost around thirty men, and the SAS lost several of their regiment.

Once liberated by the advancing American forces, Denis Mason returned to England in early 1945 and he was posted to serve out the remainder of the war with Transport Command in the Bahamas. At the end of the war, he returned to Sydney Australia, the proud recipient of the Air Force Cross, the French Resistance Medal and the Dunkirk Medal.

The focus for Bomber Command was a return to the 'Pointblank' initiative that was promulgated during the Casablanca conference attended by the Allied Commanders in June 1943. Bomber Command, its preparation of operation 'Overlord' now completed, turned its attention towards incapacitating the German's ability to produce oil. The Chief of Air Staff, Marshal of the Royal Air Force Lord Portal, proposed a new directive to destroy the German's military, industrial and economic system. The Luftwaffe

L'Hey, flying bomb site in France. *Courtesy of G/C A.J Pennington.*

Photographs of bombing missions completed by Squadron Leader Allen and Crew in chronological order.

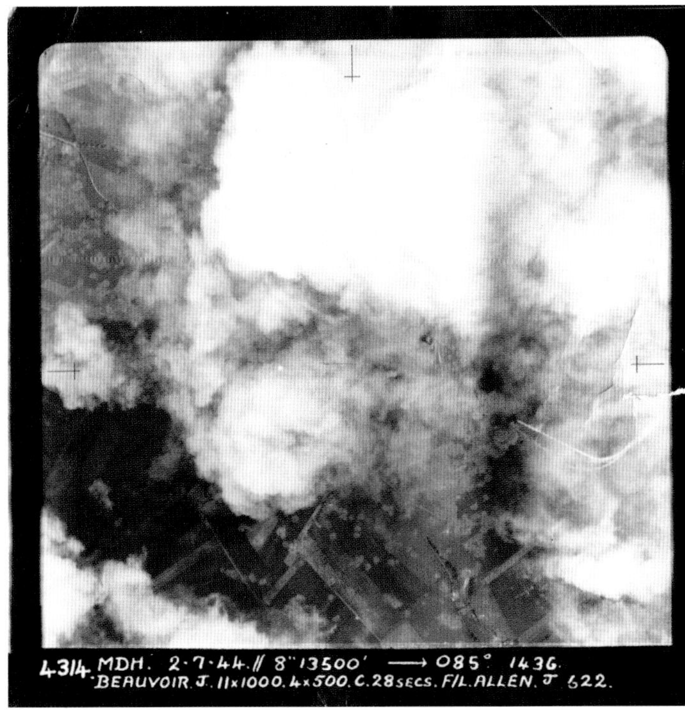

Attack on the Flying Bomb site in daylight at Beauvoir on 2nd July 1944. Aircraft hit by flak over target, returned on 3 engines. *Courtesy of G/C A. J Pennington.*

Flying bomb site at Wizernes in France was attacked on 5/6th July 1944. *Courtesy of G/C A. J Pennington.*

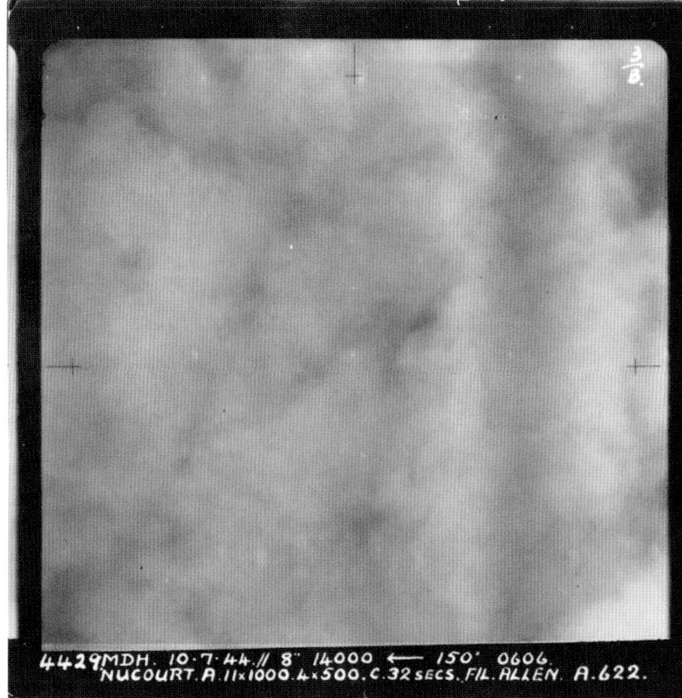

Nucourt, flying bomb site in France. *Courtesy of G/C A. J Pennington.*

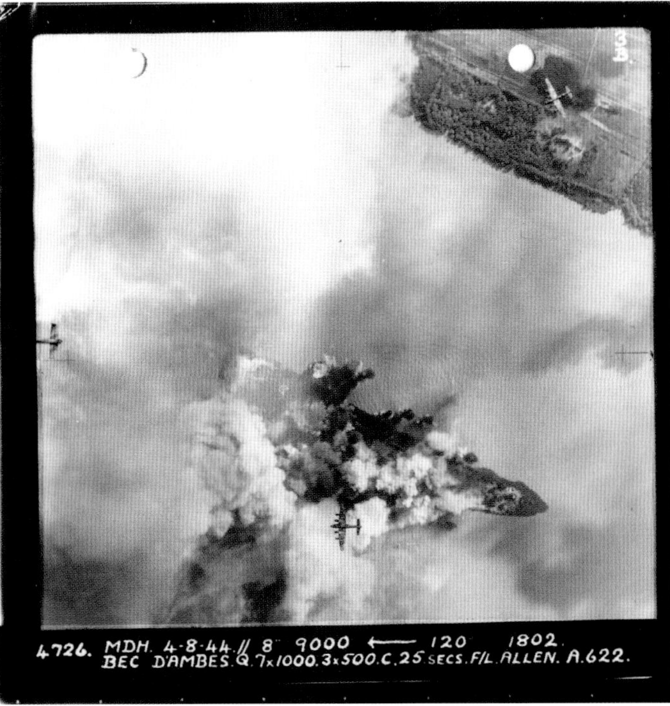

Oil storage depots at Bec d' Ambes. Radar counter measures were used for the first time in Mosquito fighters from 100 Group. *Courtesy of G/C A. J Pennington.*

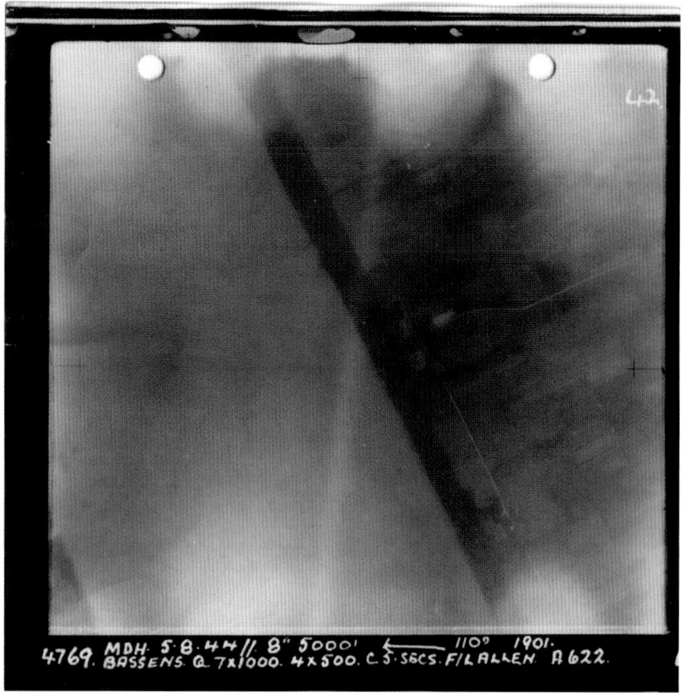

Bomb photograph depicting an attack on the oil storage depots at Bassens adjacent to the River Gironde at Blaye, Bordeaux. *Courtesy of G/C A. J Pennington.*

The railway yards at Lens in France was the target for a daylight mission on 11th August 1944. The objective was to restrict the German's capacity to refresh their front line troops with arms and equipment. *Courtesy of G/C A. J Pennington.*

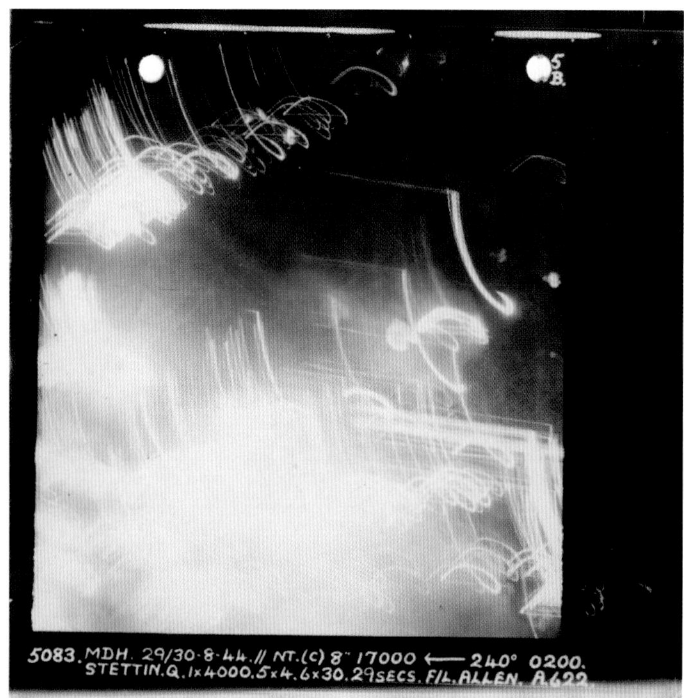

Stettin was attacked on the night of 29/30th August 1944. The crew endured an eight hour round trip to the heavily defended target. John Gray in the rear turret almost certainly shot down a single engined fighter over the target. 23 Lancasters were lost on the night. *Courtesy of G/C A. J. Pennington.*

A night mission to bomb the industrial center of Frankfurt on 12/13th September 1944. *Courtesy of G/C A. J Pennington.*

The first of two bomb photos depicting targeting the German troop positions around Calais in support of the Allied Armies. *Courtesy of G/C A. J. Pennington.*

Second photograph of the damage inflicted by the bombs falling on Calais. *Courtesy of G/C A. J Pennington*

The same target again seven days later. On this occasion, the target area was covered by cloud. The Master Bomber brought the bombers below the cloud base to bomb. *Courtesy of G/C A. J Pennington.*

On 16th November 1944, 622 Squadron supported other 3 Group squadrons by bombing the German troop positions at Heinsberg. The Allied Armies were experiencing strong resistance and asked for support from Bomber Command. The bombs falling to the target from S/Ldr Allen's Lancaster can clearly be seen. *Courtesy of G/C A. J. Pennington.*

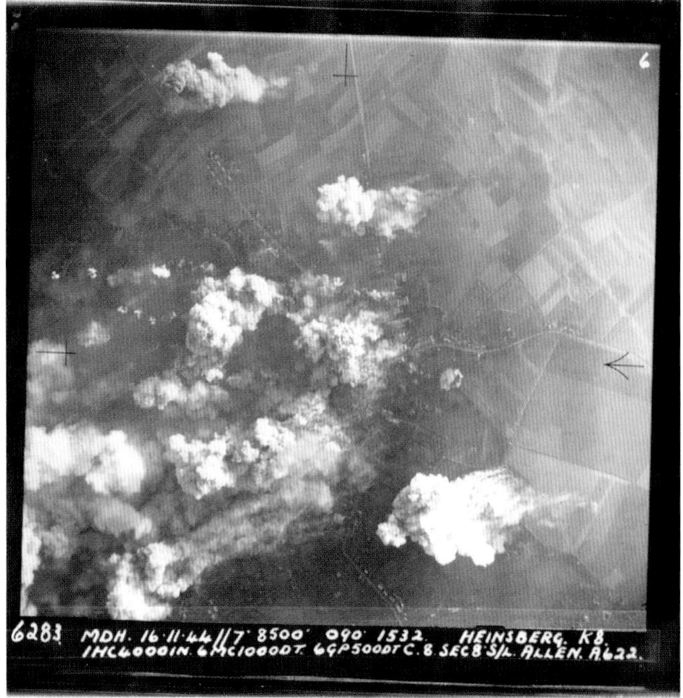

The bombs find their target at Heinsberg. *Courtesy of G/C A. J Pennington.*

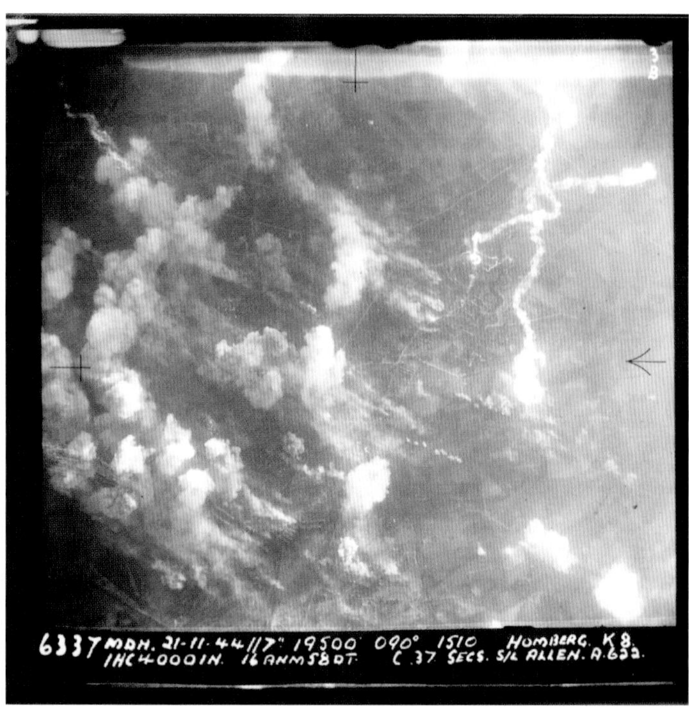

The oil refinery at Homberg received attention on 21st November 1944. Heavy, accurate flak always confronted the aircraft of Bomber Command whilst attacking this target. *Courtesy of G/C A. J Pennington.*

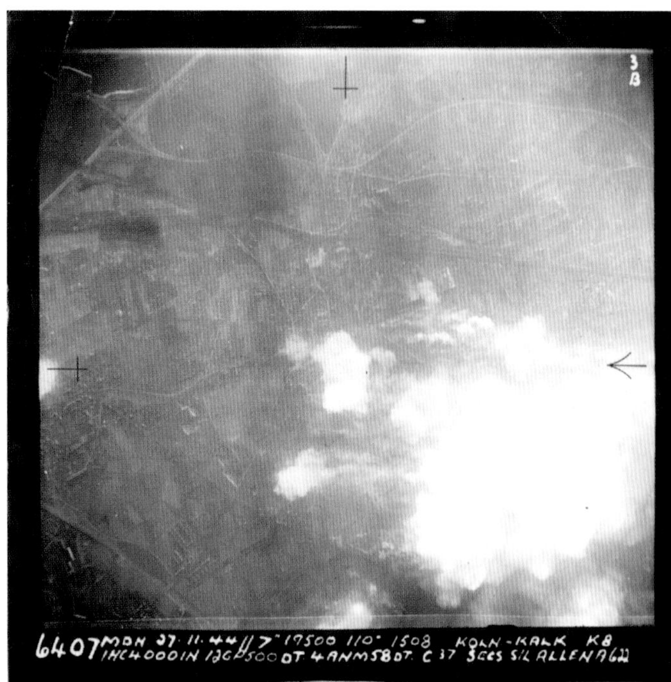

Koln Kalk (Cologne) receives attention on 27th November 1944. *Courtesy of G/C A. J Pennington.*

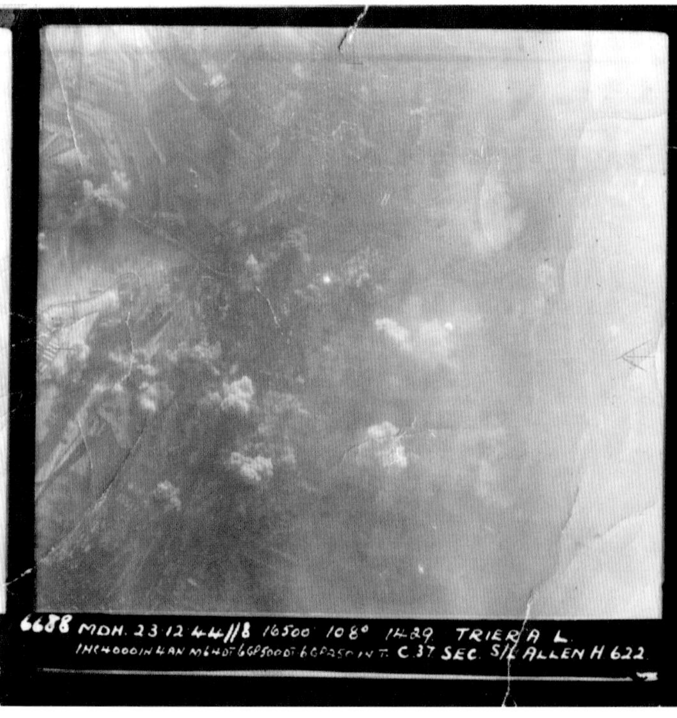

Towards the end of their 'tour', the 'Allen' crew attacked the railway yards at Trier in daylight. *Courtesy of G/C A. J Pennington.*

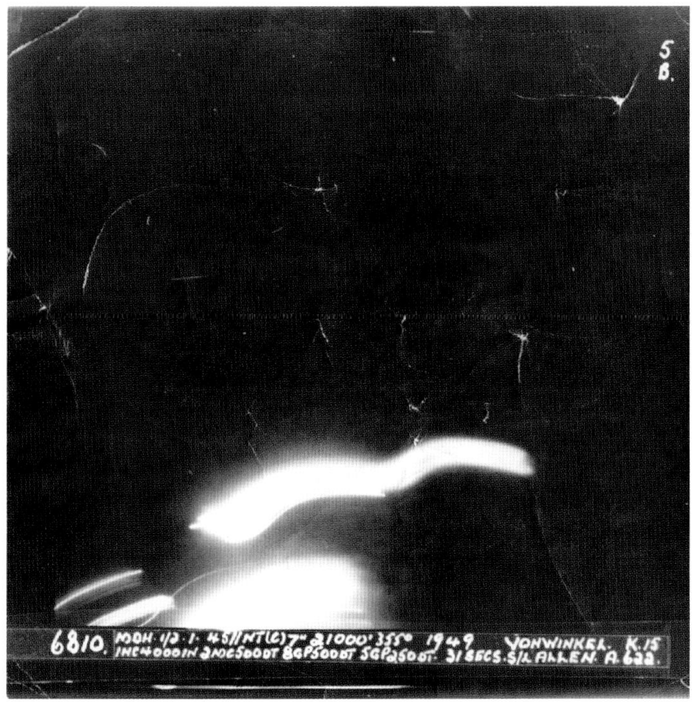

The last mission for the crew occurred on the night of 1st January 1945 when they attacked the railway yards at Vohwinkel. *Courtesy of G/C A. J Pennington.*

had been reduced to night fighter techniques and the night fighter squadrons had become accomplished at inflicting heavy losses on the bombers. The technological advances in radar meant that the bomber could no longer rely on the cloak of darkness to protect them and thus bombing Germany became a dangerous pursuit for the bomber crews. The developments with the Allied fighters such as the P51 Mustang and its long range fuel tanks meant that they could now escort the bombers in daylight to the target and back and defend the bombers with devastating effectiveness. The Allied Army advance across Belgium and Germany continued to gather momentum and on occasions faced strong resistance from the retreating German forces. Arthur Harris had promised to support the ground forces when requested and for the next few months German industrial targets and the support of the Allied forces became priorities for Bomber Command.

Operations continued thick and fast for the crew and during August 1944 they attacked, Bec d'Ambes, Bassons (Oil storage), Mare de Magnay (troop support), Foret de Lucheux (oil storage), Lens (railway marshaling yards) and Russelsheim in the Ruhr.

John Gray describes a tense mission to Stettin on 29/30th August 1944, a return trip of nearly ten hours:

> "At briefing the Commanding Officer announced the target as Stettin on the Baltic coast, a trip of nearly ten exhausting hours. Sitting cramped in the rear turret of a Lancaster for that amount of time is a daunting thought and the concentration needed to successfully defend the aircraft against attack is considerable.
>
> As a crew we were transported to the dispersal point and climbed aboard our usual Lancaster PD228, GI-A the aircraft assigned to the 'A' Flight Commander. I climbed into the rear turret having first secured my parachute on the clip in the fuselage adjacent to the rear turret doors. Once inside, I settled down to my preflight checks including plugging in my intercom, checking the ammunition tracks and their free movement, and finally the smooth operation (not firing) of the guns and turret manual rotation. The rear turrets fitted as standard on Lancasters were designed and built by Frazer & Nash, very cramped and designed specifically to be functional only. The only protection afforded to a rear gunner were four .303 Browning machine guns with an effective range of about 300 yards, anything beyond this was trial and error. Almost immediately the skipper checks that all the crew are in position and ready for take off, now is the time to report any faults and if warranted retire to the spare aircraft waiting nearby for just an eventuality. Our skipper demands strict radio protocols; only using the intercom system when necessary.
>
> Our take off was achieved with the skipper's usual aplomb and we set course for the enemy coast. Over the sea, I continually checked the turret's operation and hydraulic system; a malfunctioning turret could mean the demise of a Lancaster in battle conditions. Staring into the dark night for long periods plays tricks on the mind and I would find my mind wandering to relieve the boredom, suddenly I am given a reality check by the sight of a burning aircraft skipping across the sky and beginning its death plunge. The skipper breaks radio silence and asks us all to raise our vigilance or we could be next, whilst he weaves the Lancaster across the sky in an attempt to confuse enemy fighters trying to lock onto us. Flying a dead straight course presented the enemy night fighters radar with an easy target, as we had previously experienced the month before when we were attacked en route to Stuttgart, but that is another story.
>
> My electrically heated suit appears not to be working, although I know that it is, it is just extremely cold. I always removed the Perspex panel directly in front of my vision to allow me to search the night sky without fear of a false contact through a speck on the Perspex. The removal of the panel allowed the sub zero temperatures to penetrate the turret more easily and the cold would cut through to the bone intensified by my restricted movement in the turret. I was conscious of several other aircraft in the sky around us and considerable fighter activity, the flak was intense and the explosions buffeted us around the sky. I could see the tracer fire from the enemy fighters being pumped into the vulnerable wings of the bombers that contained the fuel and I witnessed two aircraft quite near to us fall earthwards trailing flames in a deadly plunge.
>
> Over the target the searchlights seek out targets of opportunity like beams of death waiting to suck the life out of a bomber. The result of a searchlight locking onto a Lancaster would trigger a barrage of flak guns to 'open

up' and enable the night fighters to see the target clearly. The nervous tension was unbearable as I scanned the sky for fighters approaching from the rear. Our only chance of survival would be for me to spot the fighter first and order the skipper to perform the 'corkscrew' maneuver to escape the fighter's attention. By this stage of the war, the German airborne defenses were deploying single engined fighters to infiltrate the bomber stream and shoot them down. These fighters belonged to a system called Wilde Sau (Wild Boar) where fighters used the searchlights ground fires to pick up enemy bombers without the use of a radar system. These free roaming fighters were a very effective addition to the radar guided twin engined fighters and accounted for large numbers of bombers over the target area.

The mid upper gunner broke radio silence to make us all aware that he has seen Me109 and Fw190 fighters attacking aircraft in the vicinity, his identification was assisted by the fires burning below and the pyrotechnics going on in the night sky. These aircraft are armed with formidable firepower including 20mm cannons that literally shreds open a Lancaster's thin metal structure. A fighter's range and armament could be used against a bomber from a distance that far exceeds the range of my four .303 Browning machine guns. My attention was drawn to a dark shape that was closing in from behind and the fires below allow me to identify a single engined fighter, which I know for sure is the enemy. My mind reverted to the lucky escape we had on the Stuttgart mission and I am determined that history will not repeat itself, although the pit of my stomach is telling me to get the Lancaster out of there immediately. I decide to wait for the right moment to give the skipper the order to corkscrew and he asks for a positive identification. As the fighter draws nearer I can clearly see the silhouette of a Fw190, a deadly adversary that potentially could blow us out of the sky. The fighter approaches rapidly and I was just about to give the order when his nose comes up and a stream of tracer bullets, mostly armor piercing comes towards us and narrowly flies over the top of my turret. I issued the instruction to 'dive port' and we plunged down and up in a stomach wrenching maneuver designed to lose our attacker. We level out and I search the night sky intensely for any further sign of his presence and I start to take things personally, why has he chosen us from all the aircraft in the target area he still wants to destroy us. I cannot help my thoughts drifting to my family and especially my mother who I know prays every day for my safe return.

My grip tightens on the firing handles, a natural reaction to accompany the tension and trepidation that fills my very soul. I again glimpsed a dark shape approaching and I informed the skipper to prepare for evasive maneuvers, at around 300 yards the fighter sits centrally in the gun sight and I fired a long burst of fire, willing my bullets to strike home and defend our Lancaster. The tracer bullets illuminated the night sky and I watched them drive into the fighter as I screamed 'dive port' through the intercom. The action is over in a few brief seconds and I witnessed the fighter turn away and dive down on fire. A warm sense of relief filled me and I could not help screaming 'I've got him' down the intercom, a fact that was reinforced by the mid upper gunner who saw the bullets strike home and the fighter fall away. A surreal silence filled the aircraft and my sense of smell was heightened allowing the smell of burnt cordite and

622 SQDN. MILDENHALL.

Time carried forward :— 66-37

Date	Hour	Aircraft Type and No.	Pilot	Duty	Remarks (including results of bombing, gunnery, exercises, etc.)	Flying Times Day	Flying Times Night
29-8-44	21-07	LANCASTER I 'R' P.D. 228	F/LT ALLEN	FLIGHT ENGINEER	19/ OPS. STETTIN DOCK YARD. CROSSED DENMARK + SWEDEN. SHOT DOWN FIGHTER. (POSSIBLE)		9-40

FLYING TIMES FOR AUGUST @ 622 SQDN.		DAY	NIGHT
TOTAL FOR MONTH	— FLIGHT ENGINEER :—	24-55	[illegible]
GRAND TOTAL		66-37	[illegible]

[signature] F/LT. O.C. 'A' FLT 622 SQDN.

TOTAL TIME ... 66-37

Page from the logbook of F/O J. Barker showing the recording of a possible fighter destroyed on the mission to Stettin. *Courtesy of J. Barker.*

Lancaster PD228, GI-A, the usual Lancaster assigned to S/Ldr Allen and crew. The G/H 'leader' markings are clearly visible on the tail fins. Also worthy of note is the H2S radar configuration directly under the fuselage and the gas detection patch directly behind the mid upper gunner's position. *Courtesy of J. Barker.*

hot oil to fill my nasal passage. The silence was broken by the crackling intercom and the skipper congratulated me on my efforts and promised me a few beers to celebrate if we came through the rest of the mission. The bomb aimer guided the skipper through the bomb run and we are again very vulnerable to fighter attack whilst we are flying straight and level. The intensity of the flak has not decreased and the searchlights still search the night sky for our presence. The Lancaster rose up sharply signaling that we had released the bombs and the bomb aimer called 'bombs gone' over the intercom, we had to fly a few more seconds on a straight and level path so that our photograph could be taken to record our target has been bombed. We turned for home with the skipper throwing our Lancaster into a turning dive and setting course for home and safety."

Operations continued for the 'Allen' crew under the new directives and they undertook a series of missions against industrial targets interspersed with Army support operations. Life on an operational squadron was a mixture of extreme tension and anxiety whilst on operations and an attitude of self indulgence when not on the daily battle order. One night that will always remain vivid in John Gray's memory was 20th September 1944, often referred to as the 'black day' by the squadron. The target for the day's operation was Calais to bomb the German fortified positions along the French coast to assist the Allied Armies. Richard Allen led the squadron and formed up over the base and set course for the target flying in 'V' formations, each 'V' being led by their Lancaster equipped with G/H radar apparatus. The weather was extremely bad with dense low cloud and whilst climbing through the cloud two Lancasters appeared out of the murk entwined together and spiraled down to crash near Wormington Essex. Fifteen air crewmen were killed in what was to be officially recorded as pilot error whilst in cloud. John Gray witnessed the horrific scene of the two Lancasters entwined together from his rear turret, one practically sitting on top of the other. Bits of the aircraft broke away in the collision including what appeared to be propeller blades from the lower aircraft. As if in slow motion, both aircraft peeled away slowly falling down in a deathly plunge towards the ground. The grim reality of the event has remained with John Gray to this day and he cannot comprehend the senseless loss of fifteen air crew due to an accident and not because of enemy action.

By this stage of the war 3 Group was equipped with the navigational aid entitled G/H which operated by receiving a signal from two ground stations and establishing an accurate navigational 'fix'. The advantage of G/H was that it could be used by numerous aircraft at the same time and it proved accurate enough for what was termed 'blind bombing' usually without visual identification of the target. This new device required some additional training by navigators and selected squadron navigators received the extra training, as was the case for Pilot Officer Bishop RAAF the navigator in the 'Allen' crew. Lancasters equipped with the G/H device were identified by painting their tail fins with two horizontal yellow bars. By this stage of the war, the Allies had near total control of the day skies. G/H 'leader' aircraft would lead a 'vic' formation of three Lancasters utilizing the principal of identifying the target and releasing their bomb load on the G/H signal for others to follow suit, thus ensuring a fairly accurate bomb spread onto the target.

The beginning of October saw two promotions for the crew with the skipper, Richard Allen being made up to Squadron Leader and the navigator, Wally Bishop was made a Pilot Officer. By the end of October 1944 the 'Allen' crew had built up the number of missions in their logbooks and they again visited Stuttgart on 19th October this time without incident. On 24th October Flying Officer John Gray reported to the Commanding Officer and received the news that he had been recognized as a first class gunner and that as recognition he would attend the Central Gunnery School at Catfoss to train as a Gunnery Leader. At first, he was reluctant to leave his crew and asked respectfully not to go because he wanted to finish his tour. He was assured that he would rejoin the crew on his return and that he would have the opportunity to complete his full tour of operations. He was congratulated by the rest of the crew and persuaded to attend the 'Gunnery University'.

The departure of John Gray to C.G.S allowed an opportunity for F/Lt Tom Maxwell DFC to join the crew and experience a period of continuity with the same crew. Tom Maxwell had bailed out on a mission to Stuttgart on 15th March 1944 and ventured back to the squadron where he had continued flying as a 'spare' gunner for crews that were short of a gunner. The remarkable story of Tom Maxwell's time spent in France and his return to the squadron can be found in the chapter entitled 'Behind Enemy Lines'

November 1944 commenced with a G/H mission to the oil plant at Homberg and the crew experienced heavy flak over the target area with five Lancasters eventually being lost to the

Heinsberg 16th November 1944. This remarkable photograph depicts S/Ldr Allen and crew whilst actually bombing the German town of Heinsberg in support of the American Armies. Lancaster PD228, GI-A can be clearly seen with bomb doors open and bomb impacts below. *CL1587 Courtesy of IWM.*

Flying Officer John Gray (back row 3rd from the right) at Central Gunnery School, Catfoss. Directly below F/O Gray (middle row 3rd from right) is F/Lt Wallace Macintosh DFC * DFM. F/Lt Macintosh was credited with eight and a half enemy aircraft shot down and he was the highest scoring air gunner in the RAF during the war. *Courtesy of John Gray DFC.*

German defenses. Two days later the crew was again on the battle order to attack another oil plant this time at Solingen and again it was successfully bombed.

On 16th November Bomber Command was asked to support the American first and ninth Armies in the area adjacent to Aachen and the Rhine. In total 1,188 Bomber Command aircraft from all Groups attacked the towns of Duren, Julich and Heinsberg. 3 Group specifically attacked Heinsberg with 182 of their G/H equipped Lancasters and S/Ldr Allen and crew participated in this Army support operation.

On 6th December 1944 John Gray returned to the crew from Central Gunnery School. In his absence, F/Lt Tom Maxwell had occupied the rear turret and now relinquished this position on F/O Gray's return. He had missed four missions during his time away and this was to prove impossible to rectify by the time the crew had completed their tour. However, John Gray did volunteer for a mission to Bonn on 18th October with F/O A. R Phillips to reduce the deficit slightly. Both crews were approaching the end of their respective 'tours' with Bomber Command. The Commanding Officer had resigned himself to losing S/Ldr Allen as a Flight Commander in the near future; however, this did not prevent him from restricting the number of missions the crew undertook during December 1944. John Gray used this time constructively by passing on his Central Gunnery School knowledge to all gunners on the squadron. He would arrange briefings and practical demonstrations for the gunners on the squadron and he worked closely with the squadron's Gunnery Leader in readiness for his future posting as a gunnery leader.

Subsequently the operations over enemy territory were less frequent and the crew would only complete another two missions during December 1944, bombing the Dam at Schwammenauel on the River Roer to assist the American Army in its advance. Secondly, an operation to destroy the railway yards at Trier; both operations went by without incident. On 1st January 1945 the crew completed their final mission attacking the railway yards at Vohwinkel, lifting off the runway at Mildenhall for the last time at 16:25 hours on New Year'sday and touching back down at 21:40 hours for the last time as an operational crew.

Flight Lieutenant John Gray DFC had completed a total of 27 operations against the enemy; his operational tour was cut short due to his period at the Central Gunnery School. During his 'tour', he showed courage whilst defending his aircraft and crew against enemy fighters and his Commanding Officer and his skipper recognized his accomplishments when he was awarded the Distinguished Flying Cross. At the time of writing John is now in his ninety first year and his caring and thoughtfulness shine through the emotion when he talks about his war time experiences. A great deal has been published about the bonds established with a bomber crew, and John Gray's admiration for his crew still exists to this day, evident by the framed photograph of his pilot proudly displayed amongst those of his children.

During the author's childhood he asked his grandmother (John Gray's mother) about her emotions and thoughts whilst her two sons were in Bomber Command. Her reply was short and succinct, "I prayed for the safe return of my two boys and God delivered them both back to me, there are not many mothers who could say that, my prayers were answered."

Postscript - Central Gunnery School

On 24th October 1944, F/O John Gray was posted to the Central Gunnery School at Catfoss, north-east of Beverley, Yorkshire. Five miles from the coast, the airfield was ideal as a training station. Its air gunnery and bombing range was in the North Sea area between Skipsea and Hornsea. The Central Gunnery School provided post operational training for air gunners who showed exceptional ability and leadership qualities coupled with the potential to become gunnery 'leaders' on an operational squadron. Often referred to as the 'Air Gunnery University', the emphasis was on delivering training in the latest technical developments and in particular, the gyro gun sight that was intended to revolutionize an air gunner's efficiency and accuracy. The course content was as follows:

Target practice at targets floating in the sea
Drogue firing
Photographic work
Turret familiarization and mechanical systems
Instructor and presentation skills training.

The aircraft used at the Central Gunnery School were Wellingtons, where most of the drogues were pulled by single-engine Miles Martinets. The drogues were towed by a thin wire rope and the intention was to shoot down the drogues in the most effective way.

The air gunner was trained in the art of 'deflection' shooting, a process where the gunner would fire ahead of the fighters approach in an attempt to have his bullets arrive in the same air space as the fighter, taking into account the speed and trajectory of the fighter and his own aircraft. When it comes to shooting down an enemy fighter the air gunner had to take a number of variables into consideration in order to be successful. These variables can be summarized as follows:

Distance from the target which is constantly changing.
The relative speed of your aircraft and your target.
The distance to aim ahead of the target, to allow time for the bullets to travel the required distance.
The angle at which the target is crossing one's own flight path.

The gyro gun sight was an amazing development and was developed from years of research and statistical analysis. To counter 'deflection' error the gun sight would resist movement causing a lag between the static ring of the gun sight and the gyro ring. The gun sight was designed to make the 'lag' equal to the deflection needed, for example, the faster the turret was rotated to track the fighter, more deflection would be required to be successful. The gyro resisted the greater speed of movement resulting in the

[illegible] 1st Battle Order for 1st January, 1945. No. 622 Squadron.

A/C NO.	[illegible]	CAPT. & 2ND PILOT.	NAV & W/OPERATOR.	A/B. & M.U. GUNNER.	R/GUNNER & F/ENGINEER.
PD.328	A.	S/Ldr. Allen.	P/O Bishop. P/O Paton.	F/O Pennington. P/O Maxwell.	F/O Gray. Sgt. Barker.
HK.651	B.	F/S Stille.	Sgt. Morgan. Sgt. Hewett	Sgt. Brabazon. Sgt. Dewey ~~& W.O. Hall.~~	Sgt. Jones. Sgt. Eastwood.
NF.939	D.	F/O Jordan.	F/S McDonald. Sgt. Robertson.	F/O Riley Sgt. Gregory	Sgt. Laymore. Sgt. Eyre.
PD.336	E.	F/O Flaxman.	F/O Stewart F/O Soderberg	F/O Adamson. F/S Sadler.	F/S Thurman. Sgt. Martin.
NN.709	H.	F/O Arkins.	Sgt. Colleran. F/Lt. Crocker.	Sgt. Hosegood. F/S Taskor.	Sgt. Walton. Sgt. Mountior.
HK.646	M.	F/O Thomas.	F/S Lowry F/S Charlesworth	F/S Gambell. Sgt. Kingston. & Sgt. Smith.445	Sgt. Davies. 950 Sgt. Ralph.
PD.332	N.	F/O Clark.	F/O Pantling. F/S Williams.	F/S Chaplin. Sgt. Bryant.	Sgt. Bryson. Sgt. Booth.
NG.299	O.	F/O Hussey.	F/O Simpson. F/S May.	F/S Dalton. Sgt. O'Connor.	[illegible] Sgt. Hand.
HK.617	Q.	F/O McHugh.	Sgt. Mead. Sgt. Turton.	F/O McIntee. Sgt. Harding. & F/S Chapman.	Sgt. Lee. Sgt. Pooley.
HK.614	R.	F/O Cook.	F/O Parry F/O Sherry.	F/O Gough Sgt. Savage & W.O. Friend.	Sgt. Hageety Sgt. Melaren.
NG.300	T.	F/O Gilmour.	F/O Tomsett F/SC Austin.	F/S O'Loughlin. Sgt. Davies.801	Sgt. Firth. Sgt. Davidson.
PB.795.	V.	F/O Nielsen.	F/S DeBasve. W.O. Dixon.	F/Lt. Middleton. Sgt. Morris	Sgt. Williams. Sgt. McCue.
HK.628	Y.	F/O Barnett.	Sgt. Grimsey F/S Sullivan.	P/O Hurditch. Sgt. Staplehurst	F/S Nichols. Sgt. Murrell.
HK.700	Y.	SPARE AIRCRAFT.			

Rations to be collected by F/Commanders and distributed to aircraft.
Briefing to be notified later.
F/S Darville's Crew to stand by for Radar.

(Sgd) G.K. Buckingham. W/Cdr.
Commanding No. 622 Squadron.

W/C Buckingham. F/Lt. Brignell. F/Lt. Cox. F/Lt. Johnson F/Lt. Noonan P/O Sleigh F/Lt. Berry P/O Hill.

Battle order for the last operation undertaken by Richard Allen and crew, a mission to bomb the railways yards at Vohwinkel on 1st January 1945. *Courtesy of John Gray DFC.*

End of tour photograph of S/Ldr Richard Allen & crew taken before their final mission on New Year's Day 1945. When this photograph was taken all members of the crew except the flight engineer, J. Barker were Officers and he would finish the war as a Flying Officer. Four members of the crew received the DFC for valor and devotion to duty. The keen eye will notice Tom Maxwell on the far right wearing the immediate DFC ribbon he received for evading the enemy. The crew are as follow: L to R: Ground crew, F/Lt J. Gray DFC (R/G), S/Ldr R. Allen (Pilot) DFC, F/O W. Bishop RAAF (Nav), P/O, Paton (W/op), F/Lt T.J. Maxwell DFC (MUG), Front: F/O J. Barker (F/E), F/O C. D.J. Pennington DFC (B/A), Ground crew. *Courtesy of G/C A. J Pennington.*

gyro sight showing a greater distance between the two rings and presenting the air gunner with a deflection shot.

On 6th December 1944, F/O John Gray qualified as a 'Gunnery Leader' and returned to Mildenhall to instruct other aircrew on how to become more proficient air gunners. On 1st January 1945 F/Lt John Gray DFC completed his tour of operations and he was posted to 90 Squadron at RAF Tuddenham as Squadron Gunnery Leader.

Citation for the award of the Distinguished Flying Cross for John T. W. Gray

Since his arrival on the Squadron in May 1944, Flying Officer Gray has demonstrated his skill as a Gunnery Officer with outstanding credit and distinction.

His coolness under fire is exemplified by the occasion of an attack on Stuttgart on the night of 28/29th July 1944, when the aircraft was attacked by a fighter and severely damaged.

The aircraft was precipitated into a steep dive, but notwithstanding the danger of such a situation F/O Gray held to his post and by skillful handling of his guns repelled the enemy and thus prevented further attack.

During his tour this Officer was attached to the Central Gunnery School and graduating with credit was posted to a Gunnery leader vacancy necessitating the curtailment of his operational tour, thus confirming the opinion held by his superiors that he is an Officer of more than ordinary merit.

Indeed, by his high sense of duty he commands the respect of everyone with whom he comes into contact and his handling of the situation of the night of 28/29th July typifies the sustained effort apparent throughout his operational career. For his meritorious service and outstanding devotion to duty I strongly recommend this gallant young Officer for an award of the D.F.C.

Date: 8th February 1945.
Signed S/Ldr J. A. Brignell Commanding Officer

Remarks of Officer Commanding RAF Station Mildenhall.

Strongly recommended. A fine young Officer who has set a high standard and maintained it throughout his tour. Signed W/C Buckingham.

Remarks of Air Officer Commanding No. 3 Group.

Recommended for the award of the Distinguished Flying Cross.

Signed: Air Vice Marshal Harrison.

Citation for the award of the Distinguished Flying Cross for C. D. J. Pennington

This officer has now completed an extended first operational tour throughout which he has performed his duties of Air Bomber with outstanding distinction.

Since his arrival in the Squadron in May 1944, he has been engaged against many of the enemy's important targets and by the determined application of his bombing skill has secured a number of brilliant photographic records of attacks well delivered.

On the night 28/29 July 1944 he was ordered to attack Stuttgart but on the way to the target the aircraft was attacked by a fighter, severely damaged and thrown completely out of control, but notwithstanding the hazard of the situation he maintained his position and rendered admirable support to his captain, and established himself as an outstanding member of a very fine crew.

Indeed the quiet efficiency of this officer both in preparation and attack has been a constant source of inspiration to all personnel of the Bombing Section and has contributed to a marked degree to the success of the Squadron's attacks.

His tour is noteworthy for its sustained and unsparing operational endeavor and is worthy of recognition.

23

Against Adversity
A Well Deserved D.S.O. Recipient: Pilot Officer T. Wilson

26/27th August 1944 - Target Kiel.

Distinguished Service Order. Awarded to commissioned Officers for distinguished services under fire for either general or specific acts. The order was established for rewarding individual instances of meritorious or distinguished service in war.

Pilot: P/O T. Wilson D.S.O
Nav: F/L B. Gillies D.F.C RAAF
B/A: F/O G. Harris
W/op: F/Sgt G. Whitehall
MUG: Sgt G. Harryman
R/G: Sgt A. Vaughan
F/E: Sgt H.H. Brown K.I.A.

Heroic Endeavor

On the night of 26/27th August 1944 Bomber Command dispatched 372 Lancasters and 10 Mosquitoes from 1, 3 & 8 Groups to attack the German Industrial city of Kiel. This particular city was a major supplier to the German armed forces and the Krupps engineering works was situated in Kiel. Overall the raid was a success, however for Pilot Officer Wilson and crew it was a very eventful night, during which one of the crew lost their life. Sixteen Lancasters were detailed to attack Kiel from the squadron however, one failed to take off due to a technicality.

Pilot Officer 'Tug' Wilson and crew were posted on the battle order to attack Kiel in Lancaster PA164 GI-P and they took off from RAF Mildenhall at 20.00hrs expecting strong resistance from the German defenses. Kiel is situated in the heart of the Ruhr Valley, and subsequently one of the most heavily defended targets that Bomber Command would attack. The route to the target was uneventful until they reached the target area. The crew guided the Lancaster over the target under an intense barrage of flak and searchlight beams. The bomb aimer, Flying Officer Harris guided Pilot Officer Wilson to the drop zone and they released their bombs on schedule. The moment the bombs had gone the Lancaster was hit by flak in the cockpit killing the flight engineer, Sergeant Brown instantly and hitting Pilot Officer Wilson in the head and body. The crew was now in trouble, with the Lancaster severely damaged by the flak, two engines being put out of use, and with the pilot suffering a head wound.

Fight or Flee

The crew evaluated the situation and decided to try and attempt to return to England, bailing out would surely mean that they would be taken prisoners of war. Sergeant Brown had taken the full force of a flak burst and he was clearly dead, therefore the crew was determined to take his body home to his family. The navigator, F/Lt Gillies gave P/O Wilson a course to steer for home and remained in the cockpit area assisting the pilot with flight engineer duties whilst tending to his head wound which was bleeding profusely. Fortunately the crew avoided any further attention form the German flak and fighters and they were given emergency clearance to land at Mildenhall with emergency vehicles on standby to assist.

By this stage the pilot 'Tug' Wilson was extremely weak from loss of blood; however he managed to land the Lancaster on two engines some thirty minutes behind the main force with the aide of F/Lt Gillies. Once safely down and all engines shut down the body of Sgt Brown was removed from the aircraft and Pilot Officer Wilson was rushed to hospital for medical attention.

The true extent of the damage to the Lancaster was discussed at de-briefing and the remarkable feat of bringing a badly damaged Lancaster home to Mildenhall was considerable. For his part in assisting the pilot, Flight Lieutenant Gillies RAAF was awarded an immediate Distinguished Flying Cross.

Pilot Officer Wilson was awarded an immediate Distinguished Service Order.

24

Fellowship

Pilot: F/Sgt Jim Campbell RAAF (later F/Lt DFC)
Nav: Sgt A. P. Galt
W/op: F/Sgt P. Jezzard
F/E: Sgt G. H. Hill
B/A: Sgt N. Shepley
MUG: Sgt R. Fallows DFM
R/G: Sgt William Hickling (Later W/O DFM)

From a young age William Hickling was interested in the Royal Air Force. His desire to fly was born from listening intently to aircrew experiences and stories. The lure of the RAF uniform and the associated panache was very appealing. On later reflection the reality of completing a tour of operations with Bomber Command would bear no resemblance to some of the stories that Bill heard.

William Hickling reported to the aircrew reception center at Padgate, near Warrington, Cheshire, in early 1944 and volunteered for aircrew duties. He underwent a series of aptitude tests designed to establish which aircrew position would most suit his ability. It was a mutual decision when he was accepted for air gunnery training, as there was a shortage of air gunners, and William gladly accepted as a way into the RAF.

Approximately three months later Bill received his call up papers and was told to report to No.14 Initial Training Wing at Bridlington. The accommodation at Bridlington was boarding houses and hotels that in peace time were favourite holiday destinations. Bill was billeted in a house in a street adjacent to the sea front and shared a house with eight other aircrew recruits in two rooms. The initial stages were mainly focused on discipline and square bashing and being shouted at by the Warrant Officer. Bill marched for hours on end up and down the sea front and through the town and then changed into his gym kit for running along the beach. The local people would give encouragement and their warmth was especially welcome during a difficult period. Bill and the other recruits were eventually assembled into a team worthy of being in His Majesties Royal Air Force.

With his discipline at an acceptable level, Bill progressed onto intensive classroom work on technical and air related subjects. The syllabus covered basic armament, gunnery and Morse code with a smattering of aircraft recognition. Bill recalls that there was someone on top of a tall building flashing an Aldis lamp message in Morse and they had to decipher that message. By far the hardest lessons were in navigation, maths and RAF law. Throughout the course they had to pass proficiency exams to progress, a failure equated to a 'backsquad' to complete the course again, an experience dreaded by most. Finally the course was at an end and they were dispersed to various gunnery schools around the country.

After 6 weeks of basic instruction, William Hickling was posted to Air Gunnery School to learn the fundamentals; essentially the skills required to stay alive and defend an aircraft from enemy attack. The course was interspersed with a continuation of lessons in Arithmetic and how to strip down a .303 Browning machine gun blindfolded. The instructors at the school were experienced aircrew who had completed a tour of operations. Their insight into the realities of war was a stark contrast to what he had learned before. Bill listened intently to lessons realizing that the most informed aircrew stood a better chance of survival. Eventually Bill and the other students got the opportunity to put practice into operation when they were assigned live air firing. The aircraft used were Vickers Wellingtons that were certainly past their best having completed numerous operations on various squadrons.

Bill Hickling opted for the rear gunner's turret, a position he considered one of the most important defensively and a position where a person could save the lives of his crew. Having seated himself in the rear turret, the Wellingtons took off and were quickly joined by training aircraft towing drogues that were meant to represent enemy aircraft. Each student was allocated around 200 bullets tipped with a different colored paint for identification purposes. Overall the course lasted around six weeks and William Hickling was awarded his sergeant's stripes having passed out as an above average gunner.

No.84 Operational Training Unit–Desborough

Sergeant Hickling's next posting was to No.84 OTU at Desborough Northants. It was here that he crewed up with pilot F/Sgt Jim Campbell, an Australian. At the time the RAF had an unusual method of 'crewing up'. An equal number of all aircrew designations were all thrown into a room and told to 'crew up', if they didn't they would be placed with aircrew that were left over

William Hickling proudly wearing his Flight Sergeant stripes and crown. On completion of his operational tour, he was awarded the Distinguished Flying Medal for devotion to duty. *Courtesy of W. Hickling.*

and nobody wanted to be a 'left over'. Bill Hickling states that he cannot remember how we actually crewed up, but he believes that Jim Campbell approached him with two of the other crew for company and asked him if he wanted to join the crew, to which he accepted. The three of them ventured around the packed room and collected the rest of the crew.

The OTU course content covered a mixture of the following:

Link trainer experience including bombing techniques
Gunnery combat maneuvers, air-to-air firing, fighter affiliation.
Bombing. High level bombing by day and night, bombing on cross-countries.
Navigation. DR navigation, cross countries including wireless fixes.
Operational training. Night and day exercises.
Drills. Dinghy, parachute, fire, oxygen, crash drills.

F/Sgt Campbell and crew eventually passed the course and moved onto Lancaster Finishing School at Feltwell in Norfolk.

Lancaster Finishing School

RAF Feltwell was situated in Norfolk and it was equipped with Avro Lancasters. The Lancaster required a seventh aircrew member in the form of a flight engineer and this is when Bill and crew first met Jamaican Sgt G.H. Hill.

The course started with circuits and landings in the Lancaster, an aircraft that the crew quickly came to appreciate as a delight to fly in. Each of the aircrew became proficient in their respective positions and Jim Campbell threw the Lancaster around the sky with assured confidence and a degree of mastery. The course lasted around three weeks and the crew finally received their posting to No. 622 Squadron at RAF Mildenhall a short hop down the road in Suffolk.

Squadron Life

Jim Campbell and crew arrived at RAF Mildenhall in early August 1944 at something of a turning point for Bomber Command. Due to advancing Allied forces and continuous bombing by Bomber Command they had reduced the threat to bomber aircraft, allowing them to commence daylight bombing again. In mid-August Bomber Command was removed from the control of the Supreme Commander and returned to the task set out in the Casablanca Directive. The contribution made by Bomber Command to the allied invasion and subsequent support of the land forces had been immense. By early August, the Allies were firmly lodged on the Continent and on their way to Brussels slowly pushing the Nazi war machine back into Germany. Lord Portal and chief staff agreed that the new objective would be to progressively destroy the German military, industrial and economic systems. Therefore the German oil, ball-bearing and motor transport industries would become prominent targets once more.

William Hickling provides below an account of his operational experiences and daily life whilst on the squadron:

> "Our first few days on the squadron were spent acclimatizing ourselves to Mildenhall and the luxuries of our own billets on this pre-war base. At the first opportunity we were introduced to the squadron's Commanding Officer, Wing Commander 'Blondie' Swales DSO DFC DFM who made us feel very welcome and told us that we were assigned to 'B' flight under S/Ldr Mitchell DFC, the flight commander. Blondie Swales was a charismatic character with a handlebar moustache and a charming personality. He was also highly respected among aircrew for going on operations with them on the most dangerous of enemy targets. He told Jim Campbell that he would undertake a trip as a second pilot and then the rest of us would join him for operations. One of the first duties for us as a crew was flight testing the Lancasters after the ground crews had serviced them. On one particular occasion, we took GI-P up for a flight test and we were enjoying the flight when the pilot decided to test the theory that a Lancaster could fly on one engine. Jim Campbell feathered an outboard engine and then feathered the other outboard engine leaving us with the same configuration as the 'Lancs' predecessor the Manchester. A lot of intercom chatters ensued and Jim decided to make the Lancaster into a Spitfire cutting another engine leaving us with a single Merlin to keep us in the air. On one engine the Lancaster slowly loses height and I thought that Jim had gone around the bend until he un-feathered the inboard engine followed by the other two Merlin engines. On the ground Jim explained that one of the capabilities of the Lancaster was that it could fly on one engine for a long period of time."
>
> "Life away from flying duties surrounded a surreal existence of playing hard because tomorrow could be your last day. A group of aircrew who were intense gamblers played every evening with a dice that was thrown onto

Studio photograph of Sergeant J. Campbell RAAF on successfully completing his pilot training and receiving his 'wings' brevet. By the end of his active service, Jim Campbell rose to the rank of Flight Lieutenant and was awarded the Distinguished Flying Cross. *Courtesy of W. Hickling.*

the snooker table. Each player had his own technique of throwing the dice which was a ridiculous sight, with aircrew resembling cricket bowlers. On one such evening a participant lost all his money and offered his car for sale around the room. Jim Campbell made him an offer and purchased the car there and then with the exchange of a set of keys. On another occasion a gunner who was a friend of the crew played a game and lost and I lent him £5.00 to continue. The money was never returned, as shortly afterwards he was lost on operations with the rest of his crew. I cannot remember the whole crew using the car very much; however, on occasions we would have a drive out with the skipper at the controls. By this stage of our 'tour' we were assigned our own Lancaster coded GI-P bearing the serial number PA164, with the Lancaster came a devoted ground crew who maintained the Lancaster in prestige condition. Aircrew and ground crew quickly built a mutual respect for each other and we had the utmost respect for the ground crews who worked out in all weathers to make the Lancasters serviceable for the next operation. The ground crew supplied Jim Campbell with aircraft petrol mixed with paraffin so that the tappets in the car's engine would not burn out."

Operations!

Bill Hickling continues his story:

"Our first trip was a mission to bomb a German fuel storage dump in Foret De Lucheux France. The French résistance had supplied the co-ordinates and the destruction of the fuel depot would severely disrupt the Germans. We all listened intently to our first briefing and especially to the weather and intelligence officers, followed by our individual briefing with our respective 'Leaders'. We were driven to our Lancaster GI-O, LM283 and we quickly settled into our respective positions within the aircraft and commenced preflight checks. The route to the target was uneventful and we bombed on schedule only to be immediately coned by a single searchlight that lit up our Lancaster making it almost daylight inside. The German searchlights were radar operated and once the radar had found a target the searchlight automatically locked onto its target. Being coned by searchlights was an open invitation to either the flak batteries or the night fighters to attack and crews had various methods of escaping the deadly beam. Our skipper dived down the beam and broke away at a low level into the darkness to return home alone and without the protection of the Bomber stream. Jim Campbell's quick reactions had averted danger though unfortunately our flight engineer

GI-O, LM283 the Lancaster that F/Sgt Campbell and crew took on their first mission and were coned by searchlights. *Courtesy of W. Hickling.*

had his ear drums damaged when the aircraft plunged down at top speed. He was grounded by the station doctor for the next four missions.

The mid upper gunner, Sgt Fallows and I had worked out a technique to use against the searchlights where we would instruct the skipper to take evasion action. For example if the beam was coming towards us on the port side, either one of us would give the instruction to turn to port so that we turned through the beam and subsequently lost the beam. If we had instructed Jim to turn to starboard then we would run the risk of having the beam follow us and lock on.

On the night of 9/10th August we were on the battle order to attack the flying bomb site at Fort D' Englos in France and we took another spare Lancaster this time LM167, GI-N. The Flying bomb menace had been a Bomber Command target since June when they first rained down on London with their destructive load. The flying bombs were launched from quickly assembled 'ski sites' that were erected in densely populated wooded areas making them difficult to identify. The destruction of the flying bombs on the ground was a priority to maintain the morale of the British public and the bombers continuously disrupted the German's ability to launch the weapons. After the Allied landings the launching sites were overrun and Bomber Command moved back to industrial targets deeper in the German home land. We bombed from 13,000ft and returned without incident.

On the 11th August we attacked the marshaling yards at Lens in France. The Germans were using this large marshaling yard to reinforce their front line troops with weapons and supplies. Bombing accuracy was interrupted for some of the late arriving aircraft by the smoke and dust generating by the first bombs. This was our first daylight trip and I felt extremely vulnerable to enemy fighter attack.

Our first excursion into Germany came on the night of 12th August 1944 when we appeared on the battle order to attack Brunswick in IM241, GI-G. We were loaded with one 2,000lb 'cookie' bomb and twelve 'J' type incendiary cluster bombs. The route to the target took us across Denmark, over the Baltic and then south to Brunswick returning back over Holland on the shortest possible route. This was one of our more stressful trips because of the fighter activity and the anti-aircraft fire over Brunswick which was the most intense that we had experienced. I witnessed several aircraft catching fire and continuing to fly on course for a short time and then slowly curve down until they crashed below. The Lancasters had undoubtedly been victims of the German night fighters that were equipped with upward firing cannons known as 'Schrage Müsik'. This technique proved to be lethal and took a fearsome toll of heavy bombers in the night battles. The night fighters used the technique of climbing underneath the bomber to stealthily regulate course and speed to be in exactly the right position to fire and ensure a 'kill'. When in position the night fighter would aim for the starboard inner (No.1) tank with the object of setting it on fire, to give the fighter time to get out of the way before the bomber exploded. This type of weapon favored the night fighters and to stand any chance of survival against the weapon one had to identify the approaching enemy before he could shoot at you. The German fighter always had the advantage of being below the bomber looking up into the night sky where very often a bomber would be silhouetted against the night sky. The Lancaster gunners looking down into the night sky would only see the darkness. By this time, it was practically standard policy to remove the central Perspex panel in the rear turret to improve visibility and I took the additional measure of standing up in the rear turret peering out into the night sky below. By utilizing this method I was able to instruct the skipper to take evasive action to avoid the fighters on several occasions.

Over the target our bomb aimer Sgt Shepley would issue instructions to the skipper on his course so that we could accurately bomb the target. On this occasion, we had a fault with the bomb release gear and on completion

F/Sgt Norman Shepley bomb aimer, had problems releasing the bombs over Brunswick. Seen here wearing the 'Observer' brevet that signifies that he was also trained in navigational techniques. Often aircrews were re-mustered during their training to fill vacancies in other aircrew positions. Norman Shepley was re-mustered to cover a shortfall in bomb aimer numbers. *Courtesy of W. Hickling.*

of our bombing run we found that we still had a full bomb load which meant that we would have to go around again and risk the flak and fighters once again. The skipper knew that it would have been extremely dangerous to circle back into the face of the 'bomber stream' and risk collision. With this in mind, Jim Campbell took a wide circle to the east and came behind the bomber stream which positioned us in the precarious position of being last over the target. On the second run our bomb aimer shouted 'bombs gone' and the skipper jerked on the controls which released the bombs."

"On the return journey we were introduced to our first experience of what we called 'flying onions'. The Baltic seemed infested with flak ships equipped with 40mm cannons that were very effective at lower altitudes. The shells contained tracer and it was disconcerting to watch them float up towards us in the night sky at a deceiving speed only for them to flash past at an incredible rate when they came close. The tracer also created an optical illusion that made the trajectory weave all over the sky, often appearing to go backwards to its point of origin. We later learned that the Brunswick raid was an experimental raid with no Pathfinders making the target. Each crew bombed with the assistance of its own H2S set and the results were disappointing."

Sgt G.H. Hill flight engineer in the Campbell crew seen here front row center. Originally, from Jamaica he remained in the RAF after the war serving 21 years in total. *Courtesy of W. Hickling.*

The Allies experienced fierce fighting from the German front line troops in France and on the night of 14th August the Campbell crew were briefed for a raid on Hamel in the Normandy battle area. At briefing, they informed the crews that accurate bombing was essential because the Canadian and German Armies were very close together. The Squadron dispatched 14 crews to Hamel and the Pathfinders dropped yellow target marking flares from 8,600ft. Unbeknownst to crews at the time was the fact that the Canadians sheltering in slit trenches were shooting up yellow flares identical to the Pathfinder's flares in an attempt to mark their positions. The 'Master Bomber' was made aware of the Canadian flares and tried to stop the bombing by calling over the intercom, unfortunately the Canadian positions were bombed resulting in thirteen Canadian soldiers deaths and substantial damage to Allied vehicles and equipment.

At briefing on the evening of 16th August the target was revealed as the industrial and port areas of Stettin. The target was nearly a ten hour round trip and to conserve fuel the Lancasters carried a reduced bomb load. At around 20:00 LM241, GI-Q lifted off the runway at Mildenhall and joined the bomber formation and flew to Cromer where they set course for Denmark flying over the North Sea. Once Denmark was successfully navigated they crossed over the south east corner of Sweden, a neutral country, and headed towards Berlin, later changing direction to Stettin. The constant direction changes were to confuse the German controllers and conceal the real target until the last moment in an attempt to keep the night fighters away as long as possible. The flak defenses were intense and the crew was glad to finally release their bomb load and dive out of the target area setting course for home.

Two nights later the crew was again assigned LM241, GI-Q for a raid on Bremen in which 288 aircraft took part from Bomber Command. The flight to the target was the usual hot spots of flak with Jim Campbell skillfully steering them through. As they approached the target the flight engineer Tony Hill and the skipper discovered a fault with the fuel management system. All four engines were unable to deliver full boost and subsequently the aircraft was unable to climb to the required bombing height. Reluctantly Bill and crew turned back knowing that without the photo flash photograph the trip would not count as a mission. The journey home was tainted with an air of dejection. Bill Hickling thought about the preparation that had gone into preparing the Lancaster for operations and the psychological preparation of the crew prior to take off, only for the bombs to be brought back. As Jim Campbell approached the English Channel the bomb aimer jettisoned the bombs in a designated area in preparation for landing back at base. To bring a Lancaster into land with a full bomb load was a dangerous undertaking and there was always the chance that the Lancaster had received battle damage that had gone unnoticed by the crew. The flight engineer's role was perhaps the most unsung of the crew for he had to know the mechanical side of a Lancaster inside out in case of emergencies. Throughout every flight Sgt Hill would maintain a log of fuel consumption and switch tanks in flight to balance the aircraft and ensure a steady stream of fuel to the Merlin engines. Tony Hill was of Jamaican nationality and remained in the RAF for twenty-one years.

After ditching their bombs the crew had to fly around the Channel burning off fuel to balance the fuel tanks so that they could land safely. All on board were very apprehensive about approaching England as a single aircraft because they had heard the stories of the British Navy shooting down aircraft after failing to recognize friend from foe. Pete Jezzard (W/op) gained clearance to land at Mildenhall and they touched down safely and taxied to dispersal where Jim Campbell and Tony Hill reported the engine fault. Official procedure still had to be adhered to and the crew had to endure a thorough briefing and ended up having a lonely meal in the mess.

At the end of August a new phase of the bombing campaign commenced. Bomber Command was released from the command of the Supreme Commander and this signaled a return to the doctrine of destroying the heart of industrial Germany, and in particular its oil and petroleum industry. The Chief of Bomber Command Arthur Harris and his American counterpart, Carl Spaatz agreed to place the oil and petroleum industry as number one priority followed by the ball bearing industry and thirdly the tank and motor industry. In addition the new directive would include the continued support of the armed forces and attacks on 'V' weapon sites.

F/Sgt Campbell and crew were surprised to find that they were to return to attack Stettin on the Baltic coast on 29th August in NF915, GI-U, another spare aircraft.

On this occasion the trip to Stettin would not be uneventful and the German night defenses would anticipate the intended target with

Ground crew pose with Lancaster NF915 GI-U adorned with the nose art of 'Oh 'U' Beauty' and showing 37 bombing missions. Whilst on a mission to Stettin on 29th August 1944, F/Sgt Campbell and crew were hit by flak over the target narrowly missing the Bomb Aimer and rear gunner. GI-U would be destroyed on the night of 24/25th December 1944 whilst on a mission to Bonn. F/Lt Perdue RCAF & two of the crew were KIA and four were taken POW's. *Courtesy of W. Hickling.*

Sgt R. Fallows DFM mid upper gunner. He assisted the crew over the target area by searching for fighters and bombs from above. *Courtesy of W. Hickling.*

the demise of 23 Lancasters left in ruins on German soil. Stettin was one of the most distant targets attacked by Bomber Command and took five hours to the target and five hours back. Bill Hickling in the rear turret found the vigilance and concentration required on such long trips exhausting right from crossing the French coast to the target and back. Bill picks up the story again:

"The German night fighters could attack at any time and I hardly dare take my eyes off the night sky below for fear of attack. Stealthily we arrived over Stettin and on the run in to the target the flak opened up and it was the worst that we had experienced with explosions sending shrapnel through the air and buffeting us from one side to another. Bouncing along through the flak battered sky I sometimes wondered how we could come out at the other end unscathed. We appeared to be at the tail end of the bomber stream. I looked astern and then, stood up and rotated my turret on to the beam whilst leaning forward and looking as far as I could see. There was no sign of the sky, only by looking sideways could I see gaps between the shell bursts. Most of the flak had lost their effectiveness and were just like miniature clouds; however the ones that concerned us were those bursting around us with an angry red center. These seemed to travel with us for a few split seconds and then be snatched away to the rear. Approaching the target the mid upper gunner Sgt 'Roly' Fallows and I were in charge of proceedings and on the lookout for fighter activity and any aircraft above us who may drop their bombs on us.

We both noticed a Lancaster from another squadron very near to the port side and just below. I reported its presence to the skipper. I actually waved to the rear gunner and he responded similarly. I turned my rear turret to scan to the starboard and there was a thud on the side of our plane and we were immediately pushed sideways and upwards. I swung the turret back to port and saw that the other Lancaster had disappeared; a shell burst must have made a direct hit on the bomb bay causing it to disintegrate. We had just dropped our bombs when our Lancaster was hit by flak in the nose section close to Norman Shepley the bomb aimer. A lump of shrapnel came through the nose where only moments earlier Norman had been lying marking the target. The flak left a hole in the floor about six inches in diameter, luckily Norman was unhurt. The sky was full of single engined 'wild sau' Focke-Wulf 190 fighters and aircraft were dropping out of the sky at regular intervals as a result of their attacks. The tracer from the fighters filled the sky and I was filled with trepidation and fear for our survival, by luck or miracle we arrived back safely at Mildenhall.

Back at dispersal we climbed out exhausted and very tense after our ordeal and I noticed some flak holes in the tail plane. I started to dig a piece of shrapnel out with my penknife when the Commanding Officer drove up in his car and walked over to me. He asked me how I was and then asked me if he could have the piece of shrapnel for his collection. My emotions were still running high and I told him to "Get stuffed, they were shooting this stuff at me and I'm going to keep it", he laughed and put his arm around my shoulder in a reassuring way. In other circumstances I would never have dreamt of speaking to the CO in this manner for he was much respected among aircrew. We called him 'Blondie' Swales due to his very blonde hair and handlebar moustache which were his striking features. By the end of the war he had completed three tours of operations and received the DSO, DFC & DFM for outstanding devotion to duty. Whilst Wing Commander Swales was in charge morale on the station was very high and he flew on several missions with crews as a support and guidance measure. Many Commanding Officers did the same however they chose relatively easy targets with little prospect of being shot down. 'Blondie' Swales always chose the most dangerous missions to fly and that gained him the ultimate respect, he would never expect his crews to fly anywhere that he daren't fly."

On 3rd September the crews attention was diverted to Holland and in particular, a German airfield in Eindhoven which was successfully bombed. The remainder of the month of September focused on the support of the Allied Army advance interspersed with trips to armaments factories in the Ruhr valley

Mid-Air Collision

On 20th September the Campbell crew was on the battle order to attack the German gun batteries at Calais on a daylight trip. For Bill Hickling this trip would be one of the most memorable of his operational tour for the futile and tragic waste of aircrew lives. Bill Hickling recalls the event that left fifteen members of aircrew dead on British soil:

"At briefing we were told to attack German positions around the port of Calais. Our assigned Lancaster was HK614, GI-R the usual mount of the 'B' flight Commander, S/Ldr Mitchell DFC who for some reason was not on 'ops' this day. On daylight raids we were instructed to fly in three 'vic' formations which were extremely difficult to maintain. Pilots up until this point of the campaign had never been trained in close formation flying. The degree of pilot skill necessary to keep a fully laden Lancaster in close formation was intense and physically and mentally draining. Our skipper could not see anything to his starboard side and had to rely on instructions from the mid upper gunner and the bomb aimer to keep him in position in relation to the other Lancaster on our starboard side. On instructions from both of them we were constantly moving from port to starboard. After forming up we set course for Calais and whilst climbing we entered very thick cloud which restricted our ability to keep in formation. We kept losing sight of the Lancaster on our starboard side when we veered too much to port. It was the most intense and frightening experience imaginable and it felt like ages before we finally broke through the clouds. What happened next is etched in my memory and at the time it was a surreal incident that I could not believe was happening. Two Lancasters appeared out of the clouds together in the leading formation, slightly ahead of us, clung together in a grotesque embrace after obviously colliding in the cloud. The two Lancasters appeared to hang in the air for a brief period and then fall backwards out of control and start spiraling down. All I could think was that the crews would have time to put on their parachutes and bail out, however inside the planes the crews would have been totally unprepared for an incident of this nature and the 'G' forces and panic stricken crews were unable to leave the doomed aircraft". The two Lancasters LL802, GI-M & LM167, GI-N crashed near the village of Wormingford near Colchester in Essex killing fifteen young men. Unluckily the crew of LM167 had been carrying an extra crew member who was visiting from another station."

Calais was again the target on 24th September, and they joined nine other Lancasters from 622 Squadron. The Germans were still resisting the Allied Army advance and the army requested Bomber Command's assistance. The previous trip to Calais was still fresh in the memory of Bill Hickling, and again, it would prove not to be an 'easy trip to France'. Bill explains:

"The weather conditions for the trip were atrocious with very low cloud down to 2,000ft over the target. The majority of bombers let go of their cargo on the sky markers delivered by the Pathfinder force, however several bombers including ourselves went below the cloud and bombed visually. The flak at this height was very accurate and eight bombers were shot down on this mission. As we broke through the cloud there were Lancasters on each side of us at slightly different heights and moving towards the target at slightly different angles. The greatest danger seemed to be the possibility of collision, a thought very fresh in our memories. On the bombing run Norman Shepley gave the skipper instructions and we two gunners alerted Jim Campbell to potential collisions. Through the intensity of the bombing run the crew ignored the heavy flak from below. On the return journey they were diverted to an airfield at Honeybourne due to the fact that Mildenhall was covered in mist and low cloud. Once landed, we were given a hot meal and sleeping accommodation. Unfortunately I had to sleep on the snooker table in the sergeant's mess, the luckier ones slept in armchairs. We took off for Mildenhall the following morning and the skipper decided to fly back at low level. We stacked all our gear, which we wouldn't need, such as parachutes and life jackets in the fuselage. We were all in a light hearted mood probably out of relief for surviving the previous day's mission. Norman Shepley the navigator, positioned himself in the nose of the Lancaster to map read back to base and to make sure there were no high obstructions in the path". In the rear turret, I felt naked without the bulky heated flying suit and life jackets. He was only wearing his flying boots and helmet which felt quite relaxing and enjoyable. Jim Campbell was also in a good mood and enjoying the stress free flying experience and decided to put the Lancaster through her paces. He followed a railway line and eventually crept up on a steam train with people hanging out of the windows and waving. He circled around again and repeated his actions out of sheer fun. As GI-R approached base Jim Campbell pulled the nose of the Lancaster up sharply drastically reducing the ground speed to an almost stall speed and then relaxing the Lancaster down into level flight. Jim Campbell was a very adept and confident pilot. His total command and control of the Lancaster was due to his natural strength from working as a farmer prior to joining up. Some of Jim's flying would make me float in his rear turret in a dive and then make him struggle to remain standing when pulling out of a dive. Jim Campbell's landings were another story and on occasions, he was very often too high forcing him to apply full thrust to the engines and go around again for another try."

Minelaying

Dropping mines in the waters around the Dutch, Belgian and French coasts were considered easy trips and were usually given to crews in the early stages of their tour of operations. Jim Campbell and crew undertook three mining sorties and all were not without incident. Bill Hickling hated the mining trips and considered them on a par with all other 'ops' for he particularly disliked flying over the Baltic Sea. Some of the Lancasters on 622 Squadron had been fitted with a radar navigational aid entitled H2S which was mounted in the belly of the plane roughly underneath the mid upper gunners position. The H2S radar was designed to identify

LL802 GI-M one of the Lancasters that collided en route to Calais on 20th September 1944 killing F/O James & crew. Keen eyes will notice the 'Monica' tail and wing aerials. 'Monica' was a radar device designed to warn aircrew of approaching fighters. *Courtesy of Mildenhall Register.*

targets on the ground for night and all-weather bombing and so became the first ground mapping radar to be used in combat. Its forte was identifying the difference between land and the sea and was subsequently ideal for mining trips. Sgt Galt the Navigator in the Campbell crew had received instruction on how to operate the H2S sets and this was one of the reasons that they were chosen to undertake such operations. After the war it became widely known that the H2S sets omitted a pulse that was easily picked up by the German fighters on their radar sets and subsequently tracked bombers, eventually shooting them down.

The contribution by the Royal Air Force to the battle of the oceans cannot be understated. Bomber and Costal Command laid mines to devastating effect all along the shores of Europe which virtually immobilized coastal traffic. After the war the official statistics were revealed and Germany lost 759 vessels as a result of RAF mining, a figure that equates to 32% of all the German shipping sunk during the war.

On 11th September the Campbell crew was assigned NN709, GI-H to drop mines in the Baltic at the port of Rostock. Six Lancasters were detailed to drop their 6x 1, 500lb mines and this was the first mining sortie for the Campbell crew. It was common knowledge at the time about the German fighter technique of approaching the bombers from underneath and firing up into the Lancasters wing fuel tanks. With this in mind F/Sgt Campbell would keep as low as possible to make it very difficult for a fighter to use this method of attack. Ideally this would force the fighters to come in from above and break away in a climb giving both gunners a chance to return fire. On this particular trip Sgt Pudney was the rear gunner in Flying Officer Peck's crew and deployed a similar tactic against an attacking Ju88 fighter shooting down the fighter despite his guns jamming. Fortune usually favored the vastly superior firepower of the German Ju88 with its 20mm cannons that had a far greater range in capacity. Sgt Denis Pudney was awarded an immediate DFM for his actions on this particular night. Pilot Officer Devine RAAF and crew in LM511, GI-C were not so lucky and failed to return from the mission. It was presumed that they crashed into the sea because no wreckage or bodies were recovered.

F/Sgt Peter Jezzard W/op, standing on the left. On a mission to mine Oslo Fjord he misinterpreted a code message from base instructing the crew to divert to the North of Scotland to avoid dense fog at Mildenhall. It was established later that he had not been briefed regarding a code change; however, he was 'rested' and posted away from 622 Squadron immediately. *Courtesy of Alan Martin.*

On 15th September Bomber Command sent a force of 490 heavy bombers to the German city of Kiel and home of the 'Krupps' one of the leading manufacturers of armaments. Four squadron Lancasters were dispatched to drop mines in the Kiel Estuary as soon as possible after the main bomber force, in an attempt to trick the Germans into thinking that no mining had taken place. Bill Hickling was apprehensive about this raid. Their timing over the target was particularly important to avoid stragglers from the main force dropping their bombs onto them below. En route across Denmark and some way over the Baltic, Bill Hickling contemplated the thought of barrage balloons being in place over the port and bringing down unsuspecting low flying aircraft. The last leg of the route saw the Lancasters turn through 180 degrees and run in on the eastern side of the Canal to drop their mines successfully into the canal. Bill Hickling recalls seeing a lot of flak and searchlight activity over the Kiel; luckily they appeared to have sneaked in undetected.

The third mining trip was by far the most eventful, not due to enemy activity but the adverse British weather. On 11th November 1944 Oslo Fjord was selected to be mined and two 622 crews were briefed for the mission. One being the recently commissioned Pilot Officer Jim Campbell and crew. By now the crew had a regular Lancaster assigned to them and they lifted off the runway at Mildenhall and climbed slowly with their ordnance of 3X1, 500lb and 3x1, 800lb mines. The route to the target was uneventful and they bombed after visually identifying the target at 19:42 hours. Shortly after bombing the wireless operator, F/Sgt Peter Jezzard reported to the skipper that he was receiving a coded message from base that made no sense. The whole crew felt uneasy with the uncertainty and realized that something was wrong, so Peter Jezzard kept trying to make sense of the coded message. The cause of the concern was established when they crossed the English coast and flew straight into thick fog. The navigator Jack Galt, reported that by his estimation they were flying over Mildenhall and Pete Jezzard stated that ground control reported that they had switched on all the airfield lights, although none of the crew could see anything through the dense fog. The navigator asked the skipper to fly back east over the sea and drop down lower to see if they could identify any landmarks on the coast to give him an accurate bearing. Norman Shepley the bomb aimer identified Cromer lighthouse from the nose of the Lancaster and the navigator gave the skipper a new course to steer and estimated time to Mildenhall. As they neared Mildenhall the mid upper gunner and bomb aimer saw the airfield lights after asking for the 'Drem' system to be activated. Ground control talked Jim Campbell onto a landing course and they aborted their first landing attempt because they were too high. On the second attempt the Lancaster landed safely to the relief of all the crew. The odds of landing safely were stacked against them considering the weather conditions. At the end of the runway, there were ambulance and fire crews on readiness, luckily not needed on this occasion. On investigation the coded message sent to the crew was meant to inform them to divert to the north of Scotland, either

Serial No. ....190. 1st Battle Order for 5th ~~October~~ Nov. 1944. No. 622 Squadron.

A/C NO.	LETTER.	CAPTAIN & 2ND PILOT	NAV. & W/OPERATOR.	A/B & M.U.GUNNER.	R/GUNNER & F/ENGINEER.
HK.621	G.	F/O Curling	F/S. Murdin. W.O. Hinod	F/S Middleditch Sgt. Robinson. & F/S McRae	Sgt. Wallace. Sgt. White.
NN.709	H.	F/Lt. Armitstead.	F/S Brewster Sgt. Foulkes.	Sgt. Daniels Sgt. Keylock	Sgt. Borne. Sgt. Peck.
LL.885	J.	F/O Peck	F/S Barchard. F/O Cargill	F/O Long. Sgt. Ramsay	Sgt. Rudney. Sgt. Bowyer.
PD.229	K.	F/S Francis	F/S Steedon Sgt. Kelly	Sgt. Traylen Sgt. Baxter	F/S Stott. Sgt. Soanes.
HK.645	Z.	F/O Thomson	F/S Ward, W.O. Aland.	F/S Dalley Sgt. Smith.	Sgt. Woolloff. Sgt. Boulton.
HK.623	F.	F/O Phillips	Sgt. Lowry F/S Hopewell.	Sgt. Smart Sgt. Morgan	Sgt. York. Sgt. Barber.
HK.628	X.	F/S Waigh	F/O Briggs F/O Morrison	F/O Lister Sgt. Simmons.	Sgt. Mitchell. Sgt. Evans.
HK.644	D.	F/O Barnett	Sgt. Grimsey F/S Sullivan	F/O Hurditch Sgt. Staplehurst	F/S Nicholls. Sgt. Murrell.
PD.225	G.	F/O Baxter	Sgt. Parsons Sgt. Brooker	F/S Hopkinson Sgt. Smith. Cn.445	Sgt. Ramsey. Sgt. Rossiter.
LM.288	V.	F/S Rudenko	F/S Mekeown Sgt. Vollmer.	Sgt. Sleigh Sgt. Syvolos	F/S Ross. Sgt. Lucas-Garner.
HK.646	M.	F/S Thomas.	F/O Berry Sgt. Charlesworth	F/S Gambell. Sgt. Kingston	Sgt. Davies. Sgt. Ralph.
PA.164	P.	P/O Campbell.	Sgt. Galt. F/S Jezzard.	F/S Shepley Sgt. Fallows.	Sgt. Hickling. Sgt. Hill.
HK.614	B.	F/O Richards.	F/S Kidd Sgt. Doyle	F/O Mildren Sgt. Papps	Sgt. Nicholson. Sgt. Martin.
HK.616	W.	F/Lt. Woods.	F/S Grest. Sgt. Johnson	Sgt. Taylor Sgt. Henderson & W/O Davis.	Sgt. Gantley. Sgt. Coney.
HK.617	Y.	F/O Hussey	F/O Simpson Sgt. May	F/S Dalton Sgt. O'Connor.	Sgt. Potter. Sgt. Hand.
PD.332	N.	P/O Gilmore.	F/O Tomsett F/S Austin	F/S O'Loughlin Sgt. Davies.	Sgt. Firth. Sgt. Davidson.
LM.443	T.	F/O Richards.	F/O Lubell. F/S Martin	F/O Carter Sgt. Brierley	Sgt. Campbell. Sgt. Burnard.

Rations to be collected by F/Commanders and distributed to aircraft.

Briefing Meal 0715
Nav. 0745
Main 0815
Trans. 0830.

GUARD ROOM TO COMMENCE EARLY CALLS 0600 hours.

(Sgd) G.K. Buckingham W/Cdr.
Commanding No. 622 Squadron.

W/C Buckingham S/L Allen. F/Lt. Dean. F/L Nicholl F/Lt. Noonan F/Lt. Middleton F/Lt. Berry F/Lt. Thomson

Battle order for Solingen trip on 5th November 1944 showing that 622 Squadron put up seventeen Lancasters on this particular mission. *Courtesy of Mildenhall Register.*

Lossiemouth or Kinloss, F/Sgt Jezzard had not been informed of a code change that would occur during the flight and subsequently he was unable to decipher the coded message. Nearly the whole station had been awoken to accept them and they received a frosty reception from those expecting a good night's sleep.

In 1989 Bill Hickling was visited by his pilot Jim Campbell from Australia and he provided some more details to this story. Apparently, the Officer Commanding the whole of 3 Group, Air Vice Marshall Harrison was at Mildenhall at the time and witnessed the incident. The next day he sent for Jim Campbell and told him that he was going to have the wireless operator, Pete Jezzard court marshaled. He had endangered the lives of the crew by not listening out for messages from base. Flying Officer Campbell explained the circumstances and informed the Officer that Pete Jezzard had by this stage completed thirty six operations and should be given a rest period. The high ranking Officer agreed and Pete Jezzard was sent on leave and subsequently posted out of the squadron. F/Sgt Jezzard was most perturbed to be leaving the crew so close to them completing their tour of duty and requested to stay however his request was refused. It is appropriate at this stage to mention that Peter Jezzard started his tour of operations with the crew of F/Sgt Thompson in late 1943 and he was shot down on the night of 15th March on the return journey from Stuttgart. He successfully evaded capture and returned to the squadron and subsequently the Campbell crew. The story has a sad ending when in 1947 Pete Jezzard was lost with his crew over the sea in a Wellington bomber whilst on a training exercise.

By late September and early October 1944, all of 3 Group had been equipped with the radio aid entitled G/H. The system was a two station radio direction finder. Instruments in the bomber measured its position from one station and distance from another. It could be used by up to 80 bombers from any one pair of stations. By using more than one pair of stations, multiple targets could be attacked at the same time without the aid of Pathfinders and markers. Certain Lancasters within the squadron were equipped with the G/H system and they had their tail rudders painted with distinctive colors so that other Lancasters could format on them. The idea was to ensure that when the G/H equipped Lancaster released its bombs the others followed suit ensuring bombing accuracy. Each squadron chose a different configuration of colored marking on the tail rudders, both the squadrons at Mildenhall (15 and 622) chose two distinctive horizontal yellow bars.

Equipped with this new navigation device, the Lancasters of 3 Group commenced a series of daylight attacks on German targets without the need for the assistance of the Pathfinder force. Air Chief Marshal Harris still looked to the destruction of industrial cities and now that his Bomber force had been released from the control of the Supreme Headquarters Allied Control, he was able to return to the task of bombing the industrial cities. However, Bomber Command was to remain ready to assist the ground forces as and when required. The Allied forces were progressing steadily through Europe and the German night fighter defenses in France and Belgium had been overrun by the Army. This seriously depleted the German's ability to launch any aerial defenses against the bomber forces. In addition, the Allied fighters fitted with fuel drop tanks could now escort the bombers to the target and back.

Bill Hickling and his crew were actively involved with the bomber campaign throughout the month of October 1944, mostly daylight missions interspersed with the odd night trip. On one night mission, probably the trip to Essen on 23rd October, they were detailed to drop their bombs before the Pathfinder force, such was the reputation for accuracy of the G/H system. By now, Jim Campbell had been allocated Lancaster, PA164, GI-P that became the crew's regular aircraft right up until tour completion. On this particular night, the Lancaster was loaded with additional bundles of 'Window' radar jamming strips of tinfoil which confused the German radar systems by presenting the operators with a snowstorm picture. By dropping the 'Window' ahead of the main Pathfinder force; it prevented the German anti-aircraft gunners from utilizing the predicted flak system which was based on accurate radar target indications. Over the target, Bill Hickling and crew met no flak because it was the German policy to open fire only if the target indicator flares had been dropped in an attempt to conceal the target to the last moment. The reprieve was short lived and shortly after leaving the target area the flak opened up and it was 'predicted'. Crews at this time had been taught a diversionary tactic where on the instructions of a member of the crew, usually the gunners, the pilot changed course to avoid the next flak shell. Basically the predicted flak would follow the course and height of a bomber. Once it had accurately tracked a bomber it would predict the position of the bomber and shoot into the airspace that the bomber should fly into. Once a burst of flak exploded near to the Lancaster the gunner would count a specific number in his head and then instruct the pilot to dive 500ft to starboard to the position of the previous flak burst. The next flak burst would explode in the position that the Lancaster had just left, this basic calculation compensated for the radar controller passing the Lancaster positions to the Flak batteries. The next instruction to the pilot would be to climb to the port and so on until the Lancaster cleared the flak defenses.

On 14th October the news was promulgated that Jim Campbell had received his commission to Pilot Officer. All the crew were given a twenty four hour pass to go to Australia House in London and for Jim Campbell to officially receive his commission papers. Bill Hickling described the whole affair as low key and whilst their skipper went into Australia House, the rest of the crew hung about outside taking in the hustle and bustle of London. After a few celebratory drinks in London and an overnight stay in a dingy hotel, the crew returned to RAF Mildenhall with a commissioned officer at the helm. The remainder of October and November brought more targets to bomb in the Industrial Ruhr including two consecutive trips to the German city of Solingen. On the first trip on the 4th November the bombing was widely scattered and Arthur Harris ordered the crews back again the next night to complete the task.

Take off at Mildenhall was well organized and reduced the opportunity for Lancaster engines to overheat whilst waiting to take off. Once in the air the Lancasters could obtain their formation quicker and reduce the likelihood of collision whilst circling the airfield. It was well publicized that the two squadrons at Mildenhall (15 & 622) held the record for take off time, which was a tribute to the outstanding work of the ground crew in making ready up to twenty plus Lancasters for any one mission. On 27th November 1944 Pilot Officer Jim Campbell RAAF and crew were called into the office of the Commanding Officer and congratulated on successfully completing their tour of operations. They were offered the opportunity of a six months break from operations at an aircrew training center, which they accepted. To the crew it was a moment that they all thought would never come and somewhat of an anti-climax after the psychological strains of preparing for missions to Germany.

Like so many other aircrew members before and after him, Bill Hickling cannot accurately put into words the bonds of friendship for his crew. Whilst reading the memoirs of Wing Commander Leonard Cheshire, Bill Hickling stumbled across a passage of text that epitomized his exact feelings of his war time experiences with Bomber Command. He would like to pay this tribute to his crew through the words of Wing Commander Cheshire, perhaps the most accomplished and heroic pilot in Bomber Command, who completed over one hundred operations:

> "As the flare path disappeared below the port wing and night closed in around us, I looked at the familiar faces of my crew, dim in the glow of the cockpit lighting, I realized that here was a brotherhood which could never be destroyed and I understood why England could never be defeated."
>
> "These men have etched themselves on my memory for all time. We have lived, flown, fought experienced danger, felt elation, sorrow and fear, taken leisure and done our drinking together. We are now a closely knit aircrew who trust each other when in the air and are happiest in our own company on the ground. There is a mutual respect and a sense of comradeship that will make these days supreme in our lives, days that we will remember always, or for as long as we live."
>
> The Lord Cheshire. VC, DSO & 2 bars, DFC, OM.

25

Behind Enemy Lines

The target for tonight gentlemen is...........Stuttgart! The voice of Wing Commander 'Blondie' Swales, the Commanding Officer of 622 Squadron boomed out across the briefing room. One member of the audience listening intently to the briefing was F/Sgt Tom Maxwell, the rear gunner in the crew of F/Sgt Peter Thomson, a six feet five inch Australian. As soon as the target was revealed Tom Maxwell's stomach tightened and his mind conjured up a vision of a heavily defended target where survival relies on a high degree of kismet. Stuttgart was situated in the Ruhr basin and heavily defended with both flak and fighters to contend with. Bomber Command always experienced heavy losses against this target. Tom allowed his mind to drift from the briefing. He quickly focused his attention back on the meterology officer who explained the predicted weather over the target, which met with the usual jeers of disbelief. Tom concentrated on the route displayed on the large map of Europe in the front of the briefing room. The red silk tapes pinned to the map highlighted the route and changes to confuse the enemy defenses.

Once the full briefing was complete the aircrew designations attended another briefing given by their respective 'leader'.

F/Sgt Maxwell listened with apprehension as the Flight Lieutenant explained the latest intelligence on known flak barrages and night fighter bases. It was the rear gunners responsibility to defend the crew against night fighters by keeping a constant vigil on the night sky searching for an enemy fighter before it had chance to attack. If a German night fighter was spotted then the rear gunner's quick reactions could mean the difference between life

COMBAT REPORT

No 622 Squadron — Target : Augsburg

Aircraft: Lancaster 111 ED631

Captain : F/S Peter Thomson

Date : 25 February 1944

Position : 48.28N 10.45E Height : 20000' 01-20 hours

Visibility very good cloud nil, no moon starlight.

Rear gunner saw T/E aircraft on port quarter at 500 yards on parallel course silhouetted against searchlights and glow from target. At 450 yards rear gunner identified aircraft as a Ju 88 ordered cork-screw port and fired a two second burst. The mid upper gunner got in a two second burst during early part of corkscrew which both gunners and wireless operator saw hitting the enemy aircraft.

The enemy aircraft was then lost to view on the starboard quarter high. The rear gunner next saw the E/A closing from port quarter low at 200 yards ordered corkscrew to port and fired short burst when guns stopped. The mid-upper gunner also fired a 3 second burst at the E/A which broke a way to the starboard quarter high and was not seen again.

Rear Gunner Sgt Maxwell who trained at 26 OTU 4 AGS fired 300 rounds

MUG . Sgt Peake also from 26 OTU 11 AGS fired 800 rounds.

The combat report filed by Tom Maxwell on his return from a mission to Augsburg on 25th February 1944. *Courtesy of F/Lt Tom Maxwell DFC.*

and death for the crew. F/Sgt Tom Maxwell was an above average gunner who had qualified from No.4 Air Gunnery School and then No.26 OTU at Wing in Buckinghamshire with flying colors. Tom Maxwell's attention to detail was born from a previous encounter with a German Ju88 night fighter whilst on a mission to Augsburg on 25th February 1944. On this occasion Tom and the mid upper gunner, Sgt Peake had seen the German fighter silhouetted against the searchlights over the target. Both of them had fired off several rounds from their .303 Browning machine guns, several bullets were seen to hit the fighter by the wireless operator.

The crew had first come together at the Operational Training Unit at Wing where they had flown several training exercises. These exercises were carried out in obsolete Vickers Wellington bombers that were ex-squadron aircraft that had seen considerable squadron service. The crew quickly built up a respect for each other and they enjoyed each other's company. The crew were as follows:

Pilot: F/Sgt Peter Thomson RAAF
Nav: Doug Gray RAAF
W/op: Peter Jezzard
B/A: Bruce Hyde RCAF
F/E: Frank Harmsworth
MUG: Gwilliam (Taffy) Peak
R/G: F/Sgt Tom Maxwell

After successfully completing their training at 'Wing' the crew was posted to an operational bomber station in late 1943. The crew's destination was 622 Squadron at RAF Mildenhall in Suffolk, a pre-war station that included purpose built houses for crews. On their arrival at Mildenhall the crew was introduced to the Commanding Officer and undertook a series of familiarization exercises before commencing operations against the enemy.

RAF Mildenhall was the home of XV and 622 Squadrons and operated approximately 20 Short Stirling four engined bombers, ten in each squadron. 622 Squadron had only recently been formed on 10th August 1943 from XV Squadron and 'C' flight personnel and aircraft were immediately assigned to form the new squadron. The Battle of Berlin was well under way when the crew arrived, although the Stirling bombers had been withdrawn from front line missions due to their high attrition rates. The Short Stirling suffered at the hands of the enemy, as it was unable to gain an altitude over 17,000 feet when fully laden and the flak and fighter defenses took a heavy toll on the aircraft. Peter Thomson and crew undertook two mine laying exercises in late November 1943 to the Frisian Isles and Bayonne and then during the month of December 1943, the squadron converted to the much improved Avro Lancaster, a revolutionary development in aircraft engineering.

Further conversion training took place during January 1944 and the winter weather was particularly bad with heavy snowfalls throughout January. However by the third week of January the weather had improved and the squadron commenced operations against the enemy in their new Lancasters on 20th of the month. Six missions occurred in quick succession for F/Sgt Thomson and crew to heavily defended places in the Ruhr Valley, including Berlin, Schweinfurt, Augsburg and Stuttgart on 1st March 1944.

On 15th March 1944, the crew's second trip to Stuttgart was promulgated on the daily battle order. Tom Maxwell's reaction to the news of the intended target is described in the first part of this narrative therefore the story will continue with the events leading up to the crew 'bailing out' over France. The Lancaster assigned to the crew for the Stuttgart mission was LL828, with the squadron markings of GI-J. With all the necessary preflight checks completed the crew lifted off the runway at Mildenhall at 19:20 hours and set a course for the liaison point with the bomber stream just off the Norfolk coast. The trip to the target was uneventful, the bomb aimer could clearly identify the target indicators over Stuttgart and the crew successfully released their bombs at 20,000ft. The flak over the target was in box formation which made it very difficult to avoid and almost immediately after the words "bombs gone" were spoken the Lancaster received a direct hit by flak in the port wing, crippling the bomber and ruining the crew's chances of returning home.

F/Sgt Thomson fought with the Lancaster's controls, however the entire port wing fuel tanks had been ruptured and fuel was lost. Thomson tasked the W/op Peter Jezzard to assess the condition of the Lancaster. He reported that the radio receiver was out of action and there was a large hole in the fuselage, which he nearly fell through. Corsica was a neutral country and crews were advised to fly to the Country if they were in trouble. Peter Thomson decided to head for Corsica and attempt a crash landing. The navigator and flight engineer worked out the route and fuel consumption respectively and initially the signs were good for reaching neutral territory. Further calculations ensued and Frank Harmsworth the flight engineer, reported that the Lancaster could reach base if it continued to lose fuel at its current rate. The crew was unhappy with this decision because of the condition of the Lancaster and the thoughts of crash landing in the cold English Channel were very daunting. Peter Thomson set course for Paris with the moans and groans of the crew ringing in his ears. Shortly after, the flight engineer reported that the fuel tanks were losing fuel at a faster rate than anticipated and it was expected that the aircraft would reach the south coast of England. By this stage the pilot was slowly losing height to maintain fuel and at 15,000ft Peter Thomson gave the order to lighten the aircraft to preserve fuel. All unnecessary equipment such as guns and ammunition were thrown out of the aircraft and Peter Jezzard attempted to send a radio message on an emergency frequency to give RAF Mildenhall the Lancaster's position. It was later discovered that Mildenhall received the transmission and it was recorded in the squadron's operational record book.

On the approach to Paris the flight engineer reported that the Lancaster would not reach England and the thought of 'ditching' in the Channel was a distinct possibility. Just north of Paris the engines started to cut out and Peter Thomson wished the crew good luck and told them to 'bail out' of the stricken aircraft. The crew systematically 'bailed out' with the flight engineer passing Peter Thomson his parachute on his way out. The pilot's first attempt to leave the controls resulted in the Lancaster's engine spluttering and cutting out which meant that he had to return to the controls and 'feather' the propellers to allow the Lancaster to glide, enabling

Left: Pilot F/Sgt Peter Thomson RAAF & Navigator Doug Gray RAAF. Both men were Australians. One stood at 6'5" and the other a shade over 5' 2". During the crew's enforced wait at OTU to transfer to 622 Squadron, Doug Gray took part in a fitness exercise and fell from the top of a high wall badly injuring himself. He was replaced by P/O Gordon Stevens. *Courtesy of F/Lt Tom Maxwell DFC.*

F/Sgt Tom Maxwell (later F/Lt DFC), rear gunner in the crew of F/Sgt Thomson RAAF. Tom would bail out and evade back to the squadron with the help of the French résistance. On his arrival back on 622 Squadron, Tom completed his tour of 30 operations and he was awarded a well deserved DFC for his evasion from the enemy. *Courtesy of F/Lt Tom Maxwell DFC.*

him to 'bail out'. By the time F/Sgt Thomson left the stricken Lancaster the height on the altimeter registered 2,000 feet.

Tom Maxwell relays his account of the fateful night below:

"The take off, in a Lancaster with full fuel and a full bomb load totaling anything up to 65,000 lbs+ (one third of the weight was fuel) was not always *straight* forward and the aeroplane could be wayward in strong crosswinds.

Serial No.........29. 1st Battle Order for 15th March, 1944. STUTTGART. No. 622 Squadron.

No.	LETTER.	CAPTAIN AND 2ND PILOT.	NAV. AND W/OPERATOR.	AIR BOMBER AND M/U/GUNNER.	REAR GUNNER AND F/ENGINEER.
[illegible]430	A	P/O. Curling.	F/Sgt. Featherstonhaugh. F/Sgt. Smith.	F/Sgt. Short. Sgt. Harris 308.	Sgt. Russell. Sgt. Humphries.
[illegible]691	D	F/Sgt. Tremouth.	Sgt. West. Sgt. King.	F/O. Good. Sgt. Tulman.	F/Sgt. Harvey. Sgt. Francis.
[illegible]812	G	F/Sgt. Kerr. F/Sgt. Cowsey.	F/Sgt. Casey. Sgt. Weale.	F/Sgt. Blair. F/Sgt. McDougall.	F/Sgt. Wright. Sgt. Schott.
J[illegible]876	E	F/Lt. Stoddart.	F/O. Burrows. P/O. Wright.	F/O. Ashton. F/Sgt. Smith 585.	F/Lt. Dorry. Sgt. Mocburn.
[illegible]	F	P/O. Rowsthorn.	F/Sgt. Grant. Sgt. Ward.	F/Sgt. Payne. Sgt. Craggs.	Sgt. Lowes. Sgt. Grosvenor.
L[illegible]443	G	P/O. Taylor.	F/O. Woodall. Sgt. Johnston.	Sgt. Harriott. Sgt. Shaw.	Sgt. Hutchinson. Sgt. Gregson.
LL.782	H	S/Ldr. Tilton.	F/O. Pawlyshyn. P/O. Chapman.	S/Ldr. Legge. F/Sgt. Pidgen.	W/O. Jones. P/O. Birkett.
LL.[illegible]	J	F/Sgt. Thomson.	P/O. Stevens. Sgt. Jezzard. Baled out France	F/Sgt. Hyde. Sgt. Peake.	Sgt. Maxwell. Sgt. Harmsworth.
L[illegible]376	K	F/Sgt. Hall.	F/Sgt. Smith. Sgt. Till.	F/Sgt. Morris. Sgt. Cunningham.	Sgt. Mayhead. Sgt. Jarvie.
LM477	L	P/O. Hargreaves.	Sgt. Urwin. Sgt. Crawford.	F/Sgt. Burns. Sgt. Malpass.	Sgt. Glynn. Sgt. Williams.
[illegible]	N	F/Lt. Murgatroyd.	F/O. Musson. Sgt. Emmott.	F/O. McConnac. Sgt. Reid.	Sgt. Howe. Sgt. Hargreaves.
[illegible]	P	P/O. Dorisley. F/Sgt. Lyle.	F/Sgt. McCrone. Sgt. Hollins.	Sgt. Harrison. Sgt. Crow.	Sgt. Bright. Sgt. Terry.
LL.[illegible]	Q	P/O. Sutter. F/Sgt. Burrows.	F/Sgt. McClean. Sgt. Read.	F/Sgt. Laberge. F/Sgt. Jarvis.	Sgt. Richardson. Sgt. Mason.
ED[illegible]	R	F/Sgt. Horton.	F/Sgt. Maxwell. Sgt. White.	F/Sgt. Gray. Sgt. Dye.	Sgt. Grant 367. Sgt. Parsons.
[illegible]186.	S	Sgt. Walker.	Sgt. Atkinson. Sgt. Anderson. Returned Early	F/Sgt. Hodgson. F/Sgt. Pearce.	Sgt. Brown. Sgt. Herbert.
W[illegible]	T	F/Sgt. Struthers.	F/Sgt. Andrewes. Sgt. Brooke. Landed Woodbridge	F/Sgt. Milford. Sgt. Wilt.	Sgt. Joy. Sgt. Dawkins.
[illegible]059	U	F/Sgt. Harris.	W/O. Kelly. Sgt. White.	F/Sgt. Blackmore. Sgt. Notley.	F/Sgt. Campbell. Sgt. Warcham.

Officer i/c. Flying Rations : F/O. RANSOM. (report to Adjutant) (sgd.) I.C.K. SWALES. DFC. DFM. Wing Commander, Commanding No.622 Sqdn.
Briefing to be notified later.
The following to [illegible] to Radar Officer 1400 hours :- Sgts. Purton, Waters, Mayes, Pratt and Poynter.

Battle Order for the night of 15th March 1944. 19 Lancasters from 622 Squadron took part in the mission. *Courtesy of F/Lt Tom Maxwell DFC.*

This remarkable photograph shows F/Lt Tom Maxwell assisting on the farm of his French helpers whilst awaiting further help from the local résistance force. They provided civilian clothing and made him feel welcome. The risks that the French people took assisting the Allies cannot be underestimated. The discovery of this photograph by the Germans would have meant certain death for the French family. The photo was taken at Bazancourt France in March 1944. L-R: Medard Maertens, Tom Maxwell & Tancrède Maertens. *Courtesy of F/Lt Tom Maxwell DFC.*

The clearance to take-off came from the Runway Caravan by a steady green Aldis lamp signal and meant only that the aeroplane ahead was safely airborne. The usual group of well-wishers from WAAF's to Wing Commanders huddled together in the driving rain and were just visible in the green glare, the same faithful would be there to give a 'thumbs-up' whatever the weather conditions.

'Snaking' on take off or when taxiing may have been seen as 'normal' and 'under control' by the pilot and other crew up front, but in the darkness of the rear turret, sitting almost over the tail wheel it was something different! It sometimes felt as if the tail wheel was made of wood everything at the back end strained, banged, shook and rattled, and it was a tense *hold on to everything few* moments, including the stomach. Ammunition jostled and rattled in the fuselage as the turret swayed shook and vibrated it was the closest one could get to being airsick on the ground. When the tail of the aeroplane lifted into the air one could then relax.

A 'trip' to the southern German target of Stuttgart on October 19th 1944 had a touch of the déjà vu about it, well not so much a touch, more of a gnawing apprehension, compared to the previous visit. This was my third visit to this engineering city, which produced diesel engines for enemy Tanks and 'U' Boats etc. The times taken to get to the same target and back to base would nearly always be similar if one was to navigate as the crow flies, but it was never like that. Targets were reached and bombed from various compass points. Bombers were routed sometimes towards 'spoof 'targets and then turned away towards the intended area. Sometimes a mission would be flown towards a specific target, and then flown past only to return from a different and hopefully unsuspected heading, hoping if nothing else to confuse the enemy defenses on the ground. Constant adjustment to planned tracks was the Navigators task because of head or tail winds, forecast or not, engine malfunctions, airframe icing, known flak areas, or new ones, searchlights and evasive action and not forgetting 'Gremlins'. Gremlins were wee fellas, like Pixies, and they were invisible. They could get into everything and cause terrible trouble. Their current equivalents would be called bugs or glitches.

The bomb aimer often sat in the right hand seat beside the pilot, if a second or screen pilot wasn't carried. On this gremlin occasion both the navigator and the pilot were getting edgy because of apparently unnecessary and too frequent track deviations called dog legs (if a delay was needed, or cutting a corner if behind time). The navigator could not understand it, and the pilot swore that he was flying the headings precisely as instructed. Known pinpoints were not where they should have been or were being reached late or too early. The atmosphere up front was not normal and a bit tense. The intercom provided the running commentary and it appeared that 'time on target' was going to be a hit or miss affair. Someone asked if the compass had been "swung" recently. Bombing too early or late brought additional hazards and being a 'straggler' was not recommended. The navigation errors were ultimately resolved when the pilot remarked to the bomb-aimer 'What's that?' pointing to his left boot. The bomb-aimer had been sitting since take off with a heavy metal torch stuck down the side of his left flying boot virtually within inches of the P4 compass. The air was a dark shade of blue for a short period. Gremlins had obviously put this metal object in the flying boot near the compass when the owner wasn't looking.

The three ops to Stuttgart in my logbook are logged in red ink as follows (all night flying was entered into crew logbooks in red and day flying in black):

March 1st 7 hrs 30 mins: March 15th 6 hrs 10 mins: October 19th 7 hrs 10 mins.

The difference in over an hour for the March 15th trip is significant for two reasons. The time of 6 hrs 10 mins was entered in a strange hand and the logbook was annotated: **'FAILED TO RETURN'**.

The thing about baling out, in total darkness at night, from a crippled aircraft or splashing your 25 ton Lancaster into a raging sea swell was that you didn't get any practice lessons beforehand, so it was a bit of a new thing. The nearest one got was about a year before, jumping off the top diving board in the warm water and brightly lit baths in Brighton in a flying suit and Mae West.

Then the water had loads of noisy laughter and PT life-saving instructors to help if one got into difficulty. It was 1.30 in the morning and pitch black, the top board was about 8000 feet vibrating and descending rapidly, and spewing fuel and oil from ruptured fuel tanks. No friendly life-savers etc, but the reality that our fuel was being exhausted even faster than calculated had now replaced the 'ditching' idea and baling out, (and pretty soon at that) was the only option left. We, or certainly I, was already well into a personal life preservation situation. I was personally totally disenchanted when the channel rowing exercise in total darkness was muted as a possibility. I never found the idea of hitting the English Channel at 100mph in total darkness, with sea and swell conditions unknown, and with an indeterminate amount of fuel, to be in the least, appealing. The idea did nothing for my morale at all. My lack of enthusiasm for swimming, anywhere, but especially in the dark would appear to have been quite realistic.

Six of the crew all landed in an area 40 miles north east of Rouen and all reasonably close, within a kilometer or so of each other, but when they left the aircraft I was already *on the way down* some 20 kilometers further back, representing several minutes. The reason for their delay will never be known, but after 57 years almost to the day it has just been established that the aeroplane crashed within a couple of miles from where some of the crew were taken POW.

Of the four who returned to England on May 22nd on a DC3 from Gibraltar to Bristol (Whitchurch), I only met up later with Peter Jezzard. Both of us returned to operational flying with our original Squadron, Peter finishing his 'tour' in November 1944 on 35 'trips' and myself on 32, finishing on New Year's Day 1945.

Emergency exit from the Lancaster was usually made from either the front escape hatch or the main entrance door. The procedure when leaving from the rear door was to dive out with your head down to avoid hitting the tail plane (I was definitely there and awake the day they told us that), but there were a lot of 'ifs and buts'. To exit by the main door was going to take time, which I/we didn't have, and I was just as much averse to queuing as swimming. I was quickly getting my wits together. Get the parachute! Quick glance!

Yes its there in the fuselage, an arm's length away Okay, open turret doors and hope they don't jam (they sometimes did) that's it - drag the chute carefully into the turret (it wouldn't have been the first time a parachute had accidentally deployed inside an aircraft) - consternation! There's no room to put it on. This situation wasn't in the design and Hey! You know your lower harness is loose; well you can't do anything about it now so get on! Rotate the turret 90 degrees; otherwise you'll be bailing out into the fuselage.

I flew sometimes with lower parachute harness straps loose because:

I often developed leg cramp if harnessed too tightly after a few hours in the rear gun turret.

I was never going to have to bail out, it was always going to happen to someone else.

The systems and the training were working ok , but they didn't tell us there was no room to get the chute onto the harness inside the turret, with the turret now at right angles to the fuselage, the slipstream gale was grabbing, tearing and tugging at the flapping parachute back pack. The spewing fuel whipping past me and there was nothing now but Hobson's choice, go back into the pitch black fuselage or stick your rear end into this 120 knot growling wind. They always used phrases like keep a cool head, it's dead easy, it's a piece of cake don't worry, its dead easy. I was thinking what's all this dead stuff? I'm only nineteen maybe they knew something and didn't tell, and I wondered how many times they had ever been in this situation. I didn't want to know about *dead* but I did know this wasn't easy. There was no spare space. I had one parachute hook engaged but with the 'chute' at 45 degrees. The gun sight and controls were blocking any progress to get close to getting the remaining clip engaged. I edged an inch or two into the howling blackness and just as I was about to make fast the other parachute clip I was gone! A sharp chug that felt like a broken neck reminded me about the helmet and intercom lead, and I tumbled into the night clutching the parachute in my left arm.

When they told us that baling out was dead easy it's that dead bit again they said count 'seventy-one, seventy-two seventy.' So that you wouldn't hit some part of the aeroplane, or its trailing aerial, stupid I thought there's nothing behind me but blackness. Almost immediately after the Indian neck massage I pulled the D ring (rip cord) in the only knowledge that Long John Silver managed with one hook and one was better than none. Life is simplified when there are no options. The crunch as the drag-chute came out and parachute 'woofed' into its canopy above was great to feel, and it felt that I was being taken back up. I did say 'thanks'. The dangling harness strap found its mark.

The loose harness caught more than my breath but the fear that I was spinning brought an added urgency to the situation as I tried to turn myself in the opposite direction. To this day I don't know whether I pulled myself up to the pack and hooked it or I pulled the parachute down towards me, but I was relieved that I was now descending in a more controlled manner with both parachute hooks now firmly in place. Adrenaline achieves great things. It is easy now in old age to make light of some of the, what was it? It wasn't fear or terror, more awe, consternation or dread.

All of this sequence, from the moment I aligned the rear turret with the fuselage, reached for the parachute until now when I began for the first time to feel safe, seems, as I write, to have taken ages. In fact the whole sequence of events could not have taken more than half a minute. Many things were going in and out of the brain so quickly - but a recurring apprehension of becoming impaled on a church spire, landing in a river lake or a reservoir (it was that swimming thing again) marshy ground or getting hung up on some tall building or electricity pylons or wires. You had to think of something and I was a born pessimist. As I was falling I was oddly glad of the darkness. I was definitely thinking that I should have gone to church more often, or even occasionally but I would fix it and that I should have written home more often. I will put that right as well, I promise! Things were definitely better now, and I must be down to about 3000 feet or so, onwards downwards nicely. There was just a bit of moonlight now, and instead of being rent by the roof of some French Parish church, or drowning in somebody's swimming pool, I was dumped unceremoniously into a ploughed field and a relatively soft landing. I felt nauseous and wished I had tolerated the tighter parachute harness. There was moonlight, now it was mid March in 1944, still a bit frosty in the early morning, it was about 01:40 and the piles of manure were in the fields ready for spreading.

There is a saying: "It matters not whether you're in the ***t or out of it, it's only the depth that varies." At this point, I was quite happy to be 'in it'.

The territory was enemy but the ground smelt fresh and friendly in the early hours. Two days later I was told by my French helpers that there was a German garrison just 500 meters away from where I landed. 37 broken and bent Lancasters and Halifaxes were lying on the ground scattered about Germany and France that night - lost as were many young lives. I reflected on my situation some days later and how things might have subsequently turned out for us. I was told by the French family who sheltered me, and took great risks in doing so, that Nuremberg had been bombed and 97 aircraft of Bomber Command had been lost. I thought how lucky I was. I returned to Stuttgart again seven months later and though not uneventful, this trip was by comparison dead easy."

Tom Maxwell eventually returned to the Squadron in early July 1944 along with a commission to Flying Officer and the award of the DFC for his evasion from the enemy. Unfortunately,

'It was early twilight and a magical moment'. In 1981 Pilot Peter Thompson visited the exact spot where GI-J crashed (16/3/44) assisted by local information. The location is near Llanoy Rheims & Rouen France. *Courtesy of F/Lt Tom Maxwell DFC.*

The V1 'flying bomb' rained down terror on London and the south coast of England during June and July 1944. Named by the Germans as the 'revenge' weapon the warhead contained 1, 000lbs of explosive and was launched from ramps that resembled 'ski' sites in the Pas de Calais area of France. *Author's Collection.*

Tom found himself without a crew and now considered a 'spare' gunner with experience to be exploited by every new crew that came along. The situation was far from ideal for Tom however, he was determined to finish his tour of 30 missions in whatever format his future took. F/O Maxwell's first mission after bailing out over France in March that year was on 5th July 1944 as a spare gunner in the crew of S/Ldr Hank Tilson, a Canadian pilot .The target that night was Wizernes, a V1 rocket site in France. Tom Maxwell's arrival back on the squadron coincided with the continuation for Bomber Command of destroying the launching sites of the V1 rockets, codenamed operation 'Crossbow'. The build up to the 6th June and D day landing in Normandy had been considered a diversion by ACM Harris and he reluctantly agreed to divert his bombers from bombing German cities. The second diversion for Harris was now the flying bomb menace and Eisenhower, the Allied Supreme Commander, gave priority to the task of destroying the flying bomb launching sites. The launching sites were hidden in the countryside of the Pas de Calais usually hidden in the center of wooded areas. Although woods offered perfect concealment they also acted as a beacon to bomber crews who were trying to identify launching sites. If the V1 sites had been built in open countryside then the bombers would have found it extremely difficult to locate them. Bomber Command attacked flying bombs targets right up until late August 1944 when the launching sites were captured by advancing Allied troops.

Tom would fly another four missions with this crew. Several other trips took place with other pilots including four with F/Lt Gill, a flight commander nearing his tour completion. Eventually, Tom Maxwell was chosen to fly with the new 'A' flight commander S/Ldr Richard Allen DFC who had been selecting spare gunners ever since his mid upper gunner bailed out on another Stuttgart raid in July 1944. An opportunity arose when one of the original gunners, F/Lt John Gray DFC was selected to attend the Central Gunnery School at Catfoss for a three week period. This was the opportunity for Tom Maxwell to endure a prolonged period with an established crew and Tom seized the opportunity with both hands.

The focus for Bomber Command was now a return to the 'Pointblank' initiative that was promulgated during the Casablanca conference attended by the Allied Commanders in June 1943. Bomber Command, its preparation of operation 'Overlord' now completed, turned its attention towards incapacitating the German's ability to produce oil. The Chief of Air Staff, Marshal of the Royal

Air Force Lord Portal, proposed a new directive to destroy the German's military, industrial and economic system. The Luftwaffe had been reduced to night fighter techniques and the night fighter squadrons had become accomplished at inflicting heavy losses on the bombers. The technological advances in radar meant that the bomber could no longer rely on the cloak of darkness to protect them and thus bombing Germany became a dangerous pursuit for the bomber crews. The developments with the Allied fighters such as the P51 Mustang and its long range fuel tanks meant that they could now escort the bombers in daylight to the target and back and defend the bombers with devastating effectiveness. The Allied Army advance across Belgium and Germany continued to gather momentum and on occasions faced strong resistance from the retreating German forces. Arthur Harris had promised to support the ground forces when requested and for the next few months German industrial targets and the support of the Allied Army became priorities for Bomber Command.

Operations continued for Tom Maxwell under the new directives and he undertook a series of missions against industrial targets interspersed with Army support operations. Life on an operational squadron was a mixture of extreme tension and anxiety whilst on operations and an attitude of self indulgence when not on the daily battle order. One night that will always remain vivid in Tom Maxwell's memory was 20th September 1944, often referred to as the 'black day. Tom was not selected to fly on the day's operation to Calais to bomb the German fortified positions along the French coast and that stroke of luck probably saved his life. As a spare gunner he was still standing in as a 'spare' gunner in crews that had a shortfall and on this particular mission all Lancaster crews had a full complement. Shortly after the squadron had formed up over the base they set course for the target flying in 'V' formations that contained three Lancasters in each 'vic' being led by a Lancaster equipped with G/H radar apparatus. The weather was not ideal with dense low cloud. Whilst climbing through the cloud two Lancasters appeared out of the murk entwined together and spiraled down to crash near Wormington Essex, killing fifteen aircrew in what was to be officially recorded as pilot error whilst in cloud.

With the sadness of the day's events hanging over them, Tom Maxwell and the majority of aircrew that had not been on operations decided to attend a dance in the nearby town of Soham. After an enjoyable evening where alcohol helped to null the feelings of sadness, Tom and his companions jumped into their car and headed back to Mildenhall. After a short while they came to a sharp bend in the road where an American Army truck was broadside across the road. There had obviously been an accident and Tom jumped out of the car to see if he could help in any way. As he approached the scene, he could see a mangled motorbike lying in the road with two airmen lying beside it. The scene was horrific and the lorry was full of girls returning home after a night out. The girls were screaming and crying hysterically. Tom approached the first casualty and recognized him as Flight Lieutenant Johnny Forster a squadron pilot and Tom instantly knew that he was dead. He then approached the second airman and also recognized him as a bomb aimer with the squadron namely, Flying Officer D. Smith, who was seriously injured. Tom tried to move him to help and he quickly realized that it was too late, the lorry had driven right across his chest and he was taking his last breath when Tom arrived. Both of the dead airmen had completed several missions against the enemy and to lose their lives in a tragic accident was a devastating blow to the squadron and their families. In total the squadron lost seventeen airmen on 20th September 1944, a day that will be remembered in the history books for all the wrong reasons.

By the end of October 1944 Tom Maxwell had built up the number of missions in his log book to twenty six and on 19th October he completed another mission to Stuttgart in the crew of S/Ldr Richard Allen DFC. This mission was the start of a period of continuity for Tom and he would complete the remainder of his operations with the 'Allen' crew. By this stage of the war 3 Group was equipped with the navigational aid entitled G/H which operated by receiving a signal from two ground stations and establishing an accurate navigational 'fix'. The advantage of G/H was that it could be used by numerous aircraft at the same time and it proved accurate enough for what was termed 'blind bombing' usually without visual identification of the target. This new device required some additional training by navigators and selected squadron navigators received the extra training, as was the case for Flying Officer W. Bishop RAAF the navigator in the 'Allen' crew. Lancasters equipped with the G/H device were identified by painting their tail fins with two horizontal yellow bars. The Allies had near total control of the day skies and G/H 'leader' aircraft would lead a 'vic' formation of three Lancasters. By utilizing the principal of identifying the target and releasing their bomb load on the G/H signal for others to follow suit thus ensuring an accurate bomb spread onto the target.

November 1944 commenced with a G/H mission to the oil plant at Homberg and the crew experienced heavy flak over the target area with five Lancasters eventually being lost to the German defenses. Two days later the crew were again on the battle order to attack another oil plant this time at Solingen and again it was successfully bombed.

On 16th November, Bomber Command was asked to support the American first and ninth Armies in the area adjacent to Aachen and the Rhine. In total 1,188 Bomber Command aircraft from all Groups attacked the towns of Duren, Julich and Heinsberg. 3 Group specifically attacked Heinsberg with 182 of their G/H equipped Lancasters and S/Ldr Allen and crew participated in this Army support operation.

By December 1944 Tom Maxwell and his newly adopted crew were both approaching the end of their respective 'tours' with Bomber Command. Subsequently the operations over enemy territory were less frequent and Tom would only complete another two missions during December 1944, bombing the Dam at Schwammenauel on the River Roer to assist the American Army in its advance. Secondly, the squadron carried out an operation to destroy the railway yards at Trier; both operations for Tom went by without incident. On 1st January 1945 the crew completed their final mission attacking the railway yards at Vohwinkel, lifting off the runway at Mildenhall for the last time at 16:25 hours on New Year's day and touching back down at 21:40 hours for the last time as an operational crew. Tom Maxwell, now a commissioned officer and proudly wearing the DFC ribbon on his chest had completed 34 operations and survived bailing out and evading back to 622 squadron as far back as March 1944.

Flight Lieutenant Tom Maxwell is a man of great integrity and who was devoted to the task of defeating the enemy. He set himself high standards and led by example through his own efficiency and example to others, commanding the respect of everyone. On his return to the squadron after his experiences in France, he imparted his knowledge freely to others.

I have no doubt that his experience was invaluable in saving the lives of several other crews. His personal story is worthy of inclusion in the history books and typifies the courage and bravery of aircrew fighting for their Country against Nazi tyranny.

Postscript

The fate of the crew of LL828 does not have a happy ending. After bailing out behind enemy lines on 16th March 1944 the crew were split up, each forced to take their own chances of evading back to England. Tom Maxwell's personal story is within the narrative of this story and the fate of the other members of the crew was as follows:

Pilot Peter Thomson- POW in Stalag Luft VII, rose to the position of Allies deputy camp leader. Nav G. Stevens- POW Stalag Luft 9C- Never seen again. MUG G. Peake- Stalag Luft L1- Never seen again. W/op P. Jezzard, evaded back to 622 Squadron with Tom Maxwell and completed his tour of operations in various crews. He was removed from flying duties after 35 missions; when he unfairly received the blame for misinterpreting a radio message from Group to divert to Scotland due to fog over Mildenhall. The crew eventually landed safely at Mildenhall, however a senior officer was at Mildenhall at the time and he ordered F/Sgt Jezzard to be 'rested'. In 1947 Pete Jezzard was at an operational training unit flying Wellington bombers as a wireless operator instructor. The Wellington bomber crashed in the sea with the loss of all on board, the bodies of the crew were never found.

Bomb aimer D. Hyde, evaded and never seen again. Flight engineer F. Harmsworth, evaded and was never seen again.

Citation for the immediate award of the Distinguished Flying Cross for Thomas John Maxwell

Pilot Officer Maxwell is now well advanced with his first tour of operations throughout which he had displayed resourcefulness, courage and devotion to duty of outstanding merit.

His resourcefulness and courage were never shown to better advantage than on the night of 15/16th March 1944 when the aircraft in which he was dispatched on an operational mission to Stuttgart, was so severely damaged by enemy action that the crew were ordered to bail out. From this ordeal, Pilot Officer Maxwell made a successful escape and upon his return to this country in May 1944, immediately applied for reposting to the Squadron for further operational duty as an Air Gunner.

It was as a non-commissioned Officer that he made his successful escape, since when he has been appointed to Commissioned rank and completely vindicated the knowledge held by his Leader that he is a member of aircrew of exceptional ability, whose zeal and energy are an inspiring example to everyone with whom he comes into contact.

Reported missing on his sixth operational flight, this Officer has, during the short time since he rejoined the Squadron carried out a further 18 sorties, against Stuttgart and other heavily defended German targets, displaying throughout a fine offensive spirit and applying his skill as a Gunnery Officer with outstanding ability.

With a successful escape from the enemy as background, this operational tour is noteworthy for its sustained endeavor, and the complete disregard to personal safety and outstanding gallantry of this young Officer is worthy of the best traditions of the Royal Air Force. I strongly recommend an award of the D.F.C.

Date: 25th October 1944.

Signed W/C Buckingham Commanding Officer

Remarks of Officer Commanding RAF Station Mildenhall

An exceptionally keen, determined and capable gunner who has shown courage and devotion to duty of a high order. Award recommended. Signed Commanding Officer RAF Station Mildenhall.

Remarks of Air Officer Commanding No. 3 Group

Recommended for the immediate award of the Distinguished Flying Cross.

Signed: Air Vice Marshal Harrison.

The crash site of GI-J, LL828 in 1981. The new growth in the area hides the scars of war and the young French girl poignantly picks bluebells, 37 years after the event. *Courtesy of F/Lt Tom Maxwell DFC.*

26

A Great Injustice

Pilot: F/Lt R.H.Armitstead
Nav: F/Sgt D.L. Brewster
B/A : F/Sgt C. Daniels
W/op: F/Sgt J.D. Foulkes
MUG: F/Sgt E.A. Keylock
R/G: F/Sgt Vincent F. Borge
F/E: Sgt E. B. Peck

The author is greatly indebted to Edward (Ted) Peck for allowing him to use material from his personal memoirs, 'No Medals for Bravery'.

Edward Peck left school in August 1939 aged fourteen and a half. He immediately commenced work in a large tool warehouse in Whitechapel in the heart of London's East End. By mid 1940 the Luftwaffe were making determined attacks against London and in particular the dock area. This period of the war would become known as 'The Blitz' and Londoners had to live with the daily bombing and the associated fear, sights and smells of death and destruction. Edward Peck lived close to the Victoria Docks with his mother and father. He remembers vividly the barges laden with sugar set on fire from the bombing with the air rich for several days with the smell.

To a young boy the adventure of going to war was an exciting prospect and on a daily basis young men 'joined up' and went to war. On one occasion a young clerk volunteered for the RAF from Edward's workplace and trained as an air gunner. After his training had finished he visited his old firm and he looked splendid in his uniform with sergeant's stripes and air gunner's brevet. From this moment on Edward Peck, Ted to his family and friends wanted to join the Royal Air Force in whatever capacity. The Luftwaffe's relentless bombing during the Blitz was Ted's particular motivation and he was keen to deliver similar punishment to Hitler as revenge for his home and school being obliterated. At just sixteen Ted Peck asked his father if he could join the Air Training Corps and met with a flat refusal, his father considered him to be too young to help the war effort, and of course paternal protection played a part in his decision. However, Ted was determined to join up as a boy entrant. When the opportunity arose to accompany another boy with his father to an Air Training Corp (ATC) joining ceremony, Ted's father reluctantly agreed. Subsequently Ted became a member of No.1014 Squadron attached to RAF North Weald, a front line fighter station in Battle of Britain days. Ted revelled in the experience of ATC life and undertook courses in aircraft recognition, elementary engines, drill, map reading and more drill. The culmination of all this training resulted in Ted receiving a proficiency award and being granted the rank of Corporal.

Once Edward Peck had reached the age of seventeen and a half, he became eligible to volunteer for service with the RAF. His enthusiasm resulted in him being invited to attend an Aircrew Selection Board in Euston London. Ted Peck attended the selection board in his ATC uniform complete with Corporal stripes and faced the daunting task of being interviewed by a Squadron Leader and two Flight Lieutenants, all of whom were experienced aircrew. Ted had a natural ability towards practical elements of learning and although it was every boy's dream to be a pilot, navigator or bomb aimer, Ted knew that Mathematics was not his strong subject. To give him a realistic chance of being selected he would opt for flight engineer training. The selection board went well and Ted's honesty and desire to become a flight engineer must have impressed the board, because shortly after the medical examination, he learned that he had been selected as aircrew under training. This enabled him to wear the white flash in his uniform cap, a very proud moment.

What followed next was a series of training ventures to various camps including a stay at the prestigious RAF apprentice-training establishment at Halton. Renowned for producing the best personnel the RAF had to offer. It was whilst Ted was at Halton undertaking the A.T.C annual camp, that he received an official letter informing him to report to the Aircrew Reception Center at Lords Cricket Ground on 6th September 1943. This was to commence the first stages of his aircrew training. In typically British fashion a cricket match was being played when Ted arrived and although a war was being fought throughout Europe the 'Britishness' of a game of cricket brought a surreal moment to his thoughts. Ted and his associates were all billeted in flats that had been commandeered for the purpose in St. Johns Wood. Whilst at the Aircrew Reception Center, all potential aircrew were issued with their uniform, given numerous medical inoculations and had essential dental work carried out by a dentist aptly named Mr. Savage. The essence of service life was a considerable amount of drill and parading in full dress uniform with polished boots. This was intended to instill discipline into the new recruits and knock any rough edges away.

After approximately one month Ted Peck received his instructions to report for flight engineer training at Initial Training Wing at Usworth County Durham, No.7 flight. On arrival he was allocated a billet with another 20 men and his training commenced almost immediately. The training comprised more physical fitness and discipline drill as a part of an extensive package of activities aimed at preparing the men both physically and mentally. Ted's spell at ITW was interrupted and the entire unit was relocated to Bridlington on the Yorkshire coast to complete their training. Being a seaside town, the course participants were billeted in large civilian houses presumably boarding houses in peacetime and for the remaining two weeks of Ted's training it rained, making the surroundings appear miserable. Fortunately, the training only lasted a further two weeks and Ted received seven days leave prior to his next posting to St. Athan in South Wales for technical training.

For the next six months, Edward Peck would be striving hard to gain the coveted brevet with the letter 'E' in laurel wreath. The associated promotion to sergeant on successful completion of his trade training would follow. The intense training at St. Athan was somewhat of a challenge to Ted and he made a slow start with the technical elements of the course. Eventually he began to absorb the information and he became proficient in the function of the Merlin and Hercules aero engines. The role of a flight engineer cannot be underestimated and to achieve the coveted brevet, a person had to understand practically all the mechanical systems. It was essential to have a working knowledge on how to repair and maintain them in case of emergency. Ted's eventual posting to a Lancaster squadron would see him controlling a Lancaster's fuel and engine management systems, an extremely important role and a great asset to the overburdened pilot.

Gradually Edward Peck began to master the technicalities of the course, although his nemesis was propellers and constant speed units (CSUs). The mere mention of fine pitch, coarse pitch, variable pitch etc, brought Ted out in a cold sweat. The instructors were very patient and supportive and eventually he passed the various trade tests associated with the dreaded CSUs. Towards the end of the course, Ted was posted to A.V. Roes works at Woodford near Manchester on a 'makers course' designed to familiarize new flight engineers with the Avro Lancaster. The week at Woodford was informative and the students received instruction via lectures and films regarding the Lancaster's capabilities and viewed the production line and design team. Ted was impressed with the row upon row of fuselage, wing, tail plane and undercarriage sections under preparation and the various stages of a Lancaster production line culminating in a complete Lancaster taxiing out. The week at A.V. Roes ended all too quickly for Ted and he returned to St. Athan to complete the final stages of his training. By this stage, the course was concentrating on the elements associated with flying duties and bringing all previously gained knowledge to practical assessments. By late April 1944 the course had almost been completed and the dreaded trade tests were imminent. Everyone on the course had revised intensely to be well prepared. For the final trade tests all the students were shown into a large workshop equipped with sectional engines, parts of airframes, a mock up fuel system, hydraulics and numerous other flight support systems. Ted's worse fear was realized when he spotted a section on propellers, his Achilles heel. He performed well until the inevitable happened, the propeller test in which he stumbled and needed some pointers from the Sergeant instructor. However, nerves got the better of Ted and the instructor sent him away for an hour's additional revision and told him to return with a clear head and retake the propeller test. Ted was devastated at having to retake a test and the fear of failure and ultimately failing his flight engineer training was a sobering thought. He crammed in all the revision he could in that long hour and he retook the test again with the instructor asking the same questions but in a different sequence just in case Ted had memorized his answers. On this occasion Ted mastered the test and successfully completed the course allowing him to wear the flight engineer brevet and promotion to sergeant.

Following the customary 'passing out' parade it was time for everyone to say their goodbyes and throughout the training Ted had made two good friends who had helped each other through

Sgt Edward. B Peck. A fully qualified flight engineer, proudly showing his sergeant stripes and flight engineer's brevet. *Courtesy of Ted Peck F/E 622 Sqdn.*

their mutual support. His close friends were posted to different units with one sent to a Halifax unit and another to a Lancaster unit. They all said their final goodbyes at Bristol railway station with a firm handshake of friendship promising to stay in touch with each other. That was the last time that the three of them would ever meet.

Heavy Conversion Unit

In the early summer of 1944 Edward Peck reported to the Heavy Conversion Unit at RAF Stradishall in Suffolk, a part of 3 Group and operating the enormous Short Stirling four engined bomber. The role of the Heavy Conversion Units was to continue specialist training and to convert aircrew to four engined heavy bombers. Throughout the course aircrew would learn to become proficient in their respective roles and prepare them for life on an operational squadron.

In a short space of time Ted was educated in both ground and flight procedures and he obtained a better understanding of his responsibilities as a flight engineer in a four engined bomber. In comparison to the early aircraft he had seen, the Stirling was a monster standing on an elongated undercarriage and some 30 feet tall to the cockpit. Inside the Stirling the controls for the flight engineer fell easily to hand including those for fuel tanks and fuel transfer, controls for operating the superchargers on the four engines and various other functions. All these controls were operated by means of large control wheels. A fundamental part of a flight engineer's duty in a Stirling was to check that the landing gear was locked into place and this meant scrambling all the way down the 87 feet fuselage to wind down the rear wheel by hand. Once all the wheels had been locked into position the pilot would see green lights appear on the control panel. With HCU successfully completed the next posting for Ted Peck was just down the road to RAF Methwold, a satellite station to Stradishall and it was here that he would join an already established crew of six. A flight engineer's training took them through a different route to all other aircrew duties and it was only necessary to assign flight engineers to aircrew duties when it was time to join a crew ready to commence operational missions. In general the flight engineer had the least amount of time in the air with the other crew members, pilot, navigator, wireless operator and gunners already having flown together at operational training units. Ted found the process of 'crewing up' a simplistic affair that was done on a mutual basis. He assembled outside the training section huts and mingled with the various trades who were chatting to one another in a very casual manner. Ted noticed a crew standing around perhaps hoping that a flight engineer would approach them, however it was the wireless operator, John Foulkes who approached Ted and asked "are you looking for a crew mate?" Of course Ted was and replied "yes." The wireless operator immediately burst into a description of all the crew members finishing with an introduction to the pilot and the rest of the crew. The pilot was Richard Armitstead (Dick) a pilot officer who originated from Yorkshire. Pilot Officer Armitstead introduced Ted to the rest of the crew who were all sergeants like him. The navigator was Dave Brewster, an Australian, noticeable by his slightly darker uniform and the rear gunner, Vincent Borge hailed from Gibraltar and was subsequently nicknamed 'Gib'.

This was the first meeting for Ted of six men that he would never forget. Unwittingly all the crew had made a conscious decision that would be a matter of life or death. Some crews would not survive their respective 'tours' and some would be dead in a matter of weeks. How could men tell by looking at each other who would survive and who would not and whether or not they had made the right choice? Some trusted their first impressions or judgment. However, the majority survived due to fate and the bond of total confidence in each other's abilities. This would secure them to a bond of friendship that would last a lifetime. Ted Peck was not alone in believing that he had joined the best crew in Bomber Command, an assumption that would hold some relevance by the time their tour of operations was complete.

It was as a crewmember that Edward Peck was posted to RAF Shepherds Grove, No. 1657 Heavy Conversion Unit for initial training in mid-June 1944. The ageing Short Stirling provided the basis for that training. Pilot Officer Armitstead was subjected to a series of flights with a tour expired instructor on board. The intention was to make him conversant with the Stirling's idiosyncrasies. Richard Armitstead quickly mastered the Short Stirling displaying his natural pilot abilities resulting in the crew 'going solo' in double quick time. The solos included circuits and bumps and Ted was kept busy with his management systems and of course the landing procedure of winding down the rear wheel. After about ten hours the crew graduated onto short cross country flights, high level practice bombing, fighter affiliation and air to sea firing. Eventually the crew were assigned a cross country flight of considerable duration at night on 25th July 1944.

This would test all the crews' ability to the utmost and create some realization of actual night operations when on a squadron. Just prior to take off all the crew members had received a separate briefing which included call signs and communication procedures. It was with some trepidation that the crew walked out to board the Short Stirling III, albeit they had faith in each other's ability to successfully complete the test. The flight was to be the fine tuning required to complete their training, what happened next is described in detail by Ted Peck:

> "Once airborne we did not see any other aircraft, it was almost dark when we took off at around 22.00 hrs, so perhaps that wasn't too surprising. The aircraft behaved well, we seemed to be working well as a crew, in fact, thanks to Dick's skillful piloting, the whole thing for me was proving quite enjoyable. The inky blackness of the night seemed to throw a protective cloak around us–we were cocooned in this large metal shell and felt safe. We were well around Lands End and up the coast of North Cornwall when we were hit by bad weather and we found ourselves enmeshed in the most terrific storm. Lightning was all around us, blue streaks were dancing round the propeller blades, some flying instruments were not working properly due to the storm. Fortunately the

engines were functioning smoothly with the four Hercules power plants producing a steady beat of reassurance. Survival was now our priority and to get ourselves and the aircraft to safety was paramount in our minds. The lightning subsided revealing a pitch black night and the fact that during the confusion and the storm, we had been thrown off course. The navigational equipment was malfunctioning and the storm had buffeted us into losing considerable height. For some time we flew on not ready to admit defeat to the elements, looking for land marks or any recognisable point. At this point the skipper was flying by instinct alone and the rest of us were straining our eyes into the blackness. Suddenly 'Gib,' the rear gunner broke radio silence announcing that he had seen a red light to the starboard, verified by us all once we looked in that direction seeing a flashing beacon. The pilot, Dick Armitstead pulled hard on the control column and the Stirling surged up into the darkened sky, he had realized that the flashing light was a beacon on a cliff top and in fact we were flying dangerously low just above the sea. Dick broke radio silence and called 'mayday' on the R/T, the recognized distress call. Within seconds a very welcome reply came over the air and guided us to the nearest airfield within minutes of our position luckily. Despite the traumatic experience that we had all been through our pilot put the Stirling down on the runway at RAF St. Eval in Cornwall with his usual aplomb. We had experienced and survived the worst situation known to a bomber crew, lost in the night sky without instruments. It was an experience that made us realize how easy it would have been to fly into the sea and been lost forever without parents receiving the dreaded 'missing in action' telegram."

The next morning Ted Peck and crew returned to Shepherds Grove and after essential aircraft maintenance had been carried out, the crew successfully navigated back to base after one and a half hours flying time. An important lesson had been learned during the exercise, one of reliance on each other and the ability to trust each other's ability in times of crisis, attributes that would bode well during their operational tour of duty. After de-briefing it was recognized that as a crew they had performed well in difficult conditions and they were moved on to the next stage in their preparation for war. Lancaster production was significant and as a result Lancasters had been delivered to training units as a part of the final training for Lancaster crews. So it was in August 1944 that the crew were posted to RAF Woolfox Lodge Finishing School to experience the mighty Avro Lancaster, the aircraft that they would take to war. After a series of familiarization flights it became apparent that the Lancaster was far different from the Stirling. For Ted the flight engineer's duties were totally different with new fuel management systems and the Merlin engines to get used to. On Lancasters the pilot and flight engineer had a reliance on each other at crucial times during flight. For example, on take off and landing their respective checks were conducted by means of a mnemonic code which had to be remembered. The initial letter of each check was used to form a word or short sentence e.g. fuel pumps on would equate to the letter 'F'. A full series of preflight checks were carried out including engine warm up, fuel control, tank selector and booster pump and supercharger gear control plus various other important tasks. In the cockpit, Dick Armitstead was the 'governor' and particularly on take off when he was in full control of a dangerous situation. As he advanced the throttles against the brakes, Ted Peck followed the lever movement with his left hand just applying slight pressure to prevent them falling back with disastrous consequences. Once airborne and having reached a safe height, the throttles were eased back into a gentle climb and

Serial No. ....165. 1st Battle Order for 5th October, 1944. No. 622 Squadron.

A/C NO.	LETTER	CAPT. & 2ND PILOT.	NAV & W/OPERATOR.	A/B & M.U.GUNR.	R/GUNR. & F/ENGINEER.
HA.228	A.	[illegible]	F/Sgt. Ward F/S Aland	F/S [illegible] Sgt. [illegible]	Sgt. Woolcoff. Sgt. Boulton.
NF.939	B.	F/O Jones	W.O. Roberts W.O. Morison	F/ Pidley Sgt. Rogers	Sgt. Smith. Sgt. Hills.
HK.621	C.	W.O. Hanson.	Sgt. Holden F/S Drummond	F/S Stewart Sgt. Abbott F/S [illegible]	Sgt. Crawford. Sgt. Armstrong.
[illegible]	[illegible]	F/O Phillips	Sgt. Lowry Sgt. Burton	Sgt. Smart Sgt. Morgan	Sgt. York. Sgt. Barbor.
LM.577	E.	F/S Francis	Sgt. Stoodon Sgt. Kelly	Sgt. Traylon Sgt. Baxter	Sgt. Burton. Sgt. Soanes.
LM.235	G.	F/O Baxter	Sgt. Parsons Sgt. Brocker	F/S Hopkinson Sgt. Scouller	Sgt. Bressey. Sgt. Rositor.
NN.709	H.	F/O Armitstead F/O Flaxman	F/S Brewster Sgt. Foulkes.	Sgt. Daniels Sgt. Keylock	Sgt. Borgo Sgt. Peck.
LL.885	J.	F/O Peck	F/S Burchard F/O Gargill	F/O [illegible] Sgt. Tracey	Sgt. Rudney. Sgt. Bowyer.
NF.964	L.	F/S Richards	F/S Kidd Sgt. Doyle	F/O Mildren Sgt. Papps	Sgt. Nicholson. Sgt. Martin.
PD.332	N.	F/O Bonner.	F/S Brocker. F/S Vaughan	F/C Ward. F/S Lothian	F/S Hogan. Sgt. [illegible]
LM.283	O.	F/Lt. Orton	F/O Simpson Sgt. Collins	F/O Humphreys Sgt. Strong	W.O Prince. Sgt. Davis.
[illegible]164	P	F/S Campbell	Sgt. Galt F/S Jozzard	F/S Shepley Sgt. Fallows	Sgt. Hickling. Sgt. Hill.
HK.614	R.	F/O Cox	F/C. Taylor F/S Shino	F/O Titchener Sgt. Matthews.	Sgt. Gilroy. Sgt. Hughes.
LL.803	S.	F/Lt. Bean F/Lt. Cass	P/C Mead Sgt. MacFarlane	F/S Bullock Sgt. Harland	Sgt. Brown. Sgt. Willicombe.
NF.935	U.	F/O Nicholls	F/S Ponder Sgt. Cross.	F/S Wraith Sgt. Bond	Sgt. Smith. Sgt. Lawson.
LM.292	V.	F/O Richards	F/O Imboll Sgt. Martin	F/O Carter Sgt. Bryley	Sgt. Campbell. Sgt. Burnard.
HK.616	W.	F/C Woods	F/S Crest Sgt. Johnson	Sgt. Taylor W.O. [illegible] Sgt. Henderson	Sgt. Gentley. Sgt. Gooney.
HK.617	Y	F/O Hussey.	F/O Simpson Sgt. May	F/S Dalton F/S McRae Sgt. Potter	Sgt. O'Connor. Sgt. Hand.
HK615	Z	F/S Clarke	F/C Pentling F/S Williams	F/S Chaplin Sgt. Bryant	Sgt. Bryson. Sgt. Booth.

Officer i/c Flying Rations. :) F/C Dawson.(Rations obtainable from Discip Office Key in Guardroom.)
F/C Dawson's Crew to stand by for Endr.

(Sgd) I.C.K. Swales DSO DFC DFM
Wing Commander, Commanding No. 622 Squadron.

W/C Swales S/Ldr. Allen S/Ldr. Mitchell F/Lt. Nicholl. F/Lt. Middleton. F/Lt. Turner. F/C Chapman. F/Lt. Ward.

Example of Battle Order for the raid to Saarbrucken on 5th October 1944. F/O Armitstead can be clearly seen assigned to Lancaster NN709, GI-H. The keen eye will note that the crew was assigned Pilot Officer Flaxman as a 'second dickey' crew member. *Courtesy of Ted Peck F/E 622 Sqdn.2*

Dick Armistead trimmed the aircraft to give the Lancaster a stable feel in the air. Towards the end of August 1944, with just eleven hours flying time on Lancasters, Ted Peck and crew were posted to an operational squadron.

Down To Business

RAF Mildenhall was a pre-war station that had better facilities for aircrew than the hastily built war stations. By August 1944 the Allied fighters had achieved almost total air superiority by day and dealt the Luftwaffe a bloody nose with long range fighters able to escort bombers to the target and back. In addition, Allied troops were pushing the German forces into retreat and further back into their homeland. Ted Peck and his crew's arrival coincided with a change in strategy for Bomber Command, one that would require the crew to concentrate on oil installations, lines of communication, industrial nerve centers and finally enemy troop concentrations.

Ted Peck and his crew were assigned to 'A' flight under the leadership of S/Ldr Richard Allen DFC, their flight commander. As a crew they soon found their way around the station and in particular the Sergeant's mess and bar. By far the most important area of the mess was the area that displayed the notice board. It was here that the battle orders were posted with the names of the crews detailed to take part in the operation and also the code letter of the aircraft in which they would fly. The pilots name came immediately after the aircraft details.

It was customary for pilots to undertake a 'second dickey' trip with an experienced crew to have first hand knowledge of what to expect once in the hot seat. Dick Armitstead was quickly on the Battle Order to fly as 'second dickey' on the night of 18th August, target Bremen. Aircrew were extremely superstitious and these trips that were seen as unlucky and potentially fatal. This was due to a practiced routine being interrupted by what some considered to be an additional, untried crew member. Thankfully, F/O Armitstead returned safely to a barrage of questions from the crew. Further training flights were undertaken to practice bombing and to get used to the location of the airfield. Finally, they appeared on the battle order on a 'bullseye' to Bristol as a diversionary measure to fool German radar. This exercise came as a disappointment to the crew, although they would not have to wait long for a real taste of the Ruhr Valley and its defenses.

First Mission

On 26th August 1944 the crew's tour of operations commenced in earnest with a five and a half hour trip to Kiel dock installations at night. At briefing, the crew was made aware that Kiel was a heavily defended target with considerable Anti-aircraft fire and searchlights, a real baptism of fire for a 'fresh crew'. The early fears, butterflies and dry mouths were overcome and the crew bombed the target and returned without incident-29 to go! At de-briefing Ted Peck was offered a cup of coffee by a WAAF and his first taste of rum to go with it. Ted was not accustomed to drinking rum and the large dose added to his coffee made his legs wobbly on the walk back to the billet, however, he slept soundly without reliving his first operation over again in his mind.

Operations came thick and fast including an attack on a V1 dump at Port Remy in France and several trips in support of the Allied troops who were resurgent on their march through France. Ted Peck aptly describes the experience of an actual bombing mission in the following passage:

> "Any member of aircrew who say that they were not at some time scared are being sparing with the truth. I know that I was scared quite a few times, but it was something that you had to live with. What was the alternative, letting your squadron down, letting yourself down, or worse of all letting your crewmates down. One incident remains clear in my mind, the actual date or time is not of great importance but I recall that it took place on a night raid into the Ruhr. We had encountered some flak on the run in to the target but luckily had sustained no damage.
>
> Over the target all hell broke loose with flashes of AA shell burst to near for comfort, leaving a black puff of smoke visible against the light of the fires on the ground. Searchlights were swinging a finger of light, probing the sky to illuminate a plane moving slowly towards its target. Tracer shells rising, it seemed, loomed lazily

End of 'tour' photograph taken in December 1944. The Lancaster is NN709, GI-H, the aircraft that F/Lt Armitstead and crew completed most of their missions within. The crew are as follows: L to R: F/Sgt Daniels (B/A), F/Sgt Borge (R/G), F/Sgt Brewster RAAF (Nav), F/Lt Armitstead (Pilot), F/Sgt Keylock (MUG), F/Sgt Foulkes (W/op), Sgt E.B. Peck (F/E). *Courtesy of Ted Peck F/E 622 Sqdn.*

towards us. Great orange swells of light as high explosive bombs burst in the target area. Other aircraft in trouble, flames streaming behind them with little hope for their salvation, it was a very frightening sight and one that will stay with me forever.

Over the target it was my job to stand beside the pilot and give any help needed, to watch for enemy fighters and any of our own aircraft in the bomber stream coming too close. In the event of what I was witnessing, I became overcome with what can only be described as fear. My legs began to shake violently and uncontrollably, I had heard about knees knocking but this was different. The flight engineer on a Lancaster had the use of a small seat which folded down from the side of the fuselage. I quickly dropped the seat down and used it to lean against without actually sitting down and braced my legs against the floor. In this way I was able to control the shivering in my legs and get on with the job without anyone noticing my predicament."

Ted Peck knew that the chances of surviving a full tour of operations was in the lap of the gods and the crew would often witness the station police removing the personal effects from aircrews lockers if they failed to return. There was seemingly no lack of courage among aircrews' although it was difficult to judge a man's true inner feelings when faced with danger every operation. The RAF had a term for aircrew who could not face the danger any longer and this was recorded as ' Lack of moral fiber' (LMF). During the war, there was little sympathy for anybody who refused to fly and they would be stripped of their rank and flying badges often in front of a full parade, and finally posted away. Today medical knowledge has improved dramatically and sheer fear and mental health is now recognized as a genuine illness that needs treatment not ridicule. Ted would reflect on his own vulnerability when he saw other aircraft going down over enemy territory. It was a terrible sight to see a crippled bomber spiraling to earth knowing that its crew stood only a minimal chance of survival.

During a daylight raid Ted and the crew were on the receiving end of a nasty shock. The bomber stream was tightly packed with aircraft flying close together, not in formation but close enough to be able to read identification markings clearly. The flak wasn't heavy by any means, a few bursts which seemed to be well below the Lancasters as they flew on towards the target. Suddenly the Lancaster in front must have received a direct hit in the bomb bay for it exploded killing the crew instantly leaving only a black patch of smoke. Ted Peck knew the flight engineer well, a tall black haired Welshman whom he got along with well. To protect themselves from fate aircrew would carry good luck mementoes in the form of stockings, scarves or garments that are even more intimate. Ted's father kept rabbits and he asked his father to keep a rabbit's foot for him when he next slaughtered a rabbit and Ted carried this rabbit's foot with him on all operations that followed.

In any operation there were three periods of heightened tension, take off, the bombing run into the target and landing. Take off with full fuel and bomb bays was a tense experience setting out often in total darkness. At the end of the runway the pilot increased the engines to full power, against the brakes until the green aldis light from the controller's caravan gave the all clear for take off. The Lancaster screamed down the runway until it reached take off speed and gently lifted off the tarmac into the night sky, this was an extremely tense moment for everyone knew that a mechanical error at a crucial time could have fatal consequences. The run into the target and over it, while the pilot was holding the aircraft steady, in level flight was particularly tense. It was at this point that the Lancaster was at the most vulnerable to attack from flak and fighters.

Throughout the run into the target, the gunners were at constant readiness watching for enemy fighters and their quick reflexes saved many crew lives. The rest of the crew kept a watchful eye out for attackers from their respective positions. The navigator usually stuck to his charts ready to give the pilot a new course to steer once the bombs had been dropped. The wireless operator took up position in the astro dome and the bomb aimer was transfixed with his bombing sight ready to release the bombs. The magic words 'bombs gone' coincided with the Lancaster lifting almost in relief from losing the extra weight. The navigator gave an immediate course to steer away from the danger area, although no one could relax until usually over the North Sea, approaching home. The third period of tension was the landing and the possibility of night fighters laying in wait for the returning bombers. There was a code that ground controllers used to advise returning aircraft of the presence of enemy fighters. In the majority of cases, it was a case of cruising around at a height given by the controller, whilst keeping a lookout for prowling fighters until it was an aircraft's time to land. The instructions for landing were transmitted by a WAAF Officer and would take the form of the aircraft's code letter; in this case; 'H' How Pancake. Pancake was the signal to begin the landing circuit and line up with the appropriate runway.

Flight engineer Sgt Peck would check that all systems were functioning correctly especially that the undercarriage was down and locked in position. The pilot would then be in full control of the landing whilst the flight engineer would operate the flaps control as instructed by the pilot. Finally going around the airfield on the down wind leg the pilot would call up the ground controller on the R/T and advise that he was 'downwind'. The next call to the ground would be 'funnels' when the aircraft had moved round the circuit and entered the funnel of lights which would eventually lead the aircraft down to land. The majority of the landings went without incident except for one occasion when the Lancaster had a 500lb bomb hung up in the bomb bay. The pilot tried every maneuver to try and dislodge the bomb over the North Sea, however it would not budge. On approach for landing the crew tried to lower the undercarriage and noticed that the green locked light did not flash up indicating that all was not well. Whenever the undercarriage was reluctant to lock down the Lancaster would be thrown around the sky in an attempt to lock the landing gear. On this occasion this maneuver was not possible due to the 'hang up' in the bomb bay and Dick Armitstead reported the situation to the ground controller. Emergency air was pushed through the hydraulic system designed to give the undercarriage the final push it required, alas to no effect. Landing permission was given and emergency vehicles were on standby by the edge of the runway as Pilot Officer Armitstead carried out a measured landing and the Lancaster was pulled onto the grass without the need of the emergency vehicles. The 500lb bomb had stayed in place and the undercarriage carried the full weight of the Lancaster. At briefing, searching questions were asked and Lancaster NN709 was placed into maintenance for repair to the hydraulic system.

As September gave way to October 1944 the crew had completed eleven operations and Dick Armitstead had been promoted to Flying Officer. The crew flew mainly daylight raids some of which were in support of Allied troops fighting their way forward in France. There were a number of pockets of resistance and also a few heavy gun emplacements which came in for a pounding at the request of the Army. On one occasion, the crew carried out a daylight raid to bomb German troop positions in Le Harve with very little degree of error expected. The aiming point was very close to Allied troop positions and any error may have seen the bombers release their bombs on allied troops, which unfortunately did occur from time to time.

Bombing strategy at this stage of the war was in an experimental stage and the crews commenced formation flying practice. This training was very unpopular with crews and the concentration required for a pilot to stay in formation was extremely tiring. This particular type of training was to assist the new G/H leader type of bombing where one Lancaster had G/H radar fitted and a specially trained navigator to operate the equipment. Once the G/H equipped Lancaster released its bombs then the others in the formation would follow suit. This tactic was successfully deployed by 3 Group on all daylight operations towards the latter half of 1944.

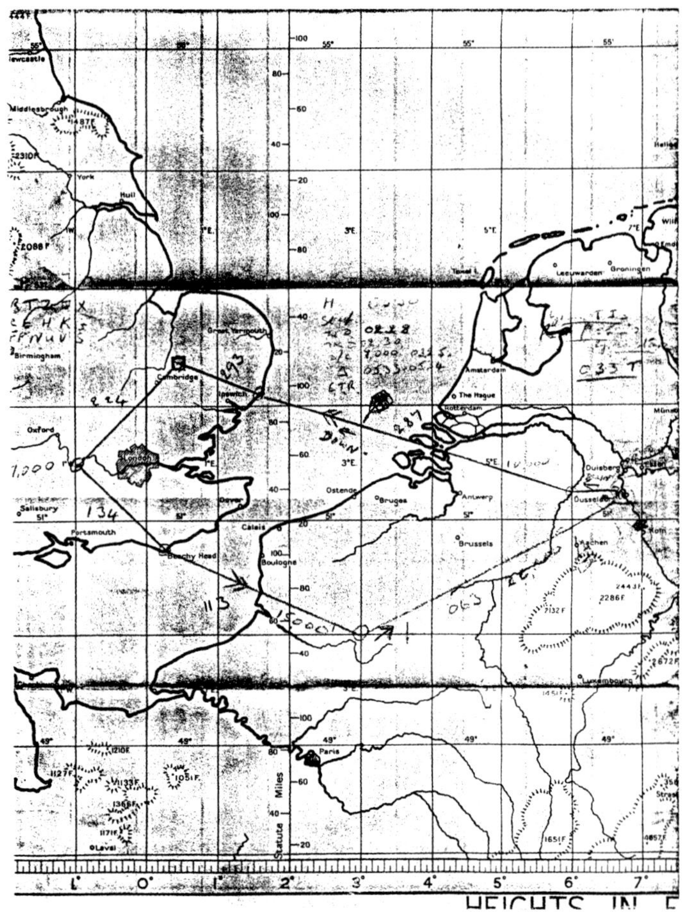

The flight plan drafted by F/Lt Armistead to map his route to Neuss in the Ruhr. Mildenhall is marked with a square and the target is shown as a triangle. Rendezvous was over Reading. Time over target was estimated at 05.33 to 05.34 hrs. Bombing was on green target indicators, red and green stars. Take off was at 02.37 and landing was 4 hrs 40 minutes later at 07:17 hrs. The course and heights can be seen, the bombing height appears to be 26,000ft. After the target, the crew were to lose height to 10,000 ft across Holland and then gradually reduce height to base. *Courtesy of Ted Peck F/E 622 Sqdn.*

Bombing photograph for a mission to attack German troop positions at Le Harve on 10th September 1944. This photograph was presented to Ted Peck by his pilot at 'tour' completion. *Courtesy of Ted Peck F/E 622 Sqdn.*

During October the crew engaged in an equal number of day and night missions in their usual Lancaster NN709, GI-H an aircraft that the crew would have an affinity with. All the raids during October were on targets in the Ruhr and in particular German industrial centers with four plus hours by day and five plus by night when visiting targets deeper inside Germany.

On 14th October Flying Officer Armitstead and crew carried out two missions to the same target within twenty four hours. The target was the city of Duisberg and its communication, factories and railway facilities. Take off on the first trip was 06.30 hrs and the crew bombed the target without incident landing at around 11.00hrs. The second trip take off was scheduled for 22.30hrs with a landing back at Mildenhall the following day at 04.20hrs. The night raid did not go without incident and the mid upper gunner spotted a German night fighter so close to the aircraft it could have been undertaking formation flying. Through whatever stroke of luck the fighter did not engage the crew. This raid was to become known on the squadron as the 'Double Duisberg' and everyone

The actual operations board in the operations room at RAF Mildenhall. The details depict a mission on the marshaling yards at NEUSS by XV and 622 Squadrons. F/O Armitstead and crew feature on the battle order in Lancaster 'H'. *Courtesy of Ted Peck F/E 622 Sqdn.*

was proud of the squadron's achievement of putting so many Lancasters over the same target twice in one day.

November came around and Dick Armitstead was promoted to Flight Lieutenant in recognition of his professionalism and experience after completing 22 operations. As a crew they were now relatively experienced and believed that they could navigate into 'Happy Valley' without navigational aids, a confidence born from visiting the Ruhr valley on numerous occasions. The crew visited Homberg on three separate occasions to destroy the huge oil installation which was now a priority for Bomber Command. It had been recognized that without fuel the German war machine would grind to a halt, and subsequently this came to fruition through constant bombing.

Approaching the end of a tour of operations is probably the most tense and vulnerable time for a crew. Crews tended to relax a little and 'got the chop' when the end was in sight. The crew was determined that this would not happen to them and they maintained their efficient standards in the air right up until they had completed their final mission. Towards the end of November 1944 the time came for the crew to carry out a mission without their skipper in order for them to finish on an equal 30. F/Lt Armitstead had completed a 'second dickey' trip and therefore he was one ahead of the rest of the crew. On the last day of November the crew was on the battle order to attack the steel works at Bottrop with the new squadron Commanding Officer at the helm. Wing Commander Buckingham was an experienced pilot and he appreciated the professionalism that the crew showed during the mission, a fact that was fed back to the crew.

On 6th December 1944 the Armitstead crew was briefed for their last mission to attack Mersberg deep inside German territory. The crew's usual Lancaster NN709, GI-H was in for servicing so the crew was allotted GI-Q. The squadron lost more Lancasters with the markings of 'Q' than any other alphabetical letter, and the superstition among the crew was intense. Their last mission and they were assigned the dreaded 'Q'. True to speculation, the mission was jinxed from the start with the engine radiator grills not operating correctly causing over heating to the engines. This fault was fixed and the result was a late take off alone. A lone aircraft stands out to German radar controllers and is sure to attract German fighters. Shortly after take off the rear turret developed a fault disabling the turret's ability to swing from side to side. With an unserviceable rear turret F/Lt Armistead was not going to risk the lives of the crew and he reluctantly took the decision to return to base and possibly saved their lives. Two nights later the crew was on the battle order to attack the marshaling yards at Duisberg at night. This particular marshaling yard was orchestrating a great deal of supplies to the German forces. Over the target the crew were coned by a searchlight for the first time whilst on the bombing run. Almost immediately F/Lt Armitstead threw the Lancaster across the sky losing the searchlight in the process. Luckily for the crew the searchlight was not one of the blue light master beams which triggered all others to locate the same target and lock on. The remainder of the trip went without incident and the crew touched down for the final time at Mildenhall with an enormous sense of relief.

Edward Peck had come a long way from the time of his first thoughts of joining the RAF. He had achieved his aim of becoming a flight engineer and trained to the highest standard with the RAF in that role. The crew commenced operational flying in August 1944 and had completed a total of thirty operations by early December, a remarkable feat of endurance and professionalism by any standards. In total, the crew had known each other for around five months and individual personalities had been harnessed into an efficient and effective bomber crew. What started out as a group of highly trained young individual men was turned into a family of brothers who would have laid down their lives for each other. Such was the respect for each other that would last a lifetime. The saddest part was the splitting up of the crew to their respective new duties and the fact that some of them would never see each other again.

It was as a crew in December 1944 that they paraded outside the flight offices at Mildenhall in one of the big hangars that is still

End of 'tour' photograph, Ground crew and aircrew, taken on 'A' flight dispersal on December 9th 1944. Left to right: Johnnie Claff (FME), Sgt Ted Peck (F/E), LAC Alf Griffin (FME), F/Sgt Danny Daniels (B/A), LAC Ron Branham (FME), F/Sgt 'Gib' Borge (R/G), F/Sgt Dave Brewster (Nav), F/Lt Dick Armitstead (pilot), LAC Jack Heaton (FMA), F/Sgt Eric Keylock (MUG), LAC Bill Ellis (FME), F/Sgt Johnnie Foulkes (W/op), LAC Cliff Ward (FME), Sgt Chalky White, i/c ground crew. *Courtesy of Ted Peck F/E 622 Sqdn.*

there today. The whole crew was congratulated, thanked and then dismissed, somewhat of an anti-climax to end proceedings. There were 'no medals for bravery' for the Armitstead crew in light of all the trials and tribulations of completing a tour of operations against a determined enemy. In some respects this was a grave injustice on behalf of the RAF; here was a crew that had carried out their duties in a competent and assured manner without drawing the notoriety to themselves that would have surely resulted in medals for at least some of the crew. F/Lt Armitstead had finished his tour as a flight commander and he was the only flight commander to serve with the squadron and not receive a D.F.C. at the end of tour, an oversight too damning to contemplate. Edward Peck has often evaluated his period with the Royal Air Force and remembers fondly the period in his life when the RAF gave him six brothers.

Tribute to All

"Whenever aircrews talk about life on an operational bomber squadron, great affection is always shown towards the members of the ground crew staff. Without the diligence and professionalism shown by the ground crew, a great number of aircraft would not have reached the target and back. The Lancaster was a mass of mechanical engineering that required various specialists such as engine and airframe fitters, armorers and electrical engineers. Working in all weathers the ground crew ensured that the aircraft was in first class condition on every sortie into enemy territory and maximized the chances of survival for the aircrew. The ground crew showed considerable distress at the loss of a crew and its aircraft; and a great many aircrew owe their lives to these unsung heroes of Bomber Command."

"We never forgot the devotion of the Ground Crew to our aircraft and to us." E. B. Peck.

27

My Time at Mildenhall F/Sgt E. J Taylor

Eric Taylor, the flight engineer in the crew, has provided the following account of his time on the squadron during the first half of 1945:

"I was very apprehensive when I walked into the recruiting office in Norwich and volunteered for aircrew training. I was initially accepted and duly arrived for my medical and assessment at RAF Cardington near Bedford. After passing various assessments I was eventually called up to Lords Cricket Ground and spent three weeks being kitted out and being injected with all sorts of potions. Once the initial pleasantries were over I was dispatched to the initial training wing at Newquay and in particular to the Beachcomber Hotel for the next few weeks. My training included theory of flight, King's regulations, NCO duties and Morse code for approximately six weeks. My personal attributes appeared to favor the role of flight engineer, being the practical type, I was assessed as suitable for flight engineer training. For my specialized training I was sent to the operational training unit at St Athens, which focused on flight engineers among other things. The course lasted for around 26 weeks and I learned just about everything associated with engines and fuel systems and mechanical engineering in general. It was at St Athens that I qualified and I was awarded my sergeant's stripes. My next posting was to Heavy Conversion Unit at Stradishall where I joined the crew of Johnnie Fiedler who wore the slightly darker uniform of the Royal Australian Air Force, the rest of the crew had a similar route to aircrew. It was unusual for the skipper and the W/op to have consecutive service numbers. The majority of the time at Stradishall was centered on the conversion to four engined bombers and their particular handling characteristics. We completed numerous circuits and bumps in the Short Stirling and molded ourselves into an efficient crew by the end of the course. The Short Stirlings that we flew had completed many hours and this often reflected in their flying capabilities. In December 1944 we were posted to Lancaster Finishing School at Methwold to familiarize ourselves with the formidable Lancaster and then we received the news of our posting to RAF Mildenhall and 622 Squadron. In early January 1945, we arrived at Mildenhall, a pre-war station with brick built permanent buildings, a far cry from some airfields that had been purpose built for the war with corrugated house blocks. In comparison Mildenhall was luxury and we were assigned to a house where we all could be together as a crew.

To place things into perspective our arrival at Mildenhall coincided with our Allied forces having made

Flying Officer Fiedler RAAF & crew commenced flying operationally in January 1945 and remained with the squadron until the end of hostilities. Crew: F/O Fiedler RAAF pilot, F/S Elliott Nav, F/S Doherty B/A, W/O Fitch RAAF W/op, Sgt Palmer MUG, Sgt Smith R/G, F/Sgt Taylor F/E. *Courtesy of E. J Taylor, Flight Engineer.*

considerable inroads into the German army, pushing them further back into their homeland. The overall bombing strategy was in the hands of General Eisenhower, the Supreme Allied Commander. The 'air armada' was being directed at strategic targets, especially on the enemy's fuel-supply in an attempt to starve the Germans aircraft and armored vehicles of vital fuel. Many crews had quickly finished their operational tours of 30 trips on short trips to the French coast, sometimes more than one trip a day, preparing for, and supporting the Normandy landings on June 6th 1944. The continuous support of the ground forces resulted in a need for more bomber crews and we were a replacement crew for the crews who had completed their 'tour' of operations in double quick time over French targets.

Our first flight from the runway at Mildenhall was on 10th January 1945 and it was in the form of a familiarization flight. It may be assumed that on an operational squadron crews only flew bombing raids. Quite wrong, for a start further training flights were scheduled when they could be fitted in, especially if there was a change in tactics or if new equipment became available. Then there were test flights after repairs or engine changes when ground crews were on board. There were also weather flights, and ferrying trips to fit into the busy programme. On one such occasion we flew a spare crew to Woodbridge to recover one of our Lancasters. Woodbridge was termed as a 'crash drome'; it was where aircraft in trouble were directed to land on the very wide and long runway. Whilst I was there I witnessed two spitfires take off side by side not down, but across the runway. When it was our turn to leave we reciprocated the spitfires by taking off side by side, although it took us slightly longer to become airborne and we took the full length of the runway. RAF Woodbridge was in the hands of the Americans and they were not as strict as the RAF controllers. The sky was always dotted about with aircraft and it was the time of the V1 'Doodlebug' rockets. It was always necessary to keep a keen lookout to avoid collision and the modern controllers would have been most perturbed if similar situations occurred today.

Fighter affiliation trips were always welcome to new crews because it was on these exercises that a crew honed its defensive tactics in case of enemy fighter attack. On these exercises we usually flew with a second crew of pilot and gunners to share the experience. The actual exercise involved being attacked by two American fighters who would simulate mock attacks from all angles and the gunners would record their results on a gun camera, and the pilots would practice their corkscrew manoeuvers. On this particular day, I had digested apricots for dessert as a part of the preflight meal. The pilots really threw the Lancaster around the sky to avoid the fighters and I regurgitated my meal of apricots during a bout of airsickness. During another exercise an instructor pilot who had been on a fighter aircraft course accompanied us. He took the pilot's controls and after getting permission to land proceeded to land after completing a tight circuit almost as if he was in a fighter. His approach to the runway was all wrong and he was too high and too fast which resulted in him hitting the runway very hard causing the Lancaster tail wheel to break off and we bounced. Instead of giving the engines a burst he let the Lancaster bounce again which resulted in our skipper giving the Lancaster a burst of power from the Merlins, which allowed the Lancaster to settle in. When the tail wheel came down on the wheel stud a shower of sparks ensued. Usually, on landing the tail gunner comes forward as a safety precaution, but because of having two sets of gunners on board, the other gunner had stayed in the rear turret and suffered a broken vertebra in his back as a result of the awful landing.

On 28th January 1945 we were on the battle order for our first operation, which was a daylight mission in formation to Cologne. I had no idea that the RAF was doing daylight raids like our American Allies. Dominance of the skies over Germany had been achieved due to the escorting fighters that could now accompany the bombers deep into Germany and back. The continuous

Great shot of three 622 Squadron Lancasters en route to the target during a daylight mission in early 1945. The aircraft nearest the camera is GI-K, PD819 with GI-A, PD228 in close formation. Completing the trio is GI-Z, HK615. Lancasters equipped with G/H radar would lead 'vic' formations of three aircraft to the target and when they released their bombs the other aircraft in the formation would follow suit. *Courtesy of James McCahill.*

bombardment of Germany's industry had resulted in fewer fighters to put up against us and the losses they were experiencing resulted in fewer pilots to fly what planes they had available.

We had certainly not practiced formation flying since I joined the crew at HCU, but here we were all assembling over Kings Lynn in flights and in 'V' formation. We found our position in the bomber stream using colored flares to maintain radio silence and then proceeding out to sea. By this stage of the war 3 Group had mastered the art of the G/H bombing technique. Several of the Lancasters were equipped with the navigational aid of G/H, which provided a topographical picture of the ground from a rotating radar dish positioned under the fuselage of the Lancaster. These Lancasters were given distinctive yellow bar markings on the tail fins so that crews were able to distinguish them. When these Lancasters released their bombs, it was the signal for the rest of the 'Lancs' in formation to drop their load also. The Lancaster depicted below is displaying the G/H markings on the tail fins and we flew several missions in this particular aircraft."

"In addition to G/H we had the wonderful navigational direction finder entitled Oboe. This was a system that utilized three ground radar stations that were strategically placed. These stations could transmit radar beams that crossed directly over the target and sent out a continuous radar pulse, which indicated the exact point to release the bombs. Oboe had been used for quite some time by this stage of the war and it had produced some amazingly accurate results. On one of the initial missions that used Oboe bombing over the industrial Ruhr, the bombing of factories was so accurate that Hitler ordered all the surrounding building to be searched, because he was convinced that a secret agent using a transmitter had guided the bombers to the target. The Germans did not establish the true accuracy of Oboe until they retrieved an Oboe transmitter from a crashed bomber some time later.

Our bomb load for this mission was a mixture of 1,000lb bombs and en route to the target my job was to push 'window' out of a shoot near my flight engineer's position. Window was metal foil strips cut to an exact length, which confused the German radar systems. As we neared the target I couldn't see our escorting fighters and there was a long queue of bombers ahead of us and we could see a formation of bombers about 200 feet above us converging from behind right. This sight brought alarm to us because we feared that the bombers above us would drop their bombs on top of us, however they forged ahead of us thankfully. There were black dots of flak peppering the sky in front of us which was commonly known as box barrage and I was sure that one of those flak burst would hit our aircraft, it was that dense and concentrated. The cloud below us broke up and the weather forecasters had wrongly predicted the weather over the target. The air is incredibly turbulent and as we hit air pockets or slipstreams, we dropped like a stone down two or three hundred feet due to our all up weight. The skipper and I had to fight with the controls to maintain formation. I was suddenly aware of the realities of war compared to the theory and practice. My role evolved into dropping 'window' at the same time as trying to record the management of the four Merlin engines and log down the different engine settings as they occur, the practice was certainly different from the theory!

We reached the target area unharmed and we watched the formation leader (Oboe and G/H equipped) when he opened his bomb doors, we would follow suit. We bombed on his actions and released our bombs a split second behind seeing his bombs released, the Lancaster pulled up through the sky relieved of its bomb load and we turned for home. I have to admit the sense of relief at achieving our aim and I allowed myself to laugh at the sight of the flight leaders 'cookie' bomb going down. The so called 'cookie' is an impact bomb much like a tar barrel and it looked incongruous as it pitched and rolled before headed down. I visited Cologne in 1947 and saw the cathedral standing virtually unscathed although I saw a blue quarry-paving tile that had partially melted obviously, when an incendiary bomb had burned itself out.

The daylight raids at this time of the winter were dirty weather jobs and often the cloud base at home was dangerously low. Descending through cloud to land was a frightening experience and comparable to the bombing run. Accidents were all too often occurring and every field on descent looked like an airfield. During August 1944, Mildenhall put up 39 fully fuelled and bombed up Lancasters at forty seven second intervals, which is quite a feat. Take off and landing was a testing time and one incident could result in considerable loss of life. At Mildenhall, there was always a scattering of well wishes at the take off end of the runway, always a heartening sight, probably not very wise all things considered."

The month of February began in dramatic fashion for another Australian pilot, Flying Officer Geoff Conacher and his all English crew. The target was a daylight trip to Mönchengladbach bombing with the aid of G/H radar. The crew were assigned Lancaster HK617, GI-Q for their first mission over enemy territory. Rather unusually F/O Conacher had not completed a '2nd dickey' trip with an experienced pilot prior to this mission, an oversight in retrospect that could have prevented the aircraft from crashing. Geoff Coancher describes in his own words what occurred:

"The aircraft we were allocated had provision (a hole in the floor between the mid upper and rear turrets) for a .5 machine gun, requiring a spare gunner to be carried. Sergeant Edward Baxter was assigned to the crew for what would have been his thirtieth and final mission.

Shortly after take-off and before crossing the coast, we noticed a small oil leak on the front edge of the port main plane at the inner engine. The engine was behaving perfectly so we continued. As we progressed the leak began spreading slowly over the wing. The flight engineer could detect no fault, but it was becoming worrying, although we were still keeping our position in the stream. However, over Europe the situation quickly worsened, with the main plane covered, and oil now hitting the rear turret, we began to lose our position in the stream. Before long, we were 3000 feet below the stream and falling behind. I made the decision to turn back about 20 minutes before the target and feather the engine. When this was attempted the propeller ran away, so with the engine shut down the propeller then began to windmill at around 4000 r.p.m. The aircraft soon began to vibrate excessively and despite efforts to reduce the wind milling, flames were seen to be coming from the port inner. Attempts to douse the fire were not successful. Our main fear was, of course the fire, and this quickly spread to the fuselage. The aircraft was now becoming increasingly difficult to control, and after we had crossed into liberated France, I decided to abandon the aircraft, and advised the crew accordingly. We all landed at a place in France called Vitry en Artois near Rheims.

The normal drill was for the two gunners and the wireless operator to leave by the back door. Because we had the extra gun, however, it was ok for the mid-under gun to be jettisoned, and the three gunners and the wireless operator, leave through the floor. The mid under gunner had difficulty in jettisoning the gun despite assistance from the others. I instructed them to stop trying and use the back door. They advised they were in position (last one out maintains contact with the pilot). I gave the order to jump. I could view the back door from my seat, and when I saw no one was left, I called up on the intercom and there was no answer. I assumed everyone had gone and proceeded to follow the bomb aimer, navigator and flight engineer out of the front hatch.

When we met up on the ground we quickly learned that Sgt. Baxter was dead. It was revealed by the others that he seemed reluctant to leave by the rear door, obviously because of what appears to be the uncertainty of striking the tail plane. Unfortunately, Sgt. Baxter must have returned to his gun position in the floor and again tried to jettison the gun. Because of the main spar, that gun position cannot be seen from the pilot's seat and with no intercom response, I made my exit.

Sgt. Baxter appeared to have jumped eventually, but it was seen by people on the ground that his parachute was on fire. It was a tragic episode, and although we, as a crew, did not really know him, he has never been forgotten.

It could be said that the flight engineer and myself, for that matter, should have realized the oil must have been coming from the constant speed unit. However in our defence, it was our first trip, my mechanical knowledge was, and never has been great."

Eric Taylor picks up the story again:

"The month of February 1945 saw us complete seven daylight operations and one trip at night to Dortmund. We suffered no real damage other than a little hole or two and some chipped Perspex, fortunately we saw no enemy fighters. The Normandy landings had made our job easier and the continuous push by the Allied Armies further and further into Germany overrunning the German fighter airfields based in France. Hitler's hatred for the Russians had resulted in him making the tactical error of opening up two war fronts against the Allies and the Russians. This stretched his army and Luftwaffe to breaking point and placed Hitler and his armed forces on the back foot. During the latter part of 1943 and even leading up to the 'D' Day invasion in early June 1944. The Luftwaffe had inflicted heavy losses on the British and American air forces through effective fighter tactics and the electronic air radar war. In fact that we had come very close to losing the bomber war over Germany. During the latter half of 1944, the Americans developed their fighter escorts inflicting considerable losses on the Luftwaffe and also allowing the bombers to become more effective on the targeting of oil installations and aircraft factories. A major contributory factor in turning the tide in the bombers favor was the introduction of the American Mustang long-range fighter escort. On its initial entry into active service the Mustang was a very average fighter with poor performance at high altitude due to its American power plant. To improve performance it was fitted with the Rolls Royce Merlin engine, the same engine that powered the Spitfire and the Lancaster. The American Packard Company produced the Merlin under licence and it completely transformed the Mustang into a world-beater. The Mustang was able to out perform the German fighter in every aspect and with the addition of 'drop tanks' that could be jettisoned allowing bombers to go deeper into Germany unmolested."

On 13th February 1945, the crew were detailed to attack the German city of Dresden. This particular mission would become infamous for the number of civilian lives lost. Eric Taylor's account of this mission can be found in Chapter 28. Eric contines with his story:

"On February 22nd 1945, we completed the first of three trips to Gelsenkirchen in 'A' for apple PD228, to attack the coking plant there that was supplying the enemy with vital fuel to make armaments. On all three occasions the target was under heavy cloud. On the first occasion we approached the target and were enveloped by dark black thunderclouds up to 23,000ft and beyond our operational ceiling. The bomber leader continued into the cloud in a dangerous manoeuver due to the fact we were in formation and the likelihood of collision was very high. We followed the leader into the thundercloud and almost immediately we were being tossed about like a cork in a rough sea. The skipper was fighting to maintain control of the Lancaster whilst flying blind and hoping not to collide with other aircraft in the same predicament. Due to not being able to identify the target we ditched the bombs on another target and set course for home. I later learned that there was no secondary target planned which seems ludicrous considering the unpredictable weather during the month of February. The second and third trip to Gelsenkirchen went without incident and we bombed on the G/H leaders mark.

The appalling losses suffered by the early British and Allied aircrews has never been fully recognized or their contribution to the war effort. At the peak of RAF losses in early 1944, a crew reported to an airbase in Lincolnshire and eventually reported to the sergeant's mess. On entering the room they asked the question "what happens when crews have completed their tours", the reply was "nobody knows it has never happened". Over 55,000 aircrew lost their lives and at the peak of the losses an airman had a less than a one in two chance of surviving a full tour of thirty missions.

Early in March 1945 our skipper was commissioned to Pilot Officer and moved into the Officers mess. We continued daylight bombing using Oboe radar and a few memories stick in my mind. On one daylight operation we were in formation behind a stream when one of the vector leaders in front received a direct flak hit. There was an almighty flash and the Lancaster just disintegrated leaving a puff of smoke, the nearest bomber had bits knocked off from the resulting explosion and we witnessed it go down in flames with no parachutes evident. Shortly after, another Lancaster lost an engine due to flak and feathered the propeller resulting in a considerable loss of height. It transpired that the vector leader was the commanding officer of No.90 Squadron at Tuddenham just down the road from Mildenhall.

During my training I was supposed to pass a night vision test, and I remember thinking that I had failed because in the blacked out hut where model aeroplanes were pulled round on a overhead line, I couldn't see a thing and I somehow passed the test. Our crew was trained well and we all appreciated the training that we had been given as a crew and its key to our survival. When we were in that Lancaster we were totally focused on procedure and our skipper never engaged the autopilot sometimes referred to as 'George'. We never indulged in idle chat over the intercom, for these reasons we were now considered an experienced crew.

Similarities can be drawn from the length of the Dresden raid to another night trip we undertook to Dessau on 7th March 1945. We were again on our maximum all up weight, whilst climbing for height to burn off fuel, we experienced a loud thump, and we knew that we had been hit. I was frantically searching the wing tops as much as I could see when a 'vortex' developed from a vapor trail issuing from the starboard flap hinge. I was on my knees at this time looking for clues to the area of damage from any fluctuations on my instrument panel. The rear gunner, a replacement for the sick Sgt.Smith, asked for permission to leave the rear turret to try to ascertain the damaged area. The mid upper gunner told the skipper to feather the starboard engine and I was in a position to say that the engine was performing perfectly. I was drawing my own conclusions and decided that the No.1 fuel tank must be leaking, when the vapor trail faded and stopped. Shortly afterwards we could smell petrol fumes through our oxygen masks and on the return journey heading for home, we took off our masks to the unbearable smell of petrol fumes. On landing, as soon as the tail came down, petrol cascaded from the wing so we shut down the engines and we were towed into the dispersal. The next day we went to see what had hit us and the petrol tank had been exposed. There was a groove cut along the outer rear wall of the petrol tank and the inner layer of the self-sealing tank had been penetrated at the very top. There was a big piece of shrapnel embedded in the wing strut. It transpired later that the enemy had devised a different way of attacking our bombers. The German night fighters were equipped with upward firing cannons known as 'Schräge Musik', a German nickname given to the Nachtjagd night fighter planes. This mode of attack proved to be lethal and took a fearsome toll of heavy bombers in the night battles. The night fighters used the technique of climbing underneath the bomber to stealthily regulate course and speed to be in exactly the right position to fire and ensure a 'kill'. When in position the night fighter would aim for the starboard inner (No.1) tank with the object of setting it on fire, to give the fighter time to get out of the way before the bomber exploded.

Crews were never briefed about this danger lurking in the dark, probably to maintain morale and also to protect intelligence on the enemy's activities gathered by reading their coded transmissions. At the time bombers were mysteriously blowing up in mid flight over the target and this was attributed to something known as 'scarecrows', a supposedly new type of flak weapon developed by the German defenses. In retrospect we now know that the cause of the majority of the bombers demise was the 'schräge musik' weapon fitted to the German night fighters.

On 18th April 1945, we were on the battle order to attack Heliogland and its naval and airfield deployments.

We had completed an air test earlier in the day in the Lancaster that we were assigned for the night raid. We discovered a fault with one of the engines during the test and reported it immediately on landing. When we reported to dispersal for take off we were told that no fault could be discovered with the engine so therefore with apprehension we boarded ready for take off. We received the green light to take off and we raced down the runway on full power to the Merlin engines. When we had reached the point of no return one of the engines began to 'run away' with its revs passing the 3,000 maximum. We were now totally committed to take off and any attempt to abort the takeoff would surely see us crash off the end of the runway and explode the fuel and bomb load that we were carrying. On this rare occasion we were using the short runway at Mildenhall and we staggered into the air just clearing the roof of the Sergeant's mess, I later joked that they needed to sweep the chimneys, we were that close.

The pilot of a Lancaster had the four throttles that powered the Merlin engines within reach of his right hand. On take off initially the pilot would increase the throttles on the engines to gather speed down the runway, however at speed the pilot would need both hands to steer and control the Lancaster during the final stages of take off. It was my responsibility at this point to take over the operation of the throttles ensuring that we were at optimum engine speed for take off and to ensure that the boost did not fall off which could result in catastrophe. Attached to the throttles was what we described as a 'panic handle' that would push the throttles through an additional boost and revs in the eventuality of an emergency, we were in such an emergency. After using this extra boast the engines had to be returned to Rolls Royce for a refurbishment. We immediately landed and raced to the spare 'kite' which was fuelled and bombed up ready to go. We were now behind the main bomber force and we would have to play catch up, although very thankful for the opportunity to still be able to take part. The mission was executed as per plan and we set course for home. On the way home the skipper wanted a drink from his flask so he switched on the vacuum pump and waited the required minute and then engaged 'George' the automatic pilot. The nose of the Lancaster went straight down; we had the beginnings of a loop the loop before the realization set in, and the skipper gained control again.

During April 1945 our wireless operator, Warrant Officer Fitch, was commissioned and moved into the Officer's mess. Shortly before our venture to Munich on 19th April, a new crew of entirely non commissioned officers moved into our billet and we were able to share some of our experiences with them. We had very little time to really get to know them because one morning shortly after they arrived we awoke to find that their beds had been stripped and their lockers emptied. A few days later I went on leave proudly wearing my Flight Sergeant's crown that I had been awarded for completing 15 operations. My next-door neighbor, Paddy Barnard a chief petty officer in the Royal Navy was also on leave from his mine sweeping duties operating out of Lowestoft. Paddy persuaded me to go to Lowestoft with him for the day and we visited one of his relatives who fed us lunch out of her rations, a charitable act that she could ill afford. Our next port of call was the local Suffolk pub where Paddy left me for a while to visit his sailor mates in another room. As I sat quietly with my pint an old gent came into the bar and approached me and said "I see that you are a flyer, where are you based". I replied that we are not supposed to talk about that. "Quite right he replied, we have just lost our Grandson flying out of Mildenhall". I sympathized with him but I could not bring myself to tell him that I thought that I was in the same billet a few days ago. Ronnie Fitch was following some sort of correspondence course on his beloved subject of architecture and he was infatuated with his girlfriend Lorna and cherished her picture. We used to joke with him that by the time he got back home Lorna would have married an American and have a couple of children. On his return home after nearly four years Ronnie did marry Lorna and he became a very rich architect. Another very interesting thing about my Aussie crewmates was the fact that although coming from different areas of Australia, they met at the same recruiting center, and were issued consecutive forces numbers. They were trained at different stations and then met up again on the ship over to America. Amazingly, they crossed America on different trains and re-met on the ship to Liverpool. They decided they would fly together and the rest is history.

Our final operational trip was to bomb a small power station in Munich, which powered the electric railway in and around the city. Our bomb aimer, Hughie was excited about this because it was our only visual bombing mission. I remember vividly the snow-capped mountain en route to the target and somehow drifted a million miles away from the fact that we were on a mission to bomb a target the other side of this natural wonder. At briefing prior to the raid we were informed that the cloud would be five tenths and the target had to be positively identified, if this meant repeating the bombing run, then so be it. This mission was shortly after the furor of the Dresden raid and we assumed that indiscriminate bombing of civilians was very topical. Having arrived over the target we identified the final turning point and commenced our bombing run only to be foiled by dense cloud over the target. We closed the bomb doors and went round for another try. Second time the target was clearly identified and our bomb aimer directed the skipper to the release point. Hughie pressed the 'tit' to release the bombs but nothing happened, there was a malfunction with the release gear. I had a theory the cause of the malfunction was a tiny switch, which operated the rams to the bomb doors. This switch would not let the bombs be released unless the bomb doors were fully open and my theory was that because it had been exposed to the extreme cold on two occasions it was probably frozen. The switch was situated on the bulk head adjacent to the bomb aimers little peep hole which was there to allow him to check all the bombs had dropped as expected. I anticipated that a smart rap on the bulk head was all that was required to solve the problem. The skipper refused me permission to leave my seat because of other aircraft in the cloudy conditions and my 'look-out' was crucial. We set course for home with the bombs still on board and when we were in radio contact with Mildenhall we reported our circumstances. To my surprise we were given permission to land. The next day our Lancaster was given a full inspection by the ground crew who discovered no apparent fault with our aircraft which confirmed my theory of the frozen switch.

Shortly after our trip to Munich in April, my name could be put forward for promotion and my skipper suggested I apply for a commission. At the time the RAF was very class orientated and to be commissioned the establishment preferred its Officers to have a high degree of education. I suggested the alternative of applying for my Warrant Officers badge instead. The promotion never materialized whether due to delay or the armistice I know not. About this time we were informed that we were likely to be transferred to the Pathfinder force."

Manna Operations

By April 1945 the Canadian Army had liberated much of the Netherlands but 120,000 well armed enemy soldiers were cut off in the western part of the country. The Allies did not have enough troops available to conquer the area without terrible losses. After making the decision not to invade, the Allied commanders faced the problem of how to help the 3.5 million Dutch citizens who were starving after four years of occupation.

3 Group Lancasters drop supplies to the enthusiastic Dutch people. *Author's Collection.*

The Crew of F/O Done RAAF, pose for a photograph shortly before taking off as a part of operation 'MANNA'. The crew are: Back L-R: F/Sgt F. M. Goody (B/A), F/O S. C. Done RAAF (pilot), F/Sgt A. G. Henderson (Nav). Front: Sgt W. Percival (F/E), Sgt J. G. 'Swifty' Swallow RCAF (R/G), Sgt W. B. Wraith (MUG), F/Sgt D. Hoare (W/op). *Courtesy of 'Swifty' 622.*

Operation Manna took place from 28th April to 8th May 1945. The operation was named after the food, which miraculously appeared for the Israelites in the book of Exodus, called Manna.

Eric Taylor picks up the story again:

"On the first day of May we were sent on a 'Manna' food-dropping mission to Holland. For this exercise the bomb bay doors were half shut, sacks of flour, peas, beans, etc were loaded in and turned till as much as possible was crammed in, then the bomb doors hand pumped to partially close. We were given instructions to fly to a certain flare marked turning point in Holland, fly very low and dump the cargo on a sports field at The Hague. The Germans had agreed a cease-fire by the remnants of their army occupying Holland, who were probably trapped there anyway. As we approached the sports field at The Hague and prepared for the food drop it was apparent by the reaction of the crowds including a great many children, that this was not the first occurrence of this kind. The crowds were waving madly with every kind of flag with the exception of the Germans. There were German soldiers stationed at the edges of the field, no doubt to keep excited people and those who would pilfer out of harm's way.

There was a tremendous feeling of satisfaction among the crew knowing that we had delivered a cargo that would save lives and not take them, although we had no regrets that we had dropped bombs on enemy targets."

Operation Exodus

RAF MILDENHALL — 622 Sqdn — Time carried forward: 161.40 | 67.48

Date	Hour	Aircraft Type and No.	Pilot	Duty	Remarks (including results of bombing, gunnery, exercises, etc.)	Flying Times Day	Flying Times Night
18.4.45		LANC III D	F/O DONE	AG	OPS HELIGOLAND 10x1000 4x500	5.05	
20.4.45		E	F/O DONE	AG	OPS REGENSBURG 6x1000 8x500	7.25	
29.4.45		K	F/O DONE	AG	X CTY	2.35	
					SUMMARY FOR APRIL 1945		
					UNIT 622 SQDN		
					DATE 1.5.45		
			B Morrison F/Lt for O.C. 'A' FLT. 622		SIGNATURE		
					TOTAL	20.30	
					OPERATIONAL	15.30	
MAY	1	E	F/O DONE	AG	HAGUE	2.20	
MAY	2	LANC I BY	F/O DONE	A.G.	FOOD DROPPING TO DUTCH (HAGUE)	2.30	
MAY	4	X	F/O DONE	A.G.	X CTY	2.40	
MAY	7	E	F/O DONE	AG	FOOD DROPPING TO DUTCH (HAGUE)	2.45	
MAY	10	E	F/O DONE	AG	JUVINCOURT RETURNED 24 POW WING	3.45	
MAY	11	E	F/O DONE	AG	(FRANCE) and Base	3.50	
MAY	14	G	F/O DONE	AG	JUVINCOURT (24 POW) TO [illegible] and [illegible]	3.30	
MAY	15	G	F/O DONE	AG	JUVINCOURT (FRANCE) 24 POW TO WESTCOTT and BASE	4.40	

Copy of a logbook page from Sgt 'Swallow, the rear gunner in the crew of F/O Done RAAF. The entries show that the crew took part in operation MANNA on 1st, 2nd and 7th May 1945. *Courtesy of 'Swifty' 622.*

"We landed on the grass airfield at Juvincourt, which had been reinforced with metal grills to withstand the weight of Lancasters. We were allocated 20 passengers who had to sit on the floor behind the main spar and we had to brief them about the dangers of letting the straps of their 'Mae wests' foul the control rods. The unusual cargo upset the balance of the Lancasters in so much as that on take off when enough speed was reached to get the tail up the aircraft was airborne. The soldiers all looked relatively fit, if a little on the slim side. Many of them were sun tanned and some said that they were on remote German farms helping the women to run them."

"As soon as the soldiers touched familiar ground again they approached trestle tables manned by Army Officers who were handing out money, travel vouchers and ration cards. They then immediately headed for the station and the train home. In total, we made six trips to Juvincourt and on one occasion we were stranded there due to fog over England.

The massive American trucks that brought the potential passengers took them away again, however one of the trucks took the aircrews into the town for a night out. There were women camp followers aplenty and wine for those who could pay. I had cleared my pockets as was the ritual before flying so the crew retired early to sleep in our Lanc. Breakfast took the form of emergency packs dished out from a vehicle; I managed to catch a

F/O Fiedler & crew stand proudly against GI-H, HK805. The Lancaster has been suitably adorned with messages from those awaiting the trip home. *Courtesy of E. J Taylor, Flight Engineer.*

622 Squadron Lancasters lined up at Juvincourt waiting to repatriate POW's. *Courtesy of J. Willis.*

Left to right: W/O Fitch RAAF, F/O Fiedler RAAF & an unknown soldier shortly before repatriation back to England. *Courtesy of E. J Taylor, Flight Engineer.*

few packs due to my height. Intermingled between the trip to Juvincourt we completed a couple of 'cooks tours', two fighter affiliation training trips, a cross country navigation exercise using H2S and air to sea firing. Finally an incident packed bomb jettison journey. The 'cooks tours' were especially arranged trips to the Ruhr with the ground crews on board so that they could see the extensive damage caused by our bombers. We saw these trips as appreciation of the ground crew who worked day and night to keep the bombers flying. The bomb jettison flight was to dump unwanted 500lb bombs in a specific area in the wash. Having located the area and dumped our cargo, Jonnie out skipper said to me "you don't live too far from here, do you"? I confirmed that it was very close and the skipper took us down the coast to Southwold and then inland to my village of Spexhall and ultimately my house. The skipper had been advised that he would soon be sent home so a little rule bending was in order. We did a couple of tight low turns over my house and my father who happened to be home called to my mother to come outside and look at the low flying Lancaster. My father did not initially realize that it was his son up above; however my mother soon realized it was me. In her rush to get outside she stepped down from her decorating chair and put her foot into a pot of whitewash trailing white footprints all the way outside whilst waving furiously. Very shortly after the aerobatics I was sent on leave and received a fair amount of ribbing from the locals in various guises. Our final trip in a 622 Squadron Lancaster was on the last day of May 1945 when we conducted another fighter affiliation exercise."

Many years of captivity for the soldiers came to an end with the repatriation from Juvincourt. The prospect of the trip home to family and friends was a welcome relief. Soldiers expressed their feelings of finally going home by adorning many Lancasters with lighthearted messages. Here F/O Fiedler's Lancaster GI-H, HK805 is suitably marked ready for the trip over the channel. *Courtesy of E. J Taylor, Flight Engineer.*

Another example of the creativity of the soldiers waiting for the flight home to England and freedom. *Courtesy of E. J Taylor, Flight Engineer.*

28

Dresden

Operation Thunderclap

The advance of the Allied Armies into Germany met with stiff resistance from the Germans who were fighting for their very lives. The Air Ministry contemplated ways of assisting the Red Army advance into eastern Germany and the result was a numbers of heavy raids on German cities. The Allies knew that the war was practically over however, they were still experiencing considerable resistance and they had to assist their new Allies, namely the Russians. The Germans reinforced the Eastern cities by drafting in troops from the west; Hitler did not want to surrender to the Russians for he knew that they would show no mercy. After much deliberation, the Air Ministry came up with operation Thunderclap, the attacks against the cities of Dresden, Leipzig and Chemnitz.

622 Squadron dispatched 13 crews to Dresden with one turning back due to their special navigation equipment malfunctioning. All crews bombed successfully with the exception of Flying Officer Thorbecke in GI-G, PD225, who experienced difficulty when his port inner engine caught fire necessitating it to be feathered.

Eric Taylor, the flight engineer in the crew of F/O Fiedler RAAF recalls the Dresden raid vividly:

> "On 13th February 1945 we were on the battle order for what we considered to be just another mission into Germany. The target on this night was Dresden, a target that was to become infamous due to the incredibly high casualties on the ground. Dresden had endured minor bombing before as it was a beautiful city full of rich agricultural history. Behind the façade was an industrial city that was producing components for the Nazi war effort and in particular for the German radar industry. The attack on Dresden has been described as the raid that went horribly right, weather conditions were perfect, there was little German fighter resistance and the Pathfinders positively marked the target. Many crews were extremely superstitious about replacement aircrew and on the Dresden raid we had a replacement gunner. Our rear gunner Jock Smith was in hospital with appendicitis in nearby Ely and he was replaced by a spare gunner. Our mid upper gunner took the rear gunner's position for the mission and the new gunner took up position in the upper turret. After take off we were tucked up in the bomber stream en route to the target and hoped that the radar counter measures produced by depositing 'window' into the night sky would conceal us. Suddenly I spotted an aircraft that was not a four-engined bomber and we considered it to be an enemy aircraft. We were already wearing our oxygen masks due to the altitude that we had reached and I switched on my mike 'engineer to skipper, fighter 10 O'clock high on the starboard beam'...'skipper to mid upper do you see it'...'yes, I've got it, prepare to corkscrew'. Almost immediately, the next transmission was 'Starboard go'. In practice, corkscrews are expected and calculated, in actual war situations with a full bomb and fuel load they are very different and inherently more frightening. The skipper threw the Lancaster down into a steep dive with the engines screaming on full power, pulling up and then down into another evasive turn. Soon the gunner reported contact broken, the skipper wrestled the Lancaster back to straight and level, when, despite our training, all hell broke loose with everybody on the intercom at once asking, 'did you see it', 'what was it'. 'Did you fire at it', 'where is it?" I could see it ahead and a bit lower on the port side and due to the intercom chatter; I tapped the skipper on the shoulder and desperately pointed to the enemy aircraft. The skipper altered course and we evaded the attention of the enemy fighter.
>
> At briefing for the Dresden raid, we were told to take off in darkness and cross into Germany over the Ruhr. Ground fire was expected to be intense due to the fact that we were so heavily laden and we would be under operational height. We were to head for Brunswick to induce the German defenses into thinking that the target was actually Brunswick and deploy additional defenses there. Just short of Brunswick we altered course and headed for Berlin. We approached Berlin near enough to witness the massive array of searchlights on its approaches, and then we swung south for Dresden. On this short leg the thinning cloud was fast disappearing and we soon saw target markers going down. Despite the incident with the enemy fighter, we were practically on time over target and as we approached the target bombs and photoflashes were lightening up the clear sky. The intention here was

to create a firestorm in this city of tall medieval buildings in narrow streets, which would be self-generating partly due to the old wooden buildings.

It was bright moonlight when we approached the drop point and we started our bombing run only to hear the master bomber change his instructions from bomb the greens to bomb the center of the fires. Our bomb aimer F/S Doherty was calling out instructions to the skipper along the lines of left a bit, right a bit, when suddenly he declared that the run had to be aborted and we would have to go around again. At this point our Navigator F/S Elliott asked the skipper if he could come out from his station point to witness the bombing run. On seeing the chaos around and below us he said "hells bells" and quickly ducked back behind his screen. Despite the armada of planes going through the target area we did a tight circuit and came in on our new run, opened the bomb doors again and bombed as instructed. An unusual feature was the instruction to leave the target on the course for home, but to quickly lose height by six thousand feet, taking care to protect our eardrums in an attempt to lose any night fighters that may be loitering, but of course, there were none. We did however see explosions, which we reported, as 'scarecrows' a description of fireworks sent up by the Germans to scare us. It was much later that we discovered that the Germans never used such devices and that what we witnessed was our own bombers blowing up. On leaving the target, the fires were visible to us for something like 100 miles from the target. Official records of the raid could not put an accurate figure on the number who died during the raid, however it is known that there was a strong contingent of refugees fleeing from the Russian army who were fast approaching Germany. It is however recorded that thousands of people died from oxygen starvation. The bombs creating a vacuum that sucked out all the air causing many to be found in perfect condition with no signs of harm.

The controversy surrounding this raid will continue, however we were briefed that Dresden was a vital part of the German industrial machine with an important road and rail network from which supplies were being sent to the army on the Eastern front. We were airborne for nine and a half hours on the trip, at least seven of which we had to endure an oxygen mask stuck to our faces. As we approached the briefing room, a WAAF was dispensing coffee and navy rum. Our mid upper gunner, who was a temporary replacement, went back for a second helping of rum and during briefing gave a colorful account of the mission."

796 heavy bombers delivered their deadly cargo on Dresden in two waves. The result was that the ancient buildings made predominately from wood, created a firestorm that sucked the very oxygen from the air. Estimates of the dead focus around 50,000 people with the American B17 bombers adding to the death toll the following day.

Chemnitz

With the success of the bombing of Dresden still being debated by Allied Command, the city of Chemnitz was another target identified under Operation Thunderclap. Therefore, Allied Air Command issued the instruction to bomb the city on the night of 14th February 1945. Chemnitz was an eight and a half hour return trip that was exhausting for the bomber crews and when the target was announced at squadron briefings around the country, gasps of derision rang out across the rooms.

When the battle order was promulgated there were fourteen Lancasters and crews assigned to the mission. F/Lt W. K. Thomas was assigned the spare aircraft, GI-H, NN709 due to his usual mount GI-M, HK646 undergoing essential maintenance. F/Lt Thomas and his crew had arrived on the squadron in September 1944 and they were about half way through their 'tour', and were a well respected crew among the squadron.

After briefing F/Lt Thomas and crew boarded their Lancaster and signed the ground crew inspection form. All the crew readied themselves for the long trip to Chemnitz. The four Merlin engines were 'run up' and the flight engineer, Sgt Ralph monitored his dials and engine pressures. Almost immediately the starboard outer engine was problematic and only producing 2, 800 revs instead of the required 3,000. This was the usual sign that the flame traps were beginning to block up. After a quick discussion with the crew, the decision was made to continue with the mission in the hope that the engine would perform better once airborne.

F/Lt Thomas coaxed GI-H into the air at 20:19 hours and set course for the target. En route to the target the starboard outer engine continued to cause concern and eventually caught fire fifteen minutes before the target resulting it having to be feathered. The whole process sounds routine, however, nothing could have been further from the truth as described by Sgt Bill Ralph the flight engineer below. His position beside the pilot gave him an eyewitness account of proceedings:

> "Approximately four and a half hours after take off we were approaching the target, when the starboard outer engine caught fire. Feathering procedure was carried out, fuel switched off, mags switched out, throttle closed, props feathered and the fire extinguisher operated putting out the fire.
>
> A few moments later, to our amazement, we noticed the starboard inner engine was also feathered. How this happened is still not clear, but the instant reaction was to press the feathering button to get the engine started again. During this procedure, the airflow caught the props, and the engine sprang to life, with all the controls in maximum power and boost. The roar was frightening and we wondered how it stayed on the wing. The bomb aimer called up from the nose, 'What the hell is going on up there?' Similarly, the mid upper gunner shouted

'Hello Russia here we come'. All this added more to our embarrassment. During the confusion, we lost height from 19,000 to 17,000 feet.

It must be recorded that for the brilliant flying of Ken, who somehow kept the starboard wing from dropping, thus avoiding a spiral dive to certain death, this story could not be told. On composing ourselves we continued to bomb the target at 00:35 hrs and set off home on three engines."

The Chemnitz raid did not achieve the degree of success attributed to the Dresden raid the previous night. This was due mainly to the cloud over the target and poor target marking.

F/Lt Ken Thomas touched down on the runway at Mildenhall at 04:59 hours with an exhausted crew on board. The journey home on three engines meant that they had fallen further behind the bomber stream and therefore vulnerable to night fighter attack. Fortunately, they were unmolested on the route home. On completion of his tour of operations, F/Lt W. K. Thomas was awarded the Distinguished Flying Cross for numerous encounters with the enemy. During his flying career, he had to change his navigator on at least three occasions. His first navigator Sgt J. O' Toole was sent back for additional training before he flew operationally. His second navigator, Flying Officer Surender Berry of Indian origin, had commenced flying with the squadron back in 1943 whilst the squadron was operating the Short Stirling bomber. He contracted Tuberculosis and subsequently hospitalized in early 1944. Whilst he was in hospital his pilot, (F/Lt J. A. Watson RCAF M.I.D.) was killed in action on the night of 27/28th April 1944, when he stayed at the controls of the doomed Lancaster to allow the rest of the crew to parachute to safety. Unfortunately all the crew were taken prisoners of war.

On 8th November 1944, the crew attacked the oil plant at Homberg and received a direct hit by flak in the navigator's position over the target, resulting in the starboard inner engine being hit and rendered useless. The flak explosion seriously wounded F/O Berry and injured Sgt J. Kingston in the mid upper turret. Fragments of shattered windscreen sprayed F/Lt Thomas in the pilot's seat. Despite his serious injuries, F/O Berry continued to navigate the aircraft back to England and due to his injuries and the damage to the aircraft, Ken Thomas decided to land at the emergency landing field at Woodbridge.

Flying Officer Berry was given the immediate award of the Distinguished Flying Cross. By the time his medal citation appeared in the London Gazette he was a Flight Lieutenant.

Flight Lieutenant Surender BERRY (133715) R.A.F.V.R., 622 Sqn.

This officer has set a fine example of devotion to duty. He has participated in numerous sorties and has proved himself to be a most able and resolute navigator. In November, 1944, he took part in an operation against Homberg. During the sortie, the aircraft sustained much damage.

Flight Lieutenant Berry was badly wounded. Although unable to move he maintained a fine spirit and, under his direction, other members of the crew were enabled to navigate the damaged aircraft home. This officer set an example of a high order.

Courtesy of the London Gazette.

The question of morality and the justification for area bombing has raged on after the war with ACM Harris being vilified by many as a mass murderer. At the time, the political perspective was to end the war quickly and ACM Harris and the Americans saw Dresden as a legitimate strategic target. The whole bombing campaign at the time was specifically directed to dislocate the transport and communication systems of the enemy and Dresden with its 'Ikon' optical factory and Siemens glass factory were prime targets. Dresden has often been described as the raid where everything went right. No bombers were lost, the weather was perfect and the navigation was spot on. The controversy over Dresden will continue to fuel political debate for many years to come.

29

'Kind' Analysis

Pilot: F/O J. Ingram RAAF
Nav: Sgt S.S. Kind
B/A: F/O W.G. Carruthers
W/op: F/Sgt E. L .Millard
MUG: Sgt D.E. Nicholson
R/G: Sgt K. Nutton
Co-Pilot-F/E: F/Sgt R.R. Davie

The author is indebted to Roy Davie for allowing him to include his personal aircrew experiences and to Mr. Alan Kind for allowing him to include his father's personal and published material to enhance this narrative. The author relies heavily on material from 'The Sceptical Witness' by Stuart Kind.

The 'Bluey' Ingram crew were by all accounts the cream of the Commonwealth youth, brought together to fight against tyranny and dictatorship. Several factors made this particular bunch of men stand out from the crowd. The two members of the crew featured herein bear testimony to what can be achieved in life with application and endeavor.

Stuart Stanley Kind was born on 21st January 1925 in the 'Meadows' district of Nottingham. The youngest of three boys, he was born into a working class family and by the end of his working life, he would be known worldwide for his contributions to the field of forensic science. For the purpose of this particular reference it will be necessary to concentrate on Stuart's RAF career. However, the lifetime achievements of Stuart Kind must be included to make the story complete.

In February 1943, shortly after his 18th Birthday, Stuart Kind walked into the Aircrew Reception Center (ACRC) at St. John's Wood in London to embark on a career in the Royal Air Force. Stuart's initiation period was cut short due to almost immediately being struck down with Influenza. The Medical Officer at the time was a non-compassionate man and reluctantly referred Stuart to the sick bay after seeing the extent of his illness. Fully recovered, AC2 Kind joined the other aircrew under training and participated in the usual high jinks associated with a large group of men thrust together.

Eventually, as the first stage of RAF life was drawing to a close, discipline and self-assurance had begun to make a mark on all the aircrew who were awaiting their next progressive move.

The famous RAF fighter station at Hornchurch in Essex was the next posting for Stuart Kind to undertake the Initial Training Wing course. The training included theory of flight, King's regulations, NCO duties and Morse code for approximately six weeks. Ultimately, the ITW determined which aircrew was suited to which position within an aircraft and Stuart's intellectual ability appeared to be best suited to the role of navigator. Hornchurch was an unusual setting for the training of Bomber Command aircrew,

A poor quality photograph of the 'Bluey' Ingram crew who arrived at RAF Mildenhall in early 1945. Back L-R:F/Sgt E. Millard (W/op), Sgt K. Nutton (R/G), Sgt D. Nicholson (MUG). Front L-R: W/O R. Davie (F/E), F/O W. Carruthers (B/A), F/O J. Ingram RAAF (Pilot), F/Sgt S. Kind (Nav). *Courtesy of Roy Davie.*

Warrant Officer Roy Davie who joined the crew at No.1668 Heavy Conversion Unit at RAF Bottesford in January 1945. W/O Davie was a fully trained pilot and very much wanted to fulfil the role on an operational squadron. Bomber Command's losses were reducing drastically and the delays for new aircrew to be posted to a squadron were long and monotonous. Roy Davie wanted to get into the war before it was all over and when he and others were approached to re-muster to flight engineer's, he jumped at the chance. Therefore, he fulfilled the role of flight engineer in the crew of F/O Ingram RAAF. *Courtesy of Roy Davie.*

Stuart Kind was profoundly affected by the death of his brother. As a result, he decided to become a navigator, rather than a pilot. LAC S.S. Kind seen here with the 'white flash' in his cap denoting aircrew under training. *Courtesy of A. D Kind.*

and unbeknownst to Stuart Kind he was being trained there due to his acceptance into the RAF at a very young age. A posting to a mainstream ITW would have raised suspicion and caused some unrest amongst other aircrew due to the potential for Stuart to jump the queue. Stuart Kind spent twelve months at Hornchurch and in addition to classroom lectures he learned to operate the machine gun clusters that were in place around the airfield perimeter.

It was whilst at Hornchurch that Stuart learnt of the death of his brother Alan in a Halifax bomber from 158 Squadron. The Halifax was returning form a mission to Nuremberg on 11th August 1943 and had been airborne for seven and a half hours. The aircraft was running low on fuel and the wireless operator (Alan Kind) tried frantically to obtain a directional fix via the radio to steer the Halifax to the nearest airfield. Just as the aircraft crossed the English coast, the fuel situation became critical and the captain gave the order to abandon the aircraft. All seven crew members bailed out successfully, however, the strong winds blew all the crew members except the pilot out to sea.

Four hours later the navigator was plucked from the sea tired and exhausted, the other crew members would be given up by the sea during the following weeks. The body of Sergeant Alan William Kind was never found and he is commemorated on the Royal Air Force memorial at Runnymede.

The decision to re-muster to a navigator speeded up training for Stuart Kind and he was posted to air navigation school on the Isle of Man in early March 1944. This distinctive little island lies centrally in the Irish Sea midway between England, Ireland, Scotland and Wales. A major part of the landscape is mountainous apart from a small northern plain where RAF station Jurby was situated. It was an ideal place to learn air navigation because for much of the time the aircraft flew in sight of distinctively shaped coast or island, which established one's position. This was a welcome aide to navigating an aircraft back to base. The course was however far more intricate than just simple map reading and bearings on lighthouses or other geographical points where required, coupled with sextant sights upon the stars all recorded within a student's flight log. The technique used was always the same, set off from base and fly to a prearranged route under certain specified conditions with the aim of arriving back successfully without running out of fuel or flying into a mountain top. LAC Kind spent most of 1944 on the Isle of Man studying air navigation and acquiring a mind for investigative knowledge.

In its simplistic form, Stuart Kind described the art of air navigation:

> "The routine task of the air navigator is to work out the direction and speed his aircraft is traveling over the ground. This he does from a knowledge of how fast, and in what direction, the aircraft is traveling through the air and then, by combining this with the direction and speed of the wind, he obtains a resultant 'track' over the ground and his ground speed. From this he can tell the pilot what the aircraft's position is at any given time, what is the required course to steer to any required destination and

No 1 AN&BS JURBY. Time carried forward :—

Date	Hour	Aircraft Type and No.	Pilot	Duty	Remarks (including results of bombing, gunnery, exercises, etc.)	Flying Times Day	Flying Times Night
19/3/44	0930	ANSON	P/O CRAWFORD	2nd NAVIGATOR	MAP READING EXERCISE. BASE – – PORTPATRICK – AYR – CASTLE DOUGLAS – MOFFAT – WISTON – – BASE	2-15	
19/3/44	1330	ANSON	P/O CRAWFORD	1st NAVIGATOR	MAP READING EXERCISE. BASE – – DUNGANNON – BUSHMILLS – – PORTADOWN – BALLYHALBERT – – MULL of GALLOWAY – BASE.	2-10	
24/3/44	1015	ANSON		2nd NAVIGATOR	MAP READING EXERCISE.	1-20	
24/3/44	1415	ANSON		1st NAVIGATOR	MAP READING EXERCISE. BASE – – DOWNPATRICK – OMAGH – NEWRY – OERVOCK – LURGAN – BASE	2-35	
27/3/44	1345	ANSON	F/S REDBURN	2nd NAVIGATOR	MAP READING EXERCISE – BASE – ARMAGH – NEWTON STEWART – DOWNPATRICK – MAGHERA – – DUNGANNON – BASE. DIVERTED TO NUTTS CORNER. N IRELAND.	1-35	
28/3/44	1226	ANSON	F/S REDBURN	1st NAVIGATOR	NUTTS CORNER TO BASE	45	
					TOTAL TIME ...	10-40	

Logbook page showing reference to Stuart Kind's time at RAF Jurby Air Navigation School. The training was intensive and some of the best on offer in the RAF at the time. *Courtesy of A. D Kind.*

No. 1. Navigator Course.

Held at Air Navigation & Bombing School, R.A.F. Jurby, Isle of Man. From 14 MAR 1944 ... 30 JUL 1944.

SUBJECTS	MARKS. Possible.	Obtained	NAVIGATION Flying Times of Course.	DAY.	NIGHT
Practical Air Work.	800	525			
Navigation (D.R.T.)	300	237	As 1st Navigator		
Navigation Theory	300	246	As 2nd Navigator		
Signals D/F. W/T.	100	88			
TOTAL	1,500	1096	Total Flying Hours.	84.10	29.40
TOTAL % OBTAINED	73.64				

REMARKS: PASSED ~~FAILED~~

Bush F/LT.
Chief Navigation Instructor.

Marks accrued by Stuart Kind at the final assessment stage of his training at RAF Jurby. *Courtesy of A. D Kind.*

Interior shot of aircrew accommodation, the dreaded Nissen hut at RAF Jurby. The heating was by means of a coke burning stove in the middle of the room. These stoves gave off intoxicating fumes making the danger of asphyxiation a real possibility. *Courtesy of A. D Kind.*

Stuart Kind standing far right in the picture, poses with other trainees whilst at Jurby. *Courtesy of A. D Kind.*

All the members of one particular Nissen hut pose for a group photograph, Stuart Kind included. *Courtesy of A. D Kind.*

the estimated time of arrival (ETA) there. He also learns a miscellany of other techniques such as whether, at any given moment in flight, it is quicker to return to base or to continue on to the destination. This sort of information can be of value when something goes wrong".

In early September 1944, the first stage of Stuart Kind's training had finished, next he was posted to No. 26 Operational Training Unit at Wing to 'crew up' with five other airmen to form a six man bomber crew training on the Vickers Wellington. The Wellington bomber was a twin engined bomber designed by Barnes Wallis whose genius found fame by designing the bomb that breached the German dams in the Ruhr. The crewing up procedure was an informal affair where aircrew of different denominations were thrust into a large room and told to 'crew up'. It was a very hit and miss affair with no criteria or misconceptions of who or what, made a good crew. Stuart Kind was chosen to join the crew of an Australian called 'Bluey' Ingram who had already spent time in the Australian Army fighting for two years in the Far East.

In many ways the role of the navigator in a bomber was possibly the most important of all. Many crews strayed off course and found themselves flying directly over heavily defended targets. It was the navigator's responsibility to ensure that the aircraft kept on the correct course to the target and back. Fuel allowances were sacrificed for extra bombs and there was no room for error by crews straying away from set course. A lost aircraft would come up against numerous problems, more often than not shot down or having to bail out due to lack of fuel. After eight weeks of practice flying machines of war, the 'Ingram' crew successfully graduated.

The next stage of training for the newly formed crew took them to No.1668 Heavy Conversion Unit at Bottesford in Nottinghamshire in February 1945. The role of the Heavy Conversion Units was to convert aircrew to the four-engined aircraft that they would take to war. In this case the Avro Lancaster,

Stuart Kind at RAF Jurby. Little did he know at this stage that his RAF navigator training would have a profound effect on his amazing, future career. *Courtesy of A. D Kind.*

Kitted up in full flying gear. Stuart Kind is standing far right in the photograph. *Courtesy of A. D Kind.*

the mainstay of Bomber Command and capable of carrying nearly 22,000lb of bombs deep into enemy territory. The Lancaster was crewed by seven crew members, and therefore it was necessary to have a flight engineer join the already established crews. The flight engineer's role was to ensure that the engine and fuel management systems were operating correctly within the Lancaster and this involved switching fuel tanks in flight once they had been drained by the four Rolls Royce Merlin engines. And so it was that F/Sgt Roy Davie joined the Bluey Ingram crew as flight engineer. Roy Davie was no ordinary aircrew member; he was also a qualified pilot who was directed to the flight engineer role to speed up his entry into the war. At the time of his training, there was a surplus of trained pilots and F/Sgt Davie considered that the flight engineer route would ensure that he experienced some operational flying.

Whilst at HCU the crew took part in high-level bombing, fighter affiliation and cross-country exercises during the day and night. These exercises were designed to test each aircrew specialist in turn, however the most challenging role was that undertaken by the navigator who had to ensure that the aircraft flew to the rendezvous point and back again without running out of fuel. Shortly before the end of Stuart Kind's training, the crew was detailed to take part in a diversionary flight over the North Sea to a point 50 miles from the north German coast. The purpose of the flight was to mislead the German air defenses into believing that the target was somewhere other than it was and draw the night fighter force away from the main bomber stream. The five hour flight centered on midnight on the 20/21st February 1945 and passed without incident, with Stuart navigating successfully back over the English coast at Cromer, on schedule.

On 2nd March 1945 the crew of Flying Officer Ingram arrived at RAF Mildenhall to join 622 Squadron, 'B' flight. On initial arrival, the crew met the Commanding Officer, Wing Commander Buckingham who welcomed them to the squadron and told them to settle into squadron life. The Officers amongst them were members of Officer Mess, but Officers and NCO's were allocated a house together on the periphery of the airfield.

The 'Ingram' crew had entered the war at a time when the odds of completing a tour of operations were better than at any time of the war. At this stage of the war, the advantage had swung in favor of the Allied Forces. The D-Day landings in early June 1944 had seen the start of the end for German forces. After initial strong opposition from the Germans, the Allied bombing campaign concentrated on supporting the Allied armies advance and on the destruction of industrial centers, in particular the oil industry. The skies had practically been cleared of German fighters and daylight missions were a common practice with fighter support just in case they did send up a few fighters. By far the greatest threat was from the flak guns that claimed so many aircraft during the Second World War and daylight missions increased the accuracy of the German flak gunners.

In late 1944, 3 Group was tasked with utilizing the navigational aid called G-H almost extensively on daylight missions. G/H was a two-station radio direction finder. Instruments in the bomber measured its position from one station and distance from another. It could be used by up to 80 bombers from any pair of stations. By using more than one pair of stations, multiple targets could be attacked at the same time without the aid of Pathfinders and markers. Once a major part of Bomber Command had been fitted with G/H, it became a most useful blind-bombing device. With the Allies creeping further towards the German capital, new G/H stations were placed on the continent.

622 Squadron utilized 'OBOE' and G/H radar navigational devices to good effect from late 1944 to the end of the war. In practice, it was usual for a select few Lancasters in each squadron to have G/H fitted and navigators were trained in how to operate the system. The G/H equipped Lancasters had their tail rudders marked with two yellow horizontal bars to distinguish them allowing for deeper daylight penetration into enemy occupied areas.

On 5th March 1945, the crew was promulgated on the battle order to attack Gelsenkirchen for their first operational sortie. The mission went without incident and over the next three months, the crew would undertake both daylight and night missions against the enemy.

Stuart Kind described his operational tour within his book 'The Sceptical Witness', in the extract that features below:

> "At Mildenhall I experienced three months of a life lived under conditions of emotional high tension, all the time wondering how it was that the other six members of my crew appeared so unaffected by it all. None appeared to be terrified as I was and I fervently hoped they did not notice what a craven navigator they had as a crewmate. Our Australian skipper was cool, calm and competent in everything he did.
>
> Our operational flights were, like all such flights, tense experiences. We bombed both at night and during the day. I preferred the night time. At night, we were on our own and the pilot flew the course I plotted for him.

F/Sgt Stuart S.S. Kind poses for a studio photograph as a fully qualified navigator. *Courtesy of A. D Kind.*

Lancaster NG301, GI-S, one of the Lancasters flown by the crew whilst at Mildenhall. *Author's Collection.*

Survival was very much an individual affair. During the day time things were different. The Lancaster had been designed as a night bomber and was only lightly armed and thus easy prey for German fighters under most circumstances during daylight.

Because of this factor, we flew in close formations with my function being reduced to that of checking the work of the lead navigator, and of issuing instructions to the bomb aimer as we bombed on the information on my radar screen.

Our three months operational experience was completed by dropping food supplies to the starving civil population of Holland at the end of April 1945. Then during May, we made a group of trips to France to pick up released British prisoners of war." (Kind 1999, 68).

Victory in Europe brought great euphoria across the whole country and the end of the need to have war machines and personnel in abundance. Great numbers of men were clamoring to be released from the RAF and Stuart Kind had to wait 18 months before it would be his time to be de-mobbed. The Commonwealth aircrew went home first leaving the British aircrew to ponder their future in 'civvy' street. The end of the war brought a realization to F/Sgt Kind that he needed to be better educated to make a success of himself in civilian life. With this in mind, he started to educate himself up to university entrance level taking every opportunity to find an empty room and study hard.

NO 622 SQDN. MILDENHALL.

Date	Hour	Aircraft Type and No.	Pilot	Duty	Remarks (including results of bombing, gunnery, exercises, etc.)	Flying Times Day	Flying Times Night
					Time carried forward :—	147.55	82.50
2/3/45		Lancaster B	F/L A. Hush P/O Ingram	Nav.	Local Flying.	·20	
5/3/45		Lancaster U	P/O Ingram	Nav	Operations on Gelsenkirchen	5·30	
8/3/45		Lancaster T	F/O Thurn P/O Ingram	Nav	Fighter Affiliation	·45	
9/3/45		Lancaster Z	P/O Ingram	Nav	Operations on Datteln	5·15	
					Summary for Period Ending 9th March 1945. S. S. Kind Sgt.	11·50	·/·
SPECIAL NAV FLT					FELTWELL.		
14/3/45	0902	Lancaster B	P/O Ingram	Nav	Special Nav Photography. (Error 180°.)	2·45	
15/3/45	1331	Lancaster E	P/O Ingram	Nav	Special Nav Photography.	2·55	
					Summary for Course: 10/3 – 16/3 1945. Unit: Special Nav Training Flt Feltwell. Date: 16/3/45 Signature: S. S. Kind	5·40	·/·
					Signed. C.I. Spec Nav Flt. Total Time ...	165·25	82·50

Page from the logbook of Stuart Kind showing his first days on 622 Sqn and the subsequent posting to RAF Feltwell for electronic navigational aid training. *Courtesy of A. D Kind.*

While waiting to be discharged, Sergeant Kind was posted to RAF Folkingham in Lincolnshire where he joined the ranks of the physical training instructors, molding personnel into some degree of fitness.

In 1946 Stuart Kind was discharged from the RAF and he sat the entrance exam for Nottingham university, which he successfully passed and spent the next four years studying. From university, Stuart Kind built a career that made him a world renowned figure in the field of forensic science. The following extract written by Angela Gallop at the time of Stuart Kind's death pays tribute to him and highlights his numerous achievements that enriched his field of expertise:

> "Stuart was undeniably one of the leading forensic scientists of our time. He was unique in that he contributed so effectively to the development of the profession at so many different levels. At one and the same time he was philosopher and visionary, skilled caseworker, research scientist and innovator, organizer and leader. In casework, he developed a reputation for being able to cope with whatever was thrown at him, and most things were in those relatively early days of forensic science when labs were small and staff were few. His ability as a scientist ideally complemented an intensely practical and common sense approach to crime investigation, to the extent that he was often able to add extra dimensions to the understanding of what had gone on and to the evidence arising from it.
>
> Take, for example, the case of the young woman asleep in her flat and who was viciously attacked by a man wielding a broken milk bottle. She drove him off by striking him repeatedly with her alarm clock. Stuart not only demonstrated an exchange of victim's and suspect's blood on their clothing, but on the suspect he found two kinds of glass–one type matching the milk bottle, and the other the broken alarm clock, down feathers like those in the damaged eiderdown from the victim's bed, and he even showed that a nondescript stain on the sleeve of the suspect's jacket that might well have gone unnoticed, contained cow protein and lactose from milk residues in the milk bottle.
>
> Stuart's research was largely applied, tending to focus on providing immediate and tangible improvements to operational practice. His work on the biochemistry of semen enabled him to revolutionize the way in which clothing for example was searched for seminal stains, something that forensic scientists unfortunately spend a lot of time doing. Reducing it all to its bench application, he developed the simple color test that, 40 years on, remains the method of choice in forensic science labs all over the world.
>
> He made species determination more robust, enabling animal blood to be confidently identified and distinguished from human blood in dirty, difficult samples. And those of us old enough to have been involved in ABO blood grouping will also have been particularly grateful to Stuart's pioneering work which gave us the absorption-elution technique following ammonia extraction of blood stains. This combined a more straight forward handling procedure, and batch processing without loss of either sensitivity of accuracy.
>
> But Stuart's prowess was not restricted to the development of specific tests-however complex they might have been. His intellectual reach facilitated the introduction of entirely new disciplines to forensic science. Perhaps the best example of this relates to some of his work in the late 1970's on the serial killer dubbed the Yorkshire Ripper. Stuart was seconded to the 'Ripper' police investigative team- an acknowledgement in itself of his pre-emergence as a superb operational forensic scientist. During that time, and using navigator skills acquired and honed within the RAF in World War II, he essentially 'invented' forensic science geographical profiling. His early calculations, hastily carried out in the small hours of one morning in a hotel 'somewhere in England', led him to pinpoint with chilling accuracy the radius within which Peter Sutcliffe, the Ripper, lived.
>
> Then there are Stuart's achievements as an organizer. The best known of these must be his founding in 1959 of the Forensic Science Society of which I have great honor to be the current President. The badge of office that I wear with pride today is the one that Stuart himself wore during his own Presidency from 1970 to1981.
>
> Stuart established the Society, as a means of encouraging communication between scientists working in the different Home Office labs so that they could learn from one another instead of constantly having to re-invent wheels- or "make the mistakes" was how he put it. Contact between the labs in those days was restricted to occasional meetings of the lab directors, but they seldom all attended and nothing of what was discussed filtered down to scientists themselves.
>
> Stuart explained that the directors were all former academics. They viewed one another with utmost suspicion, and each preferred to keep his laboratory "as a little kingdom independent of the others". The success of the Society in bringing scientists not just from the UK- a big enough task, but from all around the world, is a tribute to Stuart's vision, his infectious enthusiasm and his sheer hard work. This was manifest not least in his single-handedly launching, and continuing to edit and produce (from his kitchen table in the early days) the Journal of the Forensic Science Society, now known as Science and Justice. Never one to pass up a practical opportunity, many colleagues will recall the ease with which Stuart turned an expression of faint interest into a lasting commitment to lending a hand. Proofreaders, abstract editors, peer reviewers, editorial writers, book reviewers, all unpaid-acknowledging the importance of what he was doing, and admiring the craftsmanship of a consummate wordsmith.

There was a time when anything destined for publication from the pen of a forensic scientist had to be vetted. Anonymous editorials were, by default, taken to be the work of the editor, so there was apparently no hiding place. But have a look at some of the journals of Stuart's early days and note the conclusion, we see authors' perhaps unfamiliar initials: Jo, NA, TH, AN and so on. Carried to conclusion, we see the hand of Jonathan Wild, thief-taker of the eighteenth century. Stuart never directly admitted to me that it was he, but I and others are satisfied that he had discovered there were more ways than one to skin that particular cat.

During his career, Stuart was Director of three forensic science laboratories including the prestigious Central Research Establishment at Aldermaston. Staff remember him as a source of endless encouragement and enthusiasm- but with an abhorrence of imprecision and inaccuracy. One of his favorite sayings was to become "what I said was not what you thought I meant." As with many bright people, Stuart was impatient and did not suffer fools- gladly or otherwise. But he was always, always inspirational and always, always true and supportive to his work colleagues and to his principles of fairness and honesty and straight dealing, even if this meant that he sometimes had to go against the herd.

Stuart and Alan Clift worked tirelessly together to put on one of the most successful meetings of the International Association of Forensic Sciences in Oxford in 1984. Stuart's presidency is still remembered as a high point in the Association's history, and the meeting regarded as the touchstone by which subsequent triennial meetings continue to be judged.

Stuart was nothing if not his own man. No stranger to the 'edge', he would sometimes take a risk for the sheer fun of it. Traveling to chair a meeting in a European country whose inhabitants are not noted for their natural sense of humor, Stuart was strongly advised not to open the proceedings with a joke. He did, and recounted the story about a man who, not knowing the difference between arson and incest, set fire to his sister. Save for muffled cries of pain from his English colleague, doubled up in the aisle, there was a stony silence. On another occasion, things were no better when; having thanked his European host for their warm welcome, he remarked that he had received an even warmer one on his last visit in his Lancaster bomber in 1945!

Stuart has left us a rich heritage, not just in terms of knowledge, but also of approach and attitude, and the emphasis that needs to be placed on plain common sense. It goes without saying, and at this point Stuart would have retorted, "Then why say it?" that the forensic science profession is and will remain greatly in his debt. We are indeed grateful for his life."

Angela Gallop

Roy Davie RAFVR

In February 1942 at the age of eighteen, Roy Davie walked into the recruiting office in Stirling, Scotland, and was selected for pilot/observer aircrew training. He had no real expectations other than a strong possibility that he would be selected as an air gunner due to spending twelve months in the Home Guard handling guns. The recruiting officer emphasized his academic qualifications and recommended that he undertake pilot training instead of air gunner. Psychological and medical exams followed in Edinburgh, which Roy Davie sailed through only to be placed on the deferred waiting list, attending the Air Cadet schooling due to a surplus of candidates. Eventually he was called up in September 1942 and reported to the Aircrew Reception Center at Lords Cricket ground in London. From Lords he was posted to Ludlow in Shropshire for RAF regulations and an introductory course in discipline and fitness. His training began in earnest when he was posted in the same month to No.5 Initial Training Wing in Torquay for pilot/observer training. The course at Torquay was intensive and included lessons in air navigation, meteorology, aerodynamics, armory and gunnery, theory of internal combustion engines, Air Force law and King's regulations. In addition, there was an expectation that candidates should acquire competence in Morse code and signaling. Roy Davie's school qualifications in mathematics meant that he was excused a high proportion of the math lessons and he came through the course with excellent marks. At the completion of the course he was interviewed by a group of Officers for a commission in the RAF. By his own admission, he fluffed the interview through being blasé about the event.

January 1943 took Roy Davie to No.22 Elementary Flying Training School (EFTS) in Caxton Gibbet a satellite field near Cambridge. It was there that he was introduced to his first spell of flying and experienced Ab-Initio flying instruction on the De Havilland Tiger Moth biplane. Roy Davie quickly showed an aptitude for flying and after approximately four weeks he qualified as suitable for further pilot instruction. What followed was a holding period at Heaton Park Manchester before he sailed in March 1943 to Newport Virginia via Bermuda and then finally Moncton, New Brunswick, Canada, for flying training.

The next stage of training was a posting to No.32 Elementary Flying Training School (EFTS, March- Aug) in Bowden, Alberta. The Fairchild PT26 Cornell single engined monoplane was the main aircraft that aircrew used for training. The usual routine was morning flying, afternoon ground school and vice versa on alternate days. In September further flying instruction was carried out at No.32 SFTS (Service Flying Training School) Moose Jaw, Saskatchewan on 'Oxford' twin engine monoplanes. Eventually Roy Davie reached the degree of competence to take his 'wings' test with F/Lt Reed just prior to Christmas day. On successful completion of the 'wings' test, Roy Davie was promoted to Sergeant Pilot. To the dismay of all on course No.89, the course was extended for another month into January 1944, which was spent learning the fundamentals of Standard Beam approach blind flying. This instruction took place both in the air and on the 'Link' trainer on the ground.

In February 1944, Sgt Davie was posted to a holding unit at Moncton N.B, 31 P D and spent a long time waiting for transport to return him to England. Eventually, in March 1944, he set sail aboard the 'Nieuw Amsterdam' from Halifax Nova Scotia to Gourock Scotland. In late March, he attended yet another holding unit in Harrogate Yorkshire awaiting further training. The time dragged at Harrogate and to relieve the boredom the whole course were sent on an Army style Commando course in Whitley Bay in Northumberland for six weeks. In May 1944 the posting to Battlestead Hill, Burneston near Derby for PAFU/AFU training was a welcome relief. At this point Davie realized that there was a surplus of trained pilot aircrew and he was again posted back to Harrogate to await posting to an Operational Training Unit. At this stage of the war, Bomber Command's losses were minimized due to the Allies gradually gaining command of the skies and the Allied forces advance through Europe. In October 1944, the requirement arose for aircrew to train as flight engineers due to a shortage of this trade and a number of pilots were directed to this option to speed up their entry into the war. In October 1944, twenty-four pilots from Davie's course took up the option of becoming flight engineers and they were posted to RAF St. Athan in Wales. The option of having two trained pilot in the cockpit was a luxury that the RAF could afford and also solved a part of the problem of having numerous bored young men waiting around who were keen to enter the war.

The majority of pilots approached the flight engineer's course with limited enthusiasm. Sergeant Davie undertook the course whilst relishing the content, and he excelled in the practical approach associated with the course. Towards the end of November 1944 the course was successfully completed and the participants were sent on extended leave prior to their posting to a Heavy Conversion Unit.

In mid-January 1945, Sgt Roy Davie was posted to No.1668 H.C.U at Bottesford where he was approached by Pilot Officer 'Bluey' Ingram to join his crew. The bond between all crew members was immediate and a mutual respect grew between Sgt Davie and the skipper who had both been through the same amount of pilot training and welcomed a second pilot as support in the cockpit. The weather in January 1945 was severely cold and therefore the crew did not commence flying until 2nd February. The crew was billeted in the standard RAF Nissen huts which were extremely cold and heated only by two coke burning stoves that were inadequate for the job. The beds were arranged contrary to regulations in a circle around the stoves, and occasionally one person would nudge too near the stove and have his bed catch fire. Successful completion of the course at HCU was achieved in late February 1945 and the crew received news of their posting to No.622 Squadron. On initial arrival, the crew familiarized themselves with this pre-war, well equipped station and undertook local flying including loaded climbs and fighter affiliation. Whilst carrying out fighter affiliation with the new Meteor jets at Colerne. Flying Officer Ingram threw the Lancaster across the sky and landed to discuss tactics with the jet pilots. Another forty five minutes of 'corkscrew' and other avoidance tactics ensued with both pilots learning the capabilities of their respective machines.

The operations conducted by the 'Ingram' crew were relatively routine; however, F/Sgt Davie recalls the crew's first mission to Gelsenkirchen and the first taste of concentrated flak gun defenses over the target. By his own admission, Roy Davie admits that this was the most unnerving experience that he encountered and the relief when clear of the barrage was immense. On another night mission to Kiel on 9/10th April the whole crew were amazed at the inferno blazing below with its reddish yellow glow, interspersed with searchlight beams. Over the target, a Junkers 88 night fighter made an abortive pass at the aircraft from 1.0'clock starboard and about fifty feet below the Lancaster. Fortunately, either through lack of ammunition, fuel or some unexplained reason, the Ju88 did not return for combat.

In late April Bomber Command sent over 700 aircraft to Bremen in support of the Allies who were experiencing strong resistance from the Germans. Flying Officer Ingram lifted off the runway at dusk in Lancaster HK805, GI-H and quickly formed up in a 'vic' formation that was being led by F/Lt Cook in HK770, GI-T. As the formation flew over Holland, just north of the Ruhr, the

Sgt Roy Davie proudly displaying his newly acquired pilot wings in Moose Jaw Saskatchewan Canada. To his left in the photograph is Sgt Derbyshire another course participant. *Courtesy of Roy Davie.*

Lancasters of 622 Squadron taxi out in readiness for take off on another mission. The Lancaster in the foreground is HK615, GI-Z the aircraft in which the 'Ingram' crew flew on seven occasions during their time with 622 Squadron. *Author's Collection.*

formations experienced heavy flak and suddenly the aircraft being flown by F/Lt Cook received a direct hit. Roy Davie watched as all the crew in GI-T bailed out safely and later discovered them to be prisoners of war. Incidentally, F/Lt Cook and crew were on their thirtieth and last mission.

At the end of the hostilities, F/O Ingram was sent home to Australia and Roy Davie found himself posted to another crew with a F/Sgt pilot who had no operational experience. F/Sgt Davie was determined to revert to his original training as a pilot and requested a meeting with the Commanding Officer. At the time of undertaking the flight engineers course, Roy Davie was promised the opportunity to form his own crew at the appropriate time, and F/Sgt Davie considered that the time had come. Although the war in Europe was over, the war in the Far East was still raging and several bomber squadrons were assembled at Mildenhall to prepare for transfer to the Far East. The preparations included some major changes, and the Lancasters from 617, 44, 7, 15 & 622 Squadrons being painted white during the months of June and July 1945. Roy Davie reminded the commanding Officer of his pilot training and his desire to finally become a skipper of his own crew. The odds of converting to a pilot in Bomber Command were remote and therefore Roy Davie asked the Officer if he could transfer to the Fleet Air Arm which was seeking pilots to fly the B25 Mitchell bombers. The Officer approved F/Sgt Davie's request and sent it off to the Fleet Air Arm for processing. Events in the Far East gathered pace and two days before the Atom Bomb was dropped the Navy cancelled the transfer request.

Flying continued with the squadron right up until the squadron's disbandment in late August 1945 and Warrant Officer Davie left Mildenhall in October 1945 on transfer to Fighter Command, 12 Group as a 'Link' training instructor. Thereafter Davie found himself at Church Fenton on a Mosquito squadron teaching others how to handle the Link trainer.

After a few months at Church Fenton, Davie was posted to a formal Link Trainer Instructors course at Boreham Wood, Elstree; eventually taking charge of the 'Link' section at 1660 H.C.U. 5 Group, Bomber Command, RAF Swinderby. It was whilst at Swinderby that the Station Commander, Group Captain Thompson, gave Roy Davie an 'above average' final assessment as a pilot and with this his period in the Royal Air Force came to an end.

30

Dreams Fulfilled

Eric Willis always had a dream to fly, especially as a pilot. At the outbreak of the Second World War he was in a reserved occupation working on the family farm in Biloela, Queensland Australia. The journey towards finally joining the Royal Australian Air Force would not be a smooth transition and only by sheer persistence and endeavor would he fulfill his dream. Eric's mother was totally against him enlisting, already having one son serving in the armed forces. In addition, the family lived on a working farm that required Eric's services to make it sustainable. However, Eric was determined to contribute to the war effort by following in his brother's footsteps. Against his mother's wishes he applied to join the RAAF and after the initial educational and medical assessments he was categorized as suitable for aircrew as either a navigator, wireless operator or air gunner.

This came as a great disappointment to Eric and he asked for an explanation. During the eyesight test it was discovered that he had a 'lazy' eye and therefore not suitable to be a pilot. Undeterred Eric Willis returned home and spent several months exercising his 'lazy' eye and spending up to four hours a day on educational studies. Some months later, he received a telegram telling him to report for duty and this time he passed the eyesight and education tests resulting in him being classified fit for pilot training, the beginning of the dream.

The author picks up Eric's life story at the point when he was sent to an operational training unit to form a bomber crew ready to take to war.

The road to operational status for Eric Willis and crew began in earnest when the crew were formed at No.84 Operational Training unit at Desborough in Northamptonshire. Eric Willis had completed his pilot training in Canada as a part of the Commonwealth Air Training plan and he graduated as an above average pilot. The RAF 'crewing up' process was haphazard to say the least and crews were formed on instinct and first impressions. Flying Officer Eric Willis reported to a large hangar on the airfield that contained an equal number of all aircrew designations and was told to 'crew up'. Various introductions took place and the final crew took the flowing format:

Pilot: F/O E. J. Willis RAAF
Nav: F/Sgt G. Walters RAAF
B/A: P/O H. Pam
W/op: F/Sgt L. R. Robinson RAAF
MUG: Sgt R. W. Hawkins
R/G: Sgt R. Farthing
F/E: Sgt C. Campbell

The crew were typical of a Bomber Command crew comprising the cream of the Commonwealth youth all thrown together to fight

Studio portrait of Flying Officer Eric Willis RAAF. *Courtesy of J. Willis*

The crew photographed in front of a Vickers Wellington bomber, the type utilized at RAF Desborough, Operational Training Unit. *Courtesy of J. Willis*

The newly formed crew shortly after arrival on 622 Squadron in early 1945. *Courtesy of J. Willis.*

tyranny and dictatorship. The crew quickly established a mutual respect for each other and they successfully completed the training at Desborough on 31st January 1945 and were informed of their posting to 622 Squadron.

Mildenhall had been a pre-war station therefore domestic facilities were very good. What had been married quarters was now used by the NCOs and officers were billeted within their mess.

The Willis crew entered the war at a time when the odds of completing a tour of operations were better than at any time of the war, the advantage had swung towards that of the Allied forces. The D-Day landings in early June 1944 had seen the start of the end for German forces. After initial strong opposition from the Germans, the Allied bombing campaign concentrated on supporting the Allied Armies advance and on the destruction of industrial centers, in particular the oil industry. The skies had practically been cleared of German fighters and daylight missions were a common practice with fighter support just in case they did send up a few fighters. By far the greatest threat was from the German flak guns that claimed so many aircraft during the Second World War and daylight missions increased the accuracy of the German flak gunners. In addition the new German Jets had entered the war with a vengeance and their air speed totally outclassed the best of the Allied fighters. However, the jets were unpredictable and difficult to fly which meant only the most experienced German pilots got their hands on this potent weapon.

F/Sgt Robinson, the wireless operator in the crew was a gifted artist. An example of his talent can be seen here in the 622 Squadron crest that he painted whilst with the squadron. *Courtesy of J. Willis.*

Everybody had nicknames on the squadron; they usually went ahead of the crew's postings so when they arrived at a new station everybody already knew the various nicknames. When Eric Willis arrived at Mildenhall and walked into the Operations Room, 'Wheeler Willis' was up on the board, someone had obviously read his record sheet and this was a reference to him recently landing a Wellington bomber on one wheel whilst at Desborough. However, on this occasion 'Wheeler' did not stick and was soon forgotten. 'Mammy' Moore was another 'Aussie', whose father incidentally owned the pub at Moree, got his nickname more by way of default. There was another chap on the Squadron 'Pappy' Moore, who had earned his nickname by always addressing his crew as 'Sonny', they retaliated by naming him 'Pappy'. Therefore, when another Moore turned up on the Squadron, he naturally had to be given the nickname 'Mammy'. 'Sack' McHugh, who liked sleeping, always wanting to get into the sack. Yet another one was 'Death Ray'. Air force aircrew were a superstitious lot and F/O Willis disapproved of this nickname.

When F/O Willis and crew arrived at Mildenhall they were assigned to 'A' Flight, which was commanded by Squadron Leader J. A. Brignell and issued with 'F' for Fox, as their aircraft.

It was a new aircraft and had the best fuel consumption of all the squadron. There were always two crews to an aircraft; as one crew would nearly always be on leave, sick, etc. Flying Officer C.B. ('Mammy') Moore was the other pilot who flew 'F' for Fox. Therefore, Eric Willis shared 'F' with 'Mammy' who had a little more seniority than he having been at Mildenhall slightly longer. Because of 'Mammy's' seniority and because S/Ldr Bignell was to take a dislike to F/O Willis, he always gave 'Mammy' F' for Fox when both he and Willis were on a raid together. Every aircraft had its own ground crew, who looked after it on a day to day basis, barring major damage where it would have to be sent on for this repair work or extensive overhauls. This crew had their own dispersal bay and hut. When back from an op, the Flight Sergeant in charge of the crew went over the aircraft with the pilot, looking for damage; holes from shrapnel. After which, they immediately started to service the aircraft, refueling it, rearming it, checking the tyres, in readiness for the next raid. F/O Eric Willis wrote the following diary entries:

> Saturday 3rd February 1945. We have put in our first day on the squadron, chasing signatures. I went to briefing after lunch. It was a beautiful day, the first for many a day I have been out of doors without a coat.
>
> Sunday 4th February. Went to Mass and confession, then went to lectures on flying control and intelligence and got our escape aids. We did a short local stooge after dinner. We were up for about half an hour, we couldn't go far as George hasn't any maps yet.
>
> Monday 5th February. Just sat in the Flight Office all morning. Got paid after dinner then packed, transport lift after 4 O'clock and here we are back at Feltwell again much to my regret.

Having reached an operational Squadron, F/O Willis and crew were again posted back to G/H Training Flight, RAF Feltwell to do a short familiarization course on G/H bombing. 622 Squadron as part of three Group, specialized in this type of navigational technique. F/O Henry Pam recalls:

> "We were again posted, this time to Feltwell onto a G/H course. This was an extension of 'Gee' which enabled the navigator to help the bomb aimer to bomb more accurately even without seeing the target, blind bombing."

Willis continued his diary entries:

> Tuesday 6th February. Had lectures all morning and after dinner no one turned up to give us anything so Laurie and I went down to the village and had tea and toast.
>
> Wednesday 7th February. George and I went down to the village for morning tea before going to the 'Link' trainer. We did 12 runs and got two direct hits and would have made a record if it had not been for one run on which we got 150 yds.
>
> Thursday 8thFebruary. Laurie and I went down the village this morning and had morning tea. I did my last 6 runs in the 'Link'. We got an average error of 46 yards over the 18 runs.
>
> Friday 9th February. On the early detail in the morning but didn't get airborne. They put us on the afternoon detail, we got airborne but one of the ground stations was u/s so we just wasted our time.
>
> Saturday 10th February. On early detail we managed to get 12 photos. The weather was beautiful and I really enjoyed the trip. We had a very good a/c. Laurie, Ron and I went to the pictures in the village. Saw 'The Case of the Frightened Lady'.
>
> Sunday 11th February. On the early detail again, so couldn't get to Mass. Left at 8.15, we managed to get photos before the weather closed and we had to return to base. Returned to the squadron this afternoon.
>
> Monday 12th February. Did some H2S ground training this afternoon. Spent all morning sitting around the Flight. They are all against giving us any leave. Had supper in the boys' billet.
>
> Tuesday 13th February. Just sat around the office all morning. This was a real damp morning with some rather heavy rain but improved during the afternoon. We are on a cross country tonight so hope it isn't too bad.
>
> Friday 16th February. Nothing doing all day. Laurie, Henry, Ron and I went to the pictures and saw 'Little Nelly Kelly' and it was very good .We are on the battle order for the first time tonight. We are on for tomorrow.
>
> Saturday 17th February. Our name has appeared on the battle order again. We are on a daylight tomorrow. The one today didn't get off. I got so excited last night when I saw my name on the battle order that I couldn't get to sleep for about an hour or more after going to bed. I kept thinking of all the things that could happen.
>
> Sunday 18th February. We dropped our bombs on Germany today for the first time. Our 'Cookie' and delayed action bomb both hung up. We managed to jettison the 'Cookie' before leaving the triangle area but had to bring the delayed action job back to the jettison area in the North Sea. As a result, we were one hour overdue on our first!

First Operational sortie - Target Wesel

F/O Willis and crew were promulgated on the battle order for 18th February 1945 to attack Wesel in daylight, navigating by means of G/H radar. Wesel was on the front line, and the Allied Army had asked Bomber Command to bomb the city to prevent troop movement, concentrating mainly on the railway installations. The crew was allocated to fly aircraft HK628, GI-X a Lancaster that had been modified to carry a .5 calibre machine gun in the mid under gun position.

To operate this position an extra gunner, F/Sgt E.B. Boyce RCAF, was listed with the crew. This 'modification' was developed as a countermeasure to the threat of the German fighters who attacked from the blind spot under the aircraft by using a development called 'Schräge Musik'. This configuration comprised two 20mm upward firing cannons in the mid fuselage which were sighted by a periscope in the cockpit. The Germans had also developed rockets to fire up at aircraft. Another frightening development that needed to be countered. The Lancaster's modification was simply a hole cut near the rear door with a .50 calibre machine gun fixed with a swivel, poking through the floor. It was a basic affair, no turret nothing; the gunner sat facing backwards. A new model Lancaster was being rushed from the drawing board, with a bottom turret, but the war was to end before it got into production.

Up to three aircraft per mission had the mid under turret fitted which was considered sufficient to defend the squadron's bomber formation. In reality, this arrangement was no match for the sophisticated German night fighter radar technology and armament. Lancaster GI-X was one of them. From historical documents it can be discerned that aircraft 'B', 'E', 'F', 'M', 'W', 'Y' & 'Z' had all been modified.

With mounting apprehension, the crew gathered for their pre-raid meal. With some raids lasting anything up to 9 hours, it was essential the crews were fed before setting out on a bombing mission

Briefings

At the briefing the crew was told their target was Wesel, a small town on the Rhine close to the Allied frontline with the objective of destroying its railway and road infrastructure. F/O Willis noted down the following on his flight plan:

Window to Platerack, Fly out Dec 4", Call sign 'Gedan', form Up-Green yellow. Taxi -out time was set for 10:43, and his take off time for 10:52.

Attached to airmen's battle dress was an escape whistle, in case the crew went down in the water and were lucky enough to get into their dingy. The objective was to blow like hell on the whistle in the hope of attracting some attention from the rescue launches. Shortly before ditching, the wireless operator would send out a SOS message with the last known co-ordinates. After briefing crews were handed their escape kit, a plastic container about 6 inches by 3 inches, which contained edible escape maps, a compass, and a tiny torch along with rations. The colored escape maps, with routes out of Germany, were printed on thin, but strong

Bert Boyce RCAF KIA on a mission to Cologne, 2nd March 1945. *Courtesy of J. Willis.*

soluble paper, which were supposed to be eaten if aircrew were captured. This would stop the latest escape routes falling into German hands. Most crews slipped their escape kit into one of their flying boots; you had to hand them back in when you returned from a mission along with all your other gear. Later as the weather warmed up F/O Willis abandoned his flying boots on 'ops' for shoes. He found the boots too hot and the Lancaster kept out the cold draughts.

In addition, crews would be issued with four escape photos, for false papers. If the 'underground' were lucky enough to pick you up, these documents could be used. These photos had been taken before operational sorties commenced and whilst individuals were dressed in nondescript clothes, so that they could pass as a worker in any of the occupied countries.

Without doubt, the most stressful and thought provoking time for aircrew was whilst waiting for the transport to take crews out to their dispersal points. F/O Willis was no different to all his predecessors in this regard, and having got dressed, he would get quite uptight with his stomach churning. He always had to empty his bladder just before getting on the transport to take them out to the dispersal area. Trying not to dwell on the coming raid and its inherent dangers was hard to achieve however, the aircrew training focused the mind on the job in hand.

The one and a half hours between the briefing and take off was when Willis was the most frightened, there was always a time lag while they made sure everybody was in position and ready. Once they started everything had to go like clockwork. A truck would then pick them up and ferry the crew out to their individual dispersal where their aircraft would be armed, fuelled and waiting. The crew would say hello to the 'erks' standing by, in case there was any last minute troubles with the aircraft. They would go over and warm their hands by the fire and have a yarn. Being outdoors

Lancaster GI-F, the discerning eye will notice the mid under gun emplacement protruding from the underside of the fuselage. Lancasters with the .5 calibre machine gun fitted carried an eighth member of the crew as an additional gunner. *Courtesy of J. Willis.*

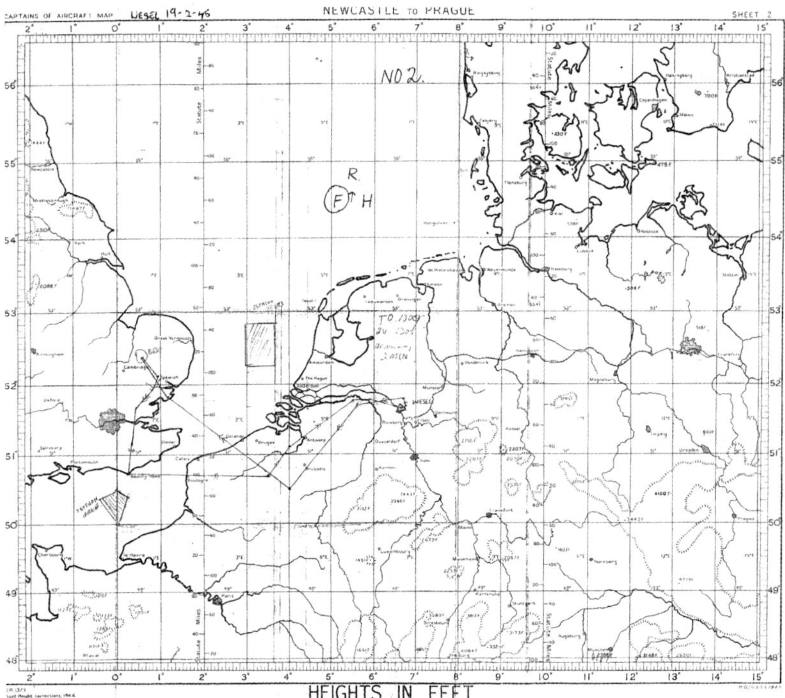

Actual pilot's flight map plotted by F/O Willis for the target of Wesel on 19th February 1945. *Courtesy of J. Willis.*

in mid February in England was not much fun. Only the worst of the winter weather would prevent the 'erks' from still being there awaiting their return at the end of the mission. Just before boarding the aircraft the crew put on their 'Mae West' and parachute harness, having to cross the English Channel going and coming home, not wanting to take the risk of having to get into it when one crashed, crews flew the whole mission wearing their Mae West. Once F/O Willis got to the plane he was too busy to be frightened; he had to work hard doing the checks. Even though the ground staff would have checked everything out, it was still the pilot's responsibility to check it out again before signing the E-700 form subsequently accepting the aircraft as fit to fly.

Both Colin Campbell (flight engineer) and Willis would walk around the aircraft together, giving it a thorough check out, in case one missed something. Two pairs of eyes were better than one. While the pilot and engineer were doing the inspection, the gunners job was to climb up onto the top of the Lancaster and take the canvas covers off the gun turrets and windscreen, which were there as protection against the elements.

Once at the aircraft, crews would go around checking their tyres. With the heavy loads the tyres wore very fast and developed deep surface cracks. A key carried specifically for the job was inserted into the tyre cracks to gauge their depth, if it went in too far, Eric Willis would have refused to take the machine up. They would then make sure the chocks were out of the ailerons. When the aircraft were towed the ground crew would put wooden chocks in to prevent the ailerons being damaged, flapping about in the breeze. Taking the 'peto' head canvas covers off facilitated the serviceability of the airspeed indicator. The pilot would then inspect the wings. Once the outside checks were complete, the crew would get in and start on the various bits of equipment. When crews climbed in, the 'erks' would take away the ladder as the door closed whilst the air gunners checked the ammunition trays as they made their way forward in the aircraft. Once seated, Flying Officer Willis would commence his instrument checks and satisfy himself that everything was working. The battery trolley was brought into position and plugged in allowing the four Merlin engines to burst into life. The wheel chocks were left in place to counter the torque from the engines and relieving the pressure on the brakes. The engine start up sequence began with the starboard inner first, as this engine charged the pneumatics and hydraulics operating the brakes, flaps and radiator shutters. After this each engine was run up, checking its two magnetos for correct operation. If the magnetos displayed more then a 300 revolution drop, then the aircraft was not to be flown and declared u/s, facilitating the use of a standby aircraft. The consequences of not applying this principle was a loss of power with a fully loaded aircraft on take off, which could result in fatalities.

The inconceivable occurred, a magneto was not operating within set parameters resulting in the crew decanting to the spare Lancaster ME383, GI-R which was ready for just such an eventuality. The resultant mad scramble to go through the pre-flight checks again on the new aircraft did little to settle the nerves, everything was timed to the second and you could not afford to cause a hold up to the schedule. During their operational 'tour' the crew would utilize the spare aircraft on three occasions. Crews learnt the importance of completing the preflight checks as soon as they got to the aircraft, to earn valuable time in case this eventually took place. On occasions, take off would be delayed and crews would warm themselves by the fire in the 'erks' hut if it was cold weather, or simply wander around near the aircraft. These delays only increased the nervous tension and the clock watching as the time ticked closer to take off. When the four Merlin engines had been satisfactorily run up, the pilot would signal the ground staff

Flight Sergeant Hawkins removes the gun covers prior to a daylight fighter affiliation exercise on 20th Feb 1945. This particular Lancaster is HK700, GI-Y. *Courtesy of J. Willis.*

to remove the wheel chocks and the brakes were released with the resultant surge of forward momentum. Twenty 622 Squadron Lancasters taxiing out to take their nominated place in line was an impressive sight and they would fall in one behind the other travelling towards the designated runway assigned for take off.

Taxiing out to the caravan at the end or the runway, a red light would tell the pilot to stop and wait, and full brakes were applied and the final engine magneto check. The green flashing light was the indication to proceed on to the runway, where the brakes were released and F/O Willis would taxi out and turn to line up with the runway. The brakes were applied again and the "Merlins" were taken up to take off speed of 1, 800 revolutions, and finally the flight engineer would release the brakes and the Lancaster would surge down the runway. Full squadron take-offs were always a delicate operation with three aircraft on the runway at the one time, one would be at the far end just taking off, one in the middle of the run way and one just given the green light and starting down the runway.

The engine revolutions gradually built up to 23, 24 hundred to allow the practiced rule of not becoming airborne until the Lancaster had reached speeds of 110m.p.h and above. The most critical time for a motor was on take off because they were usually under maximum power with heavy winds and a heavy load of petrol, Lancasters would bounce down the runway giving the rear gunner a good shake up. At 110mph F/O Willis would ease back the stick and the aircraft would lift off steadily climbing up to 1000 feet to achieve straight and level flying whilst synchronizing the motors and trimming the aircraft.

During training, an important edict was drummed into pilots that you had to be doing 110m.p.h., on take-off as a minimum. If an engine malfunctioned during take off doing under that speed, it was usually fatal. Lancasters were fine aircraft that could fly on two motors with sufficient speed. Repeatedly it was hammered into recruits that you cannot fly at 90mph and yet the foolish constantly did just that, they ignored safety rules that led them straight to an early grave.

The difference between 90m.p.h. and 110m.p.h was death if an engine was lost on take off. Lancasters simply would not fly on three motors under 110m.p.h. Once Eric Willis reached 110m.p.h. he would ease the tail back down resulting in a fast and efficient take off with the extra speed and lift enabling the aircraft to climb up to 500 feet in no time. Eric Willis witnessed two crews who lost motors on take off, the first pilot was one of these take off early types who wanted clearance. He got up to 500 feet, lost a motor and he rolled over and went in, killing all the crew. The replacement pilot was Flying Officer G.Thurn RAAF and about a week later on his first mission, he also lost an engine on take off. About a week later the replacement crew, also on their first mission took off and lost a motor. However, because the pilot was doing the recommended 110m.p.h. he was able to do a circuit on the three motors, come back in, and land.

Having taken off they climbed and headed to their forming up point, where the squadron came together. At the briefing they would be given the forming point over Lakenheath, the height, and 'S/C' Colors. Once over the forming point the Lancasters would circle around and around until they were all together before setting off on the mission. With so many planes, circling crews had to have their eyes peeled out for other planes, there were accidents where fully bomb-laden planes collided. The Squadron's forming up point was over the Lakenheath airfield. On daylight raids, the aircraft would fly in formation which was extremely exhausting for the pilot. On night operations, all that was required was to fly alone in a stream. Formation flying was a different exercise altogether.

Having formed up as a group, the squadrons then flew south, passing to the east of London, before crossing the coast over Beachy Head, then, turning east hitting the French coast below Boulogne. At this point the bomb aimer Henry Pam would start throwing out bundles of 'window'. Then, performing a number of doglegs to try to throw the German fighters off, making in a north east direction, before turning east for the approach on their target, Wesel. By this stage of the war, the Allies had overwhelming air

Flying Officer Eric Willis and flight engineer Colin Campbell in the cockpit of their usual aircraft GI-F, HK 787. The co-operation between these two members of the crew on take off was essential to enable the fully laden Lancaster to become airborne. *Courtesy of J. Willis.*

superiority. The bombing of German aircraft factories, and fuel manufacturing plant had severely curtailed the German's ability to respond to the continued bombing campaign. Nevertheless there were still German fighters looking for 'kills'. The German flak defenses were still very active and still bringing down aircraft. On this, the crew's first operation, 3 Group had assembled 160 aircraft for the raid. 160 aircraft with 8 guns apiece, capable of firing 1, 500 rounds a minute from each barrel, that's a hell of a veil of lead to fly through, it was a brave German who would try. Consequently, the crew never saw a German fighter on this operation, or for that matter on any of its other 'ops', with the exception of the night raid on Potsdam.

Bombing Run

The operation to Wesel consisted of 160 Lancasters of No.3 Group, carried out by G/H attack, through cloud. There were no Lancasters lost on this raid. Nine minutes out from the target area, George Walters the navigator handed control of the aircraft over to Henry Pam the bomb aimer. He recalls: "Our usual load was one 4000 pounder, with 12 five hundred general-purpose bombs. Our targets were mostly oil resources in or near the Ruhr."

On reaching the designated target area, and making their bomb-run the 4000 lb bomb wouldn't drop, neither would the delayed action bomb. One of the wires had shorted, causing the problem. After a bit of trouble the crew managed to jettison the 'Cookie' over the target area but they couldn't get rid of the delayed action bomb. The target area being a somewhat unhealthy place to loiter over, they headed for home. Crews were ordered not to drop 'hung-ups' and munitions over occupied territory; Belgium, Holland or France, for fear of killing some of their Allies. The alternative was to fly them to a designated dumping area in the North Sea, north of the English Channel and try and dump them there.

The crew's course home though still doglegged, was a more direct route, passing to the south of Antwerp, hitting the coast below Ostend, then turning on a north west course for their final leg home. 622 Squadron had the record for the fastest squadron to come home in the group. When the crew reached the Channel the navigator F/Sgt Walters, was anxious to get rid of the hung up bomb, Eric Willis knew that they were on their gradual descent and rejected this idea with some authority. He knew that they were crossing over a convoy of English ships with a half a dozen destroyers guarding them. The Navy were notoriously trigger happy, if they had seen him beginning to open up his bomb doors they would have let fly at him and shot him out of the sky. At that altitude, they would have been sitting ducks to the Destroyers. When they got to the designated dropping area, the bomb aimer had to filter his way back into the aircraft's fuselage to the bomb bay area. Kneeling down on the floor, he lifted the flap above where the bomb hooks were and using a screwdriver prized the bomb away.

Consequently, following this nerve-racking foul-up, they were an hour late getting back on their first raid. Having taken off at 10.52 am, they safely touched down back at Mildenhall 5 hours 50 minutes later, at 4.42 PM.

Apart from really bad winter weather, the crew of faithful 'erks' would be there waiting for their return to greet them, and they would receive a report on how the aircraft preformed and if anything needed looking at. On this occasion, the bomb aimer had something to say about the bomb release mechanism. A tender would be utilized to ferry the crew back where the first thing they did was hand in their flying kit, harness and parachute, before heading to the debriefing room. The debriefing room was a big hall with about 20 tables and chairs in it and at maximum capacity with a full squadron of 20 aircraft, 140 aircrew members would cram in. There would be Intelligence Officers accompanied by the main briefing Officers and on occasions the Wing Commander would wander around the tables. Crews would gather around a table, with each crew to a separate table assigned an intelligence officer who would conduct the de-briefing. The tables were dispersed to prevent cross talking with other tables. The questioning would take anything up to thirty minutes. Starting with what happened at take off, going right through the mission and any problems with the aircraft, what was the weather like etc. All the time the Intelligence Officer would ask questions and take notes of the individual answers. Did you see anyone go down? Did you hit the target? Did you encounter any problems? What happened on the way back? Everyone would be questioned in turn to see if they had seen or heard anything different than the rest of the crew.

The Intelligence section had the bombing photos developed and printed up to see how accurate each aircraft was on its bombing run. Copies of these photos were available after the raid so the pilots could see the results for themselves. Most of the photos were poor quality only showing 10/10 cloud, as on this raid. Eric Willis obtained copies that showed a clear image. After the de-briefing, the usual bacon and eggs were served up in the mess. It was the only time crews got bacon and eggs in the Air Force; it

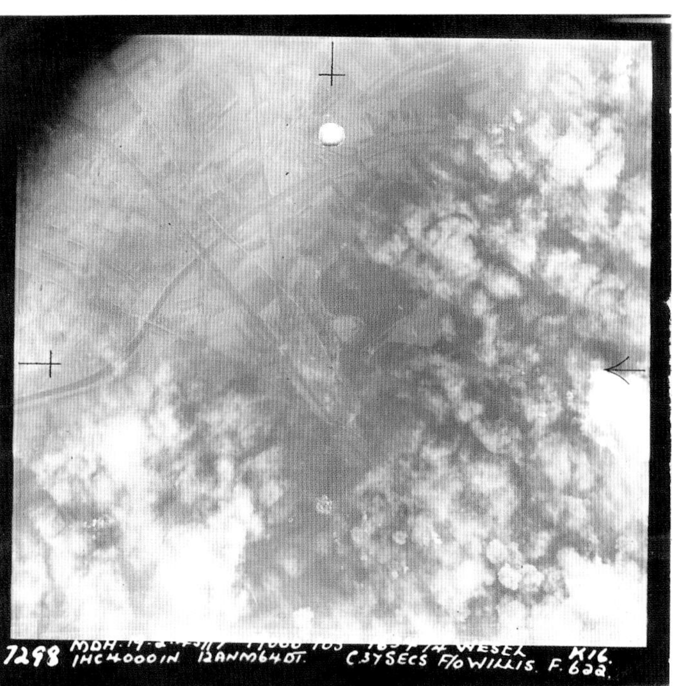

Bomb photo taken by F/O Willis & crew on their mission to Wesel on 19/2/1945. *Courtesy of J. Willis.*

Serial No. ....40. 1st. Battle Order for 18th. February, 1945. No. 622 Squadron.

A/C. NO.	LETTER.	CAPT. & 2nd. PILOT.	NAV. & W/OPERATOR.	A/B. & M/U. GUNNER.	R/GUNNER & F/ENGINEER.
HK. 651.	B.	F/S. Medler	F/S. Elliott F/S. Hitch	F/S. Doherty Sgt. Palmer & F/S. Boone	Sgt. Smith 498 Sgt. Taylor.
PD. 366.	E.	F/O. Darville	F/S. Liale F/S. Keough	F/S. Pearce Sgt. Dunn	Sgt. Beckwith Sgt. Godfrey
HK. 787.	F.	F/S. Bay	F/O. Boyle F/S. [illegible] CRAGo	F/S. Lewis Sgt. Heywood	Sgt. Armitage Sgt. Ormshaw
PD. 225.	G.	F/O. Thorbecke	F/L. Westbrock Sgt. Adams	F/O. Villiers Sgt. Staals	Sgt. Smith 445 Sgt. Hogan
LL. 885.	J.	F/O. Morrison	F/S. Orr Sgt. Totman	F/O. Pollard F/S. Stock	Sgt. West Sgt. Chambers
PB. 819.	K.	F/O. Mills 3	Sgt. Morgan Sgt. Hewett	Sgt. Brabazon Sgt. Dowey	Sgt. Jones Sgt. Eastwood
HK. 628.	X.	F/O. Willis	F/S. Walters F/S. Robinson	F/O. Pym Sgt. Hawkins & F/S. Boyce	Sgt. Farthing Sgt. Campbell
PA. 218.	L.	F/Lt. [illegible]	F/S. [illegible] F/O. Dixon	F/S. Brown Sgt. Morris	Sgt. Williams Sgt. McCue
HK. 646.	M.	F/Lt. Thomas	F/S. McKay F/S. Charlesworth	F/S. Cambell F/S. Kingston & Sgt. Mitchell 222.	F/S. Davies 930 Sgt. Ralph
NG. 299.	O.	F/Lt. Ogilby	F/Lt. [illegible] F/O. [illegible]	F/O. Tanner Sgt. Reed	Sgt. Watkins Sgt. Burton
PA. 164.	P.	F/Lt. Cook	F/O. Parry F/O. Sherry	F/O. Gough Sgt. Savage 610	Sgt. Hagerty Sgt. McLaren
NG. 447.	U.	F/O. [illegible]	Sgt. [illegible] Sgt. Burren	Sgt. Wood Sgt. Stone	Sgt. Savage 800 Sgt. Gough
PB. 795.	V.	F/Lt. [illegible]	F/S. McKeown F/S. Weller	F/O. Sleigh F/S. [illegible]	F/S. Ross. Sgt. Lucas-Garner
HK. 615.	Z.	F/O. [illegible]	Sgt. [illegible] Sgt. Bailey	Sgt. Cross Sgt. Pearce & F/S. Chapman	Sgt. Nairne Sgt. Chittock

Rations to be collected by F/Commanders and delivered to Aircraft.
Briefing to be notified later.
F/O. Robbins & Crew to stand by for Radar. G.H. Air craft. E. K. L. V.

(SGD) J.A. Brignell. S/Ldr.
Commanding, No. 622 Squadron.

F/L. Arkins. F/L. McHugh. F/L. Johnson. F/O. Arben. F/L. Noonan. F/O. Gowan. P/O. Hills. P/O. [illegible]. P/O. Glasspool.

Copy of the exact same battle order obtained by F/O Willis immediately after briefing. *Courtesy of J. Willis.*

was considered a rare treat. The ration was one egg and one strip of bacon, which was well received.

With the first mission under his belt, Flying Officer Willis obtained the order of battle sheet from the wall with the details of his first raid on it. He wanted it as a keepsake, regardless of the fact it was an infringement of security regulations to take it. Now the raid was completed he could not see the harm.

Monday 19th February
Briefing notes

Much to the crew's surprise, Wesel was again the daylight target the next day. 3 Group 244 Lancs, Total 976 Aircraft, 622 Squadron, 18 aircraft, 5 vics. Fighters 12 Squadron's Mustangs 10 Squadrons Spitfires. Start 12:56 Taxi out 12:59 Take off 13:02 Runway 3. Group rend. 'Cromer'. Forming up point 6000-6400 Climb rate 135 knots level out 145 knots. Bombing height 17000ft.Bombing tract 169T. Controled ground marking. All up weight 64120 [which was just about maximum weight] Point 'A 'Rednose'. Main force, Hookey.

Route:Base 5222 0029, Cromer H, 5430 0300, 5500 0600 5440 0740, Δ5411 0753, 5405 0755, 5400 0740, 5425 0700 , 5415 0300, Cromer , Base. Squadron colours 90 SQD. 4 Reds, 10 Sqd. 2 Green, 149Sqd, 4 Yellow, 15Sqd. Red Yellow, 622 Sqd. Green Yellow. VHF 'D', 1196 B.

Aircraft W, N, C, Y, L, T, O, A, D, V, P, F.

Usually the highest ranking officers taking part always led the group. However, at the briefing crews were informed that 90 Squadron had the honor of leading 3 Group that day, as they had a new Wing Commander, P.F. Dunham flying his first raid. This was quite unusual as Wing Commanders were invariably seasoned pilots. In fact he had already successfully completed two tours but what was unusual, the first as a wireless operator, the second as a navigator. So not only was it his first raid as a Wing Commander but also as a pilot. Two 'tours' usually meant the end of operational life, but he was keen and wanted to remuster as a pilot; eventually completing his pilot training in Canada. The squadron's place in 3 Group's formation that day was to fly behind 90 Squadron and below it in order to keep out of their slipstream. As the bombers approached the target the anti-aircraft fire started up. By this stage in the war the Germans were running out of ammo and they were selective when targeting. The Germans fired marker shots to judge the bombers airspeed and height. One German gun was firing on the first aircraft over the target, that of Wing Commander Dunham and at least five shots were counted, exploding adjacent to the lead bomber. Flying on a straight and level course whilst under scrutiny from the gunners below was practically suicide and experienced crews would vary their course slightly to throw the marksmen below off target. Inevitably, the flak gunners found their target with a direct hit presumably in the bomb bay of W/C Dunham's aircraft which just disintegrated. F/O Willis flying directly behind and below him flew straight through the debris whilst overcome with emotion and sorrow for the loss of the seven crew members.

At approximately nine minutes from the target the bomb aimer took control of the aircraft from the navigator. With nothing to do F/Sgt George Walters stood up, opened the blackout curtains, and ventured into the cockpit to see what was going on. In a case of unfortunate timing he witnessed the aircraft in front of them explode and quickly retreated to the perceived safety of the navigator's compartment. F/O Willis made the following diary entry for this day:

> Monday 19th February. Well we did our second today. It was Wesel again and the route was almost the same. We flew 'Fox' today. I did not get half as tired as I sat further away from my leader. One a/c blew up in front of us on the bombing run. He was hit by predicted flak. It was an awful sight. The flak was very light but very accurate.

Tuesday 20th February. Did fighter affiliation this morning. The weather has been marvelous all day. We are not on the battle order tonight.

Wednesday 21st February. Got up to flight at 08:30 to go to G/H bombing practice. Eventually got airborne about 10:15 after climbing to 18,000ft and spending 20 minutes finding a A.P.I., wind the stations were u/s .and we had to return. Made another attempt this afternoon but after waiting around for two hours it was scrubbed. Got four airgrams from Irene and two from Jack.

Thursday 22nd February.

Our third raid was promulgated on the battle order on 22nd February and it would prove to be a 'memorable' one attacking an oil refinery raid at Gelsenkirchen. The crew had been assigned Lancaster HK787, GI-F with F/Sgt Cane as the mid under gunner. The route to the target went without incident and we bombed on the 'leader' at 15.59 from 20, 500ft on a heading of 112T. The flak was relatively accurate and our aircraft was hit in the starboard outer engine causing it to be feathered.

Photograph taken by a member of the 'Willis' crew showing their usual Lancaster HK787, GI-F in flight. *Courtesy of J. Willis.*

The diary entries continue:

Monday 26th February. Did our fifth today and went to Dortmund. There was plenty of flak about and we had two holes, one in the starboard wing and one in the port outer, which lost all its coolant and was u/s. Rear turret hydraulics also damaged.

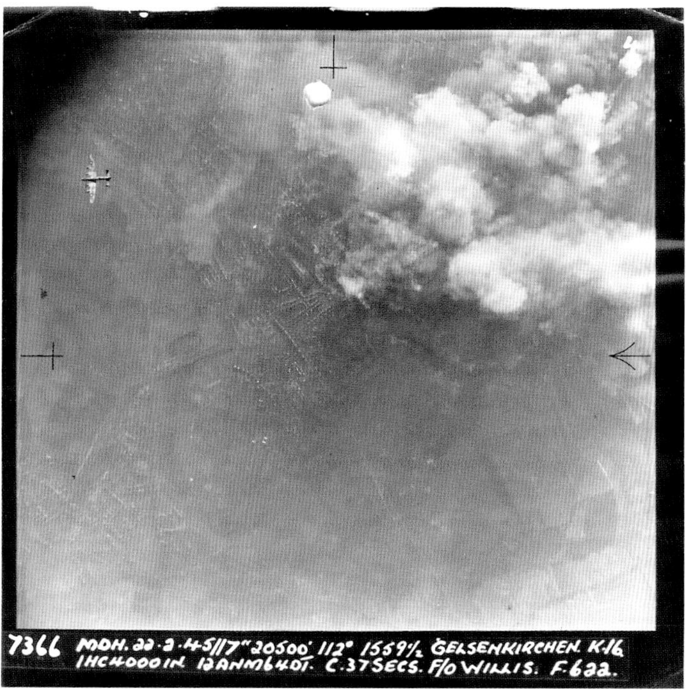

Gelsenkirchen Briefing notes: All up weight 64, 300 lbs, Petrol 1, 716 gallons, distance 800 miles. Δ [Target] 5136 0701 Form up over Lakenheath at 9000 feet. Climb to bombing height 15, 000 feet, Fighter rend. 5°East 1523. 7 Squadrons Spitfires, 4 Squadrons Mustangs as fighter cover. Forming up Colors red green. (Squadron Leader to fire very pistol colors red, green at form up point over Lakenheath to indicate the squadron was to 'set course' for mission)] Target -86 a/c on Δ [target]. 7, 000ft French Coast, coming back 3, 000ft English Coast. *Courtesy of J. Willis.*

The story continues:

Wing Commander Buckingham led the first' vic' with F/Lt 'Sack' McHugh leading F/O Willis's 'vic' formation with him positioned on his left as wing man, flying the aircraft 'E' for Easy. W/C Buckingham, on nearing home, always wanted to put on a show with a display of tight formation flying. Over the radio came the message "Move in closer, Easy". Thinking it was his 'vic' leader 'Sack' McHugh, F/O Willis told him to "Get stuffed." It was a clear sunny day with lots of cumulous clouds, which caused the aircraft to rise and dip all the time. Trying to fly formation under those conditions was sheer hard work. Back home, Eric Willis walked into the briefing room, got his first inkling of trouble. Flight Sergeant Ray said "Here's the man that told the Wing Commander to get stuffed." Eric Willis watched Buckingham wandering around the room talking to crews, when he got to him he said, "By the way Willis, were you flying Easy?" Knowing all he had to do was go look up a roster, Eric looked him in the eye and said "Yes, Sir". Buckingham turned and walked away. He could have charged Eric with insubordination in the air, quite a serious charge, but this never materialized.

Monday 26th February. We did our 6th trip today, it was on Dortmund and easy. Very little flak and no fighters.

When not flying or otherwise on duty, all the pilots and Flight Commanders congregated at the flight office, in the squadron headquarters building. At the end of the month, crews brought their logbook up to date and put it on S/Ldr Brignell's desk to sign off. Brignell's office was in one corner of the flight office with

F/O Willis hangs out of the cockpit window of an unknown Lancaster. The impressive 80 bomb symbols strongly suggest that this is HK787, GI-F, the usual Lancaster flown by the crew. *Courtesy of J. Willis.*

a window looking straight at the control tower. S/Ldr McDonald Commander of 'A' Flight had his office adjoining.

On 2nd March Eric Willis and crew were enjoying a spot of leave, Bomber Command sent 620 aircraft to Cologne. This raid was designed to block the retreat of elements of the German Army making for the bridges and ferries across the Rhine. The heavy damage inflicted during the raid helped significantly in disorganizing enemy resistance and thus contributing to Cologne's capture by the American VII Corps four days later, on the 6th March.

Even though he did not take part on this raid, Eric Willis remembers this particular raid as being the one on which Flying Officer Ray (Death-Ray), a pilot who had not been with the squadron very long, was killed. At the briefing for the raid the crews were told to aim for Cologne Cathedral as the aiming point. 'Death-Ray' stood up and said, "My bombs won't be falling on the Cathedral". This took considerable courage to voice his opinion, tragically he was the only one from the squadron shot down by flak that night.

Flight Lieutenant Jim McCahill RAAF, in Lancaster GI-K, PB819, was leading the 'vic' formation that contained Flying Officer Ray's Lancaster on his port side and F/Lt Arkins on his starboard side. Over the target area, the Germans opened up with very accurate flak bursts exploding shrapnel over a wide area. F/Lt McCahill remembers the sound of the shrapnel hitting 'K' King and equated the sound to stones being thrown onto a tin roof. F/O Ray in HK769 was hit by a flak burst in the port outer engine which burst into flames sending his aircraft spiraling down. His aircraft crashed in a field where German civilians were making hay. Three of the crew including F/O Ray survived the crash by parachuting and found themselves surrounded by haymakers who pitchforked them to death and threw them into a crater. The advancing Allies found the bodies three days later. The person that nicknamed him 'Death-Ray' always felt bad about it afterwards.

Tuesday 6th March. Target Salzbergen
Briefing notes

Δ ÷ 5219 0731. 1616 Gallons petrol, A.W.U [All up weight] 64,000lbs. Distance 919 miles.

Taxi out 08:09.a.m. S/C four reds will be fired. S/C Lakenheath 12,000ft. 165m.p.h. to Beachy Head. Fighter escort 8 Squadrons Mustangs, 3 Squadrons Spits. Time on Δ [Target] approx. 12:00. 'Windfinder' broardcast 11:40. Bombing tract 115°T. Call sigh 'Geedan'.

On the back of the raid map when he returned home, F/O Willis wrote:

"Called at 04:30. Took off at 08:30, formed up over base and climbed through cloud. Broke cloud at 9,000

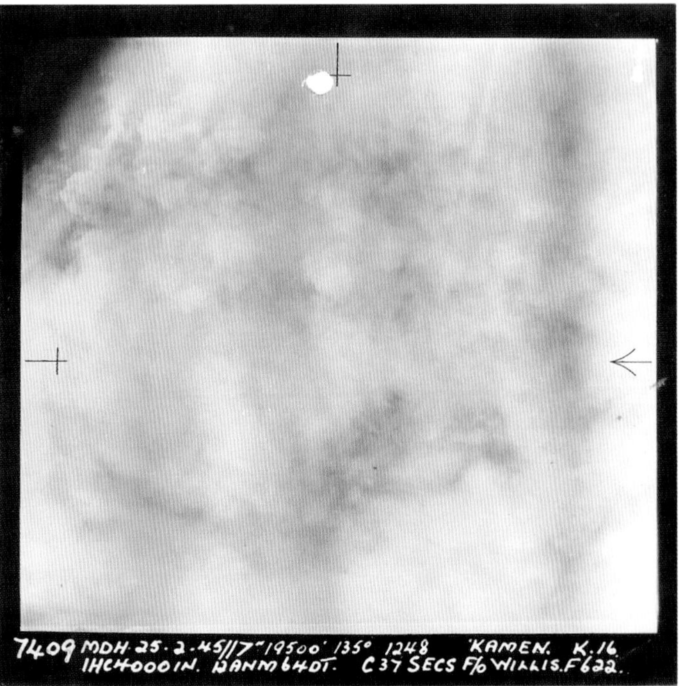

Briefing notes: Kamen. Petrol 1716 AUW. 64300, distance 920 miles. Taxi out 0830. Take off 08:35 Colors+ red-green S/C Lakenheath 9, 000ft at 170mph, 'H' Hi 1120+fighter rend. Fighters 6 spitfire squads, 11 Mustang squads. Call sin base 'Matchlight'. 154 a/c on triangle bombing tract 130 degrees. TOT 1200-1205 Route: Base 5222 0028E, Lakenheath 5203 0053 Tonbridge, Beachy Head, 503N, 0400E, 5015V 0420. *Courtesy of J. Willis.*

Serial No. ....62. 1st. Battle Order for 11th. March. 1945. No. 622 Squadron.

[illegible] NO.	LETTER.	CAPT. & 2nd. PILOT.	NAV. & W/OPERATOR.	A/B. & M.U. GUNNER.	R/GUNNER & F/ENGINEER.
PD. 228.	A.	F/O. Riedler	F/S. Elliott W/O. Fitch	F/S. Doherty Sgt. [illegible]	Sgt. Smith 408 Sgt. Taylor
HK. 651.	B.	F/O. Arnfield	Sgt. Last F/S. Atkins	Sgt. Aygan Sgt. Rivett	Sgt. Pavey Sgt. Ellison
HK. 623.	C.	F/O. Willis	F/S. Walters F/S. Robinson	F/O. Fox Sgt. Hawkins	Sgt. Farthing Sgt. Campbell
HK. 787.	F.	F/O. Moore. C.B.	F/S. Patterson Sgt. Potkins	Sgt. Cowap Sgt. Cochrane	Sgt. Carter Sgt. Sutcliffe
NN. 709.	H.	F/O. Thorbecke	F/L. Westbrock Sgt. Adams	F/O. Villiers F/S. Staols	F/S. Chapman Sgt. Hogan
LL. 885.	J.	F/S. O'Connor	F/S. O'Neill F/S. McKenzie	F/S. Williamson Sgt. Featherstone	Sgt. Goodall F/S. Wilps.
PB. 819.	K.	F/L. Stille	Sgt. Morgan F/S. Hewett	Sgt. Brabazon Sgt. Dewey	Sgt. Jones Sgt. Eastwood
PA. 164.	P.	F/O. Conechor	F/S. Thompson F/S. Edwards	F/S. Green Sgt. Llewellyn	Sgt. Marlbrough Sgt. Hogan 558.
HK. 615.	Z.	F/L. Smith	W/O. Wood W/O. Clark	Sgt. McCabe Sgt. Walsh	Sgt. Dodson Sgt. Ross.
HK. 646.	M.	F/O. Ford	F/O. Weaver Sgt. Bradley	F/S. Greenwood Sgt. Kane	Sgt. Dodman F/S. Hall
ME. 383.	R.	F/L. Robbins	Sgt. Dietrichson F/O. Smith	F/O. Scott Sgt. Hulland	Sgt. Parker Sgt. Reid.
HK. 770.	T.	F/O. Crowe	Sgt. Lawson F/S. Barron	Sgt. Wood Sgt. Stone	Sgt. Savage Sgt. Gough
PB. 795.	V.	F/L. Molson	F/S. DeBeauvo W/O. Dixon	F/S. Brown 768. Sgt. Harding. 288.	F/S. Williams Sgt. McCue
NG. 299.	G.	S/Ldr. McDonald.	F/S. Kerruish F/S. Sinclair	F/S. Brown 048. Sgt. Harding 450.	Sgt. Hermansson F/O. Chandler.

[illegible] to be collected by F/Commanders and delivered to aircraft. (SGD) G.K. Buckingham. W/Cdr.
[illegible] and Crew to stand by for Radar. G.H. aircraft. C. V. T. K. A. Commanding, No. 622 Squadron.
[illegible] S/L. Brignell. F/L. McHugh. F/L. Johnson. F/L. Noonan. F/L. Arbon. F/O. Harris. F/L. Turner. F/O. Tronnery. F/O. Lowry.

Battle order for the raid to Essen on 11th March 1945. F/O Willis has clearly been allocated Lancaster HK623, GI-C. *Courtesy of J. Willis.*

feet. S/L over Lakenheath at 12,000 feet. No top cloud at all. Good formation all the way, although a bit slow at times. It was great to see the Mustangs as we crossed the line.

10/10 cloud all the way and over the target, which was a Benzol plant. Only about half a dozen flak puffs, which was inaccurate. Although there was one a/c burning a long way back in the stream. Our squadron led the Group. Only 130 odd a/c. No fighters. Saw two V-2 trails. No eggs for our meals when we got back.

After the raid, F/O Willis filled in his diary entry:

Tuesday 6th March. Did No.7 today on Saltzberg; it was really easy. Wouldn't mind if they were all as easy. Only about half a dozen puffs of flak near us and that was after we'd dropped our bombs. The formation today was excellent.

Friday 9th March. Did our 8th today on Datteln. One went down in flames, it was an awful sight. No one got out. On the back of his raid map, Eric Willis wrote, 3/10 cloud en route until about 20 miles from the target after which we had 10/10 cloud. Both 'Brignell' and the 'Wingco' went. Flak was moderate and accurate. Saw one go down in flames. He caught fire and flew on, and then the tail assembly burned off, no one got out.

Sunday 11th March. Did our ninth today as part of 1,000 a/c raid on Essen, there was very little flak which was inaccurate."

This raid set records for the largest number of aircraft and largest tonnage of bombs dropped through the war up to now. All of Bomber Command's 'Groups' contributed aircraft for this daylight raid. The total force of 1079 aircraft, including 750 Lancasters,

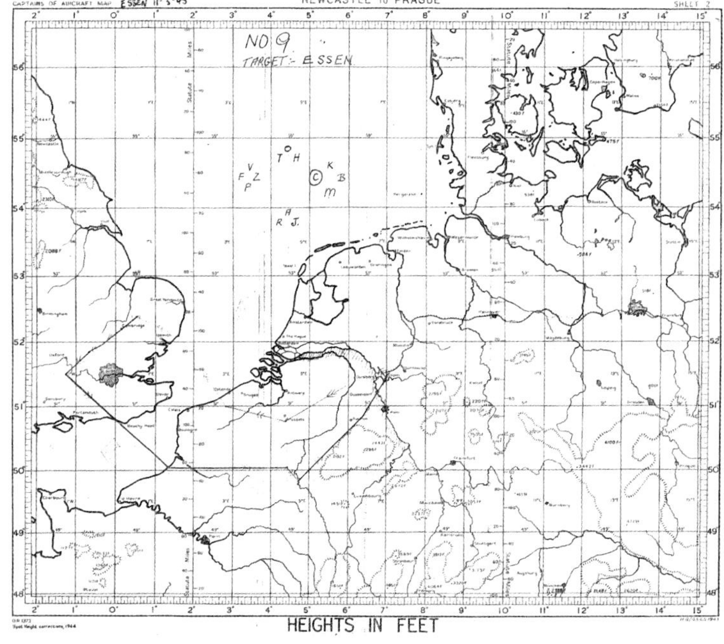

Actual pilot's flight map for the target of Essen on 11th March 1945. *Courtesy of J. Willis.*

3 of which were lost. This record was then broken the following night when 1108 aircraft, including 746 Lancasters dropped 4851 tons on Dortmund.

After making his report to the briefing officer, Eric Willis decided it was time for a bath, F/Sgt Robinson, who had also been on the raid, went for one too. They were big baths, deep and seven feet long, with a black ring running around the thing, about three inches from the bottom, denoting the level of water you could use, which nobody took any notice of. When Eric Willis got out he was completely pink, when getting dressed Laurie Robinson noticed his color, but Eric Willis wasn't too concerned, he didn't feel sick, and it certainly didn't hurt so just thought he had an overall body rash. Unconcerned they went off to the pictures. The next morning Laurie asked him "how it was?" When he admitted it was still there Laurie insisted that he went to see a doctor. At first, the diagnosis was Scarlet Fever and not wanting to risk the infection spreading. The medical officer quickly shunted him well away in to a private isolation hospital at Newmarket. On further investigation, it turned out to be German measles. F/O Willis filled in his diary:

Monday 12th March .Reported sick and was sent down to the isolation hospital at Newmarket with German Measles.
Tuesday 13th March. Hospital.
Wednesday 14th March. In Hospital, had egg for breakfast.
Thursday 15th March. In Hospital.
Friday 16th March. In Hospital.
Saturday 17th March. Had an egg for breakfast.

Sat 28th Jan. One of Eric Willis' companions through the English part of his training was a fellow Australian named F/O Geoffrey Elliot Darville. He had completed his training and also been posted to 622 Squadron where he was awarded a D.F.C. He piloted a badly damaged aircraft back from a raid on the Gremberg marshaling yards in Cologne on 28th January 1945. F/O Darville was coming back from the bombing raid and through lack of concentration he went down to 13,000 feet. Rather than go around as he should have, he took a shortcut across a heavily defended patch of flak. At that range, he was a sitting duck for the big guns and his aircraft was hit by shrapnel and lost a motor.

A Short Hospitalization, Then Back to the Fray

Whilst Flying Officer Willis was away in hospital Wing Commander Buckingham took his aircraft and crew, when he flew his monthly raid. W/C Buckingham did not have his own crew because he did not fly often enough. There was always surplus aircrew when someone was sick; pilots took one from the pool. The bomb aimer Henry Pam recalls:

> "The Wing Commander was not very popular as he seemed to fly only on easy targets. He took our skipper's place with us on the 20th March to Hamm marshaling yards. We took 2 x 1000 plus 16x5000 pound bombs and were airborne for 5 hours 40 minutes. I remember it clearly, because he complained when I operated my gun turret. Saying he could not fly straight if I moved in front of him. Near the target, we could see, some distance to starboard a lot of flak over the Ruhr so someone was catching a packet. Flight Commander McDonald flew on the same raid, which in itself was quite unusual, as the two men did not normally fly on the same missions. McDonald's navigator was the squadron's 'Navigation Leader'. During the raid, Buckingham queried F/Sgt Walters (Willis's navigator) about the course he was on. As senior man on flight, the rest of the squadron should, by all rights have been following behind Buckingham, flying in 'Vic's', but McDonald was flying 500 yards on a parallel course. His navigator was obviously thinking that F/Sgt Walters was on the wrong course and thought that he knew best."

W/C Buckingham questioned the course and navigational heading that they were flying with a tendency to believe the other navigator. F/Sgt Walters had faith in his calculations and argued his case profusely. W/C Buckingham, to his credit decided to stick with 'Walters' course. When they came to bomb the target, Buckingham's bombs fell on target and McDonald's and all that had chosen to follow him, approximately half the Squadron, fell in open fields.

McDonald's navigator had the decimal point wrong. It proved to be the first time Buckingham's bombs had hit the target and he was consequently really pleased with F/Sgt Walters. F/O Willis championed a promotion for George Walters because he stuck with his course rather than fall in with the squadron's Navigator Leader's course. W/C Buckingham later actually congratulated Eric Willis on the proficiency of his crew.

By mid-March the pace of the war began to hot up, as the Allies pessimism created by the winter battles in the Ardennes were put behind them. The Military leaders began to see a speedy end to the war was inevitable. It started with the First American Army seizing the Ludendorff rail bridge at Ramagen on the 7th March, creating the first bridgehead across the Rhine. The Germans committed main elements of 11 divisions for two weeks trying to hold them, all of which suffered under unrelenting air attack.

On the 15th March General Patton crossed the lower Moselle, charging his armored units through Hunsruck, forcing a second crossing over the Rhine at Oppenheim on the 22nd March. These crossings occupied and tied up German forces, assisting the main drive across the lower Rhine by General Montgomery at Wesel. Bomber Command was heavily involved in major softening up operations leading up to the crossing on the night of the 23rd March.

Eric Willis was discharged from the Isolation Hospital on 23rd March 1945 after being given a clean bill of health.

During the week ending 25th March, Bomber Command made numerous attacks to prepare for the Allied crossing of the Rhine. The final devastating blows were delivered on the 23rd March in two attacks on the little town of Wesel. On the first attack 77 aircraft from 3 Group attacked at 15:30 hours because of the precision bombing required for the attack. With Allied soldiers massed on the other bank of the Rhine, only G/H bombing aircraft were used.

April '45 Diary Entries
Sunday 1st April.
Monday 2nd April. Did 30 minutes 'Link' revision.
Tuesday 3rd April. Willis's Logbook records he flew Lancaster 'F' on a 45 minute fighter affiliation flight.
Wednesday 4th April. Eric Willis did 30 minutes 'Link' revision.
Friday 6th April. Flew Lancaster 'C' on a 2 hour 20 minute G/H bombing exercise.

Sergeant Bob Farthing completed his basic gunnery training whilst becoming accustomed to the latest Frazer Nash Turret. On arrival on the squadron, the older type turrets were in the process of being replaced. The Squadron's 'Gunnery Leader' knew nothing about this new turret, so he utilized the skills and knowledge of Sgt Farthing to give conversion lectures to gunners on the squadron. Sgt Farthing had been a building contractor before the war and he was used to handling men and did a thorough job of it. The 'Gunnery Leader' was very impressed with him and wanted to give him a promotion for it and so recommended him for one. Squadron Leader Buckingham refused his request. This enraged F/O Willis and he immediately attended the Wing Commander's office and demanded to see him.

When he was told to go into Buckingham's office, he found the Wing Commander sitting behind his desk and Eric Willis remonstrated with him. He was in a pensive mood and he got up, lit a cigarette, and paced up and down collecting his thoughts. Buckingham's response was based on class and not ability, which enraged Flying Officer Willis. "Unlike 'your' Air Force, we look at a man's background before we give a man his commission and after all 'Farthing' was only in the building trade." Willis replied "Oh really, what about Squadron Leader McDonald's two gunners, they were only on the wharves?"

Squadron Leader McDonald's two gunners were Flying Officers that were a couple of Liverpool dockers by trade, drank like fish, but drank with McDonald and he couldn't drink with them in the Sergeant's mess so he put them in for promotion wanting Flying Officers in his crew. Buckingham's response was, "That was Squadron Leader McDonald's business, I had nothing to do with it." Buckingham was McDonald's boss and even though he did not agree with it, he did not stop it either. He would have had to rubber stamp the promotions. It was quite within his powers not to approve these promotions.

Sunday 8th April. F/O Willis' Logbook records that he and F/O Armfield flew Lancaster PB819 'K' on a 30 minute supply dropping practice flight.

Monday 9th April. A late evening combined attack on Kiel by 1, 3 and 8 Groups with 591 Lancasters and 8 Mosquitoes leaving extensive damage to its shipyards and port areas. Damage to the Deutsche Werke U-boat yard was severe and the pocket battleship

Bombing photograph taken by the 'Willis' crew over Potsdam. *Courtesy of J. Willis.*

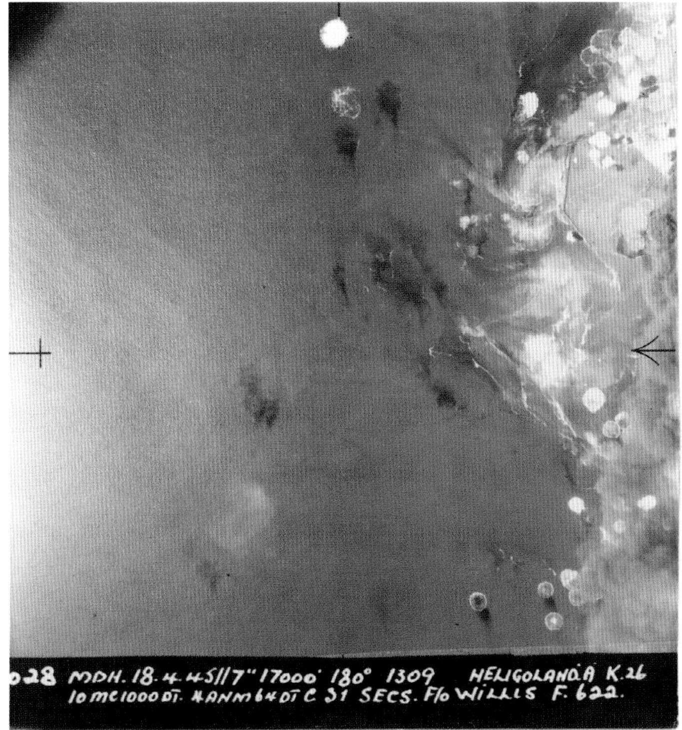

18th April 1945-Target Heligoland.1, 000 bombers. Excellent bombing photograph of the naval base at Heligoland. This mission was complicated with the crew losing an engine en route and narrowly escaping being bombed from above. *Courtesy of J. Willis.*

Admiral Scheer was hit and capsized, the Admiral Hipper and the Emden were also badly damaged. Three Lancasters were lost, including 622's NG447 flown by F/L Hodge. It was shot down by a night fighter over Germany, resulting in the deaths of all but one of the crew members.

Thursday 12th April. Logbook entry records crew flew Lancaster LM235 'X' for a 10 minute air test. Log book also records 50 minute 'link' training, which is recorded as Maltese Cross training.

Saturday 14th April log entry records the crew flew aircraft Lancaster HK787, 'F' on an 8 hour 50 minute night operations flight to Potsdam.

This was the first raid on Berlin since the Battle of Berlin, its purpose was aimed at preventing reinforcements and easing the Russian army's passage to the center of Berlin, it turned out with much of Germany now in Allied hands, and with the Luftwaffe smashed, the raid was something of a milk-run, and only one Lancaster was lost. This raid on Potsdam was the first and last night bombing raid Eric and his crew took part in. It was noteworthy also for being part of the last of Bomber Command's sustained series of attacks on Berlin. The attacks would continue on till the 23rd April. Willis and his crew would have differing memories on that one, they would come within a hairs breadth of being a second Lancaster lost that night.

The rear gunner, Sgt Farthing was unavailable for this operation and he was replaced by F/Sgt Cheeseman. Having formatted over Lackenheath they turned south. Normally they flew south, skirting around London before crossing the southern coast finally turning east and heading towards France and then their target for that particular day.

For some unknown reason the authorities decided this day to allow the force to fly over London, shortening the flying time. The rationale behind the decision was that the war was getting very close to being finished and it was not as if the Londoners would think it was the German Luftwaffe. Therefore, Flying Officer Willis flew HK787, GI-F across London for the first time in broad daylight. The next day all the papers were full of complaints about the Air Force disturbing their peace. The Air Ministry was flooded with complaints.

In order to reach Potsdam, a suburb on the far side of Berlin, the bombers had to fly over the heart of Berlin. Their target for the night was the largest staging area for the German Army at this late stage in the war. The Germans were marshaling all their reinforcements for the Russian front in Potsdam adjacent to the city's outer suburbs. Historians would later claim that it was a civilian target due to its proximity to the suburbs.

En route to the target Eric Willis decided to engage the automatic pilot system called 'George'. His reasoning was to rest for part of the eight and a half hours flying time. You could use the automatic pilot over the channel and over some of recaptured France. You would not dare use it over occupied Europe, the night fighters could attack at any time and instant reactions would very often mean the difference between life and death. On this occasion the automatic pilot was malfunctioning which was a common occurrence in many Lancasters.

Approaching the target the crew spotted a night fighter and the replacement rear gunner, F/Sgt Cheeseman screamed out a warning "fighter" just as it commenced turning away. The sky was heavily congested with bombers and obviously the night fighter wanted an easier target and not one sat centrally in the bomber stream. Whilst over the target the crew's Lancaster was caught in a master searchlight, the second plane over the target. It was one minute past midnight and he was not getting any benefit from 'Window' because the wind was blowing it behind them. Because it was cloudy, just as they got over target the Pathfinder aircraft crossed underneath them and dropped the target flares. The master searchlight came on, catching their aircraft. From the time the searchlight came on, one had about eight seconds before the first shells arrived. The master searchlight controlled the master anti-aircraft gun. When the master searchlight came on, all the other manually operated searchlights came on as well, the whole sky lit up like day.

Eric Willis instantly threw the Lancaster into a corkscrew, putting it into an 80 degree bank. Extensive fighter affiliation training had accustomed F/O Willis to the capabilities of the Lancaster and he had no hesitation in pushing the boundaries in a violent corkscrew maneuver. Unfortunately the machine wasn't the only thing sustaining punishment, the bomb aimer Henry Pam was looking through his bombsights and not strapped in, which resulted in him becoming pinned to the roof. He suffered ear damage which caused considerable deafness later. As they flattened out on the bottom of the first turn, the bomb aimer somehow managed to release their bomb load calling out "Bombs gone", at which point they shot up 500 feet adding an extra dimension to their already violent corkscrew.

Eventually the searchlight went out, obviously some bombs landed on it and as soon as that happened all the little searchlights lost him, darkness was never so beautiful! The gunners would have still been firing but 500 feet below the guns operated on four dials connected to a radar screen. The first giving height, the second one gave direction, the third gave speed, and the fourth was the one variable, giving wind speed. The 'Met' crews took wind speed, and gave it to the gun crew, if the wind speed changed in the meantime, then the gun crews could not fire accurately. On this occasion the wind speed was the only calculation they had wrong, all the others were right. It was a very close thing.

On the way home Eric Willis fell asleep momentarily, but long enough for the nose to drop. It gave the rest of the crew a hell of a fright. The navigator always carried 'wakey-wakey' tablets (Benzedrine) in his pocket and persuaded the skipper to take one. The only time in the war, he did so. The tablet was supposed to keep one going for 8 hours.

When at last the crew landed safely back at Mildenhall they attended debriefing, then had breakfast and went to bed. This was the crew's only night raid, all the others were daylight raids, which number 3 Group concentrated on. Diary entries:

Sunday 15th April. Logbook entry records that the crew flew Lancaster HK628 'D' on a 40 minute fighter affiliation practice flight.

Monday 16th April. Logbook entry records that crew flew Lancaster HK805, 'H' on a 3 hour 50 minute G/H bombing practice flight.

Tuesday 17th April. Logbook entry records that crew flew Lancaster PD225, 'G' on a 2 hour 10 minute G/H bombing practice flight.

Wednesday18th April. Logbook entry records crew flew Lancaster HK787, 'F' on a 5 hour 5 minute raid on Heligoland.

On the 18th April, the squadron carried out a raid on the Heligoland naval base in the Baltic Sea. Vivid memories remain of the raid because the crew lost an engine on the way to Heligoland, over the North Sea. They came down to 13,000 feet, but pressed on, but because of their reduced speed fell behind. They managed to restart the motor and were able to catch up with their squadron just before the target. By the time they were over the target the motor was overheating badly and pouring out smoke.

This was a big raid with a thousand bombers being used and because of the numbers involved streams of bombers flew in layers over the target. On this raid F/O Willis was just commencing his bombing run when his upper gunner Ron Hawkins, yelled out "Skipper the plane about six feet above us has opened his bomb doors." Because he was just above them, Eric Willis could not do a bank turn, so he kicked the rudder and skidded out, with the first bomb dropping behind the main wing; between it and the tailplane. It was a close thing; they were almost blown to smithereens. After their bombing run, Eric Willis stopped the overheating motor and the squadron turned and made for home. They fell behind once more and they were an hour overdue getting home. Diary entries:

Thursday 19th April. Logbook entry records the crew flew Lancaster PD819, 'K' on a 2 hour 10 minute H2S cross country flight.

Friday 20th April. Logbook entry records crew flying Lancaster PD819, 'K' on a 3 hour H.2.S cross-country flight.

Sunday 22nd April. Logbook entry records 6 of crew with F/Lt Arben flying Lancaster HK 787, 'F' on a 5 hour 15 minute mission to Bremen carrying 1x4000lbs:14x500 lbs bombs.

On the morning of the raid to Bremen Henry Pam woke up feeling sick so he went to the Medical Officer to get something to settle his stomach. He was examined and told he had a form of food poisoning so the M.O. grounded him for 48 hours. Although he protested about missing a mission with his crew, the M.O. pulled rank and phoned the 'Bombing Leader', F/Lt Douglas Arben informing him of his decision. On hearing the news F/Lt Arben volunteered to take his place. When he went to inform his skipper of what had transpired, he joked about it being their 13th mission, and being superstitious, would sit this one out. Consequently, the squadron bomb leader flew with the Willis crew on this trip. They did not know it then but Bremen was 622 Squadron's last Bomber Command Raid of the war. Fourteen aircraft from the squadron were dispatched on the raid, another of the 1000 plane raids that the crew participated in. One of the squadron's aircraft was shot down.

A point of interest, on this raid one of 622 Squadron's veteran aircraft, the Mark 1, LL885 'J' for 'Jig', clocked up its 113th operational sortie. It had commenced its service with the squadron on the night 30th /31st March 1944 on a sortie against Nuremberg. Eric Willis would fly this particular aircraft on May 10th ferrying back Allied prisoners from Juvincourt.

By now, the RAF had total dominance of the air and arrogantly used Heligoland as a turning point; turning to head down the Bremen river and follow it to Bremen itself. Bremen being one of Germany's industrial cities, with a large ship building industry, essential to the German war effort. On this raid, Fight Lieutenant Cook was hit by flak over the target, losing an engine and bailed the crew out. He headed back on three motors attempting to maintain height. Crossing the front line at 3,000 feet, he lost another motor to ground fire. Now down to an altitude of 1200 feet he bailed out and watched his Lancaster crash in a German occupied area on the Dutch Coast. All the crew survived the ordeal and were arrested by the Germans. A few days later Germany surrendered. Diary entries:

Monday 23rd April. Logbook entry records the crew flew Lancaster HK651, 'B' on a 35 minute fighter affiliation flight.

Wednesday 25th April. Logbook entry records crew flew Lancaster PD228, 'A' on a 3 hour 35 minute H2S cross country and height level bombing practice flight.

Thursday 26th April. Logbook entry records crew flew Lancaster PD366, 'E' on a 45 minute low level formation cross country practice flight.

Sunday 29th April. Eric Willis's logbook entry records the crew flew Lancaster HK787, 'F' on a 2 hour 25 minute operation flight, that of supply dropping food to Rotterdam.

The Dutch food trips were officially credited as 'ops' because of the truce with the Germans being of such a doubtful nature. For although the truce was arranged with the Germans to allow the food drop to take place, several 'Lancs' were fired on and each aircraft flew fully crewed and armed just in case. The mission had been put off for three days because of atrocious weather, but the conditions in Holland were so acute that Bomber Harris said "It's either them or you, so it's got to be you." He made a command decision to risk his aircrews' lives for the sake of the starving Dutch population. The weather was appalling, it was pouring all the way to the Dutch coast. It was very heavy rain and the visibility was just about zero. They flew the channel at about 20 feet. As the crew got to the coast, the winds hitting the coast pushed the rain clouds up and the rains stopped and they got ahead of the front.

Getting to the coast, they went up to 500 feet. The Germans had said they were not to fly under 500 feet, for fear of them spying on their armaments; they had threatened to shoot anyone who did so. Once they had crossed the coast and over the gun batteries, they dropped down to 300 feet, gradually reducing height as they flew further inland. As they neared the airport, which was the 'target area' for their food drop, they flew across a road. The crew were flying at around 100 feet and looked down into the eyes of three German soldiers on one side of the road. On the other side of the road were a group of Dutch people happily waving Union Jack flags and crowds of people with Union Jacks waiting at the airfield.

Some of the Lancasters came back with bullet holes in their wings from individual German soldiers who had fired on them; just some hotheads really, nothing organized. The Germans had covered the airfield with concrete posts to guard against any aircraft landing. The Germans had the airfield cordoned off, holding back the crowds until the food began to tumble out of the bomb bays and the crowds surged forward. The Germans did not have a hope in Hades of holding the crowd back. They claimed they wanted to see the food was distributed properly, but realistically they really meant to get their share.

This would have been reasonable and fair; they were supposedly the governing body after all and had been cut off for months from their supply lines. On their return journey, the rain had given up, and they did not have any difficulty getting home. They had the pleasure of reading all about this 'op' in the paper the next day. After this mission, the Willis crew completed another two to The Hague. Diary entries:

> Monday 30th April. Logbook entry records crew flew Lancaster BP670, 'G' on a 5 minute air test, then flew Lancaster HK623, 'C'on a 15 minute air test.
>
> May '45
>
> Tuesday 1st May. Logbook entry records crew flew Lancaster HK787, 'F'on a 2 hour 25 minute operations flight, that of supply dropping food to The Hague. They did a second drop later in the day, again to The Hague, and remarkably in the same time, 2 hours 25 minutes.
>
> Friday 4th May. Logbook entry records crew flew Lancaster 'X' on a 3 hour 15 minute H2S cross country bombing practice flight.
>
> Monday 7th May 1945. Seventeen Lancasters from 622 Squadron took part in the Squadron's last mission of the war, dropping supplies to the Dutch at Leider, an airfield S.E. of The Hague. The crew took part in this raid, flying Lancaster HK787, 'F' on yet another food supply drop operation to The Hague, which took 2 hours 45 minutes.

Wednesday 9th May - Germany Surrenders

Thursday 10th May. Logbook entry records crew flew Lancaster LL885 'J' to pick up 24 Allied prisoners at Juvincourt, and to fly them back to Westcott Base where there was a Hospital nearby. Flying time of 3 hours 40 minutes was recorded.

At the cessation of hostilities, the Willis crew ferried ex-prisoners of war from France to England. This was part of operation 'Exodus' where 74,000 British ex-POWs were repatriated from Juvincourt and Brussels in an incredible 26 days. The Americans picked them up in Dakotas from Germany and Austria and flew them into, usually Juvincourt, forty miles from Paris, where the Lancasters picked them up for the return to England. They could carry up to twenty five ex- prisoners per trip. They flew three trips to Juvincourt, on May 10th May 12th and lastly on May 24th.

One vivid memory remains with Willis whilst flying over France when an English Officer came and stood beside the pilot and asked him "Do you mind if I stand here, so I can see the White Cliffs of Dover when they come up?" Nothing gave Eric Willis greater pleasure. At about ten thousand feet, you could see them from forty miles from the channel. Tears ran down his face as they came into view, he'd been captured at Dunkirk and sent to Saltsburg in Austria to work in the salt mines. He hadn't seen daylight for six years, the prisoners were sent down before daylight and didn't come up again before nightfall, he never thought that he'd see home again.

The 'business end'. The cockpit of Lancaster HK787, GI-F. *Courtesy of J. Willis.*

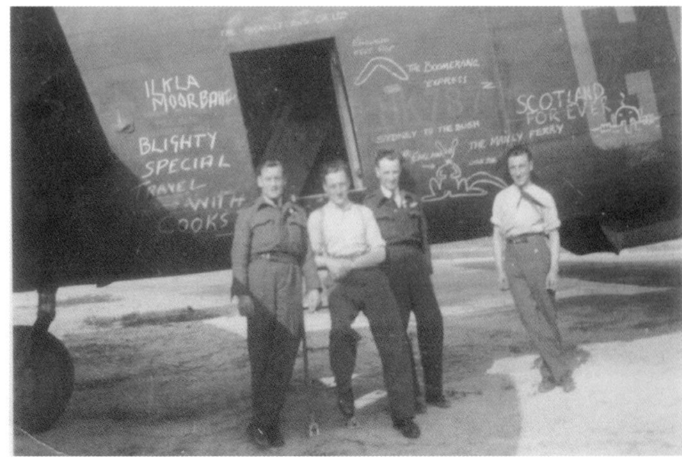

The crew pose near to their suitably adorned Lancaster before departure from Juvincourt. *Courtesy of J. Willis.*

On Saturday 12th May 1945, Flying Officer Eric Willis wrote to his sister in Australia:

Dear Irene,

Well our little war is over and everyone in England is celebrating the 'End of the War". I went to the races on my half day Victory Holiday. It was quite a change. We were late getting away so only saw three races. After that we had a meal in Newmarket and then Bob and I went to Exning Hospital. It was where I was when I had the measles. I have a standing invitation to call anytime I am in Newmarket.

We had supper there and walked into town to catch the liberty bus home.

I brought 24 ex P.O.W.s home from France today and I got more satisfaction out of the trip then I have out of anything I have done in my life. It was really grand to see how happy they were when they stepped on to English soil once again. Some of them almost cried when they saw the English cliffs loom up ahead, some had been prisoners for 6 years. We had one A.I.F. Officer in our bunch. He was from N.S.W and was so excited he couldn't sit still for a moment. He was down in the bomb hatch with Henry so was able to see everything.

Ron says those down the fuselage took it in turns in his turret (mid-upper) so they could see what was going on. When we landed they couldn't thank us enough. Now that the war is over I suppose it is quite in order to tell you I am flying Lancasters. My own particular aircraft is 'F' for Fox, but as I share it with another chap I sometimes fly odd aircraft.

Well Irene this is all for now so cheerio and lots of love.

Your loving brother, Eric.

Friday 11th May. Logbook entry records crew flew Lancaster PD819, 'K' on a 2 hour 40 minute H2S cross country bombing practice.

Tuesday 29th May. The entry in Eric Willis's logbook records he flew Lancaster HK787, 'F' with crew, taking five ground chaps as passengers on a 4 hour 10 minute flight over Germany. What wasn't stated in the logbook entry was the ground crew chaps were those who had serviced his aircraft during the war. When approaching their first city, Koln (Cologne) they were all staggered to see the extent of the bomb damage, just the Cathedral was left standing.

On returning back to base the crew had one more quick flight, lasting ten minutes, they did an air-test in Lancaster HK628, GI-D.

Letter postmarked 11 AM 31st May 1945 Bury St Edmunds, Suffolk:

My Dear Mother,

Just a short note to say "Hello" and to let you know I am still kicking.

I had a very interesting trip today. I went on an aerial tour of Germany, taking 5 ground chaps as passengers so that they could see what had been done to Germany largely as a result of their efforts.

It was about a four and a half hour trip and we visited Koln, Essen, Karmen, Dortmund, Wesel, and other places which had been targets of our squadron at some time. We went over at 1500 to 2000 feet so had a good look, it is really amazing the amount of damage done. Koln, Essen and Wesel were just rubble. The German air raid casualties must have been enormous. It amazed me how they put up with it for so long.

Wesel was the worst of the lot. It was a very small town and yet hardly a bomb missed it. There are only a few buildings standing and not a single one intact.

I went to the pictures on Sunday and saw 'The Falcon in Danger'. It wasn't a bad show. The weather is much better today. We were afraid it was going to spoil our tour but it cleared up and we had a beautiful day.

Well mother, this is all for now.

Your loving son Eric.

Wednesday 30th May. Logbook entry records again flew 'F' for Fox on a bombing practice over Rushford, total time one hour, bombing practice after the war was over was a bit of an anti-climax.

Friday 1st June. The crew flew their fourth mission ferrying ex-prisoners back from Juvincourt. They flew aircraft 'M' from base to Juvincourt, the flight taking one hour thirty minutes.

On landing, one of the other Lancasters, LL.885 'J' struck a wingtip slightly damaging it. Because of this, the pilot was not allowed to fly his own aircraft home, so Flying Officer Willis and his crew were ordered to. The flight went without complications, taking 1 hour 10 minutes, but rather than return to Mildenhall he flew the damaged aircraft to Manston, which was the procedure. Manston of course was one of the main aerodromes where damaged aircraft went to land, having extra wide and long runways specifically for that purpose. It started on the beach so you could fly in at sea level.

On the landing approach damaged aircraft could be seen dispersed all around the runway. It was a real revelation seeing all the damaged aircraft. There were crashed Allied aircraft scattered all around the perimeter; those that had crashed on their emergency landing. One of the damaged aircraft in particular caught his attention, a Mosquito in a hell of a mess, one wing had a few feet shot off it, it also had one engine virtually shot off, which was precariously hanging down under the wing. There also was a Lancaster with about nine feet shot off one wing and with two of its motors knocked out.

Apart from the drama of this last flight in a slightly damaged aircraft, this flight is worth recording because it is the last flight recorded for Eric Willis and crew in his logbook, and hence the last of his war service.

Saturday 2nd June 1945. Mildenhall held a Victory Dance, by the kind permission of Group Captain K.S. Batchelor. A souvenir programme was printed up with the back page left blank for autographs. Eric's programme had many scrawled signatures of his mates, the easiest to read by far was L.R. Nottage.

Eric Willis submitted his log book for an update on the 2nd June at the completion of his flying with the squadron, to be signed by Wing Commander Buckingham as correct as well as the Officer Commanding 'A' flight. It records that F/O Eric Willis RAAF had flown a total of 86 hours 35 minutes on Day operational flying and 8 hours 50 minutes night operational flying. 41 hours 25 minutes on day non operational flying and 6 hours 40 minutes night non operational flying. Cumulatively, the crew had flown a total of 128 hours Day time and 15 hours 30 minutes night flying with the squadron.

The End of Squadron Life

With Germany defeated, one night in the mess Eric Willis made the comment that they should continue with the war and finish off the Russians. Even at this stage Stalin was making it clear he intended to keep all the territories the Russian Army currently occupied. This caused quite a furore in the mess and Eric Willis was howled down, "Uncle Joe" was the Ally and friend, and his anti Communist stance won him no friends. After this incident Eric had a black mark against him, was cold shouldered and made to feel quite unwelcome in the mess. Understandably after six years of total war, in which England had taken a hell of a battering and sustained huge casualties, the economy was geared totally to war production. With all the shortages and rationing that war produced is it not surprising that England was war weary and had enough of fighting.

The word came through that the war was over in Europe. The Squadron's Commanding Officer, Wing Commander Buckingham, called everyone together to a meeting to see who wanted to keep flying, and who wanted to go home. Over half of the pilots were Australian, and most of them were keen to get home after long years away from home. A vote was called for. The pilots had the casting vote; the other crew did not get much say. In the speech given before the vote was taken, Buckingham had said that it would be six months before they would be sent home. He made it

Souvenir Programme

Royal Air Force, Mildenhall

Victory Dance

(by kind permission of Group Captain K. S. Batchelor, D.F.C.)

Saturday, June 2nd, 1945, at 20.00

Front cover of the RAF Mildenhall victory dance programme. *Author's Collection*

Let us celebrate our hard-won victory and, in our joy, let us not forget all our comrades who operated from this station. In particular let us salute those who failed to return to be with us on this festive occasion.

To all who have contributed to the Great Effort from Mildenhall I say "Well done!"

This is also an occasion for bidding farewell to our many Oversea friends, and we take this opportunity to wish them "God speed." May the bonds that have united us so closely in War be continued in the years of Peace.

K. S. BATCHELOR,
Group Captain.

The inside cover pays tribute to all who served at Mildenhall. *Author's Collection*

The crew pose for one last photograph together before going their separate ways. This end of tour photograph was taken in front of HK787 GI-F. *Courtesy of J. Willis.*

quite plain that he wanted the Squadron to go on. Only two voted to keep going, Eric Willis was one of the two and voted to stay on. He wanting to go on flying because he felt cheated not having finished his tour. After the near unanimous vote, Buckingham, in a fit of anger, roared out "I hope you all rot in hell." You can't keep a squadron operating with most of its pilots gone. Eric was the only Australian who voted to stay, all other Commonwealth crews were just as keen as the Australians to get home to their families.

Within a few days, the squadron was wound up. In that time before everybody departed Mildenhall, the official squadron photographer took official photos of the remaining crews. In the past, it was the norm for an official photo to be taken of crews who had successfully completed the required 30 'ops' of their tour. They did not waste photos on the dead, so you had to complete a tour before getting an official photo taken.

On the day that everybody was leaving, the Officers were called to the bar where Wing Commander Buckingham bought them a drink, wishing them the usual farewell and good luck.

31

"Ton Up"
Lancaster LL885, GI-J

The chances of any Lancaster bomber reaching 100 operational missions were less than favorable, in fact out of the 7, 366 Lancaster built 3, 400 were lost on operations and 200 were destroyed in crashes. Only 35 Lancasters went on to complete 100 operations. 622 Squadron was to produce a centurion Lancaster which proudly displayed the GI-J squadron marking and the individual serial number of LL885. This Lancaster completed 114 operational missions by the end of the war.

The first 622 Squadron Lancaster to display the 'J' squadron marking was LL828 which was lost to flak over Stuttgart on the night of 15/16th March 1944 with all the crew parachuting into occupied France. The pilot, F/Sgt Peter Thompson, and two others were taken prisoners of war and four crew members evaded with the help of the French résistance.

The loss of LL828 was a shock to the squadron, however a replacement soon arrived bearing the serial number LL885 and the ground crew soon painted the GI-J squadron markings on the fuselage.

The first operational sortie undertaken by LL885 was on the fateful night of 30/31st March 1944 to Nuremberg when Bomber Command lost 97 bombers due to high winds and German night fighter activities. The pilot with the honor of taking a brand new Lancaster on its first sortie was Pilot Officer Jack Lunn who over this tour of operations would fly GI-J on no less than 15 occasions and receive the DFC at the end of his tour. Pilot Officer Lunn recalled that he wanted to fly higher than any other Lancaster on this night to avoid the danger of being hit by falling bombs from aircraft above. Having a brand new Lancaster meant that the aircraft would presumably have better performance than older aircraft and be able to attain a greater altitude than most. His theory did not work and the aircraft was hit by falling incendiaries over the target which cracked the main spar, making the Lancaster extremely difficult to control all the way back to Mildenhall. LL885 was out of action until May when it resumed operations against French targets as a part of Bomber Command's support for the impending invasion force on 'D' Day 6th June.

Uneventful missions continued for GI-J throughout May, June and most of July until the night of 28/29th July en route to Stuttgart. This particular night was blessed with bright moonlight and the crew knew that it was ideal night fighter conditions and their apprehension grew prior to the raid. Many crews were convinced that the raid would be cancelled. The mission was not cancelled and Bomber Command lost 39 bombers to night fighter activity. GI-J had a lucky escape when a Ju88 night fighter attacked it near Orleans in France. An experienced German pilot called Heinz Rökker, who would go on to achieve 65 kills before the end of the war and be awarded the Knights Cross with Oak leaves, was flying the night fighter.

The pilot on this particular mission was F/Lt Richard Allen DFC, a Flight Commander and an experienced pilot. The rear gunner F/Lt John Gray DFC had not seen the night fighter approach and the first he knew about the attack was when the bullets from

LL885 photographed shortly before the Lancaster's first operation on 30/31st March 1944-target Nuremberg. *Author's Collection.*

the German fighter were shredding the metal in and around his rear turret. He immediately ordered the pilot to 'corkscrew' and F/Lt Allen threw the Lancaster down hard into the night sky. Due to the damage sustained in the attack the Lancaster proved very difficult to pull out of the dive and F/Lt Allen instructed the crew to put on parachutes. The mid upper gunner F/Lt D. Mason must have misheard the pilot's instruction for he bailed out into the night sky thinking that the bomber was destined to crash. (F/Lt Mason's experiences with the French résistance would earn him the Air Force Cross before his liberation at the hands of the advancing American Army).

The Lancaster lost considerable height and at 2,000ft, F/Lt Allen finally managed to gain control again and take stock of the damage inflicted. The aircraft was difficult to control and the rear ailerons were extensively damaged. The bombs were jettisoned and a course was set for Mildenhall. The endeavors of the bomb aimer, rear gunner and the pilot were recognized when they all received the DFC for bringing home the Lancaster.

GI-J underwent another period of repairs and returned to operations on 25/26th August against Russelsheim. The very next night on an operation to Kiel, the aircraft would suffer the tragic loss of the rear gunner Sgt P.S. Withers to a fighter attack. Ken Boulton was the flight engineer in the crew and he recalls from memory the tragic circumstances:

The grave of Sgt Percy Stanley Withers in the churchyard of St. John's Church Beck Row Mildenhall. In tribute, Wing Commander I.C.K. Swales DSO DFC DFM wrote: "You will always treasure the thoughts and indeed the knowledge that your son engaged in action against the common enemy, gave his life in the cause of freedom which you may be sure will not be in vain". *Author's Collection.*

> "The battle order went up and we were on it for our first operation. It was only a small force of 26 aircraft. We went to briefing and were assigned aircraft 'J'. The target was to be the Naval dock at Kiel.
>
> We took off at 20:05 flying over Denmark, as we approached the target the Pathfinders has already marked it with flares, we bombed on markers. The intelligence report; a close grouping of bombs and fires burning. The anti-aircraft fire was intense but we received no damage.
>
> We turned for home base and were attacked by a night fighter coming in from the starboard bow. The opening fire went between myself and the navigator, turning over my head, over the wireless operator, under the mid upper gunner and out through the rear turret. The mid upper gunner got a good burst in and the fighter broke off and did not return. We descended rather rapidly to get out of the light from the target fires.
>
> The skipper then called round the crew and received an OK reply from all except the rear gunner. He then asked the bomb aimer and I to go back and find out what was wrong. We could see there were numerous bullet holes in the turret and using the axe provided in the aircraft, broke the latch. It was obvious that there was no hope for Percy, he lay forward and to his right. We lifted him out and placed him on the floor of the fuselage.
>
> As the only member of the crew with a car (we were allowed 5 gallons of petrol each leave) I had promised to take Percy the next Sunday to Ely Cathedral for the service and to look at this beautiful building, but this was not to be. Percy and I had previously been to see the Abbey at Bury St. Edmunds. It was Percy's hobby to tour around these ancient buildings. Percy Withers is in the roll of honor book in Ely Cathedral under the date 26th/27th August 1944. He was layed to rest in the church yard at Beck Row adjacent to Mildenhall airfield."

Sgt Percy Withers was just 18 years old when he died and he was a popular character on the squadron. At the time of his death there was a famous American film actress called Jane Withers and Sgt Withers was nicknamed 'Jane'.

The Lancaster continued to build up its number of missions during September, October and November 1944 on targets in France and deep into Germany. It was not until 11th December 1944 on a daylight trip to Osterfeld that GI-J sustained some flak damage in the port wing and F/Sgt Stille successfully brought the Lancaster back trailing fuel from a ruptured fuel tank in the wing. On 1st February 1945 on a sortie to Munchen-Gladbach the starboard outer engine feathered of its own accord and would not stay un-feathered resulting in an aborted mission.

On 6th March 1945, it flew its 100th mission on a daylight trip to a Salzbergen oil refinery, and at the helm was a proud Flying

Officer C.B. Moore RAAF. On 14th and 21st March GI-J sustained further minor flak damage and on both occasions the ground crews patched her up. Six Manna missions were added and three Exodus trips to the 113 operational sorties bringing her total to 122 missions in total.

On 27th August 1945 the Lancaster was moved to No.44 Squadron and after a short period with No.39 MU, GI-J LL885 was eventually struck off charge on 4th March 1947.

Full Mission Log For Lancaster GI-J, LL885

LL885 Completed 114 Operations, 6 'Manna' And 3 'Exodus Trps, Totaling 123 Missions.

Date	Crew	Target	Comments
30/31st March 44	P/O J. M Lunn	Nurnberg	Hit by falling bombs from above
1/2nd May	P/O A. R Taylor	Chambly	
7/8th May	P/O J. M Lunn	Chateau Bourget	
8/9th May	P/O J. M Lunn	Cap Gris Nez	
10/11th May	P/O J. M Lunn	Courtrai	
11/12th May	P/O J. M Lunn	Louvain	
19/20th May	F/Lt R. G Godfrey	Le-Mans	
21/22nd May	P/O J. M Lunn	Duisberg	
22/23rd May	P/O J. M Lunn	Dortmund	
24/25th May	P/O J. M Lunn	Aachen	
27/28th May	P/O J. M Lunn	Gironde (mining)	
28th May	P/O E. H Cawsey RCAF	Angers	
31/1st June	F/O A. Smith	Trappes	
5/6th June	P/O J.N. Lunn	Ouistreham	
6/7th June	P/O A. B Robbins RAAF	Lisieux	
8/9th June	P/O A. B Robbins RAAF	Fougeres	
12/13th June	P/O J.E. A Pyle	Gelsenkirchen	
13/14th June	P/O J. M Lunn	Brest (mining)	
14/15th June	P/O J.M. Lunn	Le Harve	
15/16th June	F/Lt R. W Trenouth RAAF	Valenciennes	
17/18th June	P/O J. M Lunn	Montdidier	
23/24th June	P/O J. M Lunn	L'Hey (V1 site)	
30th June	P/O J. M Lunn	Villers-Bocage	
2nd July	F/Lt R. G. Allen	Beauvoir (V1 site)	Aircaft hit by AA fire over target
9th July	P/O J. M Lunn	Linzeux (V1 site)	
10th July	F/O J. W Stratton	Nucourt (V1 site)	
17th July	F/Lt R. W Trenouth RAAF	Vaires (V1 site)	
18th July	F/O N. V Gill	Caen	
18/19th July	P/O A. B Robbins	Aulnoye	
20/21st July	P/O A. B Robbins	Homberg	
23rd July	P/O A. B Robbins	Mont Condon	
24th July	P/O A. B Robbins	Prouville	
24/25th July	F/O A. T Wheate	Stuttgart	
25/26th July	P/O A. B Robbins	Stuttgart	
28/29th July	F/Lt R. G Allen	Stuttgart	Attacked by fighter, MUG bailed out.
25/26th August	P/O A. B Robbins	Russelheim	
26/27th August	F/O A. H Thompson RAAF	Kiel	R/G killed
20th September	F/O H. P Peck RAAF	Calais	
23/24th September	F/O H. P Peck RAAF	Neuss	
24th September	F/Lt Brignell	Calais	
25th September	F/O H. P Peck RAAF	Calais	
26th September	F/Sgt G. Myles	Calais	
27th September	P/O M. G Baxter	Calais	
5/6th October	F/O H. P Peck RAAF	Saarbrucken	
6th October	F/O H. P Peck RAAF	Dortmund	

Date	Crew	Target	Comments
7th October	F/O H. P Peck RAAF	Kleve	
14th October	F/O H. P Peck RAAF	Duisberg	
14/15th October	F/O H. P Peck RAAF	Duisberg	
18th October	F/O H. P Peck RAAF	Bonn	
19th October	F/O N. G. Flaxman	Stuttgart	
22nd October	F/O H. P Peck RAAF	Neuss	
23rd October	F/O H. P Peck RAAF	Essen	
25th October	F/O H. P Peck RAAF	Essen	
28th October	F/O H. P Peck RAAF	Cologne	
30th October	P/O D. C Barnett RAAF	Cologne	
4th November	F/O R. Curling RAAF	Solingen	
5th November	F/O H. P Peck RAAF	Solingen	
8th November	F/O N. G Flaxman	Homberg	
11th November	F/O N. G. Flaxman	Castrop	
15th November	F/O H. P Peck RAAF	Dortmund	
16th November	F/O H. P Peck RAAF	Heinsberg	
20th November	F/O H. P Peck RAAF	Homberg	
21st November	F/O H. P Peck RAAF	Homberg	
23rd November	F/O H. P Peck RAAF	Gelsenkirchen	
26th November	F/O H. P Peck RAAF	Fulda	
27th November	F/O R. Curling RAAF	Cologne	
28th November	F/O H. P Peck RAAF	Neuss	
30th November	F/O W. H Thorbecke	Bottrop	
2nd December	F/O W. H Thorbecke	Dortmund	
8th December	F/Sgt L. Stille	Duisberg	
11th December	F/Sgt L. Stille	Osterfeld	
12th December	F/O N.G Flaxman	Witten	
15th December	F/O N. G Flaxman	Siegen	
16th December	F/O N. G Flaxman	Siegen	
24th December	F/Sgt G. E Darville RAAF	Bonn	
28th December	F/Sgt G. E Darville RAAF	Cologne	
29th December	F/O N. Jordan RCAF	Koblenz	
2nd January 45	F/O W. H Thorbecke	Nuremberg	
3rd January	F/O N. Jordan RCAF	Dortmund	
5th January	F/O N. Jordan RCAF	Ludwigshaven	
6th January	F/O N. Jordan RCAF	Neuss	
7/8th January	F/O A. S. W Waigh	Munich	
29th January	F/O N. Jordan RCAF	Krefeld	
1st February	F/O B. Morrison RCAF	Munchen Gladbach	
3/4th February	F/O B. Morrison RCAF	Dortmund	
7th February	F/O N. Jordan RCAF	Wanne Eickel	
9th February	F/O N. Jordan RCAF	Hohenbudberg	
13/14th February	F/O N. Jordan RCAF	Dresden	
14/15th February	F/O N. Jordan RCAF	Chemnitz	
15th February	F/O W. H Thorbecke	Kattegat (mining)	
18th February	F/O B. Morrison RCAF	Wesel	
19th February	F/O B. Morrison RCAF	Wesel	
20/21st February	F/Lt N. Jordan RCAF	Dortmund	
22nd February	F/O B. Morrison RCAF	Gelsenkirchen	
23rd February	F/O A. G Moore RAAF	Gelsenkirchen	
1st March	F/O B. Morrison RCAF	Kamen	
2nd March	F/O J. B Cameron RCAF	Cologne	
4th March	F/O B. Morrison RCAF	Wanne Eickel	
5th March	F/O B. Morrison RCAF	Gelsenkirchen	

Date	Crew	Target	Comments
6th March	F/O C. B Moore RAAF	Salzbergen	
9th March	F/Sgt L. W O'Connor RAAF	Datteln	
10th March	F/O B. Morrison RCAF	Gelsenkirchen	
11th March	F/Sgt L. W O'Connor RAAF	Essen	
12th March	F/O B. Morrison RCAF	Dortmund	
14th March	F/Lt N. Jordan RCAF	Emscher	
18th March	F/O B. Morrison RCAF	Hattingen	
20th March	F/Sgt C. Malcolm	Hamm	
21st March	F/O B. Morrison RCAF	Munster	
27th March	F/O C. B Moore RAAF	Konigsborn/Hamm	
29th March	F/O J. W Armfield	Hallendorf	
9/10th April	F/Lt N. Jordan RCAF	Kiel	
13/14th April	F/Lt N. Jordan RCAF	Kiel	
14/15th April	F/O W. M Scriven RAAF	Potsdam	
22nd April	F/O W. M Scriven RAAF	Bremen	
1st May	F/O B. Morrison RCAF	'Manna'/The Hague	
2nd May	F/O C. B Moore RAAF	'Manna'/The Hague	
3rd May	F/O J. H Fiedler RAAF	'Manna'/The Hague	
4th May	F/O B. Morrison RCAF	'Manna'/The Hague	
7th May	S/Ldr C. A Ogilvy	'Manna'/The Hague	
8th May	F/O F. W Connolly	'Manna'/The Hague	
10th May	F/O E. J. Willis RAAF	'Exodus'/Juvincourt	
11th May	F/Lt J. B Cameron RCAF	'Exodus'/Juvincourt	
13th May	F/Sgt L. W. O O'Connor RAAF	'Exodus'/Juvincourt	

On 27th August LL885 joined No.44 (Rhodesia) Squadron and then No.39 Maintenance Unit on 3rd January 1946. LL885 was finally struck off charge on 4th March 1947.

Plane No LL 885 GIJ
Date 10 May 45

Nationality - BRITISH
Service - ARMY

Service No	Surname	Initials	Rank	Unit	POW No.
4278524	BLACKETT	J	Sgt	R.N.F.	3591
2698577	HINSCOUGH	E	Gdsm.	Scots Gds.	18539
5509677	BIGGS	L.J.	Pte	R.W. Kent	18597
5729758	BONFIELD	A.H.	Pte	Queens Royal	18606
4396883	BRUNTON-SANKEY	T	Pte	Buffs.	267426
171413	CALDER.	R.	Dvr.	RASC	265250
6054778	CARELESS	G	Pte	Sherwood Foresters	8588
7926850	CARPENTER	E.T.H.	Tpr.	7th Hussars	259485
14553320	CHAMBERS	S.	Pte	2nd North Staffs.	278338
1500013	CONNOR	J	L/Bdr.	R.A.	2226
5254134	CLARK	W H	Pte	ACC	8388
4751857	CONSTABLE	R.C.	Pte	Green Howards	8405
2659232	COX	J D	L/Cpl.	Coldstream Guards.	18594
14295044	EDWARDS	L.T.	Gnr.	RA	274050
14358031	DARE	F H.	Pte	1/4 Hampshire	18562
3528835	FAHEY	E	Gnr.	RA	
1780926	FAHEY	J	Gnr	RA	266356
5440175	FOSSEY	E	L/Cpl.	KOYLI	266357
6659661	FREEDMAN	M	Dvr.	RASC	18598
2721362	GALLAGHER	J	Gdm.	IRISH Gds.	3400
156883	BARNICOT	J.M.	Lieut.	R.A.	3365
NX 12382	BRICE	FED	Lieut	AIF	3595
—	BISSONETTE	A.L.	Lieut.	FMR	3555
70713	BISSET	J G.	Capt.	R Sigs	4060
					1198

Operation Exodus – 10th May 1945. List of POWs returned to England by F/O E. J Willis RAAF. *Courtesy of J. Willis.*

Appendix I:
A Brief History of RAF Mildenhall

The author is indebted to Mr. H Dring for allowing him to use material from his father's (Mr. C. Dring) book entitled 'A History of RAF Mildenhall' in this account.

RAF Mildenhall was established in 1934; however, people living in the area had long been accustomed to the sight of aircraft in the skies overhead. The Army had for many years made use of the extensive Breckland area to the northeast of Mildenhall for military training.

In 1929 it became known locally that Mildenhall had been selected to be the site of the first of the new-style bomber bases. The town was suffering the effects of the agricultural depression and the local people welcomed the thought of some much needed employment. Work began in earnest in October 1930 when the first building, a large office for the construction staff; was erected. The Ministry of Transport laid down concrete roads and in 1931 a London based building firm took over the main contract.

The first phase of construction lasted for some 3 years and most of the buildings of this period are still in existence, although now with different uses. The original hangars No's 1 and 5 were designed to such a high specification that they are in use today with the USAF. The first control tower, a small bungalow type building between hangars 2 and 3 has long since disappeared.

The airfield when finished had 3 grass runways, the longest being the NE-SW runway at 1300 yards. The first aircraft that is known to have landed at Mildenhall touched down at about 11.am on 19th March 1931 and stayed only briefly. The station was officially opened on 16th October 1934 and Wing Commander Linnell OBE became the first station commander.

The England to Australia Air Race

Starting from Mildenhall on 20th October 1934, the MacRobertson England to Australia Air Race was in celebration of the centenary of the foundation of the Australian state of Victoria. The race was sponsored by Sir MacPherson Robertson with a prize fund of £15,000.

64 entrants registered for the race but by start day only 20 presented themselves. Three British crews each raced in De Havilland DH88 Comets especially designed for the race. Each Comet was powered by two 232-hp Gipsy six R race engines driving variable pitch propellers.

The race was won by pilots Charles W.A. Scott and Tom Campbell Black, flying a de Havilland DH88 comet named "Grosvenor House" serial no. G-ACSS. The Comet crossed the finish line at 5:34 AM on 23 October 1934, completing the 11, 333 miles to Flemington Race Course, Melbourne in 70 hours, 54 minutes and 18 seconds.

A second all green Comet, G-ACSR, flown by Ken Waller and Owen Cathcart-Jones finished fourth and returned to the UK with film and photographs of the finish. In doing so they set a new there-and-back record of 13 days 6 hours and 43 minutes.

The War Years

Partial mobilization was ordered on 1st August 1939 and on the following day the station received orders to assume a state of readiness for war. Fuel storage tanks were filled to capacity, emergency rations were brought up to war strength and identity discs and field dressings were issued to all personnel. At the beginning of the war 149 and 99 Squadrons were stationed at Mildenhall and the Wellington bombers of 149 Squadron were dispersed around the airfield perimeter to minimise the effect of any enemy action. Almost immediately No.99 Squadron was dispatched to the satellite airfield on Newmarket Heath where it was to operate from still under the control of RAF Mildenhall for the first eighteen months of the war.

War was declared at 11:00 hrs on 3rd September 1939 and within hours it was reported that the German fleet was moving out of Wilhelmshaven. Three aircraft from 149 Squadron were dispatched from Mildenhall in an attempt to intercept the fleet but bad weather made the mission impossible and all returned safely to base. Bombing operations began in earnest in December 1939 when W/Cdr. Kellett of 149 Squadron led a formation of Wellingtons in an attack on the German fleet off Heligoland on the 3rd December. Although the Wellingtons were attacked by enemy fighters they still managed to sink a minesweeper by means of a bomb passing right through the ship without exploding. The 18th December saw the biggest air battle since the 1st World War when W/Cdr Kellett led a force of 24 Wellingtons from 3 squadrons again against Wilhelmshaven. German fighters had been alerted to the bombers' approach by an experimental early-warning radar system and made a classic interception of the raiding force. The forty minute battle which followed resulted in disaster for the Wellingtons and ten were shot down, two ditched on the way home and three of the ten which managed to return to England were badly damaged when they had to force land away from base. 149

Squadron was comparatively lucky in that it lost only two aircraft and made claims to shooting down anywhere from two to seven aircraft. W/Cdr Kellett was awarded the DFC for his leadership on this ill fated mission. It was obvious that losses of this magnitude could not be sustained and the RAF High Command suspended all daylight bombing raids until further notice except for the routine sweeps over the North Sea.

January 1940 saw the resumption of night time 'nickel' operations with both the Mildenhall squadrons participating in the dropping of 'nickel' (propaganda leaflets) over Germany. The wisdom of risking lives on such missions over enemy territory has been widely debated over the years and aircraft and crews continued to be lost on what many considered pointless exercises.

In March 1940, the headquarters of No. 3 Bomber Group moved from RAF Mildenhall to Harraton House at Exning, near Newmarket, not to return to Mildenhall again until January 1947.

On 17th June 1940 149 Squadron was joined at Mildenhall by 218 (Gold Coast) Squadron which had been evacuated from France where it had been operating since the outbreak of war. The union was only shot lived and 218 Squadron was posted to RAF Oakington in July where it exchanged its Fairy Battles for Blenheim IVs.

Throughout the remainder of 1940 and 1941 the two squadrons continued to play an active part in the bombing campaign and acts of endeavor and heroism were common place. A slight relief to the bombing war came around this time in the form of Mildenhall being chosen to take part in the making of a propaganda film. The film was the famous 'Target for Tonight' featuring the Wellington 'F' for Freddie and captained by Gp. Capt P.C. Pickard DSO DFC. He was later to lose his life leading the legendary attack on Amiens prison in 1944 whilst piloting a Mosquito fighter bomber.

Four engined Short Stirling bombers were assigned to 149 Squadron at the end of 1941 and it was quickly established that the large bombers were unsuitable for the grass runways. To remedy this problem the Stirlings were operated from the newly prepared concrete runways at Lakenheath a short distance down the road. The squadron's first operation with the new aircraft was against the battleship 'Tirpitz' although the poor weather restricted any real attempt at an attack. Although 149 Squadron was still under the command of RAF Mildenhall, it operated exclusively from Lakenheath and its place at Mildenhall was taken by 419 Squadron RCAF which operated Wellington bombers. The new squadron was formed at Mildenhall on 15th December 1941 and its first operational sortie took place on 11th January 1942 during an attack on Brest. No.419 Squadron operated from Mildenhall until November 1942 when it was posted to RAF Middleton St. George as a part of No.6 RCAF Group. The Canadians had become popular figures in and around Mildenhall and their high spirits and free spending was missed when they departed. With the Canadians departure came the arrival of two more Wellington squadrons in the form of No's 115 and 75 Squadrons the latter having New Zealand aircrew and formed the first Commonwealth squadron in Bomber Command.

RAF Mildenhall closed temporarily for operational flying at the end of 1942 whilst its first concrete runways were laid. The base continued to control its three squadrons even though none were now at the parent airfield. No.149 Squadron, by now one of three squadrons in Bomber Command to have trained for Gas bombing, continued to fly from the Lakenheath satellite whilst 75 Squadron converted to Short Stirlings and remained at Newmarket. No.115 Squadron was dispersed to East Wretham and in March 1943 converted from Wellingtons to Lancasters. All three squadrons took part on 12th March 1943 in the outstandingly successful raid on the Krupp armament works at Essen that heralded the start of Bomber Command's Battle of the Ruhr. At the end of March 1943 RAF Mildenhall handed over control of its three squadrons to their various airfields and now with concrete runways, a new control tower and Drom approach lighting was ready to receive the heavy bombers. In April 1943 No.15 Squadron was posted from Bourn in Cambridgeshire to Mildenhall and two Airspeed Horsa gliders towed by Whitley Vs facilitated the movement of equipment and personnel. On it second day at Mildenhall XV Squadron sent eighteen Stirlings to bomb Essen with the loss of one Stirling that crash landed on return.

622 Squadron

On 10th August 1943 No.15 Squadron detached its 'C' flight to form 622 Squadron, this being the only RAF squadron ever stationed at Mildenhall that had not had an earlier existence in the previous war. Seven Stirlings were assigned the new squadron code letters of GI and they were in operation on there first day of formation when they attacked Nuremberg all returning safely. The Stirling was the oldest and least effective of the four-engined bombers and due to the high loss rate of the bombers, they were utilized on increasing mine laying operations.

The two squadrons converted to Lancasters in December 1943, No. 622 Squadron flying its last Stirling mission; mine laying in the Frisians on the 20th December and No.15 squadron flying its last similar mission on 22nd December. By this time XV Squadron had flown the Stirling operationally for longer that any other squadron. One of its aircraft, Stirling N3669 LS-H had flown 67 missions, believed to be a record for the Stirling Bomber. This aircraft was exhibited outside St. Paul's Cathedral during the Wings for Victory week in February 1944. Both squadrons flew their first mission in Lancasters on a raid to Brunswick on 14th January 1944.

Throughout the Battle of Berlin the two squadrons continued to put on a maximum effort in support of Bomber Commands directives. In March 1944 the Battle of Berlin was halted and the impetus switched to attacks on German communications and defenses in preparation for the Normandy invasion. On D-Day 6th June 1944, 35 Lancasters from RAF Mildenhall attacked the gun emplacements on the French coast near Caen at 0500hrs, just before the Allied landings. The V1 flying bombs were now menacing Britain and the launching sites were frequently attacked. 14 aircraft from each of the Mildenhall squadrons took part in such attacks on the 23rd June and in addition operations were flown in support of the Allied armies. On one such mission to Heinsberg on 16th November 1944, the Commanding Officer of XV Squadron, W/C W. Watkins, was shot down by flak and taken POW. On 28th November 1944, Lancaster's from both squadrons took part in an attack on Neuss and important German supplies center. This was the first time that Lancasters from Mildenhall dropped the 12,000lb 'tallboy' bomb.

In the autumn of 1944 the important navigation aide 'G-H' was fitted to several of the Lancasters. The G-H system was based on a blind bombing technique governed by radar and the Lancasters had their tail rudders painted with yellow strips to distinguish them as G-H leaders. These specially adapted Lancasters were used extensively as formation leaders on massed daylight raids with the G-H equipped Lancaster flying in three 'vic' formations. When the leader released his bombs at the designated point, this was the trigger for the others to follow suit.

February 1945 was an extremely busy month, 222 sorties being flown by XV Squadron and 229 by 622 squadron. Attacks were now being made on tactical targets in preparation for the Allied crossing of the Rhine and on 23rd March, a Lancaster from 622 Squadron led 16 aircraft from Mildenhall in an attack on Wesel, the aiming point being 1500 yards in front of Allied troops.

The last bombing mission from Mildenhall came on 22nd April when 14 aircraft from each squadron took part in a raid on Bremen and one Lancaster from 622 Squadron was lost due to flak. Operation 'Manna' began on 29th April, a series of flights made to the Netherlands to drop food supplies to the starving civilian population. Finally, on 3rd May 1945 two Lancasters from each squadron took off to lay mines in the Kattegat to try to trap a convoy that had been seen leaving Kiel. Bad weather resulted in the aircraft returning to base and this proved to be the last offensive of the war flown from RAF Mildenhall.

VE-Day, 8th May 1945 passed quietly at Mildenhall with both squadrons busy dropping food to the Dutch and this prevented a general stand-down. RAF Mildenhall had figured prominently in the bombing offensive throughout the war and over 200 aircraft- Wellingtons, Stirlings & Lancasters- had been lost. The Station 'Roll of Honor' records the names of over nineteen hundred officers and men killed on active service, seventy six of whom are buried in the beautifully kept Military Cemetery at the back of St. John's Church in Beck Row.

622 Squadron had dropped 10, 469 tons of bombs since its formation in 1943 and XV squadron had dropped 13, 124 tons since changing to Lancasters in December 1943. Both squadrons were also heavily involved in mine laying operations.

Each of the squadrons could boast a Lancaster that had completed over 100 missions, a very rare feat when considering that the average number of missions completed by a Lancaster was 21. LL885 GI-J of 622 Squadron completed 113 operational sorties and LL806, also 'J' of XV Squadron completed 134. The latter's record was surpassed by only two other aircraft and in both cases they had been flown by more than one squadron whereas LL806 J-Jig completed all her missions with the one squadron.

Appendix II:
622 Squadron History

Motto: Bellamus Noctu - We Wage War By Night

Badge: A long-eared owl volant affrontée, carrying in the claws a flash of lightning. The design is symbolic of the nocturnal activities of the squadron. Authority: King George VI, October 1944.

622 Squadron was formed at Mildenhall, Suffolk on 10th August 1943 from 'C' flight of XV Squadron as a bomber squadron equipped with Stirling Bombers. The formation of the squadron came about due to the expansion of Bomber Command after the successful campaign against the Ruhr and Hamburg. Its formation also coincided with the beginning of the long and costly 'Battle of Berlin' which would see the Stirling Bomber withdrawn from front line operations due to unsustainable losses.

Seven Stirling bombers and their crews were immediately transferred from XV Squadron to 622 Squadron to form 'A' flight and the squadron code letters were changed to GI. Among the transferred crews was S/Ldr Martin who took immediate charge of the squadron for the first ten days. The squadron was in action on the first day of its formation when it dispatched seven Short Stirlings to Nuremberg. Over a period of 21 months the squadron dropped 10, 469 tons of bombs. The first Stirling lost with casualties was on 24th August 1943 when BF521, piloted by F/Sgt. N.C. Rollett, was shot down by a night fighter on an operation to Berlin with the loss of all the crew. Seven Short Stirling bombers were lost with casualties.

The squadron was re-equipped with Lancasters during December 1943 and January 1944 and carried on its operations in Germany and France. Forty two Lancasters were lost with casualties. The final Lancaster lost with casualties was PA285 piloted by F/Lt Robbins who was shot down by flak on an operation to Regensberg on 20th April 1945.

The squadron was disbanded on 15th August 1945 but appeared briefly again from 15th December 1950 as part of the Royal Auxiliary Air Force at Blackbushe operating Valettas in a transport role. Its new role was short-lived and the squadron was disbanded again on 30 September 1953.

Appendix III: Commanding Officers

S/Ldr J. Martin August 1943
W/Cdr G.H.N. Gibson August 1943–February 1944
W/Cdr I.C.K. Swales February 1944-October 1944
W/Cdr G.K. Buckingham October 1944-May 1945
W/Cdr R.H. McIntosh December 1950-September 1953

Wing Commander Ian Clifford Kirby Swales Swales DSO, DFC, DFM

In February 1944 one of the most respected operational leaders of Bomber Command took up his post at RAF Mildenhall as Commanding Officer of 622 Squadron. Already a veteran of two operational tours in Bomber Command including one with XV Squadron, W/C Swales was an inspirational leader who imparted his knowledge to others readily. Swales was a Yorkshire man and a Halton 'brat' who completed his first tour on Wellingtons with 38 Squadron winning the DFM. For his second tour he joined XV Squadron and at tour completion he was awarded the DFC. 622 Squadron was his third tour of operations all of which were completed within 3 Group. At the cessation of his final tour he was awarded the DSO.

On one occasion, W/C Swales was at 1651 Heavy Conversion Unit at Waterbeach, Suffolk after his first tour of operations. Here he took part in the 1,000 bomber raid on Cologne in May 1942. Piloting a Mark 1 Short Stirling the crew successfully bombed the target and on the return journey was attacked by a Me.110 which resulted in the aircraft being chased from 15,000ft to 2,000ft. The Stirling was hit four times on the way down and had a 20mm shell actually explode in the rear turret. The shell blew out all the Perspex, setting fire to the gunner's incendiary ammunition, which he was able to throw out. Fortunately, no one else was hit in spite of 90 different strike hits and the starboard inner engine being set on fire. Eventually the fire was put out by feathering the

Wing Commander 'Blondie' Swales, Commanding Officer of 622 Squadron seen here on the right. To his left is the C/O of XV Squadron, Wing Commander Watkins. *Author's Collection.*

Wing Commander R.H. McIntosh DFC, AFC was assigned as the Commanding Officer of the newly formed 622 Squadron in December 1950. The squadron was attached to the Royal Auxiliary Air Force (Transport Command). The Vickers Valetta twin engined aircraft was utilized whilst being based at RAF Blackbushe in Hampshire England. The squadron's new role was short lived and it was again disbanded in September 1953. Wing Commander R.H. McIntosh DFC, AFC (2nd from left) had an illustrious career in the RAF spanning 54 years from 1917-1971. Author's collection.

engine. In addition, the port inner engine was only running on half power and the Stirling belly landed at RAF Coltishall on grass. An inspection revealed an unexploded 500lb bomb with its nose poking through the step to the nose. The durability of the Short Stirling was severely tested on this night.

Stories attributed to aircrew who served under him portray a passionate and considerate man. He treated everyone as an equal and took it personally when a bomber crew failed to return from a mission. The one thing that set him apart from all others was his insistence to fly on dangerous missions into the Ruhr industrial areas with nearly every new crew who joined the squadron. Crews looked up to him as a guiding figure and their belief in him was a reassuring factor in many crews completing their full tour of 30 operations.

The paragraph below epitomizes the respect that aircrew had for Wing Commander Swales and was relayed to me by an air gunner who served under W/C Swales during 1944. The story begins back at dispersal after a grueling mission into Germany's industrial Ruhr valley, at the time the most heavily defended target in the world. Bill Hickling pays his tribute to W/C Swales:

> "Back at dispersal we climbed out exhausted and very tense after our ordeal and I noticed some flak holes in the tail plane. I started to dig a piece of shrapnel out with my penknife when the Commanding Officer drove up in his car and walked over to me. He asked me how I was and then asked me if he could have the piece of shrapnel for his collection. My emotions were still running high and I told him to "get stuffed, they were shooting this stuff at me and I'm going to keep it", he laughed and put his arm around my shoulder in a reassuring way. In other circumstances, I would never have dreamt of speaking to the C/O in this manner for he was much respected among aircrew. We called him 'Blondie' Swales due to his very blonde hair and handlebar moustache which were his striking features. By the end of the war, he had completed three tours of operations and received the DSO, DFC & DFM for outstanding devotion to duty. Whilst Wing Commander Swales was in charge morale on the station was very high and he flew on several missions with crews as a support and guidance measure. Many Commanding Officers did the same however they chose relatively easy targets with little prospect of being shot down. 'Blondie' Swales always chose the most dangerous missions to fly and that gained him the ultimate respect, he would never expect his crews to fly anywhere that he daren't fly."
> Warrant Officer William 'Bill' Hickling DFM.

'Holy of Holies'

The respect between a Commanding Officer and the aircrew under his command was essential if he was to inspire young men to go on dangerous operations, often when they knew it could be their last. This mutual respect was built upon solid leadership and by Commanding Officers going on some of the same missions as the inexperienced aircrew. In the air, the crew of a Lancaster was a team and relied on each other to successfully bomb the target and evade the German defenses. However, there were lighter moments that are memorable for their sheer audacity. Flight Lieutenant Ray Trenouth RAAF and crew exploited the good will of their commanding officer in the following story supplied by the rear gunner Don Harvey:

> "It was a balmy Sunday evening and Trenouth's crew had been asked to fly the Station Commander, Group Captain Young, to the RAF College at Cranwell, where he was attending a staff course in readiness for promotion to Air Commodore.
>
> The Group Captain perched on the flight engineer's seat beside the Skipper and map read them across, flying quite low, at about 1,000 feet. They admired the beauty of the countryside in the softness of the twilight and fields of tulips in bloom made a spectacular sight. Flying over these pretty fields makes up for a lot of other times, thought the rear gunner, who was always interested in flying over castles and country estates, with their parks and lakes.
>
> We landed on the grass airfield and taxied over to the control tower where he stood watching. Also watching was a crowd of trainees, intent on getting a good look at Lancaster GI-B 'Beer', with a row of bombs painted below a foaming pot of beer.
>
> Our rear gunner reported that the Group Captain was still watching as we taxied away. By the time F/O Ray Trenouth lined the Lancaster up for take off, he had been persuaded that it was expected of him to put on a bit of a show. Once airborne, the skipper held 'B' Beer down as long as possible, then pulled up in a steep climb, back in what was almost a stall turn and roared across the field, before pulling up at the last moment to clear the control tower. Almost immediately the skipper was full of remorse and contrition. The Group Captain was waving his fist; now look at the trouble you chaps have got me into. Shooting up Cranwell, the holy of holies, we must have been mad.
>
> Back at Mildenhall, the skipper hurried to the mess and confessed to tale to Flight Commander, S/Ldr 'Hank' Tilson, a highly respected and well liked Canadian. "You shot up Cranwell, Trennie. Oh my God" he said. "The holy of holies." Tilson seemed well informed of the incident, perhaps via a previous telephone call and perhaps the Group Captain was secretly pleased with the show one of his crews had put on for him.
>
> Squadron leader Tilson turned to Ray Trenouth and grinned at him whilst tapping two fingers on his shoulder, the unofficial nod that he had been promoted to Flight Lieutenant."

Appendix IV: Cutaway Drawing of the Avro Lancaster

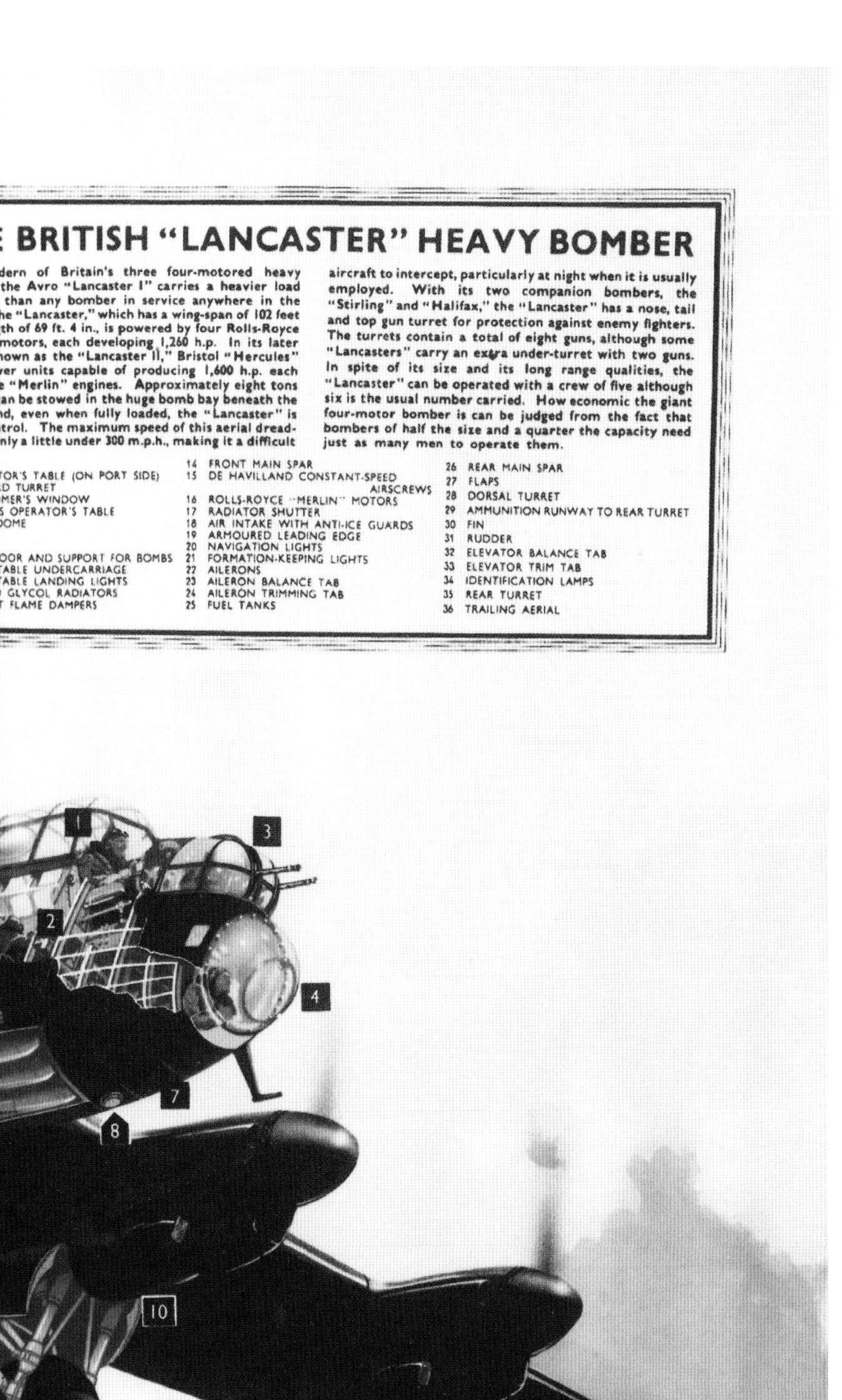

E BRITISH "LANCASTER" HEAVY BOMBER
odern of Britain's three four-motored heavy
, the Avro "Lancaster I" carries a heavier load
s than any bomber in service anywhere in the
The "Lancaster," which has a wing-span of 102 feet
gth of 69 ft. 4 in., is powered by four Rolls-Royce
motors, each developing 1,260 h.p. In its later
known as the "Lancaster II," Bristol "Hercules"
wer units capable of producing 1,600 h.p. each
he "Merlin" engines. Approximately eight tons
can be stowed in the huge bomb bay beneath the
and, even when fully loaded, the "Lancaster" is
ntrol. The maximum speed of this aerial dread-
only a little under 300 m.p.h., making it a difficult
aircraft to intercept, particularly at night when it is usually
employed. With its two companion bombers, the
"Stirling" and "Halifax," the "Lancaster" has a nose, tail
and top gun turret for protection against enemy fighters.
The turrets contain a total of eight guns, although some
"Lancasters" carry an extra under-turret with two guns.
In spite of its size and its long range qualities, the
"Lancaster" can be operated with a crew of five although
six is the usual number carried. How economic the giant
four-motor bomber is can be judged from the fact that
bombers of half the size and a quarter the capacity need
just as many men to operate them.
ATOR'S TABLE (ON PORT SIDE)
RD TURRET
AIMER'S WINDOW
SS OPERATOR'S TABLE
DOME
LOOR AND SUPPORT FOR BOMBS
TABLE UNDERCARRIAGE
TABLE LANDING LIGHTS
D GLYCOL RADIATORS
ST FLAME DAMPERS
14 FRONT MAIN SPAR
15 DE HAVILLAND CONSTANT-SPEED AIRSCREWS
16 ROLLS-ROYCE "MERLIN" MOTORS
17 RADIATOR SHUTTER
18 AIR INTAKE WITH ANTI-ICE GUARDS
19 ARMOURED LEADING EDGE
20 NAVIGATION LIGHTS
21 FORMATION-KEEPING LIGHTS
22 AILERONS
23 AILERON BALANCE TAB
24 AILERON TRIMMING TAB
25 FUEL TANKS
26 REAR MAIN SPAR
27 FLAPS
28 DORSAL TURRET
29 AMMUNITION RUNWAY TO REAR TURRET
30 FIN
31 RUDDER
32 ELEVATOR BALANCE TAB
33 ELEVATOR TRIM TAB
34 IDENTIFICATION LAMPS
35 REAR TURRET
36 TRAILING AERIAL
1
3
2
4
7
8
10
22
11

Courtesy of IWM

Appendix V: Lancasters Lost Serving with 622 Squadron

SerialNo.	Sqn Code.	Date.	Target	Cause of Demise	Pilot
ED364	GI-O	30/01/44	Berlin	Flak	F/Lt Brown
ED619	GI-T	30/03/44	Nuremberg	Night Fighter	P/O Sutton
ED624	GI-G	28/01/44	Berlin		F/Sgt Craig
KH617	GI-Q	01/02/45	Munchengladbach	Engine Fire	F/O Conacher
HK621	GI-C	06/11/44	Koblenz	Flak	F/O Stephens
HK644	GI-D	06/11/44	Koblenz	Flak	F/O Leake
HK769	GI-D	02/03/45	Cologne	Flak	F/O Ray
HK770	GI-T	22/04/45	Bremen	Flak	F/Lt Cook
L7576	GI-K	28/07/44	Stuttgart	Night Fighter	F/O Peabody
LL782	GI-H	31/05/44	Trappes	Flak	1st Lt Braithwaite
LL793	GI-Q	21/05/44	Duisberg	?	P/O Harris
LL802	GI-M	20/09/44	Calais	Collision	F/O Hogg
LL803	GI-S	02/11/44	Homberg	Flak	F/Lt Cass
LL812	GI-Z	12/06/44	Gelsenkirchen	Night Fighter	P/O Rattle
LL828	GI-J	15/03/44	Stuttgart	Flak	F/Sgt Thomson
LL859	GI-Q	20/07/44	Homberg	?	F/L Smith
LM108	GI-N	28/05/44	Angers	Flak	F/Sgt Teague
LM138	GI-N	23/06/44	L'Hey	?	F/Sgt Cooke
LM167	GI-N	20/09/44	Calais	Collision	F/O James
LM241	GI-Q	25/08/44	Russelsheim	?	F/O Holdsworth
LM283	GI-O	19/10/44	Stuttgart	?	F/O Orton
LM291	GI-F	12/09/44	Frankfurt	?	F/O Alexander
LM442	GI-P	24/02/44	Schweinfurt	?	F/Lt Doig

SerialNo.	Sqn Code.	Date.	Target	Cause of Demise	Pilot
LM466	GI-P	12/08/44	Russelsheim	?	F/O Busby
LM477	GI-L	24/07/44	Stuttgart	?	F/Sgt Vercoe
LM491	GI-E	08/06/44	Massey Palaiseau	?	P/O Hall
LM511	GI-C	11/09/44	Kattgart	?	F/Sgt Devine
LM595	GI-O	20/07/44	Homberg	?	F/O Pyle
ME693	GI-F	24/04/44	Karlsrule	?	F/Lt Jameson
ND765	GI-C	08/06/44	Masset Palaiseau	?	F/Lt Godfrey
ND767	GI-D	30/03/44	Nuremberg	Night Fighter	F/Sgt Pickin
ND781	GI-R	27/04/44	Friedrichshafen	Night Fighter	F/O Watson
ND926	GI-D	31/05/44	Trappes	Fighter	F/Lt Randall
NE146	GI-F	24/07/44	Stuttgart	?	F/O Thomas
NF915	GI-U	09/04/44	Bonn	?	F/Lt Perdue
NF939	GI-D	06/01/44	Danzig Bay	?	F/O Francis
NF964	GI-L	03/01/44	Dortmund	Night Fighter	F/Lt Dean
NF965	GI-S	12/09/44	Frankfurt	?	F/O Owen
NG447	GI-U	09/04/44	Kiel	Night Fighter	F/Lt Hodge
PA285	GI-O	20/04/44	Regensberg	Flak	F/Lt Robbins
R5483	GI-D	20/01/44	Berlin	?	F/Lt Cladon
R5625	GI-B	09/07/44	Lisieux	?	W/O Bamford
R5915	GI-P	20/01/44	Berlin	Flak	F/Sgt Deacon
W4163	GI-A	14/01/44	Berlin	Fighter	S/Ldr Martin
W4268	GI-A	15/02/44	Berlin	?	F/Lt Welch
W4272	GI-C	15/02/44	Berlin	Night Fighter	F/Lt Griffiths

46 Lancasters lost plus 3 in accidents. Raids flown with Lancasters, 227

Appendix VI:
List of Honors and Awards for No. 622 Squadron

The following list has been complied from various historical documents, in particular the London Gazette. It is by no means complete and the author apologises if he has missed any awards and honors attributed to 622 Squadron personnel. The awards were given to 622 members for their endeavors whilst on 622 sqdn. Ranks as per time of award.

Name	**Air Force**	**Rank**	**Award**
Allen R. G	RAF	S/Ldr	DFC
Allwright J.S. E	RAAF	F/O	DFC
Andrews E. P	RAAF	F/O	DFC
Bailey J.C	RCAF	Sgt	CGM (Immediate)
Bell J	RAF	F/Sgt	DFM
Belson A.F	RAF	Sgt	AFC
Berry L. F	RAF	F/Lt	DFC
Berry S.	RAF	F/O	DFC (Immediate)
Bould G.E	RAF	S/Ldr	DFC
Brignell J.A	RAF	S/Ldr	DFC
Buckingham G.K	RAF	W/C	DFC
Campbell J	RAAF	F/Lt	DFC
Chapman R.G	RAF	F/O	DFC
Chorley C.R	RAAF	P/O	DFC
Clark A.N	RAAF	F/Lt	DFC
Cole A.C	RAF	F/Sgt	CGM (Immediate)
Cook E.G	RAF	F/Lt	DFC
Cox J.L	RAF	F/Lt	DFC
Curling R	RAAF	P/O	DFC
Darville G.E	RAAF	F/O	DFC
Derisley K.J	RAF	F/Lt	DFC
Farquarson	RCAF	W/O	DFC (Immediate)
Fallows R	RAF	F/Sgt	DFM (Immediate)
Gill N.V	RAF	F/Lt	DFC
Gillies R.I	RAAF	F/Lt	DFC (Immediate)
Gilmour G.S	RAAF	F/Lt	DFC
Glynn D.F	RAF	F/Sgt	DFM (Immediate)
Good B.L	RAAF	F/O	DFC
Gray J.T.W	RAF	F/Lt	DFC
Hargreaves T	RAF	F/Lt	DFC
Harris E.H.W	RAF	F/O	DFC
Hickling W	RAF	F/Sgt	DFM
Hopswell W.H	RAF	F/Sgt	DFM
Hughes C.H	RAF	Sgt	DFM
Hussey R.T	RAF	F/Lt	DFC
Jezzard P	RAF	F/Sgt	DFM
Jones J.H	RAF	F/O	DFC
Lunn J.M	RAF	P/O	DFC
Malpass H.R	RAF	F/Sgt	DFM (Immediate)
Marr H.J	RAF	F/Sgt	DFM
Mason D.B	RAF	F/Lt	AFC. Dunkirk medal, Résistance Medal.

Name	Air Force	Rank	Award
Martin J	RAF	S/Ldr	DFC
Maxwell T.J	RAF	F/Lt	DFC (Immediate)
McDonald F.C	RAF	S/Ldr	DFC
McGuinness J	RAF	W/O	DFC
Middleton M.H (DFM)	RAF	F/Lt	DFC
Mitchell G.E	RAF	S/Ldr	DFC
Morgan J.W	RAF	F/Sgt	DFM
Murgatroyd D.L	RAF	F/O	DFC
Neilsen A.K	RAAF	F/Sgt	DFM
O' Brien W.G	RNZAF	F/O	DFC
Pantling R.W.L	RAF	F/O	DFC
Pawlyshyn J	RCAF	F/O	DSO
Peck H.P	RAAF	F/Lt	DFC
Pennington C.D.J	RAF	F/O	DFC
Pittaway R.W	RAF	Sgt	DFM
Phillips F.A	RAAF	P/O	DFC
Pudney D.C	RAF	Sgt	DFM (Immediate)
Rawsthorn R.J	RAAF	F/O	DFC
Richards A.C	RAF	F/O	DFC
Richards I.G	RNZAF	F/Lt	DFC
Robbins A.B	RAAF	F/Lt	DFC
Rumsey	RAF	Sgt	DFM (Immediate)
Rust G.	RAF	F/Sgt	DFM
Shorter D.H	RAF	F/O	Bar to DFM
Simpson R.L	RAAF	F/O	DFC
Stoddart J.K	RAF	F/Lt	DFC
Stratton J.W	RAF	F/Lt	DFC
Struthers H.C	RAAF	F/O	DFC
Swales J.C.K (DFM DFC)	RAF	W/C	DSO
Taylor A.R	RAF	F/O	DFC
Thomas W.K	RAF	F/Lt	DFC
Thorbecke W.H	RAAF	F/O	DFC
Tilson H. (DFC)	RCAF	S/Ldr	DSO
Toy G.E	RAF	F/O	MID- killed in action
Trenouth R.W	RAAF	F/O	DFC
Turner P (DFM)	RAF	F/Lt	DFC
Urwin R.L	RAF	Sgt	DFM (Immediate)
Vaughn J	RAF	F/O	DFC
Wilson T	RAF	P/O	DSO (Immediate)
Wishart G.J	RAF	F/Lt	DFC
Watson J.A	RCAF	F/Lt	MID- killed in action
Woolloff E.	RAF	Sgt	DFM

Key to Abbbreviations

AE-Air Efficiency Award
AFC-Air Force Cross
AFM-Air Force Medal
Bar-Second Award of a decoration
BEM-British Empire Medal
CB-Companion of the Order of the Bath
CBE-Commander of the Order of the British Empire
CdeG(B)-Croix de Guerre (Belgian)
CdeG(F)-Croix de Guerre (France)
CGM-Conspicuous Gallantry Medal
DBE-Dame Commander of the Order of the British Empire
DFC-Distinguished Flying Cross
DCM-Distinguished Conduct Medal
DFM-Distinguished Flying Medal
DSC-Distinguished Service Cross
DSO-Distinguisher Service Order
GC-George Cross
MC-Military Cross
MBE-Member of the Order of the British Empire
MID-Mentioned in Dispatches
MM-Military Medal
MSM-Military Service Medal

Appendix VII: The Short Stirling

The Short Stirling's origins were conceived as a result of Air Ministry specification B12/36, which called for a four engined heavy bomber that could deliver a substantial bomb load deep into enemy territory. The contract for building the bomber was awarded to 'Shorts' in 1939 and the Government was obviously influenced by the Short Sunderland flying boat which had entered service. The Sunderland flying boat was winning marvelous plaudits from aircrew and without the design restrictions placed on the Stirling, saw continuous RAF service throughout the war in different theatres.

One of the most striking features of the Stirling was its appearance towing 22ft 9" above the ground to its cockpit standing on what appeared to be a gangly undercarriage arrangement. At the initial planning stages, the Air Ministry insisted that the overall wingspan of the aircraft would be no more than 100 feet so that the bomber could fit into the standard RAF Hangar of the time. This directive was to prove to be a major operational defectiveness with the Stirling and contributed to its short front line operational service. The reduction in the wingspan significantly reduced the operational height of the aircraft and the Stirling with a full bomb load struggled to reach 13,000ft. This factor was significant when considering the performance of the Lancaster and Halifax bombers that could operate at heights around 20,000ft with a heavier bomb load. Operating over Germany at a lower altitude meant easy pickings for the German flak and night fighter defenses. In addition the danger from falling bombs from above was ever present. The second design flaw to affect the Stirling was the undercarriage. During initial trials the undercarriage was lengthened and gave the Stirling an ungainly appearance and several undercarriages collapsed on landing. The great height above ground and the angled position of the pilot's seat made it very difficult for the pilot to accurately judge touchdown altitude and precise ground position. This resulted in many pilots producing heavy landings on a spindly undercarriage configuration and collapsed undercarriages as a result.

The first squadron to receive the Short Stirling was No.7 based at the time at Leeming in North Yorkshire. The conversion to flying the first 4 engined bomber was not without 'teething' problems; however seconded 'Sunderland' crews from Costal Command assisted in converting crews to the Stirling. The first Stirling to go into operation was the MK1 fitted with Hercules MKII engines, which suffered from extensive mechanical problems that many considered a real danger. By the end of 1940, No.7 Squadron received the Stirling with an improved engine the Hercules MK X engine. With the improved engine and all crews suitably converted, the Stirling went to war on the night of 10/11th February 1941 in an attack on oil storage tanks at Rotterdam.

622 Squadron Service

On 10th August 1943 a new squadron was formed from 'C' flight of XV Squadron. That squadron was 622 Squadron, which was initiated from Bomber Command's expansion after the battle of the Ruhr. XV squadron at the time was operating Stirling bombers and therefore 9 Stirlings and 7 crews were immediately assigned to 622 Squadron. The bombers kept the same squadron individual assigned alphabetical letter, however 'GI' was the new prefix. The new Commanding Officer was S/L Martin and he conducted his first briefing on the 10th August for a raid on Nuremberg and seven Stirlings from the squadron were dispatched to the target. Two Stirlings returned early with technical faults and the rest bombed the target and returned safely.

Berlin was soon to become a regular destination for the crews of Bomber Command with the up and coming 'Battle of Berlin', and aircrew often refer to this target as 'The Big City'. ACM Harris believed that destroying the German capital would seriously dent the morale of the German people and bring home to the people the realization that the war could be brought to them in devastating ways. Harris wanted the assistance of the American 8th Air Force and he stated the together the Allies could "Wreck Berlin from end to end". On 23rd August 1943 a force of 727 bombers set out to bomb Berlin including 622 Stirlings. The German defenses were considerable and the casualty rate was 13% including the loss of the Stirling flown by F/Sgt Rollett and serious damage to another Stirling by a night fighter. Remarkably the damaged Stirling was skillfully brought back to base by its crew. The Stirling losses continued to mount and on the 27/28th August Bomber Command attacked the city of Nuremberg. 622 Squadron received no casualties on this raid however the total Stirling losses amounted to 10% of the force. Raids continued to varying targets and Berlin was again attacked on the night of 31st/1st September 1943 with the loss of two 622 Stirling crews piloted by F/O Toy and F/Sgt Young. A massive 47 crews paid the price for a disappointing raid and the Stirling loss rate was a massive 16%. The catalyst for the withdrawal of Stirlings from front line service was the Berlin raid on the night of 22/23rd November 1943, when 50 Stirlings were part of the bomber force and 10% of those were lost. The Stirling piloted by F/Lt Denham and crew was hit by flak near Hanover and the crew parachuted into captivity. ACM Harris knew that the Stirling losses could not be sustained and relegated the Stirling to secondary roles.

The mid upper gunner in F/Lt Denham's crew was F/Sgt Donald Shellock and his respect for the stirling remains to this day. The following is his account of his experiences and operations in the Short Stirling whilst with 622 Squadron:

> "When the news came through that we were posted to join the newly formed 622 Squadron at RAF Mildenhall, we were ready to join a front line squadron. We had endured just about all the training we could stomach and we were ready to do our bit for King and Country. We knew nothing about 622 Squadron but quickly found out that it was formed from 'C' flight out of XV Squadron who were also based at Mildenhall. The squadron was equipped with the short Stirling, an aircraft that we had become accustomed to during our training. At its initial formation seven Stirlings were immediately transferred from 'C' flight of XV Squadron with an expectation that the squadron would reach 16 operational Stirlings with 4 in reserve. We had hoped that we would be joining a Lancaster squadron for we knew that in comparison the Stirling was an inferior aircraft to the Lancaster. We had heard the stories about the Stirling struggling to gain the sufficient altitude over the target and the stories about how they were shot out of the sky by fighters and flak because of their low operational height. The official statistics confirm the stories, the Stirling suffered considerably more at the hands of the Germans than its counterparts the Lancaster and Halifax, in fact the night we were shot down over Berlin (22/23rd November 1943) was the last time Stirlings went to Berlin. They were withdrawn from front line service due to their poor attrition rates."

The Short Stirling was the first of the four engined 'heavies' that was restricted by the officialdom at the Air Ministry. The original design allowed for a wingspan of 112 feet; however the wingspan would have to be reduced to 100 feet to allow the Stirling to fit into the standard RAF hangar. The Stirling suffered from developmental and operational problems from the start and the majority of the problems can be attributed to a lack of operational experience and political interference. Officials criticized the Stirling's maximum operating height of 17,000 feet with a payload of just 3, 500lbs of bombs, compared with 2, 350lb of bombs carried by the Lancaster, in addition the bomb bay would not cater for the large 4,000lb 'cookie' blast bomb which was the mainstay of the RAF's arsenal. Don Shellock continues:

> "From a personal point of view, I considered the Stirling to be a majestic looking aircraft that took the war to Germany at a time when the country needed a boost after defeat at places like Dunkirk. I never flew in a Lancaster to compare the characteristics of each; however as a crew we came to love the Stirling and appreciated the aircraft's maneuverability and rugged design. Our skipper would throw the Stirling around the sky on fighter affiliation trips and very often turn inside some of the fighters on our tail. After our demise in November 1943, the Stirling was relegated to second line duties, which mainly concerned special operations. The Stirling was very maneuvrable at low altitude and it could conduct covert operations in the dead of night with ease. Towards the end of the war later versions of the Stirling were used to tow troop-carrying gliders into the fray during operation Overlord, Market Garden and Varsity, the Allied invasion of France. At the end of the war, the Stirling proved invaluable as a troop carrier, bringing back POWs from the European theatre."

During December 622 Squadron began its conversion to the Avro Lancaster and on 1st January 1944 the last of the Stirlings was flown out of Mildenhall destined for training units.

622 Squadron Stirling Service:

OPERATIONS	SORTIES	AIRCRAFT LOSSES	% LOSSES
41	195	7	3.6

Category of Operations undertaken:

BOMBING	MINING
21	20

Appendix VIII: Cutaway Drawing of the Short Stirling

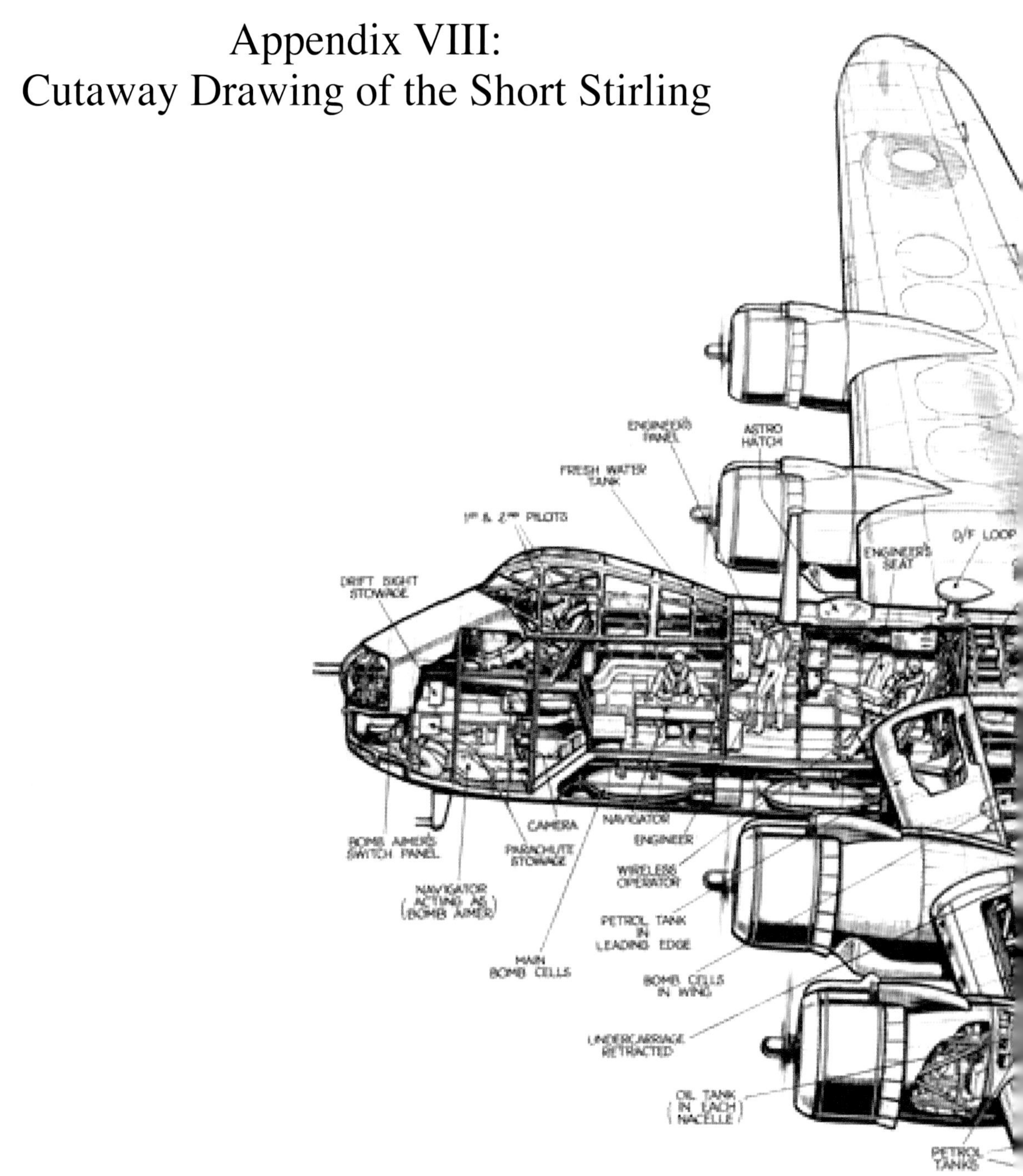

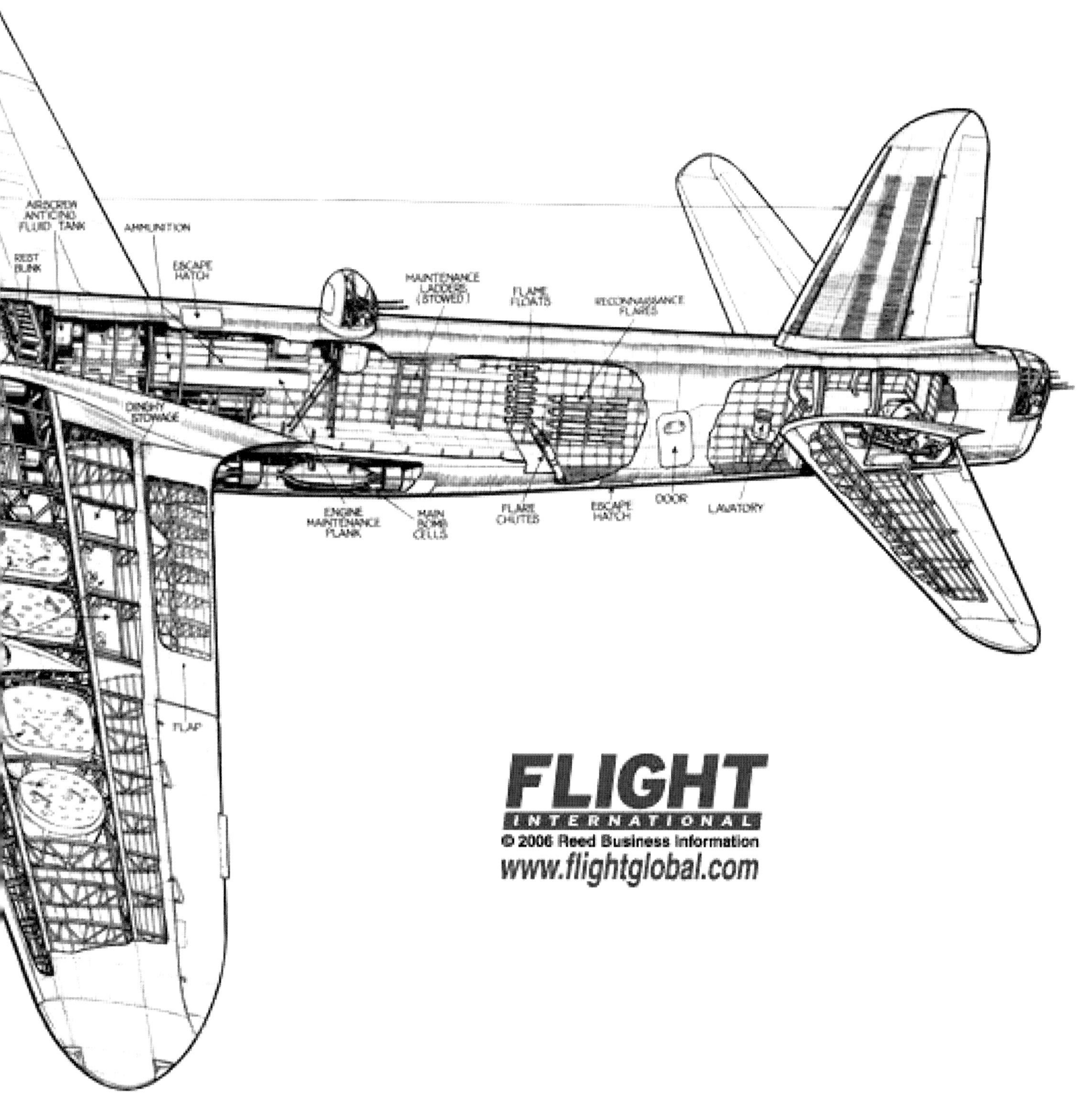

AIRSCREW ANTICING FLUID TANK
AMMUNITION
REST BUNK
ESCAPE HATCH
MAINTENANCE LADDERS (STOWED)
FLAME FLOATS
RECONNAISSANCE FLARES
DINGHY STOWAGE
ENGINE MAINTENANCE PLANK
MAIN BOMB CELLS
FLARE CHUTES
ESCAPE HATCH
DOOR
LAVATORY
FLAP
FLIGHT
INTERNATIONAL
© 2006 Reed Business Information
www.flightglobal.com

Appendix IX: The Avro Lancaster

622 Squadron converted to the Avro Lancaster in December 1943 after a four month spell of operating the Short Stirling. Once equipped with the Lancaster the squadron went on to complete 227 raids utilizing the Lancaster and would lose 44 during active service.

Lancaster Origins

The Avro Lancaster was undoubtedly the most famous bomber of World War II. The aircrafts initial design specification was almost perfect. The Lancaster went on to surpass many milestones including having its bomb bay modified to enable the aircraft to carry the massive 22,000lb 'Grand Slam' bomb.

The Lancaster's development was born out of the unsuccessful Manchester bomber programme. Two Rolls Royce Vulture engines that were prone to overheating and unexpected failure, powered the Manchester. The designer, Roy Chadwick knew that the airframe was a winning formula and after the Manchester's failure to meet expectations, he went back to the drawing board with his design team at Avro. The re-design work undertaken by Roy Chadwick resulted in Manchester's airframe and wing section being modified to allow for four Rolls Royce Merlin engines, the same power plant that powered the Spitfire and Hurricane fighters. The result of the modifications was a bomber that exceeded expectations on all fronts and won the hearts of many aircrews. Of all the superlatives heaped on the Lancaster, perhaps the finest accolade was delivered by Sir Arthur Harris, Commander In Chief of Bomber Command in a letter to the Lancaster production team. ACM Harris included the following statement in his letter. "As the user of the Lancaster during the last three and a half years of bitter, unrelenting warfare, I would say this to those who placed that shining sword in our hands. Without your genius and your effort, we would not have prevailed the Lancaster was the greatest single factor in winning the war". (Garbett & Goulding, 1979, 14). The Lancaster's defensive capabilities focused around eight .303 Browning machine guns in three turrets. The front turret manned by the bomb aimer if needed was armed with two .303 machine guns as was the mid upper gun turret. The most favored attack point for any fighter was from behind therefore the rear gun turret was armed with four .303 Browning guns to defend the aircraft from fighter attacks from the rear elevation.

Service Life

Night after night thousands of Lancasters droned across into Germany to deliver their substantial bomb load on German industrial cities. The Lancaster MK1 was an immediate operational success and from the initial stages of its service life it was clear that there was the potential to improve its capabilities even further. The Mk1's were fitted with Rolls Royce XX engines that delivered 1280 horse power on take off and this version was replaced by the Merlin 22 that delivered 1640 horse power and was capable of carrying a greater bomb load into Germany. The MkII Lancaster was fitted with the Bristol Hercules XVI engine that produced 1735 horse power. The Rolls Royce Merlin was such a success that it could not be produced fast enough to satisfy demand and therefore the 'Bristol' company was given the contract of producing engines for the MKII Lancaster to maintain momentum in aircraft production. The performance of the Bristol Hercules engine was virtually identical to that of the Merlin however it was slightly faster but burned more fuel and lacked the reliability of the Rolls Royce power plant. The MKII Lancasters were mainly used by the Canadian squadrons. The Rolls Royce general manager Claude Johnson was initially adamant that no other company would build their engines, however he conceded to demand and in 1941 the Packard Company in Detroit began to produce Merlin engines under license and the MKIII Lancaster was born. Various other marks of Lancaster were developed during the war but the Mk I, II & III were by far produced in greater numbers.

The Dambusters

The most famous raid of all conducted by the Lancaster was the attack on 16/17th May 1943 against the Ruhr Dams. The specific targets were the Mohne, Eder and Ennepe dams in the heart of Germany's industrial center. The mission would require low flying at night and some considerable skill to navigate and deliver a bomb accurately on the target. To achieve this aim a new squadron (617) was formed and W/C Guy Gibson was chosen to command the squadron and select the finest aircrews from bomber squadrons with the proviso of low flying in mind. Initially several Lancasters were drafted into the new squadron to enable flying practice to commence immediately. These Lancaster's would suffice whilst the especially adapted aircraft were being modified in the factories.

ED437 (AJ-N) was one of the aircraft posted in and eventually formed a tenuous link with 622 Squadron. During time with 617 Squadron, legendary pilots who undertook the mission on 16th May 1943 flew low level practice flights in ED437. For aficionados of the 'Dambusters' the pilots' names of Les Knight, Lew Burpee, Bill Townsend, Joe McCarthy, Les Munro, John Hopgood, Henry Maudsley and Mick Martin will need no introduction. Wing Commander Guy Gibson completed the famous list to grace the pilot's seat in this particular aircraft.

Shortly before the mission, ED437 was relegated to secondary duties and re-coded with the squadron markings of AJ-V. In January 1944 the Lancaster was posted to 622 Squadron and took on the identity of GI-D. Active service with 622 was very eventful and during the eight months with the squadron it endured being shot up twice and shot down enemy fighters.

Twenty-three especially adapted Lancaster MkIII's were delivered to RAF Scampton in Lincolnshire with the capacity to carry a cylindrical bomb hung outside the fuselage that weighed 6,600lbs. Almost immediately a programme of arduous low flying at night was commenced.

The destruction of the Ruhr Dams would severely disrupt German hydro-electric power plants in the Ruhr area and cause serious flooding in the adjoining industrial valleys. The 'bouncing bomb', as it would come to be known, was designed by Barnes Wallis. It was designed to bounce over the submarine torpedo nets that protected the Dams and sink under water to a specified depth where a hydrostatic plunger would trigger the bomb to explode. The bombs had to be dropped precisely at 60ft above the water and 400-450 yards from the dam(s) whilst being spun before being dropped by a belt driven mechanism, which would spin the bomb at 500 rpm. The degree of accuracy and skill required by the aircrew was immense and after several weeks of practicing low flying over the reservoirs in England the crews were ready. The bombs had to be dropped when the reservoirs were at their fullest, and this was around the new moon period in late May. On 16th May 1943 it was considered that the target had reached its optimum capacity and 19 aircraft took off in three waves to attack the dams. The first wave had nine Lancasters in formation and was led by W/C Gibson; the other two waves comprised five aircraft each. The first wave was to attack the most vital targets of the Mohne and Eder dam. The second wave was to attack the secondary target of the Sorpe dam. The third wave, used as a reserve wave, was also given the Sorpe as its provisional target, with the Ennepe and Lister dams as secondary objectives. En route to the dams' one Lancaster of the first wave was shot down by ground fire leaving the remaining eight to attack the targets. On reaching the Mohne dam Guy Gibson was the first to attack and eventually dropped his bomb under defence machine gun fire from the dam's towers and scored a direct hit. The next Lancaster was hit by the German machine guns whilst on the bomb run causing the Lancaster to crash with the loss of all the crew. W/C Gibson decided to fly alongside the remaining Lancasters whilst they delivered their bomb in an attempt to draw enemy fire away from the bombing aircraft. The fifth bouncing bomb to be dropped on the Mohne breached the dam caused a torrent of water to flood the valley below. Gibson sent the aircraft home that had dropped their bombs and continued onto the Eder dam with the remaining two Lancasters with their bomb intact. The second bomb dropped by F/Lt Les Knight and crew breached the Eder dam as well and although damaged the Sorpe and Ennepe dams were not breached. In total eight of the nineteen Lancasters were lost with the death of 53 of the aircrew. The raid was a tremendous morale boast for the country and demonstrated that severe damage could be inflicted on the German war machine. The success of the dams' raid was spread around the world and met with particular favor in America who Britain was attempting to bring into the war.

Lancasters took part in every major night attack on Germany. They soon showed their superiority by dropping 132 long tons of bombs for each aircraft lost, compared with 56 (later 86) for the Halifax and 41 for the Stirling. They carried a heavier load of bigger bombs than any other aircraft in the European theatre. The 12,000lb AP bomb was used to sink the battleship Tirpitz, and the 22,000 lb "Grand Slam" weapon finally shook down the stubborn viaduct at Bielefeld in March 1945. Around Caen, Lancasters were used en masse in the battlefield close-support role, and they finished the war dropping supplies to starving Europeans during operation Manna.

Lancaster specifications
Crew: seven
Maximum speed: 287 mph (462 km/h) at 11, 500 feet (3505 meters)
Ceiling height: 24, 500 feet (7470 meters)
Range: 2, 530 miles (4072 km)
Armament: eight x 0.303 machine guns.
Maximum bomb load of one x 22,000 lb Tall Boy bomb. (9979 kg) or 14,000 lb (6350 kg) of smaller bombs.

Appendix X:
622 Squadron Prisoners of War

Name	Rank	Aircraft	Date.	Target.	POW Camp	POW No.	Comments
Acworth G.F	Sgt	LL803 Lanc	02/11/44	Homberg	L7	1128	
Bamford F.B	Sgt	LM108 Lanc	28/05/44	Angers	L7	649	
Bartholomew J	Sgt	EF150 Stir	22/11/43	Berlin	4B	263561	
Benham R.P	F/Sgt	EF119 Stir	31/08/43	Berlin	4B/LB	222572	
Braithwaite J.E	1st Lt	LL782 Lanc	31/05/44	Trappes	Not Known		
Browich A.C	Sgt	LM442 Lanc	24/02/44	Schweinfurt	L6/357	2104	
Carter J	F/O	EF150 Stir	22/11/43	Berlin	L1	1582	
Caseley A.R	F/O	NF915 Lanc	24/12/44	Hangelair Airfield	L1		
Chapman R.J	F/Sgt	LM138 Lanc	23/06/44	L'Hey	L7	254	
Cloran T.H	Sgt	LL782 Lanc	31/05/44	Trappes	L7	151	
Cohen S	F/Sgt	LM108 Lanc	28/05/44	Angers	9C/L7	53401	
Collins M.W.G	F/Sgt	LM283 Lanc	19/10/44	Stuttgart	L7	1133	
Cook E.G	F/Lt	HK770 Lanc	22/04/45	Bremen		None.	Bailed out and held in transit camps. Released War coming to an end.
Cowan J.P.C	Sgt	LM466 Lanc	12/08/44	Russelsheim	L7		
Davis H.A	Sgt	LM283 Lanc	19/10/44	Stuttgart	L7	1101	
Denham K.H	F/Lt	EF150 Stir	22/11/43	Berlin	L1		
Durrant T	F/Sgt	LM138 Lanc	23/06/44	L'Hey	L7	258	
Gough P.D	F/O	HK770 Lanc	22/04/45	Bremen	Transit camps.		
Hagerty R.C	Sgt	HK770 Lanc	22/04/45	Bremen	Transit camps.		
Hansford R.J	F/Sgt	LM138 Lanc	23/06/44	L'Hey	L7		
Harper R	Sgt	EF128 Stir	18/11/43	Mannheim	L3	8094	
Hayes R.J	Sgt	ND781Lanc	27/04/44	Friedrichshafen	L6/356	3553	
Hoggan W	Sgt	EF150 Stir	22/11/43	Berlin	4B	263590	
Humphrey S.J	F/O	LM283 Lanc	19/10/44	Stuttgart	L7		
Ingham B	F/O	LL803 Lanc	02/11/44	Homberg	Not Known		
Irwin P.J	F/Sgt	R5915 Lanc	20/01/44	Berlin	L6/357	923	wounded, knocked unconscious when plane exploded.
Jeary G.H	Sgt	LM477 Lanc	24/07/44	Stuttgart	L7	460	
Johnson E	Sgt	EF150 Stir	22/11/43	Berlin	4B	263594	
Kenley C.J	F/Sgt	LM108 Lanc	28/05/44	Angers	L7	852	
Kerslake R.J	Sgt	LM442 Lanc	24/02/44	Schweinfurt	L6/357	2185	
Lamb B.D	F/O	NF915 Lanc	24/12/44	Hangelar Airfield	L1		
Lewis W.I	Sgt	NG447 Lanc	9/05/44		Kiel	Not known	

Name	Rank	Aircraft	Date.	Target.	POW Camp	POW No.	Comments
Littlewood A	Sgt	EF150 Stir	22/11/43	Berlin	4B	117119	
MacKinnon M.D	F/Sgt	ND781 Lanc	27/04/44	Friedrichshafen	L6/357	3693	
McKee W.S.J	F/Sgt	ND781 Lanc	27/04/44	Friedrichshafen	L6/357	3681	
McLaren T	Sgt	HK770 Lanc	22/04/45	Bremen	None, transit camps.		
Meese D	Sgt	LM138 Lanc	23/06/44	L'Hey	L7		
Miller K.R	F/Lt	R5915 Lanc	20/01/44	Berlin	L3	3378	
Nichol J	F/Sgt	MZ2264 Stir	31/08/43	Berlin	4B/L3	222753	
Odle A.C	F/Lt	LM442 Lanc	24/02/44	Schweinfurt	L3	3582	
Parker E	F/Sgt	PA825 Lanc	20/02/44	Regensberg	Not known		
Parry M	F/O	HK770 Lanc	22/04/45	Bremen	None.Transit Camps.		
Peake G	Sgt	LL828 Lanc	15/03/44	Stuttgart	L7	3650	
Poyser F	Sgt	EF119 Stir	31/08/43	Berlin	4B	222629	
Pratt R.H.M	F/Sgt	LM442 Lanc	24/02/44	Schweinfurt	L6/357	2116	
Prince J	W/O	LM283 Lanc	19/10/44	Stuttgart	L7	1119	
Ransom W.V	F/O	ND781 Lanc	27/04/44	Friedrichshafen	L3	4468	
Ritson G.F	F/O	EF119 Stir	31/08/43	Berlin	L3	2384	
Russell W.H	P/O	ND781 Lanc	27/04/44	Friedrichshafen	L3		
Selwyn E.G	Sgt	LM108 Lanc	28/05/44	Angers	L7		
Shellock D.W	F/Sgt	EF150 Stir	22/11/43	Berlin	4B/L3	263623	
Sherry R.W	F/O	HK770 Lanc	22/04/45	Bremen	none. Transit Camps.		
Simmond A.W	F/O	LM138 Lanc	23/06/44	L'Hey	L3	6507	
Simpson G.W	F/O	LM283 Lanc	19/10/44	Stuttgart	Not known		
Smith P.H.M	F/Sgt	EF119 Stir	31/08/43	Berlin	4B/L3	222843	
Smith W.B.R	F/Sgt	LL803 Lanc	02/11/44	Homberg	L7	1167	
Sproule G.G	F/O	ED624 Lanc	27/01/44	Berlin	L3	3458	
Stevens G	P/O	LL828 Lanc	15/03/44	Stuttgart	9C	1853	
Strange J.C	F/Sgt	LM283 Lanc	19/10/44	Stuttgart	L7	1122	
Sutherland G.B	F/Sgt	ED624 Lanc	27/01/44	Berlin	L6/357	1084	
Teague T.R	F/Sgt	LM108 Lanc	28/05/44	Angers	L7	240	
Thomson P.A	F/O	LL828 Lanc	15/03/44	Stuttgart	L7	100	
Wishart G.J	F/O	L7576 Lanc	28/07/44	Stuttagrt	Not known		
Woodward D.G	F/O	EF150 Stir	22/11/43	Berlin	L1	1614	
Yeardley H.M	Sgt	NF915 Lanc	24/12/44	Hangelar Airfiled	?		

Total: 65 Prisoners of war.

Key to German POW Camps:
4B: Stalag IVB Muhlberg (Elbe) 9C: Stalag Muhlhausen L1:Stalag Luft Barth Vogelsang L3:Stalag Luft Sagan and Belaria L6:Stalag Luft Heydekrug L7:Stalag Luft Bankan, Near Kreulberg, Upper Silesia. 357: Stalag Kopernikus.

Appendix XI:
622 Squadron Roll of Honor

622 Squadron was formed at Mildenhall, Suffolk on 10th August 1943 from 'C' flight of 15 Squadron as a bomber squadron equipped with Stirling Bombers. Over a period of 21 months the squadron dropped 10, 469 tons of bombs. The first Stirling lost with casualities was on 24th August 1943 when BF521, piloted by F/Sgt. N.C. Rollett was shot down by a night fighter on an operation to Berlin with the loss of all the crew. Seven Short Stirling bombers were lost with casualties.

The squadron was re-equipped with Lancasters during December 1943 and January 1944 and carried on its operations in Germany and France. Forty two Lancasters were lost with casualties. The final Lancaster lost with casualties was PA285 piloted by F/Lt Robbins who was shot down by flak on an operation to Regensberg on 20th April 1945.

There were over three hundred airmen who lost their lives serving with 622 Squadron:

215 of the Royal Air Force.
20 of the Royal New Zealand Air Force.
32 of the Royal Canadian Air Force.
37 of the Royal Australian Air Force.
1 of the Royal Norwegian Air Force.

56 airmen have no known grave and are commemorated on the Runnymede Memorial.

16 airmen are buried in Belgium.
2 airmen are buried in Scotland.
25 airmen are buried in Holland.
77 airmen are buried in France.
25 airmen are buried in England.
103 airmen are buried in Germany.

Name	Rank	Crew	Force	Died	Circumstances
Adams J.M	F/Sgt	A/G	RNZAF	20/09/44	Collision with friendly aircraft
Aldred F.G	Sgt	A/G	RAF	27/01/44	Night Fighter
Alexander E.D	F/O	Pilot	RAAF	12/09/44	Shot Down over Frankfurt
Allan J.M	Sgt	A/G	RAF	11/04/44	Came down over France
Allen B.J	Sgt	B/A	RAF	15/04/44	Came down on 'ops' to Berlin
Allsop A	Sgt	F/E	RAF	15/04/44	Night Fighter
Armitage P.S	Sgt	A/G	RAF	02/03/44	Flak
Austin G.H	Sgt	W/op	RAF	18/11/43	On 'ops' to Mannheim
Bache D.F	Sgt	B/A	RAF	20/01/44	Came down on 'ops' to Berlin
Bamford P.E	W/O	Pilot	RAF	09/07/44	Shot down on 'ops' to Lisieux
Barlow D.V	Sgt	F/E	RAF	09/07/44	Shot down on 'ops' to Lisieux
Barnes D	Sgt	W/op	RAF	01/09/43	Shot down over Schaepe.
Barr P	Sgt	W/op	RAF	26/08/44	Shot down over France
Baxter E	Sgt	A/G	RAF	01/02/45	Parachute on fire.
Bell P.E	Sgt	Nav	RAF	06/11/44	Came down on 'ops' to Koblenz
Bernhart D.P	F/Sgt	A/G	RCAF	01/06/44	Flak on 'ops' to Trappes
Betts S	LAC	G/C	RAF	18/11/43	Died of injuries in accident
Binns S	F/Sgt	Nav	RAF	01/06/44	Night Fighter
Blackmore D.G	P/O	B/A	RNZAF	22/05/44	Shot down on 'ops' to Duisberg
Blaubaum M.B	B/A	F/Sgt	RAAF	12/09/44	Shot down on 'ops' to Rostock
Blyth J	Sgt	W/op	RAF	08/07/44	On 'ops' to Lisieux
Boyce E.B	P/O	A/G	RCAF	02/03/45	Flak-on 'ops' to Cologne
Boyd R.G	F/Sgt	Nav	RNZAF	24/08/43	Shot down over Berlin
Boyle C.P	F/O	Nav	RCAF	02/03/45	Flak-on 'ops' to Cologne

Name	Rank	Crew	Force	Died	Circumstances
Bramley F.P	Sgt	B/A	RAF	15/02/44	Night Fighter
Bramley R	Sgt	A/G	RAF	13/06/44	Shot down over Holland
Brandon F.D	F/Sgt	W/op	RAF	21/07/44	Shot down over Holland
Brodie W.J.T	Sgt	F/E	RAF	30/01/44	On 'ops' to Berlin
Broome D.C	Sgt	B/A	RAF	25/07/44	Shot down over France
Brown C.A	Sgt	A/G	RAF	15/02/44	Shot down over Holland
Brown G.W	Sgt	A/G	RAF	03/01/44	Shot down over Dortmund
Brown H.H	Sgt	F/E	RAF	27/08/44	Killed by Flak over target
Brown R.J	F/Lt	Pilot	RAF	30/01/44	Shot down over Germany
Browne G.W	F/O	W/op	RNZAF	24/12/44	Shot down over Germany
Buckman H.E	Sgt	F/E	RAF	01/09/43	Shot down Scaepe Germany
Buckley P.W	Sgt	A/G	RAF	29/07/44	Night Fighter 'ops to Stuttgart
Bullock V.C	P/O	B/A	RCAF	03/01/45	Shot down over Dortmund
Burgess A	Sgt	A/G	RAF	02/11/44	Shot down over Germany
Burrows F.R	P/O	Pilot	RAAF	11/04/44	Shot down on 'ops' to Rostock
Burton R	Sgt	A/G	RAF	12/09/44	Shot down on 'ops' to Rostock
Busby J.H	F/O	Pilot	RAAF	13/08/44	On 'ops' to Russelsheim
Butcher N	F/Sgt	Nav	RAF	11/04/44	On 'ops' to Laon
Butler N	Sgt	Pilot	RAF	20/01/44	Hit by Flak
Campbell R.H	F/Sgt	A/G	RAAF	22/05/44	On 'ops' to Duisberg
Carter F.M	F/O	Nav	RCAF	01/09/44	Night Fighter
Cass R.F	F/Lt	Pilot	RAF	02/11/44	Came down over Germany
Challis N.D	Sgt	A/G	RAF	26/08/44	On 'ops' to Russelsheim
Chandler J.J	F/O	Nav	RCAF	28/09/43	On 'ops' to Hanover
Chapman F.E.W	Sgt	F/E	RAF	15/02/44	On 'ops' to Berlin
Chigwidden J.J	F/Sgt	Nav	RAAF	21/07/44	On 'ops' to Homberg
Chirghin C.D	F/O	B/A	RAF	08/06/44	Night Fighter over France
Christie P.A	F/Sgt	A/G	RAF	07/01/45	On 'ops' to Danzig
Clark R.E	Sgt	A/G	RAF	26/08/44	On 'ops' to Russelsheim
Claydon D.A	F/Lt	Pilot	RCAF	20/01/44	On 'ops' to Berlin
Cochrane J	Sgt	W/op	RAF	25/04/44	On 'ops' to Karlsruhe
Collins G.R	Sgt	A/G	RAF	31/03/44	Collided with Halifax
Comber D.R	Sgt	B/A	RAF	18/11/43	On 'ops' to Mannheim
Conley G.R	F/Sgt	W/op	RAAF	02/03/45	Flak over Belguim
Connor A.C	Sgt	F/E	RAF	01/06/44	Flak on 'ops' to Trappes
Davies W.H	F/O	Nav	RAF	20/01/44	On 'ops' to Berlin
Dea M	Sgt	A/G	RAF	13/06/44	On 'ops' to Gelsenkirchen
Deacon R.A	P/O	Pilot	RAF	20/01/44	On 'ops' to Berlin
Dean W.E.M	S/Ldr	Pilot	RAF	03/01/45	Flak 'ops' to Dortmund
De Angelis J.A	Sgt	F/E	RAF	20/09/44	Collision with friendly aircraft
Dench F.K	Sgt	A/G	RAF	25/02/44	Night Fighter over Germany
Devine E.N	P/O	Pilot	RAAF	12/09/44	Shot down on 'ops' to Rostock
Dineen B.P	F/Sgt	W/op	RAF	27/01/44	Night Fighter over Germany
Doe J.H	F/O	Nav	RCAF	29/07/44	Night Fighter over France
Doig P.H	F/Lt	Pilot	RCAF	25/02/44	Night Fighter over Germany
Drewett W.A	Sgt	F/E	RAF	12/09/44	On 'ops' to Frankfurt
Dryland E.J	Sgt	F/E	RAF	20/09/44	Collision with friendly aircraft
Duffield R.A	Sgt	A/G	RAF	25/07/44	On 'ops' to Stuttgart
Dumaresque J.A	Sgt	A/G	RAF	20/09/44	Collision with aircraft
Edgar F.S	Sgt	A/G	RNZAF	24/08/43	Night Fighter over Berlin
Edwards P.J	F/Lt	B/A	RAF	26/08/44	On 'ops' to Russelsheim
Fairburn N.J	F/O	Nav	RAF	25/04/44	On 'ops' to Karlsruhe
Ferguson G.R	F/Sgt	W/op	RAAF	12/09/44	Shot down on 'ops' to Rostock
Fitness G.W	F/Sgt	A/G	RNZAF	20/09/44	Collision with friendly aircraft

Name	Rank	Crew	Force	Died	Circumstances
Fletcher J.A	F/O	B/A	RAF	09/07/44	Shot down on 'ops' to Lisieux
Flower F.W	Sgt	A/G	RAF	27/01/44	Night Fighter over Berlin
Forde F.M	Sgt	W/op	RAF	30/01/44	On 'ops' to Berlin
Forrest D.T	Sgt	A/G	RAF	12/09/44	On 'ops' to Frankfurt
Forster J	F/Lt	Pilot	RAF	20/09/44	Motorcycle accident
Foster J.J.W	F/Sgt	Nav	RAF	13/08/44	On 'ops' to Russelsheim
Francis E.S	F/O	Pilot	RAAF	07/01/45	On 'ops' to Danzig Bay
Garbutt J.R	F/Sgt	Pilot	RNZAF	15/02/44	Night Fighter over Berlin
Gardiner G.E.J	F/Sgt	A/G	RNZAF	08/06/44	Night Fighter over France
Gardner H.C	Sgt	W/op	RAF	13/08/44	On 'ops' to Russelsheim
Geddes P.I	Sgt	A/G	RAF	20/09/44	Collision with friendly aircraft
Gell G.W	F/O	B/A	RCAF	10/04/45	Shot down on 'ops' to Kiel
Gibson J	F/Sgt	B/A	RAF	20/09/44	Collision with friendly aircraft
Gill A.T	F/O	B/A	RAF	20/09/44	Collision with friendly aircraft
Godden D.A	Sgt	F/E	RAF	26/08/44	On 'ops' to Russelsheim
Godfrey R.G	F/Lt	Pilot	RAAF	08/06/44	Night Fighter over France
Graham H	F/Sgt	F/E	RAF	20/01/44	On 'ops' to Berlin
Green W.M.L	W/O	Nav	RCAF	10/04/45	Shot down on 'ops' to Kiel
Grice H	Sgt	F/E	RAF	12/09/44	On 'ops' to Frankfurt
Griffiths J.W	Sgt	W/op	RAF	15/02/44	Shot down over Holland
Griffiths T.L	F/Lt	Pilot	RAAF	15/02/44	Shot down over Holland
Gronow	K.E	Sgt	A/G	RAF	25/07/44 Shot down over France
Hale D.W	Sgt	A/G	RAF	02/11/44	On 'ops' to Homberg
Hall A.H	Sgt	F/E	RAF	21/07/44	Shot down over Holland
Hall J.E	P/O	Pilot	RAF	08/06/44	Shot down over France
Hall J.W.K	P/O	B/A	RCAF	28/09/43	On 'ops' to Hanover
Hannah C.W	F/Sgt	Nav	RNZAF	19/11/43	Crashed in fog, Descending
Harland R	F/Sgt	A/G	RAF	03/01/45	Shot down over Dortmund
Harris J.A	P/O	Pilot	RAAF	22/05/44	Shot down on 'ops' to Duisberg
Harris R. B.V	P/O	A/G	RAF	25/07/44	Came down over France
Hawkes R.G	Sgt	A/G	RAF	06/11/44	Came down on 'ops' to Koblenz
Hewitt	D.A	Sgt	W/op	RAF	24/08/43 Night Fighter over Berlin
Heywood W.F	Sgt	A/G	RAF	02/03/45	Flak on 'ops' to Cologne
Hodge L.A.S	F/Lt	Pilot	RAF	10/04/45	Shot down on 'ops' to Kiel
Hogan E.A	W/O	B/A	RAAF	12/09/44	Shot Down over Frankfurt
Hogg M.L	F/O	Pilot	RAF	20/09/44	Collision with friendly aircraft
Holden R.P.P	F/Sgt	W/op	RAAF	13/06/44	Night Fighter, Gelsenkirchen
Holdsworth D.H	F/O	Pilot	RAF	28/08/44	On 'ops' to Russelsheim
Hooker E.L	F/O	W/op	RAF	20/09/44	Collision with friendly aircraft
Hoy A	F/Sgt	W/op	RAF	06/11/44	Came down on 'ops' to Koblenz
Hughes P.F	P/O	Pilot		19/11/43	Crashed in fog, Descending
Hugill N	Sgt	A/G	RAF	01/09/43	Shot down over Schaepe.
Hulland J.E	F/Sgt	A/G	RAF	20/04/45	Flak over Regensberg
Hunt W.J	P/O	Pilot	RAAF	28/09/43	On 'ops' to Hanover
Hunter R	Sgt	A/G	RAF	06/11/44	On 'ops' to Koblenz
James C.R	F/O	Pilot	RAF	20/09/44	Collision with friendly aircraft
James S.E	P/O	Pilot	RAAF	20/01/44	On 'ops' to Berlin
Jameson A	F/Lt	Pilot	RAF	25/04/44	On 'ops' to Karlsruhe
Jamieson J.R.U	F/O	Nav	RAAF	12/09/44	On 'ops' to Frankfurt
Jarvis B.W	Sgt	F/E	RAF	08/06/44	Shot down over France
Javis E.F	F/Sgt	A/G	RCAF	31/03/44	On 'ops' to Nuremberg
Jones H.F	F/O	A/G	RAF	06/11/44	Came down on 'ops' to Koblenz
Joyce L	F/Sgt	W/op	RAAF	19/11/43	Crashed in fog, Descending
Kearney A.M	F/Sgt	A/G	RAAF	18/11/43	On 'ops' to Mannheim

Name	Rank	Crew	Force	Died	Circumstances
Keatley R.S	Sgt	W/op	RAF	20/09/44	Collision with friendly aircraft
Keeling H.V	Sgt	F/E	RAF	02/11/44	On 'ops' to Homberg
Kelly L.J	P/O	Nav	RAAF	22/05/44	On 'ops' to Duisberg
Kelly S.L.W	Sgt	F/E	RAF	01/06/44	Night Fighter 'ops' to Trappes
Kelly W	F/Sgt	W/op	RAF	07/01/44	On 'ops' to Danzig
Kidman J.H	Sgt	A/G	RAF	20/01/44	Flak on 'ops' to Berlin
King J.J	Sgt	W/op	RAF	11/04/44	On 'ops' to Laon
Knight G.E	Sgt	A/G	RAF	24/08/43	Night Fighter 'ops' to Berlin
Laberge D.J	W/O	B/A	RCAF	31/03/44	Night Fighter 'ops' Nuremberg
Lanceley S.E	Sgt	A/G	RAF	09/07/44	Shot down on 'ops' to Lisieux
Leake R.D	F/O	Pilot	RAAF	06/11/44	Came down on 'ops' to Koblenz
Leaney F.M	Sgt	F/E	RAF	13/06/44	Night Fighter, Gelsenkirchen
Lewis D.G	F/Sgt	B/A	RAF	02/03/45	Flak 'ops' to Cologne
Lewis R.I	Sgt	F/E	RAF	21/07/44	On 'ops' to Homberg
Lock W.E	F/Sgt	A/G	RAF	25/04/44	On 'ops' to Karlsruhe
Lothian T.J	P/O	A/G	RCAF	12/02/45	Domestic accident-fall
MaCfarlane J	F/Sgt	W/op	RAF	03/01/45	Shot down over Dortmund
MaCgibbon P.A	F/Sgt	Nav	RAF	21/07/44	On 'ops' to Homberg
MaCgugan I.F	F/Sgt	Nav	RAAF	12/09/44	On 'ops' to Frankfurt
Mackrell S	Sgt	A/G	RAF	01/09/43	Night Fighter, Berlin
Maclean A	Sgt	A/g	RAF	25/04/44	On 'ops' to Karlsruhe
Maher P.J	F/Sgt	A/G	RCAF	20/01/44	On 'ops' to Berlin
Marks S.J	Sgt	Nav	RAF	01/09/43	On 'ops' to Berlin
Mayhead J.M	P/O	A/G	RAAF	08/06/44	Shot down over France
Mead L.G	F/O	Nav	RAF	03/01/45	Shot down over Dortmund
Meadow L	Sgt	W/op	RAF	28/09/43	On 'ops' to Hanover
Merritt J.P	P/O	Nav	RCAF	31/03/44	Collision 'ops' Nuremberg
Meyer R.C.M	Sgt	F/E	RAF	21/09/44	Shot down on 'ops' to Rostock
Minnis S	Sgt	A/G	RAF	12/09/44	On 'ops' to Frankfurt
Mitchell T.D	Sgt	A/G	RAF	24/12/44	On 'ops' to Bonn
Montgomery F.C	F/O	B/A	RCAF	21/07/44	On 'ops' to Homberg
Moore R.J.W	F/Sgt	Nav	RAAF	13/06/44	Night Fighter, Gelsenkirchen
Moore R.S	F/Sgt	B/A	RAF	25/04/44	On 'ops' to Karlsruhe
Morecombe W.J	P/O	Pilot	RAAF	18/11/43	On 'ops' to Mannheim
Morral H	F/Sgt	Pilot	RAF	15/02/44	2nd Pilot, on 'ops' to Berlin
Moseley F	Sgt	A/G	RAF	20/01/44	On 'ops' to Berlin
McClean J.A	F/Sgt	Nav	RAF	31/03/44	Night Fighter 'ops' Nuremberg
McFadden C.H	Sgt	A/G	RAF	25/02/44	On 'ops' to Schweinfurt
McGriffen H	Sgt	A/G	RAF	11/04/44	On 'ops' to Laon
McLeod K.G	F/Sgt	F/E	RAF	28/09/43	On 'ops' to Hanover
McRae W	W/O	A/G	RAF	07/01/45	On 'ops' to Danzig Bay
McSpayden J	Sgt	A/G	RAF	15/02/44	Night Fighter, Berlin
Napier H	Sgt	A/G	RAF	01/09/43	On 'ops' to Berlin
Neilsen K.M	F/Sgt	W/op	RNZAF	15/02/44	Night Fighter, Berlin
Nesvold M.L	F/Sgt	A/G	RCAF	18/11/43	On 'ops' to Mannheim
Newman P	Sgt	F/E	RAF	31/03/44	Night Fighter 'ops' Nuremberg
Norris D.M	P/O	B/A	RCAF	08/06/44	Shot down over France
Norris S	W/O	A/G	RAF	01/06/44	Flak 'ops' to Trappes
Notley A	F/Sgt	A/G	RAF	22/05/44	On 'ops' to Duisberg
O'Connor E.A	Sgt	A/G	RAF	21/07/44	On 'ops' to Homberg
O'Connell T.B	Sgt	F/E	RAF	06/11/44	Came down on 'ops' to Koblenz
Oliver F	Sgt	A/G	RAF	24/06/44	On 'ops' to L'Hey
Ormshaw W.J	Sgt	F/E	RAF	02/03/45	Flak, 'ops' to Cologne
Orton E	F/Lt	Pilot	RAF	23/11/44	Flak, 'ops' to Stuttgart-died in Hospital

Name	Rank	Crew	Force	Died	Circumstances
Ough A.A	Sgt	A/G	RAF	18/11/43	On 'ops' to Mannheim
Owen G.W	F/O	Pilot	RAF	12/09/44	On 'ops' to Frankfurt
Owen S	P/O	Pilot	RAF	18/11/43	On 'ops' to Mannheim
Page H.F	Sgt	F/E	RAF	31/03/44	Collision 'ops' Nuremberg
Parsons W.A	Sgt	A/G	RAF	10/04/45	On 'ops' to Kiel
Paterson W	F/O	Nav	RCAF	24/12/44	On 'ops' to Bonn
Payton A	Sgt	W/op	RAF	29/07/44	Night Fighter, 'ops' Stuttgart
Peabody H.S	F/O	Pilot	RCAF	29/07/44	Night Fighter, 'ops' Stuttgart
Pearce W.C	Sgt	F/E	RAF	25/04/44	On 'ops' to Karlsruhe
Pearson M.S	F/Sgt	A/G	RAF	15/02/44	Night Fighter, Berlin
Pepper D.R	F/Sgt	Nav	RNZAF	25/07/44	Night Fighter, 'ops' Stuttgart
Perdue R.N	F/Lt	Pilot	RCAF	24/12/44	On 'ops' to Bonn
Pezaro L	Sgt	F/E	RAF	18/11/43	On 'ops' to Mannheim
Piche J.L	F/Sgt	A/G	RCAF	30/01/44	On 'ops' to Berlin
Pickin E	P/O	Pilot	RAF	31/03/44	Collision 'ops' Nuremberg
Polkinghorne H.C	F/O	Nav	RAF	09/07/44	'Ops' to Lisieux
Pool W.H	P/O	A/G	RCAF	21/07/44	On 'ops' to Homberg
Pritchard H.E	F/O	W/op	RNZAF	20/09/44	Collision with friendly aircraft
Proulx R.G	F/Sgt	A/G	RCAF	29/07/44	Night Fighter, 'ops' Stuttgart
Pyle J.E.A	F/O	Pilot	RAF	21/07/44	On 'ops' to Homberg
Randall F.R	F/Lt	Pilot	RAF	01/06/44	Night Fighter, 'ops' to Trappes
Ratcliffe P.J	F/Sgt	B/A	RAAF	19/11/43	Crashed in fog, Descending
Rattle W.F.H	F/O	Pilot	RAAF	13/06/44	Night Fighter, Gelsenkirchen
Ray M.E.M	F/O	Pilot	RAF	02/03/44	Flak, 'ops' to Cologne
Read L.E	F/Sgt	W/op	RAF	31/03/44	Night Fighter 'ops' Nuremberg
Rees S.G	Sgt	Nav	RAF	15/02/44	Night Fighter, Berlin
Reid R.W	Sgt	F/E	RAF	20/04/45	Flak, 'ops' to Regensberg
Richards H.L.R	F/Sgt	Pilot	RNZAF	18/11/43	On 'ops' to Mannheim
Richardson J.F	Sgt	A/G	RAF	31/03/44	Night Fighter 'ops' Nuremberg
Robbins V.S	F/Lt	Pilot	RAF	20/04/45	Flak, 'ops' to Regensberg
Robertshaw R.W	P/O	B/A	RCAF	30/01/44	On 'ops' to Berlin
Robertson J.D	F/Sgt	B/A	RAF	06/11/44	Came down on 'ops' to Koblenz
Robinson F	F/Sgt	Nav	RAF	20/09/44	Collision with friendly aircraft
Rollett N.C	F/Sgt	Pilot	RNZAF	24/08/43	Night Fighter, Berlin
Ross W	F/Sgt	A/G	RAF	08/06/44	Shot down over France
Rust K.W	F/Sgt	W/op	RAAF	12/09/44	On 'ops' to Frankfurt
Ryder A.W	Sgt	F/E	RAF	08/06/44	Shot down over France
Schmidt C.J	F/Sgt	B/A	RAAF	31/03/44	Collision 'ops' Nuremberg
Scott B.F	F/O	W/op	RNZAF	20/04/45	Flak, 'ops' to Regensberg
Sewell F.S	P/O	W/op	RNZAF	08/06/44	Shot down over France
Seymour A.S	F/O	W/op	RAF	10/04/45	On 'ops' to Kiel
Shields W.G.J	P/O	W/op	RAF	20/01/44	On 'ops' to Berlin
Schute M.R	F/O	Nav	RAF	25/07/44	Night Fighter, 'ops' Stuttgart
Simpson T.J	Sgt	F/E	RAF	25/07/44	Night Fighter, 'ops' Stuttgart
Sinclair G.A	F/Sgt	A/G	RNZAF	25/07/44	Night Fighter, 'ops' Stuttgart
Sly A.E	Sgt	F/E	RAF	18/11/43	On 'ops' to Mannheim
Small E.G	F/Sgt		RAF	01/06/44	Night Fighter, 'ops' to Trappes
Smith A.L	F/Lt	Pilot	RAF	21/07/44	On 'ops' to Homberg
Smith D.F.A.F	F/O	Nav	RAF	20/09/44	Domestic road accident
Smith D.S	F/Sgt	Nav	RAF	18/11/43	On 'ops' to Mannheim
Smith H.A	F/O	W/op	RAF	20/04/45	Flak, 'ops' to Regensberg
Smith R.M	P/O	Nav	RCAF	08/06/44	Shot down over France
Soanes R.C	Sgt	F/E	RAF	07/01/45	On 'ops' to Danzig Bay
Spaven J.L	Sgt	A/G	RAF	21/07/44	On 'ops' to Homberg

Name	Rank	Crew	Force	Died	Circumstances
Spencer J	Sgt	A/G	RAF	21/07/44	On 'ops' to Homberg
Stanley T.J	Sgt	F/E	RAF	11/04/44	On 'ops' to Laon
Steeden A.D	F/Sgt	Nav	RAF	07/01/45	On 'ops' to Danzig Bay
Stewart A.H	P/O	Nav	RAF	08/06/44	Shot down over France
Strange J.B	Sgt	F/E	RAF	20/01/44	Flak 'ops' to Berlin
Strevens F.C	Sgt	B/A	RAF	24/08/43	Night Fighter 'ops' Berlin
Sutton J	P/O	Pilot	RAF	31/03/44	Night Fighter 'ops' Nuremberg
Tanner W.R	F/O	B/A	RAAF	13/06/44	Night Fighter, Gelsenkirchen
Taylor A	Sgt	F/E	RAF	19/11/43	Crashed in fog, Descending
Taylor R.C	F/O	Nav	RCAF	15/02/44	On 'ops' to Berlin
Taylor R.S.C	Sgt	Nav	RAF	25/02/44	On 'ops' to Schweinfurt
Taylor S.G	Sgt	A/G	RAF	10/04/45	On 'ops' to Kiel
Tebbutt W	Sgt	A/G	RAF	28/09/43	On 'ops' to Hanover
Tetlow R	F/O	Nav	RAF	26/08/44	On 'ops' to Russelsheim
Thomas C.F	F/Sgt	A/G	RAF	19/11/43	Crashed in fog, Descending
Thomas H.S	F/Sgt	W/op	RAF	01/06/44	Night Fighter, 'ops' to Trappes
Thomas M.T	F/O	Pilot	RAAF	25/07/44	On 'ops' to Stuttgart
Thomas S.A	Sgt	W/op	RAF	18/11/43	On 'ops' to Mannheim
Thomson R.J	F/Sgt	Pilot	RAAF	18/11/43	On 'ops' to Mannheim
Thorogood W.C	Sgt	A/G	RAF	12/09/44	On 'ops' to Frankfurt
Tidmas F.E	Sgt	Nav	RAF	30/01/44	On 'ops' to Berlin
Till A.E	Sgt	W/Op	RAF	08/06/44	Shot down over France
Tofield P.J	F/O	B/A	RAF	12/09/44	On 'ops' to Frankfurt
Tomlinson L	F/Sgt	B/A	RAF	21/07/44	On 'ops' to Homberg
Toy G.F	F/O	Pilot	RAF	01/09/43	Night Fighter, 'ops' Berlin
Tozer R.H	Sgt	F/E	RAF	24/08/43	Night Fighter, 'ops' Berlin
Traylen G.R	F/Sgt	Nav	RAF	07/01/45	On 'ops' to Danzig Bay
Troake R.H.C	Sgt	A/G	RAF	13/08/44	On 'ops' to Russelsheim
Vercoe P.N	F/Sgt	Pilot	RNZAF	25/07/44	On 'ops' to Stuttgart
Vieritz C.A	F/Sgt	W/op	RAAF	12/09/44	On 'ops' to Frankfurt
Wareham B.E	Sgt	F/E	RAF	22/05/44	On 'ops' to Duisberg
Watson J.A	F/Lt	Pilot	RCAF	28/04/44	Night Fighter, Friedrichshafen
Weatherhead E.A	Sgt	A/G	RAF	12/09/44	On 'ops' to Frankfurt
Weaving L.G.H	Sgt	A/G	RAF	28/09/43	On 'ops' to Hanover
Welch G.A	F/Lt	Pilot	RAF	15/02/44	Night Fighter, Berlin
White D.B	Sgt	W/op	RAF	22/05/44	On 'ops' to Duisberg
White W.R	Sgt	A/G	RAF	09/07/44	Shot down on 'ops' to Lisieux
Whittington F.H	Sgt	F/E	RAF	25/07/44	On 'ops' to Stuttgart
Westbrook R.H	Sgt	Nav	RAF	20/09/44	Collision with friendly aircraft
Willets S	F/O	Nav	RAF	18/11/43	On 'ops' to Mannheim
Willicombe H.R	Sgt	F/E	RAF	03/01/45	Flak 'ops' to Dortmund
Wilson G.W	Sgt	A/G	RAF	13/08/44	On 'ops' to Russelsheim
Withers P.S	Sgt	A/G	RAF	27/08/44	Night Fighter 'Ops' to Kiel
Woodcock A.W	Sgt	W/op	RAF	20/01/44	Flak, 'ops' to Berlin
Woolhouse A.T.W	F/Sgt	Pilot	RAF	30/01/44	2nd Pilot 'ops' Berlin
Wooten W.F.S	Sgt	A/G	RAF	30/01/44	On 'ops' to Berlin
Wragg A	F/Sgt	B/A	RAF	11/04/44	On 'ops' to Laon
Wright P.W	Sgt	A/G	RAF	15/02/44	On 'ops' to Berlin
Young J.M	P/O	Pilot	RAF	01/09/43	On 'ops' to Berlin

Glossary & Abbreviations

Bulls eye - Training run by crews at OTU to undertake practice bombing run.

Casablanca Directive - Approved by the Combined Chiefs of Allied Staff on 21st January 1943. The directive set out a series of priorities for the strategic bombing of Germany by the Allies.

Circuits & Bumps - Training exercise where a pilot takes off and circles an airfield and lands repeatedly

Cookie - Standard 4,000lb blast bomb.

Corkscrew - Maneuver deployed by the heavy bombers to avoid enemy fighter attack.

DR - Dead reckoning - Basic navigation without electronic aids.

ETA - Estimated time of arrival.

Exodus - The operation to repatriate POWs back to England from French airfields.

FTR - Failed To Return.

FIDO - Fog intensive dispersal operation. Pipes laid either side of the runway that had petrol pumped through them under pressure. Once lit, it was intended that the heat would disperse the fog allowing the returning bombers to land safely.

Gee - Bomber navigation radar, received radar pulses sent from ground Stations in England.

George - Automatic pilot.

G/H - Navigation/bombing aid. Used predominantly by 3 Group Bomber Command.

Grand Slam - 22,000lb bomb. Designed by Barnes Wallis, largest bomb designed in WWII.

H2S - Radar device built into aircraft. Worked by producing a topographical picture of the ground onto a cathode - ray tube.

IFF - Identification friend or foe. Device to transmit signal from aircraft to aid Identification.

Kammhuber Line - Defensive line of searchlights, flak guns and ground controllers who would scramble German night fighters the entire length of the Kammhuber line stretched from Denmark down across the entire length of the enemy coast. The system comprised grid of boxes each with its own ground controller who would vector a night fighter into the box once a bomber was identified.

'Kriegie' - German term for Prisoner Of War - Kriegsgefangener.

LFS - Lancaster finishing school.

Lichtenstein - Luftwaffe radar system fitted to their night fighters.

LMF - Lack of moral fiber. Acronym assigned to aircrew that could no longer face

the rigors of operational flying.

MANNA - Operation Manna took place from 28th April to 8th May 1945. The operation was named after the food, which miraculously appeared for the Israelites in the book of Exodus, called Manna. The Dutch people were cut off from food supplies and they were starving. The Allies agreed a ceasefire with the Germans allowing the bombers to drop food supplies to the starving Dutch population.

Maquis - French resistance (named after the Corsican scrub).

Monica - Electronic detection system fitted to bombers to detect approaching enemy fighters.

Oboe - Radio beam navigation system.

OTU - Operational Training Unit. All aircrew had to spend around 4 - 8 weeks at OTU. Course comprised 'crewing up' and familiarization with the equipment that would be utilized by all crew members.

Pointblank Directive - A revised directive issued by the Combined Chiefs of Allied Staff on 14th June 1243. The primary directive was to "impose heavy loses on the German day fighter force and to attack industrial targets that were producing materials to assist the German Air and Ground war".

POW - Prisoner Of War.

RDF - Radio Direction Finding.

R/T - Radio telephone.

SABS - Stabilised automatic bomb sight.

SBA - Standard Beam Approach.

Second 'dickey' - co - pilot, gaining experience prior to flying operational alone.

Schräge Musik (slanting music), a German nickname given to the Nachtjagd 'Night Fighter Planes' equipped with two MG ff's or MG 151/20s 20mm cannons mounted in the cabin or fuselage at a 70 - 80 angle which were aimed by a second Revi C 12/D or 16B gun sight mounted on the canopy roof.

SOC - Struck Off Charge.

TI - Target Indicators.

Tour - Name describing 30 operational missions with Bomber Command. Crews had to complete this number of missions to become 'tour expired' and take a rest from operational flying.

U/S - Unserviceable.

WAAF - Women's Auxiliary Air Force.

Wild Boar (Wild Saur) - German single engined night fighters which chose targets of opportunity in amongst the bomber stream.

Window - Metal strips of tin foil cut to the same length as the wavelengths of German ground radar receivers. Bundles were dropped by bombers and initially totally deceived the German radar screens into giving false and numerous contacts.

Wurzburg - German ground station radar control systems. Usually comprised of two units, the larger would detect individual bombers. The smaller unit would direct the searchlights onto the bombers.

Ranks:
AC: Aircraftman
AG: Air Gunner
AOC: Air Officer Commanding
AOC in C: Air Officer Commanding-in-Chief
B/A: Bomb Aimer
CO: Commanding Officer
Cpl: Corporal
F/E: Flight Engineer
F/O: Flying Officer
F/Lt: Flight Lieutenant
F/Sgt: Flight Sergeant
G/C: Group Captain
LAC: Leading Aircraftman
MUG: Mid Upper Gunner
Nav: Navigator
NCO: Non-Commissioned Officer
P/O: Pilot Officer
R/G: Rear Gunner
S/Ldr: Squadron Leader
Sgt: Sergeant
SWO: Station Warrant Officer
W/C: Wing Commander
W/op: Wireless Operator

<sub>Units
AGS: Air Gunners School
B&GS: Bombing & Gunnery School
CU: Conversion Unit
EFTS: Elementary Flying Training School
HCU: Heavy Conversion Unit
ITW: Initial Training Wing
MU: Maintenance Unit
(O)AFU: Observers Advanced Flying Unit
OUT: Operational Training Unit
PFF: Pathfinder Force
PNB: Pilot/Navigator Bomb Aimer Training Scheme
SHQ: Station Headquarters
AAF: Auxiliary Air Force
RAF: Royal Air Force
RAAF: Royal Australian Air Force
RCAF: Royal Canadian Air Force
RNZAF: Royal New Zealand Air Force
USAAF: United States Army Air Force
WAAF: Women's Auxiliary Air Force

Bibliography

Chorley, W.R. *Bomber Command losses 1943-45*. Leicester England*:* Midland Publishing 1992-97

Clarke M.B.E., Don. *The Mildenhall Register Newsletters:* Bedford England 1981-2008.

Clutton Brock, Oliver. *Footprints on the Sands of Time*: London, England. Grub Street 2003

Delve Ken & Jacobs, Peter.*The Six Year Offensive*: London, England. Arms & Armour 1992

Dring, Colin. *A History of RAF Mildenhall:* Mildenhall England. Mildenhall Museum Publications 1980

Falconer, Jonathon. *Stirling at War*: Surrey, England. Ian Allan 1991

Freeman, Roger. *Raiding The Reich:* London, England. Arms & Armour Press 1997

Ford Jones, Martyn R. *Oxfords Own, Men & Machines of 15/XV Squadron*: Atglen PA, USA. Schiffer Publishing1999.

Ford Jones, Martyn R. *Bomber Squadron- Men who flew with XV Squadron*: London, England. W. Kimber 1987

Golding, Brian & Garbett, Mike. *Lancaster At War Vols 1-5*. Ian Allen publishing 1971-95

Harris, Arthur. Sir. *The Bomber Offensive*: London, England. Greenhill Books 1990

Hastings M. *Bomber Command*. London, England. Michael Joseph 1979

Kind, Stuart. *The Sceptical Witness:* Harrogate, Yorkshire, England. Hodology Ltd 1999

Foreman, John. Matthews, Johannes. Parry, Simon. *Luftwaffe Night Fighter Claims 1939-1945*: Surrey, England. Red Kite 2004

Hall, Grace. 'Archie'. *We Also Were There*: Braunton, Devon, England. Merlin Books 1985

Middlebrook Martin & Everit, Chris. *The Bomber Command War Dairies:* London, England. Viking Publishing 1985

Middlebrook Martin. *The Berlin Raids*: London, England. Viking Publishing 1988

Neilands Robin. *The Bomber War:* London, England. John Murray 2001

Parsons Leslie. *Over Hell & High Water*: Bognor Regis, England. Woodfield Publishing 2001

Pichon. Josselyne. L. *Nous Combattons de nuit an Squadron 622* :Rambouillet France. Imprimé en France. 2000

Price, Alfred. *Battle Over The Reich:* Surrey, Engand. Ian Allen Publishing 1973

Price, Alfred. *The Bomber in World War II:* Abingdon, Oxon, England. Charles Schribner & Sons 1976

Public Records Office. 622 Squadron Operational Records books, Air 27

Richards Denis.*The Hardest Victory*: London, England. Hodder & Stoughton 1994

Saunders H. *The Fight Is Won:* London, England. HMSO. 1954

Taylor Geoff. *The Nuremberg Massacre*: London, England. Sidgwick & Jackson 1980

Walley B. *Silk and Barbed Wire:* Warwick, Western Australia. 2000

Ward. Chris. *622 Squadron Profile*: Lutterworth, England. Copy Cats 1999

Willis James J. *My Dream To Fly Fulfilled*: Rockampton, Australia. University Publishers Australia 2009

Index

Personnel

Index

Index

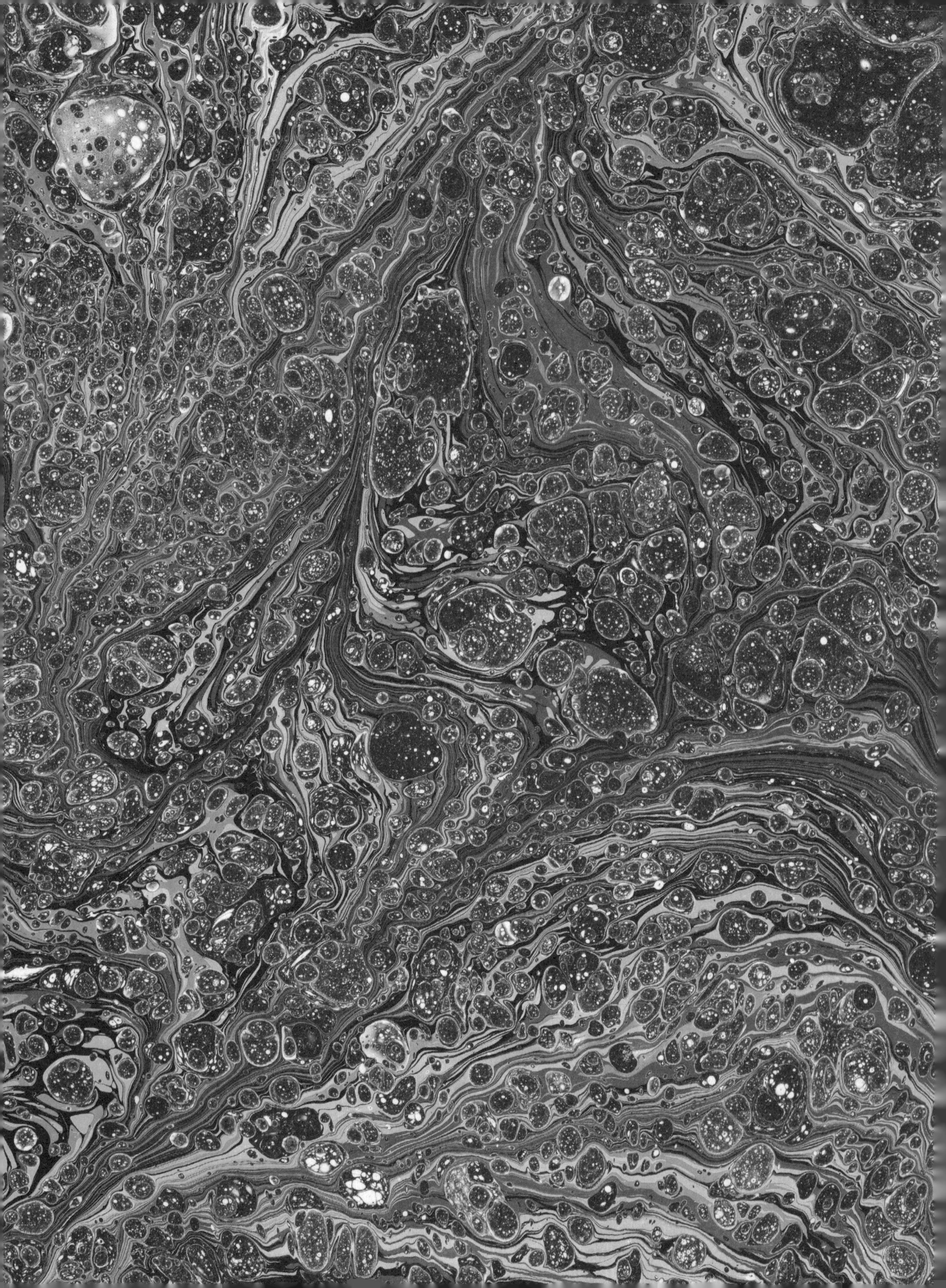